Toward Self-Understanding / Studies in Personality and Adjustment

Toward Self-Understanding

STUDIES IN PERSONALITY AND ADJUSTMENT

LAWRENCE C. GREBSTEIN   University of Rhode Island

To My Parents

Library of Congress Catalog Card Number 76-75130
Copyright © 1969 by Scott, Foresman and Company, Glenview, Illinois 60025.
Philippines Copyright 1969 by Scott, Foresman and Company.
All Rights Reserved. Printed in the United States of America.
Regional Offices of Scott, Foresman and Company are located in Atlanta,
Dallas, Glenview, Palo Alto, Oakland, N.J., and London, England.

PREFACE

Students often complain of being frustrated in their attempts to achieve greater self-understanding. They frequently claim that existing psychology courses, particularly at the introductory level, are of limited practical value. Specifically, students protest, with varying degrees of justification, that courses in the area of personality and adjustment often include material which is irrelevant, overly technical, excessively complex, uninteresting, too research-oriented, or, at the other extreme, oversimplified and unchallenging.

Ironically, this discontent is shared by many psychology instructors who realize that they have a double task. First, they must bring together in a single course instructional materials which adequately reflect the diverse methods, theories, and research findings related to the study of personality. Second, they must present material which is relevant to the lives of their students. The failure of many existing textbooks to present the subject matter meaningfully and in depth makes the task of the instructor even more difficult. In many cases, the need for textbook authors to cover a wide range of topics in a manner comprehensible to students of quite different backgrounds results in superficiality. This collection of readings has been influenced considerably by these common complaints from both students and faculty. It is intended to provide a selective but penetrating inquiry into problems of personality and adjustment in ways that will be meaningful to students in the context of their life experiences.

The specific contents of the present volume have evolved from a course of the same title which I have taught at the University of Rhode Island since 1964. The readings are divided into seven sections which deal with psychological issues of interest and concern to young adults. In addition to the discussion of traditional topics, such as the definition of psychology, motivation, personality development, and psychological stress, there are sections devoted to love and sexual behavior, identity and alienation, and man's basis for self-judgment. In most of the sections, there is at least one selection dealing specifically with problems of the college student. While the majority of the articles are written by psychologists, emphasis has been placed on a multidisciplinary approach to the topics. Essays have been selected from the fields of anthropology, child development, education, psychiatry, sociology, and theology in an attempt to expose the reader to a variety of viewpoints on a particular issue.

All the readings are of the essay type and emphasize content rather than methodology. They have been selected primarily for their ability to convey information and provoke thought. To the best of my knowledge, most of the articles have not been reprinted in comparable collections, and an effort has been made to include primarily contemporary selections. The articles are of varying difficulty and can be read profitably by persons with different amounts of training and sophistication. Some readings have been included which are relatively advanced for an introductory level. These few articles have been deliberately chosen to illustrate the complexity of some of the problems. Hopefully, their relevance, frequent use of examples, and clarity of style will help the reader to overcome any difficulty encountered in understanding them.

Although some of the readings refer to research findings to illustrate particular points, there are no research reports or descriptions of experimental investigations per se included in the book. There are no graphs, charts, or mathematical equations in the entire volume to bore or confuse the inexperienced student. This characteristic is not intended to diminish the importance of research. On the contrary, it is my belief that exposing students to stimulating discussions of interesting and relevant topics will motivate them to seek out additional information on their own. The presentation of research findings as a didactic technique seems more appropriate at an advanced level when the student has a clearer understanding of the problem.

Since the major purpose of the book is to stimulate students to think critically about their behavior and the reasons for it, the articles have been deliberately chosen to provide conflicting points of view on a given topic. Many of the selections reflect the present state of incomplete knowledge about human behavior. In order to minimize confusion, however, each group of readings is preceded by a lengthy introduction which attempts to provide a meaningful context for the articles that follow. The section introductions discuss the nature of the problem, selectively review the existing theory and research in the area, and attempt to point out some of the unanswered questions. In addition, brief introductions to each article relate the readings to the section introductions and give some biographical information about the author. All the introductions are designed to reveal existing controversies and encourage the reader to develop new perspectives on the subject.

The success of any readings book is to a large extent dependent upon the availability of suitable articles. I wish to thank all the authors, editors, and publishers for their kind permission to reproduce the selections included in the present volume. In all cases, the articles have been reprinted in their original form to preserve the author's intent and accuracy of thought. Many of my colleagues and students have contributed indirectly to this volume through their stimulating comments and questions. However, I am particularly grateful to Leila Cain for her many helpful comments for the introductions to sections three and seven and to Albert Silverstein for his critical appraisal of the introduction on motivation. My wife, Ellen, has read the entire manuscript more times than is reasonable to ask and has helped me not only to clarify my writing but to complete it.

LAWRENCE C. GREBSTEIN

Kingston, Rhode Island

CONTENTS

1

THE PROBLEM OF DEFINITION

We live in an age where television, magazines, and other mass media constantly document our social problems, psychological difficulties, and the general plight of the human condition. The American public is continually reminded of the importance of being well adjusted. It is not surprising, therefore, that many persons seek definite explanations of their behaviors and are prone to accept oversimplified interpretations of why they act as they do. Unfortunately, the complexity of human behavior cannot be reduced to simple explanations. Professional psychologists disagree considerably, not only about what kinds of human experiences should be included within psychology, but also about the most effective ways of studying these experiences. Beginning students of psychology are often confused by the discovery that some psychologists question or reject many familiar and commonly used terms, such as mind, unconscious, and self. The introductory student may experience considerable frustration upon discovering that the very concepts he wants to study are dismissed as unscientific, undefinable, or meaningless. Although it is often those concepts related to the study of personality and adjustment that are the most controversial and questionable, the problem cannot be restricted to a specific area of psychology. The purpose of this section is to discuss some of the issues related to the definition of psychology.

At a very basic level, psychologists can be classified into two groups: those who believe that man's behavior is ordered and lawful and those who do not. The former point of view has been succinctly stated by Farber (1964).

The basic assumption of behavioral scientists is that behavior is a function of its antecedents. These antecedents are natural events in the natural world, and the laws relating behavior to its antecedents can be discovered in the manner of other natural sciences, by the observation and analysis of empirical events. These laws of behavior are, at least in principle, susceptible of discovery. Not all will, as a matter of fact, be known at any given time, since they are exceedingly complex, and new information tends to uncover new complexities. But this is merely a recognition of pragmatic difficulties. It does not make a virtue of obscurantism nor elevate ignorance of ultimate causes to the status of a scientific principle. Once the laws of behavior, or enough of them, are known, the behavior can be predicted. And if the determinants, or enough of them, are manipulable, the behavior can be controlled (Farber, 1964, p. 6).

It follows from this position that the methods of the psychologist should approximate the methods of the natural scientist. That is, the study of human behavior would be based on the precise measurement and control of variables through the use of the experimental method. In the history of American psychology, this approach has been most enthusiastically advocated by the psychologists called *behaviorists*. As Lundin (1963) states:

. . . from the standpoint of the behaviorist, any theory which incorporates propositions not open to verification through objective observation is "mentalistic." Any theory, no matter how elegantly and logically stated, which in the final analysis depends upon such ineffable concepts as "psychic energy" or "unconscious processes" is, in the behavioral view, prescientific (Lundin, 1963, p. 257).

Although there is not universal agreement among the behaviorists about the appropriate data for psychological inquiry, their insistence that behavior must be observable and subject to precise measurement places certain restrictions on what is defined as acceptable content for study. In other words, the method to a large extent determines the content, and what is not amenable to objective observation is not acceptable data for psychology.

At the other extreme are those psychologists who do not assume that human behavior is ordered and lawful. On the contrary, their basic assumption is that each man is a unique individual who cannot be completely understood in terms of general laws of behavior. As a result, psychologists who believe in man's essential individuality place less emphasis on the importance of the scientific method and more emphasis on understanding the totality of man's behavior. Schlien (1963) presents one aspect of this point of view as follows:

If the mind could not think silently; if there were outwardly audible and visible signs directly indicating specific mental activities, we would all be rank behaviorists, and the history of psychology, to say

the least, would be hinged on a very different set of data. But this is not the case. As things stand, we have both internal and external events experienced by the total organism; experienced, recorded at some level of awareness, and in some cases, given meaning. The phenomenologist is convinced that much goes on "inside," and that the behavioristic concept of the "empty organism" is narrow, and largely spurious. Most of our experience and its meanings exist in "private worlds," not expressed on pointer readings (Schlien, 1963, p. 291-292).

The advantage of this and similar approaches is that it places fewer restrictions on what can be studied by the psychologist because it does not make the meaningfulness or significance of behavior subservient to the scientific status of the method used to study the behavior. The disadvantage of perspectives which stress the importance of man's inner experience is that they provide less opportunity for their hypotheses to be substantiated. It is more difficult to agree about the nature of internal, nonobservable events than it is to confirm external, observable ones.

In order to deal more efficiently with the diversity and complexity of the varieties of human experience, psychologists create abstract concepts to categorize and account for behavior. Simply stated, these abstractions or *constructs* can be described as educated guesses about what is going on inside the person, and they are usually combined into a logical and consistent theory. A theory, according to Rychlak (1968), is "a process of abstraction based upon observations of a set of phenomena (p. 12)." Psychological theories vary considerably, particularly in terms of how much they abstract from the data. For example, theories of personality are perhaps the most ambitious because they try to account for a variety of complex behaviors. As a result personality theories often contain highly abstract hypotheses about nonobservable entities. Terms such as ego, conscience, and mind are examples of these abstract constructs. They are not directly observable but are inferences based on the observation of behavior. At the same time, they attempt to account for behavior. Other theories, like those of the behaviorist, deal with more restricted units of behavior, and therefore do not require constructs as abstract as those of the personality theorist.

One of the purposes of a theory is to facilitate communication and encourage clarification. Sometimes, in our enthusiasm to get on with the business of understanding man, we fail to distinguish theory from fact. Consequently, we may accept constructs as realities, forgetting that they are man-made fictions created for our convenience. The validity and utility of both a theory and its constructs are generally determined by how well they correspond to observed behavior. For this reason, many popularly used terms are not universally accepted by psychologists. In fact, many psychologists recommend eliminating the use of these terms altogether. In addition to causing a good deal of frustration and confusion on the part of the beginning psychology student, as we noted earlier, this may be an academic instance of throwing out the baby with the bath.

While we have attempted to relate psychologists' failures to agree in their definitions to differences in their basic attitudes, it would be a misleading oversimplification to suggest that all psychologists are rigidly divided into one or the other of two opposing orientations. It might appear that the issue is one of science versus nonscience, but it cannot be reduced exclusively to one of scientific orientation even though it is frequently characterized as such. As Falk (1956) indicates, there is no essential conflict between these two approaches in terms of their merit as scientific methods. Those who emphasize the importance of man's uniqueness provide useful hypotheses about his behavior. Psychologists who maintain that man's behavior is lawful provide the means for verifying these hypotheses through the use of precise methods of experimentation.

To the extent that definitions tend to terminate investigations rather than to initiate them, they are not useful. In approaching the topic of self-understanding, it is as important to be aware of the factors that are involved in reaching a conclusion as it is to be concerned with the correctness of the conclusion itself. This first group of readings presents some of the problems involved in defining the realm of psychology and points to some of the factors that interfere with the conclusion-making process.

References

Falk, J. L. Issues distinguishing idiographic from nomothetic approaches to personality theory. *Psychol. Rev.*, 1956, 63, 53-62.

Farber, I. E. A framework for the study of personality as a behavioral science. In Worchel, P. & D. Byrne (Eds.) *Personality Change*. New York: Wiley, 1964, 3-37.

Lundin, R. W. Personality theory in behavioristic psychology. In Wepman, J. M. & R. Heine (Eds.) *Concepts of Personality*. Chicago: Aldine, 1963, 257-290.

Rychlak, J. F. *A Philosophy of Science for Personality Theory*. Boston: Houghton Mifflin, 1968.

Schlien, J. M. Phenomenology and personality. In Wepman, J. M. & R. Heine (Eds.) *Concepts of Personality*. Chicago: Aldine, 1963, 291-330.

Behavior: datum or abstraction [1]

ROLLAND H. WATERS

Historically, the development of psychology as a formal discipline has been characterized by considerable disagreement about both its content and its method of inquiry. This article describes some of the problems encountered by psychologists in their attempts to define their subject matter. Using the concept of behavior as a basis for his discussion, the author points out the many ambiguities and controversies that can develop in the search for a precise definition of the term. This article provides a concise review of earlier definitions of psychology, as well as the objections to these definitions, and illustrates the close relationship between the content and methods of psychology.

Before his death in 1967, R. H. Waters, Ph.D., was Professor of Psychology at the University of Florida and had been Professor Emeritus since 1964.

The problem of the subject matter of psychology and its implications has recently taken on renewed interest (3, 4, 8). This may be because of the reference to studies of the rat as appropriate for a rodentology but not for a psychology of human behavior. But another reason may be that contemporary textbook writers give insufficient attention to the problem of defining and delimiting psychology's field of study. This is reflected in the uncritical assertion that the subject matter of psychology is behavior, a term which is then characteristically left undefined and, hence, ambiguous. An example from a current textbook illustrates the situation. The writer says:

If you ask almost any psychologist to define his subject, the chances are that he will say, "The study of behavior." He takes it for granted, of course, that you know he is talking about human and animal behavior, not the behavior of stars or machines or atoms . . . [If one asks] why is psychology the study of behavior? the answer is . . . straightforward. You can study only what you can observe, and behavior is the only aspect of a person that is observable. We know very well that there are events going on within a person—events that can be called "thought," "feelings," or more generally, "mental activities." We can and do make fairly trustworthy inferences about these events, but we always make them from the way a person behaves. It is what he says, does, and writes that we as scientists can observe and record. Hence it is only behavior that we can study. A person who cannot talk, write, move a muscle, or behave in some way might very well have a "mind," "thoughts," and "feelings," but we could never know what they were, because we would have no access to them. These inner processes are brought to light only through a person's behavior. That is why we say psychology is the study of behavior (7, p. 3).[2]

This statement raises a series of questions. What is the meaning of the term "behavior"? Is the term appropriately applied to the movements of machines, stars, and atoms? How

From *American Psychologist*, XIII (1958), 278-282. Reprinted by permission of the American Psychological Association and Mrs. R. H. Waters.

[1] Address of the President at the Annual Meeting of the Florida State Psychological Association, Miami Beach, Florida, May 3, 1957.
[2] Quotation reprinted by permission from *Introduction to Psychology* by C. T. Morgan. Copyright, 1956. McGraw-Hill Book Company.

would an animal have to behave to be a star? Or a machine to be human? How are we to know that "he is talking about human and animal behavior, not the behavior of stars or machines or atoms?" The last question requires some criterion by which we can distinguish the movements of atoms from those of the human individual. Is this criterion *external* to the movements themselves, such as being exhibited by living things? If so, what about plants? Are their movements to be described as "behavior"? Does this external criterion limit the applicability of the term "behavior" to living animal forms? Then does "behavior" include all the movements and activities carried out by the animal or only certain specified activities, activities that exhibit certain characteristics? If this latter is true, then the criterion must be an internal one, that is, one based on the intrinsic or inherent features of the various acts performed. Such an internal criterion is not described. But unless we know what these differentiating characteristics are, I doubt our ability to distinguish between the "behavior" of man, animal, plants, stars, machines, or atoms.

Again the author says:

We know very well that there are events going on within a person—events that can be called "thoughts," "feelings," or more generally, "mental activities."

Now when he, by implication at least, asserts that "you cannot observe these events within a person," does he mean that you, as experimenter, cannot observe them in another, as subject, or does he mean they cannot be observed by either experimenter or subject? If the latter, how can he accept their existence without question? If the former, what is the justification for accepting the subject's behavior as an index of their existence? I would agree that their presence in the experimental subject is, in part, inferential and based, as he tells us, on the character of the subject's responses. However, our belief in the *existence* of such processes is certainly *not* based only on responses we observe. Such a belief is based on our observations of those processes taking place within ourselves. If what we call "behavior" is only a partial basis for accepting their existence, must we not once more ask for the differen-

tiating characteristics of those activities which we can class as "behavior"? Is it not also legitimate to ask: What is the status of these inner processes? Do they not, in their own right, possess those characteristics which justify their being included, along with other activities, in the class "behavior"?

This illustration should be sufficient indication of the need for a definition of the term, behavior, when used to refer to the subject matter of psychology. Such a definition should specify those characteristics of psychology's "behavior" that set it off or serve to differentiate it from the physicist's "behavior of atoms," the botanist's "behavior of plants," the astronomer's "behavior of the stars," and similar usages. The definition must be broad enough to include within its scope three classes of events: the movements of the organism through space, his manipulative and adaptive responses, all of which may be referred to as molar in nature; the subjectively reported, experiential processes; and the neurophysiological activities occurring in conjunction with the molar and experiential processes. Finally, such a definition or, perhaps better, such a conception of behavior must provide *Lebensraum* not only for the comparative psychologist but for the phenomenologist, the clinician, the sensory and physiological psychologist, the experimentalist, the theoretician, and all the rest.

We are all familiar with the statement Woodworth credits to some "wag" to the effect that psychology first lost its soul, then its mind, then consciousness, but that, strangely enough, it still behaves. This characterization is supposed to be descriptive of the change in the subject matter, or content, of psychology throughout its history. We can readily think of a similar characterization of psychology's methodology. For example, the mind has been exorcised, mesmerized, hypnotized, analyzed, psychoanalyzed, cauterized, and is now being tranquilized. It's a wonder the poor thing has survived!

Along with these shifts in content and method there has been a change in the kind of laboratory subject employed. Thus, as substitutes for the adult human individual, we are accustomed to find psychologists using children, the ape, the monkey, the dog, cat, rat, pig, pigeon, hamster, fish, porpoise, paramecium, and the ant lion in his investigations.

Psychology has thus had a curious and interesting history with respect to its subject matter, its correlated methodologies, and experimental subjects. It started with the conception of a dualism between an immaterial substance, spirit, soul, or mind, and a material substance, matter or body. Then came the first division of labor among the original philosopher-scientists. The study of the changes and phenomena of material things was given over to one group who became the physicists, chemists, physiologists, and neurophysiologists of our day. The study of the phenomena of immaterial substance was taken on by another group from whom we present-day psychologists trace our line of descent. But there is an important point to notice in the present context. The first group claimed to be studying matter; the second, the soul. Matter for the first, soul for the second, was the underlying reality manifesting itself in the phenomena under investigation.

From this early beginning, and we shall now confine ourselves to psychology, the above series of changes were rung on this object of study. The soul was found to be heavily freighted with theological connotations and hence was abandoned by the psychologist. This occurred in spite of the stand taken by Aristotle who, according to McDougall

. . . rejected the traditional notion of the soul, and regarded it rather as the sum of the vital functions . . . to say that a thing possessed a soul was for him but a convenient way of saying that it exhibited some or all of these peculiarities (peculiarities that distinguish living beings from inert things) (5, p. 12).

Following the rejection of the term, soul, as an adequate designation or label for the subject matter of psychology, the term, mind, was introduced. But this term was too reminiscent of the soul as an active agent, an entity or substance that carried on its activities "behind the scenes" as it were, and hence did not serve as a satisfactory name for that which could actually be brought into the laboratory. At best it could only be used as a class name for all the concrete "thoughts and feelings" that could be empirically observed. Mind thus lost favor, and the term, consciousness, was introduced in its place. This concept in its turn was

discarded and for much the same reason. To paraphrase James' statement made with reference to the Transcendental Ego: mind and consciousness turned out to be but "cheap and nasty editions of the soul" (2, p. 365). Thus, we come finally to the "modern" notion, at least it is as modern as Aristotle, that the proper subject matter of psychology is behavior. And is there now evidence that this term is being rejected, although for what reason is not clear, by the phenomenologists?

These changes imply a shifting conception of the essential nature of psychology's subject matter. This is not necessarily so. It might as easily be argued that the true nature of that subject matter has not changed. There has been a change in emphasis, a shift in the relative value placed upon different components of this subject matter, or, if you will, a broadening in some respects; but all this gives belated recognition to the fact that no basic change in the conception of psychology's subject matter has taken place. The verbal tag or label attached to that subject matter has changed. But the successive changes in this label reflect only a continuing attempt on the part of psychologists to arrive at a better descriptive term for that which they abstract from the data at hand.

Thus the fundamental reason for the rejection of soul, mind, and consciousness was the fact that, as conceptions abstracted from the raw data, they took on the status of entities, of obscure agencies determining behavior. And this sort of construct was out of harmony with the developing scientific temper of the time. They were not discarded because they were looked upon simply as names for a given class of phenomena. In this respect they might have been discarded later when the emphasis on psychology's data shifted to what was called behavior. Perhaps the longevity of this term, behavior, is due to the fact that it cannot be easily conceived of as an agent or entity. It remains simply a term referring to a group of phenomena. In any other sense it is in no better logical status than was Wundt's "consciousness" or Titchener's "mind."

As we all know, McDougall, for all his being described as a purposivist and interactionist, was the first to use the term, behavior, in the title of a textbook in psychology. True enough, he, as did the man who spat out his first drink of beer, regretted it ever afterward. This regret, for McDougall, stemmed from the fact that behaviorism denied the validity of introspection as a method and hence ignored data which were available to the psychologist through this source. McDougall was thus led to modify his 1912 definition of psychology, as ". . . the positive science of behaviour of living things" (5, p. 19), in such a way as to leave the psychologist room for the use of ". . . the observed facts of experience, facts of his own experience observed introspectively and facts of others' experience described and recorded by them (6, p. 38).

There are few of us who would disagree with the formal definition of psychology as the positive and empirical science of behavior, providing, of course, that the meaning of behavior can be agreed upon. We will return to this question in a moment. More of us would hesitate to accept introspection as a method on a par with objective observation. In a recent historical review, however, Boring (1) says that "introspection is still with us, doing business under various aliases, of which *verbal report* is one." He enumerates other places in which the method is used:

. . . the sensory experience of psychophysics, the phenomenal data of Gestalt psychology, the symbolic processes and intervening variables employed by various behaviorists, the ideas, the manifest wishes, the hallucinations, delusions, and emotions of patients and neurotic subjects, and the many mentalistic concepts which social psychology uses.

In this sense, and in some one or more of these areas, who of us does not use that method of observation? But what is it that we are observing or that the subjects of our experiments are observing? Are they states of consciousness, of a consciousness that is wholly separate, distinct, and independent of bodily activities taking place at the same time? In other words, when we make such use of introspection, are we still operating under a dualistic point of view that has been with us throughout our history? Are we, as Boring seems to be saying in his historical review, simply using the verbal reports, the language responses, as well as behavioral responses as the basis for making consciousness "an inferred construct, a concept as inferential as any of the other psychologist's realities" (5, p. 187)? May it

not be that in the introspective or verbal reports, we are being given an account of the components of an act or bit of behavior that we can not know in any other way? In any other way, that is, except through something the subject, human or animal, does or says? When the clinician observes, either by reading or hearing, what the client sees in the Rorschach Test, when the physiological psychologist observes a human subject discriminating between two brightness values, or a comparative psychologist sees the rat doing the same task, the three of us immediately assume that these several reactions, linguistic or grossly behavioral, are telling us something about what is taking place beyond our ken, simultaneously and as part and parcel of the behavioral manifestations that can be observed from the outside and by an independent observer. In other words, we base our inferences of the inner, subjective side of the activity on these outer, objective components of the act. We need these reports, these revelations of the subjective components of the act, to achieve an understanding of the entire act. We need them even more when the external components of the performance are either absent or present in such a manner as not to be open to our own observation. This is the situation when reasoning, thinking, subtle affective, attitudinal, and motivational processes are under examination and study. True, were we clever enough, we assume that instrumental means would reveal that minute neurophysiological and muscular events were likewise taking place. But lacking these instrumental devices, or even with them, the verbal report or some other aspect of the subject's behavior would be necessary to make our knowledge of the entire performance sure. True enough, the subject's verbal report may not be accurate, it may mislead the investigator, but just so may the handshake or complimentary statement be mistakenly interpreted by the recipient.

This seems to me to be the point at which Titchener, and possibly Boring, have missed something important. The dualism between consciousness or mental process and bodily activity was so deeply entrenched in their thinking that they did not see what introspective observation and theory plainly revealed: that the activity of the organism was not properly divisible into two or three distinct parts, but that the parts constituted a single unitary performance. This unit presented certain phenomena that were observable by an external observer and other phenomena that were observable only by the subject himself.

The act that psychology studies is a unitary act. It is not made up of different kinds of reality that run in parallel lines or courses or that interact with each other. No, the act is a complex totality, composed of elements, parts, or phases of which some are open to the observation of an outsider, with or without instruments, and some can be observed only by the subject and reported in linguistic or other expressive movements. Whether the act is a sensory discrimination, a perceptual reaction, a flight of fancy, or a laborious act of reasoning, these components are present within and through it. It is because of this complexity that we need and use, as Boring has so clearly shown, both objective and subjective observation. Both approaches are necessary if we are to arrive at an understanding of the act or bit of behavior we are examining.

Of course it is true that both approaches are not open to us if there is not a common language between subject and experimenter. Some may seize upon this fact and argue that there is no place in psychology for comparative or animal work since the lack of a common language is here obvious. But remember that the subject's report may not be perfectly correlated with the inner side of his behavior— and the human animal is the only animal we know that may deliberately attempt to mislead the experimenter. Predictions of behavior can be made even though we are not in a position to know all the details of that act. I can predict that my car will start when I twist the key, although I know nothing about the operation of the carburetor or its ignition system. The comparative psychologist must grant that what the subjective side of the animal's behavior may be is unknown to him. But this does not prevent most of us from engaging in a bit of judicious anthropomorphizing.

But now we must come to some conclusion to the question with which we started. What is this "behavior" that the psychologist studies? Can we formulate a conception of behavior, the subject matter of psychology, that will be acceptable to our modern temper? Presumably such a conception should utilize only those criteria that can be referred to behavior itself. That is, the conception should be delineated in terms of the essential properties of behavior and not in terms of some extrabehavioral characteristics. For these criteria or attributes which characterize an act as behavior, I favor the following, with grateful acknowledgment to McDougall, Carr, Tolman, and others who have contributed them: The term *behavior* refers to those activities which exhibit (*a*) spontaneity or autonomy, that is, that are not always or completely controlled by conditions external to the organism itself, (*b*) persistence, (*c*) variability, and (*d*) docility. I would be quite willing to add a fifth characteristic, purpose, but do not do so for two reasons. First, purpose is implied, in any reasonable sense, in the four given; and, second, it might be misunderstood as involving an objectionable brand of teleology.

These, then, are the characteristics, properties, or attributes of those activities that form the subject matter of psychology, that is, behavior. Must they all be present in any given instance, or will the presence of one alone mark the action as behavior? Neither situation may hold. The earmarks need not be present simultaneously, nor does the presence of one alone justify our classifying the act as behavior. In the latter instance, I would argue that somewhere along the line, in the history of the act, the other earmarks have been exhibited. Thus the question might be raised as to the docility of a well learned or habitual performance. To settle such an issue we would ask: "Has the early history of this act exhibited docility?" If so, and to that extent, it qualifies as a bit of behavior. And so we would proceed to apply these criteria to all those actions or activities that present themselves as candidates for psychological study. Those failing to meet the criteria would be excluded; those meeting them would be included.

When I submitted the title for these comments, I proposed to discuss the following question: Does the term "behavior" as used in psychological jargon refer to something we observe, examine, and manipulate in the laboratory or to something abstracted from the observed phenomena? When the subject, or client, responds to an experimental or interview situation, is this response—whether it be partly overt, partly covert, objective or subjective—a bit of behavior; or is it an activity or response possessing characteristics which justify its being a member of a class of phenomena to which the term "behavior" refers?

An analogy may help. The physicist notes and records the readings on his thermometer, his voltmeter, or his pressure gauge. Were we to ask him what he is studying, would he say that he was studying the variation in the readings these instruments exhibit or would he say that he was studying heat, electricity, light, and so on? I think he would say the latter and then add that these terms are the class names or labels for particular groups of phenomena. Any given phenomenon is assigned to this or that category in terms of the characteristics that are held in common with other members of the class.

My contention is that psychology's "behavior" is analogous to the physicist's heat, that the psychologist uses the term to refer to a class of activities that possess certain characteristics, those referred to by the criteria outlined above. This means that "behavior" is an abstraction, not a datum. The data are the specific responses exhibited by the human or animal subject. Some of these specific responses can be classed as "behavior" for and by the psychologist; others presumably exist that do not belong to that class and hence are not data for psychology.

I think that what I am suggesting is not particularly novel in any way. Throughout its his-tory, psychology has continually used such terms as mind, consciousness, adaptation, or adjustive activities to refer to its subject matter. And has not this usage always implied an abstracting of common characteristics from the specific and concrete activities studied? In a more restricted area, are not such terms as learning, retention, intelligence, aptitude, one's perception of his "self," and a host of other terms used in this abstract sense?

References

1. Boring, E. G. A history of introspection. *Psychol. Bull.,* 1953, 50, 169-189.

2. James, W. *Principles of psychology.* Vol. I. New York: Holt, 1890.

3. Johnson, E. On readmitting the mind. *Amer. Psychologist,* 1956, 11, 712-714.

4. McClelland, D. C. The psychology of mental content reconsidered. *Psychol. Rev.,* 1955, 62, 297-302.

5. McDougall, W. *Psychology: The study of behavior.* New York: Holt, 1912.

6. McDougall, W. *Outline of psychology.* New York: Scribner's, 1923.

7. Morgan, C. T. *Introduction to psychology.* New York: McGraw-Hill, 1956.

8. Nuttin, J. Consciousness, behavior, and personality. *Psychol. Rev.* 1955, 62, 349-355.

On readmitting the mind[1]

E. PARKER JOHNSON

This brief essay further illustrates the problem of defining psychology by discussing the validity of the mind as a meaningful psychological concept. The author, who is Dean of the Faculty and Professor of Psychology at Colby College, observes that nonpsychologists are often surprised and confused by their discovery that some psychologists refuse to acknowledge the existence of the mind. Professor Johnson explores the rationale behind this attitude and discusses the difficulties of establishing a scientifically acceptable definition of the mind. He uses examples from the biological sciences to illustrate that definition problems are not unique to psychology, but are a continuing dilemma for all disciplines oriented toward greater precision of meaning.

On discovering that I am a psychologist, people sometimes ask, "What is psychology?" More often, instead of asking, they tell me what it is. "Oh, yes, that's the study of the mind, isn't it?" I usually agree and let it go at that. But the question is not one which should be shrugged off so easily.

The problem of a definition for psychology has bedeviled psychologists for years. Practically everyone who is *not* a psychologist knows that it is the science or study of the mind, and anyone with a dictionary may easily confirm this. He will discover that psychology derives from the Greek words *psyche* and *logos*. *Logos* means word or discourse. From it has developed the English suffix used to denote the doctrine, theory, or science of something or other. *Psyche* refers to a sort of "inner spirit" of things and is translatable either as soul or as mind. With the distinction which has developed between these two English words, the transla-

tion "mind" is employed for its lack of specifically religious connotations. Etymologically then, psychology is certainly the science of the mind.

But, oddly enough, many modern psychologists refuse to accept this definition. Why? It is probably the word science—and their conception of what a science is—that has created the difficulty. To them, indeed to most of us, science is identified with concreteness. The word mind, on the other hand, connotes something different from our bodies and their functions . . . something immaterial, impalpable, quite beyond observation . . . something placed, by very definition, beyond the ken of science which, by *its* definition, is built on the observation of recordable events.

The psychologist understands that what he actually studies is people and their behavior. Thus, during the last fifty years, psychologists have developed a strong reluctance to refer to psychology as the science of the mind. While continuing to make use of this ancient concept as a criterion to determine what is, or what is not, psychology, psychologists have adopted many devious circumlocutions to avoid any reference to the word mind itself. Many protest, indeed, that scientifically speaking there is no such thing as the mind to be studied!

To the nonpsychologist such a remark appears to be utter nonsense; there is certainly a mind, and a glance at the topics covered in

From *American Psychologist*, XI (1956), 712-714. Reprinted by permission of the American Psychological Association and the author.

[1] This argument was first presented before the Maine Psychological Association at its annual meeting on May 21, 1955.

any psychology book shows that psychologists are studying it. Now, as a psychologist, I wish to state that there are certainly many definitions of the mind, either relics of the past or representations of current lay thinking, which are scientifically unacceptable or meaningless; but I would like to go on record as agreeing with the layman's judgment that psychologists are certainly studying the mind, that they neither can nor should get out of it, and that it behooves them to stop exclaiming how insufferable most definitions of mind are and to mention, instead, some definition which they will accept. The question is this: In *what sense of the word mind* may modern psychology be correctly described as the *study of the mind?* And I refuse to accept the answer, "In no sense."

To the problem, then:

In the scientific exploration of the natural world we find that men of scientific habit accept a certain necessary division of labor. Thus, within the unity of science, we find a multiplicity of sciences, each concerned with some roughly demarcated segment of the whole field and each with a special identifying name. Most scientists agree that such divisions and distinctions within science are arbitrary, that the lines are drawn where they are through a combination of historical accident and simple convenience. In many cases the boundaries are but lightly sketched in, but the divisions are real and serve a function. As one moves from physics through physical chemistry to organic chemistry, to biochemistry, to cell physiology and to physiology proper one is aware of the continuity or unity of science but one is also aware of some diversity. One cannot but remark occasional changes in terrain. The borders are, of course, hardest to see when one is nearest to them. Standing on the beach it is hard to say where the land ends and the sea begins, what with the surge and mixture of elements. But proceed far enough in one direction and one is indubitably in the sea while, with a reverse motion, one may reach what is just as certainly the land. Thus the several sciences are defined: so that one may for practical purposes (though in no absolute sense) distinguish between them.

Some sciences are easier to define than others. Astronomy is the study of the stars and of their companions in the sky, with meteorites about the only source of confusion (though when biologists land on Mars and start to interest themselves in forms of life there, we shall have to decide whether their findings represent advances in astronomy or in biology; the best prediction is that the problem will be neatly dodged by the simple founding of a new science of "astrobiology").

Mention of biology leads us to consider the interesting problem biologists have encountered in defining *their* science. Biology is, etymologically, the study of *life*. But what is life? The experience of biologists in their attempts to define life offers a valuable introduction to the problem faced by psychology in defining its field, the mind. While astronomers or geologists can point to certain objects that they are studying—stars, stones, or whatever—neither the biologist's *life* nor the psychologist's *mind* exists in such concrete form. Neither life nor mind may be identified as a "thing." Neither biologist nor psychologist can discover any "object" to study which is not equally available to the physicist or chemist as an object for physical or chemical study and analysis. How, then, *do* the biologists and the psychologists define their scientific fields?

Biologists long since abandoned the notion of a special "vitalistic" ingredient in living things, distinguishing the living from the nonliving. They are willing to allow, in advance of proof, that every event occurring in the process of life very likely occurs in full accordance with physical and chemical principles which apply equally to the living or to the nonliving; and that—no matter what definition of "life" or "living" one chooses—there exist, in all probability, agglomerations of matter in such intermediate stages of physical-chemical organization as will confound the definition. The biologist's problem, then, is not to determine what life *is,* but to state what he will *have it be.* The definition will be selected for its convenience to him in consolidating his science and in making useful generalizations.

In accordance with this principle he lays down criteria: irritability, growth, ability to reproduce, metabolic interchange with the environment, etc. All of these criteria are subject to abandonment or change in the event that other, more useful, criteria should be enunciated with sufficient force and cogency.

There is one restriction on the biologist's

freedom to define: he must not move too far nor too fast. Whatever his definition it must, in application, embrace most of what we commonly call living and rule out most of what we commonly call nonliving; else he would be under obligation to find another name for his concept, and something besides the word *biology,* the science of life, as a name for his discipline.

In some sciences we have observed name changes which have served to warn the layman of the scientist's determination to abandon certain ideas commonly associated with his central enterprise. Students of the heavens calling themselves astronomers were free to take whatever they wished from the lore of the astrologers without inheriting a host of misconceptions as to their aims and endeavors. Chemistry has similarly dissociated itself from alchemy. Within the past half century some psychologists have desired, for like reasons, to throw the *psyche* out of psychology. They have felt that both the Greek *psyche* and the English *mind* were so cluttered with scientifically objectionable connotations that they could no longer be borne. One new name proposed has been that of anthroponomy [2] (a system of laws about man). There is doubt, however, that the lay concept of psychology is so at variance with the scientific that a name change is required. If most people connected psychology with mind-reading and the occult we might, with good conscience, desert the word. The evidence is, however, that most people think psychologists are scientists who study what people do and how they do it, how the world looks to them, and how to help them get along better in it. If this is not the truth it is near enough; and it is hard to see how changing the name of the science would improve anything.

Actually the word *psyche* is no worse a burden than is the word *bios.* The problem of definition, moreover, may be met in much the same way. Biologists have defined living things, but have refused to probe the "essence" of "life." They consider it to have no "essence." So psychologists may decline to grant "mind" any independent existence or "essence," outlining, nevertheless, criteria for determining when an organism is displaying mental behavior—which places it within the purview of psychology.

Recognizing that psychologists may wish to argue about the exact details of the definition (in accordance with our previous statement that such definitions cannot be absolute but must represent working agreements among those in the field) I shall offer not "the" definition but—to make clear the arbitrariness of definition and the latitude of choice—several definitions. Whether they agree with one another or disagree will, of course, depend on how the terms used in the definitions are themselves understood.

We might say, for instance, that we are dealing with mental activity whenever we observe the *adjustment* of individual *organisms* to the *world about them,* or when we study the *responses* of *organisms* to *stimulation* or, for a third try, whenever we are dealing with the *integrated behavior* of *organisms.*

We allow the biologist to conceive of life as embodied in the special *organization* of living matter. Thus he avoids its representation as a "stuff." So we may allow the psychologist to define *mind* as the *organization* of the individual's behavior in his responses or adjustments to the world. To state our definition in its briefest form: *Mind is the organization of behavior.*

It is my belief that the intelligent layman, given a little explanation of the philosophical implications of dualism and a bit of briefing on the methods and limitations of scientific endeavor, would readily concede the advantages, to science, of such a definition of mind. Indeed, he would very likely claim that something like this was what he really meant all along. He would disavow any connection with the impalpable mystic conceptions with which the scientific psychologist has felt himself to be contending. He would tell the psychologist to forget this straw man, that the difference between the lay concept of mind and that of the behavior scientist was merely a matter of speaking. I believe that it is, and that when introducing newcomers to the subject matter of psychology one may perfectly well start in boldly with the statement: Psychology is the science of the mind.

---

[2] W. S. Hunter attempted to popularize this term, beginning with his paper, "General anthroponomy and its systematic problems," *Amer. J. Psychol.,* 1925, 36, 286-302.

The psychology of mental content reconsidered[1]

DAVID C. McCLELLAND

David McClelland, Ph.D., is Professor of Psychology in the Department of Social Relations at Harvard University and was formerly Chairman of the Staff of the Center for Research in Personality at Harvard. He has written six books and approximately sixty articles on personality but is best known for his theory and research on achievement and motivation. His books include *Personality, The Achieving Society,* and *The Roots of Consciousness.*

In this essay Professor McClelland discusses the topic of mental content. He suggests that American psychology has been concerned with understanding the mechanics of how people think and has neglected to study what they think about. The article traces this neglect of mental content to certain historical traditions in the development of American psychology. The author cites examples of how content-oriented research has been used to study the personality and suggests how these techniques might be more widely applied to other areas of psychological investigation.

Psychologists used to be interested in what went on in people's heads. In fact, for thousands of years this was practically all they were interested in. Psychologists from Aristotle to John Stuart Mill were concerned primarily with ideas and associations between ideas, but with the rise of modern scientific psychology we lost interest in ideas, by and large. The history of this development is well known, but let us review it for a moment. The psychology of mental content collapsed in the United States under the impact of two heavy blows. First, introspectionism seemed to run into a dead end. Titchener had argued manfully for a scientific study of the contents of mind, a kind of mental chemistry in which the basic elements would all be discovered and sorted out, but his laboratories simply failed to produce enough data to back up his theoretical position. It was not so much that his position was untenable. It was just that the data collected by the introspectionists did not seem to lead anywhere—to fruitful hypotheses, for example, which would serve to make theoretical sense out of the flux of mental events.

The second blow was even more devastating. It was, of course, the behavioristic revolution. Particularly in the United States, psychologists began to argue that conscious content could never form the basis of a science, whereas behavior could. J. B. Watson led the revolt in the name of scientific objectivity. After all, could you see or touch or feel or record with a machine a thought or a feeling? Now, a muscular contraction—an eye blink, a foot withdrawal, a right turn in a maze—that was something else again. That could be seen and touched and felt and often recorded entirely automatically by an impersonal, mechanical gadget. Here was the stuff of which a real science could be made!

Looking back with the perspective of 30 years we can begin to see why this movement was so appealing. In the first place, it did provide the kind of objectivity, methodologically speaking, that psychology had never had before and it could, therefore, lend real support to psychology's claim that it was a science. Secondly, it fit in with the traditional American

From *Psychological Review,* LXII (1955), 297-302. Reprinted by permission of the American Psychological Association and the author.

[1] This paper was delivered at the Fourteenth International Congress of Psychology in Montreal, June 9, 1954.

pragmatic bias in favor of action rather than thought or feeling which were generally considered to be old-fashioned European concepts. After all, in the United States it is what a man does that counts, not what he says or thinks or feels. This tendency in American psychology is still so prevalent that to many of us prediction of behavior means *only* predicting gross motor behavior rather than predicting thoughts, conflicts, doubts, imaginings, feelings, etc., as reflected in verbal behavior. Thirdly, behaviorism tended to focus attention on problems which were of vital topical interest to a new country in which many of its citizens were attempting to adjust to new ways of life. In fact, adjustment or *learning* became the key concept. And this was natural in a country in which so many immigrants or their children had to give up traditional European ways of behaving for new American habit patterns. It was at this point that psychology became almost exclusively interested in "process variables," in how people went about doing things rather than in what they did. This was the time when Woodworth was stressing that we should rewrite psychology in terms of "ing" words—e.g., perceiving, emoting, thinking, learning, etc. No one was interested in *what* people thought, *what* they perceived, *what* they learned, etc. Instead, we were to be concerned only with the laws which governed the *process* of perceiving, learning, etc.

Even personality and social psychology, which by definition are content-oriented and which, therefore, should have resisted this trend, fell under the spell of this widespread movement. In personality psychology we were primarily interested in self-descriptive inventories in which the subject answered a lot of questions about his aches, pains, and anxieties. But, mind you, we did not look at his answers. We added them up to get a neuroticism score or dominance score or what not. We were not interested even here in *what* he said about himself, in *what* his ideas were. We were only interested in the extent to which his answer contributed to a total score which meant something else. To be sure, an individual clinician sometimes went so far as to look at the actual answers a person had given on a personality inventory, but then, he was not a scientist! In social psychology, too, we managed to get along without much concern with content, although here, too, it was a little difficult. The problem was solved with the help of the attitude concept. An attitude is essentially what I have been calling a process variable. We are interested in *how* attitudes get set up, in how we can measure them, in their consistency, in their rigidity, their generality or specificity, etc.—all process variables. But we are not interested in *what* they are, particularly. Any old attitude will do for our purpose, just as in studying learning, any old task will do for our purpose—a maze, a bar to press, a list of nonsense syllables, or what not. So social psychologists chose as the attitudes to be investigated whatever happened to be of current interest at the moment—e.g., internationalism, feminism, pacifism, race prejudice, and so on. Few if any people thought it was even worth asking which attitudes were the "important" ones to use in describing a person or his culture. Many people probably would have wondered whether such questions really fell within the province of psychology at all.

It is against the background of this widespread social movement in psychology that we can see the beginnings of the projective testing movement as the source of a change in attitude which is finally beginning to be felt today, possibly in large part because of the success of projective tests. But certainly projective testing did not start as a conscious revolt against this interest in process. Quite the contrary. The Rorschach test, as one of the oldest of these new instruments, probably gained as wide acceptance as it did in the United States largely because it became primarily process-oriented. It became concerned with *how* people perceive and only secondarily with *what* they perceive. Quantitative indices could be computed according to how many responses were determined primarily by form, by color, by movement, and the like. Nevertheless, the good clinicians often found that the particular content of the association given by the patient was of value to them in understanding the person. And this has always been the case with a good clinician. He *has* to be interested in *what* his patient thinks as well as in how he thinks it. Even though his formal psychological training gives him very little assistance at this level, he knows that in order to handle this particular person he has to be interested in the patient's ideas.

This, it seems to me, has been the great and continuing contribution of the clinic and the projective test in a time when psychological theorists have talked themselves out of being interested in content altogether. I am reminded here of a comment made to me once by one of my more cynical colleagues who claimed that no new ideas of importance ever appeared in the universities. Usually they appear outside first and then are only gradually claimed by the universities. Certainly if we think for a minute of men like Descartes, Darwin, Freud, or Einstein, there would seem to be something in what he said. And this development seems to be a case in point. The projective testing movement grew up largely *outside* the conservative academic tradition and, finally, because of its clinical success, has managed to dent the calm assurance with which many theoretical psychologists have discarded all problems of mental content.

But to continue with my story: The real change came with the development by Murray and his associates of the Thematic Apperception Test about 20 years ago. Now for the first time we had an instrument in which the primary concern was not form but content. The person interpreting a TAT record must ask such questions as: *What* motives activate this person? *What* conflicts plague him? *What* modes of defense does he adopt? *What* characteristics does the world have for him? No longer are we concerned primarily, as in the Rorschach, with *how* he approaches his task, although some have attempted to analyze the TAT in these terms. To help us in our analyses of such content, we have drawn heavily on psychoanalysis, the one system of content psychology which, isolated in the clinic, survived the mass attack of behaviorism in the laboratory. Murray in his original system of analysis for the TAT attempted to provide us with a much broader vocabulary for the analysis of content, but, by and large, in our analyses we draw upon relatively few general psychoanalytical concepts such as sex, aggression, parent-child relationships, and the like. This, to my way of thinking, is an impoverished set of concepts for dealing with mental content, but it is, nonetheless, the one real and vital one in the United States today.

What evidence is there that this tendency to concern oneself with mental content is of grow-ing influence? In the first place, we must not underestimate the conservative resistance to the belief that such a psychology is possible. Even Freud's generalizations about the importance of certain basic conflicts such as those involved in the Oedipus complex are under constant attack. To some extent the attacks are motivated by the conviction that generalizations about content are really impossible. The argument runs that there are no general concepts which can serve to describe the human situation at *any* place or time in history. What about cultural relativism? After all, individuals differ widely in what they think and so do cultures. Some have an Oedipus complex and some do not. How can we generalize about anything except the process by which individuals arrive at their ideas? The ideas themselves are completely relative. One can perhaps be literary about them, but not scientific. This is the argument and there is no answer to it, except to prove that it can be done fruitfully. Many of us are convinced already, for example, that despite individual and cultural variations, it is a major scientific achievement to have focused attention on the framework of the mother-son relationship as of primary importance in the development of the individual, and to have worked out some of the taxonomy of this and the allied relationship with the father.

Meanwhile, there have been some new developments which would encourage us to believe that perhaps a psychology of content is possible. Take the research report on *The Authoritarian Personality* (1), for example. I would contend that the essential issues raised by this research are issues in the psychology of content. It represents to some extent a fusion of psychoanalytic structural concepts with certain concepts drawn from political ideology. Whether we like the fusion or not does not really matter too much. From the methodological point of view it represents an exciting step forward since its authors have drawn on political ideology as well as psychoanalysis to help explain the structure of personality. When our science has matured to the point where we can draw not only on political ideology, but on economic, religious, esthetic ideologies, and the like, then we will be on the way toward developing a really full-blown psychology of mental content.

Our own research on *The Achievement Mo-*

tive (2) has contributed as much to these conclusions as anything else. We started with the relatively simple task of identifying those types of imagery in a TAT-type record which indicated the presence of a motive to achieve or succeed. After we were able to identify reliably this item of mental content, we were able to select individuals whose thought processes contained a lot of such items and other individuals whose thought processes contained few such items. We were then faced with the question of how these people differed. Do they behave differently? Yes, they do. The ones with a lot of achievement imagery tend to learn faster, to perform better, to set different levels of aspiration, to have a better memory for incompleted tasks, to perceive the world in different terms, etc. Perhaps even more interesting was the question of how they got that way. How is it that some people tend to think more often in achievement terms? We were led back to the mother-son relationship and found that independence training seems to be associated with achievement motivation. That is, those mothers who encouraged their sons to develop independently, to learn their way around by themselves, seemed to have sons with higher achievement motives. But we pushed the question one step further back. How is it that some mothers favor independence training more than others? This raised the question of values, and values raised the question of religious ideology. Then we found that attitudes toward independence training were not randomly distributed through various population subgroups. Instead, Protestant and Jewish parents were much more likely to favor early independence training than were Catholic parents and this, in turn, seemed to fit into the belief systems and emphases of these three religions (3). And if this is so, we can begin to trace some of the details of the connection between Protestantism and the rise of capitalism as originally outlined by Max Weber (5) and R. H. Tawney (4).

So our recent research has led us into the relationships between religious values, independence training, achievement motivation, and economic development. We think we are beginning to discover some connections among these phenomena which can be traced out with a fair degree of scientific confidence. But whether we succeed or not, the point I am trying to make is that by concentrating on one item of mental content, namely achievement imagery, we have opened up a whole new set of problems in social science that can be investigated by psychology.

Now let us pause a minute and try to reconsider what has happened. The "new look" in the study of mental content really involves neither introspection nor projective testing in their pure forms. Instead I prefer to call it "thought sampling," and to use the analogy of the "blood count" from the medical laboratory to explain what I have in mind. Just as we need a sample of blood to make a white cell count, we want a sample of thoughts or ideas to make our imagery counts. In general, we get these samples by asking the subject to write stories to certain cues, usually verbal or visual. Having gotten our thought sample, we have to learn to recognize certain types of imagery, just as the medical technician has to learn to recognize a white blood cell when he sees one. This involves a great deal of preliminary work so that we can define the characteristics of the imagery carefully and then train individuals to recognize what they are looking for. It does require training, but probably no more training than a medical technician needs to be able to distinguish one type of blood cell from another. That is, it does not involve high-level judgment, but is essentially a "pointing" operation which is a little, but not much, more difficult to make than pointing to an animal's right turn in a maze. Watson need not have feared for the objectivity of this kind of analysis. The record is permanent. The same person can look at it again and again, or several people can analyze it. It is quite possible to get a reliable and objective result.

If we put the "new look" in mental content in these general terms, it is immediately clear that we have a number of problems to solve. For example, there is the sampling problem. Under what conditions should we get our thought samples? What cues should we use? Should we get long samples or short samples? What about the subject's set? How does it influence content? Here it becomes obvious that traditional projective testing elicits only a very small segment of the possible types of mental content. To the extent that we stay within the limited framework of the traditional TAT cards, for example, we are bound to have a biased sample of what goes on in a man's mind.

An even more important problem has to do with the decision as to what categories for content analysis we use. This is the heart of the problem, since we will get theoretically meaningful results, or generalizations that hold for a wide variety of situations, only if we choose the right categories to begin with. How does one discover the right categories? The literature of social science is strewn with content analyses of everything from open-ended interviews to "soap operas"—analyses which are purely *ad hoc*—for the immediate practical purpose in hand. I am certainly not arguing for more of this industrious busy work. The categories must be meaningful; they must be related to theory; they must be trans-situational —i.e., applicable to more situations than the one to which they are first applied. It takes inspiration or luck or hard work or something to discover such a category, just as it did in biology to discover what was the most useful of many possible ways to classify blood cells. The only concrete suggestion I have as to how to proceed, which comes from our own experience, is to choose those categories which show significant shifts as a result of experimental operations. Whether this is an unnecessarily restrictive rule, I do not know. At any rate it certainly eliminates many possible categories, and it seems to be roughly the one which the chemists have used in setting up the classification of elements.

This brings us back to Titchener. Looking back with the perspective of history, we can now see that Titchener's structural psychology failed for two reasons. In the first place, the content categories he chose did not turn out to be fruitful. They were not related to experimental operations on the one hand or to other types of behavior on the other. For these or other reasons, they simply did not lead to theoretical development. Therefore they were the wrong categories. In the second place, and this is of major methodological importance, his students categorized their own data. The essence of introspection is that the same person serves both as a source of data and as a categorizer of them. This has an obvious weakness, a weakness which has been perpetuated in self-descriptive personality inventories. It is simply that the subject may have a very imperfect or incorrect idea of what categories his thoughts belong in. This may be because his

categories are different from the ones we as scientists want to use or because he may really misperceive himself. The great contribution that both Freud and the projective testing movement made was that neither asked the subject to pass judgment on his thoughts as they appeared to him. Both simply asked for a sample of those thoughts and then left the categorization process to an outside observer. This was an important methodological advance, the significance of which I think we are only just beginning to appreciate.

If psychologists are to re-enter the field of mental content and start classifying it according to categories of genuine theoretical fruitfulness, I fear they will have to return to disciplines they have long neglected. In the twenties, in the heyday of behaviorism, we were proud that we knew nothing of religion, of art, of history, of economics, or politics (except in a personal, often naive way). We didn't need to know about these things if we were only interested in process variables. We could make our own choice of a task situation—for example, the rat in a maze—and what we found out there about how the rat learned the maze would apply equally well to *all* (including human) learning situations. We could afford to be ignorant of many things that man has thought about. But if the psychology of content develops as I think it will, we shall have to go back to getting a broad, general education. Certainly nothing in my training *as a psychologist* prepared me to handle problems in religious belief systems or economic development. Yet these are typical of the problems which I think will begin to arise increasingly often in the new psychology of content, and we simply cannot afford to be naïve and pretend that research scholars in these fields have nothing to tell us.

If my analysis is correct, we are on the brink of an important new development in psychology. Because of methodological improvements, we are about to take up again some of the problems in mental content that formerly were considered to be an essential part of psychology. And it is my conviction that the projective testing movement is to be thanked for keeping an interest in content alive in an era when most theoretical psychologists were otherwise occupied, and for providing us with the methodological advance that enabled us to escape from the blind alley into which introspection had led us.

References

1. Adorno, T. W., Frenkel-Brunswik, Else, Levinson, D. J., & Sanford, R. N. *The authoritarian personality*. New York: Harper, 1950.

2. McClelland, D. C., Atkinson, J. W., Clark, R. A., & Lowell, E. L. *The achievement motive*. New York: Appleton-Century-Crofts, 1953.

3. McClelland, D. C., Rindlisbacher, A., & deCharms, R. Religious and other sources of attitudes toward independence training. In D. C. McClelland (Ed.), *Studies in motivation*. New York: Appleton-Century-Crofts, 1955. Pp. 389-397.

4. Tawney, R. H. *Religion and the rise of capitalism*. New York: Harcourt, 1926.

5. Weber, M. *The Protestant ethic*. (Trans. by Talcott Parsons.) New York: Scribner's, 1930.

2

SOME PERSPECTIVES ON HUMAN MOTIVATION

The task of trying to explain what makes man behave as he does has long been a burdensome one for philosophers, psychologists, sociologists, and other behavioral scientists. Many persons define this task as understanding human motivation. However, if you ask different psychologists what characteristics of behavior suggest that a person is motivated, you are very likely to get different answers. This is not surprising when one realizes that psychologists base their ideas on many different kinds of observations. An inference based on evidence originating from the psychoanalyst's couch is likely to vary considerably from ideas emanating from the observation of a white rat solving a maze. Nevertheless, even hypotheses derived from such divergent sources can be consistent. The essential point is that motivation is an inference based on the observation of behavior. As such, it falls into the category of educated guesses we previously labeled *constructs*. In this section we shall review some of the different constructs that have been suggested to explain motivation, indicate specific difficulties and sources of disagreement psychologists have encountered in using these constructs and, finally, document a few particular viewpoints in greater detail.

One of the most fundamental approaches to the analysis of motivation is to examine it from the standpoint of its source. The basis for motivation can be located *within* the organism or *outside* the organism. When motivation is described as originating from within the organism, this situation is usually described in terms of a *drive state* which impels the organism to action. Psychologists who attribute the primary responsibility for motivation to some aspect of the environment outside the organism generally refer to these sources as *incentives*. The difference between these two basic orientations has been simply and clearly described by Bolles (1967), who states: "Drives push and incentives pull; the two complement each other in providing a motivational explanation of behavior. The question is how much of motivation is push and how much is pull" (p. 332). Of the two approaches, the concept of drive has received more diversified and detailed attention in the psychological literature. Typically, the concept of drive has been associated with the idea of reduction in drive as the basis of reward. Let us review some of the different ideas that have been offered, using drive-reduction as the basis for explaining motivation.

All the drive-reduction theories share a

simple and appealing strategy. First, the individual is assumed to have certain internal tensions, usually based on physiological needs, which require reduction. Second, the individual is motivated to behave in ways which will effectively reduce these tensions. Third, tension reduction results in the organism's achieving pleasure, relief, or some other form of positive experience. The greater the amount of tension, the more motivated an individual will be to find appropriate outlets for the tension. Although the basic idea of drive-reduction is clear enough, its advocates disagree on several issues, such as the nature of the drives, the number of drives, and the kinds of behavior involved. For example, in the first case, we find some psychologists emphasizing the purely biological nature of the drives (e.g., hunger), while others expand the concept to include social phenomena, such as achievement. Still others advocate the inclusion of emotional experiences like fear. In terms of the number of drives we find relatively short lists which include only the basic physiological needs and more lengthy lists of perhaps several hundred drives. Finally, the drive-reduction model has been used to account for various kinds of behavior from simple learning experiences to the more complex processes involved in personality development. The specific behaviors which psychologists investigate or discuss are often only reflections of the particular interests of the individuals studying them. As an illustration, Dollard and Miller (1950), two of the best-known and influential drive-reductionists, have clearly demonstrated the importance of learning in personality formation. Their research has shown that motivational constructs developed on the basis of observing one kind of behavior clearly have relevance for other types of behavior. Thus, it would be a misleading oversimplification to assume that there is no overlap between the motivational principles underlying different kinds of behavior.

Despite its well-established stature as an explanatory principle, the drive-reduction model has been challenged from several points of view. Typically, the challenge has appeared in the form of behavioral observations which appear to be incompatible with a drive-reduction explanation. Festinger (1954) has noted that even casual observation reveals that people exert a great deal of energy in an attempt to

find out more about the world in which they live. While this behavior might be more conspicuous in children, it is equally apparent in adults, particularly when they are placed in an unfamiliar situation. Technically, we usually refer to this behavior as curiosity or exploratory behavior. The same kinds of observations have been made about animals. For example, monkeys will learn to open the door of an opaque cage just to see what is outside (Butler & Miller, 1954). Similarly, rats will consistently choose a path leading to a complex maze rather than one leading to a dead end (Montgomery, 1955). From the opposite direction, interesting changes in behavior occur when the opportunity for sensory contact with the environment is minimized or reduced. Heron (1957) found that sensory-deprived college students increased their effort to obtain stimulation. Deprived of the usual amount of sensory stimulation, college students willingly listened to senseless conversation and volunteered to take dull psychological tests. Their thinking processes showed a marked decline and few of the students could tolerate the situation for more than a few days despite excellent care and pay for participating.

It is important to note that this research by itself does not constitute incontrovertible proof against a drive-reduction explanation. On the contrary, some psychologists have interpreted the results of these experiments as evidence for an exploratory drive which exists independently of the other physiological drives (Berlyne, 1960). However, White (1959), after a detailed review of the literature, has pointed out some of the serious disadvantages of considering exploration as a drive in the same sense that we talk about physiological drives. As an alternative to the drive-reduction explanation of exploratory behavior, White (1959) has suggested that the organism is motivated to achieve *competence,* which he defines as the "organism's capacity to interact effectively with its environment" (p. 297). According to White, competence is learned in man and the higher animals but is inborn in the lower animals. In this view, man's active behavior results from either inactivity or mild stimulation from the environment rather than from the need to reduce some drive-producing tension.

Another source of evidence which raises

questions of the drive-reduction hypothesis stems from experiments that provide the organism with a choice between a drive-reducing and non-drive-reducing source of stimulation. As an illustration, Harlow (1958), in his experiments on the development of love in infant monkeys, found that baby monkeys preferred to cling to a soft, cloth-covered mother-surrogate rather than hug a metal wire mother-surrogate even though the monkeys had been fed from the wire mothers. The monkeys spent only as much time on the wire mother-surrogate as was required by the feeding. In another experiment, Sheffield and Roby (1954) demonstrated that food-deprived rats learned to perform a task when the reward consisted of a sweet-tasting but nonnutritive saccharine solution. Using sexual behavior as a means of studying motivation, Sheffield, Wulf, and Backer (1951) and Kagan (1955) found that male rats were able to learn when they were rewarded by being allowed to copulate with a female rat even though the male rats were not allowed to reach ejaculation. Although the male rats learned faster when ejaculation was allowed, the findings still suggest that motivation can exist in the absence of physiological drive satisfaction.

A different source of evidence challenging the drive-reduction model has come from psychologists studying brain functioning. Several theorists have hypothesized that man has an arousal mechanism in his brain which activates him in the absence of high drive states (Duffy, 1957; Hebb, 1955; Malmo, 1957). Destruction or malfunction of this neurological arousal mechanism in animals leads to a marked reduction in both activity and responsivity (Lindsley, 1957). Other research in this area has led to the postulation of "pleasure centers" in the brain which produce prolonged and heightened activity in response to electrical stimulation. Hungry rats will work harder to obtain mild electrical stimulation of their brain than they will to obtain food. In some cases, the animals will continue bar-pressing activity until they reach a state of total exhaustion (Olds, 1956; Olds & Milner, 1954). These findings suggest the possibility of additional explanations for motivation and indicate the undesirability of maintaining a drive-reduction model exclusively.

When one tries to understand human behavior, the question of motivation becomes even more difficult to answer because the behavior itself is more complex and, consequently, harder to study. Since many human activities are not easily investigated in the laboratory, it is often necessary to make inferences on the basis of information which is crude by comparison with laboratory standards of precision. As the scientist moves further away from his laboratory, he can be less sure of the accuracy of his observations. Personality theorists and applied psychologists often defend the adequacy of their formulations by citing the need to deal with the important practical problems of everyday living before the results of the slow research process become available. In their attempt to account for the motivation of human behavior, personality theorists, clinical psychologists, and psychiatrists have on occasion been the objects of extensive criticism from some of their colleagues because of their willingness to speculate about the motives underlying human behavior. These speculations, although not always models of scientific caution, have stimulated much useful research. Because of the level at which they operate, personality theorists and researchers must deal with relatively large and complex units of behavior that defy detailed analysis. As a result, students of personality are often interested in and frustrated by problems that are of less concern to other psychologists investigating motivation. Let us consider a few of these problems.

One of the optimistic assumptions made by many psychologists is that findings from the laboratory can be applied to the behavior that occurs outside the laboratory. If this assumption is true, there are two implications. First, we should be able to generalize the findings based on one area of research to another. Second, we should be able to use principles that explain one type of behavior to explain a different kind of behavior. There is reason to believe that neither of these implications is completely accurate. Consider the first, generalizing from one area of research to another. Bolles (1967) gives reason for caution by citing the empirical work of the ethologists. These scientists, who study animal behavior by observing it in its natural habitat, have consistently documented the fact that much animal behavior is specific to a particular species. According to Bolles (1967): "We cannot expect the psychology of the rat to apply immediately to the stickleback, or to the jackdaw, or to man. The psychologist, with his great haste to generalize, can learn a valuable lesson from the ethologist's respect for the diversity of behavior" (p. 102). This comment raises serious questions about the utility of many of the research findings from animal research for the understanding of human motivation. It clearly counsels caution in drawing conclusions about man from the study of animals. A more detailed discussion of this issue as it relates to sexual behavior appears in the article by Hardy.

The practice of generalizing from one kind of behavior to another is also questionable. It has not been established that the same motivational constructs can account for different behaviors. As Hall and Lindzey (1957) point out, personality theorists differ considerably in their estimates of the number of motives that influence man's total behavior. Some theorists speculate that there are many motives, and some say there are only a few basic motives. Specifically, the theories of Allport, Cattel, Lewin, Murphy, and Murray, among others, all emphasize the multiplicity of man's motivation. Freud, Jung, Adler, Rogers, and Sullivan, on the other hand, discuss many fewer motivational variables. While each theorist cites evidence to support his particular point of view, our present state of knowledge is much too incomplete to reach any firm decisions about the correctness of the theories.

The issue of conscious versus unconscious motivation has been debated by psychologists ever since Freud suggested that the major determinants of behavior lie outside of awareness. Whether or not man is aware of the reasons for his behavior has been one of the most important and controversial issues in the study of human motivation. Most psychologists agree that at times we do things that we are not aware of. However, not all psychologists accept the idea that there is an unconscious part of the mind which contains our "real" motives. The evidence to date, both from the laboratory and clinic, is mixed, and there does not appear to be any final resolution to the argument in the near future.

The question of inborn versus acquired motives is another problem area. Unfortunately, many lay persons are still under the misconception that certain individuals behave as they do because "they were born that way." Despite its popular appeal, the attempt to explain human motivation by reducing it to innate or inherited characteristics is a gross oversimplification. Most psychologists today agree that the interaction of heredity and learning must be taken into consideration in understanding man's behavior, and the issue of heredity versus environment is largely of historical significance only.

Finally, clinical psychologists have been particularly interested in the various forms of maladaptive and antisocial behavior. Most personality theorists have made some attempt to account for the factors leading to personality disorder and socially unacceptable behavior, and some have been criticized for basing too much of their theory on the observation of pathological behavior. One of the most frequent criticisms of psychologists who deal with behavior disorders is that they too readily generalize their impressions about the underlying causes of behavior. It is certainly true that the observation of persons with behavior disorders may provide a misleading basis for understanding the motivation of healthy persons. Unfortunately, psychologists, like policemen, tend to be sought out only by people in trouble, actual or imagined. Persons without difficulties seldom seek the services of psychologists or psychiatrists.

Our introductory discussion of the theory and research on motivation has been, of necessity, incomplete. The papers following are also incomplete in their coverage. They are intended to reflect some of the questions that have been raised about motivation and some of the solutions that have been offered. They are not representative of the entire field and do not support a particular point of view. On the contrary, they have been selected to illustrate a few of the different approaches to the problem and to raise questions about a fundamental area of human behavior.

References

Berlyne, D. E. *Conflict, arousal, and curiosity.* New York: McGraw-Hill, 1960.

Bolles, R. C. *Theory of motivation.* New York: Harper, 1967.

Butler, R. A. & H. M. Alexander. Daily patterns of visual exploratory behavior in the monkey. *J. comp. physiol. Psychol.,* 1955, 48, 247-249.

Dollard, J. & N. E. Miller. *Personality and psychotherapy: An analysis in terms of learning, thinking, and culture.* New York: McGraw-Hill, 1950.

Duffy, E. The psychological significance of the concept of "arousal" or "activation." *Psychol. Rev.,* 1957, 64, 265-275.

Festinger, L. Motivations leading to social behavior. In M. R. Jones (Ed.), *Nebraska symposium on motivation 1954.* Lincoln: University of Nebraska Press, 1954, 191-219.

Hall, C. S. & G. Lindzey. *Theories of personality.* New York: Wiley, 1957.

Harlow, H. F. The nature of love. *Amer. Psychologist,* 1958, 12, 673-685.

Hebb, D. O. Drives and the CNS (Conceptual nervous system). *Psychol. Rev.,* 1955, 62, 243-254.

Heron, W. The pathology of boredom. *Scientific Amer.,* 1957, 196, 52-56.

Kagan, J. Differential reward value of incomplete and complete sexual behavior. *J. comp. physiol. Psychol.,* 1955, 48, 59-64.

Lindsley, D. B. Psychophysiology and motivation. In M. R. Jones (Ed.), *Nebraska symposium of motivation 1957.* Lincoln: University of Nebraska Press, 1957, 44-105.

Malmo, R. B. Anxiety and behavior arousal. *Psychol. Rev.,* 1957, 64, 276-287.

Montgomery, K. C. The relation between fear induced by novel stimulation and exploratory behavior. *J. comp. physiol. Psychol.,* 1955, 48, 254-260.

Myers, A. & N. E. Miller. Failure to find a learned drive based on hunger; evidence for learning motivated by "exploration." *J. comp. physiol. Psychol.,* 1954, 47, 428-436.

Olds, J. Pleasure centers in the brain. *Scientific Amer.,* 1956, 195, 105-116.

Olds, J. & P. Milner. Positive reinforcement produced by electrical stimulation of septal area and other regions of the rat brain. *J. comp. physiol. Psychol.,* 1954, 47, 419-427.

Sheffield, F. D., Wulf, J. J. & R. Backer. Reward value of copulation without sex drive reduction. *J. comp. physiol. Psychol.,* 1951, 44, 3-8.

Sheffield, F. D. & T. B. Roby. Reward value of a non-nutritive sweet taste. *J. comp. physiol. Psychol.,* 1950, 43, 471-481.

White, R. W. Motivation reconsidered: the concept of competence. *Psychol. Rev.,* 1959, 66, 297-333.

Man has no "killer" instinct

GEOFFREY GORER

One of the most frightening aspects of human behavior is man's tendency to destroy himself and others. Observers of human nature do not disagree about the evidence of man's capacity for aggressive behavior, but they do argue about the reasons for it. At one extreme are theorists like Freud who argue that man has an inherent, biological tendency toward self-destruction which he must learn to control. Other more optimistic motivational theorists deny any such inborn tendency and attribute man's aggressive behavior to the effects of frustration, learning, or provocation. In this article,

Dr. Gorer, a British social anthropologist who has written books on American, Russian, and English character, reviews the historical and anthropological evidence of man's aggressive and peace-loving behavior. He describes some common characteristics of societies who do not exhibit any signs of hostility, and challenges the view that man's aggressive behavior is motivated by a "killer" instinct.

One of the most persistent and widespread beliefs about "human nature" held by men of goodwill in most of the advanced societies in the world is that human beings are "naturally" peaceful and gentle, considerate of their fellow human beings, and unwilling to hurt or kill them save under the (assumedly) exceptional conditions of war.

This belief in the essential gentleness of "human nature" can only be maintained by a willful blindness that refuses to recognize the evidence which history, social anthropology, the daily newspapers, and television so constantly provide of man's willingness to hurt and kill his fellows, and to take pride and pleasure in so doing.

In recent months we have read detailed accounts and seen gruesome pictures of Ibos and Hausas gleefully slaughtering one another in Nigeria, of massacres of Indonesians and Chinese in Java and other islands of the archipelago, of Chinese youngsters with red armlets self-righteously humiliating their elders, not to mention both sides in Vietnam. If we try to console ourselves by claiming that most of these slaughters and humiliations were the acts of people who were not civilized and not Christian, this consolation should be short-lived. The Boers and white Rhodesians claim Christian justification for the ill-treatment of their fellow citizens with darker skins; the pictures of the school at Grenada, Miss., are surely not forgotten; and no recorded "uncivilized" nation has equaled the systematic humiliation and slaughter practiced by Christian Germany and her allies a bare generation ago.

All known societies make a distinction between murder—the killing of a member of one's own group—and the killing of outsiders. We can understand murder for jealousy, or gain, or safety, however much we reprobate and punish it; we think it "rational." But when somebody kills without a "rational" motive— nurses in a dormitory, students from a university tower, policemen in a street—we are puzzled, disturbed, and fascinated. The murder of eight nurses or three policemen will hold our attention over longer periods and with more intensity than the slaughter of masses of Javanese.

Contemporary psychological science is at a loss to account for people killing one another without a "rational" motive, according to our standards; an implicit hypothesis in all Western thinking, both scientific and popular, is that man has built-in instincts against killing except under extreme provocation. When people in our own societies kill without a "good reason" we tend to use the term "psychopath"; but this is really a scientific-sounding confession of ignorance and impotence.

Sometimes this pseudo-explanation is applied to killers by other societies, but more frequently the Malayan term "running amok" is used. In Malaya, and some other societies, individuals may suddenly start killing strangers, and amok is the Malayan term for this kind of behavior. This is, however, a description, not an explanation.

Some people reject the hypothesis that man is naturally peaceable and instead, invoke the hypothesis of a "killer" instinct as an aspect of man's hereditary endowment. This "instinct" is held to be normally under strong restraint in "civilized societies" but capable of erupting in "psychopathic" individuals and nearer the surface in "savage" societies. Were there evidence for such an "instinct" it would offer a sort of explanation for the joy of killing, for which there is such plentiful evidence; but I will argue that this is an unnecessary hypothesis.

The most important statement, almost without question, about this aspect of human nature made in this century is that contained in the recent book of the ethologist Konrad Lorenz, translated into English under the title, "On Aggression." He shows that all the carnivores, the mammals which kill other species for their food, have innate inhibitions (instincts, if the term be preferred) against killing members of their own species, with two exceptions—rats and men. The animals with potentially lethal teeth, claws, or horns can be automatically stopped from pressing an attack on a fellow member of the species by signs of submission, either flight or some physical analogue to raising the hands or showing the white flag. Once the species-specific signs of submission are made, the attacker automatically halts; he literally *cannot* kill his defeated rival.

Dr. Lorenz argues that there is an evolutionary connection between the larger carnivores' lethal physical equipment and the innate inhibitions against using this physical equipment on fellow members of the same species. In comparison, man is physically ill-equipped;

his teeth and nails are not adapted to killing large animals of other species; and even his strong and clever hands could seldom be used on healthy beasts. It has indeed been argued that very early man, away from the seacoasts, relied on carrion for his protein. Since man is so physically ill-equipped for killing, he did not acquire the built-in inhibitions against killing other men as part of the evolutionary protection of the species, as wolves or tigers did for their co-specifics. And then he invented weapons.

To avoid confusion, it should be emphasized that for all carnivores, including man, killing other species of animals for food is innately of a different nature from killing members of the same species for rivalry or jealousy or pleasure. In animals, there is no connection between hunting and ferocity toward members of their own species; ethology gives no support to the arguments of tender-minded human beings that man would be less ferocious if he abstained from eating meat.

The Latin proverb, *homo homini lupus*— man is a wolf to man—has been taken over by nearly every society which derives customs, laws, or language from ancient Rome. This is a libel on the wolf, which is a gentle animal with other wolves. Ethologically more appropriate would be *homo homini Mus rattus*— man is a rat to man—for, exceptionally among carnivores, rats do sometimes kill other rats. In his mating and child-rearing patterns, in his vision, and in some other aspects, man resembles birds more than he does other mammals; but in his treatment of his own species there is an uncomfortably close analogy with rats.

Rats live in packs or hordes; and (still following Dr. Lorenz) they do not fight seriously with, much less kill, members of the same pack. But they are quite merciless to members of alien packs; they kill them slowly and painfully and (if one wishes to be anthropomorphic) they seem to get pleasure from so doing. They share our lack of built-in inhibitions against killing members of the same species.

The analogy with human beings is almost total. Human beings also live in packs (in most cases the pack is the society), and the killing of other members of the pack is always forbidden (save, occasionally, under carefully defined rules) and typically subject to very severe sanctions; but this ban and these sanctions do not usually apply to members of other packs. As is well known, very many primitive tribes have only a single word to designate members of the tribe and human beings; they alone are fully human, members of other packs are (so to speak) subhuman, and killing them is not murder. This primitive type of rat-thinking is never far below the surface, even among the civilized and sensitive.

Where human beings differ from rats is in their very varying definitions of who shall be included within the pack. Usually, the pack is the society or tribe, people who speak the same language (typically unique to the tribe) and between whom real or suppositious bonds of kinship can be traced; but there are variants in both directions.

The smallest packs known to me are those described by Dr. and Mrs. Ronald M. Berndt, who studied four contiguous language groups in the Eastern Highlands of New Guinea. Here the people one should not kill are certain specified kinfolk and a few relations of one's wife or wives. Everyone else, irrespective of ancestry or language, was fit prey for the "deadly game" of death, for only by killing can a man earn power and prestige. The dead were eaten and, in the case of women, raped either before or after death.

The only reason why these packs had not exterminated one another before the Australians pacified the area a bare decade ago is that they practiced a policy of preservation of human game. They seldom killed more than they could eat, and left the temporarily weak in peace to breed. The gleeful, guiltless accounts that Dr. and Mrs. Berndt gathered from the participants in these orgies of slaughter, cannibalism, and rape read like a nightmare vision of human savagery.

New Guinea also contains one of the relatively few tribes described by anthropologists in which the joy of killing seems to be completely absent. These are the Arapesh, studied by Dr. Margaret Mead and Dr. Reo Fortune. They will be discussed in more detail subsequently.

For most of humanity, the tribe is the unit within which killing is considered murder, and outside which, killing may be a proof of manhood and bravery, a pleasure, and a duty. Such killing may be done by individuals—headhunters, scalp-collectors, as part of a vendetta or raid—or by groups; in the latter case the killing is called "warfare." The differences in quality and scope between tribal warfare and modern war between nation-states are so great that it might be useful if different words were used for the two activities.

The nation-state was invented after the Neolithic revolution, less than 10,000 years ago; and this is a very short period in man's evolutionary history. One of the advantages of the nation-state was that it greatly extended the area within which killing would be murder; a number of tribes were brought under the same law and equally protected from mutual slaughter. This amalgamation is not now an easy one, as the sad condition of contemporary Nigeria or Indonesia demonstrates; and it probably was no less difficult in the past. There are no reliable contemporary records of the establishment of the first nation-states, mostly along the great rivers of Asia and North Africa; by the time adequate historical records commence, a dominant group had succeeded in preserving peace among the component tribes. The pack was successfully extended to include and protect most of the inhabitants of a given geographical area, even though slaves and captives were usually excluded.

The nation-state is really the last successful human invention for extending the size of the pack, within which killing is murder. In the past 4,000 years a number of religions have been founded which would include all believers inside the pack; but no religion has commanded worldwide allegiance; and regularly the outcasts, infidels, untouchables, heathen, or heretics could all be humiliated or killed with added pleasure and self-righteousness, because they were members of the devil's pack.

The founders of the great world religions, Gautama Buddha, Jesus, Lao-Tzu, Mohammed, all seem to have striven for a worldwide brotherhood of man; but none of them could develop institutions which would include the enemy, the unbeliever, and give him the same protection from anger, hatred, and the lust for killing which they decreed within their own congregations.

Within the last century and a half, various millennial ideologies—democracy, Socialism, the Communist internationals, the United Nations—have taken over the goal of the

traditional religions: the establishment of a worldwide brotherhood of man, a single pack. They have been no more successful than their predecessors in protecting the enemy, the unbeliever, from the horrible results of righteous anger.

In recent centuries, most men of goodwill have at least paid lip service to the ideal of a universal brotherhood with equal protection for all, whatever might be their actual behavior or that of their compatriots. But this century has seen a most sinister recrudescence of rat-pack ideology, in which human status is denied to all persons who do not share one's hypothetical ancestry or visible skin color: Fascism, Nazism, white supremacy, black power, all justify hatred and contempt for those outside the pack; and recent history shows how easily, how very easily, this justified hatred and contempt develop into humiliation, torture, and killing.

The evidence could be endlessly multiplied to demonstrate that man, as a species, has no inhibitions against killing his fellow men who do not belong to the same pack, however the pack may be defined, and often gets intense pleasure and a sense of pride from so doing. But to admit this is not the same as positing a "killer" instinct as part of man's hereditary endowment. There is no logical reason for hypothesizing such an instinct, and some arguments, to be advanced shortly, against doing so.

Because men have no innate instinctual inhibitions against hurting and killing other members of their species, this offers some human beings a potential source of intense pleasure, as do incest, homosexuality, and other sexual deviations. Man has no built-in inhibitions against these sources of pleasure either; did he possess them, laws would be unnecessary. Whether any of these pleasures will be sought, how frequently, and by whom, depends on the values of a specific society at a given time and the vicissitudes of individual lives.

Because man can and does gain intense pleasure from humiliating, hurting, and killing his fellows, the speculative novels of the Marquis de Sade are extremely important documents, whatever their literary qualities. Save in a directly sexual situation (when he relished flagellation), de Sade was an affectionate, humane, and very courageous man. In his 13-year-long solitary confinement he looked without flinching into the deepest recesses of his unconscious fantasies and reported, in fictional form, the pleasures to be derived from the unfettered exercise of power over one's fellow men and women.

De Sade linked these pleasures with the pleasures of sex; this was the only metaphor which contemporary science made available to him, and it was congenial to his temperament. Even so, there are many episodes in the novels when power is used for its own sake—power to humiliate, hurt, or kill—without any overt sexual gratification. De Sade wished to portray "the spasms of man's loathsome heart and fearful passions" because he was convinced that only by acknowledging the truth about human nature, as he saw it, could a safe and just society be built.

Classical psychoanalysis has in good part confirmed de Sade's pessimistic diagnosis of "man's loathsome heart." Freud always maintained the central position in his theory of the Oedipus complex; and the little Oedipus had murder in his heart, the killing of his father —a point which many contemporary psychoanalysts tend to gloss over. According to the findings of the late Melanie Klein and her followers, the inchoate hatred and rages of very young children produce wishes which, when translated into verbal metaphors, parallel the fantasies of de Sade: cannibalism, poisoning, evisceration, castration, murder.

The history of civilized nations in the century and a half since de Sade's death also confirms his pessimistic diagnosis of human behavior. Although he placed no bounds on his imagination, we have been witnesses to far greater horrors than de Sade could dream of; man can be an even more savage monster than he guessed.

It is possible that, had de Sade's diagnosis of human potentialities been taken consistently into account, the fanatics, torturers, and murderers would have had less impunity in the indulging of their fearful passions.

There are, however, a few rays of hope, a few societies where men seem to find no pleasure in dominating over, hurting, or killing the members of other societies, where all they ask is to be at peace and to be left in peace. These societies are, of course, small, weak, technologically backward, and reside in inaccessible country; only so could they survive the power-seeking of their uninhibited neighbors.

Among these gentle societies are the Arapesh of New Guinea, mentioned earlier; the Lepchas of Sikkim in the Himalayas (whom I studied); and, most impressive of all, the pygmies of the Ituri rain-forest in the Congo, studied by Colin Turnbull. These small societies (there are several others), living in the most inaccessible deserts and forests and mountains of four continents, have a number of traits in common, besides the fact that they do not dominate over, hurt, or kill one another or their neighbors, though they possess the weapons to do so. Many of them, including the pygmies and the Lepchas until a couple of generations ago, rely almost exclusively on hunting for their protein food.

What seem to me the most significant common traits in these peaceful societies are that they all manifest enormous gusto for concrete physical pleasures—eating, drinking, sex, laughter—and that they all make very little distinction between the ideal characters of men and women, particularly that they have no ideal of brave, aggressive masculinity.

Men and women have different primary sexual characteristics—a source of endless merriment as well as more concrete satisfactions—and some different skills and aptitudes. No child, however, grows up with the injunctions, "All real men do . . ." or "No proper woman does . . . ," so that there is no confusion of sexual identity: no cases of sexual inversion have been reported among them. The model for the growing child is of concrete performance and frank enjoyment, not of metaphysical symbolic achievements or of ordeals to be surmounted. They do not have heroes or martyrs to emulate or cowards or traitors to despise; their religious life lacks significant personalized gods and devils; a happy, hard-working, and productive life is within the reach of all.

As far as the history of these small tribes can be reconstructed, they have always chosen to retreat into ever more inaccessible country rather than stand their ground and fight with invaders. There is no reason to suppose that their psychological or physiological potentialities are different from those of their more aggressive neighbors, but their values certainly are; for them peace and the absence of quarreling and jealousy are far more important than a reputation for bravery and virility. And while the tribes are not broken up, it is likely that these values will continue to prevail. When the tribes are broken, individuals, unsupported by the traditional ethics, might easily revert to rat-pack mentality. Save that they have so far survived, these small tribes have not been conspicuously successful in the struggle for existence and terrain against more ruthless neighbors. Nevertheless, they may offer a paradigm of ways to diminish the joy of killing in the uninhibited human race.

By contrast, the cannibals in the New Guinea Highlands have a highly aggressive ideal of masculinity; and so, in general, do all the peoples who prize the martial virtues and self-righteously kill their enemies or their "inferiors." The New Guinea Highlanders frankly enjoy sex, especially if it approximates to rape; but many other martial societies repudiate all sensual pleasure as unworthy of a "real man." If our gods and heroes are killers—Lords of Hosts, warriors, successful revolutionaries—and if masculinity is demonstrated by the willingness to give and take "punishment," then the joy of killing is always likely to re-emerge.

It seems possible that the youth international, which has developed, nearly the whole world over, in the last generation, has inarticulately sensed the necessity to redefine the concepts of "a real man" and "a true woman" if we are not to destroy ourselves completely. The long hair, dandified dress, and pleasantly epicene features (which so infuriate their elders) are a physical repudiation of the ideal of aggressive masculinity which has been traditional in all their societies in recent generations, and which is still maintained by the conventional and the neo-Fascists (white supremacists, Empire loyalists, Birchites, and the like) in the same societies.

Even idiotic slogans such as "Make love, not war" (as if the two activities had ever been incompatible!) and the use of drugs make the same point. Mankind is safer when men seek pleasure than when they seek the power and the glory.

If the members of the youth international—the beats and the swingers, the *provos* and the *stilyagi*—maintain the same scale of values and the same sex ideals 20 years hence when they themselves are middle-aged and parents, then they may, just possibly, have produced a permanent change in the value systems and sex roles of their societies, which will turn the joy of killing into an unhappy episode of man's historic past, analogous to human sacrifice, which ascribed joy in killing to the gods also.

The attempts to devise a social unit more inclusive than the nation-state, a brotherhood of man, have all been unsuccessful to date. It is just possible that the youth international, with its emphasis on shared sensual pleasure and its repudiation of the ideal of truculent "manliness," may succeed where the grandiose schemes of idealists have always failed. For man has no "killer" instinct; he merely lacks inhibitions.

A theory of human motivation

ABRAHAM H. MASLOW

Abraham Maslow, Ph.D., is a past president of the American Psychological Association and former chairman of the Psychology Department at Brandeis University, where he is presently Professor of Psychology. He is the author of more than eighty articles on research and theory in psychology, and his books include *Motivation and Personality; Toward a Psychology of Being; Religions, Values and Peak Experiences; Eupsychian Management: A Journal;* and *The Psychology of Science: A Reconnaissance.*

In this selection Professor Maslow challenges theories of motivation which are based entirely on principles of physiological drive reduction and presents an alternative theory. He describes most people as motivated by a hierarchy of needs but suggests that this sequence can be altered by an individual's life circumstances. The article questions the validity of theories of motivation derived exclusively from laboratory experiments with animals and describes some of the limitations inherent in generalizing from animal to human behavior.

I. Introduction

In a previous paper (13) various propositions were presented which would have to be included in any theory of human motivation that could lay claim to being definitive. These conclusions may be briefly summarized as follows:

1. The integrated wholeness of the organism must be one of the foundation stones of motivation theory.

2. The hunger drive (or any other physiological drive) was rejected as a centering point or model for a definitive theory of motivation. Any drive that is somatically based and localizable was shown to be atypical rather than typical in human motivation.

3. Such a theory should stress and center itself upon ultimate or basic goals rather than partial or superficial ones, upon ends rather than means to these ends. Such a stress would imply a more central place for unconscious than for conscious motivations.

4. There are usually available various cultural paths to the same goal. Therefore conscious, specific, local-cultural desires are not as fundamental in motivation theory as the more basic, unconscious goals.

5. Any motivated behavior, either preparatory or consummatory, must be understood to be a channel through which many basic needs may be simultaneously expressed or satisfied. Typically an act has *more* than one motivation.

6. Practically all organismic states are to be understood as motivated and as motivating.

7. Human needs arrange themselves in hierarchies of prepotency. That is to say, the appearance of one need usually rests on the prior satisfaction of another, more prepotent need. Man is a perpetually wanting animal. Also no need or drive can be treated as if it were isolated or discrete; every drive is related to the state of satisfaction or dissatisfaction of other drives.

8. *Lists* of drives will get us nowhere for various theoretical and practical reasons. Furthermore, any classification of motivations must deal with the problem of levels of specificity or generalization of the motives to be classified.

9. Classifications of motivations must be based upon goals rather than upon instigating drives or motivated behavior.

10. Motivation theory should be human-centered rather than animal-centered.

From *Psychological Review,* L (1943), 370-396. Reprinted by permission of the American Psychological Association and the author.

11. The situation or the field in which the organism reacts must be taken into account, but the field alone can rarely serve as an exclusive explanation for behavior. Furthermore, the field itself must be interpreted in terms of the organism. Field theory cannot be a substitute for motivation theory.

12. Not only the integration of the organism must be taken into account, but also the possibility of isolated, specific, partial, or segmental reactions.

It has since become necessary to add to these another affirmation.

13. Motivation theory is not synonymous with behavior theory. The motivations are only one class of determinants of behavior. While behavior is almost always motivated, it is also almost always biologically, culturally, and situationally determined as well.

The present paper is an attempt to formulate a positive theory of motivation which will satisfy these theoretical demands and at the same time conform to the known facts, clinical and observational, as well as experimental. It derives most directly, however, from clinical experience. This theory is, I think, in the functionalist tradition of James and Dewey, and is fused with the holism of Wertheimer (19), Goldstein (6), and Gestalt Psychology, and with the dynamicism of Freud (4) and Adler (1). This fusion or synthesis may arbitrarily be called a "general-dynamic" theory.

It is far easier to perceive and to criticize the aspects in motivation theory than to remedy them. Mostly this is because of the very serious lack of sound data in this area. I conceive this lack of sound facts to be due primarily to the absence of a valid theory of motivation. The present theory then must be considered to be a suggested program or framework for future research and must stand or fall, not so much on facts available or evidence presented, as upon researches yet to be done, researches suggested perhaps by the questions raised in this paper.

II. The basic needs

The "physiological" needs.—The needs that are usually taken as the starting point for motivation theory are the so-called physiological drives. Two recent lines of research make it necessary to revise our customary notions about these needs, first, the development of the concept of homeostasis, and second, the finding that appetites (preferential choices among foods) are a fairly efficient indication of actual needs or lacks in the body.

Homeostasis refers to the body's automatic efforts to maintain a constant normal state of the blood stream. Cannon (2) has described this process for (1) the water content of the blood, (2) salt content, (3) sugar content, (4) protein content, (5) fat content, (6) calcium content, (7) oxygen content, (8) constant hydrogen-ion level (acid-base balance), and (9) constant temperature of the blood. Obviously this list can be extended to include other minerals, the hormones, vitamins, etc.

Young in a recent article (21) has summarized the work on appetite in its relation to body needs. If the body lacks some chemical, the individual will tend to develop a specific appetite or partial hunger for that food element.

Thus, it seems impossible as well as useless to make any list of fundamental physiological needs for they can come to almost any number one might wish, depending on the degree of specificity of description. We can not identify all physiological needs as homeostatic. That sexual desire, sleepiness, sheer activity, and maternal behavior in animals, are homeostatic, has not yet been demonstrated. Furthermore, this list would not include the various sensory pleasures (tastes, smells, tickling, stroking) which are probably physiological and which may become the goals of motivated behavior.

In a previous paper (13) it has been pointed out that these physiological drives or needs are to be considered unusual rather than typical because they are isolable, and because they are localizable somatically. That is to say, they are relatively independent of each other, of other motivations, and of the organism as a whole, and secondly, in many cases, it is possible to demonstrate a localized, underlying somatic base for the drive. This is true less generally than has been thought (exceptions are fatigue, sleepiness, maternal responses) but it is still true in the classic instances of hunger, sex, and thirst.

It should be pointed out again that any of the physiological needs and the consummatory behavior involved with them serve as channels for all sorts of other needs as well. That is to say, the person who thinks he is hungry may actually be seeking more for comfort, or dependence, than for vitamins or proteins. Conversely, it is possible to satisfy the hunger need in part by other activities such as drinking water or smoking cigarettes. In other words, relatively isolable as these physiological needs are, they are not completely so.

Undoubtedly these physiological needs are the most prepotent of all needs. What this means specifically is, that in the human being who is missing everything in life in an extreme fashion, it is most likely that the major motivation would be the physiological needs rather than any others. A person who is lacking food, safety, love, and esteem would most probably hunger for food more strongly than for anything else.

If all the needs are unsatisfied, and the organism is then dominated by the physiological needs, all other needs may become simply nonexistent or be pushed into the background. It is then fair to characterize the whole organism by saying simply that it is hungry, for consciousness is almost completely preempted by hunger. All capacities are put into the service of hunger-satisfaction, and the organization of these capacities is almost entirely determined by the one purpose of satisfying hunger. The receptors and effectors, the intelligence, memory, habits, all may now be defined simply as hunger-gratifying tools. Capacities that are not useful for this purpose lie dormant or are pushed into the background. The urge to write poetry, the desire to acquire an automobile, the interest in American history, the desire for a new pair of shoes are, in the extreme case, forgotten or become of secondary importance. For the man who is extremely and dangerously hungry, no other interests exist but food. He dreams food, he remembers food, he thinks about food, he emotes only about food, he perceives only food and he wants only food. The more subtle determinants that ordinarily fuse with the physiological drives in organizing even feeding, drinking, or sexual behavior, may now be so completely overwhelmed as to allow us to speak at this time (but *only* at this time) of pure hunger drive and behavior, with the one unqualified aim of relief.

Another peculiar characteristic of the human organism when it is dominated by a certain need is that the whole philosophy of the future tends also to change. For our chronically and extremely hungry man, Utopia can be defined very simply as a place where there is plenty of food. He tends to think that, if only he is guaranteed food for the rest of his life, he will be perfectly happy and will never want anything more. Life itself tends to be defined in terms of eating. Anything else will be defined as unimportant. Freedom, love, community feeling, respect, philosophy, may all be waved aside as fripperies which are useless since they fail to fill the stomach. Such a man may fairly be said to live by bread alone.

It cannot possibly be denied that such things are true but their *generality* can be denied. Emergency conditions are, almost by definition, rare in the normally functioning peaceful society. That this truism can be forgotten is due mainly to two reasons. First, rats have few motivations other than physiological ones, and since so much of the research upon motivation has been made with these animals, it is easy to carry the rat picture over to the human being. Secondly, it is too often not realized that culture itself is an adaptive tool, one of whose main functions is to make the physiological emergencies come less and less often. In most of the known societies, chronic extreme hunger of the emergency type is rare, rather than common. In any case, this is still true in the United States. The average American citizen is experiencing appetite rather than hunger when he says, "I am hungry." He is apt to experience sheer life-and-death hunger only by accident and then only a few times through his entire life.

Obviously a good way to obscure the "higher" motivations, and to get a lopsided view of human capacities and human nature, is to make the organism extremely and chronically hungry or thirsty. Anyone who attempts to make an emergency picture into a typical one, and who will measure all of man's goals and desires by his behavior during extreme physiological deprivation is certainly being blind to many things. It is quite true that man lives by bread alone—when there is no bread. But what happens to man's desires when there *is* plenty of bread and when his belly is chronically filled?

At once other (and "higher") needs emerge and these, rather than physiological hungers, dominate the organism. And when these in turn are satisfied, again new (and still "higher") needs emerge and so on. This is what we mean by saying that the basic human needs are organized into a hierarchy of relative prepotency.

One main implication of this phrasing is that gratification becomes as important a concept as deprivation in motivation theory, for it releases the organism from the domination of a relatively more physiological need, permitting thereby the emergence of other more social goals. The physiological needs, along with their partial goals, when chronically gratified cease to exist as active determinants or organizers of behavior. They now exist only in a potential fashion in the sense that they may emerge again to dominate the organism if they are thwarted. But a want that is satisfied is no longer a want. The organism is dominated and its behavior organized only by unsatisfied needs. If hunger is satisfied, it becomes unimportant in the current dynamics of the individual.

This statement is somewhat qualified by a hypothesis to be discussed more fully later, namely, that it is precisely those individuals in whom a certain need has always been satisfied who are best equipped to tolerate deprivation of that need in the future, and that, furthermore, those who have been deprived in the past will react differently to current satisfactions than the one who has never been deprived.

The safety needs.—If the physiological needs are relatively well gratified, there then emerges a new set of needs, which we may categorize roughly as the safety needs. All that has been said of the physiological needs is equally true, although in lesser degree, of these desires. The organism may equally well be wholly dominated by them. They may serve as the almost exclusive organizers of behavior, recruiting all the capacities of the organism in their service, and we may then fairly describe the whole organism as a safety-seeking mechanism. Again we may say of the receptors, the effectors, of the intellect, and the other capacities that they are primarily safety-seeking tools. Again, as in the hungry man, we find that the dominating goal is a strong determinant not only of his current world outlook and philosophy but also of his philosophy of the future. Practically everything looks less important than safety (even sometimes the physiological needs which being satisfied, are now underestimated). A man in this state, if it is extreme enough and chronic enough, may be characterized as living almost for safety alone.

Although in this paper we are interested primarily in the needs of the adult, we can approach an understanding of his safety needs perhaps more efficiently by observation of infants and children in whom these needs are much more simple and obvious. One reason for the clearer appearance of the threat or danger reaction in infants is that they do not inhibit this reaction at all, whereas adults in our society have been taught to inhibit it at all costs. Thus even when adults do feel their safety to be threatened, we may not be able to see this on the surface. Infants will react in a total fashion and as if they were endangered, if they are disturbed or dropped suddenly, startled by loud noises, flashing light, or other unusual sensory stimulation, by rough handling, by general loss of support in the mother's arms, or by inadequate support.[1]

In infants we can also see a much more direct reaction to bodily illnesses of various kinds. Sometimes these illnesses seem to be immediately and *per se* threatening and seem to make the child feel unsafe. For instance, vomiting, colic, or other sharp pains seem to make the child look at the whole world in a different way. At such a moment of pain, it may be postulated that for the child the appearance of the whole world suddenly changes from sunniness to darkness, so to speak, and becomes a place in which anything at all might happen and in which previously stable things have suddenly become unstable. Thus a child who because of some bad food is taken ill may, for a day or two, develop fear, nightmares, and a need for protection and reassurance never seen in him before his illness.

Another indication of the child's need for safety is his preference for some kind of undisrupted routine or rhythm. He seems to want

---

[1] As the child grows up, sheer knowledge and familiarity as well as better motor development make these "dangers" less and less dangerous and more and more manageable. Throughout life it may be said that one of the main conative functions of education is this neutralizing of apparent dangers through knowledge, e.g., "I am not afraid of thunder because I know something about it."

a predictable, orderly world. For instance, injustice, unfairness, or inconsistency in the parents seems to make a child feel anxious and unsafe. This attitude may be not so much because of the injustice *per se* or any particular pains involved, but rather because this treatment threatens to make the world look unreliable, or unsafe, or unpredictable. Young children seem to thrive better under a system which has at least a skeletal outline of rigidity, in which there is a schedule of a kind, some sort of routine, something that can be counted upon, not only for the present but also far into the future. Perhaps one could express this more accurately by saying that the child needs an organized world rather than an unorganized or unstructured one.

The central role of the parents and the normal family setup are indisputable. Quarreling, physical assault, separation, divorce, or death within the family may be particularly terrifying. Also parental outbursts of rage or threats of punishment directed to the child, calling him names, speaking to him harshly, shaking him, handling him roughly, or actual physical punishment sometimes elicit such total panic and terror in the child that we must assume more is involved than the physical pain alone. While it is true that in some children this terror may represent also a fear of loss of parental love, it can also occur in completely rejected children who seem to cling to the hating parents more for sheer safety and protection than because of hope of love.

Confronting the average child with new, unfamiliar, strange, unmanageable stimuli or situations will too frequently elicit the danger or terror reaction, as, for example, getting lost or even being separated from the parents for a short time, being confronted with new faces, new situations or new tasks, the sight of strange, unfamiliar, or uncontrollable objects, illness, or death. Particularly at such times, the child's frantic clinging to his parents is eloquent testimony to their role as protectors (quite apart from their roles as food-givers and love-givers).

From these and similar observations, we may generalize and say that the average child in our society generally prefers a safe, orderly, predictable, organized world which he can count on, in which unexpected, unmanageable, or other dangerous things do not happen, and in which, in any case, he has all-powerful parents who protect and shield him from harm.

That these reactions may so easily be observed in children is in a way a proof of the fact that children in our society feel too unsafe (or, in a word, are badly brought up). Children who are reared in an unthreatening, loving family do *not* ordinarily react as we have described above (17). In such children the danger reactions are apt to come mostly to objects or situations that adults too would consider dangerous.[2]

The healthy, normal, fortunate adult in our culture is largely satisfied in his safety needs. The peaceful, smoothly running, "good" society ordinarily makes its members feel safe enough from wild animals, extremes of temperature, criminals, assault and murder, tyranny, etc. Therefore, in a very real sense, he no longer has any safety needs as active motivators. Just as a sated man no longer feels hungry, a safe man no longer feels endangered. If we wish to see these needs directly and clearly we must turn to neurotic or near-neurotic individuals, and to the economic and social underdogs. In between these extremes, we can perceive the expressions of safety needs only in such phenomena as, for instance, the common preference for a job with tenure and protection, the desire for a savings account, and for insurance of various kinds (medical, dental, unemployment, disability, old age).

Other broader aspects of the attempt to seek safety and stability in the world are seen in the very common preference for familiar rather than unfamiliar things, or for the known rather than the unknown. The tendency to have some religion or world philosophy that organizes the universe and the men in it into some sort of satisfactorily coherent, meaningful whole is also in part motivated by safety-seeking. Here too we may list science and philosophy in general as partially motivated by the safety needs (we shall see later that there are also other

---

[2] A "test battery" for safety might be confronting the child with a small exploding firecracker, or with a bewhiskered face, having the mother leave the room, putting him upon a high ladder, a hypodermic injection, having a mouse crawl up to him, etc. Of course I cannot seriously recommend the deliberate use of such "tests" for they might very well harm the child being tested. But these and similar situations come up by the score in the child's ordinary day-to-day living and may be observed. There is no reason why these stimuli should not be used with, for example, young chimpanzees.

motivations to scientific, philosophical, or religious endeavor).

Otherwise the need for safety is seen as an active and dominant mobilizer of the organism's resources only in emergencies, *e.g.,* war, disease, natural catastrophes, crime waves, societal disorganization, neurosis, brain injury, chronically bad situations.

Some neurotic adults in our society are, in many ways, like the unsafe child in their desire for safety, although in the former it takes on a somewhat special appearance. Their reaction is often to unknown psychological dangers in a world that is perceived to be hostile, overwhelming, and threatening. Such a person behaves as if a great catastrophe were almost always impending, *i.e.,* he is usually responding as if to an emergency. His safety needs often find specific expression in a search for a protector, or a stronger person on whom he may depend, or perhaps, a Fuehrer.

The neurotic individual may be described in a slightly different way with some usefulness as a grown-up person who retains his childish attitudes toward the world. That is to say, a neurotic adult may be said to behave "as if" he were actually afraid of a spanking, or of his mother's disapproval, or of being abandoned by his parents, or having his food taken away from him. It is as if his childish attitudes of fear and threat reaction to a dangerous world had gone underground, and untouched by the growing up and learning processes, were now ready to be called out by any stimulus that would make a child feel endangered and threatened.[3]

The neurosis in which the search for safety takes its clearest form is in the compulsive-obsessive neurosis. Compulsive-obsessives try frantically to order and stabilize the world so that no unmanageable, unexpected, or unfamiliar dangers will ever appear (14). They hedge themselves about with all sorts of ceremonials, rules, and formulas so that every possible contingency may be provided for and so that no new contingencies may appear. They are much like the brain-injured cases, described by Goldstein (6), who manage to maintain their equilibrium by avoiding everything unfamiliar and strange and by ordering their restricted world in such a neat, disciplined, orderly fashion that everything in the world can be counted upon. They try to arrange the world so that anything unexpected (dangers) cannot possibly occur. If, through no fault of their own, something unexpected does occur, they go into a panic reaction as if this unexpected occurrence constituted a grave danger. What we can see only as a none-too-strong preference in the healthy person, *e.g.,* preference for the familiar, becomes a life-and-death necessity in abnormal cases.

The love needs.—If both the physiological and the safety needs are fairly well gratified, then there will emerge the love and affection and belongingness needs, and the whole cycle already described will repeat itself with this new center. Now the person will feel keenly, as never before, the absence of friends, or a sweetheart, or a wife, or children. He will hunger for affectionate relations with people in general, namely, for a place in his group, and he will strive with great intensity to achieve this goal. He will want to attain such a place more than anything else in the world and may even forget that once, when he was hungry, he sneered at love.

In our society the thwarting of these needs is the most commonly found core in cases of maladjustment and more severe psychopathology. Love and affection, as well as their possible expression in sexuality, are generally looked upon with ambivalence and are customarily hedged about with many restrictions and inhibitions. Practically all theorists of psychopathology have stressed thwarting of the love needs as basic in the picture of maladjustment. Many clinical studies have, therefore, been made of this need, and we know more about it perhaps than any of the other needs except the physiological ones (14).

One thing that must be stressed at this point is that love is not synonymous with sex. Sex may be studied as a purely physiological need. Ordinarily sexual behavior is multi-determined, that is to say, determined not only by sexual but also by other needs, chief among which are the love and affection needs. Also not to be overlooked is the fact that the love needs involve both giving *and* receiving love.[4]

The esteem needs.—All people in our so-

---

[3] Not all neurotic individuals feel unsafe. Neurosis may have at its core a thwarting of the affection and esteem needs in a person who is generally safe.
[4] For further details see (12) and (16, Chap. 5).

ciety (with a few pathological exceptions) have a need or desire for a stable, firmly based, (usually) high evaluation of themselves, for self-respect, or self-esteem, and for the esteem of others. By firmly based self-esteem, we mean that which is soundly based upon real capacity, achievement, and respect from others. These needs may be classified into two subsidiary sets. These are, first, the desire for strength, for achievement, for adequacy, for confidence in the face of the world, and for independence and freedom.[5] Secondly, we have what we may call the desire for reputation or prestige (defining it as respect or esteem from other people), recognition, attention, importance, or appreciation.[6] These needs have been relatively stressed by Alfred Adler and his followers and have been relatively neglected by Freud and the psychoanalysts. More and more today, however, there is appearing widespread appreciation of their central importance.

Satisfaction of the self-esteem need leads to feelings of self-confidence, worth, strength, capability, and adequacy of being useful and necessary in the world. But thwarting of these needs produces feelings of inferiority, of weakness, and of helplessness. These feelings in turn give rise to either basic discouragement or else compensatory or neurotic trends. An appreciation of the necessity of basic self-confidence and an understanding of how helpless people are without it can be easily gained from a study of severe traumatic neurosis(8).[7]

The need for self-actualization.—Even if all these needs are satisfied, we may still often (if not always) expect that a new discontent and restlessness will soon develop, unless the individual is doing what he is fitted for. A musician must make music, an artist must paint, a poet must write, if he is to be ultimately happy. What a man *can* be, he *must* be. This need we may call self-actualization.

This term, first coined by Kurt Goldstein, is being used in this paper in a much more specific and limited fashion. It refers to the desire for self-fulfillment, namely, to the tendency for him to become actualized in what he is potentially. This tendency might be phrased as the desire to become more and more what one is, to become everything that one is capable of becoming.

The specific form that these needs will take will, of course, vary greatly from person to person. In one individual it may take the form of the desire to be an ideal mother, in another it may be expressed athletically, and in still another it may be expressed in painting pictures or in inventions. It is not necessarily a creative urge, although in people who have any capacities for creation, it will take this form.

The clear emergence of these needs rests upon prior satisfaction of the physiological, safety, love, and esteem needs. We shall call people who are satisfied in these needs, basically satisfied people, and it is from these that we may expect the fullest (and healthiest) creativeness.[8] Since in our society basically satisfied people are the exception, we do not know much about self-actualization, either experimentally or clinically. It remains a challenging problem for research.

The preconditions for the basic need satisfactions.—There are certain conditions which are immediate prerequisites for the basic need satisfactions. Danger to these is reacted to almost as if it were a direct danger to the basic needs themselves. Such conditions as freedom to speak, freedom to do what one wishes so long as no harm is done to others, freedom to express one's self, freedom to investigate and seek for information, freedom to defend one's self, justice, fairness, honesty,

---

[5] Whether or not this particular desire is universal we do not know. The crucial question, especially important today, is "Will men who are enslaved and dominated inevitably feel dissatisfied and rebellious?" We may assume on the basis of commonly known clinical data that a man who has known true freedom (not paid for by giving up safety and security but rather built on the basis of adequate safety and security) will not willingly or easily allow his freedom to be taken away from him. But we do not know that this is true for the person born into slavery. The events of the next decade should give us our answer. See discussion of this problem in (5).

[6] Perhaps the desire for prestige and respect from others is subsidiary to the desire for self-esteem or confidence in oneself. Observation of children seems to indicate that this is so, but clinical data give no clear support for such a conclusion.

[7] For more extensive discussion of normal self-esteem, as well as for reports of various researches, see (11).

[8] Clearly creative behavior, like paintings, is like any other behavior in having multiple determinants. It may be seen in "innately creative" people whether they are satisfied or not, happy or unhappy, hungry or sated. Also it is clear that creative activity may be compensatory, ameliorative, or purely economic. It is my impression (as yet unconfirmed) that it is possible to distinguish the artistic and intellectual products of basically satisfied people from those of basically unsatisfied people by inspection alone. In any case, here too we must distinguish in a dynamic fashion the overt behavior itself from its various motivations or purposes.

orderliness in the group are examples of such preconditions for basic need satisfactions. Thwarting in these freedoms will be reacted to with a threat or emergency response. These conditions are not ends in themselves but they are *almost* so, since they are so closely related to the basic needs which are apparently the only ends in themselves. These conditions are defended, because without them the basic satisfactions are quite impossible, or at least, very severely endangered.

If we remember that the cognitive capacities (perceptual, intellectual, learning) are a set of adjustive tools which have among other functions the satisfaction of our basic needs, then it is clear that any danger to them, any deprivation or blocking of their free use, must also be indirectly threatening to the basic needs themselves. Such a statement is a partial solution of the general problems of curiosity, the search for knowledge, truth, and wisdom, and the ever-persistent urge to solve the cosmic mysteries.

We must therefore introduce another hypothesis and speak of degrees of closeness to the basic needs, for we have already pointed out that *any* conscious desires (partial goals) are more or less important as they are more or less close to the basic needs. The same statement may be made for various behavior acts. An act is psychologically important if it contributes directly to satisfaction of basic needs. The less directly it so contributes, or the weaker this contribution is, the less important this act must be conceived to be from the point of view of dynamic psychology. A similar statement may be made for the various defense or coping mechanisms. Some are very directly related to the protection or attainment of the basic needs, others are only weakly and distantly related. Indeed if we wished, we could speak of more basic and less basic defense mechanisms, and then affirm that danger to the more basic defenses is more threatening than danger to less basic defenses (always remembering that this is so only because of their relationship to the basic needs).

The desires to know and to understand.—So far, we have mentioned the cognitive needs only in passing. Acquiring knowledge and systematizing the universe have been considered as, in part, techniques for the achievement of basic safety in the world, or, for the intelligent man, expressions of self-actualization. Also freedom of inquiry and expression have been discussed as preconditions of satisfactions of the basic needs. True though these formulations may be, they do not constitute definitive answers to the question as to the motivation role of curiosity, learning, philosophizing, experimenting, etc. They are, at best, no more than partial answers.

This question is especially difficult because we know so little about the facts. Curiosity, exploration, desire for the facts, desire to know may certainly be observed easily enough. The fact that they often are pursued even at great cost to the individual's safety is an earnest of the partial character of our previous discussion. In addition, the writer must admit that, though he has sufficient clinical evidence to postulate the desire to know as a very strong drive in intelligent people, no data are available for unintelligent people. It may then be largely a function of relatively high intelligence. Rather tentatively then, and largely in the hope of stimulating discussion and research, we shall postulate a basic desire to know, to be aware of reality, to get the facts, to satisfy curiosity, or as Wertheimer phrases it, to see rather than to be blind.

This postulation, however, is not enough. Even after we know, we are impelled to know more and more minutely and microscopically on the one hand, and on the other, more and more extensively in the direction of a world philosophy, religion, etc. The facts that we acquire, if they are isolated or atomistic, inevitably get theorized about, and either analyzed or organized or both. This process has been phrased by some as the search for "meaning." We shall then postulate a desire to understand, to systematize, to organize, to analyze, to look for relations and meanings.

Once these desires are accepted for discussion, we see that they too form themselves into a small hierarchy in which the desire to know is prepotent over the desire to understand. All the characteristics of a hierarchy of prepotency that we have described above, seem to hold for this one as well.

We must guard ourselves against the too easy tendency to separate these desires from the basic needs we have discussed above, *i.e.,* to make a sharp dichotomy between "cognitive" and "conative" needs. The desire to know and to understand are themselves conative, *i.e.,* have a striving character, and are as much personality needs as the "basic needs" we have already discussed (19).

III. Further characteristics of the basic needs

The degree of fixity of the hierarchy of basic needs.—We have spoken so far as if this hierarchy were a fixed order, but actually it is not nearly as rigid as we may have implied. It is true that most of the people with whom we have worked have seemed to have these basic needs in about the order that has been indicated. However, there have been a number of exceptions.

(1) There are some people in whom, for instance, self-esteem seems to be more important than love. This most common reversal in the hierarchy is usually due to the development of the notion that the person who is most likely to be loved is a strong or powerful person, one who inspires respect or fear, and who is self-confident or aggressive. Therefore such people who lack love and seek it, may try hard to put on a front of aggressive, confident behavior. But essentially they seek high self-esteem and its behavior expressions more as a means to an end than for its own sake; they seek self-assertion for the sake of love rather than for self-esteem itself.

(2) There are other apparently innately creative people in whom the drive to creativeness seems to be more important than any other counter determinant. Their creativeness might appear not as self-actualization released by basic satisfaction, but in spite of lack of basic satisfaction.

(3) In certain people the level of aspiration may be permanently deadened or lowered. That is to say, the less prepotent goals may simply be lost and may disappear forever, so that the person who has experienced life at a very low level, *i.e.,* chronic unemployment, may continue to be satisfied for the rest of his life if only he can get enough food.

(4) The so-called "psychopathic personality" is another example of permanent loss of the love needs. These are people who, according to the best data available (9), have been starved for love in the earliest months of their lives and have simply lost forever the desire and the ability to give and to receive affection (as animals lose sucking or pecking reflexes that are not exercised soon enough after birth).

(5) Another cause of reversal of the hierarchy is that when a need has been satisfied for a long time, this need may be underevaluated. People who have never experienced chronic hunger are apt to underestimate its effects and to look upon food as a rather unimportant thing. If they are dominated by a higher need, this higher need will seem to be the most important of all. It then becomes possible, and indeed does actually happen, that they may, for the sake of this higher need, put themselves into the position of being deprived in a more basic need. We may expect that after a long-time deprivation of the more basic need there will be a tendency to reevaluate both needs so that the more prepotent need will actually become consciously prepotent for the individual who may have given it up very lightly. Thus, a man who has given up his job rather than lose his self-respect, and who then starves for six months or so, may be willing to take his job back even at the price of losing his self-respect.

(6) Another partial explanation of *apparent* reversals is seen in the fact that we have been talking about the hierarchy of prepotency in terms of consciously felt wants or desires rather than of behavior. Looking at behavior itself may give us the wrong impression. What we have claimed is that the person will *want* the more basic of two needs when deprived in both. There is no necessary implication here that he will act upon his desires. Let us say again that there are many determinants of behavior other than the needs and desires.

(7) Perhaps more important than all these exceptions are the ones that involve ideals, high social standards, high values, and the like. With such values people become martyrs; they will give up everything for the sake of a particular ideal or value. These people may be understood, at least in part, by reference to one basic concept (or hypothesis) which may be called "increased frustration-tolerance through early gratification." People who have been satisfied in their basic needs throughout their lives, particularly in their earlier years, seem to develop exceptional power to withstand present or future thwarting of these needs simply because they have strong, healthy character structure as a result of basic satis-

faction. They are the "strong" people who can easily weather disagreement or opposition, who can swim against the stream of public opinion and who can stand up for the truth at great personal cost. It is just the ones who have loved and been well loved, and who have had many deep friendships who can hold out against hatred, rejection, or persecution.

I say all this in spite of the fact that there is a certain amount of sheer habituation which is also involved in any full discussion of frustration tolerance. For instance, it is likely that those persons who have been accustomed to relative starvation for a long time are partially enabled thereby to withstand food deprivation. What sort of balance must be made between these two tendencies, of habituation on the one hand, and of past satisfaction breeding present frustration tolerance on the other hand, remains to be worked out by further research. Meanwhile we may assume that they are both operative, side by side, since they do not contradict each other. In respect to this phenomenon of increased frustration tolerance, it seems probable that the most important gratifications come in the first two years of life. That is to say, people who have been made secure and strong in the earliest years tend to remain secure and strong thereafter in the face of whatever threatens.

Degrees of relative satisfaction.—So far, our theoretical discussion may have given the impression that these five sets of needs are somehow in step-wise, all-or-none relationships to each other. We have spoken in such terms as the following: "If one need is satisfied, then another emerges." This statement might give the false impression that a need must be satisfied 100 per cent before the next need emerges. In actual fact, most members of our society who are normal are partially satisfied in all their basic needs and partially unsatisfied in all their basic needs at the same time. A more realistic description of the hierarchy would be in terms of decreasing percentages of satisfaction as we go up the hierarchy of prepotency. For instance, if I may assign arbitrary figures for the sake of illustration, it is as if the average citizen is satisfied perhaps 85 per cent in his physiological needs, 70 per cent in his safety needs, 50 per cent in his love needs, 40 per cent in his self-esteem needs, and 10 per cent in his self-actualization needs.

As for the concept of emergence of a new need after satisfaction of the prepotent need, this emergence is not a sudden, saltatory phenomenon but rather a gradual emergence by slow degrees from nothingness. For instance, if prepotent need A is satisfied only 10 per cent, then need B may not be visible at all. However, as this need A becomes satisfied 25 per cent, need B may emerge 5 per cent, as need A becomes satisfied 75 per cent, need B may emerge 90 per cent, and so on.

Unconscious character of needs.—These needs are neither necessarily conscious nor unconscious. On the whole, however, in the average person, they are more often unconscious rather than conscious. It is not necessary at this point to overhaul the tremendous mass of evidence which indicates the crucial importance of unconscious motivation. It would by now be expected, on *a priori* grounds alone, that unconscious motivations would on the whole be rather more important than the conscious motivations. What we have called the basic needs are very often largely unconscious although they may, with suitable techniques and with sophisticated people, become conscious.

Cultural specificity and generality of needs. —This classification of basic needs makes some attempt to take account of the relative unity behind the superficial differences in specific desires from one culture to another. Certainly in any particular culture an individual's conscious motivational content will usually be extremely different from the conscious motivational content of an individual in another society. However, it is the common experience of anthropologists that people, even in different societies, are much more alike than we would think from our first contact with them, and that as we know them better we seem to find more and more of this commonness. We then recognize the most startling differences to be superficial rather than basic, *e.g.,* differences in style of hairdress, clothes, tastes in food, etc. Our classification of basic needs is in part an attempt to account for this unity behind the apparent diversity from culture to culture. No claim is made that it is ultimate or universal for all cultures. The claim is made only that it is relatively *more* ultimate, more universal, more basic, than the superficial conscious desires from culture to culture, and makes a somewhat closer approach to common-human characteristics. Basic needs are *more* common-human than superficial desires or behaviors.

Multiple motivations of behavior.—These needs must be understood *not* to be *exclusive* or single determiners of certain kinds of behavior. An example may be found in any behavior that seems to be physiologically motivated, such as eating, or sexual play, or the like. The clinical psychologists have long since found that any behavior may be a channel through which flow various determinants. Or to say it in another way, most behavior is multi-motivated. Within the sphere of motivational determinants any behavior tends to be determined by several or *all* of the basic needs simultaneously rather than by only one of them. The latter would be more an exception than the former. Eating may be partially for the sake of filling the stomach, and partially for the sake of comfort and amelioration of other needs. One may make love not only for pure sexual release, but also to convince one's self of one's masculinity, or to make a conquest, to feel powerful, or to win more basic affection. As an illustration, I may point out that it would be possible (theoretically if not practically) to analyze a single act of an individual and see in it the expression of his physiological needs, his safety needs, his love needs, his esteem needs and self-actualization. This contrasts sharply with the more naïve brand of trait psychology in which one trait or one motive accounts for a certain kind of act, *i.e.*, an aggressive act is traced solely to a trait of aggressiveness.

Multiple determinants of behavior.—Not all behavior is determined by the basic needs. We might even say that not all behavior is motivated. There are many determinants of behavior other than motives.[9] For instance, one other important class of determinants is the so-called "field" determinants. Theoretically, at least, behavior may be determined completely by the field, or even by specific isolated external stimuli, as in association of ideas, or certain conditioned reflexes. If in response to the stimulus word "table," I immediately perceive a memory image of a table, this response certainly has nothing to do with my basic needs.

Secondly, we may call attention again to the concept of "degree of closeness to the basic needs" or "degree of motivation." Some behavior is highly motivated; other behavior is only weakly motivated. Some is not motivated at all (but all behavior is determined).

Another important point [10] is that there is a basic difference between expressive behavior and coping behavior (functional striving, purposive goal seeking). An expressive behavior does not try to do anything; it is simply a reflection of the personality. A stupid man behaves stupidly, not because he wants to, or tries to, or is motivated to, but simply because he *is* what he is. The same is true when I speak in a bass voice rather than tenor or soprano. The random movements of a healthy child, the smile on the face of a happy man even when he is alone, the springiness of the healthy man's walk, and the erectness of his carriage are other examples of expressive, non-functional behavior. Also the *style* in which a man carries out almost all his behavior, motivated as well as unmotivated, is often expressive.

We may then ask, is *all* behavior expressive or reflective of the character structure? The answer is "No." Rote, habitual, automatized, or conventional behavior may or may not be expressive. The same is true for most "stimulus-bound" behaviors.

It is finally necessary to stress that expressiveness of behavior and goal-directedness of behavior are not mutually exclusive categories. Average behavior is usually both.

Goals as centering principle in motivation theory.—It will be observed that the basic principle in our classification has been neither the instigation nor the motivated behavior, but rather the functions, effects, purposes, or goals of the behavior. It has been proven sufficiently by various people that this is the most suitable point for centering in any motivation theory.[11]

Animal- and human-centering.—This theory starts with the human being rather than any lower and presumably "simpler" animal. Too

---

9 I am aware that many psychologists and psychoanalysts use the term "motivated" and "determined" synonymously, e.g., Freud. But I consider this an obfuscating usage. Sharp distinctions are necessary for clarity of thought and precision in experimentation.

10 To be discussed fully in a subsequent publication.

11 The interested reader is referred to the very excellent discussion of this point in Murray's *Explorations in Personality* (15).

many of the findings that have been made in animals have been proven to be true for animals but not for the human being. There is no reason whatsoever why we should start with animals in order to study human motivation. The logic or rather illogic behind this general fallacy of "pseudo-simplicity" has been exposed often enough by philosophers and logicians as well as by scientists in each of the various fields. It is no more necessary to study animals before one can study man than it is to study mathematics before one can study geology or psychology or biology.

We may also reject the old, naive, behaviorism, which assumed that it was somehow necessary, or at least more "scientific" to judge human beings by animal standards. One consequence of this belief was that the whole notion of purpose and goal was excluded from motivational psychology simply because one could not ask a white rat about his purposes. Tolman (18) has long since proven in animal studies themselves that this exclusion was not necessary.

Motivation and the theory of psychopathogenesis.—The conscious motivational content of everyday life has, according to the foregoing, been conceived to be relatively important or unimportant accordingly as it is more or less closely related to the basic goals. A desire for an ice cream cone might actually be an indirect expression of a desire for love. If it is, then this desire for the ice cream cone becomes extremely important motivation. If however the ice cream is simply something to cool the mouth with, or a casual appetitive reaction, then the desire is relatively unimportant. Everyday conscious desires are to be regarded as symptoms, as *surface indicators of more basic needs.* If we were to take these superficial desires at their face value we would find ourselves in a state of complete confusion which could never be resolved, since we would be dealing seriously with symptoms rather than with what lay behind the symptoms.

Thwarting of unimportant desires produces no psychopathological results; thwarting of a basically important need does produce such results. Any theory of psychopathogenesis must then be based on a sound theory of motivation. A conflict or a frustration is not necessarily pathogenic. It becomes so only when it threatens or thwarts the basic needs, or partial needs that are closely related to the basic needs (10).

The role of gratified needs.—It has been pointed out above several times that our needs usually emerge only when more prepotent needs have been gratified. Thus gratification has an important role in motivation theory. Apart from this, however, needs cease to play an active determining or organizing role as soon as they are gratified.

What this means is that, *e.g.,* a basically satisfied person no longer has the needs for esteem, love, safety, etc. The only sense in which he might be said to have them is in the almost metaphysical sense that a sated man has hunger, or a filled bottle has emptiness. If we are interested in what *actually* motivates us, and not in what has, will, or might motivate us, then a satisfied need is not a motivator. It must be considered for all practical purposes simply not to exist, to have disappeared. This point should be emphasized because it has been either overlooked or contradicted in every theory of motivation I know.[12] The perfectly healthy, normal, fortunate man has no sex needs or hunger needs, or needs for safety, or for love, or for prestige, or self-esteem, except in stray moments of quickly passing threat. If we were to say otherwise, we should also have to aver that every man has all the pathological reflexes, *e.g.,* Babinski, etc., because if his nervous system were damaged, these would appear.

It is such considerations as these that suggest the bold postulation that a man who is thwarted in any of his basic needs may fairly be envisaged simply as a sick man. This is a fair parallel to our designation as "sick" of the man who lacks vitamins or minerals. Who is to say that a lack of love is less important than a lack of vitamins? Since we know the pathogenic effects of love starvation, who is to say that we are invoking value questions in an unscientific or illegitimate way, any more than the physician does who diagnoses and treats pellagra or scurvy? If I were permitted this usage, I should then say simply that a healthy man is primarily motivated by his needs to develop and actualize his fullest potentialities and capacities. If a man has any

---

[12] Note that acceptance of this theory necessitates basic revision of the Freudian theory.

other basic needs in any active, chronic sense, then he is simply an unhealthy man. He is as surely sick as if he had suddenly developed a strong salt hunger or calcium hunger.[13]

If this statement seems unusual or paradoxical the reader may be assured that this is only one among many such paradoxes that will appear as we revise our ways of looking at man's deeper motivations. When we ask what man wants of life, we deal with his very essence.

IV. Summary

(1) There are at least five sets of goals, which we may call basic needs. These are briefly physiological, safety, love, esteem, and self-actualization. In addition, we are motivated by the desire to achieve or maintain the various conditions upon which these basic satisfactions rest and by certain more intellectual desires.

(2) These basic goals are related to each other, being arranged in a hierarchy of prepotency. This means that the most prepotent goal will monopolize consciousness and will tend of itself to organize the recruitment of the various capacities of the organism. The less prepotent needs are minimized, even forgotten or denied. But when a need is fairly well satisfied, the next prepotent ("higher") need emerges, in turn to dominate the conscious life and to serve as the center of organization of behavior, since gratified needs are not active motivators.

Thus man is a perpetually wanting animal. Ordinarily the satisfaction of these wants is not altogether mutually exclusive, but only tends to be. The average member of our society is most often partially satisfied and partially unsatisfied in all of his wants. The hierarchy principle is usually empirically observed in terms of increasing percentages of nonsatisfaction as we go up the hierarchy. Reversals of the average order of the hierarchy are sometimes observed. Also it has been observed that an individual may permanently lose the higher wants in the hierarchy under special conditions. There are not only ordinarily multiple motivations for usual behavior, but in addition many determinants other than motives.

(3) Any thwarting or possibility of thwarting of these basic human goals, or danger to the defenses which protect them, or to the conditions upon which they rest, is considered to be a psychological threat. With a few exceptions, all psychopathology may be partially traced to such threats. A basically thwarted man may actually be defined as a "sick" man, if we wish.

(4) It is such basic threats which bring about the general emergency reactions.

(5) Certain other basic problems have not been dealt with because of limitations of space. Among these are (a) the problem of values in any definitive motivation theory, (b) the relation between appetites, desires, needs, and what is "good" for the organism, (c) the etiology of the basic needs and their possible derivation in early childhood, (d) redefinition of motivational concepts, i.e., drive, desire, wish, need, goal, (e) implication of our theory for hedonistic theory, (f) the nature of the uncompleted act, of success and failure, and of aspiration level, (g) the role of association, habit, and conditioning, (h) relation to the theory of interpersonal relations, (i) implications for psychotherapy, (j) implication for theory of society, (k) the theory of selfishness, (l) the relation between needs and cultural patterns, (m) the relation between this theory and Allport's theory of functional autonomy. These as well as certain other less important questions must be considered as motivation theory attempts to become definitive.

References

1. Adler, A. *Social interest.* London: Faber & Faber, 1938.

2. Cannon, W. B. *Wisdom of the body.* New York: Norton, 1932.

3. Freud, A. *The ego and the mechanisms of defense.* London: Hogarth, 1937.

[13] If we were to use the word "sick" in this way, we should then also have to face squarely the relations of man to his society. One clear implication of our definition would be that (1) since a man is to be called sick who is basically thwarted, and (2) since such basic thwarting is made possible ultimately only by forces outside the individual, then (3) sickness in the individual must come ultimately from a sickness in the society. The "good" or healthy society would then be defined as one that permitted man's highest purposes to emerge by satisfying all his prepotent basic needs.

4. Freud, S. *New introductory lectures of psycho-analysis.* New York: Norton, 1933.

5. Fromm, E. *Escape from freedom.* New York: Farrar and Rinehart, 1941.

6. Goldstein, K. *The organism.* New York: American Book Co., 1939.

7. Horney, K. *The neurotic personality of our time.* New York: Norton, 1937.

8. Kardiner, A. *The traumatic neuroses of war.* New York: Hoeber, 1941.

9. Levy, D. M. Primary affect hunger. *Amer. J. Psychiat.*, 1937, 94, 643-652.

10. Maslow, A. H. Conflict, frustration, and the theory of threat. *J. abnorm. (soc.) Psychol.*, 1943, 38, 81-86.

11. ——. Dominance, personality and social behavior in women. *J. soc. Psychol.*, 1939, 10, 3-39.

12. ——. The dynamics of psychological security-insecurity. *Character & Pers.*, 1942, 10, 331-344.

13. ——. A preface to motivation theory. *Psychosomatic Med.*, 1943, 5, 85-92.

14. ——, & Mittelmann, B. *Principles of abnormal psychology.* New York: Harper & Bros., 1941.

15. Murray, H. A., *et al. Explorations in personality.* New York: Oxford University Press, 1938.

16. Plant, J. *Personality and the cultural pattern.* New York: Commonwealth Fund, 1937.

17. Shirley, M. Children's adjustments to a strange situation. *J. abnorm (soc.) Psychol.*, 1942, 37, 201-217.

18. Tolman, E. C. *Purposive behavior in animals and men.* New York: Century, 1932.

19. Wertheimer, M. Unpublished lectures at the New School for Social Research.

20. Young, P. T. *Motivation of behavior.* New York: John Wiley & Sons, 1936.

21. ——. The experimental analysis of appetite. *Psychol. Bull.*, 1941, 38, 129-164.

The functional autonomy of motives

GORDON W. ALLPORT

The late Gordon Allport, Ph.D., was Professor of Social Relations at Harvard University, past president of the American Psychological Association, and recipient of the Distinguished Scientific Contribution Award of the APA in 1964. His numerous books and articles cover a variety of topics, including personality theory, prejudice, public opinion, religion, and rumor.

In this essay Dr. Allport discusses the issue of individual motivation. Although committed to the viewpoint of dynamic psychology which tries to answer the question of why men behave as they do, he is critical of those theories which attempt to reduce all human behavior to a few basic motives. The article defends the position that current behaviors of the adult are derived from but not determined by prior experiences. Dr. Allport concludes with a discussion of the limitations of his point of view and considers some of the objections raised by alternative theories.

For fifty years *The American Journal of Psychology* has served both as a rich repository for research and as a remarkably sensitive record of the psychological temper of the times. These two services are of great historical value. Since there is no reason to doubt that the *Journal* will continue to hold its position of leadership in the future, one wonders what new currents of psychological interest its pages will reflect in the coming half-century. With what problems will psy-

From *American Journal of Psychology*, L (1937), 141-156. Reprinted by permission of the publisher.

chologists be chiefly concerned? What discoveries will they make? What types of scientific formulation will they prefer?

To predict at least one of these trends accurately requires no clairvoyance. On all sides we see the rising tide of interest in problems of personality. Up to a few years ago the somewhat segregated field of clinical psychology alone was concerned; but now theoretical and experimental psychology are likewise deeply affected. As never before, the traditional portrait of the "generalized human mind" is being tested against the living models from which it is derived. As compared with particular minds it is found to lack locus, self-consciousness, organic character, and reciprocal interpenetration of parts, all of which are essential to personality. Unless I am greatly mistaken the coming half-century will see many attempts to replace the abstract datum (mind-in-general) with the concrete datum (mind-in-particular), even at the peril of a revolutionary upset in the conception of psychology *as science*.

Some of the best-known definitions of psychology formulated in the past fifty years have given explicit recognition to the individuality of mind—that is, to its dependence upon the person. But these definitions have not as yet noticeably affected the abstractive tendency of psychological research—not even that of their authors. Wundt, James, and Titchener serve as examples. The first wrote: *"It [psychology] investigates the total content of experience in its relations to the subject."* The second: *"Psychology is the science of finite individual minds";* and the third: *"Psychology is the study of experience considered as dependent on some person."* None of these authors developed his account of mental life to accord with his definition. It is as though some vague sense of propriety guided them in framing their definitions; they *knew* that mind (as a psychological datum) exists only in finite and in personal forms. Yet their historical positions—the spirit of the times in which they worked—prevented them from following their own definitions to the end. Had any one of them done so, the psychology of personality would have had early and illustrious sponsorship.

In line with what I regard as a certain development in the psychology of the future I venture to submit a paper dealing, I think, with the one issue that above all others divides

the study of mind-in-general from the study of mind-in-particular. Motivation is the special theme, but the principle involved reaches into every nook and cranny of the evolving science of personality.[1]

Two kinds of dynamic psychology

Any type of psychology that treats *motives,* thereby endeavoring to answer the question as to *why* men behave as they do is called a *dynamic psychology.* By its very nature it cannot be merely a descriptive psychology, content to depict the *what* and the *how* of human behavior. The boldness of dynamic psychology in striking for causes stands in marked contrast to the timid, "more scientific," view that seeks nothing else than the establishment of a mathematical function for the relation between some artificially simple stimulus and some equally artificial and simple response. If the psychology of personality is to be more than a matter of coefficients of correlation, it too must be a dynamic psychology and seek first and foremost a sound and adequate theory of the nature of human dispositions.

The type of dynamic psychology almost universally held, though sufficient from the point of view of the *abstract* motives of the generalized mind, fails to provide a foundation solid enough to bear the weight of any *single* full-bodied personality. The reason is that prevailing dynamic doctrines refer every mature motive of personality to underlying original instincts, wishes, or needs, shared *by all men.* Thus, the concert artist's devotion to his music is sometimes "explained" as an extension of his self-assertive instinct, of the need for sentience, or as a symptom of some repressed striving of the libido. In McDougall's hormic psychology, for example, it is explicitly stated that only the instincts or propensities can be prime movers. Though capable of extension (on both the receptive and executive sides), they are always few in number, common in all men, and established at birth. The enthusiastic collector of bric-a-brac derives his enthusiasm from the parental instinct; so too does the kindly old philanthropist, as well as the mother of a brood. It does not matter how different these three interests may seem to be,

---

[1] What follows is drawn in part from Chapter VII of *Personality: A psychological interpretation,* 1937.

they derive their energy from the same source. The principle is that a very few basic motives suffice for explaining the endless varieties of human interests. The psychoanalyst holds the same over-simplified theory. The number of human interests that he regards as so many canalizations of the one basic sexual instinct is past computation.

The authors of this type of dynamic psychology are concerning themselves only with mind-in-general. They seek a classification of the common and basic motives by which to explain both normal or neurotic behavior of *any* individual case. (This is true even though they may regard their own list as heuristic or even as fictional.) The plan really does not work. The very fact that the lists are so different in their composition suggests—what to a naïve observer is plain enough—that motives are almost infinitely varied among men, not only in form but in substance. Not four wishes, nor eighteen propensities, nor any and all combinations of these, even with their extensions and variations, seem adequate to account for the endless variety of goals sought by an endless variety of mortals. Paradoxically enough, in many personalities the few simplified needs or instincts alleged to be the *common* ground for all motivation, turn out to be completely lacking.

The second type of dynamic psychology, the one here defended, regards adult motives as infinitely varied, and as self-sustaining, *contemporary* systems, growing out of antecedent systems, but functionally independent of them. Just as a child gradually repudiates his dependence on his parents, develops a will of his own, becomes self-active and self-determining, and outlives his parents, so it is with motives. Each motive has a definite point of origin which may possibly lie in instincts, or, more likely, in the organic tensions of infancy. Chronologically speaking, all adult purposes can be traced back to these seed-forms in infancy, but as the individual matures the tie is broken. Whatever bond remains is historical, not functional.

Such a theory is obviously opposed to psychoanalysis and to all other genetic accounts that assume inflexibility in the root purposes and drives of life. (Freud says that the structure of the Id *never* changes!) The theory declines to admit that the energies of adult

personality are infantile or archaic in nature. Motivation is *always* contemporary. The life of modern Athens is *continuous* with the life of the ancient city, but it in no sense *depends* upon its present "go." The life of a tree is continuous with that of its seed, but the seed no longer sustains and nourishes the full-grown tree. Earlier purposes lead into later purposes and are abandoned in their favor.

William James taught a curious doctrine that has been a matter for incredulous amusement ever since, the doctrine of the *transitoriness of instincts*. According to this theory—not so quaint as sometimes thought—an instinct appears but once in a lifetime, whereupon it promptly disappears through its transformation into habits. If there *are* instincts this is no doubt of their fate, for no instinct can retain its motivational force unimpaired after it has been absorbed and recast under the transforming influence of learning. Such is the reasoning of James, and such is the logic of functional autonomy. The psychology of personality must be a psychology of *post-instinctive* behavior.

Woodworth has spoken of the transformation of "mechanisms" into "drives." [2] A mechanism Woodworth defines as any course of behavior that brings about an adjustment. A *drive* is any neural process that releases mechanisms especially concerned with consummatory reactions. In the course of learning, many preparatory mechanisms must be developed in order to lead to the consummation of an original purpose. These mechanisms are the effective cause of activity in each succeeding mechanism, furnishing the drive for each stage following in the series. Originally all these mechanisms were merely instrumental, only links in the long chain of processes involved in the achievement of an *instinctive* purpose; with time and development, with integration and elaboration, many of these mechanisms become activated directly, setting up a state of desire and tension for activities and objects no longer connected with the original impulse. Activities

---

[2] R. S. Woodworth, *Dynamic psychology*, 1918. Equivalent assertions are those of W. Stern concerning the transformation of "phenomotives" into "genomotives" (*Allgemeine Psychologie*, 1935, 569), and of E. C. Tolman regarding the "strangle hold" that "means-objects" acquire by "setting up in their own right" (Psychology versus immediate experience, *Phil. Sci.*, 2, 1935, 370).

and objects that earlier in the game were *means* to an end, now become *ends* in themselves.[3]

Although Woodworth's choice of quasi-neurological terminology is not the best, his doctrine, or one like it, is indispensable in accounting for the infinite number of effective motives possible in human life, and for their severance from the rudimentary desires of infancy. Further discussion of the operation of the principle and a critique of Woodworth's position will be more to the point after a review of the evidence in favor of the principle.

Evidence for functional autonomy

We begin in a common-sense way. An ex-sailor has a craving for the sea, a musician longs to return to his instrument after an enforced absence, a city dweller yearns for his native hills, and a miser continues to amass his useless horde. Now, the sailor may have first acquired his love for the sea as an incident in his struggle to earn a living. The sea was merely a conditioned stimulus associated with satisfaction of his nutritional craving. But now the ex-sailor is perhaps a wealthy banker; the original motive is destroyed; and yet the hunger for the sea persists unabated, even increases in intensity as it becomes more remote from the nutritional segment. The musician may first have been stung by a rebuke or by a slur on his inferior performances into mastering his instrument, but now he is safely beyond the power of these taunts; there is no need to compensate further; now he loves his instrument more than anything else in the world. Once indeed the city dweller may have associated the hills around his mountain home with nutritional and erotogenic satisfactions, but these satisfactions he now finds in his city home, *not* in the mountains; whence then comes all his hill-hunger? The miser perhaps learned his habits of thrift in dire necessity, or perhaps his thrift was a symptom of sexual perversion (as Freud would claim), and yet the miserliness persists, and even becomes stronger with the years, even after the necessity or the roots of the neurosis have been relieved.

Workmanship is a good example of functional autonomy. A good workman feels compelled to do clean-cut jobs even though his security, or the praise of others, no longer depends upon high standards. In fact, in a day of jerry-building his workmanlike standards may be to his economic disadvantage. Even so he cannot do a slipshod job. Workmanship is not an instinct, but so firm is the hold it may acquire on a man that it is little wonder Veblen mistook it for one. A businessman, long since secure economically, works himself into ill-health, and sometimes even back into poverty, for the sake of carrying on his plans. What was once an instrumental technique becomes a master motive.

Neither necessity nor reason can make one contented permanently on a lonely island or on an isolated farm after one is adapted to active, energetic city life. The acquired habits seem sufficient to urge one to a frenzied existence, even though reason and health demand the simpler life.

The pursuit of literature, the development of good taste in clothes, the use of cosmetics, the acquiring of an automobile, strolls in the public park, or a winter in Miami—all may first serve, let us say, the interests of sex. But every one of these instrumental activities may become an interest in itself, held for a lifetime, long after the erotic motive has been laid away in lavender. People often find that they have lost allegiance to their original aims because of their deliberate preference for the many ways of achieving them.

The maternal sentiment offers a final illustration. Many young mothers bear their children unwillingly, dismayed at the thought of the drudgery of the future. At first they may be indifferent to, or even hate, their offspring; the parental instinct seems wholly lacking. The only motives that hold such a mother to child-tending may be fear of what her critical neighbors will say, fear of the law, a habit of doing any job well, or perhaps a dim hope that the child will provide security for her in her old age. However gross these motives, they are sufficient to hold her to her work, until through the practice of devotion her burden becomes a joy. As her love for the child develops, her earlier practical motives are forgotten. In

---

[3] "The fundamental drive towards a certain end may be hunger, sex, pugnacity, or what not, but once the activity is started, the means to the end becomes an object of interest on its own account" (Woodworth, *op. cit.*, 201). "The primal forces of hunger, fear, sex, and the rest, continue in force, but do not by any means, even with their combinations, account for the sum total of drives activating the experienced individual" (*ibid.*, 104).

later years not one of these original motives may operate. The child may be incompetent, criminal, a disgrace to her, and far from serving as a staff for her declining years, he may continue to drain her resources and vitality. The neighbors may criticize her for indulging the child; the law may exonerate her from allegiance; she certainly feels no pride in such a child; yet she sticks to him. The tenacity of the maternal sentiment under such adversity is proverbial.

Such examples from everyday experience could be multiplied *ad infinitum*. The evidence, however, appears in sharper outline when it is taken from experimental and clinical studies. In each of the following instances some new function emerges as an independently structured unit from preceding functions. The activity of these new units does not depend upon the continued activity of the units from which they developed.

(1) The circular reflex. Everyone has observed the almost endless repetition of acts by a child. The good-natured parent who picks up a spoon repeatedly thrown down by a baby wearies of this occupation long before the infant does. Such repetitive behavior, found likewise in early vocalization (babbling), and in other early forms of play, is commonly ascribed to the mechanism of the circular reflex.[4] It is an elementary instance of functional autonomy; for any situation where the consummation of an act provides adequate stimulation for the repetition of the *same* act does not require any backward tracing of motives. The act is self-perpetuating until it is inhibited by new activities or fatigue.

(2) Conative perseveration. Many experiments show that incompleted tasks set up tensions that tend to keep the individual at work until they are resolved. No hypothesis of self-assertion, rivalry, or any other basic need, is required. The completion of the task itself has become a quasi-need with dynamic force of its own. It has been shown, for example, that interrupted tasks are better remembered than completed tasks,[5] that an individual interrupted in a task will, even in the face of considerable opposition, return to that task,[6] that even trivial tasks undertaken in a casual way become almost haunting in character until they are completed.[7]

Conative perseveration of this order is stronger if an empty interval of time follows the period of work, showing that *left to itself,* without the inhibiting effect of other duties or activities, the motive grows stronger and stronger. The experiment of Kendig proves this point, as well as that of C. E. Smith.[8] The latter investigator demonstrated that there is more success in removing a conditioned fear if the de-conditioning process is commenced immediately. After a twenty-four hour delay the fear has become set and is more difficult to eradicate. Hence the sound advice to drivers of automobiles or airplanes who have been involved in an accident, that they drive again immediately to conquer the shock of the accident, lest the fear become set into a permanent phobia. The rule seems to be that, unless specifically inhibited, all emotional shocks, given time to set, tend to take on a compulsive autonomous character.

(3) Conditioned reflexes not requiring reinforcement. The pure conditioned reflex readily dies out unless the secondary stimulus is occasionally reinforced by the primary stimulus. The dog does not continue to salivate whenever it hears a bell unless sometimes at least an edible offering accompanies the bell. But there are innumerable instances in human life where a single association, *never* reinforced, results in the establishment of a lifelong dynamic system. An experience associated only once with a bereavement, an accident, or a battle, may become the center of a permanent phobia or complex, not in the least dependent on a recurrence of the original shock.

(4) Counterparts in animal behavior. Though the validity of a principle in human psychology never depends upon its having a counterpart in animal psychology, still it is of interest to find functional autonomy in the lower organisms. For example, rats, who will first learn a certain habit only under the incentive of some specific tension, as hunger, will, after learning,

---

4 E. B. Holt, *Animal Drive and the Learning Process,* 1931, esp. Chaps. VII and VIII.
5 B. Zeigarnik, Uber das Behalten von erledigten und unerledigten Handlungen, *Psychol. Forsch.,* 9, 1927, 1-86.
6 M. Ovsiankina, Die Wiederaufnahme unterbrochener Handlungen, *ibid.,* 11, 1928, 302-379.
7 I. Kendig, Studies in perseveration, *J. Psychol.,* 3, 1936, 223-264.
8 C. E. Smith, Change in the apparent resistance of the skin as a function of certain physiological and psychological factors. A thesis deposited in the Harvard College Library, 1934.

often perform the habit even when fed to repletion.[9]

Another experiment shows that rats trained to follow a long and difficult path will for a time persist in using this path, even though a short easy path to the goal is offered and even after the easier path has been learned.[10] Among rats as among human beings, old and useless habits have considerable power in their own right.

Olson studied the persistence of artificially induced scratching habits in rats. Collodion applied to the ears of the animal set up removing and cleaning movements. Four days later the application was repeated. From that time on the animals showed significantly greater number of cleaning movements than control animals. A month after the beginning of the experiment when the ears of the rats as studied by the microscope showed no further trace of irritation, the number of movements was still very great. Whether the induced habit spasm was permanently retained the experimenter does not say.[11]

(5) Rhythm. A rat whose activity bears a definite relation to his habits of feeding (being greatest just preceding a period of feeding and midway between two such periods) will, even when starved, display the same periodicity and activity. The acquired rhythm persists without dependence on the original periodic stimulation of feeding.[12]

Even a mollusc whose habits of burrowing in the sand and reappearing depend upon the movements of the tide, will, when removed from the beach to the laboratory, continue for several days in the same rhythm without the tide. Likewise certain animals, with nocturnal rhythms advantageous in avoiding enemies, obtaining food, or preventing excessive evaporation from the body, may exhibit such rhythms even when kept in a laboratory with constant conditions of illumination, humidity, and temperature.[13]

There are likewise instances where acquired rhythms in human life have taken on a dynamic character. Compulsive neurotics enter upon fugues or debauches, apparently not because of specific stimulation, but because "the time has come." A dipsomaniac, in confinement and deprived for months of his alcohol, describes the fierceness of the recurrent appetite (obviously acquired) as follows:

Those craving paroxysms occur at regular intervals, three weeks apart, lasting for several days. They are not weak, namby-pamby things for scoffers to laugh at. If not assuaged with liquor they become spells of physical and mental illness. My mouth drools saliva, my stomach and intestines seem cramped, and I become bilious, nauseated, and in a shaky nervous funk.[14]

In such states of drug addiction, as likewise in states of hunger, lust, fatigue, there is to be sure a physical craving, but the rhythms of the craving are partially acquired, and are always accentuated by the mental habits associated with it. For instance, eating in our civilized way of life takes place not because physical hunger naturally occurs three times a day, but because of habitual rhythms of expectancy. The habit of smoking is much more than a matter of craving for the specific narcotic effects of tobacco; it is a craving for the motor ritual and periodic distraction as well.

(6) Neuroses. Why are acquired tics, stammering, sexual perversions, phobias, and anxiety so stubborn and so often incurable? Even psychoanalysis, with its deepest of depth-probing, seldom succeeds in effecting *complete* cures in such cases, even though the patient may feel relieved or at least reconciled to his difficulties after treatment. The reason seems to be that what are usually called "symptoms" are in reality something more. They have set themselves up in their own right as independent systems of motivation. Merely disclosing their roots does not change their independent activity.[15]

[9] J. D. Dodgson, Relative values of reward and punishment in habit formation, *Psychobiol.*, 1, 1917, 231-276. This work has already been interpreted by K. S. Lashley as favoring Woodworth's dynamic theory as opposed to Freud's (Contributions of Freudism to psychology: III. Physiological analysis of the libido, *Psychol. Rev.*, 31, 1924, 192-202).
[10] H. C. Gilhousen, Fixation of excess distance patterns in the white rat, *J. Comp. Psychol.*, 16, 1933, 1-23.
[11] W. C. Olson, *The measurement of nervous habits in normal children*, 1929, 62-65.
[12] C. P. Richter, A behavioristic study of the activity of the rat, *Comp. Psychol. Monog.*, 1, 1922 (no. 2), 1-55.
[13] S. C. Crawford, The habits and characteristics of nocturnal animals, *Quart. Rev. Biol.*, 9, 1934, 201-214.
[14] Inmate Ward Eight, *Beyond the door of delusion*, 1932, 281.
[15] The case of W. E. Leonard, *The locomotive god*, 1927, is instructive in this regard. An intense phobia was not relieved by tracing its history backward to the start of life. Even though he could explain why he was once frightened for a very good reason (by a locomotive), the author is

(7) The relation between ability and interest.
Psychometric studies have shown that the relation between ability and interest is always positive, often markedly so. A person likes to do what he can do well. Over and over again it has been demonstrated that the skill learned for some external reason, turns into an interest, and is self-propelling, even though the original reason for pursuing it has been lost. A student who at first undertakes a field of study in college because it is prescribed, because it pleases his parents, or because it comes at a convenient hour, often ends by finding himself absorbed, perhaps for life, in the subject itself. He is not happy without it. The original motives are entirely lost. What was a means to an end has become an end in itself.

Furthermore, there is the case of genius. A skill takes possession of the man. No primitive motivation is needed to account for his persistent, absorbed activity. It just *is* the alpha and omega of life to him. It is impossible to think of Pasteur's concern for health, food, sleep, or family, as the root of his devotion to his work. For long periods of time he was oblivious of them all, losing himself in the white heat of research for which he had been trained and in which he had *acquired* a compelling and absorbing interest.

A much more modest instance is the finding of industrial research that when special incentives are offered and work speeded up as a consequence, and then these special incentives removed, *the work continues at the speeded rate.* The habit of working at a faster tempo persists without external support.

(8) Sentiments vs. instincts. Every time an alleged instinct can by rigid analysis be demonstrated not to be innate but acquired, there is in this demonstration evidence for functional autonomy. It is true enough that maternal conduct, gregariousness, curiosity, workmanship, and the like, have the tenacity and compelling power that instincts are supposed to have. If they are not instincts, then they must be autonomous sentiments with as much dynamic character as has been attributed to instincts. It is not necessary here to review all the arguments in favor of regarding such alleged instincts as acquired sentiments.

(9) The dynamic character of personal values. When an interest-system has once been formed it not only creates a tensional con-

dition that may be readily aroused, leading to overt conduct in some way satisfying to the interest, but it also acts as a silent agent for selecting and directing any behavior related to it. Take the case of people with strongly marked esthetic interests. Experiments with the word-association test have shown that such people respond more quickly to stimulus-words connected with this interest than to words relating to interests they lack.[16] Likewise, in scanning a newspaper they will observe and remember more items pertaining to art; they also take a greater interest in clothes than do nonesthetic people; and when they are asked to rate the virtues of others, they place esthetic qualities high. In short the existence of a well-established acquired interest exerts a directive and determining effect on conduct just as is to be expected of any dynamic system. The evidence can be duplicated for many interests other than the esthetic.[17]

Critique of functional autonomy

Objections to the principle of autonomy may be expected from two sides. Behaviorists will continue to prefer their conception of organic drive with its capacity for manifold conditioning by ever receding stimuli. Whereas purposivists will be unwilling to accept a pluralistic principle that seems to leave motives so largely at the mercy of learning.

The behaviorist is well satisfied with motivation in terms of organic drive and conditioning because he feels that he somehow has secure anchorage in physiological structure. (The closer he approaches physiological structure the happier the behaviorist is.) But the truth of the matter is that the neural physiology of organic drive and conditioning is no better established, and no easier to imagine, than is the neural physiology of the type of complex autonomous units of motivation here described.

Two behavioristic principles will be said to account adequately for the instances of func-

---

quite unable to explain why now he is frightened *for no particular reason.* Such neuroses, and psychotic delusional systems as well, often acquire a "strangle hold," and the task of dislodging them is usually more than therapeutic skill is equal to.

[16] H. Cantril, General and specific attitudes, *Psychol. Monog.,* 42, 1932, (no. 192), 1-109.

[17] H. Cantril and G. W. Allport, Recent applications of the study of values, *J. Abnorm. & Soc. Psychol.,* 28, 1933, 259-273.

tional autonomy previously cited, viz., the circular reflex and cross-conditioning. The former concept, acceptable enough when applied to infant behavior, merely says that the more activity a muscle engages in, the more activity of the same sort does it engender through a self-sustaining circuit.[18] This is, to be sure, a clear instance of autonomy, albeit on a primitive level, oversimplified so far as adult conduct is concerned. The doctrine of cross-conditioning refers to subtle recession of stimuli, and to the intricate possibility of cross-connections in conditioning. For instance, such ubiquitous external stimuli as humidity, daylight, gravitation, may feed collaterally into open channels of activity, arousing mysteriously and unexpectedly a form of conduct to which they have unconsciously been conditioned. For example, the angler whose fishing expeditions have been accompanied by sun, wind, or a balmy June day, may feel a desire to go fishing whenever the barometer, the thermometer, or the calendar in his city home tells him that these conditions prevail.[19] Innumerable such crossed stimuli are said to account for the arousal of earlier patterns of activity.

Such a theory inherits, first of all, the well-known difficulties resident in the principle of conditioning whenever it is made the sole explanation of human behavior. Further, though the reflex circle and cross-conditioning may in fact exist, they are really rather trivial principles. They leave the formation of interest and its occasional arousal almost entirely to chance factors of stimulation. They give no picture at all of the spontaneous and variable aspects of traits, interests, or sentiments. These dispositions are regarded as purely *reactive* in nature; the stimulus is all-important. The truth is that dispositions *sort out* stimuli congenial to them, and this activity does not in the least resemble the rigidity of reflex response.[20]

A variant on the doctrine of cross-conditioning is the principle of redintegration.[21] This concept admits the existence of highly integrated dispositions of a neuropsychic order. These dispositions can be aroused *as a whole* by any stimulus previously associated with their functioning. In this theory likewise, the disposition is regarded as a rather passive affair, waiting for reactivation by some portion of the original stimulus. Here again the variability of the disposition and its urge-like quality are not

accounted for. The stimulus is thought merely to reinstate a complex determining tendency. Nothing is said about how the stimuli themselves are *selected,* why a motive once aroused becomes insistent, surmounting obstacles, skillfully subordinating conflicting impulses, and inhibiting irrelevant trains of thought.

In certain respects the principle of autonomy stands midway between the behavioristic view and the thoroughgoing purposive psychology of the hormic order. It agrees with the former in emphasizing the acquisition of motives, in avoiding an a priori and unchanging set of original urges, and in recognizing (as limited principles) the operation of the circular response and cross-conditioning. It agrees with the hormic psychologist, however, in finding that striving-from-within is a far more essential characteristic of motive than stimulation-from-without. It agrees likewise in distrusting the emphasis upon stomach contractions and other "excess and deficit stimuli" as "causes" of mature behavior. Such segmental sources of energy even when conditioned cannot possibly account for the "go" of conduct. But functional autonomy does not rely as does hormic theory upon modified instinct, which after all is as archaic a principle as the conditioning of autonomic segmental tensions, but upon the capacity of human beings to replenish their energy through a plurality of constantly changing systems of a dynamic order.

The hormic psychologist, however, will not accept the autonomy of new motivational systems. If mechanisms can turn into drives, he asks, why is it that habits and skills as they become exercised to the point of perfection do not acquire an ever increasing driving force?[22] The mechanisms of walking, speaking, or dressing cannot be said to furnish their own motive-power. One walks, speaks, or dresses in order

---

[18] E. B. Holt, op. cit., 38.
[19] Ibid., 224.
[20] The basic fact that complex "higher" centers have the power of inhibiting, selecting, and initiating the activity of simpler segmental responses is a fact too well established to need elaboration here. It constitutes the very foundation of the psychophysiological theories advanced by Sherrington, Herrick, Dodge, Kohler, Troland, and many others.
[21] Cf. H. L. Hollingworth, *Psychology of the functional neuroses,* 1920.
[22] W. McDougall, Motives in the light of recent discussion, *Mind,* 29, 1920, 277-293.

to satisfy a motive entirely external to these learned skills.[23]

The criticism is sufficiently cogent to call into question Woodworth's form of stating the principle, viz., "mechanisms may become drives." It is not an adequate statement of the case.

Looking at the issue more closely, it seems to be neither the perfected talent nor the automatic habit that has driving power, but the imperfect talent and the habit-in-the-making. The child who is *just learning* to speak, to walk, or to dress is, in fact, likely to engage in these activities for their own sake, precisely as does the adult who has an *unfinished* task in hand. He remembers it, returns to it, and suffers a feeling of frustration if he is prevented from engaging in it. Motives are always a kind of striving for some form of completion; they are unresolved tension, and demand a "closure" to activity under way. (Latent motives are dispositions that are easily thrown by a stimulus or by a train of associations into this state of active tension.) The active motive subsides when its goal is reached, or in the case of a motor skill, when it has become at last automatic. The novice in automobile driving has an unquestionable impulse to master the skill. Once acquired, the ability sinks to the level of an *instrumental* disposition and is aroused only in the service of some other *driving* (unfulfilled) motive.

Now, in the case of the permanent interests of personality, the situation is the same. A man whose motive is to acquire learning or to perfect his craft can never be satisfied that he has reached the end of his quest, for his problems are never completely solved, his skill is never perfect. Lasting interests are recurrent sources of discontent, and from their incompleteness they derive their forward impetus. Art, science, religion, love, are never perfected. Motor skills, however, are often perfected, and beyond that stage they seldom provide their own motive power. It is, then, only mechanisms-on-the-make (in process of perfecting) that serve as drives. With this emendation, Woodworth's view is corrected, and McDougall's objection is met.[24]

Implications of functional autonomy

The principle of functional autonomy accounts, as no other principle of dynamic psy-

chology is able to do, for the concrete impulses that lie at the root of personal behavior. It is thus the first step in establishing a basis for the more realistic study of unique and individual forms for personality. "But how—" the traditionalists may cry, "how are we ever to have a *science* of unique events? Science must generalize." So it must, but it is a manifest error to assume that a general principle of motivation must involve the postulation of abstract or general motives. What the objectors forget is that *a general law may be a law that tells how uniqueness comes about.* The principle of functional autonomy is general enough to meet the needs of science, but particularized enough in its operation to account for the uniqueness of personal conduct. Its specific advantages stand out in the following summary.

(1) It clears the way for a completely dynamic psychology of *traits, attitudes, interests,* and *sentiments,* which can now be regarded as the ultimate and true dispositions of the mature personality.

(2) It avoids the absurdity of regarding the energy of life now, in the *present,* as somehow consisting of early archaic forms (instincts, prepotent reflexes, or the never-changing Id). Learning brings new systems of interests into existence just as it does new abilities and skills. At each stage of development these interests are always contemporary; whatever drives, drives *now.*

(3) It dethrones the stimulus. A motive is no longer regarded as a mechanical reflex or as a matter of redintegration, depending entirely upon the capricious operation of a conditioned stimulus. In a very real sense dispositions *select* the stimuli to which they respond, even though *some* stimulus is required for their arousal.

(4) It readily admits the validity of all other established principles of growth. Functional autonomy recognizes the products of differentiation, integration, maturation, exercise, imitation, suggestion, conditioning, trauma, and all other processes of development; and allows,

---

[23] Though this objection is usually valid, it is not always so, for there are cases where the liking for walks, for talking for the sake of talking, or for dressing, playing games, etc., seems to be a self-sustaining motivational system.

[24] This theory embraces very easily the work of K. Lewin and his associates upon the nature of "quasi-needs." The urgency of these needs is greatest just before a goal is reached, after which time the motive subsides completely.

as they do not, considered by themselves, for the preservation of these products in significant motivational patterns.

(5) It places in proper perspective the problems of the origin of conduct by removing the fetish of the genetic method. Not that the historical view of behavior is unimportant for a complete understanding of personality, but so far as *motives* are concerned the cross-sectional dynamic analysis is more significant. Motives being always contemporary should be studied in their present structure. Failure to do so is probably the chief reason why psychoanalysis meets so many defeats, as do all other therapeutic schemes relying too exclusively upon uncovering the motives of early childhood.

(6) It accounts for the force of delusions, shell-shock, phobias, and all manner of compulsive and maladaptive behavior. One would expect such unrealistic modes of adjustment to be given up as they are shown to be poor ways of confronting the environment. Insight and the law of effect should both remove them —but too often they have acquired a strangle hold in their own right.

(7) At last we can account adequately for socialized and civilized behavior. The principle supplies the correction necessary to the faulty logic of *bellum omnium contra omnes*. Starting life as a completely selfish being, the child would indeed remain entirely wolfish and piggish throughout his days unless genuine transformations of motives took place. Motives being completely alterable, the dogma of Egoism turns out to be a callow and superficial philosophy of behavior, or else a useless redundancy.

(8) It explains likewise why a person often *becomes* what at first he merely *pretends* to be —the smiling professional hostess who grows fond of her once irksome rôle and is unhappy when deprived of it; the man who for so long has counterfeited the appearance of self-confidence and optimism that he is always driven to assume it; the prisoner who comes to love his shackles. Such *personae,* as Jung observes, are often transformed into the real self. The mask becomes the *anima.*

(9) The drive behind genius is explained. Gifted people demand the exercise of their talents, even when no other reward lies ahead. In lesser degree the various hobbies, the artistic, or the intellectual interests of any person show the same significant autonomy.

(10) In brief, the principle of functional autonomy is a declaration of independence for the psychology of personality. Though in itself a general law, at the same time it helps to account, not for the abstract motivation of an impersonal and therefore non-existent mind-in-general, but for the concrete, viable motives of each and every mind-in-particular.

An appetitional theory of sexual motivation

KENNETH R. HARDY

The formal study of motivation is frequently difficult for introductory psychology students because of the many complex issues involved. The following article illustrates some of the problems encountered in studying motivation by analyzing a particular kind of behavior—sex. Dr. Hardy, Professor of Psychology at Brigham Young University and author of *The Interpersonal Game,* challenges the validity of drive-reduction theory and argues that sexual desire is primarily learned. According to him, sexual appetites, like other appetites, are specific habits that can be increased or decreased depending on the experience of the individual. Experiences which produce changes in pleasant feelings for the person are likely to increase in their motivational strength. Contrary to the prevalent opinion of many psychiatrists, psychologists, and sexologists, Professor Hardy states that periodic sexual release is not biologically essential. The last and most controversial section of the paper deals with specific recommendations for the management of premarital sexual behavior. It is important that these recommendations be considered separately from the evaluation of the earlier, more theoretical portions of the paper.

Following a brief review of evidence on the adequacy of biological explanations of sexual motivation, a cognitive-affective model of motivation is stated. The model is used to develop a conception of sexual motivation as an experientially developed appetite. Two constitutional sources of affect are proposed, each of which is sufficient to reward behavior: the pleasure of genital stimulation or arousal and the complex excitement-relaxation of orgasm. The nature of childhood sexuality and the elaboration of sexual appetite in courtship are examined. After a discussion of approach-avoidance dynamics, problems of sexual control and compatibility are considered.

The purpose of this paper is to develop a theory of human sexual motivation which may more adequately account for *human* behavior than the conceptions now prevalent in the psychological and lay literature. Despite much direct and indirect evidence to the contrary, some form of biological drive theory is dominant today, couched in terms of drive reduction, homeostatic disequilibrium, endocrine secretion, or instinctual libido.

To be proposed is a conception of sexual appetite based upon psychological hedonism or affective change. This statement owes much to the thinking and research of F. A. Beach, P. T. Young, D. C. McClelland, Kurt Lewin, D. O. Hebb, and many others. However, no previous attempt has been made, as far as is known, to systematically pursue the implications of affective theory to the development of sexual appetite. Further, the present author must remain responsible for this development, as those mentioned may wish to disown the particular formulation proposed here.

Inadequacy of organic explanations

It is beyond the scope of this paper to give a comprehensive review of evidence regarding the adequacy of biological needs in accounting for sexual motivation. Nevertheless, a brief summary of several lines of investigation may be stated:

Phyletic Comparisons. Much of the experimental work on sex motivation has been done on varous species of birds and rodents (Beach, 1951). This work demonstrates the importance of hormonal factors, particularly in the females of these species. The tendency to extrapolate from these data to humans should be strongly tempered by several considerations. In the first place, there are striking interspecies differences. For example, although testosterone propionate treatment accelerates the rate of maturation of sexual responses and produces greater than normal sexual drive and secretory activity of the accessory sexual organs in the rat, it does not do so in the guinea pig (Gerall, 1958). Also, studies of higher mammals, especially primates, show the relaxation of endocrine and genetic controls, with experience playing an increasingly prominent role as the human level is approached (Beach, 1947; Ford & Beach, 1951; Harlow, 1962; Nissen, 1953). Finally, when constitutional or hormonal interpretations of sexual motivation are tested directly upon humans, they fail to adequately account for the data, as noted in what is to follow.

Infantile and Childhood Sexuality. Cross-cultural data show the extensive elaboration of sexual behavior (masturbation, mutual masturbation, sexual games, attempted coitus, coitus itself) in cultures which are permissive, encouraging, or demanding of sexual activity prepuberally (Ford & Beach, 1951; Henry & Henry, 1953). In such societies, virtually no secrecy is associated with sex, and little or nothing is done to inhibit the sexual activity of the youngsters. Ford and Beach (1951) report that in a few cultures, regular heterosexual intercourse occurs from ages 8-10 onward; e.g., among the Chewa it is believed that youth will not mature unless intercourse begins early in life; similarly, the Lepcha believe that girls will be infertile unless they participate in coitus prepuberally.

The extent of sexual activity in childhood among the peoples mentioned above is a

---

From *Psychological Review*, LXXI (1964), 1-18. Reprinted by permission of the American Psychological Association and the author.

powerful demonstration of the hypothesis that sexual interest is not dependent upon the maturation of the sex glands.

Effects of Castration. When males are castrated postpuberally, the effects are highly variable, ranging from heightened libido to an abrupt cessation of sexual motivation (Hamilton, 1943; Tauber, 1940). Tauber, after reviewing the literature, concluded that the attitude of the patient toward the castration was a critical factor.

When females are castrated postpuberally, the effects again are variable. In Filler and Drezner's (1944) careful study of 41 cases, 36 experienced no libidinal change, 3 showed a drop in libido, and 2 showed an increase.

Data are scanty regarding the effects of prepuberal castration. Ford and Beach (1951) refer to a few cases where the male is able to voluntarily obtain an erection, copulate, and experience orgasm (of course without ejaculation); these may be atypical in our culture, however. Since prepuberal castration usually results in underdevelopment of the penis, it would bring about lessened effectiveness in copulation, as well as all of the psychological implications of masculine inadequacy that a small penis may connote to the patient.

Homosexuality. Kinsey (1941) convincingly maintains that hormonal interpretations are inadequate to account for the following facts: *(a)* homosexuality and heterosexuality are not mutually exclusive but coexist in combinations of every degree of relative preponderance; *(b)* persons may go from heterosexual to homosexual relationships and vice versa in a matter of hours; or alternatively, there may occur months or years of an exclusively heterosexual or homosexual relationship, followed by a reversal of pattern; *(c)* thus far, there is an inability to distinguish between heterosexuals and homosexuals on the basis of hormonal secretion or constitutional typologies.

In a few societies (Siwan, Aranda, Keraki, Kiwai), sodomy is virtually universal, with those not participating considered peculiar. Commonly, these relationships begin at puberty, the boy taking the feminine role at first, later assuming the masculine role (Ford & Beach, 1951). Such relations coexist, of course, with heterosexual relations. In their study of American men, Kinsey, Pomeroy, and Martin (1948) report that 37% of their sample had had at least one homosexual experience resulting in orgasm, though only 4% were exclusively homosexual.

It is true that most American men settle into a pattern of heterosexuality, while a small minority establish various degrees of bisexual orientation (Kinsey et al., 1948). Some members of this minority establish definite homosexual preferences, with an accompanying way of life which includes a special jargon, mien, and social life among those similarly disposed (Cleckley, 1957; Cory, 1961). Whether one defines homosexuality as dealing with these extreme cases, or subsumes under this term a more widespread personality predisposition, the biological interpretation is equally tenuous.

Hermaphroditism. Data on individuals with confused or mistaken sex identity show variations in sexual desire, fantasy, and social role to be a function of the person's self-conception as to which sex he is (usually this is dependent upon parental conceptions), and not upon actual sex identity as determined by gonadal tissue (Ellis, 1945; Finesinger, Meigs, & Sulkowitch, 1942; Miles, 1942; Seward, 1946). In Ellis' exhaustive review of the literature, those who were true hermaphrodites (possessing both masculine and feminine gonadal tissue) were not significantly different from the pseudo-hermaphrodites in direction of sex libido. Of the total group studied intensively by Ellis, 80% had heterosexual libido, 11% were psychosexually immature, and 9% were homosexual or bisexual in libidinal interest, percentages which are probably fairly comparable to a "normal" group. Furthermore, the only bisexuals (those having heterosexual and homosexual motivation) came from the pseudohermaphrodites, the group least expected (biologically) to produce them. In virtually every case, the sex role and libidinal interest were those expected of the sex the individual was assumed to be while growing up, with little correspondence between sex role and libidinal interest on the one hand, and somatic characteristics on the other.

More recently, Money, Hampson, and Hampson (1955a, 1955b, 1957) and Money (1961) have reported results of comprehensive medical and psychological observations on 105 hermaphroditic patients. Their results strongly confirm Ellis' findings, but are even more striking. Only five of their patients had a gender role or libidinal orientation ambiguous or deviant from that expected for the sex to which they were assigned and in which they were reared. This was true despite the fact that these patients had one or more of the following physical variables of sex which were incongruous with the assigned sex: external genital morphology, internal accessory reproductive structures, hormonal sex and secondary sex characteristics, gonadal sex, and chromosomal sex. Especially striking were cases of the same medical diagnosis (e.g., hyperadrenocortical female, cryptorchid male hypospadiac), some of whom had been reared as masculine, others as feminine. Those raised as masculine were strikingly different from those raised as feminine in gender role and libidinal orientation, which followed their assigned sex in virtually every case.

Treatment of Sexual Problems. Attempts to treat impotence and frigidity by hormonal means have proved generally unsuccessful, when the effects of suggestion (the meaning of the treatment to the patient) are controlled (Carmichael, Noonan, & Kenyon, 1941; Creevy & Rea, 1940; Seward, 1946). Seward (1946, pp. 198–200) concludes her discussion of relevant literature by maintaining that in virtually all cases of frigidity and impotence, the difficulty is psychogenic rather than organic in character, and that the efficacy of psychotherapy as against hormonal therapy substantiates this diagnosis.

Periodicity of Sex Desire. Data from Davis (1929), Dickinson and Beam (1931), Ellis (1936), Hamilton (1929), Terman (1938), Tinklepaugh (1933), indicate two peaks of sexual desire in women, one occurring immediately prior to menstruation, the other occurring just following menstruation, with desire at a low ebb during the period of peak fertility. This is exactly opposite to expectation based upon hormonal fluctuations. Benedek and Rubenstein (1939, 1942), on the other hand, report maximal heterosexual drive among patients in psychoanalysis during the follicular phase of maximum fertility. These investigators inferred drive levels from reports of fantasy obtained during psychoanalytic interviews. Further research is needed to clarify the differences in results, whether due to populations studied, relative validity of measures used, or other factors. There does seem to be general

agreement that periodic variations in sex drive are difficult for many if not most women to report. If such monthly fluctuations were of major consequence, it seems reasonable to assume that they would be more fully reflected in behavior or consciousness.

Although it is part of our folklore that, following sexual outlet, postpuberal males experience a steadily increasing sex drive which becomes more and more insistent, this belief is most probably false. In the words of Beach (1956),

No genuine tissue or biological needs are generated by sexual abstinence. It used to be believed that prolonged sexual inactivity in adulthood resulted in the progressive accumulation of secretions within the accessory sex glands, and that nerve impulses from these distended receptacles gave rise to sexual urges. Modern evidence negates this hypothesis. . . . What is commonly confused with a primary drive associated with sexual deprivation is in actuality sexual appetite, and this has little or no relation to biological or physiological needs [p. 4].

It seems warranted to conclude that the overwhelming proportion of the variance in human sexual motivation and behavior is not explicable in terms of some biological need or tension, however conceived. An alternative view is explored in this paper, one which uses a series of notions based largely on cognitive expectancy theory, Lewinian field theory, and modern hedonic or affective theory.

Principles of motivation

The present theory of sexuality is based upon several principles common to motives generally, which will be stated prior to the specific discussion of sex motivation.

1. Motives are based upon learned expectations of an affective (hedonic) change (McClelland, 1951, p. 466; Young, 1959). These expectations are aroused by cues or stimuli which are associated with affective states due to some previous learning. Such learning may be based on the actual experience of the individual; however, it may also be vicariously based on affect laden fantasies (imaginal processes) aroused either by the person's own thought processes or through some form of social influence (e.g., reading

a romantic novel). It is not implied that imaginal or vicarious experience is necessarily as potent a source of motivation as firsthand, physical experience, since the physical experience will ordinarily carry more affect, and may have a richer context of cues (Principles 4 and 5 below). However, imagined or vicarious experiences may be highly motivating. This is witnessed by common fears of ghosts, dragons, bogeymen, haunted houses; behavior following a horror movie (locking windows, insomnia, nightmares). Johnson's (1945) report of the phantom anesthetist of Mattoon is a dramatic illustration.

2. For such an expectation to motivate behavior, the person must believe that some action (symbolic or overt) on his part helps or is required to bring about the desired affective change. A motive, then, is an expectation that the pursuit of a given course of action will contribute to, or result in, a change in affective state. The explicit requirement made here that instrumental behavior is a necessary part of a motivational expectation seems to go beyond the statement of affective theory by McClelland, Atkinson, Clark, and Lowell (1953).

An example may help to clarify this point. Suppose a small boy hears the bells of an ice cream truck coming down the street; his mother buys him an ice cream bar; and he thoroughly enjoys this tasty treat. There will then be a tendency for the bells on subsequent occasions to produce in him an expectation of pleasurable affect. However, the behavior he is motivated to employ is dependent upon the way in which the thoughts or actions he engages in are conceived as mediating between the cues and the affect, or serve as affect-producing cues themselves. Thus if the boy had to do nothing to receive the ice cream bar, he would merely engage in watchful waiting upon hearing the bells. If he had to coax his mother to purchase him a bar, however, the sound of the bells would instigate vigorous action on his part.

3. The confidence one places in a given affective expectation increases each time it is confirmed through having the affect follow or accompany the cues which arouse the expectation. Conversely, the lack of confirmation (infirmation) of an expectation tends to destroy belief in it as the predicted affective changes fail to follow the associated cues (Bruner, 1951). Furthermore, the extent to which the affect and stimuli are uniquely associated determines the degree to which the affect will be aroused by only such cues and the degree to which the cues will arouse only such affect. Continuing the example of the boy, if the occasion mentioned is the only time he hears such bells and has such an ice cream bar, then it can be said that these two things have been uniquely associated. If he hears such bells subsequently and enjoys this tasty treat each time, then he will develop great confidence (faith) that when the bells are heard a pleasurable eating experience will follow. The principle of uniqueness is similar to the Bruner-Postman concept of monopoly (Bruner, 1951).

4. There is some positive relationship between the amplitude of the affective change and the intensity of the resulting motive.

5. The likelihood of arousal of a motive is a function of the variety of cues associated with the affective change, together with the associative strength of those cues to the affect (Principle 3).

The last three principles parallel rather closely the analysis by McClelland et al. (1953, pp. 68-73) of factors affecting motive strength.

6. A family of expectations is a group of expectations which tend to arouse one another or to be aroused by a similar set of cues. Confirmation of one member of a family of expectations strengthens belief in other members of that family. Conversely, infirmation of one member reduces belief in other members of the set. The amount of generalized confirmation or infirmation is a function of the organization of relationships between the confirmed member and the other members of the family (see Asch, 1952, pp. 580-582; Rokeach, 1960, ch. 2).

These statements are cognitive equivalents for phenomena often phrased in terms of stimulus generalization, discrimination, and habit family hierarchy.

7. There is a degree of habituation in some affective areas in which repetition or continuance of an activity leads to a lesser affective change than that which occurred upon initial participation in the activity. For example, viewing the Grand Canyon of the Colorado or the

Lower Falls of the Yellowstone is more thrilling the first time seen than later. Somehow the "edge of newness" is rubbed off, perhaps as a function of gratification of the cognitive need to know the environment, or of other habituating factors (see Dember & Earl, 1957).

8. Motives can be grossly categorized into three types: (*a*) *Approach,* in which the expectations are of a positive affective change; (*b*) *Avoidant,* in which the expectations are of a negative affective change; (*c*) *Ambivalent,* in which both positive and negative expectations are aroused by the same cues.

9. The tendency to act on the basis of some motive is a function of (*a*) the relative net affective strength of the alternatives aroused in a given situation; and (*b*) the subjective probability of attainment of the goals involved (see Atkinson, 1957). The net affective strength of a course of action is the algebraic sum of the positive and negative affectivity associated with it. When the difference in Factors *a* and *b* between two alternatives is great, other things equal, the decision is relatively easy; when the alternatives are about equal, decision is difficult, with vacillation and decision time increasing (Cartwright, 1940; Cartwright & Festinger, 1943).

10. Other things equal, the more immediate the affective change the more attractive or compelling is a given alternative as opposed to a change more distant; that is, as the psychological distance to a goal increases, the less motivating it is (Miller, 1951). This time-distance gradient is much steeper for children than adults, who live in a wider time perspective (Lewin, 1946). The immediacy or delay of gratification may be related to the subjective probability or certainty of attainment. For the hunter, a bird in the hand is indeed worth two in the bush because he may not get the birds in the bush.

11. The perceived permanence or transience of the anticipated affective state is relevant in assessing the net affect of a given alternative. Stealing may bring money for a temporary splurge, but may bring lengthy incarceration, distrust by friends, chronic twinges of conscience. Other things equal, affective states perceived as being relatively permanent will be more compelling than those relatively transient. Again, the differences between children and adults in time perspective should be noted.

This dimension will be less important for children because of their relative inability to foresee long-term consequences (Lewin, 1948, p. 105).

12. Another pertinent problem in the analysis of choice behavior is the problem of mutual exclusiveness. Can a person take one alternative and also, perhaps later, another; can he have his cake and eat it too? Obviously, the perception of mutual exclusiveness may make a decision much more difficult than when both goals are seen as jointly attainable.

13. Closely related to the above is the finality or irrevocability of the decision. For example, if marriage is conceived of as a permanent bond between two people, the decision to marry a given person will be a more difficult one than if marriage is seen as an arrangement to be dissolved at the convenience of one or both of the partners.

With the foregoing tentative principles stated in general form, attention can now be directed specifically to sexual motivation.

Affective foundations of sexuality

A theory which assumes that motives are learned in association with affective experience must, in order to be complete, describe those conditions which produce affective change in the first place. McClelland, recognizing this problem, has analyzed it with regard to taste. One of his generalizations is that mild states of stimulation produce pleasure (positive affect), intense states produce pain (negative affect), with the range of intensities involved dependent upon the specific sensory quality, such as sweet, sour, salty, or bitter (McClelland, 1951, pp. 467–470). Young (1959) has made a similar analysis based upon food preferences as related to concentration in solution.

It is postulated that certain conditions, which innately are affectively positive, form the constitutional base for the elaboration of sexual appetite:

1. Mild local stimulation of the genitals is innately pleasurable. This is a matter of common observation by parents. The random exploration of the body by the infant's hands soon leads to an undue amount of time spent stimulating the genital organs unless some preventive action is taken. The phenomenon is more easily noticed in the male child because of the greater accessibility to stimulation of the

penis than the vulva and because of the observability of the phenomena of tumescence and erection consequent upon such stimulation. Adults of the Atimelang tribe of Alor, Indonesia, have capitalized upon the pleasurable character of such stimulation; they may deliberately stimulate the genitals of the child to soothe and quiet him (Kardiner, 1945, p. 131). This also occurs among the Hopi, Siriono, and Kazak (Ford & Beach, 1951). The pleasure accompanying genital stimulation (arousal) continues throughout life as an affective base for motivational development. Many stimuli, once neutral, may become associated with it, as a consequence functioning as cues leading to genital arousal, even in the absence of tactual stimulation itself.

2. The phenomenon of genital climax, together with its sequel, relaxation, is highly pleasurable. It is postulated that arousal short of climax is pleasurable, though not as gratifying as arousal leading to climax (see Kagan, 1955; Sheffield, Wulff, & Backer, 1951; Whalen, 1961, for experimental evidence in rats). Ford and Beach (1951), relying largely on data from Dickinson, maintain that masturbation in women perseverates among those who experience orgasm if no feelings of guilt or disgust ensue. While those who fail to achieve orgasm tend more often to quit, some persist in the practice for years without it.

In men, the pleasures of "girl watching," voyeurism, viewing "cheesecake" photography (Clark, 1952; Mussen & Scodel, 1955), and reading suggestive literature are well known, though participation rarely culminates in orgasm. Reference is made to Beach's (1956) tentative analysis of the sexual arousal mechanism (SAM) and the intromissive and ejaculatory mechanism (IEM). He suggests these as separate and sequential mechanisms in the male, and further suggests that the IEM has changed little in the course of evolution and is under poor voluntary control, but that the unique features of human sexuality are consequent upon the great lability of the SAM. Both the SAM and the IEM are here presumed to be highly charged with positive affect.

Childhood sexuality

In some societies (e.g., Alorese, Pilaga of Argentina), masturbation develops early and is maintained unabated through the childhood years, sometimes being elaborated into mutual masturbation and other forms of sex play, both homosexual and heterosexual. These forms of erotic expression would seem to be learned through the association of the pleasurable affect with the tactual stimulation producing it. It must be noted, of course, that other sources of affect than the erotic are frequently involved in motivations toward sexual behavior. An examination of the data of Henry and Henry (1953) on Pilaga Indian children reveals the importance of several additional factors. Sex games are used to manifest hostility and dominance. Also, parental intercourse is openly viewed by the children from a very tender age. Here the child is excluded from a social experience of powerful affect, and it may well be that in both his doll play and interpersonal play, the Pilaga child is seeking to capture the warmth of inclusion in such an affect laden experience. While in the present article the primary focus is upon the erotic or lustful affect associated with sex, it must be remembered that this affective component is nearly always integrated with other sources of affect in the sexual behavior of humans of all ages.

In many societies, more or less active steps are taken to limit or prevent the masturbatory efforts of children, and to punish other presumed evidences of sexual curiosity or interest such as boy girl exploration of genitals, public nudity, use of sex words, etc. The Victorian mores of nineteenth century Vienna are generally recognized today as the basis for Freud's postulated latency period, in which a dearth of conscious or overt sexual material occurs in (approximately) the sixth through the twelfth years. In his scheme the latency period follows closely upon the heels of the "phallic" stage in which the libido is presumed to be localized for the first time in the genitalia. This sequence is understandable, for it is precisely the behavioral evidences of the phallic stage noted above which evoke social sanctions of sufficient power to provoke inhibition or concealment of sexual expression. A wide range of sanctions may be employed, far beyond the veiled or explicit castration threats deemed to be so important by Freud. Verbal judgments, vague threats, corporal punishment, shaming, teasing, isolation, denial of privileges, distraction are some of the devices used (Sears,

Maccoby, & Levin, 1957). In this way, expressions of sexual motivation may be largely prevented until the time of life deemed culturally appropriate.

From the present theoretical framework, the similarity of childhood sexuality to adult sexuality is basically a function of the comparative sophistication about sex based in affective experience, though without the potent affect associated with orgasm, a lesser childhood intensity of motivation would usually be expected. For the child to desire intercourse (e.g., with the opposite-sex parent), he would have to know about intercourse, would have to have positive affective expectations about it, and would have to perceive the person involved as a potential sex object. Among the Pilaga Indians, where such conditions seem to pertain, little difference in sexual motivation other than in intensity might be expected between children and adults. But great differences would be expected between the naïve, carefully protected United States middle-class child and his parents. To impute to the child the sexual desires of the experienced adult is entirely unwarranted unless the child has the requisite background of affective learning.

Clinical studies by Levy (1937), Goldfarb (1944, 1945), Spitz and Wolf (1949), and others have suggested that extreme social deprivation in infancy produces severe and lasting disruption of affectional (and intellectual) processes, though others dispute this (Dennis & Najarian, 1957; Pinneau, 1955). The Harlow (1962) and the Harlow and Harlow (1962) ingenious studies of the development of affectional systems in monkeys give promise of identifying the critical variables (at least for monkeys!), though it is too early for results to be definitive. In the rhesus monkey, social deprivation in infancy appears to produce lasting inability to exhibit adequate mating behavior, but lack of peer relationships seems far more critical than the absence of the mother-child relationship. It should be noted that in Dennis and Najarian's study, the infants had active peer relationships after the first six months or so, though they were almost totally deprived of relationships with adults. Although these children seemed somewhat retarded in infancy, they appeared to be normal when tested at a later age (3-5 years).

In any event, there seems to be mounting evidence that extreme social deprivation in early childhood may produce pathological effects upon the development of "normal" heterosexuality, supporting the thesis that sexuality is in large part a derivative of experiential factors.

Development of sexual appetite in dating and courtship

In order to take a closer view of the development of sexual motivation, let us assume a "normal" but reasonably unsophisticated United States boy and girl who have entered our culturally prescribed period of heterosexual activities, the dating period. By this time, say at age 15, they each have gone through a long period of largely incidental learning about such "presexual" activities as holding hands, kissing, and embracing. Exposure to the mass media, "popular" songs, to the romantic ventures of older siblings, teasing about girl friends or boy friends—indeed, myriads of influences have given rise to the development of a family of related expectations that engaging in behavior such as holding hands, walking arm in arm, kissing, and embracing with the "right" (culturally delimited) person leads to a positive affective experience. These activities are perceived as related to one another, and thus they constitute a family or system. In the absence of personal affective experience, these expectations are not very compelling in motivational strength; but they may, under the proper conditions, lead to the initiation of such behavior. These conditions would include the perception of the partner as an appropriate object for romantic interest, a social situation of privacy or intimacy where affectively negative consequences resulting from kidding, tattling, etc., are minimized, and a developing relationship between the couple such that the girl is perceived as providing encouragement to the attentions of the boy.

As the boy becomes more assured by the conditions mentioned to expect positive consequences from his attempt to hold the girl's hand, the motivations leading to such behavior will begin to outweigh those restraining such expression, and he will initiate the activity. Assuming he has appraised the situation correctly, his grasp of the girl's hand will be reciprocated by the girl. In our society the chances are excellent that this contact will produce a pleasurable emotional state, the occurrence of which confirms the previously held expectation, and also other members of the set of expectations.

Why does holding hands produce this emotional response? Obviously, it is not because of some innate connection between receptors in the hand and neural centers of affective arousal, erotic or otherwise, since equivalent stimuli from other persons do not produce this response at all. Rather, this reaction is produced because of the learned symbolic significance of holding hands with the appropriate person. And there need not be any sexual connotation attached. This special intimacy may gratify a need for psychological closeness with someone; or it may fulfill needs for status building by meriting such a relationship with a person favorably placed in the status system of adolescent culture. Simply put, it is satisfying to be able to hold hands with someone perceived as attractive (in the modern slang, "real cool"), and doubly satisfying if this person is generally so regarded by one's age-mate reference group. The importance of esteem motives in dating has been described for an earlier generation by Waller (1937), and more recently has been graphically portrayed by Margaret Mead (1949, pp. 281-295). Other motives may be involved, of course, but the point is that initial participation in hand holding and further romantic activities generally originates in nonsexual motives, and further, that the positive affect arising from the activity serves to strengthen motivation for it.

As the dating period continues, the tendency for the couple to engage in kissing is fostered by the increased motivational strength generalized from hand holding, also by the growing intimacy of the relationship which alters the distribution of positive and negative expectations, e.g., the partner permitting or encouraging such a thing. Assuming that the kiss is attempted and is mutually acceptable, a positive affective state is likely to result, with consequences comparable to those discussed above for hand holding. If the girl's lipstick tastes good, there may be another reward, which Young (1952) would call the "palatability effect"!

But an additional development is going on at the same period of time. The couple is getting more educated about things sexual through a more sophisticated exposure to the "facts of life" via reading, age-mate conversations, and a host of other sources. So a new set of expectations is established about "petting," sexual intercourse, and the like, with affect more or less vividly imagined. This new set may have only a tenuous relationship with the former set initially, a bond which will become firmer as the association value between the sets increases.

At this point, application needs to be made of the principle of habituation, which states that the gratification which comes from an initial experience occurs with lessened intensity upon subsequent occasions. The dulling of the thrill with repetition may lead the person or couple to try out new activities in order to regain the prior level of gratification. In the case of the hypothetical couple this habituation effect heightens the likelihood that they will resort to progressively more intense lovemaking, e.g., embracing, "necking," petting, as they continue to engage in amatory behavior.

The confirmation of their affective expectations, the increase of their romantic appetite with gratification, and the dulling of the thrill of any given activity with habituation all combine to move the couple along the path of more affect laden experiences.

Now at some point in this sequence there will occur a true sexual arousal (lust). The specifically sexual connotations of certain acts, e.g., kissing the ear, fondling the breasts, indeed, a host of verbal or gestural cues of affection or assent, can set off this reaction. Once this erotic arousal has occurred, bringing powerful excitement in its wake, the desire to repeat and continue the experience is greatly enhanced; thus the sexual appetite is increased. Another important event also takes place, however. A new set of associations or meanings is formed. The activities which led up to the initial erotic arousal now have a tendency to serve as cues leading to the arousal of sexual desire. Furthermore, as erotic experiences are repeated (a) the greater the association value of these cues to sexuality, and (b) the wider the range of cues to sexuality. Thus, kissing, embracing, exposure of body parts ordinarily covered, and a host of other acts may serve as sexual stimuli to the person with a history of arousal, while to the naive person they have no such significance. A 9-year-old, for example, may find intimate scenes in the movies boring while they may be highly arousing to his experienced elders.

Summarizing, the positive affect accompanying sexual arousal increases the appetite for such experiences; and the occurrence of such experiences produces an association of the preceding stimuli to the sexual affect, thereby making these stimuli cues leading to the arousal of sexual desire. These developments, together with the habituation phenomenon, tend to carry the participants toward the point where the couple may become so excited that it is virtually impossible for them to stop short of climax. In Beach's terms, the IEM may become sufficiently aroused for the male that it carries itself to completion with virtually no voluntary control. This may occur without actual intromission (petting to climax), though intercourse will tend to follow upon subsequent occasions due to the operation of the factors just mentioned.

The careful study of Ehrmann (1959) provides much data pertinent to the behavior discussed above, and also the problems of approach-avoidance and control of sexuality discussed below. His data are not sufficiently precise to confirm or deny aspects of the theory. His results are generally consistent with appetitive theory, though admittedly they are subject to alternative interpretations. To test precise details of any theory of sexual behavior, it will be necessary to go beyond his study and those of Kinsey et al. (1948, 1953) to two kinds of research: that which is more experimental in character, providing necessary control of variables, and that which studies individual cases more intensively on a longitudinal basis.

Problems of approach and avoidance

To this point, only the positive affect has been considered. However, there are several sources of negative affective expectations surrounding sexual behavior which need to be considered to give an adequate treatment of sex motivation.

One important source is the guilt arising out of moral compunctions against various expressions of sexuality. These arise in varying degree among persons in the great bulk of societies throughout the globe. A second source is the fear of discovery, of bringing disgrace to one's family and ruination to one's reputation. For the unmarried, a third source, the fear of pregnancy, is compounded from the guilt and fear already mentioned, together with the loss of freedom accompanying a forced marriage. For both the married and unmarried other anxieties attendant to pregnancy may arise: threats to health, the stress of psychological and economic adjustments to the baby. A fourth source of concern is the fear of being "used," with the loss of interest by the partner once he has gotten what he wanted. A fifth source common to women is the disgust and revulsion toward sex produced by the doctrine that sex is filthy and degrading (French Institute of Public Opinion, 1961, pp. 159-163).

The above list of sources of negative affect is not meant to be exhaustive, but to lend credence to the proposal that one or both partners in a sexual relationship may have potent ambivalent feelings toward it.

A Lewinian analysis of driving and restraining forces (Lewin, 1947) is useful in describing the approach-avoidance dynamics involved in sexual conflict and the management of sex appetite.

In American society, the burden of the responsibility for the control of sexuality rests upon the female. In the dating and courtship period, a girl may decide that she will allow a boy to go only so far, and then she will "draw the line." Thus, behavior will occur at a given level because of the balance of driving forces with restraining forces. This is an unstable equilibrium, however, and the device therefore ineffective if love-making is habitual up to this point, since the increased appetite may overbalance the restraints, causing a shift in the line. The resulting guilt, anxiety, and cognitive dissonance are then assuaged by rationalization and other available defenses.

One prevalent manifestation of ambivalence about sex is the divorcement of sexual qualities and feelings from conceptions of the "good" mate. Thus a young man may coax a girl to grant sexual favors, then lose interest in her as a prospective wife when she does, since he cannot conceive of marrying a girl who is promiscuous! Because "love is wonderful but sex is nasty" the girl, too, is likely to perceive the boy who wants to make love as one who is untrustworthy, one who is perhaps not interested in her but only in what selfish satisfaction he can obtain. Consequently, while the couple is verbally reassuring one another of their affection while they make love, they actually experience mounting doubts about the genuineness of their devotion as the frequency and intensity of the love-making increase. Both before and after marriage the enjoyment of sex may be colored by a loss of respect for the partner as one who is no longer pure and sweet. This occurs because the good person, shorn of sexual quality, is overidealized. When erotic characteristics are discovered in that person, disillusionment results.

The very personal gratification which accompanies sexual activity lies at the heart of the enigma of love and sex, since it raises the eternal question: Is the other person making love to obtain selfish satisfaction or out of a more inclusive feeling for me and an altruistic concern for my happiness? The dissociation of love and sex just discussed is one attempt to resolve this problem. Another is the doctrine that love and sex are virtually synonymous. While this theory typifies much of the wishful content of the mass media today, physical (sexual) attraction is probably not convincing to the lovers themselves as a criterion of love.

Reiss (1960), in his analysis of American premarital sex standards, suggests that there is a generally recognized distinction between sex for sex' sake (body centered coitus) and sex for love's sake (person centered coitus). Most American women reserve intercourse for lovers, as an affectionate expression of love. The quandary which exists is not merely whether the woman "really" loves the man, but whether the man really loves her. If the man is sexually opportunistic, aggressive, or demanding—and a wealth of data (e.g., Ehrmann, 1959; Kinsey, Pomeroy, & Martin, 1948; Reiss, 1960) suggests that the majority of American men are—then the woman is left to seek for nonsexual assurances that he really does love her. The more insistent he is about sexual relations, the more unsure of his love she becomes. If they are not married, the uncertainty is magnified, because of the lack of marital responsibilities assumed by the lover.

A specialized consequence of ambivalence about sex is the development of fetishism or other bizarre aberrations. The case described by Grant (1953) may be chosen as an illustration of this, though his data are insufficient to make any analysis certain. In such cases, a dissociation occurs between one's erotic desires and more legitimate, upright impulses, and a corresponding split develops between sexual and lofty qualities perceived in others. Thus, in Grant's case, the patient in earlier years could have sexual escapades with a woman of easy virtue and a platonic relationship with a good woman toward whom no erotic interest could be tolerated; and "never the twain shall meet." The patient's resolution of his problem by developing a fetish about shoes, legs, and leg movements may be interpreted as an attempt to control deep-lying feelings of guilt about licentious relationships with women. In view of this, his final solution, which consisted of viewing art films emphasizing leg displays, seems rather clever because no one else is involved, guilt is thereby minimized, and his own risk of exposure is virtually eliminated.

Cases of sexual assault, exhibitionism, and the like may result from the eruption of sexual desire through the barriers imposed by morality and reality testing. The development of such a breakthrough would be explained in the following fashion. The person engages in a period of lustful fantasy, in many cases stimulated by romantic or pornographic material. The excitement which accompanies this activity is sufficiently rewarding to increase the appetite. If such stimulation occurs over a protracted period, a greatly aggravated appetite may ensue. If socially acceptable channels of expression are denied the person, he may more or less planfully enter a social setting of erotic outlet where the chances for detection and capture are reduced. Thus the avoidance forces deterring him from such an act, reduced by lowered expectations of negative consequences, are overwhelmed by the mounting approach tendencies, which increase as the lascivious longing continues.

Valuative applications of the theory

A brief attempt will now be made to apply appetitional theory to problems of the personal and social management of sexuality, as follows: premarital relations, masturbation, control of sexual appetite, and sexual compatibility in marriage.

Premarital relations

Some observers have argued that American premarital sex mores should be made more lenient. Their argument is based upon evidence that there is widespread violation of these standards. Such a position assumes that the standards are more flexible than the behavior; therefore, the standards should be altered to conform to the realities of conduct. If one assumes that libido is a function of biological sex maturation, therefore subject to limited control, then since American culture tends to delay marriage for a number of years beyond sexual maturity, it follows that the violation of standards of permarital chastity is virtually inevitable.

However, if one assumes that biological maturation is only a minor factor in the development of sexual desire, and that sex appetite is subject to a tremendous degree of control, then other conclusions are permitted. Furthermore, if there are negative personal-social consequences of premarital indulgence which outweigh the positive consequences, as suggested by the Judeo-Christian moral code, then one might conclude that the behavior should be altered rather than the standards.

If such a conclusion be entertained, the question then follows: On what does the behavior depend, and how may it be altered? Based on the above analysis of the development of sexual appetite, several factors can be identified as contributive to the growth of libido: (a) Early dating where presexual behavior is permitted and even encouraged. (b) "Going steady" early in the courtship years, which tends to increase the likelihood of the next factor. (c) A dating pattern which is characterized by chronic love-making. (d) The bombardment of adolescents with sexually stimulating materials of many kinds, such as suggestive or obscene literature, sexy motion pictures, etc. It might be noted that the drive-in theater is called a "passion pit" not because of climatological factors which generate gonadal secretions, but because the lustful pictures frequently shown stimulate and legitimize sexual expression, and the darkened privacy of the automobile lowers other barriers to such behavior. (e) The lowering of moral standards which serve to restrain immediate gratification of impulse. Emphasis upon and idealization of glamor, physical attractiveness, and fun tend to produce a decreased concern with other values which depend upon long-term action. The absence of moral training in a setting of sex sophistication leaves a crucial void in restraining forces.

Masturbation

The use of self-stimulation as a source of erotic pleasure is reported to be very widespread among American adolescent males, and also to be common among females (Kinsey, Pomeroy, & Martin, 1948; Kinsey, Pomeroy, Martin, & Gebhard, 1953). The recognition of this has led to a curious reversal of a former position. Whereas previous generations were warned not to masturbate because they might thereby become insane or abnormal, many argue today that those who fail to indulge in this practice must somehow be unbalanced or abnormal. The limitations of such a statistical conception of normality are too well known to require comment.

The present generation would seem to be "victims" of the misconception that periodic sexual outlet is biologically required. This notion is very handy and is readily linked to the feeling that one might as well enjoy it, controlling evocation of the impulse so as to maximize pleasure.

Needless to say, where moral standards exist which forbid such gratification, approach-avoidance conflict exists. As in the case of premarital intercourse, conflict can be resolved by changing standards. However, it may be preferable to alter the behavior to fit the standards.

Control of sexual appetite

A device sometimes suggested to control sexuality is to reduce tension by displacement or sublimation, i.e., to relieve sexual drive by reading, dancing, painting, attending the theater, etc. According to appetitional theory, if the substitute activity is sexually stimulating, then the appetite will tend to increase, and the problem of control is worsened. If the activity is nonsexual in character, sexual impulses will not be relieved nor aroused. If a person finds enough such activities which are satisfying because of nonsexual reasons, his need for sexual gratification will be lessened, not because of sublimation of libido, but simply because the role of sexual gratification in the total motivational economy of the personality will be relatively minor. In contrast to Freud's view that much human activity gratifies a sublimated libido, it seems probable that sex is often indulged in as a substitute for a reasonably satisfying life in other areas.

Appetitional theory suggests a set of recommendations for the control of lust during the premarital period.

1. Participation in activities which fill one's life with abundant gratifications, so that sexual intimacies are not indulged in as an escape from boredom or emotional starvation. Athletic, intellectual, altruistic, occupational, avocational, esthetic, or social pursuits may serve this function.

2. Comprehension of the nature of sex motivation and the factors which govern it, to help the person to foresee the consequences of alternative courses of action, thus enabling him to make a knowledgeable decision in terms of his own motives and values.

3. Prevent the appetite from growing by abstinence from arousing activities until the time acceptable for sexual expression. This implies a dating-courtship pattern which is centered upon a wide variety of nonsexual activities which additionally might contribute to a more adequate prediction of marital compatibility. (See Leuba, 1954, for a related set of recommendations.)

4. Exposure to entertainment, reading material, companionship, etc., which have nonsexual connotations of intrinsic interest to the person. This will tend to prevent the recurrent arousal of sexuality.

5. Emphasis upon the long-term rewards of continence, and idealization of the ability to delay immediate gratification of impulse.

The implication should not be drawn from the preceding suggestions that an overprotective, authoritarian control of behavior is favored. The emphasis recommended is on self-selection of situations and activities. Of course, in a society as exploitative as America, some degree of social control of blatant obscenity is probably required.

Sexual compatibility in marriage

The problem of the role of sexual compatibility in marriage is another area of application of the theory. It is sometimes maintained that sexual compatibility is of central importance to a successful marriage. Based upon this argument is the notion that a couple needs to have intercourse before marriage to find out if they are compatible.

Appetitional theory supports a contrasting view. Rather than conceiving of a person's sexual drive as a relatively fixed quantity which can only be compared with that of another individual, the present theory maintains that the appetite is a variable quantity which might be adjusted over a period of time to match that of another. Thus a couple whose initial appetites are at variance may work toward a mutual adjustment of these until greater harmony exists. Their willingness to do this probably depends upon their nonsexual love for one another.

Summary

1. An appetitional theory of human sexual motivation is proposed as a needed alternative to theories based upon sex as a biological drive or instinct in view of the mounting evidence against the adequacy of physiological interpretations.

2. The theory is based upon a general motivational orientation which maintains (a) the affective consequences of behavior are central in the development of motives, through the mediation of associations between cues and affect. These cues, perceptual or cognitive, tend to arouse expectations that a given pattern of action will produce a certain affective change. For an expectation to be motivational in character, it must involve not only affective change, but also a course of behavior, symbolic or overt, which is instrumental to attaining the desired affect; (b) motives are strengthened in proportion to the degree of affective change experienced; (c) the likelihood of arousal of a motive is a function of the likelihood of occurrence of cues to the affective change and the associative strength of cues to the affect; (d) all members of a family or set of expectations are reinforced by the confirmation of one member of the set along a gradient of generalization; (e) a habituation process occurs in many affective areas wherein the repetition of a given activity produces a diminished affective change in comparison with the initial experience; (f) approach motives are based upon positive affective expectations, avoidance motives upon negative affective expectations; however, most motivated behavior is ambivalent, based upon a mixture of posi-

tive and negative components; (g) of a number of expectations aroused at any time, the one acted upon depends on the relative positive affective change anticipated over a period of time, and the subjective probability of attainment of the alternatives.

3. The affective foundations for genital sex motivation (lust) are (a) the pleasurable excitement of arousal, and (b) the intense pleasure accompanying orgasm and the relaxation which follows. Either of these sources of affect is adequate to strengthen sexual appetite. It is recognized that there are many nonlustful motives which contribute to participation in sexual behavior.

4. Childhood sexuality is based primarily upon the first affective foundation, and becomes more potent with indulgence; however, in many societies the precautions taken to prevent arousal together with various threats of negative consequences are usually adequate to keep such behavior subdued to a rather inconsequential level.

5. The burgeoning of sexual motivation usually occurs during the culturally prescribed period of courtship. Middle-class American society is used as an illustration. The person or couple engages in amatory adventures of increasing intensity due to the effect of reinforcement, generalization of reinforcement, and habituation. At some point in this sequence true genital arousal (lust) occurs, its affective power greatly heightening the motivational level. Chronic participation in arousing activity augments the appetite, which overwhelms even strong resistances composed of moral compunctions and various fears, eventually leading to intercourse.

6. The theory is applied to problems in the management of sexual appetite in premarital courtship and masturbation and to the role of sexual compatibility in marriage.

References

Asch, S. E. *Social psychology.* New York: Prentice-Hall, 1952.

Atkinson, J. W. Motivational determinants of risk-taking behavior. *Psychol. Rev.,* 1957, 64, 359-372.

Ball, Josephine, & Hartman, C. J. Sexual excitability as related to the menstrual cycle in the monkey. *Amer. J. Obstet. Gynec.,* 1935, 29, 117-119.

Beach, F. A. Evolutionary changes in the physiological control of mating behavior in mammals. *Psychol. Rev.,* 1947, 54, 297-315.

Beach, F. A. Instinctive behavior: Reproductive activities. In S. S. Stevens (Ed.), *Handbook of experimental psychology.* New York: Wiley, 1951, pp. 387-434.

Beach, F. A. Characteristics of masculine "sex drive." In M. R. Jones (Ed.), *Nebraska symposium on motivation: 1956.* Lincoln: Univer. Nebraska Press, 1956, pp. 1-32.

Benedek, Therese, & Rubenstein, B. B. The correlations between ovarian activity and psychodynamic processes. *Psychosom. Med.,* 1939, 1, 245-270; 461-485.

Benedek, Therese, & Rubenstein, B. B. The sexual cycle in women. *Psychosom. Med. Monogr.,* 1942, 3, 1-306.

Bruner, J. S. Personality dynamics and the process of perceiving. In R. R. Blake & G. V. Ramsey (Eds.), *Perception: An approach to personality.* New York: Ronald Press, 1951, pp. 121-147.

Carmichael, H. T., Noonan, W. J., & Kenyon, A. T. The effects of testosterone propionate in impotence. *Amer. J. Psychiat.,* 1941, 97, 919-943.

Cartwright, D. Decision-time in relation to the differentiation of the phenomenal field. *Psychol. Rev.,* 1941, 48, 425-442.

Cartwright, D., & Festinger, L. A quantitative theory of decision. *Psychol. Rev.,* 1943, 50, 595-621.

Clark, R. A. The projective measurement of experimentally induced sexual motivation. *J. exp. Psychol.,* 1952, 44, 391-399.

Cleckley, H. *The caricature of love.* New York: Ronald Press, 1957.

Cory, D. W. Homosexuality. In A. Ellis & A. Abarbanel (Eds.), *The encyclopedia of sexual behavior.* New York: Hawthorn, 1961, pp. 485-493.

Creevy, C. D., & Rea, C. E. The treatment of impotence by male sex hormone. *Endocrinology,* 1940, 27, 392-394.

Davis, Katharine B. *Factors in the sex life of 2200 women.* New York: Harper, 1929.

Dember, W. N., & Earl, R. W. Analysis of exploratory, manipulatory, and curiosity behaviors. *Psychol. Rev.,* 1957, 64, 91-96.

Dennis, W., & Najarian, Pergrouhi. Infant development under environmental handicap. *Psychol. Monogr.,* 1957, 71 (7, Whole No. 436).

Dickinson, R. L., & Beam, L. *A thousand marriages.* Baltimore: Williams & Wilkins, 1931.

Ehrmann, W. *Premarital dating behavior.* New York: Holt, 1959.

Ellis, A. The sexual psychology of human hermaphrodites. *Psychosom. Med.*, 1945, 7, 108-125.

Ellis, H. *Studies in the psychology of sex.* Vol. 1. New York: Random House, 1936, pp. 97-105.

Filler, W., & Drezner, N. The results of surgical castration in women under forty. *Amer. J. Obst. Gynec.*, 1944, 47, 122-124.

Finesinger, J. E., Meigs, J. V., & Sulkowitch, H. W. Clinical, psychiatric, and psychoanalytic study of a case of male pseudohermaphroditism. *Amer. J. Obst. Gynec.*, 1942, 44, 310-317.

Ford, C. S., & Beach, F. A. *Patterns of sexual behavior.* New York: Harper, 1951.

French Institute of Public Opinion. *Patterns of sex and love: A study of the French woman and her morals.* New York: Crown, 1961.

Gerall, A. An attempt to induce precocious sexual behavior in male guinea pigs by injections of testosterone propionate. *Endocrinology*, 1958, 63, 280-284.

Goldfarb, W. Infant-rearing as a factor in foster home replacement. *Amer. J. Orthopsychiat.*, 1944, 14, 162-166.

Goldfarb, W. Effects of psychological deprivation in infancy and subsequent stimulation. *Amer. J. Psychiat.*, 1945, 102, 18-33.

Grant, V. W. A case study of fetishism. *J. abnorm. soc. Psychol.*, 1953, 48, 142-149.

Hamilton, G. V. *A research in marriage.* New York: Boni, 1929.

Hamilton, J. B. Demonstrated ability of penile erection in castrate men with markedly low titers of urinary androgens. *Proc. Soc. Exp. Biol. Med.*, 1943, 54, 309-312.

Harlow, H. F. The heterosexual affectional system in monkeys. *Amer. Psychologist*, 1962, 17, 1-9.

Harlow, H. F., & Harlow, Margaret K. Social deprivation in monkeys. *Scient. American*, 1962, 207, 136-146.

Henry, J., & Henry, Zunia. Doll play of Pilaga Indian children. In C. Kluckhohn, H. Murray, & D. M. Schneider (Eds.), *Personality in nature, society, and culture.* (2nd ed.) New York: Knopf, 1953, pp. 292-307.

Johnson, D. M. The phantom anesthetist of Mattoon: A field study of mass hysteria. *J. abnorm. soc. Psychol.*, 1945, 40, 175-186.

Kagan, J. Differential reward value of incomplete and complete sexual behavior. *J. comp. physiol. Psychol.*, 1955, 48, 59-64.

Kardiner, A. *The psychological frontiers of society.* New York: Columbia University Press, 1945.

Kinsey, A. C. Criteria for a hormonal explanation of the homosexual. *J. clin. Endocrinol.*, 1941, 1, 424-428.

Kinsey, A. C., Pomeroy, W. B., & Martin, C. E. *Sexual behavior in the human male.* Philadelphia: Saunders, 1948.

Kinsey, A. C., Pomeroy, W. B., Martin, C. E., & Gebhard, P. H. *Sexual behavior in the human female.* Philadelphia: Saunders, 1953.

Leuba, C. *The sexual nature of man and its management.* New York: Doubleday, 1954.

Levy, D. M. Primary affect hunger. *Amer. J. Psychiat.*, 1937, 94, 643-652.

Lewin, K. Behavior and development as a function of the total situation. In L. Carmichael (Ed.), *Manual of child psychology.* New York: Wiley, 1946, pp. 791-844.

Lewin, K. Frontiers in group dynamics: Concept, method, and reality in social science; social equilibria and social change. *Hum. Relat.*, 1947, 1, 5-42.

Lewin, K. *Resolving social conflicts.* New York: Harper, 1948.

McClelland, D. C. *Personality.* New York: Sloane, 1951.

McClelland, D. C., Atkinson, J. W., Clark, R. A., & Lowell, E. L. *The achievement motive.* New York: Appleton-Century-Crofts, 1953.

Mead, Margaret. *Male and female.* New York: Morrow, 1949.

Miles, Catherine C. Psychological study of a young male pseudohermaphrodite reared as a female. In Q. McNemar & Maud Merrill (Eds.), *Studies in personality.* New York: McGraw-Hill, 1942, pp. 209-227.

Miller, N. E. Comments on theoretical models illustrated by the development of a theory of conflict behavior. *J. Pers.*, 1951, 20, 82-100.

Money, J. Hermaphroditism. In A. Ellis & A. Abarbanel (Eds.), *The encyclopedia of sexual behavior.* New York: Hawthorn, 1961, pp. 472-484.

Money, J., Hampson, Joan G., & Hampson, J. L. Hermaphroditism: Recommendations concerning assignment of sex, change of sex, and psychologic management. *Johns Hopkins Hosp. Bull.*, 1955, 97, 284-300. (a)

Money, J., Hampson, Joan G., & Hampson, J. L. An examination of some basic sexual concepts: The evidence of human hermaphroditism. *Johns Hopkins Hosp. Bull.*, 1955, 97, 300-319. (b)

Money, J., Hampson, Joan G., & Hampson, J. L. Imprinting and the establishment of gender role. *AMA Arch. Neurol. Psychiat.*, 1957, 77, 333-336.

Mussen, P. H., & Scodel, A. The effects of sexual stimulation under varying conditions on TAT sexual responsiveness. *J. consult. Psychol.*, 1955, 19, 90.

Nissen, H. W. Instinct as seen by a psychologist. *Psychol. Rev.*, 1953, 60, 291-294.

Pinneau, S. R. The infantile disorders of hospitalism and anaclitic depression. *Psychol. Bull.*, 1955, 52, 429-452.

Reiss, I. L. *Premarital sexual standards in America.* Glencoe, Ill.: Free Press, 1960.

Rokeach, M. *The open and closed mind.* New York: Basic Books, 1960.

Sears, R. R., Maccoby, Eleanor E., & Levin, H. *Patterns of child rearing.* Evanston, Ill.: Row, Peterson, 1957.

Seward, Georgene H. *Sex and the social order.* New York: McGraw-Hill, 1946.

Sheffield, F. D., Wulff, J. J., & Backer, R. Reward value of copulation without sex drive reduction, *J. comp. physiol. Psychol.*, 1951, 44, 3-8.

Spitz, R. A., & Wolf, Katherine M. Autoerotism. In *Psychoanalytic study of the child.* Vol. 3/4. New York: International Universities Press, 1949, pp. 85-120.

Tauber, E. S. Effects of castration upon the sexuality of the adult male: A review of relevant literature. *Psychosom. Med.*, 1940, 2, 74-87.

Terman, L. M. *Psychological factors in marital happiness.* New York: McGraw-Hill, 1938.

Tinklepaugh, O. L. The nature of periods of sex desire in women and their relation to ovulation. *Amer. J. Obst. Gynec.*, 1933, 26, 335-345.

Waller, W. The rating and dating complex. *Amer. social. Rev.*, 1937, 2, 727-734.

Whalen, R. E. Effects of mounting without intromission and intromission without ejaculation on sexual behavior and maze learning. *J. comp. physiol. Psychol.*, 1961, 54, 409-415.

Young, P. T. The role of hedonic processes in the organization of behavior. *Psychol. Rev.*, 1952, 59, 249-262.

Young, P. T. The role of affective processes in learning and motivation. *Psychol. Rev.*, 1959, 66, 104-125.

3

THE DEVELOPMENT AND INTEGRATION OF PERSONALITY

The study of personality has been a difficult task for psychologists for many years. One of the fundamental problems has been the failure of psychologists to agree on a common definition of "personality." As long ago as 1937, Allport discovered no fewer than fifty different definitions of personality in the psychological literature. Despite this clear indication that psychologists do not adhere to a single view of the personality, most agree that personality is an example of what we called in the first section a *construct*. Personality is not a "thing" but an inference based on behavior. Kagan (1968) suggests that the behavior patterns which constitute the personality must show two characteristics: they must be stable "over time and place," and they must show considerable variability when measured in a large group of people. These views are similar to those of Byrne (1966) who defines personality as "the combination of all the relatively enduring dimensions of individual differences" (p. 15) on which a person can be measured. According to Bradburn (1963), we can talk about personality more meaningfully in terms of the "generalized patterns of behavior characteristic of the individual under many different environmental conditions" (p. 353).

Sometimes the term "character" is used synonymously with personality. However, many psychoanalytic theorists use "character" to designate the "inner core" of the individual and reserve the label personality to refer to the total behavioral repertoire of the person. This distinction is not consistently accepted by psychologists and psychiatrists, and this has produced considerable confusion for both students and professional persons. In order to maintain clarity, we shall use the term personality in this section.

If we summarize the current views among psychologists, we can say that the notion of personality is based upon several general characteristics: 1) persons exhibit some degree of consistency in their responses to specific situations; 2) different persons respond to similar situations in different ways; and 3) these differences in behavior are potentially measurable. Unfortunately, the practical problems involved in measuring certain kinds of behavior are considerable. Despite the ingenuity of psychologists in developing a variety of tests, questionnaires, rating forms, and other sophisticated measuring devices, much of the behavior which is usually included under the heading of personality defies precise measurement. It is perhaps for this reason, as well as the fact that psychologists sometimes fail to agree on what constitutes adequate measurement, that Allport found so many different specific descriptions of personality.

Assuming, perhaps naively or optimistically, that these practical measurement problems can be overcome, there remains the task of combining and integrating all of the individual differences in behavior into a cohesive and meaningful description of the personality. One of the ways in which psychologists have attempted to cope with this task is by postulating general theories of personality. These theories are helpful because they allow an infinite variety of individual behavior patterns to be incorporated into more general classification systems. As Hall and Lindzey (1957) point out, one of the most distinctive characteristics of personality theories, in addition to their emphasis on understanding the whole person, is their attempt to integrate diverse findings. This serves the function of "preventing the observer from being dazzled by the full-blown complexity of natural or concrete events" (Hall and Lindzey, 1957, p. 14).

There are many different theories of personality, and they differ considerably in their scope, orientation, and basis in fact. Despite these differences, there appears to be two main areas within the study of personality which have attracted the attention of theorists, researchers, and clinicians. First, there are the enduring patterns of behavior which Hall and Lindzey (1957) call the *structure of personality*. Second, there are the qualitative aspects of the personality that we shall discuss in the context of the *acquisition of personality*.

The structure of personality

The idea that personality refers to consistent and habitual behavior patterns implies the existence of a basic personality structure with describable properties. The various theories differ in their hypotheses about: 1) the components of personality; 2) the nature of the components; and 3) how they are organized and integrated within the personality structure. Freud (1923) attempted to account for the diversity of behavior in terms of three structural units. According to Freud (1923), mental life is a function of a "physical apparatus" which consists of an *id,* an *ego,* and a *superego.* The id is the oldest part of the psychical apparatus containing the biologically based instincts. Instincts are units of energy and are similar to what we called drives in Section II. The instincts are capable of being expressed in the form of a variety of physiological and psychological tensions, but there are only two basic types: *eros,* the life instinct, and the *destructive* or *death* instinct. In practice, these two instincts can either combine or work against each other. However, in principle, the two instincts have opposite aims. Eros is oriented toward the preservation of one's own life and of the species. It is revealed primarily by man's sexual and love behavior. The death instinct has as its final aim the reduction of life to an inorganic state. It is reflected by man's aggressive behavior. The id is the basic structural component in the Freudian system, and its contents provide the basic motivational constructs within the theory. Every act is explainable in terms of an attempt to reduce the tensions originating from either of the two instincts or a combination of both.

The ego is the executive branch of the personality and includes the functions of control over physical coordination, perception, thinking, the experiencing of emotion, and memory (Brenner, 1955). It is the ego's responsibility to coordinate the different facets of the personality into a smoothly functioning whole. In this role, the ego acts as the mediator between the person and the external world and between the opposing forces arising internally from the id and the superego. It is the responsibility of the ego to help the person adapt to the demands of the external world and to keep the internal psychological forces in relatively harmonious balance.

The evaluative branch of the personality is the superego which determines the appropriateness of behavior from a moral standpoint. The superego is divided into two subsystems, the *ego ideal* and the *conscience*. The ego ideal represents the individual's idealized conception of what is morally good, right, and desirable behavior. The conscience is the internal representation of what is wrong, bad, or undesirable. The specific behaviors associated with these standards are usually learned early in life from the parents and other socializing agents responsible for teaching the child.

Freud's division of the personality into three

structural components provides us with a theme capable of many variations. A recent innovation by Berne (1964) attempts to describe the personality in terms of *child, adult,* and *parent* components. The child is characterized by intuition, creativity, and spontaneity. The adult, like Freud's ego, has a double role. It acts as a computer to process the information necessary for a successful adaptation to the world, and it serves as a mediator between the child and parent. The parent enables the person to contribute to the survival of the human race by acting as an actual parent, and it allows the individual to make many minor decisions automatically.

If we adopt a more universal attitude, Freud's id, ego, and superego can be considered functionally analogous to the relationship of the earth, man, and God. The earth, like the id, provides the natural resources and raw energy which man (the ego) must learn to harness for his own use and survival. The concept of God provides the ethical and moral standards by which man can evaluate and control his behavior. Whatever example or analogy we choose to illustrate the Freudian concepts, we must remember that the id, ego, and superego are abstractions developed by Freud to make our task of understanding the personality more manageable. These constructs are not things to be interpreted literally, even though they often are. No surgeon has ever removed or transplanted an id, ego, or superego.

A different approach to personality is presented by those theorists who postulate the self as the primary structural component. According to Jourard (1963): "The self-structure is a construction of the ego. *It refers to the beliefs, perceptions, ideals, expectations, and demands which a person has come to formulate with respect to his own behavior and experience*" (p. 156, italics in original). Different theorists emphasize different aspects of the self, such as the self-concept, the ideal self, and various public selves. The self-concept is the summation of the person's beliefs about what he *is*. The ideal self is the person's conception of what he *should be*. The public selves represent the different ways in which a person behaves in order to impress others. These three constructs taken together are usually referred to as the self-structure, and there is considera-

ble variability in the definitions of the self. For instance, Horney (1950) and Fromm (1941) describe the *real self* as the *basic inner reality,* referring to the spontaneous experiencing of thoughts, memories, wishes, and feelings. Royce (1964) defines the self-concept as "what a man thinks of himself when the facade of social living has been removed" (p. 102). For Rogers (1951), the self-structure is formed primarily out of the individual's interaction with others and is *"an organized, fluid, but consistent conceptual pattern of perceptions of characteristics and relationships of the 'I' or the 'Me,' together with values attached to the concepts"* (p. 498). The term has been used by many different psychologists to mean many different things. Hall and Lindzey (1957) cite twenty-one different theorists who have written about the self, and their list is not exhaustive.

A considerably different approach to the description of personality structure consists of what is usually referred to as *trait* theory. Both Freudian theory and self-theory describe personality structure in terms of a few major components. Trait theory, on the other hand, analyzes personality structure into a larger number of more specific behavioral patterns. A trait is any pattern of behavior which tends to persist over time and is specific enough to be a distinguishable characteristic of the person. There is considerable variability among trait theorists with regard to the definition, number, kinds, and names of traits. Cattell (1950) describes several categories of traits, but the most significant are *source traits* and *surface traits*. Source traits are the more general underlying structural characteristics of the personality. Surface traits are more specific, observable, and changeable characteristics. Cattell, like Eysenck (1947, 1952) and some other trait theorists, derives his traits from measured behavior by the complicated statistical technique of factor analysis. Consequently, the term *factor* is sometimes used synonymously with trait.

Allport (1937, 1950), like Cattell, describes two major classes of traits, *central* and *secondary* traits. For Allport, a trait is a predisposition to behavior based on both biological and psychological considerations. Central traits differ from secondary traits in several respects. They are more important, fewer in number, less specific, and more characteristic of the total functioning of the individual. Unlike Cattell, however, Allport does not base his description of the personality on large-scale measurement techniques such as factor analyses. On the contrary, Allport strongly advocates studying the individual personality in depth. The trait is a distinctly individual characteristic. No two persons can possess the same traits. However, Allport does allow for the similarities among different persons by postulating a category of *common traits*. The common traits reflect the similarities in cultural background to which individuals of the same society are exposed.

In recent years, a variety of new dimensions of the personality have been described by research psychologists. One of the most potentially rewarding areas of research deals with *cognitive style,* or the ways in which the person processes data about the world. Cognitive styles usually refer to the patterns of thinking and perceiving which are characteristic of the individual. There is increasing evidence to suggest that some persons have cognitive styles that are sufficiently distinctive to allow these people to be differentiated from others solely on the basic of how they approach problems. Much of the early work in this area was done on the *authoritarian personality* (Adorno, Frenkl-Brunswik, Levinson & Sanford, 1950). According to these authors, this type of personality is characterized by prejudice or biased attitudes towards others, usually members of some minority group. Compared with persons who are low in ethnic prejudice, authoritarian personalities tend to be more rigid in their approaches to problems, more concrete in their thinking, more likely to have inaccurate memories, and less able to tolerate uncertainty.

Rokeach (1960) describes persons in terms of whether they have open or closed minds. A social psychologist, Rokeach has investigated belief-disbelief systems. A *belief system* refers to the entire range of ideas, expectancies, beliefs, and hypotheses about the world, both conscious and unconscious, that a person accepts as true at any given time. The *disbelief system* contains all the ideas a person rejects as false. The person with an open belief system can receive, evaluate, and act on information on its own merits and in accordance with the requirements of the situation. Also, the

person with an open belief system should be better able to act on the basis of internal standards, to resist external pressures, and to avoid acting on the basis of irrational inner forces. Simply stated, the person with an open mind is able to process information more accurately and more completely, and, as a result, is free to act in a more flexible and effective manner. A number of other cognitive styles have been described in the research literature, many referring specifically to the perception and appraisal of psychological threat, anxiety, or danger. Some of these will be described in the section on stress and coping behavior.

The acquisition of personality

Many interesting hypotheses have been offered to account for how the personality acquires its distinctive qualitative features. Freudian theory describes the enduring qualitative characteristics of adult personality in terms of earlier experiences, particularly during certain phases of childhood. According to Freud's approach, there are a few universal stages of development which are biologically determined. During each of these stages, a specific part of the body assumes greater psychological significance because of an increase in its sensitivity. This increase in sensitivity is typically experienced as tension and reduction of this tension is experienced as pleasurable. Thus, during the first year of life, the mouth is the center of attention and much of the infant's behavior consists of biting, sucking, spitting, chewing, and other oral activities. The amount of oral activity is related to the circumstances surrounding feeding. The child who is able to satisfy the need for oral stimulation during the feeding procedure is less likely to seek additional stimulation than the child whose feeding is less satisfying. In the second year of life, attention shifts to the anal area with the onset of toilet training. The parents' method of toilet training is important. This stage presents the child with his first real conflict with authority and external regulation of his inner impulses. Between the ages of three and six, the child becomes more occupied with his sexual organs, and the fact of possessing or not possessing a penis is of crucial significance. Although Freud described five stages in all, these three—the oral, anal, and phallic stages—are the most important for the formation of the personality. Excessive frustration or excessive gratification during any one of these stages can retard the child's movement to the next stage. This interruption in development is called a *fixation*. When a fixation occurs, behavior characteristic of the particular stage of development tends to become permanently incorporated into the personality to an excessive degree. For example, experiences during the oral stage of development are related to characteristics of trust, security, optimism, and independence. Consequently, unsuccessful growth through this stage may result in an adult who is insecure, anxious, distrustful, and dependent. Psychoanalysts often refer to this constellation of characteristics as an *oral personality*. The *anal personality,* who is fixated at the anal stage, is identified by such qualities as orderliness, frugality, and obstinacy. These examples are grossly oversimplified but give an indication of the strategy underlying the Freudian explanation of distinctive personality characteristics.

Erikson (1963, 1968), like other modern disciples of Freud, places more emphasis on cultural and learned factors during each stage and attributes less importance to the biological basis. Erikson proposes eight stages and suggests that each stage produces specific "ego qualities" which become incorporated into the personality. For example, the adult quality of trust of others is based upon the quality of maternal care that the child receives during the first year of life. According to Erikson (1968): "Mothers create a sense of trust in their children by that kind of administration which in its quality combines sensitive care of the baby's individual needs and a firm sense of personal trustworthiness within the trusted framework of their community's life style" (p. 103). As we shall see in a later section, this first stage is also instrumental in providing the child with a rudimentary feeling of identity. The remaining seven stages in Erikson's scheme allow for the development of other important qualitative aspects of the personality. These include: autonomy versus shame and doubt (muscular-anal stage, second year); initiative versus guilt (locomotor-genital stage, ages three to five); industry versus inferiority (latency, ages six to twelve); identity versus identity confusion (puberty and adolescence); intimacy versus isolation (young adulthood); gen-

erativity versus stagnation (adulthood); and integrity versus despair (maturity). Each of these pairs of qualities represents the primary conflict that the person is confronted with at each stage. Which of the qualities becomes incorporated within the personality is a function of the individual's experiences at the time.

Personality theorists vary considerably in the amount of importance they attribute to the learning process in the formation of personality. As Hall and Lindzey (1957) point out, some theorists like Dollard and Miller offer a detailed outline on the role of learning, whereas other theorists (Freud, Jung, and Rogers) do not specifically mention or minimize the function of learning in their theories. It is sometimes difficult to evaluate the importance of learning in personality development, because different terminology is used to denote similar kinds of learning. For example, one of the most simple and efficient ways to learn to do anything is to watch some other person do it and then copy the behavior. Psychoanalytic theorists use the term *identification* to refer to this kind of observational learning that occurs when one person incorporates the characteristics of another person. Experimental psychologists use the term *imitation* to refer to similar behavior. Other psychologists (Moreno, 1934; Sarbin, 1954) use the term *role-playing* to identify essentially the same behavior. Ethologists use the term *imprinting* to refer to the kind of imitation behavior in which the young of many species follow the first moving object they see.

Another point on which psychologists differ is whether or not the kinds of learning that are important for personality acquisition are special cases of more general principles or whether they represent different kinds of learning. Dollard and Miller (1941, 1950) treat imitation as a special case of instrumental conditioning. However, Bandura and Walters (1964) suggest that imitation cannot be adequately accounted for by the more traditional principles of learning.

Some of the most valuable formulations about the acquisition of personality have come not from psychologists or psychiatrists but from other behavioral scientists, notably sociologists and anthropologists. Their impact has been two-fold. First, they have made their own specific formulations about the development of personality; and second, they have stimulated many personality theorists to revise their theories to incorporate more information about the impact of society and culture on the individual. Ralph Linton, an anthropologist whose writings have contributed a great deal to our understanding of how culture influences personality development, introduced the concepts of the *basic personality type* and the *status personality* (Linton, 1945). The basic personality type represents the many personality characteristics that members of a society will have in common and includes the shared values and understandings of the larger society. In addition, each society has status personalities which represent the more specific behavior patterns that are associated with particular subgroups of the society. These vary from one society to another. In our society, for instance, men are expected to behave differently from women, adults differently from adolescents, and Northerners differently from Southerners. Status personalities are both superimposed upon and integrated within the basic personality type. Linton (1945) clearly advocates the view that an individual's personality reflects his previous experiences in interacting with the environment. It follows that a detailed knowledge of the specific conditions that surrounded a person's upbringing are not only helpful but essential in predicting different personality configurations. Support for this point of view is presently emerging from workers in federal antipoverty projects who have observed that individuals denied exposure to opportunities taken for granted by most members of the society do develop distinctive personality characteristics.

The close relationship of personality and culture has also been described by Spiro (1951), who states: "Personality and culture then are not different or mutually exclusive entities; they are part and parcel of the same process of interaction. Both personality and culture reside in the individual or, to put it differently, they are the individual as modified by learning" (p. 43). Although we expect the individual to be influenced by the values, attitudes, and behaviors maintained by the various groups of which he is a member, Spiro (1951) points out that individual differences in learning ability will modify the internalization of cultural values. Different members of the same society may absorb considerably different aspects of the culture, resulting in the variation of individual personality patterns within the same society and even within the homogeneous subgroups of a society.

Some good examples of specific culturally influenced personality patterns have been provided in recent years by Riesman, Denney, and Glazer (1950) and Fromm (1947). Riesman *et al,* depict three types of societies which produce three corresponding kinds of personality patterns or what they call "social character." Relatively stable and unchanging societies tend to produce *tradition-directed* personalities who are behaviorally conforming individuals. Transitional societies characterized by growth and expansion are more likely to contain *inner-directed* persons whose values become internalized early in life. Contrasted with this is the *other-directed* individual who looks to his peers and others around him for guidelines and values. This type of individual is most frequently found in large, affluent, industrialized societies such as our own.

Fromm (1947) deviates from the biological orientation of traditional psychoanalytic theory by emphasizing the cultural and social bases of character. Unlike Freud, who attributed the origin of character to instinctually based patterns of libido organization within the individual, Fromm believes that character develops out of the specific ways in which man relates to the world. He presents five character types. These are ideal types, but various combinations can be found in specific individuals. The person with a *productive* orientation is concerned with work, with doing, and with producing. This kind of person is most capable of loving others and of reasoning. The other four types of personality are all subtypes of the nonproductive orientation and include the *receptive* (accepting), *exploitive* (taking), *hoarding* (preserving) and *marketing* personalities. Each type of personality has characteristic attributes reflecting both positive and negative qualities associated with it. For example, the marketing orientation is a product of modern capitalistic societies, such as contemporary America, and stresses the value of exchange rather than use. Consequently, marketing personalities look upon themselves as objects or commodities which have marketable value. This type of person places a great deal of importance on "selling himself" and tries to appear to others in whatever way he thinks will be most desirable to the "buyers." Positive aspects of this orientation include qualitics such as the ability to change, efficiency, adaptability, generosity, open mindedness, tolerance, wit, and purposefulness. Negative aspects are opportunism, childishness, lack of principles and values, lack of tact, indifference, wastefulness, and the inability to be left alone.

Our introduction has focused on a few of the questions that have attracted the attention of scholars interested in the human personality. We have not attempted to present a comprehensive or detailed summary of all the major theories and research. The papers in this section have been selected primarily to reflect the wide range of problems which exist within the area of personality.

References *

Adorno, T. W., Frenkel-Brunswik, Else, Levinson, D. J., & Sanford, R. N. *The authoritarian personality.* New York: Harper, 1950. Also available in paperback edition published by John Wiley & Sons, Inc. (N.Y.).

Allport, G. W. *Personality: a psychological interpretation.* New York: Holt, 1937.

Allport, G. W. *Becoming: basic considerations for a psychology of personality.* New Haven: Yale University Press, 1955. Also available in paperback edition.

Bandura, A. & Walters, R. H. *Social learning and personality development.* New York: Holt, 1964.

Berne, E. *Games people play.* New York: Grove Press, 1964. Also available in paperback edition.

Bradburn, N. M. The cultural context of personality. In J. M. Wepman & R. W. Heine (Ed.) *Concepts of personality.* Chicago: Aldine Press, 1963.

Brenner, C. *An elementary textbook of psychoanalysis.* New York: International Universities Press, 1955. Also available in paperback edition published by Doubleday (N.Y.).

Byrne, D. *An introduction to personality: a research approach.* Englewood Cliffs, N. J.: Prentice-Hall, 1966.

Cattell, R. B. *Personality: a systematic, theoretical, and factual study.* New York: McGraw-Hill, 1950.

Dollard, J. & Miller, N. E. *Personality and psychotherapy.* New York: McGraw-Hill, 1950. Also available in paperback edition.

Erikson, E. H. *Childhood and society.* (2nd ed.) New York: Norton, 1963. Also available in paperback edition.

Erikson, E. H. *Identity, youth and crisis.* New York: Norton, 1968.

Eysenck, H. J. *Dimensions of personality.* London: Routledge and Kegan Paul, 1947.

Eysenck, H. J. *The scientific study of personality.* London: Routledge and Kegan Paul, 1952.

Freud, S. (1940) *The ego and the id.* New York: Norton, 1962. Also available in paperback edition. [Edited by J. Strachey, translated by J. Riviera.]

Fromm, E. *Escape from freedom.* New York: Rinehart, 1941. Also available in paperback edition published by Avon (N.Y.).

Fromm, E. *Man for himself.* New York: Holt, 1947. Also available in paperback edition published by Fawcett World Library (N.Y.).

Hall, C. S. & Lindzey, G. *Theories of personality.* New York: Wiley, 1957.

Horney, K. *Neurosis and human growth.* New York: Norton, 1950.

Jourard, S. *Personal adjustment: an approach through the study of the healthy personality.* New York: Macmillan, 1963.

Kagan, J. Personality development, In P. London & D. Rosenhan (Ed.), *Foundations of abnormal psychology.* New York: Holt, 1968, 117-173.

Linton, R. *The cultural background of personality.* New York: Appleton-Century, 1945. Also available in paperback edition.

Miller, N. E. & Dollard, J. *Social learning and imitation.* New Haven: Yale University Press, 1941.

Moreno, J. L. Who shall survive? *Nervous and mental diseases monograph series,* 1934, 58.

Riesman, D., Denney, R. & Glazer, N. *The lonely crowd: a study of the changing American character.* New Haven: Yale University Press, 1950. Also available in revised paperback edition.

Rokeach, M. *The open and closed mind.* New York: Basic Books, 1960. Also available in paperback edition.

Rogers, C. R. *Client-Centered Therapy.* Boston: Houghton Mifflin, 1951. Also available in paperback edition.

Royce, J. R. *The encapsulated man.* Princeton, N. J.: Van Nostrand, 1964. Also available in paperback edition.

Sarbin, T. R. Role theory. In G. Lindzey (Ed.), *Handbook of social psychology.* Reading, Mass.: Addison-Wesley, 1954, 1, pp. 223-258.

Spiro, M. E. Culture and personality: the history of a false dichotomy. *Psychiatry,* 1951, 14, 19-46.

* Paperback editions of listed titles are by the original publishers unless otherwise stated.

Personality formation: the determinants

CLYDE KLUCKHOHN AND HENRY A. MURRAY

Current psychological research and theory on personality development tends toward increasing specialization. This emphasis on understanding specific behaviors can make it difficult for the introductory student to integrate the many aspects of the personality into a meaningful whole. This first selection provides a helpful point of departure to the study of personality by emphasizing the general as well as the specific. The authors facilitate an understanding of the total person by classifying the various factors involved in personality development into four general categories and by describing how these variables interact with each other.

Henry Murray, Ph.D., is former Director of the Psychology Clinic and Professor Emeritus of Clinical Psychology in the Department of Social Relations at Harvard University. He received the Distinguished Scientific Contribution Award of the American Psychological Association in 1961. He has authored several books and many articles in the area of personality theory and research. Before his death in 1960, Clyde Kluckhohn, Ph.D., was Professor of Anthropology at Harvard University. Two of his better known books are *Mirror for Man* and *Culture*.

EVERY MAN is in certain respects

    a. like all other men,
    b. like some other men,
    c. like no other man.

He is like all other men because some of the determinants of his personality are universal to the species. That is to say, there are common features in the biological endowments of all men, in the physical environments they inhabit, and in the societies and cultures in which they develop. It is the very obviousness

of this fact which makes restatements of it expedient, since, like other people, we students of personality are naturally disposed to be attracted by what is unusual, by the qualities which distinguish individuals, environments, and societies, and so to overlook the common heritage and lot of man. It is possible that the most important of the undiscovered determinants of personality and culture are only to be revealed by close attention to the commonplace. Every man experiences birth and must learn to move about and explore his environment, to protect himself against extremes of temperature, and to avoid serious injuries; every man experiences sexual tensions and other importunate needs and must learn to find ways of appeasing them; every man grows in stature, matures, and dies; and he does all this and much more, from first to last, as a member of a society. These characteristics he shares with the majority of herd animals, but others are unique to him. Only with those of his own kind does he enjoy an erect posture, hands that grasp, three-dimensional and color vision, and a nervous system that permits elaborate speech and learning processes of the highest order.

Any one personality is like all others, also, because, as social animals, men must adjust to a condition of interdependence with other

Reprinted by permission of the publisher from *Personality in Nature, Society, and Culture*, Second Edition, by Clyde Kluckhohn and Henry Murray. Copyright, 1948, 1953 by Alfred A. Knopf, Inc.

Note: This paper represents a complete revision of an earlier scheme published by C. Kluckhohn and O. H. Mowrer, "Culture and personality: A conceptual scheme," *American Anthropologist*, Vol. 46 (1944), pp. 1-29. The present writers gratefully acknowledge their indebtedness to Dr. Mowrer.

members of their society and of groups within it, and, as cultural animals, they must adjust to traditionally defined expectations. All men are born helpless into an inanimate and impersonal world which presents countless threats to survival; the human species would die out if social life were abandoned. Human adaptation to the external environment depends upon that mutual support which is social life; and, in addition, it depends upon culture. Many types of insects live socially yet have no culture. Their capacity to survive resides in action patterns which are inherited via the germ plasm. Higher organisms have less rigid habits and can learn more from experience. Human beings, however, learn not only from experience but also from each other. All human societies rely greatly for their survival upon accumulated learning (culture). Culture is a great storehouse of ready-made solutions to problems which human animals are wont to encounter. This storehouse is man's substitute for instinct. It is filled not merely with the pooled learning of the living members of the society, but also with the learning of men long dead and of men belonging to other societies.

Human personalities are similar, furthermore, insofar as they all experience both gratifications and deprivations. They are frustrated by the impersonal environment (weather, physical obstacles, etc.) and by physiological conditions within their own bodies (physical incapacities, illnesses, etc.). Likewise, social life means some sacrifice of autonomy, subordination, and the responsibilities of superordination. The pleasure and pain men experience depend also upon what culture has taught them to expect from one another. Anticipations of pain and pleasure are internalized through punishment and reward.

These universalities of human life produce comparable effects upon the developing personalities of men of all times, places, and races. But they are seldom explicitly observed or commented upon. They tend to remain background phenomena—taken for granted like the air we breathe.

Frequently remarked, however, are the similarities in personality traits among members of groups or in specific individuals from different groups. In certain features of personality, most men are "like some other men." The similarity may be to other members of the same socio-cultural unit. The statistical prediction can safely be made that a hundred Americans, for example, will display certain defined characteristics more frequently than will a hundred Englishmen comparably distributed as to age, sex, social class, and vocation.

But being "like some other men" is by no means limited to members of social units like nations, tribes, and classes. Seafaring people, regardless of the communities from which they come, tend to manifest similar qualities. The same may be said for desert folk. Intellectuals and athletes the world over have something in common; so have those who were born to wealth or poverty. Persons who have exercised authority over large groups for many years develop parallel reaction systems, in spite of culturally tailored differences in the details of their behaviors. Probably tyrannical fathers leave a detectably similar imprint upon their children, though the uniformity may be superficially obscured by local manners. Certainly the hyperpituitary type is equally recognizable among Europeans, African Negroes, and American Indians. Also, even where organic causes are unknown or doubtful, certain neurotic and psychotic syndromes in persons of one society remind us of other individuals belonging to very different societies.

Finally, there is the inescapable fact that a man is in many respects like no other man. Each individual's modes of perceiving, feeling, needing, and behaving have characteristic patterns which are not precisely duplicated by those of any other individual. This is traceable, in part, to the unique combination of biological materials which the person has received from his parents. More exactly, the ultimate uniqueness of each personality is the product of countless and successive interactions between the maturing constitution and different environing situations from birth onward. An identical sequence of such determining influences is never reproduced. In this connection it is necessary to emphasize the importance of "accidents," that is, of events that are not predictable for any given individual on the basis of generalized knowledge of his physical, social, and cultural environments. A child gets lost in the woods and suffers from exposure and hunger. Another child is nearly drowned by a sudden flood in a canyon. Another loses his mother and is reared by an aged grandmother, or his father remaries and his education is entrusted to a stepmother with a psychopathic personality. Although the personalities of children who have experienced a trauma of the same type will often resemble each other in certain respects, the differences between them may be even more apparent, partly because the traumatic situation in each case had certain unique features, and partly because at the time of the trauma the personality of each child, being already unique, responded in a unique manner. Thus there is uniqueness in each inheritance and uniqueness in each environment, but, more particularly, uniqueness in the number, kinds, and temporal order of critically determining situations encountered in the course of life.

In personal relations, in psychotherapy, and in the arts, this uniqueness of personality usually is, and should be, accented. But for general scientific purposes the observation of uniformities, uniformities of elements and uniformities of patterns, is of first importance. This is so because without the discovery of uniformities there can be no concepts, no classifications, no formulations, no principles, no laws; and without these no science can exist.

The writers suggest that clear and orderly thinking about personality formation will be facilitated if four classes of determinants (and their interactions) are distingusihed: *constitutional, group-membership, role,* and *situational.* These will help us to understand in what ways every man is "like all other men," "like some other men," "like no other man."

1. Constitutional determinants

The old problem of "heredity *or* environment" is essentially meaningless. The two sets of determinants can rarely be completely disentangled once the environment has begun to operate. All geneticists are agreed today that traits are not inherited in any simple sense. The observed characters of organisms are, at any given point in time, the product of a long series of complex interactions between biologically-inherited potentialities and environmental forces. The outcome of each interaction is a modification of the personality. The only pertinent questions therefore are: (1) which of the various genetic potentialities will be actualized as a consequence of a particular series of life-events in a given physical, social, and cultural environment? and (2) what limits

to the development of this personality are set by genetic constitution?

Because there are only a few extreme cases in which an individual is definitely committed by his germ plasm to particular personality traits, we use the term "constitutional" rather than "hereditary." "Constitution" refers to the total physiological make-up of an individual at a given time. This is a product of influences emanating from the germ plasm and influences derived from the environment (diet, drugs, etc.).

Since most human beings (including scientists) crave simple solutions and tend to feel that because simple questions can be asked there must be simple answers, there are numberless examples both of overestimation and of underestimation of constitutional factors in theories of personality formation. Under the spell of the spectacular success of Darwinian biology and the medicine of the last hundred years, it has often been assumed that personality was no less definitely "given" at birth than was physique. At most, it was granted that a personality "unfolded" as the result of a strictly biological process of maturation.

On the other hand, certain psychiatrists, sociologists, and anthropologists have recently tended to neglect constitutional factors almost completely. Their assumptions are understandable in terms of common human motivations. Excited by discovering the effectiveness of certain determinants, people are inclined to make these explain everything, instead of something. Moreover, it is much more cheerful and reassuring to believe that environmental factors (which can be manipulated) are all important, and that hereditary factors (which can't be changed) are comparatively inconsequential. Finally, the psychiatrists, one suspects, are consciously or unconsciously defending their livelihood when they minimize the constitutional side of personality.

The writers recognize the enormous importance of biological events and event patterns in molding the different forms which personalities assume. In fact, in the last chapter personality was defined as "the entire sequence of organized governmental proccsscs in the brain from birth to death." They also insist that biological inheritance provides the stuff from which personality is fashioned and, as manifested in the physique at a given time-point, determines trends and sets limits within which variation is constrained. There are substantial reasons for believing that different genetic structures carry with them varying potentialities for learning, for reaction time, for energy level, for frustration tolerance. Different people appear to have different biological rhythms: of growth, of menstrual cycle, of activity, of depression and exaltation. The various biologically inherited malfunctions certainly have implications for personality development, though there are wide variations among those who share the same physical handicap (deafness, for example).

Sex and age must be regarded as among the more striking constitutional determinants of personality. Personality is also shaped through such traits of physique as stature, pigmentation, strength, conformity of features to the culturally fashionable type, etc. Such characteristics influence a man's needs and expectations. The kind of world he finds about him is to a considerable extent determined by the way other people react to his appearance and physical capacities. Occasionally a physically weak youth, such as Theodore Roosevelt was, may be driven to achieve feats of physical prowess as a form of over-compensation, but usually a man will learn to accept the fact that his physical make-up excludes him from certain types of vocational and social activities, although some concealed resentment may remain as an appreciable ingredient of his total personality. Conversely, special physical fitnesses make certain other types of adjustment particularly congenial.

2. Group-membership determinants

The members of any organized enduring group tend to manifest certain personality traits more frequently than do members of other groups. How large or how small are the groupings one compares depends on the problem at hand. By and large, the motivational structures and action patterns of Western Europeans seem similar when contrasted to those of Mohammedans of the Near East or to Eastern Asiatics. Most white citizens of the United States, in spite of regional, ethnic, and class differences, have features of personality which distinguish them from Englishmen, Australians, or New Zealanders. In distinguishing group-membership determinants, one must usually take account of a concentric order of social groups to which the individual belongs, ranging from large national or international groups down to small local units. One must also know the hierarchical class, political or social, to which he belongs within each of these groups. How inclusive a unit one considers in speaking of group-membership determinants is purely a function of the level of abstraction at which one is operating at a given time.

Some of the personality traits which tend to distinguish the members of a given group from humanity as a whole derive from a distinctive biological heritage. Persons who live together are more likely to have the same genes than are persons who live far apart. If the physical vitality is typically low for one group as contrasted with other groups, or if certain types of endocrine imbalance are unusually frequent, the personalities of the members of that group will probably have distinctive qualities.

In the greater number of cases, however, the similarities of character within a group are traceable less to constitutional factors than to formative influences of the environment to which all members of the group have been subjected. Of these group-membership determinants, culture is with little doubt the most significant. To say that "culture determines" is, of course, a highly abstract way of speaking. What one actually observes is the interaction of people. One never sees "culture" any more than one sees "gravity." But "culture" is a very convenient construct which helps in understanding certain regularities in human events, just as "gravity" represents one type of regularity in physical events. Those who have been trained in childhood along traditional lines, and even those who have as adults adopted some new design for living, will be apt to behave predictably in many contexts because of a prevailing tendency to conform to group standards. As Edward Sapir has said:

All cultural behavior is patterned. This is merely a way of saying that many things that an individual does and thinks and feels may be looked upon not merely from the standpoint of the forms of behavior that are proper to himself as a biological organism but from the standpoint of a generalized mode of conduct that is imputed to society rather than to the individual, though the personal genesis of conduct is of precisely the same nature, whether we choose to call the conduct "individual" or "social." It is impossible to say what an individual is doing unless we have tacitly accepted the essentially arbitrary modes of interpretation that social tradition is constantly suggesting to us from the very moment of our birth.

Not only the action patterns but also the motivational systems of individuals are influenced by culture. Certain needs are biologically given, but many others are not. All human beings get hungry, but no gene in any chromosome predisposes a person to work for a radio or a new car or a shell necklace or "success." Sometimes biologically given drives, such as sex, are for longer or shorter periods subordinated to culturally acquired drives, such as the pursuit of money or religious asceticism. And the means by which needs are satisfied are ordinarily defined by cultural habits and fashions. Most Americans would go hungry rather than eat a snake, but this is not true of tribes that consider snake meat a delicacy.

Those aspects of the personality that are not inherited but learned all have—at least in their more superficial and peripheral aspects—a cultural tinge. The skills that are acquired, the factual knowledge, the basic assumptions, the values, and the tastes, are largely determined by culture. Culture likewise structures the conditions under which each kind of learning takes place: whether transmitted by parents or parental substitutes, or by brothers and sisters, or by the learner's own age mates; whether gradually or quickly; whether renunciations are harshly imposed or reassuringly rewarded.

Of course we are speaking here of general tendencies rather than invariable facts. If there were no variations in the conceptions and applications of cultural standards, personalities formed in a given society would be more nearly alike than they actually are. Culture determines only what an individual learns as a member of a group—not so much what he learns as a private individual and as a member of a particular family. Because of these special experiences and particular constitutional endowments, each person's selection from and reaction to cultural teachings have an individual quality. What is learned is almost never symmetrical and coherent, and only occasionally is it fully integrated. Deviation from cultural norms is inevitable and endless, for

variability appears to be a property of all biological organisms. But variation is also perpetuated, because those who have learned later become teachers. Even the most conventional teachers will give culture a certain personal flavor in accord with their constitution and peculiar life-experiences. The culture may prescribe that the training of the child shall be gradual and gentle, but there will always be some abrupt and severe personalities who are temperamentally disposed to act otherwise. Nor is it in the concrete just a matter of individuality in the strict sense. There are family patterns resultant upon the habitual ways in which a number of individuals have come to adjust to each other.

Some types of variation, however, are more predictable. For example, certain differences in the personalities of Americans are referable to the face that they have grown up in various sub-cultures. Jones is not only an American; he is also a member of the middle class, an Easterner, and has lived all his life in a small Vermont community. This kind of variation falls within the framework of the group determinants.

The values imbedded in a culture have special weight among the group membership determinants. A value is a conception, explicit or implicit, distinctive of an individual or characteristic of a group, of the desirable which influences the selection from available modes, means, and ends of action. It is, thus, not just a preference, a desire, but a formulation of the *desirable,* the "ought" and "should" standards which influence action.

The component elements of a culture must, up to a point, be either logically consistent or meaningfully congruous. Otherwise the culture carriers feel uncomfortably adrift in a capricious, chaotic world. In a personality system, behavior must be reasonably regular or predictable, or the individual will not get expectable and needed responses from others because they will feel that they cannot "depend" on him. In other words, a social life and living in a social world both require standards "within" the individual and standards roughly agreed upon by individuals who live and work together in a group. There can be no personal security and no stability of social organization unless random carelessness, irresponsibility, and purely impulsive behavior are restrained in terms of private and group codes. If one asks the question, "Why are there values?" the reply must be: "Because social life would be impossible without them; the functioning of the social system could not continue to achieve group goals; individuals could not get what they want and need from other individuals in personal and emotional terms, nor could they feel within themselves a requisite measure of order and unified purpose." Above all, values add an element of predictability to social life.[1]

Culture is not the only influence that bears with approximate constancy upon all the members of a relatively stable, organized group. But we know almost nothing of the effects upon personality of the continued press of the impersonal environment. Does living in a constantly rainy climate tend to make people glum and passive, living in a sunny, arid country tend to make them cheerful and lively? What are the differential effects of dwelling in a walled-in mountain valley, on a flat plain, or upon a high plateau studded with wide-sculptured red buttes? Thus far we can only speculate, for we lack adequate data. The effects of climate and even of scenery and topography may be greater than is generally supposed.

Membership in a group also carries with it exposure to a social environment. Although the social and cultural are inextricably intermingled in an individual's observable behavior, there is a social dimension to group membership that is not culturally defined. The individual must adjust to the presence or absence of other human beings in specified numbers and of specified age and sex. The density of population affects the actual or potential number of face-to-face relationships available to the individual. Patterns for human adjustment which would be suitable to a group of five hundred would not work equally well in a group of five thousand, and vice versa. The size of a society, the density of its population, its age and sex ratio are not entirely culturally prescribed, although often conditioned by the interaction between the technological level of the culture and the exigencies of the physical environment. The quality and type of social interaction that is determined by this social dimension of group membership has, likewise, its consequences for personality formation.

Before leaving the group-membership determinants, we must remind the reader once more that this conception is merely a useful abstraction. In the concrete, the individual personality is never directly affected by the group as a physical totality. Rather, his personality is molded by the particular members of the group with whom he has personal contact and by his conceptions of the group as a whole. Some traits of group members are predictable—in a statistical sense—from knowledge of the biological, social, and cultural properties of the group. But no single person is ever completely representative of all the characteristics imputed to the group as a whole. Concretely, not the group but group agents with their own peculiar traits determine personality formation. Of these group agents, the most important are the parents and other members of the individual's family. They, we repeat, act as individuals, as members of a group, and as members of a sub-group with special characteristics (the family itself).

3. Role determinants

The culture defines how the different functions, or roles, necessary to group life are to be performed—such roles, for example, as those assigned on the basis of sex and age, or on the basis of membership in a caste, class, or occupational group. In a sense, the role determinants of personality are a special class of group membership determinants; they apply to strata that cross-cut most kinds of group membership. The long-continued playing of a distinctive role, however, appears to be so potent in differentiating personalities within a group that it is useful to treat these determinants separately.

Moreover, if one is aware of the role determinants, one will less often be misled in interpreting various manifestations of personality. In this connection it is worth recalling that, in early Latin, *persona* means "a mask"— *dramatis personae* are the masks which actors wear in a play, that is, the characters that are represented. Etymologically and historically, then, the personality is the character that is

---

[1] Fuller treatment of the concept of values will be found in C. Kluckhohn, "Values and value-orientations in the theory of action: An exploration in definition and classification," in T. Parsons and E. Shills (Eds.), *Toward a general theory of action*, Cambridge: Harvard University Press, 1951.

manifested in public. In modern psychology and sociology this corresponds rather closely to the role behavior of a differentiated person. From one point of view, this constitutes a disguise. Just as the outer body shields the viscera from view, and clothing the genitals, so the public personality shields the private personality from the curious and censorious world. It also operates to conceal underlying motivations from the individual's own consciousness. The person who has painfully achieved some sort of integration and who knows what is expected of him in a particular social situation, will usually produce the appropriate responses with only a little personal coloring. This explains, in part, why the attitudes and action patterns produced by the group-membership and role determinants constitute a screen which, in the case of normal individuals, can be penetrated only by the intensive, lengthy, and oblique procedures of depth psychology.

The disposition to accept a person's behavior in a given situation as representative of his total personality is almost universal. Very often he is merely conforming, very acceptably, to the cultural definition of his role. One visits a doctor in his office, and his behavior fits the stereotype of the physician so perfectly that one says, often mistakenly, "There indeed is a well-adjusted person." But a scientist must train himself to get behind a man's cultivated surface, because he will not be able to understand much if he limits his data to the action patterns perfected through the repeated performance of the roles as physician, as middle-aged man, as physician dealing with an older male patient, etc.

4. Situational determinants

Besides the constitutional determinants and the forces which will more or less inevitably confront individuals who live in the same physical environment, who are members of a society of a certain size and of a certain culture, and who play the same roles, there are things which "just happen" to people. Even casual contacts of brief duration ("accidental" —i.e., not foreordained by the cultural patterns for social interrelations) are often crucial, it seems, in determining whether a person's life will proceed along one or another of various possible paths. A student, say, who is undecided as to his career, or who is about equally drawn to several different vocations, happens to sit down in a railroad car next to a journalist who is an engaging and persuasive advocate of his profession. This event does not, of course, immediately and directly change the young man's personality, but it may set in motion a chain of events which put him into situations that are decisive in molding his personality.

The situational determinants include things that happen a thousand times as well as those that happen only once—provided they are not standard for a whole group. For example, it is generally agreed that the family constellation in which a person grows up is a primary source of personality styling. These domestic influences are conditioned by the cultural prescriptions for the roles of parents and children. But a divorce, a father who is much older than the mother, a father whose occupation keeps him away from home much of the time, the fact of being an only child or the eldest or youngest in a series—these are situational determinants.

Contact with a group involves determinants which are classified as group-membership or situational, depending on the individual's sense of belongingness or commitment to the group. The congeries of persons among whom a man accidentally finds himself one or more times may affect his personality development but not in the same manner as those social units with which the individual feels himself allied as a result of shared experiences or of imaginative identification.

5. Interdependence of the determinants

"Culture and personality" is one of the fashionable slogans of contemporary social science and, by present usage, denotes a range of problems on the borderline between anthropology and sociology, on the one hand, and psychology and psychiatry, on the other. However, the phrase has unfortunate implications. A dualism is implied, whereas "culture *in* personality" and "personality *in* culture" would suggest conceptual models more in accord with the facts. Moreover, the slogan favors a dangerous simplification of the problems of personality formation. Recognition of culture as one of the determinants of personality is a great gain, but there are some indications that this theoretical advance has tended to obscure the significance of other types of determinants. "Culture and personality" is as lopsided as "biology and personality." To avoid perpetuation of an over-emphasis upon culture, the writers have treated cultural forces as but one variety of the press to which personalities are subjected as a consequence of their membership in an organized group.

A balanced consideration of "personality in nature, society, and culture" must be carried on within the framework of a complex conceptual scheme which explicitly recognizes, instead of tacitly excluding, a number of types of determinants. But it must also not be forgotten that any classification of personality determinants is, at best, a convenient abstraction.

A few illustrations of the intricate linkage of the determinants will clarify this point. For example, we may instance a network of cultural, role, and constitutional determinants. In every society the child is differently socialized according to sex. Also, in every society different behavior is expected of individuals in different age groups, although each culture makes its own prescriptions as to where these lines are drawn and what behavioral variations are to be anticipated. Thus, the personalities of men and women, of the old and the young, are differentiated, in part, by the experience of playing these various roles in conformity with cultural standards. But, since age and sex are biological facts, they also operate throughout life as constitutional determinants of personality. A woman's motivations and action patterns are modified by the facts of her physique as a woman.

Some factors that one is likely to pigeonhole all too complacently as biological often turn out, on careful examination, to be the product of complicated interactions. Illness may result from group as well as from individual constitutional factors. And illness, in turn, may be considered a situational determinant. The illness—with all of its effects upon personality formation—is an "accident" in that one could predict only that the betting odds were relatively high that this individual would fall victim to this illness. However, when the person does become a patient, one can see that both a constitutional predisposition and membership in a caste or class group where sanitation and medical care were substandard are causative factors in this "accidental" event. Similarly, a constitutional tendency towards corpulence

certainly has implications for personality when it is characteristic of a group as well as when it distinguishes an individual within a group. But the resources of the physical environment as exploited by the culturally transmitted technology are major determinants in the production and utilization of nutritional substances of various sorts and these have patent consequences for corpulence, stature, and energy potential. Tuberculosis or pellagra may be endemic. If hookworm is endemic in a population, one will hardly expect vigor to be a striking feature of the majority of people. Yet hookworm is not an unavoidable "given," either constitutionally or environmentally: the prevalence and effects of hookworm are dependent upon culturally enjoined types of sanitary control.

Complicated interrelations of the same sort may be noted between the environmental and cultural forces which constitute the group membership determinants. On the one hand, the physical environment imposes certain limitations upon the cultural forms which man creates, or it constrains toward change and readjustment in the culture he brings into an ecological area. There is always a large portion of the impersonal environment to which men can adjust but not control; there is another portion which is man-made and cultural. Most cultures provide technologies which permit some alterations in the physical world (for example, methods of cutting irrigation ditches or of terracing hillsides). There are also those artifacts (houses, furniture, tools, vehicles) which serve as instruments for the gratification of needs, and, not infrequently, for their incitement and frustration. Most important of all, perhaps, culture directs and often distorts man's perceptions of the external world. What effects social suggestion may have in setting frames of reference for perception has been shown experimentally. Culture acts as a set of blinders, or series of lenses, through which men view their environments.

Among group-membership determinants, the social and cultural factors are interdependent, yet analytically distinct. Man, of course, is only one of many social animals, but the ways in which social, as opposed to solitary, life modifies his behavior are especially numerous and varied. The fact that human beings are mammals and reproduce bi-sexually creates a basic predisposition toward at least the rudiments of social living. And the prolonged helplessness of human infants conduces to the formation of a family group. Also, certain universal social processes (such as conflict, competition, and accommodation) are given distinct forms through cultural transmission. Thus, while the physically strong tend to dominate the weak, this tendency may be checked and even to some extent reversed by a tradition which rewards chivalry, compassion, and humility. Attitudes towards women, towards infants, towards the old, towards the weak will be affected by the age and sex ratios and the birth and death rates prevalent at a particular time.

The social and cultural press likewise interlock with the situational determinants. There are many forces involved in social interaction which influence personality formation and yet are in no sense culturally prescribed. All children (unless multiple births) are born at different points in their parents' careers, which means that they have, psychologically speaking, somewhat different parents. Likewise, whether a child is wanted or unwanted and whether it is of the desired sex will make a difference in ways in which it will be treated, even though the culture says that all children are wanted and defines the two sexes as of equal value.

A final example will link the constitutional with both the group-membership and situational determinants. Even though identical twins may differ remarkably little from a biological standpoint and participate in group activities which are apparently similar, a situational factor may intrude as a result of which their experiences in social interaction will be quite different. If, for instance, one twin is injured in an automobile accident and the other is not, and if the injured twin has to spend a year in bed, as the special object of his mother's solicitations, noticeable personality differences will probably develop. The extent to which these differences endure will depend surely upon many other factors, but it is unlikely that they will be entirely counteracted. The variations in treatment which a bed-ridden child receives is partly determined by culture (the extent to which the ideal patterns permit a sick child to be petted, etc.), and partly by extra-cultural factors (the mother's need for nurturance, the father's idiomatic performance

of his culturally patterned role in these circumstances, etc.).

6. Similarities and differences in personality

In conclusion, let us return for a moment to the observed fact that every man is "like all other men, like some other men, like no other man." In the beginning there is (1) the organism and (2) the environment. Using this division as the starting point in thinking about personality formation, one might say that the *differences* observed in the personalities of human beings are due to variations in their biological equipment and in the total environment to which they must adjust, while the *similarities* are ascribable to biological and environmental regularities. Although the organism and the environment have a kind of wholeness in the concrete behavioral world which the student loses sight of at his peril, this generalization is substantially correct. However, the formulation can be put more neatly in terms of field. There is (1) the organism moving through a field which is (2) structured both by culture and by the physical and social world in a relatively uniform manner, but which is (3) subject to endless variation within the general patterning due to the organism's constitutionally determined peculiarities of reaction and to the occurrence of special situations.

In certain circumstances, one reacts to men and women, not as unique organizations of experience, but as representatives of a group. In other circumstances, one reacts to men and women primarily as fulfilling certain roles. If one is unfamiliar with the Chinese, one is likely to react to them first as Chinese rather than as individuals. When one meets new people at a social gathering, one is often able to predict correctly: "That man is a doctor." "That man certainly isn't a businessman, he acts like a professor." "That fellow over there looks like a government official, surely not an artist, a writer, or an actor." Similarities in personality created by the role and group-membership determinants are genuine enough. A man is likely to resemble other men from his home town, other members of his vocation, other members of his class, as well as the majority of his countrymen as contrasted to foreigners.

But the variations are equally common.

Smith is stubborn in his office as well as at home and on the golf course. Probably he would have been stubborn in all social contexts if he had been taken to England from America at an early age and his socialization had been completed there. The playing of roles is always tinged by the uniqueness of the personality. Such differences may be distinguished by saying, "Yes, Brown and Jones are both forty-five-year-old Americans, both small-business-men with about the same responsibilities, family ties, and prestige—but somehow they are different." Such dissimilarities may be traced to the interactions of the constitutional and situational determinants, which have been different for each man, with the common group-membership and role determinants to which both have been subjected.

Another type of resemblance between personalities cuts across the boundaries of groups and roles but is equally understandable within this framework of thinking about personality formation. In general, one observes quite different personality manifestations in Hopi Indians and in white Americans—save for those common to all humanity. But occasionally one meets a Hopi whose behavior, as a whole or in part, reminds one very strongly of a certain type of white man. Such parallels can arise from similar constitutional or situational determinants or a combination of these. A Hopi and a white man might both have an unusual endocrine condition. Or both Hopi and white might have had several long childhood illnesses which brought them an exceptional amount of maternal care. While an over-abundance of motherly devotion would have had somewhat different effects upon the two personalities, a striking segmental resemblance might have been produced which persisted throughout life.

In most cases the observed similarities, as well as the differences, between groups of people are largely attributable to fairly uniform social and cultural processes. When one says, "Smith reminds me of Brown," a biologically inherited determinant may be completely responsible for the observed resemblance. But when one notes that American businessmen, for example, have certain typical characteristics which identify them as a group and distinguish them from American farmers and teachers it can hardly be a question of genetic constitution. Likewise, the similarities of personality between Americans in general as contrasted with Germans in general must be traced primarily to common press which produces resemblances in spite of wide variations in individual constitutions.

To summarize the content of this chapter in other terms: The personality of an individual is the product of inherited dispositions and environmental experiences. These experiences occur within the field of his physical, biological, and social environment, all of which are modified by the culture of his group. Similarities of life experiences and heredity will tend to produce similar personality characteristics in different individuals, whether in the same society or in different societies.

Although the distinction will not always be perfectly clear cut, the readings which follow will be organized according to this scheme of constitutional, group-membership, role, and situational determinants, and the interactions between them. It is believed that this will assist the reader in keeping steadily in mind the variety of forces operative in personality formation and the firm but subtle nexus that links them.

Some observations on the organization of personality[1]

CARL R. ROGERS

Psychotherapy is a form of psychological treatment which is based on the assumption that talking about one's problems helps the person to learn to cope more successfully with them. It is also a valuable source of information, and much of our own knowledge about the personality has been derived from observations of persons undergoing psychotherapy. This paper illustrates how a particular method of psychotherapy, the client-centered approach, can facilitate increased understanding of the personality. The author points out that by adopting the client's internal frame of reference the therapist can create an atmosphere of empathic understanding, and this enables the client to describe more clearly his self-perceptions, behavior, and perception of reality. The article presents some of the author's hypotheses about the nature of personality functioning which are derived from his observations as a therapist.

Carl Rogers, Ph.D., is a former president of the American Psychological Association and recipient of its Distinguished Scientific Contribution Award in 1956. He is the author of many journal articles and several books on psychotherapy and personality theory including *Counseling and Psychotherapy: New Concepts in Practice, Client-Centered Therapy,* and *On Becoming a Person.*

In various fields of science rapid strides have been made when direct observation of significant processes has become possible. In medicine, when circumstances have permitted the physician to peer directly into the stomach of his patient, understanding of digestive processes has increased, and the influence of emotional tension upon all aspects of that process has been more accurately observed and understood. In our work with nondirective therapy we often feel that we are having a psychological opportunity comparable to this medical experience—an opportunity to observe directly a number of the effective processes of personality. Quite aside from any question regarding nondirective therapy as therapy, here is a precious vein of observational material of unusual value for the study of personality.

Characteristics of the observational material

There are several ways in which the raw clinical data to which we have had access is unique in its value for understanding personality. The fact that these verbal expressions of inner dynamics are preserved by electrical recording makes possible a detailed analysis of a sort not heretofore possible. Recording has given us a microscope by which we may examine at leisure, and in minute detail, almost every aspect of what was, in its occurrence, a fleeting moment impossible of accurate observation.

Another scientifically fortunate characteristic of this material is the fact that the verbal productions of the client are biased to a minimal degree by the therapist. Material from client-centered interviews probably comes closer to being a "pure" expression of attitudes than has yet been achieved through other means. One can read through a complete recorded case or listen to it, without finding more than a half-dozen instances in which the therapist's views on any point are evident. One

---

From *American Psychologist,* II (1947), 358-368. Reprinted by permission of the American Psychological Association and the author.

[1] Address of the retiring President of the American Psychological Association delivered at the September 1947 Annual Meeting.

would find it impossible to form an estimate as to the therapist's views about personality dynamics. One could not determine his diagnostic views, his standards of behavior, his social class. The one value or standard held by the therapist which would exhibit itself in his tone of voice, responses, and activity is a deep respect for the personality and attitudes of the client as a separate person. It is difficult to see how this would bias the content of the interview, except to permit deeper expression than the client would ordinarily allow himself. This almost complete lack of any distorting attitude is felt, and sometimes expressed by the client. One woman says:

"It is almost impersonal. I like you—of course I don't know why I should like you or why I shouldn't like you. It's a peculiar thing. I've never had that relationship with anybody before and I've often thought about it. . . . A lot of times I walk out with a feeling of elation that you think highly of me, and of course at the same time I have the feeling that 'Gee, he must think I'm an awful jerk' or something like that. But it doesn't really—those feelings aren't so deep that I can form an opinion one way or the other about you."

Here it would seem that even though she would like to discover some type of evaluational attitude, she is unable to do so. Published studies and research as yet unpublished bear out this point that counselor responses which are in any way evaluational or distorting as to content are at a minimum, thus enhancing the worth of such interviews for personality study.

The counselor attitude of warmth and understanding, well described by Snyder (9) and Rogers (8), also helps to maximize the freedom of expression by the individual. The client experiences sufficient interest in him as a person, and sufficient acceptance, to enable him to talk openly, not only about surface attitudes, but increasingly about intimate attitudes and feelings hidden even from himself. Hence in these recorded interviews we have material of very considerable depth so far as personality dynamics is concerned, along with a freedom from distortion.

Finally, the very nature of the interviews and the techniques by which they are handled give us a rare opportunity to see to some extent through the eyes of another person—to perceive the world as it appears to him, to achieve at least partially, the internal frame of reference of another person. We see his behavior through his eyes, and also the psychological meaning which it had for him. We see also changes in personality and behavior and the meanings which those changes have for the individual. We are admitted freely into the backstage of the person's living where we can observe from within some of the dramas of internal change, which are often far more compelling and moving than the drama which is presented on the stage viewed by the public. Only a novelist or a poet could do justice to the deep struggles which we are permitted to observe from within the client's own world of reality.

This rare opportunity to observe so directly and so clearly the inner dynamics of personality is a learning experience of the deepest sort for the clinician. Most of clinical psychology and psychiatry involves judgments *about* the individual, judgments which must, of necessity, be based on some framework brought to the situation by the clinician. To try continually to see and think *with* the individual, as in client-centered therapy, is a mindstretching experience in which learning goes on apace because the clinician brings to the interview no predetermined yardstick by which to judge the material.

I wish in this paper to try to bring you some of the clinical observations which we have made as we have repeatedly peered through these psychological windows into personality, and to raise with you some of the questions about the organization of personality which these observations have forced upon us. I shall not attempt to present these observations in logical order, but rather in the order in which they impressed themselves upon our notice. What I shall offer is not a series of research findings, but only the first step in that process of gradual approximation which we call science, a description of some observed phenomena which appear to be significant, and some highly tentative explanations of these phenomena.

The relation of the organized perceptual field to behavior

One simple observation, which is repeated over and over again in each successful therapeutic case, seems to have rather deep theoretical implications. It is that as changes occur in the perception of self and in the perception of reality changes occur in behavior. In therapy, these perceptual changes are more often concerned with the self than with the external world. Hence we find in therapy that as the perception of self alters, behavior alters. Perhaps an illustration will indicate the type of observation upon which this statement is based.

A young woman, a graduate student whom we shall call Miss Vib, came in for nine interviews. If we compare the first interview with the last, striking changes are evident. Perhaps some features of this change may be conveyed by taking from the first and last interviews all the major statements regarding self, and all the major statements regarding current behavior. In the first interview, for example, her perception of herself may be crudely indicated by taking all her own statements about herself, grouping those which seem similar, but otherwise doing a minimum of editing, and retaining so far as possible, her own words. We then come out with this as the conscious perception of self which was hers at the outset of counseling.

"I feel disorganized, muddled; I've lost all direction; my personal life has disintegrated.

"I sorta experience things from the forefront of my consciousness, but nothing sinks in very deep; things don't seem real to me; I feel nothing matters; I don't have any emotional response to situations; I'm worried about myself.

"I haven't been acting like myself; it doesn't seem like me; I'm a different person altogether from what I used to be in the past.

"I don't understand myself; I haven't known what was happening to me.

"I have withdrawn from everything, and feel all right only when I'm all alone and no one can expect me to do things.

"I don't care about my personal appearance.

"I don't know *anything* anymore.

"I feel guilty about the things I have left undone.

"I don't think I could ever assume responsibility for anything."

If we attempt to evaluate this picture of self from an external frame of reference various diagnostic labels may come to mind. Trying to perceive it solely from the client's frame of reference we observe that to the young woman herself she appears disorganized, and not herself. She is perplexed and almost unacquainted with what is going on in herself. She feels unable and unwilling to function in any responsible or social way. This is at least a sampling of the way she experiences or perceives herself.

Her behavior is entirely consistent with this picture of self. If we abstract all her statements describing her behavior, in the same fashion as we abstracted her statements about self, the following pattern emerges—a pattern which in this case was corroborated by outside observation.

"I couldn't get up nerve to come in before; I haven't availed myself of help.

"Everything I should do or want to do, I don't do.

"I haven't kept in touch with friends; I avoid making the effort to go with them; I stopped writing letters home; I don't answer letters or telephone calls; I avoid contacts that would be professionally helpful; I didn't go home though I said I would.

"I failed to hand in my work in a course though I had it all done; I didn't even buy clothing that I needed; I haven't even kept my nails manicured.

"I didn't listen to material we were studying; I waste hours reading the funny papers; I can spend the whole afternoon doing absolutely nothing."

The picture of behavior is very much in keeping with the picture of self, and is summed up in the statement that "Everything I should do or want to do, I don't do." The behavior goes on, in ways that seem to the individual beyond understanding and beyond control.

If we contrast this picture of self and behavior with the picture as it exists in the ninth interview, thirty-eight days later, we find both the perception of self and the ways of behaving deeply altered. Her statements about self are as follows:

"I'm feeling much better; I'm taking more interest in myself.

"I do have some individuality, some interests.

"I seem to be getting a newer understanding of myself. I can look at myself a little better.

"I realize I'm just one person, with so much ability, but I'm not worried about it; I can accept the fact that I'm not always right.

"I feel more motivation, have more of a desire to go ahead.

"I still occasionally regret the past, though I feel less unhappy about it; I still have a long ways to go; I don't know whether I can keep the picture of myself I'm beginning to evolve.

"I can go on learning—in school or out.

"I do feel more like a normal person now; I feel more I can handle my life myself; I think I'm at the point where I can go along on my own."

Outstanding in this perception of herself are three things—that she knows herself, that she can view with comfort her assets and liabilities, and finally that she has drive and control of that drive.

In this ninth interview, the behavioral picture is again consistent with the perception of self. It may be abstracted in these terms.

"I've been making plans about school and about a job; I've been working hard on a term paper; I've been going to the library to trace down a topic of special interest and finding it exciting.

"I've cleaned out my closets; washed my clothes.

"I finally wrote my parents; I'm going home for the holidays.

"I'm getting out and mixing with people; I am reacting sensibly to a fellow who is interested in me seeing both his good and bad points.

"I will work toward my degree; I'll start looking for a job this week."

Her behavior, in contrast to the first interview, is now organized, forward-moving, effective, realistic and planful. It is in accord with the realistic and organized view she has achieved of her self.

It is this type of observation, in case after case, that leads us to say with some assurance that as perceptions of self and reality change, behavior changes. Likewise, in cases we might term failures, there appears to be no appreciable change in perceptual organization or in behavior.

What type of explanation might account for these concomitant changes in the perceptual field and the behavioral pattern? Let us examine some of the logical possibilities.

In the first place, it is possible that factors unrelated to therapy may have brought about the altered perception and behavior. There may have been physiological processes occurring which produced the change. There may have been alterations in the family relation-

ships, or in the social forces, or in the educational picture, or in some other area of cultural influence, which might account for the rather drastic shift in the concept of self and in the behavior.

There are difficulties in this type of explanation. Not only were there no known gross changes in the physical or cultural situation as far as Miss Vib was concerned, but the explanation gradually becomes inadequate when one tries to apply it to the many cases in which such change occurs. To postulate that some external factor brings the change and that only by chance does this period of change coincide with the period of therapy, becomes an untenable hypothesis.

Let us then look at another explanation, namely that the therapist exerted, during the nine hours of contact, a peculiarly potent cultural influence which brought about the change. Here again we are faced with several problems. It seems that nine hours scattered over five and one-half weeks is a very minute portion of time in which to bring about alteration of patterns which have been building for thirty years. We would have to postulate an influence so potent as to be classed as traumatic. This theory is particularly difficult to maintain when we find, on examining the recorded interviews, that not once in the nine hours did the therapist express any evaluation, positive or negative, of the client's initial or final perception of self, or her initial or final mode of behavior. There was not only no evaluation, but no standards expressed by which evaluation might be inferred.

There was, on the part of the therapist, evidence of warm interest in the individual, and thoroughgoing acceptance of the self and of the behavior as they existed initially, in the intermediate stages, and at the conclusion of therapy. It appears reasonable to say that the therapist established certain definite conditions of interpersonal relations, but since the very essence of this relationship is respect for the person as he is at that moment, the therapist can hardly be regarded as a cultural force making for change.

We find ourselves forced to a third type of explanation, a type of explanation which is not new to psychology, but which has had only partial acceptance. Briefly it may be put that the observed phenomena of change seem most adequately explained by the hypothesis that *given certain psychological conditions, the individual has the capacity to reorganize his field of perception, including the way he perceives himself, and that a concomitant or a resultant of this perceptual reorganization is an appropriate alteration of behavior.* This puts into formal and objective terminology a clinical hypothesis which experience forces upon the therapist using a client-centered approach. One is compelled through clinical observation to develop a high degree of respect for the ego-integrative forces residing within each individual. One comes to recognize that under proper conditions the self is a basic factor in the formation of personality and in the determination of behavior. Clinical experience would strongly suggest that the self is, to some extent, an architect of self, and the above hypothesis simply puts this observation into psychological terms.

In support of this hypothesis it is noted in some cases that one of the concomitants of success in therapy is the realization on the part of the client that the self has the capacity for reorganization. Thus a student says:

"You know I spoke of the fact that a person's background retards one. Like the fact that my family life wasn't good for me, and my mother certainly didn't give me any of the kind of bringing up that I should have had. Well, I've been thinking that over. It's true up to a point. But when you get so that you can see the situation, then it's really up to you."

Following this statement of the relation of the self to experience, many changes occurred in this young man's behavior. In this, as in other cases, it appears that when the person comes to see himself as the perceiving, organizing agent, then reorganization of perception and consequent change in patterns of reaction take place.

On the other side of the picture, we have frequently observed that when the individual has been authoritatively told that he is governed by certain factors or conditions beyond his control, it makes therapy more difficult, and it is only when the individual discovers for himself that he can organize his perceptions that change is possible. In veterans who have been given their own psychiatric diagnosis, the effect is often that of making the individual feel that

he is under an unalterable doom, that he is unable to control the organization of his life. When, however, the self sees itself as capable of reorganizing its own perceptual field, a marked change in basic confidence occurs. Miss Nam, a student, illustrates this phenomenon when she says, after having made progress in therapy:

"I think I do feel better about the future, too, because it's as if I won't be acting in darkness. It's sort of, well, knowing somewhat why I act the way I do . . . and at least it isn't the feeling that you're simply out of your own control and the fates are driving you to act that way. If you realize it, I think you can do something more about it."

A veteran at the conclusion of counseling puts it more briefly and more positively: "My attitude toward myself is changed now to where I feel I *can* do something with my self and life." He has come to view himself as the instrument by which some reorganization can take place.

There is another clinical observation which may be cited in support of the general hypothesis that there is a close relationship between behavior and the way in which reality is viewed by the individual. It has been noted in many cases that behavior changes come about for the most part imperceptibly and almost automatically, once the perceptual reorganization has taken place. A young wife who has been reacting violently to her maid, and has been quite disorganized in her behavior as a result of this antipathy, says "After I . . . discovered it was nothing more than that she resembled my mother, she didn't bother me any more. Isn't that interesting? She's still the same." Here is a clear statement indicating that though the basic perceptions have not changed, they have been differently organized, have acquired a new meaning, and that behavior changes then occur. Similar evidence is given by a client, a trained psychologist, who after completing a brief series of client-centered interviews, writes:

"Another interesting aspect of the situation was in connection with the changes in some of my attitudes. When the change occurred, it was as if earlier attitudes were wiped out as completely as if erased from a blackboard. . . . When a situation which would formerly have provoked a given type of response occurred, it was not as if I was tempted to act in the way I formerly had but in some way found it easier to control my behavior. Rather the new type of behavior came quite spontaneously, and it was only through a deliberate analysis that I became aware that I was acting in a new and different way."

Here again it is of interest that the imagery is put in terms of visual perception and that as attitudes are "erased from the blackboard" behavioral changes take place automatically and without conscious effort.

Thus, we have observed that appropriate changes in behavior occur when the individual acquires a different view of his world of experience, including himself; that this changed perception does not need to be dependent upon a change in the "reality," but may be a product of internal reorganization; that in some instances the awareness of the capacity for reperceiving experience accompanies this process of reorganization; that the altered behavioral responses occur automatically and without conscious effort as soon as the perceptual reorganization has taken place, apparently as a result of this.

In view of these observations a second hypothesis may be stated, which is closely related to the first. It is that *behavior is not directly influenced or determined by organic or cultural factors, but primarily,* (and perhaps only) *by the perception of these elements.* In other words the crucial element in the determination of behavior is the perceptual field of the individual. While this perceptual field is, to be sure, deeply influenced and largely shaped by cultural and physiological forces, it is nevertheless important that it appears to be only the field as it is *perceived* which exercises a specific determining influence upon behavior. This is not a new idea in psychology, but its implications have not always been fully recognized.

It might mean, first of all, that if it is the perceptual field which determines behavior, then the primary object of study for psychologists would be the person and his world *as viewed by the person himself.* It could mean that the internal frame of reference of the person might well constitute the field of psychology, an idea set forth persuasively by Snygg and Combs in a significant manuscript as yet unpublished. It might mean that the laws which govern behavior would be discovered more deeply by turning our attention to the laws which govern perception.

Now if our speculations contain a measure of truth, if the *specific* determinant of behavior is the perceptual field, and if the self can reorganize that perceptual field, then what are the limits of this process? Is the reorganization of perception capricious, or does it follow certain laws? Are there limits to the degree of reorganization? If so, what are they? In this connection we have observed with some care the perception of one portion of the field of experience, the portion we call the self.

The relation of the perception of the self to adjustment

Initially we were oriented by the background of both lay and psychological thinking to regard the outcome of successful therapy as the solution of problems. If a person had a marital problem, a vocational problem, a problem of educaitonal adjustment, the obvious purpose of counseling or therapy was to solve that problem. But, as we observe and study the recorded accounts of the conclusion of therapy, it is clear that the most characteristic outcome is not necessarily solution of problems, but a freedom from tension, a different feeling about, and perception of, self. Perhaps something of this outcome may be conveyed by some illustrations.

Several statements taken from the final interview with a twenty-year-old young woman, Miss Mir, give indications of the characteristic attitude toward self, and the sense of freedom which appears to accompany it.

"I've always tried to be what the others thought I should be, but now I am wondering whether I shouldn't just see that I am what I am."

"Well, I've just noticed such a difference. I find that when I feel things, even when I feel hate, I don't care. I don't mind. I feel more free somehow. I don't feel guilty about things."

"You know it's suddenly as though a big cloud has been lifted off. I feel so much more content."

Note in these statements the willingness to perceive herself as she is, to accept herself "realistically," to perceive and accept her "bad" attitudes as well as "good" ones. This realism seems to be accompanied by a sense of freedom and contentment.

Miss Vib, whose attitudes were quoted earlier, wrote out her own feelings about counseling some six weeks after the interviews were over, and gave the statement to her counselor. She begins:

"The happiest outcome of therapy has been a new feeling about myself. As I think of it, it might be the only outcome. Certainly it is basic to all the changes in my behavior that have resulted." In discussing her experience in therapy she states, "I was coming to see myself as a whole. I began to realize that I am *one* person. This was an important insight to me. I saw that the former good academic achievement, job success, ease in social situations, and the present withdrawal, dejection, apathy and failure were all adaptive behavior, performed by *me*. This meant that I had to reorganize my feelings about myself, no longer holding to the unrealistic notion that the very good adjustment was the expression of the real "me" and this neurotic behavior was not. I came to feel that I am the same person, sometimes functioning maturely, and sometimes assuming a neurotic role in the face of what I had conceived as insurmountable problems. The acceptance of myself as one person gave me strength in the process of reorganization. Now I had a substratum, a core of unity on which to work." As she continues her discussion there are such statements as "I am getting more happiness in being myself." "I approve of myself more, and I have so much less anxiety."

As in the previous example, the outstanding aspects appear to be the realization that all of her behavior "belonged" to her, that she could accept both the good and bad features about herself and that doing so gave her a release from anxiety and a feeling of solid happiness. In both instances there is only incidental reference to the serious "problems" which had been initially discussed.

Since Miss Mir is undoubtedly above average intelligence and Miss Vib is a person with some psychological training, it may appear that such results are found only with the sophisticated individual. To counteract this opinion a quotation may be given from a statement written by a veteran of limited ability and education who had just completed counseling and was asked to write whatever reactions he had to the experience. He says:

"As for the counseling I have had I can say this, It really makes a man strip his own mind bare, and when he does he knows then what he really is and what he can do. Or at least thinks he knows himself pretty well. As for myself, I know that my ideas were a little too big for what I really am, but now I realize one must try start out at his own level.

"Now after four visits, I have a much clearer picture of myself and my future. It makes me feel a little depressed and disappointed, but on the other hand, it has taken me out of the dark, the load seems a lot lighter now, that is I can see my way now, I know what I want to do, I know about what I can do, so now that I can see my goal, I will be able to work a whole lot easier, at my own level."

Although the expression is much simpler, one notes again the same two elements—the acceptance of self as it is, and the feeling of easiness, of lightened burden, which accompanies it.

As we examine many individual case records and case recording, it appears to be possible to bring together the findings in regard to successful therapy by stating another hypothesis in regard to that portion of the perceptual field which we call the self. It would appear that *when all of the ways in which the individual perceives himself—all perceptions of the qualities, abilities, impulses, and attitudes of the person, and all perceptions of himself in relation to others—are accepted into the organized conscious concept of the self, then this achievement is accompanied by feelings of comfort and freedom from tension which are experienced as psychological adjustment.*

This hypothesis would seem to account for the observed fact that the comfortable perception of self which is achieved is sometimes more positive than before, sometimes more negative. When the individual permits all his perceptions of himself to be organized into one pattern, the picture is sometimes more flattering than he has held in the past, sometimes less flattering. It is always more comfortable.

It may be pointed out also that this tentative hypothesis supplies an operational type of definition, based on the client's internal frame of reference, for such hitherto vague terms as "adjustment," "integration," and "acceptance of self." They are defined in terms of perception, in a way which it should be possible to prove or disprove. When all of the organic perceptual experiences—the experiencing of attitudes, impulses, abilities and disabilities, the experiencing of others and of "reality"—when all of these perceptions are freely assimilated into an organized and consistent system, available to consciousness, then psychological adjustment or integration might be said to exist. The definition of adjustment is thus made an internal affair, rather than dependent upon an external "reality."

Something of what is meant by this acceptance and assimilation of perceptions about the self may be illustrated from the case of Miss Nam, a student. Like many other clients she gives evidence of having experienced attitudes and feelings which are defensively denied because they are not consistent with the concept or picture she holds of herself. The way in which they are first fully admitted into consciousness, and then organized into a unified system may be shown by excerpts from the recorded interviews. She has spoken of the difficulty she has had in bringing herself to write papers for her university courses.

"I just thought of something else which perhaps hinders me, and that is that again it's two different feelings. When I have to sit down and do (a paper), though I have a lot of ideas, underneath I think I always have the feeling that I just can't do it. . . . I have this feeling of being terrifically confident that I can do something, without being willing to put the work into it. At other times I'm practically afraid of what I have to do. . . ."

Note that the conscious self has been organized as "having a lot of ideas," being "terrifically confident" but that "underneath," in other words not freely admitted into consciousness, has been the experience of feeling "I just can't do it." She continues:

"I'm trying to work through this funny relationship between this terrific confidence and then this almost fear of doing anything . . . and I think the kind of feeling that I can really do things is part of an illusion I have about myself of being, in my imagination, sure that it will be something good and very good and all that, but whenever I get down

to the actual task of getting started, it's a terrible feeling of—well, incapacity, that I won't get it done either the way I want to do it, or even not being sure how I want to do it."

Again the picture of herself which is presented in consciousness is that of a person who is "very good," but this picture is entirely out of line with the actual organic experience in the situation.

Later in the same interview she expresses very well the fact that her perceptions are not all organized into one consistent conscious self.

"I'm not sure about what kind of a person I am— well, I realize that all of these are a part of me, but I'm not quite sure of how to make all of these things fall in line."

In the next interview we have an excellent opportunity to observe the organization of both of these conflicting perceptions into one pattern, with the resultant sense of freedom from tension which has been described above.

"It's very funny, even as I sit here I realize that I have more confidence in myself, in the sense that when I used to approach new situations I would have two very funny things operating at the same time. I had a fantasy that I could do anything, which was a fantasy which covered over all these other feelings that I really couldn't do it, or couldn't do it as well as I wanted to, and it's as if now those two things have merged together, and it is more real, that a situation isn't either testing myself or proving something to myself or anyone else. It's just in terms of doing it. And I think I have done away both with that fantasy and that fear. . . . So I think I can go ahead and approach things— well, just sensibly."

No longer is it necessary for this client to "cover over" her real experiences. Instead the picture of herself as very able, and the experienced feeling of complete inability, have now been brought together into one integrated pattern of self as a person with real, but imperfect abilities. Once the self is thus accepted, the inner energies making for self-actualization are released, and she attacks her life problems more efficiently.

Observing this type of material frequently in counseling experience would lead to a tentative hypothesis of maladjustment, which like the other hypothesis suggested, focuses on the perception of self. It might be proposed that the tensions called psychological maladjustment exist when the organized concept of self (conscious or available to conscious awareness) is not in accord with the perceptions actually experienced.

This discrepancy between the concept of self and the actual perceptions seems to be explicable only in terms of the fact that the self-concept resists assimilating into itself any percept which is inconsistent with its present organization. The feeling that she may not have the ability to do a paper is inconsistent with Miss Nam's conscious picture of herself as a very able and confident person, and hence, though fleetingly perceived, is denied organization as a part of her self, until this comes about in therapy.

The conditions of change of self perception

If the way in which the self is perceived has as close and significant a relationship to behavior as has been suggested, then the manner in which this perception may be altered becomes a question of importance. If a reorganization of self-perceptions brings a change in behavior, if adjustment and maladjustment depend on the congruence between perceptions as experienced and the self as perceived, then the factors which permit a reorganization of the perception of self are significant.

Our observations of psychotherapeutic experience would seem to indicate that absence of any threat to the self-concept is an important item in the problem. Normally the self resists incorporating into itself those experiences which are inconsistent with the functioning of self. But a point overlooked by Lecky and others is that when the self is free from any threat of attack or likelihood of attack, then it is possible for the self to consider these hitherto rejected perceptions, to make new differentiations, and to reintegrate the self in such a way as to include them.

An illustration from the case of Miss Vib may serve to clarify this point. In her statement written six weeks after the conclusion of counseling Miss Vib thus describes the way in which unacceptable percepts become incorporated into the self. She writes:

"In the earlier interviews I kept saying such things as, 'I am not acting like myself, I never acted this way before.' What I meant was that this withdrawn, untidy, and apathetic person was not myself. Then I began to realize that I was the same person, seriously withdrawn, etc. now, as I had been before. That did not happen until after I had talked out my self-rejection, shame, despair, and doubt, in the accepting situation of the interview. The counselor was not startled or shocked. I was telling him all these things about myself which did not fit into my picture of a graduate student, a teacher, a sound person. He responded with complete acceptance and warm interest without heavy emotional overtones. Here was a sane, intelligent person wholeheartedly accepting this behavior that seemed so shameful to me. I can remember an organic feeling of relaxation. I did not have to keep up the struggle to cover up and hide this shameful person."

Note how clearly one can see here the whole range of denied perceptions of self, and the fact that they could be considered as a part of self only in a social situation which involved no threat to the self, in which another person, the counselor, becomes almost an alternate self and looks with understanding and acceptance upon these same perceptions. She continues:

"Retrospectively, it seems to me that what I felt as 'warm acceptance without emotional overtones' was what I needed to work through my difficulties. . . . The counselor's impersonality with interest allowed me to talk out my feelings. The clarification in the interview situation presented the attitude to me as a 'ding an sich' which I could look at, manipulate, and put in place. In organizing my attitudes, I was beginning to organize me."

Here the nature of the exploration of experience, of seeing it as experience and not as a threat to self, enables the client to reorganize her perceptions of self, which as she says was also "reorganizing me."

If we attempt to describe in more conventional psychological terms the nature of the process which culminates in an altered organization and integration of self in the process of therapy it might run as follows: The individual is continually endeavoring to meet his needs by reacting to the field of experience as he perceives it, and to do that more efficiently by differentiating elements of the field and re-integrating them into new patterns. Reorganization of the field may involve the reorganization of the self as well as of other parts of the field. The self, however, resists reorganization and change. In everyday life individual adjustment by means of reorganization of the field exclusive of the self is more common and is less threatening to the individual. Consequently, the individual's first mode of adjustment is the reorganization of that part of the field which does not include the self.

Client-centered therapy is different from other life situations inasmuch as the therapist tends to remove from the individual's immediate world all those aspects of the field which the individual can reorganize except the self. The therapist, by reacting to the client's feeling and attitudes rather than to the objects of his feelings and attitudes, assists the client in bringing from background into focus his own self, making it easier than ever before for the client to perceive and react to the self. By offering only understanding and no trace of evaluation, the therapist removes himself as an object of attitudes, becoming only an alternate expression of the client's self. The therapist by providing a consistent atmosphere of permissiveness and understanding removes whatever threat existed to prevent all perceptions of the self from emerging into figure. Hence in this situation all the ways in which the self has been experienced can be viewed openly, and organized into a complex unity.

It is then this complete absence of any factor which would attack the concept of self, and second, the assistance in focusing upon the perception of self, which seems to permit a more differentiated view of self and finally the reorganization of self.

Relationship to current psychological thinking

Up to this point, these remarks have been presented as clinical observations and tentative hypotheses, quite apart from any relationship to past or present thinking in the field of psychology. This has been intentional. It is felt that it is the function of the clinician to try to observe, with an open-minded attitude, the complexity of material which comes to him, to report his observations, and in the light of this to formulate hypotheses and problems which

both the clinic and the laboratory may utilize as a basis for study and research.

Yet, though these are clinical observations and hypotheses, they have, as has doubtless been recognized, a relationship to some of the currents of theoretical and laboratory thinking in psychology. Some of the observations about the self bear a relationship to the thinking of G. H. Mead (7) about the "I" and the "me." The outcome of therapy might be described in Mead's terms as the increasing awareness of the "I," and the organization of the "me's" by the "I." The importance which has been given in this paper to the self as an organizer of experience and to some extent as an architect of self, bears a relationship to the thinking of Allport (1) and others concerning the increased place which me must give to the integrative function of the ego. In the stress which has been given to the present field of experience as the determinant of behavior, the relationship to Gestalt psychology and to the work of Lewin (6) and his students is obvious. The theories of Angyal (2) find some parallel in our observations. His view that the self represents only a small part of the biological organism which has reached symbolic elaboration, and that it often attempts the direction of the organism on the basis of unreliable and insufficient information, seems to be particularly related to the observations we have made. Lecky's posthumous book (4), small in size but large in the significance of its contribution, has brought a new light on the way in which the self operates, and the principle of consistency by which new experience is included in or excluded from the self. Much of his thinking runs parallel to our observations. Snygg and Combs (11) have recently attempted a more radical and more complete emphasis upon the internal world of perception as the basis for all psychology, a statement which has helped to formulate a theory in which our observations fit.

It is not only from the realm of theory but also from the experimental laboratory that one finds confirmation of the line of thinking which has been proposed. Tolman (12) has stressed the need of thinking as a rat if fruitful experimental work is to be done. The work of Snygg (10) indicates that rat behavior may be better predicted by inferring the rat's field of perception than by viewing him as an object. Krech (Krechevsky, 3) showed in a brilliant study some years ago that rat learning can only be understood if we realize that the rat is consistently acting upon one hypothesis after another. Leeper (5) has summarized the evidence from a number of experimental investigations, showing that animal behavior cannot be explained by simple S-R mechanisms, but only by recognizing that complex internal processes of perceptual organization intervene between the stimulus and the behavioral response. Thus there are parallel streams of clinical observation, theoretical thinking, and laboratory experiment, which all point up the fact that for an effective psychology we need a much more complete understanding of the private world of the individual, and need to learn ways of entering and studying that world from within.

Implications

It would be misleading however if I left you with the impression that the hypotheses I have formulated in this paper, or those springing from the parallel psychological studies I have mentioned, are simply extensions of the main stream of psychological thinking, additional bricks in the edifice of psychological thought. We have discovered with some surprise that our clinical observations, and the tentative hypotheses which seem to grow out of them, raise disturbing questions which appear to cast doubt on the very foundations of many of our psychological endeavors, particularly in the fields of clinical psychology and personality study. To clarify what is meant, I should like to restate in more logical order the formulations I have given, and to leave with you certain questions and problems which each one seems to raise.

If we take first the tentative proposition that the specific determinant of behavior is the perceptual field of the individual, would this not lead, if regarded as a working hypothesis, to a radically different approach in clinical psychology and personality research? It would seem to mean that instead of elaborate case histories full of information about the person as an object, we would endeavor to develop ways of seeing his situation, his past, and himself, as these objects appear to him. We would try to see with him, rather than to evaluate him. It might mean the minimizing of the elaborate psychometric procedures by which we have endeavored to measure or value the individual from our own frame of reference. It might mean

the minimizing or discarding of all the vast series of labels which we have painstakingly built up over the years. Paranoid, preschizophrenic, compulsive, constricted—terms such as these might become irrelevant because they are all based in thinking which takes an external frame of reference. They are not the ways in which the individual experiences himself. If we consistently studied each individual from the internal frame of reference of that individual, from within his own perceptual field, it seems probable that we should find generalizations which could be made, and principles which were operative, but we may be very sure that they would be of a different order from these externally based judgments *about* individuals.

Let us look at another of the suggested propositions. If we took seriously the hypothesis that integration and adjustment are internal conditions related to the degree of acceptance or nonacceptance of all perceptions, and the degree of organization of these perceptions into one consistent system, this would decidedly affect our clinical procedures. It would seem to imply the abandonment of the notion that adjustment is dependent upon the pleasantness or unpleasantness of the environment, and would demand concentration upon those processes which bring about self-integration within the person. It would mean a minimizing or an abandoning of those clinical procedures which utilize the alteration of environmental forces as a method of treatment. It would rely instead upon the fact that the person who is internally unified has the greatest likelihood of meeting environmental problems constructively, either as an individual or in cooperation with others.

If we take the remaining proposition that the self, under proper conditions, is capable of reorganizing, to some extent, its own perceptual field, and of thus altering behavior, this too seems to raise disturbing questions. Following the path of this hypothesis would appear to mean a shift in emphasis in psychology from focusing upon the fixity of personality attributes and psychological abilities, to the alterability of these same characteristics. It would concentrate attention upon process rather than upon fixed status. Whereas psychology has, in personality study, been concerned primarily with the measurement of the fixed qualities of the individual, and with his past in order to explain his present, the hypothesis here suggested would seem to concern itself much more with the personal world of the present in order to understand the future, and in predicting that future would be concerned with the principles by which personality and behavior are altered, as well as the extent to which they remain fixed.

Thus we find that a clinical approach, client-centered therapy, has led us to try to adopt the client's perceptual field as the basis for genuine understanding. In trying to enter this internal world of perception, not by introspection, but by observation and direct inference, we find ourselves in a new vantage point for understanding personality dynamics, a vantage point which opens up some disturbing vistas. We find that behavior seems to be better understood as a reaction to this reality-as-perceived. We discover that the way in which the person sees himself, and the perceptions he dares not take as belonging to himself, seem to have an important relationship to the inner peace which constitutes adjustment. We discover within the person, under certain conditions, a capacity for the restructuring and the reorganization of self, and consequently the reorganization of behavior, which has profound social implications. We see these observations, and the theoretical formulations which they inspire, as a fruitful new approach for study and research in various fields of psychology.

References

1. Allport, Gordon W. The ego in contemporary psychology. *Psychol. Rev.,* 1943, 50, 451-478.

2. Angyal, Andras. *Foundations for a science of personality.* New York: Commonwealth Fund, 1941.

3. Krechevsky, I. Hypotheses in rats. *Psychol. Rev.,* 1932, 39, 516-532.

4. Lecky, Prescott. *Self-Consistency: A theory of personality.* New York: Island Press, 1945.

5. Leeper, Robert. The experimental psychologists as reluctant dragons. Paper presented at APA meeting, September 1946.

6. Lewin, Kurt. *A dynamic theory of personality.* New York: McGraw-Hill, 1935.

7. Mead, George H. *Mind, self, and society.* Chicago: University of Chicago Press, 1934.

8. Rogers, Carl R. Significant aspects of client-centered therapy. *Amer. Psychologist,* 1946, 1, 415-422.

9. Snyder, W. U. 'Warmth' in nondirective counseling. *J. abnorm. soc. Psychol.,* 1946, 41, 491-495.

10. Snygg, Donald. Mazes in which rats take the longer path to food. *J. Psychol.,* 1936, 1, 153-166.

11. Snygg, Donald and Combs, Arthur W. Book manuscript, loaned to present author. In process of publication. New York: Harper and Bros.

12. Tolman, E. C. The determiners of behavior at a choice point. *Psychol. Rev.,* 1938, 45, 1-41.

The concept of identification [1]

JEROME KAGAN

A major task for psychologists is to understand how the personality is acquired. The concept of identification was originally postulated by Sigmund Freud as an explanation of how the child incorporates particular aspects of the adult personality into his own. Many personality theorists continue to use the concept of identification, but they vary in their specific definitions of the term. This article reviews the various ways in which identification has been defined and suggests how the concept can be best understood. The analysis illustrates the complexity of the task confronting the psychologist in the search for a precise explanation of the personality.

Jerome Kagan, Ph.D., is Professor of Human Development at Harvard University. He is coauthor of several books, including *Birth to Maturity, Child Development and Personality,* and *Psychology: An Introduction* and has published a number of articles on research and theory in personality development and infant behavior.

Several years ago Sanford (20) presented an analysis of the concept of identification. In brief, Sanford suggested that the term be applied to situations in which "an individual may be observed to respond to the behavior of other people or objects by initiating in fantasy or reality the same behavior himself . . . the individual strives to behave in a way that is exactly like that of the object" (20, p. 109). Sanford further suggested that the motive for this imitative behavior was a threat to the person's self esteem. By limiting the term "identification" to those imitative behavioral sequences in which the motivation for the act was anxiety over self esteem, Sanford emphasized two points: (*a*) mere similarity in overt behavior between a subject and a model was not necessarily a measure of identification, and (*b*) the motive for the imitative behavior was one of the defining characteristics of an identificatory response.

The various behavioral phenomena which have been labeled "identification" differ in their manifest properties and motivations. The following four classes of behavior have been described as related to the process of identification because they all can lead to similarities in behavior between a subject and a model.

Imitation learning

This term refers to the initiation and practice of certain responses (gestures, attitudes, speech patterns, dress, etc.) which are not subject to prohibition by the social environment and which are assumed to be the result of an attempt to imitate a model. The behavior has been labeled either "matched-dependent behavior" or "copying" by Miller and Dollard (17). Miller and Dollard posit that initially the imitative act occurs by chance and the act can only be reinforced if some drive is reduced following the execution of the response. According to this view only direct reward from the social environment, like praise or affection, can strengthen the person's tendency to imitate a model. Mowrer (18) distinguishes between develop-

From *Psychological Review,* LXV (1958), 296-304. Reprinted by permission of the American Psychological Association and the author.

[1] This research was supported, in part, by a research grant (M-1260) from the National Institute of Mental Health of the National Institutes of Health, United States Public Health Service. The views of Wesley Allinsmith, Vaughn J. Crandall, Leonard M. Lansky, and Howard A. Moss are especially acknowledged. A major stimulus for the present essay was a workshop in parent-child relations supported by USPHS Grant 1649 and held at the Merrill-Palmer School, Detroit, Michigan, July 14-27, 1957.

mental and defensive identification. In the former process, the person imitates or reproduces the behavior of a model in order to "reproduce bits of the beloved and longed-for parent" (18, p. 615). Mowrer suggests that most imitation of a model is the result of the desire to reproduce responses which have acquired secondary reward value through association with a nurturant and affectionate model. Thus, Mowrer emphasizes the self-rewarding aspect of certain imitative acts as opposed to Miller and Dollard's emphasis on direct reward from the social environment.

Prohibition learning

This term refers to the adoption and practice of the prohibitions of the parents and parent substitutes. The acquisition of these prohibitions bears some relation to the process of superego development as described by psychoanalytic theory (2, 3, 4, 11). Several investigators have suggested that a major motivation for the acquisition of some prohibition is anxiety over anticipated loss of love (10, 11, 18, 20, 23). Sanford labeled this process "introjection" and suggested that the learning and maintenance of this class of behavior might be explained without use of the concept of identification.

Identification with the aggressor

This phrase refers to the adoption of behaviors which are similar to those of an aggressive or threatening model. The motivation for this "imitation" is assumed to be anxiety over anticipated aggression or domination by the threatening model. It is difficult to explain this behavior as a product of either prohibition or imitation learning, since the motive and reinforcement do not seem related to anxiety over anticipated loss of love or desire for a direct, social reward like praise or affection. Anna Freud (2) has labeled this phenomenon "identification with the aggressor," Mowrer has called this process "defensive identification" (as distinct from developmental identification), and Sanford has suggested that the term "identification proper" be restricted to this class of behavior.

Vicarious affective experience

This phrase refers to the experience of positive or negative affect on the part of a person as a result of an event which has occurred to a model. Salient examples of this phenomenon are (a) a child's elation or depression at learning that his parent is a success or failure, or (b) a mother's elation following the success of her child in school. This phenomenon of vicarious, affective experience has been attributed to a person's identification with a model, but this affective response has been difficult to explain and often neglected by psychologists investigating the identification process. These four phenomena (imitation learning, prohibition learning, identification with the aggressor, and vicarious, affective experience) appear to be mediated by different motives and rewards, and an analysis of each of them is one purpose of this paper.[2]

In different contexts, social scientists have used the term "identification" to refer to three different sets of variables: (a) the process of identification; (b) individual differences in the content of the behaviors, motives, and attitudes acquired as a result of the identification process; and (c) the differential effect of various models that are used during the identification process (3, 4, 5, 7, 9, 11, 13, 15, 16, 25, 26). This paper recognizes the relevance of the model and content dimensions but is primarily concerned with the process of identification and will attempt to analyze this process in behavioral terms. It is suggested that the process remains the same regardless of the models used or the specific behavioral content that is acquired as a result of an identification.

Definitions of identification

The concept of identification originated in psychoanalytic theory, and Freud made a distinction between primary and secondary identification (3, 4, 5). Primary identification referred to the initial, undifferentiated perception of the infant in which an external object was perceived as part of the self, while secondary identification began after the child had discriminated a world of objects separate from the self. Freud implied in his later writings that

[2] In an unpublished paper presented at a symposium at Harvard University in 1957, Bronfenbrenner described three types of identification: (a) anaclitic identification, (b) identification with a source of power, and (c) identification through reinforcement of a role model. These three terms are similar in meaning to the present phrases of prohibition learning, identification with the aggressor, and imitation learning, respectively.

the process of secondary identification was motivated primarily by the motives and anxieties created by the oedipal situation. In order to reduce the anxiety over anticipated aggression or rejection from the same-sex parent and obtain vicariously the affection of the opposite-sex parent, the child identified with the former. Identification was described by Freud as "the endeavor to mould a person's own ego after the fashion of one that has been taken as a model" (5, p. 63).

Mowrer's concept of "defensive identification," Sanford's definition of "identification proper," and Anna Freud's description of "identification with the aggressor" are all related to the earlier psychoanalytic hypothesis that the threat value of the same-sex parent motivated the child to identify with him in order to reduce the anxiety associated with this threat. However, it is suggested that an individual may identify with a model not only to reduce anxiety over anticipated aggression from a model but also to experience or obtain positive goal states which he perceives that the model commands. The thesis of this paper is that the motivation to command or experience desired goal states of a model is salient in the development and maintenance of an identification.[3] It will be suggested later that two major goal states involved in identification behavior are (a) mastery of the environment and (b) love and affection. However, it is not implied that these are the only goals which an individual desires to command.

Definition

Identification is defined as an acquired, cognitive response within a person (S). The content of this response is that some of the attributes, motives, characteristics, and affective states of a model (M) are part of S's psychological organization. The major implication of this definition is that the S may react to events occurring to M as if they occurred to him.

The acquisition and maintenance of an identification

Although identification has been defined as a cognitive response, it is not implied that the content of the response is available to consciousness or easily verbalized. Thus the terms "cognitive response," "belief," "wish," or "assumption" will be used in this text to include cognitive processes not always available through verbal report. Identification is not viewed as an all-or-none process. Identification is a response that can vary in strength, and there will be differences in the degree to which an S believes that the characteristics of a model, whether assets or liabilities, belong to him. In addition, the S may become identified, to differing degrees, with a variety of models. The motives and reinforcements that are involved in the acquisition and maintenance of this cognitive response are elaborated in the following assumptions.

Assumption 1

Initially the S perceives that the M possesses or commands goals and satisfactions that the S desires. This perception leads to a wish to possess these desired goal states.

Assumption 2

The wish to command the goal states of the M leads to the desire to possess the characteristics of the M, because S believes that if he were similar to the M he would command the desired goals. That is, the S assumes that the more similarity there is between the S and M the more likely S is to possess or command the desired goal states of the M.

To illustrate, let the S be a child and the M a mother, although S and M could be an adolescent boy and the leader of a group, or a girl and her older sister. The child perceives that the mother can feed the child, restrict the child, obtain articles out of the child's reach, punish the child, etc. Thus, to the S, the M appears to command desired skills and goal states. The discrepancy between the child's perception of his inability to obtain these desired goals and his perception of the more adequate adult elicits the wish to possess or control those goals which he perceives that M commands. The perceptions of the child are subject to distortion, and the child may exaggerate the degree to which M commands desired goals.

---

[3] It is assumed that anticipation of a positive goal state is associated with the anticipation of a change in affect, and thus the phrase "experience goal states of the model" will be used synonymously with the phrase "experience affective states of the model." This assumption agrees with McClelland's definition of a motive as an "anticipation of a change in affective state" (14, p. 466).

It was assumed (Assumption 2) that the wish to command these goal states led to the expectation that if S possessed M's characteristics he would also command these desired goals. There often is direct reinforcement of the belief that to "be similar to" a model is equivalent to possessing his positive attributes. Often, the social environment tells the child directly that he is similar to a parent in certain characteristics, and this communication may be contiguous in time with statements related to some of the model's desired goal states. For example, parents and relatives may tell the child, "You have your father's eyes," and often add, "You'll grow up to be big and strong just like Daddy." It is suggested that these statements which associate similarities in external attributes with command of desired goal states have an important effect on the child's learning about himself, and lead the child to the expectation that to be similar to the model is equivalent to possessing his positive and desirable attributes.

Assumption 3

The identification response (i.e., "some of the characteristics of the model are mine") is reinforced each time S perceives or is told that he is similar to the M. One type of reinforcement for the identification response occurs when an S is told directly that he and the M are similar in temperament or appearance. It is suggested that a second type of reinforcement for this cognitive response is S's own perception of similarity to the M. Once again, consider the case of the small child and his parent. Although the child may perceive marked differences in size, strength, and skills between himself and the M, he may perceive a similarity in affective states, such as joy, anger, or sadness. The importance of the perception of similarities in affective states between the S and M is stressed because a major motive for identification is a desire to experience positive affective states of the model. Thus, perception of similarity in affect is assumed to have saliency as a reinforcement. If the parent becomes angry, sad, or happy and communicates these affects to the child, the child has the opportunity to perceive that he and the M experience similar feelings. This perception reinforces the belief that there is similarity between the S and M. In addition to similarity in affective states,

perception of similarities in external characteristics will reinforce the identification response. With specific reference to the child-parent relation, it is assumed that perception of similarities in sexual anatomy, dress, amount and distribution of hair, and other external attributes are potential reinforcements of the identification. Thus, while the identification response is being learned, the major reinforcements for the response are perceptions of similarity between the S and M.[4] Freud suggested that perceptions of similarity strengthen an identification, for he wrote,

Identification . . . may arise with every new perception of a common quality shared with some other person who is not an object of the sexual instinct. The more important this common quality is, the more successful may this partial identification become, and it may thus represent the beginning of a new tie (5, p. 65).

Assumption 4

In order for the identification belief to be maintained, the S must not only perceive similarity between the S and M but he also must experience some of the desired, affective goal states of the M. Thus, if the M were successful or happy and S believed that M was experiencing positive affect, the S would also feel positive affect appropriate to the success, and this experience would reinforce his identification. The S also may experience affect appropriate to events occurring to M as a result of the expectation that the social environment will respond to him the same way it responds to the M. That is, when the S has developed some degree of identification with the M, he may anticipate that when the social environment praises or rewards the M, it will behave similarly to him. If, on the other hand, the M were sad or criticized, S might experience negative affect because of the identification belief that he and the M were similar and the

---

[4] It is suggested that the concept of identification has not yielded to a behavioral analysis because the notion of social reinforcement has been viewed as a specific action directed at an individual by a reinforcing agent. There has been a tendency to overlook the possibility that a perception, fantasy, or thought may be a potential reinforcement of a response. A recent experimental finding by Estes and Johns (1) supports the hypothesis that a person's perception of a situation, even though objectively inaccurate, can reinforce his subsequent behavior.

expectation that the environment might react to him as it did to M. However, if no vicarious command of desired goals or positive affect were experienced as a result of the identification, then the response should extinguish just as any other habit does in the absence of positive reinforcement.[5] That is, some degree of identification should be maintained as long as S perceives that the M commands desired goals. When the S no longer perceives the M in this fashion, then both the motivation for the identification and the intensity of the positive reinforcement should decrease.

The acquisition of behavior similar to a model: the motives for imitation, identification, and prohibition learning

Since perceptions of similarity between the S and M reinforce the identification response, the S may imitate the M during the acquisition phase of an identification in order to increase the degree of similarity. It is acknowledged that the social environment rewards imitative behaviors with affection and praise, and these direct, social reinforcements may strengthen the tendency to imitate adults independently of any identification motives. However, it is suggested, along with Sears et al. (23), that direct, social reinforcement of imitative behavior cannot account for all of the imitative responses that the S initiates. A four-year-old child may simulate adult behaviors when the child is alone or in situations where the parents discourage or punish the imitative response. However, despite the punishment or absence of social reward for some imitative behaviors, the behavior continues to be practiced. Sears et al. call this behavior "role practice" and assume that it is motivated by the "desire to reproduce pleasant experiences" (23, p. 370). Consider the three-year-old girl who plays the role of mother alone in her room. It is hypothesized that a potential reinforcement for this behavior is the creation, in fantasy, of perceptual similarity between the behaviors of the S and M. This perception strengthens S's identification with the M and allows S to share vicariously some of the positive goal states which M commands.

A somewhat different phenomenon is the behavior called "identification with the aggressor" by A. Freud or "defensive identification" by Mowrer. Anna Freud describes a girl who was afraid of ghosts and suddenly began to make peculiar gestures as she ran in the dark. She told her brother, "there is no need to be afraid, you just have to pretend that you're the ghost who might meet you" (2, p. 119). The present theory assumes that the child desired the threatening power of the feared object and this motive elicited the imitative behavior. The fantasied perception of similarity to the feared model gave S a vicarious feeling of power and reduced her anxiety over attack. It is suggested that "identification with the aggressor" does not differ from other identification responses with respect to the basic mechanism of acquisition but does involve a specific motive and goal state. Identification with the aggressor involves a specific relationship between the S and M in which S fears the M. Thus, S desires the aggressive power or threat value of the M in order to reduce his own anxiety over anticipated attack. It may be misleading to classify "identification with the aggressor" as qualitatively different from other identificatory behavior merely because the motive and goal differ from those involved in other identifications.

A third motive which can lead to behavioral similarity between an S and M is anxiety over anticipated loss of love or nurturance. It is suggested that many social prohibitions which the M practices are learned by the S in situations in which this anxiety motivate the acquisition and maintenance of the response. The reinforcement for the learned prohibition is continued acceptance and a consequent reduction in anxiety over rejection. The research of Sears et al. (23) suggests a relationship between "high conscience" in a child and a pattern in which the mother is nurturant and uses withdrawal of love as a disciplinary technique. In summary, any one response which is imitative of a model may be mediated by three different motive-reinforcement sequences, and in many instances all three may be involved in producing be-

---

[5] This view of identification suggests a measurement operation which differs from the usual practice of assessing similarities in behavior between an S and an M. One measure of degree of identification would be the degree to which an S's affective state or behavior was influenced as a result of events that occurred to an M. That is, praise or criticism of an M in S's presence should lead to corresponding changes in the affective state of an S who was identified with the M.

havioral similarity between an S and M.[6] Thus, "eating neatly," "getting good grades," or "being nonaggressive" could be motivated by the desire for praise as in imitation learning, by anxiety over loss of love as in prohibition learning, or by the desire to create perceptual similarity between the S and M as in identification. Thus, mere similarity in overt behavior between an S and M may not be the most sensitive measure of degree of identification.

At a more speculative level, it is suggested that the behaviors which have been called "self actualizing" (6) could be motivated and reinforced by a desire for perceptual similarity to an M and be an indication of early identification tendencies. Even the most orthodox supporters of the importance of simple imitation learning find it difficult to explain the child's initial imitations of a model. Once the child has begun to imitate a model it is likely that praise and recognition from adults could maintain this behavior. However, why does the child suddenly want to dress himself, sit on the toilet alone, or put on Daddy's shoes? It is difficult to account for the initial display of this imitative behavior, and the term "self actualization" implies that the child has some biological drive to use his potentialities. This hypothesis seems no more parsimonious than the suggestion that the initiation of these "self actualizing" behaviors is motivated by S's desire to create perceptual similarity between himself and a model.

Two goals motivating identification: mastery and love

It has been assumed that S's desire to command certain goal states motivates his identification with a model. It is suggested, for the child especially, that two important goal states that the S desires to command are (a) a feeling of power or mastery over the environment and (b) love and affection. Attainment of these goals should lead to diminution in anxiety over helplessness or loneliness. The young child perceives that he is not able to gratify all of his needs, while the parental model is perceived as more capable of dealing with the environment. This discrepancy between the S's perception of his own relative helplessness and the power that he perceives M to possess motivates the wish to have M's power and the search for perceptions of similarity between himself and the M.

Unfortunately, there are no empirical studies which directly test these hypotheses because most of the research on identification has used similarities in behavior between an S and M as the measure of identification. However, there are some results which are at least consistent with the view that the child identifies with the more powerful parent and the one who is perceived to command important sources of gratification. Payne and Mussen (19) reported that adolescent boys who perceived the father as rewarding on projective tests were more highly identified with the father (based on similar answers to a personality inventory) than boys who pictured their fathers as nonrewarding. In addition, boys with dominant and "masculine" mothers tended to be poorly identified with the father. P. S. Sears (22) reported a finding that is more difficult to explain without use of the concept of identification. She found, in a doll-play situation, that kindergarten girls used the mother doll as agent significantly more often than the father doll, while boys used both mother and father dolls with more nearly equal frequency. Since the mother is initially the major controller of gratifications for both sexes, one might expect an initial identification with her for both boys and girls. P. S. Sears (22) also reports that the kindergarten boys who used the mother doll most often had mothers who were (a) more nurturant than the father, (b) more critical of the father, and (c) more restrictive of the child's mobility outside the home. This result is consistent with the hypothesis that the child is predisposed to identify with the parental model who is perceived as controlling important goal states.

A study of Maccoby and Wilson (15) furnishes more direct support for the present hypotheses. The authors showed movies to seventh grade boys and girls and then determined the protagonist with whom the child identified. The most significant result was that a "boy's choice of screen character (the one with whom he was presumed to identify) is more closely related to the social class level *to which he aspires* than to the level his family

---

6 In a manuscript being prepared for publication, H. Kelman suggests that the response of conformity to the attitudes of another person can be mediated by three different motives. His analysis of conformity parallels the present discussion of imitative behavior.

currently occupies" (15, p. 79). This result suggests that the child identified with models who commanded desired goals.

A second goal state which may motivate identification is the desire for nurturance and affection. In addition to Freud's classical hypothesis that the child identified with the same-sex parent in order to receive vicariously the affection of the opposite-sex parent, there are situations in which nonparental models command sources of affection. The relation between siblings is such a situation, and the younger child may identify with an older sibling if the former perceives that the latter commands parental affection. The research of Helen Koch (12) indirectly supports this hypothesis. She reported that school-age boys with older sisters tended to develop more feminine attributes than boys with older brothers. On the other hand, girls with older brothers tended to be more masculine than girls with older sisters. In the experiment of Maccoby and Wilson, described earlier, the authors reported that girls were more likely than boys to recall movie content involving boy-girl interaction while boys were superior on recall of aggressive acts by the hero. If one assumes that the need for affection is stronger for girls than for boys, and that the recalled content is influenced by the model chosen for identification, then these results suggest that the specific goal states desired by the S determine the models chosen for identification.

Factors influencing the strength of identification

The strength of the identification habit, following a basic behavioral law, should be a function of the strength of the motive and the quality and frequency of the reinforcement (8). It would be predicted, therefore, that the most intense identification would occur when the S had strong needs for love and power, felt incapable of gratifying these motives through his own skills, and perceived similarity between himself and an M who commanded these goals. Utilizing this hypothesis, two generalized predictions can be made concerning the strength of identification for different ages and models.

1. The strength of identification tendencies should decrease with age because, in general, the individual's ability to gratify his needs for mastery and love through his own behavior, rather than through a vicarious mechanism, should increase with development. Thus, the identifications of a young child should be more intense than the identifications of older individuals.

2. An identification with an M with whom S was in direct contact should be stronger than with an M with whom S was not in contact, assuming that the motivation for identification was constant and the models were perceived as equally potent. This statement is based on the assumption that the reinforcements of perceived similarity are stronger when S perceives the affects and attributes of the M directly as opposed to instances in which he is merely told that he is similar to the M. Thus, degree of identification with a father with whom S was in contact should be greater than with an imagined fantasy father whom S had never seen. Only very indirect evidence is available to support this prediction. However, reports by P. S. Sears (21) and Sears et al. (24) suggest that absence of the father from the home tends to decrease the degree of "masculine" doll play in preschool boys, while this experience has little effect on the doll play of girls. The results are open to alternative interpretations but are not inconsistent with the present hypothesis.

Summary

This paper has attempted to analyze the concept of identification and place the concept within a learning-theory framework. Identification was defined as an acquired, cognitive response. The content of this response was that some of the characteristics of a model belonged to the individual, and the individual behaved as if some of the characteristics and affective states of the model belonged to him. Identification was not viewed as an all-or-none process. An identification can vary in strength and the individual can identify, to differing degrees, with a variety of models. The motive for the acquisition and maintenance of the identification response was a desire for the positive goal states commanded by the model, and mastery of the environment and love-nurturance were suggested as two important goals. The reinforcement for the acquisition of the identification was perceived similarity in attributes between the person and the model. Thus, the person may strive to imitate aspects of the model's behavior in order to create perceptual similarity between himself and the model. Once the identification was established, the individual behaved as if the goal states of the model belonged to him and the positive affect derived from this vicarious sharing of desired goal states helped to maintain the identification.

It was suggested that the usual emphasis on similarities in overt behavior between an individual and a model is not the best measure of identification, since the motives and reinforcements involved in imitation and prohibition learning could also explain similarities in behavior between two people. A differentiation of imitative behavior based on imitation learning, prohibition learning, and identification was attempted.

References

1. Estes, W. K., & Johns, Marcia D. Probability learning with ambiguity in the reinforcing stimulus. *Amer. J. Psychol.*, 1958, 71, 219-228.

2. Freud, Anna. *The ego and the mechanisms of defense.* London: Hogarth, 1937.

3. Freud, S. *New introductory lectures in psychoanalysis.* New York: Norton, 1933.

4. Freud, S. *The ego and the id.* London: Hogarth, 1935.

5. Freud, S. *Group psychology and the analysis of the ego.* London: Hogarth, 1949.

6. Goldstein, K. *The organism.* New York: American Book, 1939.

7. Gray, Susan W., & Klaus, R. The assessment of parental identification. *Genet. Psychol. Monogr.,* 1956, 54, 87-114.

8. Hull, C. L. *Principles of behavior.* New York: Appleton-Century-Crofts, 1943.

9. Kagan, J. The child's perception of the parent. *J. abnorm. soc. Psychol.*, 1956, 53, 257-258.

10. Kagan, J. Socialization of aggression and the perception of parents in fantasy. *Child Develpm.*, 1958, 29, 311-320.

11. Knight, R. P. Introjection, projection and identification. *Psychoanal. Quart.,* 1940, 9, 334-341.

12. Koch, Helen L. Attitudes of young children toward their peers as related to certain characteristics of their siblings. *Psychol. Monogr.*, 1956, 70, No. 19 (Whole No. 426).

13. Lazowick, L. M. On the nature of identification. *J. abnorm. soc. Psychol.*, 1955, 51, 175-183.

14. McClelland, D. C. *Personality.* New York: Sloane, 1951.

15. Maccoby, Eleanor E., & Wilson, W. C. Identification and observational learning from films. *J. abnorm. soc. Psychol.*, 1957, 55, 76-87.

16. Martin, W. F. Learning theory and identification: III. The development of value in children. *J. genet. Psychol.*, 1954, 84, 211-217.

17. Miller, N. E., & Dollard, J. *Social learning and imitation.* New Haven: Yale Univer. Press, 1941.

18. Mowrer, O. H. *Learning theory and personality dynamics.* New York: Ronald, 1950.

19. Payne, D. E., & Mussen, P. H. Parent-child relations and father identification among adolescent boys. *J. abnorm. soc. Psychol.*, 1956, 52, 358-362.

20. Sanford, R. N. The dynamics of identification. *Psychol. Rev.,* 1955, 62, 106-118.

21. Sears, Pauline S. Doll play aggression in normal young children: Influence of sex, age, sibling status, father's absence. *Psychol. Monogr.*, 1951, 65, No. 6 (Whole No. 323).

22. Sears, Pauline S. Child rearing factors related to playing sex-typed roles. *Amer. Psychologist,* 1953, 8, 431. (Abstract)

23. Sears, R. R., Maccoby, Eleanor E., & Levin, H. *Patterns of child rearing.* Evanston, Ill.: Row, Peterson, 1957.

24. Sears, R. R., Piniler, Margaret H., & Sears, Pauline S. Effect of father separation on pre-school children's doll play aggression. *Child Develpm.*, 1946, 17, 219-243.

25. Seward, J. P. Learning theory and identification: II. The role of punishment. *J. genet. Psychol.*, 1954, 84, 201-210.

26. Stoke, S. M. An inquiry into the concept of identification. *J. genet Psychol.*, 1950, 76, 163-189.

The changing American child—a speculative analysis [1]

URIE BRONFENBRENNER

More than one parent, in a fit of perplexity and frustration brought about by their inability to control their child's behavior, has exclaimed that "things were different" when they were children. The following article supports this statement by documenting the changes that have occurred in child-rearing patterns and methods of discipline over the last twenty-five years. Dr. Bronfenbrenner, who is Professor of Psychology and of Child Development and Family Relations at Cornell University and the author of many articles on personality development, stresses the effects of these changes on the personality development of children. The article further illustrates how changes in the parent affect the child and discusses differences in parental behavior in terms of sex and socio-economic class. The essay concludes with some speculations on future trends in the personality formation of children and adults.

A question of moment

It is now a matter of scientific record that patterns of child rearing in the United States have changed appreciably over the past twenty-five years (Bronfenbrenner, 1958). Middle class parents especially have moved away from the more rigid and strict styles of care and discipline advocated in the early Twenties and Thirties toward modes of response involving greater tolerance of the child's impulses and desires, freer expression of affection, and increased reliance on "psychological" methods of discipline, such as reasoning and appeals to guilt, as distinguished from more direct techniques like physical punishment. At the same time, the gap between the social classes in their goals and methods of child rearing appears to be narrowing, with working class parents beginning to adopt both the values and techniques of the middle class. Finally, there is dramatic correspondence between these observed shifts in parental values and behavior and the changing character of the attitudes and practices advocated in successive editions of such widely read manuals as the Children's Bureau bulletin on *Infant Care* and Spock's *Baby and Child Care*. Such correspondence should not be taken to mean that the expert has now become the principal instigator and instrument of social change, since the ideas of scientists and professional workers themselves reflect in part the operation of deep-rooted cultural processes. Nevertheless, the fact remains that changes in values and practices advocated by prestigeful professional figures can be substantially accelerated by rapid and widespread dissemination through the press, mass media of communication, and public discussion.

Given these facts, it becomes especially important to gauge the effect of the changes that are advocated and adopted. Nowhere is this issue more significant, both scientifically and socially, than in the sphere of familial values and behavior. It is certainly no trivial matter to ask

From *Journal of Social Issues*, XVII, No. 1 (1961), 8-18. Reprinted by permission of The Society for the Psychological Study of Social Issues.

[1] This paper draws heavily on results from a program of research being conducted by the author in collaboration with Edward C. Devereux and George J. Suci. The contribution of these colleagues to facts and ideas presented in this paper is gratefully acknowledged. The research program is supported in part with grants from the National Science Foundation and the National Institutes of Health.

whether the changes that have occurred in the attitudes and actions of parents over the past twenty-five years have been such as to affect the personality development of their children, so that the boys and girls of today are somewhat different in character structure from those of a decade or more ago. Or, to put the question more succinctly: has the changing American parent produced a changing American child?

A strategy of inference

Do we have any basis for answering this intriguing question? To begin with, do we have any evidence of changes in the behavior of children in successive decades analogous to those we have already been able to find for parents? If so, we could take an important first step toward a solution of the problem. Unfortunately, in contrast to his gratifying experience in seeking and finding appropriate data on parents, the present writer has, to date, been unable to locate enough instances in which comparable methods of behavioral assessment have been employed with different groups of children of similar ages over an extended period of time. Although the absence of such material precludes any direct and unequivocal approach to the question at hand, it is, nevertheless, possible, through a series of inferences from facts already known, to arrive at some estimate of what the answer might be. Specifically, although as yet we have no comparable data on the relation between parental and child behavior for different families at successive points in time, we do have facts on the influence of parental treatment on child behavior at a given point in time; that is, we know that certain variations in parental behavior tend to be accompanied by systematic differences in the personality characteristics of children. If we are willing to assume that these same relationships obtained not only at a given moment but across different points in time, we are in a position to infer the possible effects on children of changing patterns of child rearing over the years. It is this strategy that we propose to follow.

The changing American parent

We have already noted the major changes in parental behavior discerned in a recent analysis of data reported over a twenty-five-year period. These secular trends may be summarized as follows:

1. Greater permissiveness toward the child's spontaneous desires

2. Freer expression of affection

3. Increased reliance on indirect "psychological" techniques of discipline (such as reasoning or appeals to guilt) vs. direct methods (like physical punishment, scolding, or threats)

4. In consequence of the above shifts in the direction of what are predominantly middle class values and techniques, a narrowing of the gap between social classes in their patterns of child rearing.

Since the above analysis was published, a new study has documented an additional trend. Bronson, Katten, and Livson (1959) have compared patterns of paternal and maternal authority and affection in two generations of families from the California Guidance Study. Unfortunately, the time span surveyed overlaps only partially with the twenty-five-year period covered in our own analysis, the first California generation having been raised in the early 1900's and the second in the late '20's and early '30's. Accordingly, if we are to consider the California results along with the others cited above, we must make the somewhat risky assumption that a trend discerned in the first three decades of the century has continued in the same direction through the early 1950's. With this important qualification, an examination of the data cited by Bronson et al. (1959) points to still another, secular trend—a shift over the years in the pattern of parental role differentiation within the family. Specifically:

5. In succeeding generations the relative position of the father vis-à-vis the mother is shifting with the former becoming increasingly more affectionate and less authoritarian, and the latter becoming relatively more important as the agent of discipline, especially for boys.

"Psychological" techniques of discipline and their effects

In pursuing our analytic strategy, we next seek evidence of the effects on the behavior of children of variations in parental treatment of the type noted in our inventory. We may begin by noting that the variables involved in the first three secular trends constitute a complex that has received considerable attention in recent research in parent-child relationships. Within the last three years, two sets of investigators, working independently, have called attention to the greater efficacy of "love-oriented" or "psychological" techniques in bringing about desired behavior in the child (Sears, Maccoby, and Levin, 1957; Miller and Swanson, 1958; 1960). The present writer, noting that such methods are especially favored by middle class parents, offered the following analysis of the nature of these techniques and the reasons for their effectiveness.

Such parents are, in the first place, more likely to overlook offenses, and when they do punish, they are less likely to ridicule or inflict physical pain. Instead, they reason with the youngster, isolate him, appeal to guilt, show disappointment—in short, convey in a variety of ways, on the one hand, the kind of behavior that is expected of the child; on the other, the realization that transgression means the interruption of a mutually valued relationship. . . .

These findings [of greater efficacy] mean that middle class parents, though in one sense more lenient in their discipline techniques, are using methods that are actually more compelling. Moreover, the compelling power of these practices is probably enhanced by the more permissive treatment accorded to middle class children in the early years of life. The successful use of withdrawal of love as a discipline technique implies the prior existence of a gratifying relationship; the more love present in the first instance, the greater the threat implied in its withdrawal (Bronfenbrenner 1958).

It is now a well established fact that children from middle class families tend to excel those from lower class in many characteristics ordinarily regarded as desirable, such as self-control, achievement, responsibility, leadership, popularity, and adjustment in general.[2] If, as seems plausible, such differences in behavior are attributable at least in part to class-linked variations in parental treatment, the strategy of inference we have adopted would appear on first blush to lead to a rather optimistic conclusion. Since, over the years, increasing numbers of parents have been adopting the more

effective socialization techniques typically employed by the middle class, does it not follow that successive generations of children should show gains in the development of effective behavior and desirable personality characteristics?

Unfortunately, this welcome conclusion, however logical, is premature, for it fails to take into account all of the available facts.

Sex, socialization, and social class

To begin with, the parental behaviors we have been discussing are differentially distributed not only by socio-economic status but also by sex. As we have pointed out elsewhere (Bronfenbrenner, 1961), girls are exposed to more affection and less punishment than boys, but at the same time are more likely to be subjected to "love-oriented" discipline of the type which encourages the development of internalized controls. And, consistent with our line of reasoning, girls are found repeatedly to be "more obedient, cooperative, and in general better socialized than boys at comparable age levels." But this is not the whole story.

. . . At the same time, the research results indicate that girls tend to be more anxious, timid, dependent, and sensitive to rejection. If these differences are a function of differential treatment by parents, then it would seem that the more "efficient" methods of child rearing employed with girls involve some risk of what might be called "oversocialization" (Bronfenbrenner, 1961).

One could argue, of course, that the contrasting behaviors of boys and girls have less to do with differential parental treatment than with genetically-based maturational influences. Nevertheless, two independent lines of evidence suggest that socialization techniques do contribute to individual differences, *within the same sex,* precisely in the types of personality characteristics noted above. In the first place, variations in child behavior and parental treatment strikingly similar to those we have cited for the two sexes are reported in a recent comprehensive study of differences between first

---

[2] For a summary of findings on social class differences in children's behavior and personality characteristics, see Mussen, P. H., and Conger, J. J., *Child Development and Personality.* New York: Harper, 1956.

and later born children (Schachter, 1959). Like girls, first children receive more attention, are more likely to be exposed to "psychological" discipline, and end up more anxious and dependent, whereas later children, like boys, are more aggressive and self-confident.

A second line of evidence comes from our own current research. We have been concerned with the role of parents in the development of such "constructive" personality characteristics as responsibility and leadership among adolescent boys and girls. Our findings reveal not only the usual differences in adolescents' and parents' behaviors associated with the sex of the child, but also a striking contrast in the relationship between parental and child behaviors for the two sexes. To start on firm and familiar ground, girls are rated by their teachers as more responsible than boys, whereas the latter obtain higher scores on leadership. Expected differences similarly appear in the realm of parental behavior: girls receive more affection, praise, and companionship; boys are subjected to more physical punishment and achievement demands. Quite unanticipated, however, at least by us, was the finding that both parental affection and discipline appeared to facilitate effective psychological functioning in boys, but to impede the development of such constructive behavior in girls. Closer examination of our data indicated that both extremes of either affection or discipline were deleterious for all children, but that the process of socialization entailed somewhat different risks for the two sexes. Girls were especially susceptible to the detrimental influence of overprotection, boys to the ill effects of insufficient parental discipline and support. Or, to put it in more colloquial terms: boys suffered more often from too little taming, girls from too much.

In an attempt to account for this contrasting pattern of relationships, we proposed the notion of differential optimal levels of affection and authority for the two sexes.

The qualities of independence, initiative, and self-sufficiency, which are especially valued for boys in our culture, apparently require for their development a somewhat different balance of authority and affection than is found in the "love-oriented" strategy characteristically applied with girls. While an affectional context is important for the socialization of boys, it must evidently be accompanied by and be compatible with a strong component of parental discipline. Otherwise, the boy finds himself in the same situation as the girl, who, having received greater affection, is more sensitive to its withdrawal, with the result that a little discipline goes a long way and strong authority is constricting rather than constructive (Bronfenbrenner, 1960).

What is more, available data suggest that this very process may already be operating for boys from upper middle class homes. To begin with, differential treatment of the sexes is at a minimum for these families. Contrasting parental attitudes and behaviors toward boys and girls are pronounced only at lower class levels, and decrease as one moves up the socioeconomic scale (Kohn, 1959; Bronfenbrenner, 1960). Thus, our own results show that it is primarily at lower middle class levels that boys get more punishment than girls, and the latter receive greater warmth and attention. With an increase in the family's social position, direct discipline drops off, especially for boys, and indulgence and protectiveness decrease for girls. As a result, patterns of parental treatment for the two sexes begin to converge. In like manner, we find that the differential effects of parental behavior on the two sexes are marked only in the lower middle class. It is here that girls especially risk being over-protected and boys not receiving sufficient discipline and support. In upper middle class the picture changes. Girls are not as readily debilitated by parental affection and power; nor is parental discipline as effective in fostering the development of responsibility and leadership in boys.

All these trends point to the conclusion that the "risks" experienced by each sex during the process of socialization tend to be somewhat different at different social class levels. Thus the danger of overprotection for girls is especially great in lower class families, but lower in upper middle class because of the decreased likelihood of overprotection. Analogously, boys are in greater danger of suffering from inadequate discipline and support in lower middle than in upper middle class. But the upper middle class boy, unlike the girl, exchanges one hazard for another. Since at this upper level the more potent "psychological" techniques of discipline are likely to be employed with both sexes, the boy presumably now too runs the risk of being "oversocialized," of losing some of his capacity for independent aggressive accomplishment.

Accordingly, if our line of reasoning is correct, we should expect a changing pattern of sex differences at successive socioeconomic levels. Specifically, aspects of effective psychological functioning favoring girls should be most pronounced in the upper middle class; those favoring boys in the lower middle. A recent analysis of some of our data bears out this expectation. Girls excel boys on such variables as *responsibility* and *social acceptance* primarily at the higher socioeconomic levels. In contrast, boys surpass girls on such traits as *leadership, level of aspiration,* and *competitiveness* almost exclusively in lower middle class. Indeed, with a rise in a family's social position, the differences tend to reverse themselves with girls now excelling boys.[3]

Trends in personality development: a first approximation

The implications for our original line of inquiry are clear. We are suggesting that the "love-oriented" socialization techniques, which over the past twenty-five years have been employed in increasing degree by American middle class families, may have negative as well as constructive aspects. While fostering the internalization of adult standards and the development of socialized behavior, they may also have the effect of undermining capacities for initiative and independence, particularly in boys. Males exposed to this "modern" pattern of child rearing might be expected to differ from their counterparts of a quarter century ago in being somewhat more conforming and anxious, less enterprising and self-sufficient, and, in general, possessing more of the virtues and liabilities commonly associated with feminine character structure.[4]

At long last, then, our strategy of inference has led us to a first major conclusion. The term "major" is appropriate since the conclusion takes as its points of departure and return four of the secular trends which served as the impetus for our inquiry. Specifically, through a series of empirical links and theoretical extrapolations, we have arrived at an estimate of the effects on children of the tendency of successive generations of parents to become progressively more permissive, to express affection more freely, to utilize "psychological" techniques of discipline, and, by moving in these directions, to narrow the gap between the social classes in their patterns of child rearing.

Family structure and personality development

But one other secular trend remains to be considered: what of the changing pattern of parental role differentiation during the first three decades of the century? If our extrapolation is correct, the balance of power within the family has continued to shift with fathers yielding parental authority to mothers and taking on some of the nurturant and affectional functions traditionally associated with the maternal role. Again we have no direct evidence of the effects of such secular changes on successive generations of children, and must look for leads to analogous data on contemporaneous relationships.

We may begin by considering the contribution of each parent to the socialization processes we have examined thus far. Our data indicate that it is primarily mothers who tend to employ "love-oriented" techniques of discipline and fathers who rely on more direct methods like physical punishment. The above statement must be qualified, however, by reference to the sex of the child, for it is only in relation to boys that fathers use direct punishment more than mothers. More generally, . . . the results reveal a tendency for each parent to be somewhat more active, firm, and demanding with a child of the same sex, more lenient and indulgent with a child of the opposite sex. . . . The reversal is most complete with respect to discipline, with fathers being stricter with boys, mothers with girls. In the spheres of affection and protectiveness, there is no actual shift in preference, but the tendency to be especially warm and solicitous with girls is much more pronounced among fathers than among mothers. In fact, generally speaking, it is the father who is more likely to treat children of

---

[3] These shifts in sex difference with a rise in class status are significant at the 5% level of confidence (one-tailed test).
[4] Strikingly similar conclusions were reached almost fifteen years ago in a provocative essay by Arnold Green ("The Middle Class Male Child and Neurosis," *American Sociological Review*, 1946, 11, 31-41). With little to go on beyond scattered clinical observations and impressions, Green was able to detect many of the same trends which we have begun to discern in more recent systematic empirical data.

the two sexes differently (Bronfenbrenner, 1960).

Consistent with this pattern of results, it is primarily the behavior of fathers that accounts for the differential effects of parental behavior on the two sexes and for the individual differences within each sex. In other words, it is paternal authority and affection that tend especially to be salutary for sons but detrimental for daughters. But as might be anticipated from what we already know, these trends are pronounced only in the lower middle class; with a rise in the family's social status, both parents tend to have similar effects on their children, both within and across sexes. Such a trend is entirely to be expected since parental role differentiation tends to decrease markedly as one ascends the socioeconomic ladder. It is almost exclusively in lower middle class homes that fathers are more strict with boys and mothers with girls. To the extent that direct discipline is employed in upper middle class families, it tends to be exercised by both parents equally. Here again we see a parallelism between shifts in parental behavior across time and social class in the direction of forms (in this instance of family structure) favored by the upper middle class group.

What kinds of children, then, can we expect to develop in families in which the father plays a predominantly affectionate role, and a relatively low level of discipline is exercised equally by both parents? A tentative answer to this question is supplied by a preliminary analysis of our data in which the relation between parental role structure and adolescent behavior was examined with controls for the family's social class position. The results of this analysis are summarized as follows: . . . Both responsibility and leadership are fostered by the relatively greater salience of the parent of the same sex. . . . Boys tend to be more responsible when the father rather than the mother is the principal disciplinarian; girls are more dependable when the mother is the major authority figure. . . . In short, boys thrive in a patriarchal context, girls in a matriarchal. . . . The most dependent and least dependable adolescents describe family arrangements that are neither patriarchal nor matriarchal, but equalitarian. To state the issue in more provocative form, our data suggest that the democratic family, which for so many years has been held up and aspired to as a model by professionals and enlightened laymen, tends to produce young people who "do not take initiative," "look to others for direction and decision," and "cannot be counted on to fulfill obligations" (Bronfenbrenner, 1960).

In the wake of so sweeping a conclusion, it is important to call attention to the tentative, if not tenuous character of our findings. The results were based on a single study employing crude questionnaire methods and rating scales. Also, our interpretation is limited by the somewhat "attenuated" character of most of the families classified as patriarchal or matriarchal in our sample. Extreme concentrations of power in one or another parent were comparatively rare. Had they been more frequent, we suspect the data would have shown that such extreme asymmetrical patterns of authority were detrimental rather than salutary for effective psychological development, perhaps even more disorganizing than equalitarian forms.

Nevertheless, our findings do find some peripheral support in the work of others. A number of investigations, for example, point to the special importance of the father in the socialization of boys (Bandura and Walters, 1959; Mussen and Distler, 1959). Further corroborative evidence appears in the growing series of studies of effects of paternal absence (Bach, 1946; Sears, Pintler, and Sears, 1946; Lynn and Sawrey, 1959; Tiller, 1958). The absence of the father apparently not only affects the behavior of the child directly but also influences the mother in the direction of greater overprotectiveness. The effect of both these tendencies is especially critical for male children; boys from father-absent homes tend to be markedly more submissive and dependent. Studies dealing explicitly with the influence of parental role structure in intact families are few and far between. Papanek (1957), in an unpublished doctoral dissertation, reports greater sex-role differentiation among children from homes in which the parental roles were differentiated. And in a carefully controlled study, Kohn and Clausen (1956) find that "schizophrenic patients more frequently than normal persons report that their mothers played a very strong authority role and the father a very weak authority role." Finally, what might best be called complementary evidence for our inferences regarding trends in family structure and their effects comes from the work of Miller, Swanson, and their associates (1958, 1960) on the differing patterns of behavior exhibited by families from *bureaucratic* and *entrepreneurial* work settings. These investigators argue that the entrepreneurial-bureaucratic dichotomy represents a new cleavage in American social structure that cuts across and overrides social class influences and carries with it its own characteristic patterns of family structure and socialization. Thus one investigation (Gold and Slater, 1958) contrasts the exercise of power in families of husbands employed in two kinds of job situations: (a) those working in large organizations with three or more levels of supervision; (b) those self-employed or working in small organizations with few levels of supervision. With appropriate controls for social class, equalitarian families were found more frequently in the bureaucratic groups; patriarchal and, to a lesser extent, matriarchal in the entrepreneurial setting. Another study (Miller and Swanson, 1958) shows that, in line with Miller and Swanson's hypotheses, parents from these same two groups tend to favor rather different ends and means of socialization, with entrepreneurial families putting considerably more emphasis on the development of independence and mastery and on the use of "psychological" techniques of discipline. These differences appear at both upper and lower middle class levels but are less pronounced in higher socio-economic strata. It is Miller and Swanson's belief, however, that the trend is toward the bureaucratic way of life, with its less structured patterns of family organization and child rearing. The evidence we have cited on secular changes in family structure and the inferences we have drawn regarding their possible effects on personality development are on the whole consistent with their views.

Looking forward

If Miller and Swanson are correct in the prediction that America is moving toward a bureaucratic society that emphasizes, to put it colloquially, "getting along" rather than "getting ahead," then presumably we can look forward to ever increasing numbers of equalitarian families who, in turn, will produce successive generations of ever more adaptable but unaggressive "organization men." But recent signs

do not all point in this direction. In our review of secular trends in child rearing practices we detected in the data from the more recent studies a slowing up in the headlong rush toward greater permissiveness and toward reliance on indirect methods of discipline. We pointed out also that if the most recent editions of well-thumbed guidebooks on child care are as reliable harbingers of the future as they have been in the past, we can anticipate something of a return to the more explicit discipline techniques of an earlier era. Perhaps the most important forces, however, acting to redirect both the aims and methods of child rearing in America emanate from behind the Iron Curtain. With the firing of the first Sputnik, Achievement began to replace Adjustment as the highest goal of the American way of life. We have become concerned—perhaps even obsessed—with "education for excellence" and the maximal utilization of our intellectual resources. Already, ability grouping, and the guidance counsellor who is its prophet, have moved down from the junior high to the elementary school, and parents can be counted on to do their part in preparing their youngsters for survival in the new competitive world of applications and achievement tests.

But if a new trend in parental behavior is to develop, it must do so in the context of changes already under way. And if the focus of parental authority is shifting from husband to wife, then perhaps we should anticipate that pressures for achievement will be imposed primarily by mothers rather than fathers. Moreover, the mother's continuing strong emotional investment in the child should provide her with a powerful lever for evoking desired performance. It is noteworthy in this connection that recent studies of the familial origins of need-achievement point to the matriarchy as the optimal context for development of the motive to excel (Strodtbeck, 1958; Rosen and D'Andrade, 1959).

The prospect of a society in which socialization techniques are directed toward maximizing achievement drive is not altogether a pleasant one. As a number of investigators have shown (Baldwin, Kalhorn and Breese, 1945; Baldwin, 1948; Haggard, 1957; Winterbottom, 1958; Rosen and D'Andrade, 1959), high achievement motivation appears to flourish in a family atmosphere of "cold democracy" in which initial high levels of maternal involvement are followed by pressures for independence and accomplishment.[5] Nor does the product of this process give ground for reassurance. True, children from achievement-oriented homes excel in planfulness and performance, but they are also more aggressive, tense, domineering, and cruel (Baldwin, Kalhorn and Breese, 1945; Baldwin, 1948; Haggard, 1957). It would appear that education for excellence if pursued single-mindedly may entail some sobering social costs.

But by now we are in danger of having stretched our chain of inference beyond the strength of its weakest link. Our speculative analysis has become far more speculative than analytic and to pursue it further would bring us past the bounds of science into the realms of science fiction. In concluding our discussion, we would reemphasize that speculations should, by their very nature, be held suspect. It is for good reason that, like "damn Yankees," they too carry their almost inseparable sobriquets: speculations are either "idle" or "wild." Given the scientific and social importance of the issues we have raised, we would dismiss the first of these labels out of hand, but the second cannot be disposed of so easily. Like the impetuous child, the "wild" speculation responds best to the sobering influence of friendly but firm discipline, in this instance from the hand of the behavioral scientist. As we look ahead to the next twenty-five years of human socialization, let us hope that the "optimal levels" of involvement and discipline can be achieved not only by the parent who is unavoidably engaged in the process, but also by the scientist who attempts to understand its working, and who—also unavoidably—contributes to shaping its course.

References

1. Bach, G. R. "Father-fantasies and father-typing in father-separated children." *Child Development*, 1946, 17, 63-79.

2. Baldwin, A. L., Kalhorn, J., and Breese, F. H. "The appraisal of parent behavior." *Psychol. Monogr.*, 1945, 58, No. 3 (Whole No. 268).

3. Baldwin, A. L. "Socialization and the parent-child relationship." *Child Development*, 1948, 19, 127-136.

4. Bandura, A., and Walters, R. H. *Adolescent Aggression*. New York: Ronald Press, 1959.

5. Bronfenbrenner, U. "Socialization and social class through time and space." In Maccoby, E., Newcomb, T. M., and Hartley, E. L., *Readings in Social Psychology*. New York: Holt, 1958, pp. 400-425.

6. Bronfenbrenner, U. "Some familial antecedents of responsibility and leadership in adolescents." In Petrullo, L., and Bass, B. M. *Leadership and Interpersonal Behavior*. New York: Holt, Rinehart, and Winston, 1961.

7. Bronson, W. C. Katten, E. S., and Livson, N. "Patterns of authority and affection in two generations." *J. abnorm. soc. Psychol.*, 1959, 58, 143-152.

8. Gold, M., and Slater, C. "Office, factory, store— and family: A study of integration setting. *Amer. sociol. Rev.*, 1959, 23, 64-74.

9. Haggard, E. A. "Socialization, personality, and academic achievement in gifted children." *The School Rev.*, 1957, 65, 388-414.

10. Kohn, M. L., and Clausen, J. A. "Parental authority behavior and schizophrenia." *American J. Orthopsychiatry*, 1956, 26, 297-313.

11. Kohn, M. L. "Social class and parental values." *American J. of sociol.*, 1959, 44, 337-351.

12. Lynn, D. B., and Sawrey, W. L. "The effects of father-absence on Norwegian boys and girls." *J. abnorm. soc. Psychol.*, 1959, 59, 258-262.

13. Miller, D. R., and Swanson, G. E. *The changing American parent*. New York: John Wiley, 1958.

14. Miller, D. R., and Swanson, G. E. *Inner conflict and defense*. New York: Holt, 1960.

15. Mussen, P., and Distler, L. "Masculinity, identification, and father-son relationships." *J. abnorm. soc. Psychol.*, 1959, 59, 350-356.

16. Papanek, M. *Authority and interpersonal relations in the family*. Unpublished doctoral dissertation on file at the Radcliffe College Library, 1957.

17. Rosen, B. L., and D'Andrade, R. "The psychosocial origins of achievement motivation." *Sociometry*, 1959, 22, 185-217.

18. Schachter, S. *The psychology of affiliation*. Stanford, California: Stanford University Press, 1959.

---

[5] Cold democracy under female administration appears to foster the development of achievement not only in the home but in the classroom as well. In a review of research on teaching effectiveness, Ackerman reports that teachers most successful in bringing about gains in achievement score for their pupils were judged "least considerate," while those thought friendly and congenial were least effective. (Ackerman, W. I., "Teacher Competence and Pupil Change," *Harvard Educational Review*, 1954, 24, 273-289.)

19. Sears, R. R., Pintler, M. H., and Sears, P. S. "Effects of father-separation on preschool children's doll play aggression." *Child Development,* 1946, 17, 219-243.

20. Sears, R. R., Maccoby, Eleanor, and Levin, M. *Patterns of child rearing.* Evanston, Illinois: Row, Peterson, 1957.

21. Strodtbeck, F. L. "Family interaction, values, and achievement." In McClelland, D. C., Baldwin, A. L., Bronfenbrenner, U., and Strodtbeck, F. L., *Talent and society.* Princeton, N.J.: Van Nostrand, 1958, pp. 135-194.

22. Tiller, P. O. "Father-absence and personality development of children in sailor families." *Nordisk Psykologis Monograph Series,* 1958, 9.

23. Winterbottom, M. R. "The relation of need achievement to learning experiences in independence and mastery." In Atkinson, J. W., *Motives in fantasy, action, and society.* Princeton, N.J.: Van Nostrand, 1958, pp. 453-494.

Continuities and discontinuities in cultural conditioning

RUTH BENEDICT

All societies influence personality formation by expecting its members to conform to specific behavior patterns. To the extent that these social expectancies are inconsistent or contradictory, they can create strain for the individual and interfere with the successful development of the personality. The following article describes several of the inconsistencies that exist in American society and demonstrates the utility of the anthropological method of cross-cultural comparison. In the process of illustrating how the transition from childhood to adulthood is made more difficult because of discontinuities in our patterns of social learning, the author illustrates the relevance of social factors for understanding personality development.

The late Ruth Benedict, Ph.D., was Professor of Anthropology at Columbia University, and was a past president of the American Anthropological Society. She is the author of many articles and several books, including *Science and Politics.*

All cultures must deal in one way or another with the cycle of growth from infancy to adulthood. Nature has posed the situation dramatically: on the one hand, the new-born baby, physiologically vulnerable, unable to fend for itself, or to participate of its own initiative in the life of the group, and, on the other, the adult man or woman. Every man who rounds out his human potentialities must have been a son first and a father later, and the two roles are physiologically in great contrast; he must first have been dependent upon others for his very existence, and later he must provide such security for others. This discontinuity in the life cycle is a fact of nature and is inescapable. Facts of nature, however, in any discussion of human problems, are ordinarily read off not at their bare minimal but surrounded by all the local accretions of behavior to which the student of human affairs has become accustomed in his own culture. For that reason, it is illuminating to examine comparative material from other societies in order to get a wider perspective on our own special accretions. The anthropologist's role is not to question the facts of nature, but to insist upon the interposition of a middle term between "nature" and "human behavior"; his role is to analyze that term, to document local man-made doctorings of nature, and to insist that these doctorings should not be read off in any one culture as nature itself. Although it is a fact of nature that the child becomes a man, the way in which this transition is effected varies from one society to another, and no one of these particular cultural bridges should be regarded as the "natural" path to maturity.

From a comparative point of view our culture goes to great extremes in emphasizing contrasts between the child and the adult. The child is sexless, the adult estimates his virility by his sexual activities; the child must be protected from the ugly facts of life, the adult must meet them without psychic catastrophe; the child must obey, the adult must command this obedience. These are all dogmas of our culture, dogmas which, in spite of the facts of nature, other cultures commonly do not share. In spite of the physiological contrasts between child and adult these are cultural accretions.

It will make the point clearer if we consider one habit in our own culture in regard to which there is not this discontinuity of conditioning. With the greatest clarity of purpose and economy of training, we achieve our goal of conditioning everyone to eat three meals a day. The baby's training in regular food periods begins at birth, and no crying of the child, and no inconvenience to the mother is allowed to interfere. We gauge the child's physiological make-up and at first allow it food oftener than adults, but, because our goal is firmly set and our training consistent, before the child is two years old it has achieved the adult schedule. From the point of view of other cultures this is as startling as the fact of three-year old babies perfectly at home in deep water is to us. Modesty is another sphere in which our child training is consistent and economical; we waste no time in clothing the baby and in contrast to many societies where the child runs naked till it is ceremonially given its skirt or its pubic sheath at adolescence, the child's training fits it precisely for adult conventions.

In neither of these aspects of behavior is there need for an individual in our culture to embark before puberty, at puberty, or at some later date upon a course of action which all his previous training has tabued. He is spared the unsureness inevitable in such a transition.

The illustration I have chosen may appear trivial, but in larger and more important aspects of behavior, our methods are obviously different. Because of the great variety of child training in different families in our society, I might illustrate continuity of conditioning from individual life histories in our culture, but even these, from a comparative point of view, stop far short of consistency, and I shall therefore confine myself to describing arrangements in other cultures in which training, which with us is idiosyncratic, is accepted and traditional and does not therefore involve the same possibility of conflict. I shall choose childhood rather than infant and nursing situations, not because the latter do not vary strikingly in different cultures, but because they are, nevertheless, more circumscribed by the baby's physiological needs than is its later training. Childhood situations provide an excellent field in which to illustrate the range of cultural adjustments which are possible within a universally given, but not so drastic, set of physiological facts.

The major discontinuity in the life cycle is of course that the child who is at one point a son must later be a father. These roles in our society are strongly differentiated; a good son is tractable, and does not assume adult responsibilities; a good father provides for his children and should not allow his authority to be flouted. In addition the child must be sexless so far as his family is concerned, whereas the father's sexual role is primary in the family. The individual in one role must revise his behavior from almost all points of view when he assumes the second role.

I shall select for discussion three such contrasts that occur in our culture between the individual's role as child and as father: 1. responsible—nonresponsible status role. 2. dominance—submission. 3. contrasted sexual role. It is largely upon our cultural commitments to these three contrasts that the discontinuity in the life cycle of an individual in our culture depends.

1. Responsible—nonresponsible status role

The techniques adopted by societies which achieve continuity during the life cycle in this sphere in no way differ from those we employ in our uniform conditioning to three meals a day. They are merely applied to other areas of life. We think of the child as wanting to play and the adult as having to work, but in many societies the mother takes the baby daily in her shawl or carrying net to the garden or to gather roots, and adult labor is seen even in infancy from the pleasant security of its position in close contact with its mother. When the child can run about, it accompanies its parents still, doing tasks which are essential and yet suited to its powers, and its dichotomy between work and play is not different from that its parents recognize, namely the distinction between the busy day and the free evening. The tasks it is asked to perform are graded to its powers and its elders wait quietly by, not offering to do the task in the child's place. Everyone who is familiar with such societies has been struck by the contrast with our child training. Dr. Ruth Underhill tells me of sitting with a group of Papago elders in Arizona when the man of the house turned to his little three-year-old granddaughter and asked her to close the door. The door was heavy and hard to shut. The child tried, but it did not move. Several times the grandfather repeated, "Yes, close the door." No one jumped to the child's assistance. No one took the responsibility away from her. On the other hand there was no impatience, for after all the child was small. They sat gravely waiting till the child succeeded, and her grandfather gravely thanked her. It was assumed that the task would not be asked of her unless she could perform it, and, having been asked, the responsibility was hers alone just as if she were a grown woman.

The essential point of such child training is that the child is from infancy continuously conditioned to responsible social participation, while at the same time the tasks that are expected of it are adapted to its capacity. The contrast with our society is very great. A child does not make any labor contribution to our industrial society except as it competes with an adult; its work is not measured against its own strength and skill but against high-geared industrial requirements. Even when we praise a child's achievement in the home, we are outraged if such praise is interpreted as being of the same order as praise of adults. The child is praised because the parent feels well disposed, regardless of whether the task is well done by adult standards, and the child acquires no sensible standard by which to measure its achievement. The gravity of a Cheyenne Indian family ceremoniously making a feast out of the little boy's first snowbird is at the furthest remove from our behavior. At birth the little boy was presented with a toy bow, and from the time he could run about, service-

able bows suited to his stature were specially made for him by the man of the family. Animals and birds were taught him in a graded series beginning with those most easily taken, and, as he brought in his first of each species, his family duly made a feast of it, accepting his contribution as gravely as the buffalo his father brought. When he finally killed a buffalo, it was only the final step of his childhood conditioning, not a new adult role with which his childhood experience had been at variance.

The Canadian Ojibwa show clearly what results can be achieved. This tribe gains its livelihood by winter trapping, and the small family of father, mother, and children live during the long winter alone on their great frozen hunting grounds. The boy accompanies his father and brings in his catch to his sister as his father does to his mother, the girl prepares the meat and skins for him just as his mother does for her husband. By the time the boy is 12, he may have set his own line of traps on a hunting territory of his own and return to his parent's house only once in several months—still bringing the meat and skins to his sister. The young child is taught consistently that it has only itself to rely upon in life, and this is as true in the dealings it will have with the supernatural as in the business of getting a livelihood. This attitude he will accept as a successful adult, just as he accepted it as a child.[1]

2. Dominance—submission

Dominance—submission is the most striking of those categories of behavior where like does not respond to like, but where one type of behavior stimulates the opposite response. It is one of the most prominent ways in which behavior is patterned in our culture. When it obtains between classes, it may be nourished by continuous experience; the difficulty in its use between children and adults lies in the fact that an individual conditioned to one set of behavior in childhood must adopt the opposite as an adult. Its opposite is a pattern of approximately identical reciprocal behavior, and societies which rely upon continuous conditioning characteristically invoke this pattern. In some primitive cultures the very terminology

---

[1] Landes, Ruth, The Ojibwa woman, Part 1, Youth—Columbia University Contributions to Anthropology, Volume XXXI.

of address between father and son, and more commonly, between grandchild and grandson or uncle and nephew, reflects this attitude. In such kinship terminologies one reciprocal expresses each of these relationships so that son and father, for instance, exchange the same term with one another, just as we exchange the same term with a cousin. The child later will exchange it with his son. "Father—son," therefore, is a continuous relationship he enjoys throughout life. The same continuity, backed up by verbal reciprocity, occurs far oftener in the grandchild-grandson relationship or that of mother's brother-sister's son. When these are "joking" relationships, as they often are, travellers report wonderingly upon the liberties and pretensions of tiny toddlers in their dealings with these family elders. In place of our dogma of respect to elders such societies employ in these cases a reciprocity as nearly identical as may be. The teasing and practical joking the grandfather visits upon his grandchild, the grandchild returns in like coin; he would be led to believe that he failed in propriety if he did not give like for like. If the sister's son has right of access without leave to his mother's brother's possessions, the mother's brother has such rights also to the child's possessions. They share reciprocal privileges and obligations which in our society can develop only between age mates.

From the point of view of our present discussion, such kinship conventions allow the child to put in practice from infancy the same forms of behavior which it will rely upon as an adult; behavior is not polarized into a general requirement of submission for the child and dominance for the adult.

It is clear from the techniques described above by which the child is conditioned to a responsible status role that these depend chiefly upon arousing in the child the desire to share responsibility in adult life. To achieve this little stress is laid upon obedience but much stress upon approval and praise. Punishment is very commonly regarded as quite outside the realm of possibility, and natives in many parts of the world have drawn the conclusion from our usual disciplinary methods that white parents do not love their children. If the child is not required to be submissive, however, many occasions for punishment melt away; a variety of situations which call for it do not occur.

Many American Indian tribes are especially explicit in rejecting the ideal of a child's submissive or obedient behavior. Prince Maximilian von Wied who visited the Crow Indians over a hundred years ago describes a father's boasting about his young son's intractibility even when it was the father himself who was flouted; "He will be a man," his father said. He would have been baffled at the idea that his child should show behavior which would obviously make him appear a poor creature in the eyes of his fellows if he used it as an adult. Dr. George Devereaux tells me of a special case of such an attitude among the Mohave at the present time. The child's mother was white and protested to its father that he must take action when the child disobeyed and struck him. "But why?" the father said, "he is little. He cannot possibly injure me." He did not know of any dichotomy according to which an adult expects obedience and a child must accord it. If his child had been docile he would simply have judged that it would become a docile adult—an eventuality of which he would not have approved.

Child training which brings about the same result is common also in other areas of life than that of reciprocal kinship obligations between child and adult. There is a tendency in our culture to regard every situation as having in it the seeds of a dominance-submission relationship. Even where dominance-submission is patently irrelevant we read in the dichotomy, assuming that in every situation there must be one person dominating another. On the other hand some cultures, even when the situation calls for leadership, do not see it in terms of dominance-submission. To do justice to this attitude, it would be necessary to describe their political and especially their economic arrangements, for such an attitude to persist must certainly be supported by economic mechanisms that are congruent with it. But it must also be supported by—or what comes to the same thing, express itself in—child training and familial situations.

3. Contrasted sexual role

Continuity of conditioning in training the child to assume responsibility and to behave no more submissively than adults is quite possible in terms of the child's physiological endowment if his participation is suited to his strength. Because of the late development of the child's reproductive organs, continuity of conditioning in sex experience presents a difficult problem. So far as their belief that the child is anything but a sexless being is concerned, they are probably more nearly right than we are with an opposite dogma. But the great break is presented by the universally sterile unions before puberty and the presumably fertile ones after maturation. This physiological fact no amount of cultural manipulation can minimize or alter, and societies therefore which stress continuous conditioning most strongly sometimes do not expect children to be interested in sex experience until they have matured physically. This is striking among American Indian tribes like the Dakota; adults observe great privacy in sex acts and in no way stimulate children's sexual activity. There need be no discontinuity, in the sense in which I have used the term, in such a program if the child is taught nothing it does not have to unlearn later. In such cultures adults view children's experimentation as in no way wicked or dangerous but merely as innocuous play which can have no serious consequences. In some societies such play is minimal, and the children manifest little interest in it. But the same attitude may be taken by adults in societies where such play is encouraged and forms a major activity among small children. This is true among most of the Melanesian cultures of Southeast New Guinea; adults go as far as to laugh off sexual affairs within the prohibited class if the children are not mature, saying that since they cannot marry there can be no harm done.

It is this physiological fact of the difference between children's sterile unions and adults' presumably fertile sex relations which must be kept in mind in order to understand the different mores which almost always govern sex expression in children and in adults in the same culture. A great many cultures with preadolescent sexual license require marital fidelity and a great many which value premarital virginity in either male or female arrange their marital life with great license. Continuity in sex experience is complicated by factors which it was unnecessary to consider in the problems previously discussed. The essential problem is not whether or not the child's sexuality is consistently exploited—for even where such exploitation is favored in the majority of cases the child must seriously modify his behavior at puberty or at marriage. Continuity in sex expression means rather that the child is taught nothing it must unlearn later. If the cultural emphasis is upon sexual pleasure the child who is continuously conditioned will be encouraged to experiment freely and pleasurably, as among the Marquesans; [2] if emphasis is upon reproduction, as among the Zuni of New Mexico, childish sex proclivities will not be exploited for the only important use which sex is thought to serve in his culture is not yet possible to him. The important contrast with our child training is that, although a Zuni child is impressed with the wickedness of premature sex experimentation, he does not run the risk as in our culture of associating this wickedness with sex itself rather than with sex at his age. The adult in our culture has often failed to unlearn the wickedness or the dangerousness of sex, a lesson which was impressed upon him strongly in his most formative years.

Discontinuity in conditioning

Even from this very summary statement of continuous conditioning, the economy of such mores is evident. In spite of the obvious advantages, however, there are difficulties in its way. Many primitive societies expect as different behavior from an individual as child and as adult as we do, and such discontinuity involves a presumption of strain.

Many societies of this type, however, minimize strain by the techniques they employ, and some techniques are more successful than others in ensuring the individual's functioning without conflict. It is from this point of view that age-grade societies reveal their fundamental significance. Age-graded cultures characteristically demand different behavior of the individual at different times of his life and persons of a like age-grade are grouped into a society whose activities are all oriented toward the behavior desired at that age. Individuals "graduate" publicly and with honor from one of these groups to another. Where age society members are enjoined to loyalty and mutual support, and are drawn not only from the local

---

[2] Ralph Linton, class notes on the Marquesans.

group but from the whole tribe as among the Arapaho, or even from other tribes as among the Wagawaga of Southeast New Guinea, such an institution has many advantages in eliminating conflicts among local groups and fostering intra-tribal peace. This seems to be also a factor in the tribal military solidarity of the similarly organized Masai of East Africa. The point that is of chief interest for our present discussion, however, is that by this means an individual who at any time takes on a new set of duties and virtues is supported not only by a solid phalanx of age mates but by the traditional prestige of the organized "secret" society into which he has now graduated. Fortified in this way, individuals in such cultures often swing between remarkable extremes of opposite behavior without apparent psychic threat. For example, the great majority exhibit prideful and nonconflicted behavior at each stage in the life cycle even when a prime of life devoted to passionate and aggressive head hunting must be followed by a later life dedicated to ritual and to mild and peaceable civic virtues.[3]

Our chief interest here, however, is in discontinuity which primarily affects the child. In many primitive societies such discontinuity has been fostered not because of economic or political necessity or because such discontinuity provides for a socially valuable division of labor, but because of some conceptual dogma. The most striking of these are the Australian and Papuan cultures where the ceremony of the "Making of Man" flourishes. In such societies it is believed that men and women have opposite and conflicting powers, and male children, who are of undefined status, must be initiated into the male role. In Central Australia the boy child is of the woman's side and women are tabu in the final adult stages of tribal ritual. The elaborate and protracted initiation ceremonies of the Arunta, therefore, snatch the boy from the mother, dramatize his gradual repudiation of her. In a final ceremony he is reborn as a man out of the men's ceremonial "baby pouch." The men's ceremonies are ritual statements of a masculine solidarity, carried out by fondling one another's *churingas*, the material symbol of each man's life, and by letting out over one another blood drawn from their veins. After this warm bond among men has been established through the ceremonies, the boy joins the men in the men's house and participates in tribal rites.[4] The enjoined discontinuity has been tribally bridged.

West of the Fly River in southern New Guinea there is a striking development of this Making of Man cult which involves a childhood period of passive homosexuality. Among the Keraki [5] it is thought that no boy can grow to full stature without playing the role for some years. Men slightly older take the active role, and the older man is a jealous partner. The life cycle of the Keraki Indians includes, therefore, in succession, passive homosexuality, active homosexuality, and heterosexuality. The Keraki believe that pregnancy will result from post-pubertal passive homosexuality and see evidences of such practices in any fat man whom even as an old man, they may kill or drive out of the tribe because of their fear. The ceremony that is of interest in connection with the present discussion takes place at the end of the period of passive homosexuality. This ceremony consists in burning out the possibility of pregnancy from the boy by pouring lye down his throat, after which he has no further protection if he gives way to the practice. There is no technique for ending active homosexuality, but this is not explicitly tabu for older men; heterosexuality and children, however, are highly valued. Unlike the neighboring Marindanim who share their homosexual practices, Keraki husband and wife share the same house and work together in the gardens.

I have chosen illustrations of discontinuous conditioning where it is not too much to say that the cultural institutions furnish adequate support to the individual as he progresses from role to role or interdicts the previous behavior in a summary fashion. The contrast with arrangements in our culture is very striking, and against this background of social arrangements in other cultures the adolescent period of *Sturm und Drang* with which we are so familiar becomes intelligible in terms of our discontinuous cultural institutions and dogmas

[3] Henry Elkin, manuscript on the Arapaho.
[4] Spencer, B., and Gillen, F. J., *The Arunta;* N. Y.: Macmillan, 1927 (2 vols.). Roheim, Geza, Psychoanalysis of primitive cultural types. *Internat. J. Psychoanal.,* 1932, 13:1-224—in particular, Chapter III, on the Aranda, The children of the desert.
[5] Williams, Francis E., *Papuans of the Trans-Fly.* Oxford, 1936.

rather than in terms of physiological necessity. It is even more pertinent to consider these comparative facts in relation to maladjusted persons in our culture who are said to be fixated at one or another pre-adult level. It is clear that if we were to look at our social arrangements as an outsider, we should infer directly from our family institutions and habits of child training that many individuals would not "put off childish things"; we should have to say that our adult activity demands traits that are interdicted in children, and that far from redoubling efforts to help children bridge this gap, adults in our culture put all the blame on the child when he fails to manifest spon-

taneously the new behavior or, overstepping the mark, manifests it with untoward belligerence. It is not surprising that in such a society many individuals fear to use behavior which has up to that time been under a ban and trust instead, though at great psychic cost, to attitudes that have been exercised with approval during their formative years. Insofar as we invoke a physiological scheme to account for these neurotic adjustments we are led to overlook the possibility of developing social institutions which would lessen the social cost we now pay; instead we elaborate a set of dogmas which prove inapplicable under other social conditions.

Personality development during the college years

NEVITT SANFORD

Perhaps as a consequence of the pervasive influence of orthodox psychoanalytic theory on contemporary personality theory, many psychologists have neglected the significance of changes in the personality which occur after childhood. This article attempts to correct this oversight by focusing on personality growth during young adulthood. After describing some of the changes characteristic of personality development in the late teens and early twenties, the author attempts to relate these changes to aspects of the college environment. Of particular interest is his description of the difficulty inherent in achieving a detailed understanding of the impact of college life on the individual.

Nevitt Sanford, Ph.D., is a Professor of Psychology and Education at Stanford University and Director of the Institute for the Study of Human Problems. Among the books which he has authored, coauthored, or edited are Self and Society, The American College, and The Authoritarian Personality.

Psychologists have so far given relatively little attention to developmental changes occurring during the years seventeen to twenty-two. Indeed, it is a common notion among psychologists that the personality is well-formed by the age of seventeen or thereabouts, and that what happens after that is merely an expression, or an unfolding, of what has previously been established. It appears that much educational theory is based upon this notion, particularly that which assumes that the student will choose his experiences in accordance with motives that are by now basic to his personality and that the chief job of the college is to help

From Personnel and Guidance Journal, XXXV (1956), 74-80. Reprinted by permission of the American Personnel and Guidance Association and the author.

This paper was presented in a more extended form as an address before the Annual Meeting of the American College Personnel Association at the American Personnel and Guidance Association Convention, Washington, D. C., March 28, 1956.

the student acquire the means for the successful pursuit of his purposes.

There is, of course, a contrasting view of education, according to which it is argued that the concern of the college should be not so much with teaching students how to realize their values as with helping them decide what values to have, that instead of permitting students to become confirmed in patterns of motives whose determinants have been childish or accidental the college should encourage development toward patterns that are valued in our society.

The title of this paper implies that personality *does* develop during the college years, and that this development is to some extent dependent upon the stimuli which the college provides. But we cannot doubt that such growth or development takes place in people in whom more or less enduring structures have already been built up, or that it is somehow continuous with the past. The question is, what kinds of changes, in what areas or processes of the person, may reasonably be expected? What are the factors producing change, and what are the mechanisms by which their effects are wrought?

Fortunately, there exists today a certain amount of theory concerning these questions. That branch of academic psychology which accents the cognitive processes has argued all along for the importance of contemporary experiences in affecting the organization, or reorganization, of the personality. In recent years a growing number of psychoanalysts and dynamic psychologists, such as E. H. Erikson [3], Peter Blos [1, 2] and R. W. White [4] have interested themselves in the phenomena of late adolescence, and produced concepts which accent fresh developments at the college level without forsaking continuity with the past.

Robert W. White, in his "Lives in Progress" [4], has performed a distinctive service in summarizing with lucidity much recent thought about growth trends and processes in late adolescence. In our research under the Mellon Program at Vassar College we have found much guidance in his writing.[1]

White distinguishes and discusses four major growth trends: "the stabilizing of ego identity," "the deepening of interests," "the freeing of personal relationships," "the humanizing of values." In our own consideration of the matter we have thought it best to add a fifth trend: the general development and strengthening of the ego.

In this paper I wish to focus the discussion upon some of these growth trends. It will appear that they embrace many of the commonly stated aims of liberal education.

First, it is necessary to describe, in general terms, the research that we have undertaken. This research is simple enough in its design, but not so easy of execution. We wish to describe some of the changes that take place during the college years, and to discover, if we can, what factors have been mainly influential —and in what way. The program for describing changes calls for before-, intermediate-, and after-testing. And, since we wish to know whether effects wrought in college are lasting, there must be follow-up, or at least studies of graduates.

The test battery that we have used embraces some 1,100 items, true-false items comprising various personality scales (some standardized ones and some of our own recent design), adjective check-lists, and several simple projective techniques.

We have tested four incoming freshman classes, with N's of approximately 430, and four senior classes, with N's averaging a little under 300.

We are also carrying on a program of intensive interviewing with eighty subjects, a random sample of the class of 1958. They will have, we hope, at least three interviews a year throughout their college careers.

With attention to the possibly lasting effects of college education we have carried out an OSS-type personality assessment with a sample of fifty alumnae from the classes of 1930-1934. Other groups of alumnae have been tested with our standard battery.

In selecting personality variables for study, we were guided by considerations of what important features of the person might, on one hypothesis or another, be expected to change under the impact of the college experience. Our major variables may readily be grouped according to their relevance to one or another of the major growth trends listed earlier.

I propose now to take up several of these

---

[1] Our staff at the present time consists of John Bushnell, Mervin Freedman, Harold Webster, and myself.

growth trends in turn, presenting a few relevant results, and offering some hypotheses about aspects of the college situation that favor, or hamper, growth. Discussion will be limited to stabilization of ego identity, humanization of values, and general development of the ego. Deepening of interests and freeing of personal relationships will have to be left for another occasion.

Stabilization of ego identity

"The sense of ego identity," Erikson writes, "—is the accrued confidence that one's ability to maintain inner sameness and continuity (one's ego in the psychological sense) is matched by the sameness and continuity of one's meaning for others" [3, p. 216]. The emphasis, it would appear, belongs on the matching; inner sameness and continuity can hardly be maintained without some social confirmation, while reliance upon outside judgments to the neglect of personal experience puts the sense of identity at the mercy of the shifting social situation. Stabilization is achieved in the degree that the self-conception is based on the kind of ego functioning that permits the inclusion of deeper, more personal needs and that, at the same time, gives adequate attention to reality.

What shall we make of the fact that, according to our results, seniors show more disturbance with respect to identity than do freshmen? This is true. Seniors as a group show more dissatisfaction with themselves, more apparent vacillation between different patterns, more conscious conflict about what to be. Indeed it appears that seniors (we are speaking of women) often have to deal with what amounts to an identity crisis; enough inner uncertainty remains so that often they feel unprepared for the decisions which now have to be made. Many observers have commented upon the flight into marriage that so often takes place at this time. It appears that the young woman seeks to attain stable identity through intimacy, or through a well-defined external pattern. But one cannot enter into a mature affectionate and erotic relationship until after one has attained some sureness about oneself as an independent person. There is some evidence from our alumnae sample that marriages undertaken as a means for resolving identity crises did not work out very well.

But this is not the whole story. There is more to the matter of sound ego identity than that the individual have a satisfying self-conception and remain more or less unchanging in this respect. The seniors, on our view, are striving to include more in—they are on the road to becoming richer and more complex personalities; they are striving for stabilization on a higher level. What distinguishes seniors from freshmen is not just the latter's relative freedom from conflict and uncertainty, but their greater narrowness, perhaps rigidity, of identity, and their greater dependence upon external definition and support. These are the very supports which seniors have had to give up, without having as yet found adequate replacements.

For many young women, it seems, the first few years after college are crucial for identity. Now she assumes social roles that will be hers for a long time to come. The question is, will she be able to take them without giving up too much of herself. She will not find a pattern that will permit her to include all the identities which were seriously considered, or experimented with, when she was a senior. As a matter of fact, our studies of alumnae 20-25 years after college indicated that some of these women had not succeeded in finding expression of certain dispositional patterns which, during the college years, had been rather important. A more or less suitable self-conception had been achieved by the exclusion of some preferences and aspirations. But these excluded patterns were still very much alive, sometimes prompting implicit assumptions that they would some day be attended to, sometimes giving rise to guilt and regret, or even to a nagging sense of self-betrayal. But, as indicated above, the indications are that really crucial events occur during the first few years after college; this period should be made the object of special research efforts.

There are many features of the college environment which would appear to be favorable to the development of sound ego identity. Here is an opportunity for a new start away from home; in the relative anonymity of the college situation one can be free of the limiting expectations of the home community. There is the possibility that a sense of belonging to the college culture will replace older, less adequate constructions. There are opportunities for acquiring realistic knowledge of available roles, and for imagining oneself in them; opportunities for experimenting with identities, such as serious scholar, glamor girl, community leader. Feminine identity is favored by experiences with young men and by participation in a student culture that governs procedures for attracting and handling men. And finally there is the necessity for giving serious consideration to such possible future roles as marriage and career, with their implications for identity.

But at the same time, the college environment frequently presents circumstances that hamper growth in this area. There may be perpetuation of a school girl identity through over-adjustment to an all too enticing peer culture. Frequently there is pressure to hurry and establish that one is able to attract men, to get engaged, so that intimacy is sought ahead of identity, or in place of it, to the detriment of both intimacy and identity. Closely related to this is the felt necessity for remaining uncommitted, so that one can move in any one of several directions, depending upon how one conceives the requirements of marriage. On the other hand, there is sometimes over-commitment or too early commitment to a pattern that is ill-suited to one's real needs and preferences; for example, a very able student may find herself caught in a major program that she entered more or less by accident, perhaps in a momentary burst of enthusiasm or under the influence of an admired teacher, and from which she cannot now extricate herself for fear of disappointing the hopes and expectations of teachers or parents.

Finally, young women in residential colleges —perhaps all college women—often have difficulty getting a clear conception of what roles an educated woman may take in our society, and of how these may be related to a basic feminine identity.

Humanizing of values

Humanizing of values involves movement from a literal belief in rules to an attitude of greater relativity, to an inclination to see values in relation to their social purposes; it involves increasing ability to bring to bear one's own experiences and one's own motives in promoting a value system.

It is with respect to the humanizing of values that the quantitative differences between seniors and freshmen are most marked. Seniors are clearly more flexible and uncompulsive, more tolerant and impunitive, more rebellious and critical of authority, more unorthodox in religious outlook, more rejecting of traditional feminine roles, more unconventional and nonconforming, more liberal in their views on interpersonal relationships.

What happens, we may suppose, is that old, automatically accepted values are challenged by competing values, inducing conflict and hence a necessity for new perceptions and new thinking. At the same time, wider experience of one's own impulses, and of empathic reactions to other people, confront the individual with new phenomena that must be taken into account.

The college situation offers much to promote these processes of growth. There is exposure to a wide variety of values and ways, through teaching and study and through actual experience; traditional values are confronted by more general and more liberal patterns as represented by admired figures—the college as a whole, teachers, friends both female and male. The student is required to make ethical decisions but is not altogether without external support. Sexual experimentation, and participation in a community in which sexual experimentation is going on, may lead to a questioning of values. Of particular importance is teaching that brings insight into the unconscious sources of compulsively sustained values; for example, teaching that requires students to understand characters in literature before judging them in moral terms.

But, we must seek some explanation of those cases that do not go along with the majority. There are enough seniors who are not notably different in this respect from the average freshmen so that we will not lack a suitable sample to work with.

For one thing, the peer culture, from which the student does not extricate herself, may serve as a powerful support for the historical value system; for another, dependent relations with parents may be maintained throughout the college years, if the parents are clever enough and persistent enough. And again, an authoritarian conscience may find reinforcement in the college regime or in campus authority figures.

It should be noted, too, that the college setting may afford an excellent critique of traditional values without supplying the basis for a new, humanized system, so that we get either more rebellion than is necessary or else tolerance so extreme that it shrinks from any value judgments at all.

General ego growth

We turn, finally, to general development and strengthening of the ego. A general principle here is that of growth through exercise. Ego functions improve as they are performed with success in increasingly difficult situations. A major requirement is that tasks calling for a wide variety of ego performances be assigned the individual, but in situations that are not so difficult or anxiety provoking that he is forced to make use of primitive defensive devices.

Another point would be that anything that frees the individual from the necessity of defensive operations favors the growth of the ego.

It follows, then, that ego growth is hampered both by authoritarian or overprotective regimes and by permissive-chaotic ones. The former do not give the synthetic functions of the ego a chance for exercise; the latter, through too much stimulation of impulse with consequent anxiety, may put too heavy a strain upon the developing ego.

In the college situation ego development is favored by teaching that shows the student something of the variety and complexity of the social world, by teaching that shows him how people feel, what it means to be human, and particularly by teaching that forces self-awareness by inducing empathy with many kinds of people—real and fictional—and that confronts the student with some of the deficiencies of his old, automatically adopted values, inducing conflict and requiring decision. Ego development is favored by a non-academic environment that is varied and impelling enough to challenge old values, and yet protective enough to prevent too much anxiety, and it is furthered by opportunities for acquiring skills, techniques, mastery—with ensuing self-confidence.

But the college is not always a perfect culture for the ego. There may be possibilities for resistance to awareness and to breadth of experience, for example, parental support for the student's outlook or too much protection against experiences regarded as possibly dangerous. There may be effective peer group devices to prevent learning; for example, tolerance of the superficial C student, or various "inside dopester" tactics for getting grades; particularly the peer group value for avoiding issues, not permitting anything unpleasant, not "becoming involved."

There may be authoritarianism in teaching, with rewards for doing precisely what one is told or authoritarianism in the regime—perhaps in the student government—with its invitation to substitute external control for inner direction.

It would be quite discouraging if our results did not indicate positive development in ego functioning during the college years. Actually, our test results show that seniors are well ahead of the freshmen in flexibility of thinking, in capacity to suspend judgment, in tolerance of the uncertain, the indefinite, the merely probable; in skepticism, criticalness, realism. Interestingly, seniors are less cynical than freshmen in their conceptions of people, far more cynical with respect to institutions and organizations. Seniors show more self-insight, more inner life and—let's face it—they show more "neuroticism" of a certain kind. At least they show a greater willingness to admit, or perhaps to take a certain satisfaction in admitting, conflicts, worries, doubts, fears, faults, psychosomatic symptoms. Perhaps we are dealing here with response to the situation of being a senior—with that identity crisis mentioned earlier. Perhaps, for college students, the usual neuroticism scales are not so much measures of durable neurotic structures as they are measures of growing pains. But at least, it seems, seniors show fewer repressive mechanisms of defense.

In considering the several developmental trends, it seems that we have to deal with that curious state of affairs that is so marked in the case of brief psychotherapy: that those who get the most out of it are those who in a sense need it least, who are already farthest along the road to achieving what the therapists would like to bring about.

We have the strong impression that those freshmen who will get the most out of college, in the usual meanings of this expression, are those who already are the most developed in respect to ego identity, interests, personal relationships, values, and general ego functioning. If we were to undertake to predict success in college, on the basis of information collected at the time of application for admission, we would of course most heavily on measures of these growth trends. But does anyone wish to suggest that young people who are particularly backward in these respects should not be offered the opportunity to grow? There is nothing for it but to try and discover what conditions determine growth in each area. It is not inconceivable that at some future time, after dependable knowledge of these matters has been attained, there will be different educational programs which can be prescribed in accordance with the developmental status of the individual student.

To come now to a conclusion, I have indicated some ways in which personality does change, in positively valued ways, during the college years; and I have suggested some hypotheses concerning the processes and mechanisms by which the student changes, through interaction with the complex environment of the college and the larger community.

I believe the promise of research in this area is very great. We are approaching territory that is virtually unexplored by the discipline of personality research, and we have methods and techniques that are ready to hand, having proved their worth in other areas. It is practically impossible to study college students, with the use of such concepts and methods as have been indicated, without coming up with results that are new and interesting. One may say with confidence that the next decade will bring great advances in our general knowledge of personality development in late adolescence.

But with respect to research on higher education, research designed to show what policies and practices have what effects with what students, one cannot be quite so sanguine. The difficulties here are rather enormous.

It is hard to obtain measures of the environmental factors. With what independent variables, operating in the college situation, shall we correlate changes in our test scores? Variations in major subject, in certain other aspects of curriculum, in counseling experience, in living arrangements, in patterns of social relationships—the list of measures readily obtained is not extensive. Interviews, on the other hand, yield fairly clear conceptions of numerous apparently significant factors. It seems possible that many of these may eventually yield to methodological ingenuity.

The really great problem, of course, has to do with the establishment of experimental controls. How do we know that such changes in personality as we have considered would not occur just as well in people who do not go to college?

If we are struck by the fact that no college has so far produced any scientific evidence that it actually brings about the changes it hopes, and often claims, to bring about, let us remember that psychological research has so far produced no evidence that *psychotherapy* has lasting effects. No one is suggesting, however, that either colleges or psychotherapists forthwith close their activities.

The problems of research design in two areas are very similar; but research on higher education would appear to be the more difficult; it is more complex and it necessarily requires projects on a vaster scale.

In considering the determinants of personality change in college, it is our impression that the over-all culture of the college is more important, in general, than any particular factor that can be isolated within a single college environment. This means that the same measures of personality change will have to be used in various colleges whose cultures will have been defined. This will require a project of very considerable scope indeed. Still, it need be no larger than some that have been undertaken, in military or mental health research, for example; sooner or later we may expect to hear that such a project has been begun.

Finally, it is very necessary to consider that research on higher education is value-laden through and through. Any incontrovertible results that it produces may make a difference to a great many people. When we talk of changing education in the American College, we are talking about changing the American culture, within which the college is embedded and which the college in turn promotes. If one should produce conclusive evidence that system A is more effective in bringing about the culturally valued results than system B, he would have hold of a cultural hot potato.

One wonders what the great foundations, which distribute bounty among the colleges, would do if means were available for evaluating the work of the college. Does it not seem safest to assume that all colleges are equal—however much they may claim, or we may believe, that some colleges are more equal than others?

Colleges operate in an educational free market. They are at pains to acquaint the public with what they do, and students are able to choose their college with a fair knowledge of what will be offered; if they do not like what they find they are free to go elsewhere. But usually they do like, or learn to like, what they find, and years later, when asked to tell the attributes of a good college they will describe the one they attended.

It will be with some difficulty that scientific knowledge will effectively penetrate this system which has, after all, much practical wisdom to support it. As scientists, however, we should worry more about how to produce dependable knowledge than about the danger of its not being applied. In our society, knowledge tends to get around. Our history records few instances in which it has been suppressed for long.

It is safe to predict that sound knowledge of personality development in late adolescence will eventually be generally applied in the colleges, though not necessarily in ways that we may now envision.

To the argument that science, when applied to higher education, may tend to reduce the diversity that is rightly prized so highly in our society we may answer that the opposite is true. Knowledge of human behavior increases its diversity. The more we know of what determines our behavior, the more we are able to bring it under conscious control and, hence, the more we are able to increase our freedom of choice; the more freedom of choice—such is our nature—the more diversity. This is true of the college student's behavior, and it is true of the behavior of the college itself.

Plan proposed to finance college study

A plan to finance the higher education of qualified students through easily available long-term loans has been proposed by Chicago businessman Sydney M. Roth. The collateral for the loans would be the students' enhanced earning power after they are launched on their careers.

A central corporation or trust (either for profit or not for profit) could handle the main details under the plan; the loans could be insured by the government as it now insures loans in the housing field. Students would be financed on the basis of individual need and ability to repay. The universities and colleges would handle the actual details of the loans. They also could take part in the directing corporation that would attract investment funds.

The plan is being studied by scholars and businessmen interested in providing more money for education.

References

1. Blos, P. Psychological couseling of college students. *American J. Orthopsychiat.*, 16, 1946.

2. Blos, P. The contribution of psychoanalysis to the treatment of adolescents. Chap. 10 in *Psychoanalysis and Social Work*, M. Heiman (Ed.), New York: Int. Univ. Press, 1953.

3. Erikson, E. H. Crises of normal development. *In* Kluckhohn, C., & Murray, H. (Ed.), *Personality in Nature, Society, Culture*, (rev. ed.). New York: Alfred Knopf, 1955.

4. White, R. W. *Lives in Progress.* New York: Dryden Press, 1952.

4

PERSONAL ENCOUNTERS: LOVE AND SEX

"My belief is that no matter what advances we make in technology, and in the controlling of nature, and so on, the real basis of life is human relationships. It's through them that we are happy or unhappy, and that we fulfill ourselves or we don't." This statement by Henry Moore, the famous modern sculptor, simply, but elegantly, reminds us of the importance of personal relationships at a time when our preoccupation with scientific achievements carries us further into the realm of object relationships. There is no more significant or fundamental human relationship than the one resulting from the love between two people: it is our task in this section to explore the nature of love and sex.

The romantic love tradition

Historically, courtship behavior in the United States between man and woman has emphasized romantic love as an essential ingredient of a successful relationship. We are so preoccupied with love that we take it for granted. However, many persons in our society are not aware, as Havelock Ellis (1938) points out, that knowledge of love is not universal, and in many cultures there are no words in the language for it. Even though the present high divorce rate might suggest that there is something seriously wrong with the bases for many marriages, relatively few persons appear willing to question the adequacy of romantic love as a prerequisite for marriage. According to Heyns (1958), romantic love, as it is understood and accepted by most persons in our society, emphasizes the following characteristics: 1) the importance of physical attraction; 2) the desire for sexual relations; 3) the notion that the male should dominate the relationship, particularly with regard to initiating courtship; 4) the necessity of idealizing one's partner; 5) the use of separation as a test of the strength of the relationship (the "I can't live without you" phenomenon); and 6) love at first sight. The assumption underlying all of these tenets is that there is only one ideal mate in the world for any individual.

The inadequacy of these criteria as the only bases for mate selection is clearly conveyed in the following criticism by Heyns (1958):

It is exceedingly doubtful that these criteria provide the best bases for marriage. Indeed, they probably mislead people and complicate the problems of courtship as well as marriage. The signs themselves are apt to be indicative of immaturity on the part of one or both parties rather than of the presence of ingredients conducive to a successful marriage. The major indictment against the romantic-love criteria is their emphasis. None calls attention to the fact that the major ingredients of a successful marriage are learned, acquired skills. They emphasize the subjective, emotional responses that people may or may not make to each other rather than the interpersonal skills and attitudes which are of critical importance (p. 463).

Albert Ellis (1962) describes romantic love in less flattering terms. He writes:

The pattern of courtship in America and in practically all of Western civilized society is . . . that of the Sex Tease. In following this pattern, the modern woman, whether she consciously knows it or not, is forcibly striving to do two major things: First, to make herself appear infinitely sexually desirable—but finally approachable only in legal marriage. Second, to use sex as bait and therefore to set it up as something special. If she gives in too easily to sex pleasure, she loses her favorite man-conquering weapon. Hence she must retain sexuality on a special plane, and dole it out only under unusual conditions.

The idealized aspect of this philosophy of let-us-women-stick-together-and-only-employ-sex-for-special-baiting-purposes is what we usually call romantic love (p. 113).

Ellis (1962) is equally critical of romantic love but for quite different reasons than Heyns. He feels that romantic love interferes with the active and enjoyable expression of human sexuality. As evidence for his point of view, he suggests that sex is enjoyed more for its own sake in societies characterized by non-romantic types of love.

Levine (1963) cites three reasons why persons have a misperception of the love object prior to marriage. First, there is a tendency for familiarization to occur only under conditions oriented at putting each person in the most favorable light. Dating and courtship typically involve the mutual enjoyment of recreation, entertainment, or other "fun" activities which do not adequately reflect qualities such as responsibility and concern for the other

person. The dating situation usually provides a limited or even artificial basis for learning about the more significant aspects of the other person that are important within a marriage. Second, the perception of the loved one can be distorted by the need to be loved by a "perfect" person. That is, the love object may take on characteristics which are more consistent with the ideals of the loved one than with the actual personality of the love object. Third, the love object is seen as possessing either actual or wished-for characteristics of previous love objects.

Despite these criticisms, emphasis on romantic love dominates courtship patterns in America and will probably continue to do so for some time to come. Even though we all may agree about how great or important love is, we find it difficult to agree about *what* it is. For example, Montagu (1953) states the "interdependence" of two persons is the single best descriptive term for "what love really is" (p. 11). Similarly, Erich Fromm (1956) defines erotic love as the "craving for complete fusion, for union with one other person" (p. 44). Montefiore (1963) describes a *"structure of love* which includes trust and dependence, care and consideration, loyalty and faithfulness, friendship and affection, and the desire to be united with the beloved . . ." (p. 68). In an earlier work, Fromm (1947) states: "Genuine love is an expression of productiveness and implies care, respect, responsibility, and knowledge" (p. 129). Some other definitions are presented by Prescott (1952) and Foote (1953) in articles which appear in this section.

Love and sex

In discussing the topic of love there is usually no problem until the issue of sex is introduced. As English (1953) has noted: "Man's love for woman is accepted as a great unselfish thing. But man's *sexual* love for woman is regarded by almost everyone as another matter entirely" (p. 163). The major point of disagreement among different writers is the extent to which sex is of primary or secondary significance in its relationship with love. Freud (1921) said: "The nucleus of what we mean by love naturally consists (and this is what is commonly called love, and what the poets sing of) in sexual union as its aim" (p. 90). However, it is important to realize that Freud used the term sex in a much broader sense than others do. Freud attempted to clarify what he meant by sex in a letter to a friend who was a clergyman. Freud wrote: ". . . our word 'erotic' includes what in your profession is called 'love' and is not at all restricted to gross sensual pleasure" (Jones, 1955, p. 440). While it is true that Freud emphasized the importance of the sexual component, he did not advocate, as many of his less well-informed critics assume, the reduction of love to sensuality as an ideal. His real attitude has been noted by Rieff (1961): "Freud considered sensuality without affection a degrading state of affairs, and set forth his conception of a completely normal attitude in love and marriage as a fusion of tenderness with sensuality" (p. 179).

Following Freud, most experts seem to agree that sex is a part of love even if they disagree about how important a part it is. For example, Havelock Ellis (1938) suggests that: ". . . we must distinguish between *lust,* or the physiological sexual impulse, and *love,* or that impulse in association with other impulses" (p. 234). Montefiore (1963) notes: "To admit an element of sex in all human love is no more than to confess our humanity" (p. 69). It also appears that most authorities regard sex within the context of love as a desirable goal and consider sexual behavior apart from love as an unhealthy situation. Nevertheless, there is evidence that many people in our society deviate from this ideal in their actual behavior. Foote (1954) states: ". . . in the United States, what is preached and what is practiced sexually are widely discrepant" (p. 160). The following quotation from Ellis (1962) provides a good example of this discrepancy.

A man may profess to believe one thing even while he acts at variance with this profession. A man on his way to a bawdy house, and very especially a man leaving a bawdy house with his immediate desires satisfied, may profess to believe that his wife is the only woman in the world for him. Despite his profession, his acts make clear that he does not really believe this. He thinks he *should* believe it perhaps, but the fact is that he does not act accordingly. For behavioral purposes, therefore, we must assume that belief is that upon which one acts (p. 243).

Ellis is calling attention to a situation that many practicing psychologists and psychiatrists acknowledge. Namely, when a person says one thing and does another, his actions are a more accurate indication of his real feelings than his words.

A number of different observations have been offered as evidence that many persons still have difficulty coming to grips with sex. One of the most frequently cited examples of this is the extent to which sexual content has saturated our culture (Sorokin, 1956), particularly in the area of advertising (Foote, 1955) and other mass media, including motion picture films, magazines, books of fiction, newspapers, and other periodicals (Ellis, 1962). For some behavioral scientists, this sexual preoccupation indicates the inability of people in our society to deal with sex openly and honestly. From this point of view, magazines, movies, and other forms of entertainment become sources of vicarious sexual enjoyment which attempt to fill the void created by a lack of more direct sexual gratification. For other social critics, this sexual saturation indicates a general moral decay on the part of society (Sorokin, 1956). A third interpretation perceives this increase in sexual expression as an indication of emancipation from long standing, psychologically unhealthy repression of sexual interest.

In view of these diverse opinions concerning the same facts, it is clear that anyone looking for a single interpretation of this behavior is likely to be disappointed, confused, or both. The simple fact is that there is no universally accepted explanation for our strong interest in sexual behavior. Increased sexual saturation in our society does not satisfy any one motivation; on the contrary, it is likely to reflect many factors. A man or woman who seeks sexual content in a book or movie *may* do so to compensate for sexual frustrations in his or her personal life. On the other hand, this person may be free from the psychological inhibitions that prevent others from exploring sex more fully and completely. Interpretations about any specific behavior made out of the context of the person's background and without knowledge of the total situation are premature and possibly irresponsible. Nevertheless, we are too often prone to pass judgment on another person when the behavior of that person violates our own personal code. What is more likely to reveal a person's attitude toward sex is his appraisal or evaluation of sexual material rather than his willingness to be exposed to it. Unfortunately, too much of the existing literature on love and sex is characterized by the faulty generalizations and premature conclusions that often accompany prejudiced thinking.

Another example that is frequently offered as proof of our unhealthy attitude toward sex is the "double standard." Typically, this phrase refers to the fact that the sexual behavior of men and women is evaluated by different criteria. Specifically, overt sexual behavior is more acceptable for the man than for the woman, particularly before marriage. If we accept the validity of Kinsey's (1953) findings with regard to sexual behavior in the female, however, there is considerable evidence that the prevalence of the double standard is diminishing and is being replaced by greater sexual equality between the male and female. The following are just some of the findings that Foote (1954) suggests support this conclusion: 1) the increase in premarital sexual behavior by women to approximate more closely the behavior of the male; 2) the increasing number of extramarital sexual affairs by women; 3) the steady rise toward equal freedom for the male and female in premarital petting and marital sex play; and 4) the reduction in male insistence that the female be a virgin at the time of marriage. Foote (1954) interprets these changes in sexual attitudes and behavior in terms of more general changes in the role of the female in our society, such as the greater opportunity for women to get better jobs and the decline in the number of legal and political restrictions imposed upon women.

McLuhan and Leonard (1967) attribute the reduction of the double standard to the discovery of the contraceptive pill. In their own words:

The demands for new male and female ideals and actions are all around us, changing people in many a subtle and unsuspected way. But there is one specific product of modern technology, the contraceptive pill, that can blow the old boundaries sky high. It makes it possible for sexual woman to act like sexual man. Just as the Bomb instantly wipes out all the separating boundaries in a flash. The Pill makes woman a Bomb. She creates a new kind of fragmentation, separating sexual intercourse from procreation. She also explodes old barriers between the sexes, bringing them closer together. Watch for traditions to fall (p. 58).

Using this example as just one basis for their argument, McLuhan and Leonard (1967) predict not only the disappearance of the traditional double standard but suggest that "sex as we now think of it may soon be dead" (p. 56). Contrary to some social critics who interpret the increase in sexual permissiveness as potentially destructive to society, McLuhan and Leonard (1967) suggest that the revolution in sexual attitudes and changes in the roles of the male and female may lead to a decrease in socially undesirable forms of sexual behavior, such as homosexuality and prostitution.

Despite the forcefulness of McLuhan and Leonard's argument, there is reason to question the validity of their conclusions. Specifically, there is reason to doubt that any sexual revolution, at least as measured by behavior change, is in fact taking place. Reiss (1966) points out that all the available evidence from major studies does not indicate any significant change in many areas of sexual behavior (e.g., premarital coital rates). There are consistent signs, however, of changes in attitudes toward sexual behavior. As Reiss (1966) notes: "The major importance lies in the increasing acceptance of premarital coital behavior rather than in increased performance of this behavior" (p. 126).

Much of the disagreement that exists with regard to sexual behavior stems from the fact that sex can be motivated by desires other than communicating love and expressing affection. For example, Erich Fromm (1955) suggests: "Sexual desires can be the expression of fear, vanity, or of a wish for domination and they can be the expression of love" (p. 308). Montefiore (1963) writes that sex can serve as a source of "kicks" like alcohol or drugs for those who seek to escape boredom or dissatisfaction with life. According to Allan Fromme (1966), sex can serve as an outlet for tension, depression, and boredom or as a weapon to express aggression. Horney (1937) states that sex can satisfy the desire for reassurance. Persons who have a low opinion of themselves and feel that getting affection from someone else is an impossibility are likely to substitute physical sexual contact for emotional relationships. Clearly, if sex can serve such diverse purposes, any actual increase or change in the sexual behavior of a society cannot be simply explained.

The inability to love

Whenever there are indications that sex is being isolated from love, there are two general ways of understanding the situation. One is to examine the individual's capacity to love another person. The other is to consider whether the person has developed inhibitions against expressing love in the form of sexual behavior. In either case, there is good reason to believe that the capacities to love and to express this love freely are learned through previous experience. By the same token, it appears that the prohibitions and barriers against the fulfillment of sex are also learned, often early in childhood. On this point, Frank (1953) states:

Loving . . . has to be learned by experience. Thus, it is becoming clear that we can invest another with lovableness and respond with loving, only if we have earlier experienced being loved ourselves. We must have once been the focus of another's loving, have had the experience of being invested with worth, treated with tenderness, felt the warm concern and focused interest of someone, in order to be able to love another (p. 33).

Frank is suggesting that the infant or young child who is denied the experiences of intimacy, affection, and tenderness will be handicapped in establishing a love relationship as an adult. This point of view is not unique and has been expressed by other noted psychiatrists. Horney (1937) suggests that one of the basic dilemmas of the neurotic person is the inability to love accompanied by a strong need to be loved by others. According to Horney (1937): "The difference between love and the neurotic need for affection lies in the fact that in love the feeling of affection is primary, whereas in the case of the neurotic the primary feeling is the need for reassurance and the illusion of loving is only secondary" (p. 109). The interesting, if tragic, paradox is that underlying the neurotic's compulsive and insatiable need for love is a basic hostility toward others. This hostility results, according to Horney (1937), from the neurotic's early fears of being abandoned in a world perceived as hostile. Most children do not begin by separating love and sex. They learn to do this. What we tend to forget is that prohibitions against sex may be generalized by the child to include love. English (1953) warns of the consequences of instilling in our young "the conviction that sex is something dirty which man must have and woman must tolerate, albeit sadly" (p. 170).

If we accept the pronouncements of psychologists and psychiatrists that the formation of negative attitudes in childhood can have unfortunate consequences later in life, it is important to understand how these attitudes are established. Some psychologists suggest that sex has to be associated with some form of punishment in order for the child to develop negative feelings toward it. Other psychologists feel that the mere avoidance of frank discussion in the home can create an atmosphere of guilt and anxiety associated with sex. According to this rationale, the child assumes that anything which is avoided must be bad. Even though there is disagreement about the details of how these attitudes are learned or communicated, there is general acceptance of the notion that it is the parents' own attitudes that prevail. A parent who feels comfortable with love and sex is not likely to communicate anxiety or fear to the child. For the parent who has unresolved conflicts in this area, it is an entirely different matter. As Lepp (1963) suggests: "Many married women have never experienced anything in sexuality but boredom and fatigue. How can they tell their daughters that there is anything beautiful or grand about sex?" (p. 30).

Sexual attitudes and religious experience

Tracing the basis of psychological conflicts about love and sex back to what was learned from one's parents does not answer the question of where the parents got their own negative ideas. A frequent answer to this query is that certain religious beliefs are responsible for originating and maintaining the separation between love and sex. A number of writers, including theologians and clergymen of different faiths, have called attention to the traditional devaluation of sex by most organized religions (e.g., Hettlinger, 1966; Montefiore, 1963; Reiss, 1966). For example, Hettlinger (1966) writes that:

. . . the Church has succeeded in leaving its members with the unavoidable impression that sex is a regrettable necessity, and sexual sin the worst of all evils. St. Augustine denied that the sex act originally and properly involved any emotional desire, and developed the doctrine of original sin in such a manner as virtually to equate it with sexual pleasure. It is remarkable how much of the tradition has been elaborated by celibate monks who were either less highly sexed than the average man, or, having sown their wild oats as pagans and having on conversion foresworn their youthful lusts, then proceeded in later life to enforce more rigid standards on the next generation (p. 25)."

Lepp (1963), on the other hand, suggests that sometimes the church is unjustly blamed for developing puritanical attitudes within a person when these attitudes actually reflect other psychological problems of the person. He illustrates this point by citing the case of a father who was driven to incestuous sex play with his daughter as a result of a lack of sexual fulfillment with his wife. His wife's avoidance of sexual contact was, according to Lepp, due to "misguided piety." Kinsey's (1948) findings indicate that religiously active people engage in sexual behavior less frequently both before and after marriage than persons who are less active in the church.

Some observers feel that even though the church is becoming increasingly liberal in its views on sex, it has little influence on the sexual attitudes of people today, particularly young people and college students. Hettlinger (1966) notes: "There are, of course, signs of a reaction against this distortion in ecclesiastical circles; but it will be many decades before the heritage of antisexualism is erased from the image of the church. Under the circumstances it is not surprising that the student, to whom sex is among the most exciting potentialities of life, regards the official codes of Christendom as meaningless" (p. 26). Similarly, Montefiore (1963) writes: ". . . the church's condemnation does not for many people carry the weight that it would have done in former generations. For vast numbers in this country it carries no weight at all" (p. 79). To the extent that these comments are accurate, they provide an insight into the possible origins of man's present confusion regarding interpersonal intimacy. Psychiatrists claim that the separation of love and sex is unhealthy. At the same time, traditional religious values still associate sex with sin. Add to this the biological fact that sex is physiologically pleasurable and the psychological fact that love is greatly rewarding, and you have sufficient ingredients for considerable conflict.

Love, sex, and normality

Unfortunately, there are relatively few tangible bases for establishing meaningful criteria for psychologically healthy or "normal" behavior in the realm of love and sex. Psychologists and psychiatrists are often reluctant to commit themselves in these matters because love and sex are considered by many to be nonscientific, subjective issues which are more appropriate topics for the clergyman and philosopher. Those few psychologists who have written on the topic, typically in textbooks on personal adjustment, either speak in such general terms that their suggestions are of limited practical value, or they prescribe arbitrary standards of acceptable behavior representing their own personal value system. These criteria may have little relevance to someone with a different orientation. Nevertheless, for those who seek a model to follow, guidelines are available.

Maslow (1953) provides a description of some characteristics of love in self-actualizing persons, those rare individuals who are fulfilling their potential as human beings. Typically, self-actualizing behavior in the realm of love and sex involves honesty and freedom of self-expression; the improving of sexual satisfaction with the length of the relationship; the ability to love freely, easily, and naturally, but selectively; the fusion of love and sex within the person, including the tendency not to be satisfied with sex alone or to seek it by itself; greater enjoyment of sexual orgasm but less frequent requiring of it; certainty and comfort in one's respective sex role; acceptance of the loved one's individuality and respect for the other; and a detachment and individuality which includes "a healthy selfishness, a great self-respect, a disinclination to make sacrifices without good reason" (p. 86). Maslow points out that these characteristics should be considered more as impressions than as observations, since, by virtue of their greater desire for privacy, self-actualizing people are difficult to study. Nevertheless, these observations are consistent with the ideas of others such as Schwarz (1951), who describes the "perfect, fully mature human being" as having an "inseparable fusion of sexual impulse and love" (p. 21).

Guidelines for what is acceptable, healthy, or "normal" behavior with regard to sex and love are particularly appealing to those persons in our society who, according to Montefiore (1963), require "packaged morals, devised by experts, and prepared ready for use" (p. 79). It also appears, as Reiss (1966) notes, that,

. . . Basically, the issues involved in sexual relationships are moral issues. They involve the choice of one conception of the good life over another. Such a choice is ultimately a matter of personal conscience; all the social scientist can do is try to illuminate the issues involved, and clarify the consequences of various types of choices" (p. 130-131).

Hopefully, the readings in this section will provide information that will illuminate the issues and clarify what is an intricate but important aspect of man's behavior.

References

Ellis, A. *The American sexual tragedy.* (2nd ed.) New York: Lyle Stuart, 1962. Also available in paperback published by Grove Press (N.Y.).

Ellis, H. *Psychology of sex.* (1938 ed.) New York: New American Library, 1954. Also available in paperback.

English, O. S. Sexual love—man toward woman. In A. Montagu (Ed.), *The meaning of love.* New York: Julian Press, 1953. Pp. 163-178.

Foote, N. N. Sex as play. *Social Problems,* 1954, 1, 159-163.

Foote, N. N. Love. *Psychiatry,* 1953, 16, 245-251.

Freud, S. Group psychology and the analysis of the ego. (1921) In J. Strachey (Ed.), *The standard edition of the complete psychological works of . . .* London: Hogarth Press, 1955. Pp. 67-134.

Fromm, E. *The art of loving.* New York: Harper, 1956. Paperback published by Bantam Books (N.Y.).

Fromm, E. *Man for himself.* New York: Rinehart, 1947. Paperback published by Fawcett World Library (N.Y.)

Fromm, E. Sex and character: the Kinsey report viewed from the standpoint of psychoanalysis. In

Himelhoch, J. & Fava, S. F. (Ed.), *Sexual behavior in American society; an appraisal of the first two Kinsey reports.* New York: Norton, 1955. Pp. 301-311.

Fromm, Allan. *The ability to love.* New York: Farrar, Straus, & Giroux, 1955. Paperback published by Pocket Books, Inc. (N.Y.).

Hettlinger, R. F. *Living with sex: the student's dilemma.* New York: Seabury Press, 1966. Also available in paperback.

Heyns, R. W. *The psychology of personal adjustment.* New York: Holt, 1958.

Horney, K. *The neurotic personality of our time.* New York: Norton, 1937. Also available in paperback.

Jones, E. *The life and work of Sigmund Freud.* Vol. 2. *Years of maturity: 1901-1919.* New York: Basic Books, 1955.

Kinsey, A. C., Pomeroy, W. B. & Martin, C. E. *Sexual behavior in the human male.* Philadelphia: Saunders, 1948.

Kinsey, A. C., Pomeroy, W. B., Martin, C. E. & Gebhard, P. E. *Sexual behavior in the human female,* Philadelphia: Saunders, 1953. Paperback published by Pocket Books, Inc. (N.Y.)

Lepp, I. *The psychology of loving.* Baltimore: Helicon Press, 1963. (Translated by Gilligan.) Also available in paperback.

Levine, L. S. *Personal and social development.* New York: Holt, 1963.

Maslow, A. Love in healthy people. In Montagu (Ed.) *The meaning of love.* New York: Julian Press, 1953. Pp. 57-96.

McCluhan, M. and Leonard, G. The future of sex, *Look,* July 25, 1967.

Montagu, A. *The meaning of love.* New York: Julian Press, 1953.

Montefiore, H. W. Personal relations before marriage. In MacKinnon, D.M., Root, H. E., Montefiore, H. W., & Burnaby, J., *God, sex and war.* Philadelphia: Westminster Press, 1963. Also available in paperback.

Prescott, D. The role of love in human development, *J. Home Economics,* 1952, 44, 173-176.

Reiss, I. L. The sexual renaissance: A summary and analysis. *J. soc. Issues,* 1966, 22, 123-137.

Rieff, P. *Freud: the mind of the moralist.* New York: Anchor Books, 1961. (Doubleday). Also available in paperback.

Schwarz, O. *The psychology of sex,* Harmondsworth, Middlesex: Penguin Books, 1951.

Sorokin, P. A. *The American Sex Revolution.* Boston: Porter Sargeant, 1956.

Role of love in human development [1]

DANIEL A. PRESCOTT

Love has been discussed, analyzed, praised, and debated for thousands of years, but there is still disagreement about what it is. In this article the author reviews a variety of definitions of love found in the literature of the behavioral sciences in an attempt to establish whether love is a reality or a cultural delusion. He formulates several hypotheses about the nature of love and concludes by speculating on the role of love in human development.

Daniel Prescott, Ed.D., is Professor of Education and Director of the Institute for Child Study at the University of Maryland. He is the author of two books, *Emotion and the Educative Process* and *The Child in the Educative Process*.

This paper will address itself to three questions: (1) Is love a reality or a delusive romantic construct of our culture? (2) If love *is* a reality, what is its nature? If love *is* a reality, what is its role in human development? In preparing this paper, I examined several dozen books in human development, educational psychology, cultural anthropology and sociology, psychiatry, and biography. In the majority of books in human development and educational psychology the word love did not occur. When it did occur, it was used without definition for the most part. I feel that if love *is* a reality, we need seriously and scientifically to study its influence on human lives and to learn what conditions are favorable to its enhancement and fulfillment. If it is not a reality, we shall need to study the reasons for the emergence of so strong a myth, so frustrating an aspiration, so delusive a pretension. There is a remarkably small amount of scientific material now available about it.

A very brief review of the ideas found in the books examined comes first. Breckenridge and Vincent *(1)*, Strang *(2)*, and Barker, Kounin and Wright *(3)* all mention love as a reality. The general idea expressed is that love markedly influences behavior, development, and adjustment. One notes a vagueness about the nature of love as a positive force and finds much more specificity about the negative effects of lack of love and of inappropriate use of love relationships. Kluckhohn and Murray *(4)* give a great amount of material about sexual behavior and about family processes but no discussion of love as such.

James Plant *(5)* clearly regards love as a reality but does not define it. Love affords children a basic security, a sure feeling of belonging, he says. Insecure, unloved children show anxious, panicky symptoms that contrast with the aggressive overcompensation of inadequate children. He shows that confusion about their security often arises as children try to meet the learning and behavioral demands set for them by the authority of their parents and of society and again as they struggle for independence.

Harry Stack Sullivan *(6)* defines love: "When the satisfaction or the security of another person becomes as significant to one as is one's own security, then the state of love exists."

From *Journal of Home Economics*, XLIV, No. 3 (March 1952), 173-176. Reprinted by permission of the author and publisher.

[1] This paper was presented at an AHEA sectional meeting of the American Association for the Advancement of Science in Philadelphia on December 23, 1951.

Overstreet (7) says,

The love of a person implies not the possession of that person but the affirmation of that person. It means granting him gladly the full right to his unique humanhood. One does not truly love a person and yet seek to enslave him—by law, or by bonds of dependence and possessiveness. Whenever we experience a genuine love we are moved by the transforming experience toward a capacity for good will.

Fromm (8) coins the term "productive love" because the word love as popularly used is so ambiguous. The essence of love, he contends, is the same whether it is the mother's love for a child, our love for man, or the erotic love between two individuals. Certain basic elements are characteristic of all forms of productive love. They are: care, responsibility, respect, and knowledge. He says,

Care and responsibility denote that love is an activity, not a passion . . . the essence of love is to labor for something, to make something grow. . . . Without respect for and knowledge of the beloved person love deteriorates into domination and possessiveness. Respect . . . denotes the ability to see a person as he is, to be aware of his individuality and uniqueness. . . . Love is the expression of intimacy between two human beings under the condition of the preservation of each other's integrity. . . . To love one person productively means to be related to his human core, to him as representing mankind.

Fromm also contends that love of others and of ourselves are not alternatives,

The affirmation of one's own life, happiness, growth, and freedom is rooted in one's capacity to love. . . . If an individual is able to love productively he loves himself too. . . . Selfishness and self-love, far from being identical are actually opposites. . . . The selfish person does not love himself too much but too little, in fact he hates himself. . . . He is necessarily unhappy and anxiously concerned to snatch from life the satisfactions which he blocks himself from attaining. . . .

The recurring mention in the literature of the relatedness of love for self (self-respect), love for other individuals, and love for man-kind led me to examine biographies and writings of three men who have lived lives of great devotion to mankind: Kagawa, Gandhi, and Albert Schweitzer.

Kagawa (9) says,

Love awakens all that it touches . . . creation is the art of life pursued for love. . . . Love is the true nature of God. . . . In social life human beings meet and love one another through a material medium. . . . Love spins garments for itself out of matter . . . through love economic life appears as the content of the spiritual. . . . Real reconstruction of society can be accomplished only through the operation of education through love. . . . If we view economics so, the study of it changes into a science of love. . . . Art must create externally beautiful objects and internally it is itself love.

The practical social and political application of love has worked several miracles in India during our times. Gandhi (10) said,

To be truly non-violent I must love my adversary and pray for him even when he hits me. . . . We may attack measures and systems. We may not, we must not attack men. Imperfect ourselves, we must be tender towards others . . . forgiveness is more manly than punishment.

Gandhi contended that God is love and can be known only through action. "Faith does not permit of telling. It has to be lived and then it is self-propagating."

Albert Schweitzer (11) is another extraordinary international figure who has accomplished the apparently impossible during the past 50 years. He has tremendous reverence for life and respect for the dignity of all human beings and believes that love is the great force of the universe. He says,

By the spirit of the age the man of today is forced into skepticism about his own thinking in order to make him receptive to truth which comes to him from authority . . . [but] it is only by confidence in our ability to reach truth by our own individual thinking that we are capable of accepting truth from outside. . . . Man must bring himself into a spiritual relation to the world and become one with it. . . . Beginning to think about life and the world leads a man directly and almost irresistibly to reverence for life . . . the idea of love is the spiritual beam of light which reaches us from the Infinite . . . in God, the great first cause, the will-to-create and the will-to-love are one. . . . In knowledge of spiritual existence in God through love he [man] possesses the one thing needful.

Each of these three men was a man of action who accomplished the seemingly impossible during his lifetime in the first half of this our twentieth century. Each affirmed that love was a central dynamic in his accomplishment, love of other individuals, love of mankind, and love of God. Theirs certainly was "productive love." We may, therefore, regard our first question as answered in the affirmative. Love does exist. It is a potent reality.

The nature of love

Now what about the nature of love? On the basis of this little research, I have developed a number of theses about love. They will be presented with brief mention of the degree to which they seem to be supported by ideas in the material already cited.

1. *Love involves more or less empathy with the loved one.* A person who loves actually enters into the feeling of, and so shares intimately the experiences of, the loved one and the effects of experiences upon the loved one. Sullivan indicates something of how this comes about *(12):*

If another person matters as much to you as you do yourself, it is quite possible to talk to this person as you have never talked to anyone before. The freedom which comes . . . permits nuances of meaning, permits investigation without fear or rebuff which greatly augments the consensual validation of all sorts of things.

2. *One who loves is deeply concerned for the welfare, happiness, and development of the loved one.* This concern is so deep as to become one of the major values in the organized personality or "self" structure of the loving person. All sources studied seem to agree on this proposition. It is especially validated by the lives of Kagawa, Gandhi, and Schweitzer. Each of them has shown by his actions that he values the human beings whom he serves

not only as much as he values himself but even more.

3. *One who loves finds pleasure in making his resources available to the loved one,* to be used by the latter to enhance his welfare, happiness, and development. Strength, time, money, mind—indeed all resources—are happily proffered for the use of the loved one. This implies that a loving person acts with and on behalf of the loved one whenever his resources permit and the action is desired by the loved one. The loving person is not merely deeply concerned about the welfare, happiness, and development of the beloved; he *does* something to enhance them whenever possible. All sources seem to agree on this proposition, too.

4. *On the one hand the loving person seeks a maximum of participation in the activities that contribute to the welfare, happiness, and development of the loved one.* On the other hand, the loving one accepts fully the uniqueness and individuality of the loved one and accords him freedom to experience, to act, and to become what he desires. This thesis is agreed to by nearly all of our sources.

5. *Love is most readily and usually achieved within the family circle but can be extended to include many other individuals, or categories of people, or all of humanity.* For Schweitzer it also includes all living things and the Creative Force of the universe—God. In the same way a person can advantageously experience love from a limitless number of other human beings and living things. Of course, genuine full love is hard to achieve even with a few persons, as several of our sources pointed out. But this is not proof that with greater scientific understanding of its processes we cannot create conditions that will favor its broadening.

6. *The good effects of love are not limited to the loved one but promote the happiness and further development of the loving one as well.* Love is not altruistic, self-sacrificing, and limiting for the one who loves. On the contrary, it is a reciprocal dynamic which greatly enriches the lives of both. This idea is not too clearly stated in a number of our sources but seems implied where not stated in nearly all.

7. *Love is not rooted primarily in sexual dynamics or hormonal drives,* although it may well have large erotic components whether between parents and children, between children, or between adults. Fromm seems to support

this position when he says that the essence of productive love is the same no matter who is concerned.

8. *Love affords many individuals fundamental insights into and basic relationships to humanity and to the Forces that organize and guide the universe.* It gives many persons a basic orientation in the universe and among mankind. It can become the basis for faith in God. I was surprised to find support for this thesis from all sources. For example, Plant affirms that *(13)* "from early adolescence on, the Church gives a great many children a sense of belongingness which has greater continuity and certainty for the individual than anything provided by his parents." The other sources also intimated that love is a great aid in the developmental tasks of orienting the self toward the rest of mankind and within the universe toward God.

These eight theses, I hope, may be of some aid in analyzing the nature of love and the processes by which it develops. Admittedly they represent only a first and faltering attempt. But if they are sufficient to focus more scientific attention and research on love, the purposes of this paper will have been accomplished.

The roles of love in human development

Now we address ourselves to the third question. Since love does exist, it potentially can become a reality in the life of every human being. Then, if our theses regarding the nature of love are true, what roles can love play in human development? This question will be answered during the next decade, I hope, by a whole series of researches. The findings should fill many monographs and some books. In the meantime, I should like to propose a series of hypotheses as to the probable findings of these researches, in the hope of suggesting profitable research leads.

The first hypothesis is that being loved can afford any human being a much needed basic security. To feel that one is deeply valued because one is, rather than because of the way one behaves or looks, is to feel fundamentally at home whenever one can be with the person who loves one so. From earliest infancy to most advanced age this feeling of being deeply valued is an important precondition to meeting life's challenges and expectations, to doing one's best without unhealthy stress.

The second hypothesis is that being loved makes it possible to learn to love oneself and others. The capacity of infants for empathy, before language development makes more explicit communication possible, permits the feeling of the nature of love very early in life. The closeness of mutual understanding among pre-adolescent peers makes its joyous expansion natural. The hormonal creation of unrest in the presence of peers of the opposite sex pushes its further development until it is stilled by intimate sexual sharing of vivid life in marriage. The mystery and the creative fulfillment that come with the first baby begin a cycle of nurturance and guidance of a rapidly developing new personality that brings tremendous fulfillment through the years. But this wonderful growth and enrichment of life by love seems possible only to those who first were loved by others. Indeed we suspect that a person who has never been loved cannot fully respect and love himself but must always restlessly be reassuring himself as to his fundamental worth.

Our third hypothesis is that being loved and loving others facilitates winning belonging in groups. Of course, winning roles in group activities requires that the individual have knowledge and skills that are valuable in carrying on the activities of the group. Of course, conformity to group customs and codes is necessary to group belonging, and being loved contributes to none of these. But being secure through love and being able to give love, favors personality characteristics that are easy and attractive in group situations. Such a child or youth has no reason to lord it over others, to be aggressive and hostile, or to be shy and withdrawing. Such children do not need constantly to climb in status by calling attention to the failure and inadequacy of others.

A fourth hypothesis is that being loved and loving in return facilitates identifications with parents, relatives, teachers, and peers by which the culture is internalized more readily and organizing attitudes and values are established easily. When one feels loved and loves in return, it is easy to learn that which is expected; it is easy to believe that which one's objects of love believe and to aspire in the directions encouraged by one's objects of identification. The unloved child feels so much insecurity that he scarcely dares try his wings in learning. Or he is so full of hostility that he tends to reject what he is told and to refuse to meet the expectancies that face him, as a way of demonstrating his power to himself. Obviously the readiness of loving persons to provide meaningful experiences and to aid them in the learning process are further facilitations that give great advantages to loved children.

Our fifth hypothesis is that being loved and loving facilitates adjustment to situations that involve strong unpleasant emotions. When a loved child fails at something, the failure does not cut so deep as to make him doubt his basic worth because he is still secure in that love relationship. Conseqently, he is more easily reassured and encouraged to try again and again. In contrast, the unloved child who fails is in double jeopardy. To his insecurity is added the feeling of inadequacy, and the world looks blacker and blacker. When a loved child is frightened, he can literally or figuratively take the hand of the person who loves him, approach and examine the terrifying situation, learn its true dimensions, and more readily find the courage to face it. But terror to the unloved child is unfaceable and overwhelming. Punishments, penalties, and the demands of authority are bearable for loved children because they do not imply rejection or fundamental lack of worth. Consequently, they are analyzable by the loved child, who more easily can perceive their meaning and take them in stride. But to the unloved child these things may be taken as indicators of personal rejection or of unfavorable status. Resentment, rebellion against authority, hostility against peers who seem more favored, or fundamental doubts of own worth ensue.

All of our hypotheses about the role of love in human development show it as a powerful facilitator of wholesome and full self-realization. As Bruno Bettelheim has so ably pointed out, *Love Is Not Enough* to cure badly maladjusted children. But it surely is a great aid to their adjustment and, best of all, it is a great preventive of maladjustment for the children who are fortunate enough to feel it constantly as they face their evolving developmental tasks.

References

1. Breckenridge, Marian E., and Vincent, Elizabeth L. *Child development*. Philadelphia: W. B. Saunders Company, 1943.

2. Strang, Ruth. *Introduction to child study*. New York: The Macmillan Company, 1951.

3. Barker, Roger G., Kounin, Jacob S., and Wright, Herbert F. *Child behavior and development*. New York: The McGraw-Hill Book Company, 1943.

4. Kluckhohn, Clyde, and Murray, Henry A. *Personality in nature, society and culture*. New York: Alfred A. Knopf, 1948.

5. Plant, James. *The envelope*. New York: The Commonwealth Fund, 1950.

6. Sullivan, Harry Stack. *Conceptions of modern psychiatry*. Washington, D. C.: William Alanson White Psychiatric Foundation, 1947.

7. Overstreet, Harry. *The mature mind*. New York: W. W. Norton & Company, Inc., 1949.

8. Fromm, Erich. *Man for himself*. New York: Rinehart & Co., Inc., 1947.

9. Kagawa, Toyokiko. *Meditations*. New York: Harper & Brothers, 1950.

10. Fischer, Louis. *The life of Mahatma Gandhi*. New York: Harper & Brothers, 1950.

11. Schweitzer, Albert. *Out of my life and thought*. New York: Henry Holt & Co., 1949.

12. Sullivan, Harry Stack. *Op. cit.*, p. 20.

13. Plant, James. *Op. cit.*, p. 26.

Love [1]

NELSON N. FOOTE

Almost all definitions of love emphasize that it is to some extent a matter of emotional arousal. In this essay, however, the author discounts emotionally based interpretations of love and suggests that love is a function of one's competence in interpersonal relations. The views expressed provide an interesting and stimulating contrast with the hypotheses developed in the previous article. Dr. Foote reviews and evaluates some existing definitions of love and describes some of our current attitudes toward it. He postulates what kinds of conditions provide the most favorable climate for the growth of love and develops some ideas about the nature of love which deviate from the more traditional views.

Nelson N. Foote, Ph.D., is presently a sociologist with the Consumer Behavior Research Division of the General Electric Co. He was formerly Associate Professor of Sociology and Director of the Family Study Center of the University of Chicago. Dr. Foote is the co-author of two books, *Identity and Interpersonal Competence* and *Housing Choices and Housing Constraints*.

The title of this paper has provoked comments from friends and acquaintances ever since it was publicly announced. If those comments are classified according to the attitudes they express, they appear to fall into four rough categories: *cynical, joking, sentimental,* and *matter-of-fact.* Comments falling into the fourth category were least frequent, totaling three cases out of perhaps twenty. Of these three persons, two pointed out to me that love is not considered a proper subject for academic discourse: one claimed that the title would draw only a group of moralistic or sentimental listeners, lacking in scientific motive; the other claimed that the regular academics would be scornful unless I devised a more pompous and wordy title. The third merely made the cryptic remark that it takes courage to speak on this subject. This paper is aimed at drawing scientific attention to a matter-of-fact attitude toward love. Serious matter-of-factness toward love is a minority point of view even among professed social scientists. Indeed, one gains some introductory illumination of the subject from recognizing that the first three categories of comments are far more representative of the common approach to love.

Ambivalence

Cynicism, joking, and sentimentality alike bespeak a fundamental ambivalence toward love. Cynicism is the attitude of a person who is afraid that he will become the victim of illusions—illusions which he believes exist, entrap others, and are dangerous to himself. He hungers and thirsts for beliefs he can trust, but he never finds any that he can trust. Joking is the classical symptom by which the field ethnologist identifies status relationships that evoke conflicting emotions. And sentimentality is of course the lavish counterfeiting of genuine emotion that occurs when genuine emotion is deemed appropriate in a particular social situation but is not forthcoming spontaneously.

Freud believed that ambivalence was charac-

[1] This paper was presented at the Fourth Annual Symposium of the Committee on Human Development, Univ. of Chicago, January 31, 1953.

teristic of all human love, and he also appeared to believe that the characteristic complement of love was hate. There is much truth in what he says, but at the present time some refinement and qualification are required. In general, the appearance of ambivalence in love relationships is probably peculiar to our own highly competitive society and may not be characteristic of other times and places. To suggest that it may happily be made to disappear in our own time is the only preachment I would proffer in this paper.

To understand how ambivalence toward love may diminish and disappear requires more precise analysis than is implied by the simple concept of ambivalence as the concurrence of love and hate. In a competitive society, as Bacon long ago pointed out, "he that hath wife and children hath given hostages to fortune." One who entrusts himself fully to another may find his credulity and kindness exploited. His love may be rejected or betrayed. To expose oneself to another is to run the risk of getting hurt. It may take only foolhardiness, among specialists in human development, to talk about love, but it does take courage to love in a society like our own. Many dare not try; they fear involvement. In short, fear rather than hate appears to be the original rival of love in the ambivalent situations that one encounters daily.

To be sure, when the fear seems justified by some act of the other, then the sense of betrayal is keen, and hostility is at once engendered. Several years ago I formed a habit of collecting clippings about domestic crimes in which wives, husbands, and children burned, poisoned, shot, and butchered each other. These clippings mounted so fast that I soon had a manila folder full of them. I was very glad to terminate the habit by donating the whole batch to Robert Hess of the Committee on Human Development, who has been doing a study of aggression in families for the United States Public Health Service. Aggression against the other is always potential in love relationships, but it forms a secondary and conditional phase; the fear of being hurt oneself is primary and continuous. Yet to the extent that one is withheld from entering into love relationships by fear of being hurt, he is deprived of love and may crave it all the more.

This unrequited craving for love, in a so-ciety which demands the seal of love upon most interpersonal relations, leads not only to the characteristic expressions of cynicism, joking, and sentimentality, but also to a kind of self-renewing vicious circle. The signs of love are demanded, disbelieved, and demanded again. The oftener they are required, the oftener they are simulated; the more often they are distrusted, the more often further reassurance is demanded—until it is a wonder that any sound currency for conducting valid exchanges remains in use at all. The inflation of amatory declaration in this country has regularly puzzled foreign visitors. Fortunately some Americans do develop a keen and insistent ear for the real article, whereby they can detect it beneath the babble of spurious affirmations. The honored heroes of our best fiction are those who can with relentless accuracy distinguish true from false in this shadowy realm; they are sparing in terms of endearment to the point of taciturnity.

Competence

A matter-of-fact approach to the study of love requires a redefinition and even some reconceptualization of its nature. Some would doubt that anything new could be said on a subject that has been popular for so many thousands of years. Can contemporary social scientists, for instance, improve upon the old Greek distinction between *eros* and *agape,* the sexual and nonsexual types of love? Did Freud really add something to modern knowledge and insight by his many assertions that *eros* really underlies the expressions of *agape?* In attempting to answer these challenges, it may be helpful strategy to pick out the most basic innovation of modern social science and proceed from that to an appropriately contemporary redefinition of love.

The most basic finding of recent social science is undoubtedly the novel proposition that human nature, conceived in terms of personality, is a cultural product, subject to a continuous process of re-creation and development. This concept is not to be found in the Greeks or the Scholastics or even, in its present form, in the philosophers of the Enlightenment, though these last certainly turned scientific attention to processes of history, change, and progress. As late as Darwin, the notion that personality is biologically given still had sway.

The evolutionary model of thought, however, with its emphasis upon continuous creation, eventually became the basis for overthrowing so-called Social Darwinism (approximately in the 1930's in this country if we count in terms of majority sentiment). Even so, we still have with us those who fear that national intelligence is declining because the Ph.D.'s have so few children.

There is a growing number of scholars nowadays who conceive that not only personality, in general, but intelligence, in particular, are modifiable and develop differently in both kind and degree as social and cultural conditions are varied. In fact, it seems possible that purposive development of personality along optimal lines may soon become an objective of public policy. The recent report of the Midcentury White House Conference on Children and Youth carries a title, *Personality in the Making*,[2] which almost any previous decade would have found revolutionary.

In a recent article entitled, "The Role of Love in Human Development," Daniel Prescott attempted to arrive at a satisfactory definition of love in order to explore its implications for human development.[3] He reviewed critically the conceptions of love mentioned by the standard writers of the standard textbooks on child development, and also those set forth by such psychiatric thinkers as James Plant, Erich Fromm, and Harry Stack Sullivan.[4] The results of his library search are interesting, but it seems more illuminating to pursue his quest in the opposite direction. That is, it may be better to define love in terms of human development, as follows: *Love is that relationship between one person and another which is most conducive to the optimal development of both.* This optimal development is to be measured practically in the growth of competence in interpersonal relations.

Sullivan's definition is a helpful beginning: "When the satisfaction or the security of another person becomes as significant to one as is one's own satisfaction or security, then the state of love exists."[5] But his approximation is static, unilateral, and still tinged with the Christian morality which honors sacrifice of oneself to another as an ultimate good, though it may thwart the development of both. Erich Fromm's notion of productive love, and his insistence upon the legitimacy of self-love,

appear more analytically precise and valid: ". . . love is an activity and not a passion . . . the essence of love is to 'labor' for something and 'to make something grow'. . . . To love a person productively implies to care and to feel responsible for his life, not only for his physical existence but for the growth and development of all his human powers . . . without *respect* for and *knowledge* of the beloved person, love deteriorates into domination and possessiveness."[6]

Fromm might well have gone further than he did to exclude other kinds of behavior as not coming within a definition of love which emphasizes mutual development—for example, dependency, conceit, and mere tribal identification with kindred. The director of a child care agency told me recently that her agency had come to recognize that the best mother for a child was not the one who regarded the child as an extension of the parent, but the one who could regard the child as *another person,* to be respected, responded to, and understood for his own sake.

If, by definition, we love most those to whose development we contribute most, whether wittingly or unwittingly, such a definition has specific virtues over the popular conception of love as a fluctuating emotion which can only to a degree be stabilized by ritual or pretense. Rather, love is to be known by its works. The familiar emotions may be evoked intermittently by the works of love; there is nothing drab about the joys of receiving the actual evidence of love as against merely its verbal affirmation; but the more important point is that the growth of love can thus be charted as a developing process, progressive fruition of which is more to be desired than attainment and fixation of a particular state of emotional response. From this viewpoint, one values another not only for what he is at the moment but for his

[2] Helen Leland Witmer and Ruth Kotinsky (eds.), *Personality in the making: The fact-finding report of the Midcentury White House Conference on Children and Youth,* New York: Harper, 1952.
[3] Daniel A. Prescott, "The role of love in human development," *J. Home Economics* (1952) 44:173-176.
[4] James Plant, *The envelope,* New York: Commonwealth Fund, 1950. Erich Fromm, *Man for himself: An inquiry into the psychology of ethics,* New York: Rinehart, 1947. Harry Stack Sullivan, *Conceptions of modern psychiatry,* Washington, D. C.: William Alanson White Foundation, 1947.
[5] Sullivan reference footnote 3: p. 20.
[6] Fromm, reference footnote 3: pp. 98-101.

potentialities of development, and these are necessarily assessed longitudinally and not by comparison shopping. One commits himself to another not on the basis of romantic, forced illusions, but of real possibilities which can emerge with proper cultivation. Trust and appreciation accumulate through proven results as indexed in mutual personal development.

Audience

I want to turn now to the question of the precise delineation of the relationship of lover to loved one—parent and child, husband and wife, friend and friend—which is most conducive to the optimal development of each. A beginning toward the precise characterization of the ideal form of this relationship can be made by likening it to the relationship of artist and audience. There are of course all kinds of artists and all kinds of audiences. But almost every artist is acutely conscious of the bearing of his audience upon his performance and development as an artist. To attain an audience that is critical but appreciative, objective but hopeful, and neither patronizing, nor condemnatory, nor sentimentally adulatory, is the ideal his experience leads him toward. This ideal audience expects from him a performance as good or better that he has given before; it expects him to work hard for it. But it is identified with the artist, and sympathetic in an informed, understanding way. Thus it never unrealistically demands that he exceed his powers, achieve a result he never aimed for, or be something he is not. Best of all is the audience that clearly differentiates between the artist and the work of art, judging the latter as a finished product but the former as a never-fully-disclosed realm of potential productivity. Such an audience is only disappointed when its favored artist does less than his best.

Everyone knows the prodigies of creativity which are occasionally unleashed when a person discovers and is discovered by the perfect critic. Many a person can look back upon an incident in his school career when a sensitive teacher recognized at the critical moment an emerging talent and thereby permanently exalted his conception of himself and his capabilities. These are the moments of love in its sublime power to move. Such incidents are the imputed reference when a husband speaks of his wife as his "best friend and critic," although the phrase has become shopworn through sentimental usage. To be critical is thus to be neither hypercritical nor hypocritical. To achieve the delicate adjustment which is required means that criticism itself must become almost an art. Many a great artist has been intimately associated with a great critic.

The ideal audience, however, is often found among those with whom the artist tends to compare himself in measuring his own worth, as in the case of his fellow students. For it is never quite as positive a stimulus for the artist to have his creative productions praised by a teacher or master, as it is for him to have them praised by those who are themselves his potential emulators and who know intimately what these creative productions cost the artist.

Thus the relationship most conducive to development may be further described as one of social equality and of reciprocity. It cannot be a relationship of superiority and subordination. Nor can it even be the relationship of counselor and client, contrary to some present-day currents of thought, for even the most nondirective counselor-client relationship is unequal and unilateral. It is worth while to glance still more closely at what social equality and reciprocity mean between two persons.

Somewhere Durkheim contends that equality is indispensable if genuine discussion is to occur between persons; Simmel has made the same point with reference to the occurrence of sociability.[7] Discussion and sociability are two of the activities indispensable to carrying on the dialectic of creation and criticism from which comes personal development. By equality, however, is not meant sameness; quite the contrary. Let us take parents and children as the most obvious case where the persons involved are never—unless perhaps in the case of twins—of the same age or powers. The practice of equality may be exhibited by sharing alike in certain valued experiences and by such devices as taking turns—things that are familiar to everyone who ever had brothers or sisters. But obviously it would be ruinous for parents to insist that each child reach the same standard of performance. Rather, each is expected by a loving parent to move toward a standard which is reasonable for a person of his capaci-

---

7 Kurt H. Wolff (ed.), *The Sociology of George Simmel*, Glencoe, Ill., Free Press, 1950, pp. 47-49.

ties. Moreover, the most important expression of the kind of equality I am defining lies in the conception of each child as *ultimately incommensurable with any other*. He may be compared quantitatively to another child in this or that respect, but as a whole person he is unique. Also, as a whole person he is such a pregnant complex, such a rich array of potentialities, that the loving parent can always find some respects in which each child does excel. By developing these special talents or virtues, each child can outshine the others on his own grounds; the competition which is so threatening and destructive when all are judged by a single standard loses its force when each child is judged by his own.

The parent does not have to determine arbitrarily the line of development for which each child is best disposed; he has only to observe attentively the outcome of the child's own search for the notion of his particular talents which is most satisfying and promising, and then to ratify, as only a sympathetic audience can, the correctness of the discovery made. To do otherwise is to be as disruptive of orderly and optimal development as is the patron who tells the artist what he is to create. Wholeness and individuality, integrity and autonomy, are inseparable.

Reciprocity is perhaps a peculiar kind of equality, but so peculiar that it needs careful analysis. Malinowski [8] has analyzed its ubiquitous function in regulating primitive social organization. Someone of equal genius, I hope, will someday set forth in full the way it works throughout interpersonal relations. In the many books and articles on child development, reciprocity rarely gets the attention due it in terms of the scope of its influence. The child who is denied the opportunity to reciprocate according to his powers the favors conferred upon him by his parents is thwarted in the growth of those powers. Many people have no doubt witnessed the crushing effect upon a child of having a parent ignore or disparage a gift which the child has made and tendered him. Conversely, when a child has labored unstintingly to produce some offering and the parent accepts it with honest gratitude and praise, the delight of the child is sometimes almost physically convulsive.

I cannot resist mentioning the first party which my seven-year-old daughter threw for her parents. It consisted only of two pieces of pastry taken secretly from the refrigerator, a small table cloth and napkins spread carefully on her own little table, two cups of milk, and of course two chairs. It was entirely her own idea, and from a realistic point of view it was rather inappropriate, since we had only finished dinner half an hour before. She did not sit down with us after inviting our presence, but stood there giggling and squirming in ecstasy as we thanked her and praised her cooking. She has already learned the role of hostess and fancies grander successes in the future.

To deny a person opportunities for reciprocating is to forestall his respect for himself, to keep him dependent and inferior. This is one point where resentment of do-gooders arises. A person may garner flattery by surrounding himself with dependents, but flattery can hardly match the satisfaction of contributing to the growth of others by stimulating their achievement of autonomy and equality. In fact, the person who insists upon the expression of affection from dependents whom he cannot let go may not be autonomous himself—as in the case of overprotective parents. On the other hand, the encouragement of reciprocation by those of lesser powers is about as strong a medicine for stimulating their growth as is likely to be found. In competition, as studies on recreation show, stimulation is maximal when rivals are equally matched. Equality and reciprocity are not static concepts; it is hierarchy and unilateralism which are static and which hinder development.

Self-transcendence

Any present-day scholar would be loathe to say that the impulse to explore and develop individuality is natural, in the sense of being an inborn imperative. On the other hand, it is certainly an almost universal discovery that development of one's powers is the primary value in life, since these powers are the instruments which provide access to all other values. If a person is permitted freedom to play and is stimulated by a loving audience, he moves on not merely from one requisite developmental task to another, but toward self-chosen goals

---

[8] Bronislaw Malinowski, *Argonauts of the Western Pacific*, Dutton: N. Y., 1950.

which are not requisite but are autonomously affirmed.

No one has quite as well described as has James Mark Baldwin [9]—the father of genetic psychology—the dialectic of personal growth in all its intricacy and cumulative onwardness, whether vicious or benevolent in trend. It is very significant that Baldwin encouraged his wife to translate the two classical treatises on the psychology of play by Karl Groos,[10] for these works stress the importance of play as a kind of practice for the tasks of reality. Some students of human development have lately taken up where Groos left off, and in a few years may go far beyond him. It is nonetheless regrettable for progress in the discipline of human development that there was a fifty-year lapse in serious scientific analysis of the consequences of play.

Art, however, is not play, any more than it is work. It is an activity of intense seriousness and concentration, although it excites joy of a kind and degree which is neither an illusion nor a joking matter nor a hypocrisy. Perhaps art could be called the serious form of play. Both work and play at their best become art. In the best art, the artist performs at the limit of his capacities. By performing at the limit of his capacities, he continually transcends the limits of those capacities. That is, he goes beyond the point he had previously reached in the development of his capacities.

It is at this point that it may be appropriate to mention that at the Family Study Center we are engaged in working out a theory of human development based upon a concept of self-transcendence. I might stick my neck out further and add that this theory in its embryonic form is one of self-transcendence through love. By self-transcendence we have in mind an entirely secular and matter-of-fact approach.

To review briefly some ideas which are by now commonplace: Human beings, as human beings, are among other features distinguished by the acquisition of selves through experience. The self, however, is a symbolic construct postulated for certain kinds of behavior not otherwise explainable. This self develops in terms of abilities to perform various kinds of behavior. There are a number of definable abilities, growth in which may properly be taken as the measures of human development. The process by which these abilities increase

always occurs and is exhibited within a matrix of interpersonal relations.

The Family Study Center is engaged in a series of studies in the measurement and experimental development of a number of these abilities, which we designate jointly as interpersonal competence. The three we are doing research upon are empathy, autonomy, and creativity, but there are others. In order to generate desired movements in these respects, our staff has been devising a number of very specific hypotheses as to the reproducible conditions under which measurable change in the optimal direction regularly occurs. Once these conditions for the growth of interpersonal competence can be validly stated, we shall have the full description of what I have been speaking of as the relationship of love. Love so defined *is* enough.[11]

This conception of love as the interpersonal conditions optimal for self-transcendence is a hard doctrine from which many will shrink, because it puts the claim of love to the test of the results produced. It should have a cauterizing effect upon the sentimentality and falsehood by which a parent can protest that he loves a child while frustrating his development. Likewise it implies a conception of marriage, in which the success of the marriage is judged by the degree to which each partner contributes reciprocally to the continuous development of the other.

The dialectical transactions between artist and audience to which we have referred need not be limited to two persons, though it is convenient to analyze them in this manner. At one time, a child may be considered as a work of art produced by the mother, with the father as audience; at another, by the father, with the mother as audience; and at a third, as himself an aspiring artist engaged in producing some piece of work, with both parents as his audience. Most importantly, as the child increases in interpersonal competence, he becomes a successful artist in evoking desired behavior

[9] James Mark Baldwin, *Social and ethical interpretations in mental developments,* New York: Macmillan, 1899.
[10] Karl Groos: *The Play of Animals,* New York, D. Appleton & Co., 1911. *The Play of Man,* New York: D. Appleton & Co., 1912.
[11] Cf., Bruno Bettelheim, *Love is not enough: The treatment of emotionally disturbed children:* Glencoe, Ill., Free Press, 1950.

from his parents—ideally, their delight rather than their dismay.

Professor Frank H. Knight at the University of Chicago has written profoundly about the matter of love. I would particularly recommend his long essay on "Ethics and Economic Reform." [12] He has been heard to declare that if Western civilization succeeds in developing a workable society on a secular basis, it will be for the first time in history. I believe that the effort to advance human development through a matter-of-fact investigation of the relationships most conducive to self-transcendence is a reasonable and even promising experiment. And I would go further to predict that the proven attainment of desired results in this direction will be a more substantial and enduring source of joy than all the pretended ecstasies of those who still put their hope in nonrational wish-fulfillment.

It now seems in order to take another look at Freud's statement that erotic motivation underlies all other expressions of human ties. If one speaks of humans as selves, it is at least equally as plausible that *eros* is the symbol and *agape* the substance. In an age in which the substance is lacking, people in their loneliness grasp feverishly but vainly for the symbol. If by the progressive restoration of trust through proving the consequence of love in action, we are able to diminish the fear of each other which makes our love so ambivalent, then *eros* as the symbol of love becomes no longer counterfeit, and no longer properly regarded with cynicism, joking, or sentimentality.

---

[12] Frank H. Knight, *Freedom and reform: Essays in economics and social philosophy*, New York: Harper, 1947, pp. 45-128.

Sexuality and sexual learning in the child [1]

JOHN H. GAGNON

The current controversy about the merits of sex education underscores the emotionalism that still characterizes American attitudes toward sexual behavior. Although most psychologists agree that the basis for adult attitudes toward sex is established early in life, many persons are unaware of the subtle ways in which children learn about sex from their elders. This selection discusses the development of sexuality in the child. The author describes how the child's attitudes toward sex do not necessarily correspond to his knowledge about sexual matters. In addition to providing a great deal of useful factual information about sexual behavior in children and adults, the article raises some thought-provoking questions about the merits and limitations of sex education.

John Gagnon is Associate Professor of Sociology at the State University of New York at Stony Brook and was formerly a Senior Research Sociologist at the Institute for Sex Research, Inc. at Indiana University. He is coeditor of the book *Sexual Deviance* and has done research on sex offenders, homosexuality, and adolescent development.

One of the most impressive aspects of this century is its exceptional concern with chil-

[1] This is a revised version of a paper originally published in Italian as "Sessualità ed apprendimento sessuale del bambino." *Scuvola e Città* (1964), 15:249-258. This research was supported by the National Institute of Mental Health Grant No. MH-07742.

dren. This is not to say that our children are loved more intensely or that their loss is mourned more deeply than in previous times, but that there is a special awareness of them as *children*. Only occasionally in prenineteenth-century literature is a child depicted in present-day terms; rather children are represented as smaller and weaker versions of the adults surrounding them. A reading of Chaucer and Shakespeare fails to reveal a special world of the child, and it is not until the nineteenth century that such writers as Wordworth in poetry and Dickens in the novel attest a new and prepossessing concern for the life of the child,[2] and childhood becomes a unique stage during which perceptions and learning are related to age as well as to station. In contrast, the execution of the Princes in Shakespeare's *Richard the Third,* and even the labor of children in the mines and factories in the nineteenth century, were consequences of children sharing with adults the assets and dangers of their common social positions of nobility or proletariat. There was no universal dispensation for age independent of social status even in the nineteenth century, though a change of consciousness was beginning to appear in the genius of the era.

This newfound concern, not only in England, with the child as an entity unlike an adult presaged the fundamental assessment of the impact of a child's experience on his character as an adult, which was the basic contribution of Freud. While much of the discussion of childhood in the late nineteenth century was idyllic and asexual, this tendency would seem to be partially a result of the honorable desire to protect the child from the vicissitudes of adulthood. At the same time, however, the quality of protection given to any individual child often depended upon his presumed innocence. Concurrent with this increasingly prevalent image of children, which is often conceived to have been universal and wrong-headed by modern scholars reacting to "Victorian prudery," there was writing about the sexual capacity of children in British medical literature, focusing upon its dangers, but certainly not denying its existence.[3] Thus the shock for adults of Freud's discoveries was not that children might be involved in sexual activity, but that this activity was not confined to a few evil children and was, in fact, an essential pre-

cursor and component of the development of the character structure of the adult. What superficially appeared to be an aspersion on the innocence of childhood was an assault upon the antisexuality and asexuality of adults. Freud pointed out the many permutations of the sexual impulse, the most important of which was that it never failed to be manifest.

In this process of realization that there was a special character to childhood, and, indeed, that it might require a special psychology, a new consciousness of children developed. While this change has not been universal, it is a characteristic of the United States and other countries of the Western European tradition, and more than likely it will be the dominant orientation of the future.

One of the consequences of this recognition is that adults now have a greater conscious concern with the processes by which children learn about sexuality. During the nineteenth century the popular method of dealing with childhood sexuality when it intruded upon adults was either to suppress the behavior or to deny its existence, and to avoid thinking about it at all as long as it was not a public issue. These methods are to this day the most popular ways of dealing not only with the sexuality of children, but also with that of adults.

However, as sexuality has become more and more of a public concern in the United States, a growing desire has been expressed to instruct children appropriately in sexual matters. Appropriate instruction is usually considered to be that which teaches without provoking either discussion or overt behavior. In this way, it is hoped, the alleged traumas that result either from incomplete information or mislearning may be avoided, and the essential nonsexual character of the child is preserved. In addition, the development of textbooks of sexual knowledge relieves parents of the anxieties and embarrassments of talking about sexuality to their

---

[2] An analysis of this historical change, particularly in France, is the work by Phillipe Ariés, *Centuries of childhood:* New York, Knopf, 1962. For changes in attitudes toward sexuality, see especially pp. 100-127. A remarkably original work tracing from an existentialist point of view the general implications of this change in consciousness is Jan H. van den Berg, *The changing nature of man,* New York: Dell, 1964.

[3] Steven Marcus, "Mr. Acton of Queen Anne Street, or, The wisdom of our ancestors," *Partisan Review* (1964), 31:201-230.

children.[4] Part of this reluctance to talk about sexuality to one's offspring arises from the fact that such discussion may suggest to the child the sexual character of the adult. If the parent describes coitus to the child, then there is the risk that the child will make the correct supposition about parental participation. As will be discussed later in this paper, only a minority of sexual information is in fact learned by children in a legitimate, formal manner either through the school or the parents. However, when discussions are held about the methods of such instruction, it is usually these formal informational channels that are emphasized. Thus such questions as, "What, how much, by what means, and when should I tell my child about sex?," are always cognitively framed as if a rational pedagogy were the solution to the proper ordering of the sexual life, not only of the child, but of the adult. Out of these questions a small but growing literature on how to tell children about sex is appearing, oriented not only to parents but to formal youth groups; in addition, there is some interest in programs of sex education, to be carried on usually in the high schools for children of 15 to 18 years of age. It is in this mode that the majority of effort is directed, even though there is some evidence that it is misdirected and that, even if directed properly, it occurs at considerably later ages than it should.

The rest of this paper is concerned with what seem to be some of the central elements in the development of sexuality and sexual knowledge in children and the role that the formal processes of information-giving may have in this development.

The sexual value system of adults

A prerequisite in any discussion of the sexuality of children is some description of the sexual value system of the adult members of the community. The discussion here, as elsewhere in the paper, is restricted to the United States, less specifically to Western Europe, and probably not at all to non-Western cultures.

The most apparent element in the sexual culture of adults is the degree to which there is no real community of values.[5] There is a cluster of negative values that represents the total body of public sexual norms, but as Lionel Trilling says in evaluating the larger cultural significance of the book, *Sexual Behavior in the Human Male*,[6]

"Nothing shows more clearly the extent to which modern society has atomized itself than the isolation in sexual ignorance which exists among us. . . . Many cultures, the most primitive and the most complex, have entertained sexual fears of an irrational sort, but probably our culture is unique in strictly isolating the individual in the fears that society has devised." [7]

What consensus there is usually is worked out by indirection or through the behavior of sexual pairs. The public system of values in reference to sexuality is clearly supportive of only marital coitus as a legitimate expression of either virtuous or mature sexuality. However, there is a substantial body of evidence that marital coitus has not been the only source of sexuality for the majority of adults, especially males. This capacity of the system of values and the system of behavior to exist side by side not only within groups, but within the same person, is indeed remarkable, so that it is possible for the same individual to report the majority values as well as behavior contradictory to them.

An examination of the specific sexual ad-

---

[4] An example of the confused thought that results from this dilemma—that children should know about sex but not act out their knowledge—is provided by the following paragraph in a relatively sensible popular work on the sexual development of children. "Shielding children from the awareness of adult sex conduct goes without saying. Much more injurious than any play among themselves would be the observation of adult behavior and loose significant talk. As in the case of vulgarities—the greater the prudery the greater the pornography—so the greater the freedom among adults the greater the freedom among children. Also, the greater the denial of legitimate understanding among them, the greater the exploration. Far from being an abnormal or perverted or precocious entrance into heterosexuality, sex play in children is a normal, if socially unacceptable, instance of sex interest, an expression of a normal developmental need. If they are not to provide an answer to that need themselves, we must provide it for them, not only in knowledge of the life processes, but in legitimate though vicarious participation in those processes. Words alone do not satisfy." Francis Bruce Strain, *The normal sex interests of children*, New York: Appleton-Century-Crofts, 1948, p. 139.

[5] It may, in fact, be a myth of the intellectualizing classes that value consensus as an outcome of rational deliberation exists to any extent in lower-class populations. There is a strong tendency among those to whom ideas and language are important to impute the same significance to others for whom words are inadequate or unimportant.

[6] Alfred C. Kinsey, Wardell B. Pomeroy, and Clyde E. Martin, *Sexual behavior in the human male*, Philadelphia: Saunders, 1948.

[7] Lionel Trilling, "The Kinsey Report," in *The liberal imagination*, New York: Doubleday Anchor Books, 1953, p. 216.

justment of pairs of persons reveals that it is quite possible for extensive and long-term sexual relationships—even, and possibly especially, in marriage—to work out to the apparent satisfaction of the two persons involved without a word being spoken about sexual behavior and its consequent pleasure or pain. This seems to be primarily a function of the character of the male and female roles brought to the marriage. The exchange of information between males in American culture is not sexually informative except in an indirect sense. The information comes as part of tales of sexual prowess or of humor in which emphasis is placed on heterosexual expertise or exploits. What evolves from this male-to-male interaction is an image of the sexual self rather than knowledge about sexuality. Among females, on the other hand, while a certain amount of sexual information is exchanged, by far the majority of discussion is related to affection and love. Thus the male is cast in the role of the technical expert, and this expertise is related to his masculine role. Even if he is not expert, there is a substantial constraint on the female not to point this out and not to help in the sexual adjustment, because there is always the problem of revealing to the male how she acquired her knowledge and arousing his anxiety about her ability to make invidious comparisons. Consequently, the sexual relation is learned by and large through the exchange of cues and gestures rather than through discussion or direct experimentation.

This development of adult sexual consensus about acceptable overt behavior through the interaction of pairs of individuals rather than among larger social groups in the community has serious consequences for the nature of public discussion of sexuality, especially in times of controversy. The privatization of sexual consensus means that no one can be sure of the behavior of others, and this insecurity is accompanied by a belief that statements that differ from the conventional norms will be taken as evidence of sexual deviation. The only system of values that can be invoked in a time of sexual controversy is the most conservative, and this often results in the most puritan of the community defining the content of public sex education for children.[8] This lack of consensus makes it very difficult for a body of disinterested opinion about sexuality to exist. Any statement by an individual about sexuality is commonly presumed to be related to the sexual preferences and desires of that individual. In this sense all sexual statements are assumed to be ideological in character. Another consequence of this lack of knowledge and consensus is the degree to which fantasy may be projected into and then shape the sexual situation. In most areas of social activity, a reality check upon individual fantasies is provided either by interaction with other persons or by contact with the mass media; but the sexual area lacks such checks, and the proportion of fantasy probably outweighs the proportion of reality. With these conditions prevalent in the adult sexual community, it is not difficult to see some of the difficulties inherent in parent-child interaction, out of which come the primary experiences that shape character structure and sexual behavior.

Parent-child interaction

It was Freud who developed the first fully articulated theory of psychosexuality,[9] and the stages of psychosexual development, which he called the oral, anal, and genital, have now passed into what might be called the "conventional wisdom." Freud conceived of the sexual character of the child and the processual changes by which the undifferentiated drive becomes the infrastructure of adult sexual life. To a striking extent, Freud's hypotheses were put to use as part of therapeutic programs without conventional empirical testing—except as they were tested in relation to individual patients. The result of this historical accident was that instead of the ideas being adequately judged, two warring camps developed, one believing in Freud as revealed wisdom, and the other rejecting his insights as absolutely unscientific. It is only in recent years that these ideas have received serious treatment from a scientific point of view—that is, one that treats the ideas as subject to confirmation or disproof. This is, in fact, the most important honor that could be done to Freud's work.

---

[8] This is not always true, since in some communities sex education in schools has successfully weathered rather extreme conflicts. However, it is the fear of this situation that keeps most adults silent.

[9] Sigmund Freud, "Three essays on sexuality," *Standard edition of the complete psychological works* 7:135-245, London: Hogarth, 1953.

There are two primary difficulties in the Freudian scheme that are relevant to the problem of childhood sexuality. The first is the location of the instinctual energy within the child; the child is invested with initiatory capacities that would seem to be better allocated to the parent. The second is the rather over-general presumption that all contacts with or stimulation of the end organs of the infant have either a protosexual or completely sexual meaning.[10]

The first of these difficulties has been the emphasis on the instinctual character of the sexual energy source in the child. The child is seen as possessing certain sexual characteristics which express themselves regardless of parental action systems. These actions of the child are viewed, in an older sense of the concept of instinct, as rooted in the constitutional nature of the organism. It is possible to reconceptualize this notion to include that of a transactional information system which exists between the child and the mother, and, while maintaining many of the clinical insights of Freud, to abandon the psychic instinctual model.[11] To suggest this does not require that such central insights as the unconscious and the irrational bases of action be abandoned, but rather that they be reorganized into another noninstinctual theoretical system. It is interesting that Freud should have allocated certain initiatory elements in the interaction between parent and the child to the child's own "nature." This theory projects upon the child—who is less differentiated sexually and therefore less initiatory—the sexual desires of the parents, who are the primal agents in developing, promoting, or repressing the sexual behavior and attitudes of the child. In some sense this may have made it easier for the parent to accept a sexual element in the child by placing it in the realm of constitutional forces. However, it seems more likely that parents may unknowingly be sexually initiatory to their children, and may interpret nonspecific behavior as sexual and respond to it, giving it such a definition to the child.

The second difficulty is the primitive Freudian view that all actions of parents that impinge upon the child or that all of the child's actions of a specific class—for example, thumbsucking—have direct control over or stand in place of certain sexual actions or functions. It is clear that this is too general a formulation, but it does lead to fruitful considerations of the relationships between "nonsexual" parent-child interaction and the resultant sexual behavior of the child. The specific mechanisms by which the parents' behavior in reference to, say, bowel control is related to the sexual functioning of the child, and the hierarchy of significance of the various activities involved in the teaching of this earliest form of control, are currently unknown. However, there is substantial evidence that the experiences of the child early in life have certain lasting and defining influences on the way in which he conducts his sexual life.

The convergence of the early work of Spitz [12] on mother-deprived infants and that of Harlow and others [13] on the Rhesus monkey are two of the most important examples of research pointing out the significance of early learning for sexual development.[14] Spitz found that infants observed in normal homes with excellent mother-child relations had a significantly greater incidence of genital play in the first year of life than did children reared either in an institution with mother-child relations of varying emotional quality, or in a foundlings' home without mother-child relations. Spitz concluded that genital play was part of the normal pattern of development of the healthy child in contact with

[10] It is clear that not all psychoanalysts hold these positions in whole or in part. Unfortunately little effort has been devoted to redefinition. A reconstruction of the Oedipus complex by Rado bears upon the first point very directly. Sandor Rado, Psychoanalysis of behavior: collected papers, New York: Grune & Stratton, 1956, p. 197.

[11] The functions of the sex hormones as an alternative energy source in preparing the organism to receive sexual information is discussed in the following work by John Money: "Components of eroticism in man: I. The hormones in relation to sexual morphology and sexual desire," J. nervous and mental disease (1961) 132:239-248. "Sex hormones and other variables in human eroticism," in Sex and internal secretions, edited by William C. Young, Baltimore: Williams and Wilkins, 1961, pp. 1383-1400.

[12] René A. Spitz, with the collaboration of Katherine M. Wolf, "Autoeroticism; some empirical findings and hypotheses on three of its manifestations in the first year of life," in The psychoanalytic study of the child, 3/4:85-120, New York: Internat. Univ. Press, 1949.

[13] See the following works by Harry F. Harlow: "The nature of love," Amer. Psychol. (1958) 13:673-685. "Love in infant monkeys," Scientific Amer. (1959) 200:68-74. "Sexual behavior in the rhesus monkey," paper presented to the Conference on Sex and Behavior, Berkeley, Calif., 1961 (mimeographed). Harry F. Harlow and M. K. Harlow, "Social deprivation in monkeys," Scientific Amer. (1962) 207:137-146.

[14] This convergence has been noted by Spitz himself in René A. Spitz, "Autoeroticism re-examined: The role of early sexual behavior patterns in personality formation," in The psychoanalytic study of the child, 17:283-315, New York: Internat. Univ. Press, 1962.

an accepting mother. This remains rather global terminology since the acts and attitudes of the mother are not so much specified as hidden in the description; however, it still points to the importance of the early experience. The work of Harlow in rearing Rhesus monkeys in a variety of experimental situations is of equal significance, and, since the adult activities of the monkeys were observed, of even more convincing character. Some of the monkeys were reared with surrogate mothers made alternatively of wire or cloth; others were reared in various combinations of play groups and present or absent mothers. A series of powerful findings was generated by these researches. One was that adult monkeys who had been reared in isolation from both mothers and peers were completely incapable of adult heterosexual contacts, and exhibited symptoms which looked very much like human mental disease. In addition, an important element in the development of the sexual capacity of these animals was the presence of peers; when the infant monkeys were reared with peers but without mothers, the sexual capacity did not seem to be disturbed. Deprivation of peers from the age of three to six months, Harlow contends, "irreversibly blights the animal's capacity for social adjustment." [15] He further suggests, "It is apparent also that sexual activity is stimulated by the mother's grooming of the infant." [16] In this research there is specific evidence that particular patterns of activity of a mother with an infant animal have lasting and permanent impact on the sexual life of that infant when he is an adult.

Thus there exists the beginning of a body of empirical evidence that is supportive of the general Freudian presumptions about early childhood experience. Further, there is some value in viewing the original Freudian conceptions which specified basic developmental sequences as a prototype of the critical-period hypothesis. This hypothesis, which originated in ethological research, has, as pointed out by Caldwell, two possible meanings. One is that beyond a certain point in time the organism becomes immune or resistant to certain types of stimulation, and the second is that during a particular period of time the organism is especially susceptible or sensitive to certain types of modifiers.[17] This is, of course, what is involved in the Harlow findings about deprivation

of peer interaction during the period of from three to six months of age in the Rhesus monkey.

It would appear reasonable to suggest that the developmental sequences suggested by Freud might well be of the critical-period type.[18] However, at this point, while there is evidence that the early period of life is extremely significant, the systems of transactions which are causal are not as yet clearly delineated.

Much of the behavior described above may have sexual consequences for the child; however, except for a few adults who are conscious of Freud, there is little recognition of the significance of differences in parental behavior that have different outcomes for the child. Indeed, even among those who have some recognition of the current fads in childrearing, there is little evidence to suggest that conscious planning of child-parent interaction has done any more than confuse the child about what to expect next. The parent often seems to be working out fundamentally unconscious needs in a pattern of habitual response rather than planning his interaction with the child.[19]

One of the obvious areas in which the behavior of parents toward children has clear-cut sexual consequences is the separate behavioral syndromes that are related to the rearing of male and female children. The work of Money and the Hampsons [20] indicates clearly the early

---

[15] See footnote 13, Harlow and Harlow, p. 138.

[16] See footnote 15, p. 144.

[17] Bettye M. Caldwell, "The usefulness of the critical period hypothesis in the study of filiative behavior," *Merrill Palmer Quart.* (1962) 8:229-242. It is implicit that prior to a certain point in time the organism may well be resistant to learning.

[18] An alternative formulation of the findings on infant behavior from a learning theory point of view may be found in Jacob L. Gewirtz, "A learning analysis of the effects of normal stimulation, privation and deprivation in the acquisition of social motivation and attachment," in *Determinants of infant behavior,* edited by Brian M. Foss, New York: Wiley, 1961, pp. 213-290.

[19] The most thoroughgoing of the planners have been those who have used the Skinner Box with infants, but the outcomes of these experiments are still unclear.

[20] See the following papers by John Money, Joan G. Hampson, and John L. Hampson: "Hermaphroditism: Recommendations concerning assignment of sex, change of sex, and psychologic management," *Bull. Johns Hopkins Hosp.* (1955) 97:284-300. "Sexual incongruities and psychopathology: The evidence of human hermaphroditism," *Bull. Johns Hopkins Hosp.* (1956) 98:43-57. Joan G. Hampson, "Hermaphroditic genital appearance, rearing and eroticism in hyperadrenocorticism," *Bull. Johns Hopkins Hosp.* (1955) 96:265-273.

development of gender role, which they describe as ". . . all those things that a person says or does to disclose himself or herself as having the status of boy or man, girl or woman, respectively. . . . A gender role is not established at birth, but is built up cumulatively through experiences encountered and transacted—through casual and unplanned learning, through explicit instruction and inculcation, and through spontaneously putting two and two together to make sometimes four and sometimes, erroneously, five." [21] These scientists demonstrated that in their cases gender role was usually set by a little after two years of age, and attempts after this time to change the orientation in children who had been placed in the incorrect sex category because of external genital ambiguity had various negative psychic consequences for the child. Other criteria—gonadal or chromosomal—for sex assignment were of minor importance even though they have been assumed to have biological priority.

It is possible to argue, as indeed Money and the Hampsons do, that their research is antithetical and in basic contradiction to theories of innate bisexuality such as those of Freud. However, a more modest middle ground which will admit directionality based on prenatal potentiation of the organism through hormonal effects on the nervous system seems to be the one to take at present.[22] It is possible, as has been pointed out by Diamond, that the abnormal cases studied by Money and the Hampsons may have been less directed toward maleness or femaleness because of lowered hormonal levels and therefore more labile to misprinting in the sense that the latter authors use the term.[23] The biological substrate produced by prenatal hormonal effects may differentially ready the organism to receive the definitions and inputs of masculinity and femininity from the parents. The gender role and its components will then be built on the bisexual biological character, and the gender role will be a resultant of these two kinds of forces rather than the unique product of either. Further, data have been gathered that suggest that persons with anomalous genitalia who have been reared in a gender role opposite that of their biological internal structure have made successful shifts in gender role late in life, and these shifts were often made because the patients felt "something was wrong." [24] This finding suggests that the management of the sexually misidentified child should also take into account his own self-conception and desires rather than simply adhering to one or another rigid therapeutic orientation derived from a specific theory.

Since many of these inputs of information to the child occur without thought upon the part of the parent, it is clear that the actions that are involved even in the development of gender role are quite obscure; however, the fact that the parents are clear in their belief that the infant is either male or female has permanent consequences for the child.[25] Thus the vigor of play, the frequency of father-child as opposed to mother-child interaction, and the tolerance for aggression in the male as opposed to the female infant and child all contribute to the development of the self defined as masculine or feminine. Indeed, one of the purely physical elements that may be connected with the greater intensity of the Oedipus conflict when compared with the Electra conflict is the sheer frequency with which the mother handles the genitalia of the male child in contrast to the frequency with which the father handles the female, and the period in development when the contacts take place. In addition, the mother may have a more sexual definition of the phallus than she does of the vagina. The period of contact, the frequency of contact, and the psychological set of the parents can be expected to have differential consequences for gender role development.

This is an example of sets of actions which spill over indirectly into the sexual area. The phenomenon of indirect learning is probably more important in sexuality than in any other zone of development. These early experiences are primarily important in setting the capacity of the organism to respond to information that comes later on. Therefore, the child in the first years of life does not develop a fully articulated

---

[21] See footnote 20, 1955, p. 285.
[22] William C. Young, Robert W. Goy, and Charles H. Phoenix, "Hormones and sexual behavior." *Science* (1964) 143:212-218.
[23] Milton Diamond, "A critical evaluation on the ontogeny of human sexual behavior," *Quart. Review Biology* (in press).
[24] From studies cited in footnote 23.
[25] John L. Hampson and Joan G. Hampson, "The ontogenesis of sexual behavior in man," in *Sex and internal secretions*, edited by William C. Young, Baltimore: Williams and Wilkins, 1961, pp. 1401-1432.

sexual structure, but rather there are limits and parameters set, within and around which the growing child will operate. Thus the experiences of the child with nurturance and the character of his toilet training define to a greater or lesser degree his capacities to deal in the future with situations which are homologous or analogous to the early experience.

Negative labeling, nonlabeling, and rigidity

Upon examining the interaction of parents and children, one is struck by the frequency of both negative injunctions and what appear to be—at least to adults—unambiguous instructions given to children in their early years. A simple household item like the stove is an example; the toddler is taught that the stove is hot, and whether it is hot or cold at any given moment he is told not to touch it, for a single failure in learning might well be disastrous. As the child grows older, more flexible information and attitudes about fire, temperature, and the stove are learned. The stove may be touched when there is no fire, cooking may be experimented with, and finally a series of rather fine discriminations are learned in order to deal with a common household object. This new information comes in both positive and negative forms and overlays the original information about the hot stove. This form of training is necessary for the child who is operating in a complex environment where the dangers of injury are high. However, as the child grows older, explanations of negative injunctions tend to be based more and more frequently upon rational calculations. Thus the infant who has been warned only about "hot" when he approaches the stove, is informed as he grows older about the dangers of burning himself, and is given a complicated set of responses to use in dealing with the stove.

This early instruction of the child comes from adults in whom the child invests considerable affect. However, in most areas of behavior the influence of the parents, while setting limits upon the capacity of the child to respond, is made less pervasive by the impact of other and later experiences. It is in the area of sexual behavior that this body of apparently unambiguous and negative instructions is least modified by later experience. If the child exhibits behavior which the adult perceives as sexual—

and, as I have noted before, the majority of adults often do not understand the relevance of most of these behaviors to sexuality since in the adult state sexuality and genitality are usually assumed to be congruent—the adult's response is one of two types. The first is to tell the child that it is wrong to behave in that way —that is, to label the behavior as unequivocally wrong. This type of information often will not come as a shock to the child, since parents who respond in this way have already communicated some elements of this attitude to the child in nonverbal learning situations. The second type of response is to nonlabel or mislabel the behavior.[26] When the behavior is observed, the parent attempts to distract the child from what he is doing by interposing tasks which are suggested to be more enjoyable, or by pointing out negative consequences which are not related to the sexual aspect of the behavior—for example, giving hygienic reasons against kissing. As part of the process of mislabeling, the infantile words for the genitals and for the acts of excretion are only replaced fragmentarily by another vocabulary. The negative control of sexual information extends to single words, and the child is left to nonparental agencies for learning the specific informational content of sexuality.

The nonlabeling phenomenon has two major consequences. The first is that the primary negative and dichotomous informational inputs to the child are never revised. The primitive form of conditioning, which constructs only black and white consequences for behavior, maintains itself independently, since the parental figures, who create the sexual capacity of the child through both direct action and indirection, are not reassessed or newly judged. This may be partially related to Freud's discovery of the requirement of transference for successful treatment of neurosis. One of the commonplaces of our time is the ease with which people adjust to a changing technological environment; however, an even greater commonplace is the difficulty in the treatment of mental disease. Freud says in reference to this:

---

26 Robert R. Sears, Eleanor E. Maccoby, and Harry Levin, *Patterns of child rearing*, Evanston, Ill.: Row, Peterson, 1957, pp. 176-217. See pp. 215-216 for the origin of the term *nonlabeling*.

In the absence of such a transference (bearing a "plus" sign) . . . the patient would never even give a hearing to the doctor and his arguments. In this his belief is repeating the story of its own development; it is a derivative of love and, to start with, needed no arguments. Only later did he allow them enough room to submit them to examination, provided they were brought forward by someone he loved.[27]

Thus it is possible for the child to reevaluate his parents' attitudes toward politics, vocations, and religion, for in these areas the parents have interacted with the child not only in the primitive negative manner, but also in a more complex and rational way. The child, as he matures, construes the parent as a religious, political, vocational being, and therefore the original inputs to the child are modified by consequent experience. This is not to say that even such reevaluations, especially if negative, are not accompanied by pain and grief and that in many cases they never take place; however, there is little doubt that most children and most adults are unable to consciously conceive of their parents as sexual creatures. Even those persons who remember having observed the primal scene—as well as the larger numbers who have repressed all such memories—should be included in this class. This observation of parental coitus, even if it occurs more than once—which is more likely to happen to those living in poor and crowded circumstances—is not sufficient to create an articulated sexual image of the mother or the father, whatever else it might do.[28] It is very difficult for children to believe that their parents even existed prior to their birth, and this primacy of mother as only mother, and father as only father continues long into adolescence. Even after the experience of coitus, it is extremely difficult for a young man or woman to conceive of his parents in the same roles. It is of great significance that the original organization of sexual learning and attitude is never challenged in any major way, and it is not easily possible for the growing child to revise these early conceptions. Of course, in addition to the parents, other agencies of socialization serve to modify early nonsexual learning, but once again the absence of such processes in the area of sexuality should be noted.

The second consequence of nonlabeling is that of spillover from one training experience to another. As pointed out above, there is an influence on sexual behavior arising from early contact between parents and children which is not recognized as sexual by the parents, and the character of which is not clearly understood at the present time. However, there is one element which seems of greater significance than many others—the problem of the control of aggression and the manner in which training for aggression spills over into sexuality. If the sexual domain is left relatively empty and undefined by processes of nonlabeling, there seems to be a flow of aggression into this area. This has very basic consequences for both males and females, for if the sexual area is left empty, or if only the primitive forms of learning are in the child's repertoire, the differential training and control of aggression in the boy or the girl can come to characterize their sexuality as well. The fact that male children are usually more aggressive than females, and that this aggression is aided and abetted by parents, suggests that it is through the aggressive component of the personality that the male child frees himself from the repression of the sexual drive. In the case of females the sexual component is both nonlabeled and repressed, and the aggressive component is repressed as well; and so the typical adult female has a more responsive and less initiatory personality structure.[29]

This phenomenon of nonlabeling or ignoring sexuality may not always have deleterious re-

---

[27] Sigmund Freud, "Transference," *Standard edition of the complete psychological works*, 16:431-447, London: Hogarth, 1963, p. 445.

[28] The chronic use of the term "motherfucker" by American Negro slum dwellers is a case in point. Rather than being directed toward anyone's "real" mother or calling to mind coitus with her, it has an extremely abstract referent. In its use in verbal games which function as outlets for aggression and therefore social ranking among males it is clear that the reference is to womankind. See Roger D. Abrahams, *Deep down in the jungle*, Hatboro, Pa.: Folklore Associates, 1964, for examples and discussion of urban Negro folklore, and especially pp. 259-262 for the meaning of this and other obscenities.

[29] The work of Maslow supports this hypothesis. He shows that women who had higher dominance scores on a dominance-submission scale were more similar to men in other characteristics than similar to low-dominance women. It is quite likely that this shift in characteristics may have resulted from differences in the training for aggression rather than in training for sexuality. Abraham H. Maslow, "Dominance, personality and social behavior in women," *J. Soc. Psychol.* (1939) 10:3-39; and "Self-esteem (dominance-feeling) and sexuality in women," *J. Soc. Psychol.* (1942) 16:259-294.

sults for children. Since many parents have intense anxiety about their own sexuality, the manner and content of their direct instruction about sexual matters might be more damaging to the child than the nonfamilial and informal structures that actually supply the information. In addition to protecting the child from parental anxieties about giving sexual information, it is possible that lack of recognition by adults of the sexual consequences of certain kinds of contacts with children—such as cleaning the genitals or body contact—may free the adults to perform such tasks with lowered anxiety. If they did recognize the fundamentally sexual character of certain of these experiences which are necessary for the development of the child, they might be inhibited from performing them or at least be unable to do so without displaying considerable guilt and upset.

Even after infancy parents create, unawares, situations of sexual learning. Mother-daughter look-alike costumes are an example of this. The mother wears the costume because it makes her attractive, which is an ultimately sexual consideration, while the child ostensibly dresses the same way because it is "cute." The child is modeling elements of adult female sexual attributes without the conscious awareness of the parent. In this example, the linkage is relatively direct. In other situations, such as those involving cleanliness and aggression after the child is verbal, and types of handling and contact with the preverbal child and infant, the adult is even less likely to see these relationships—possibly properly so.

Adult provocation of childhood sexual experiences as actual occurrences, rather than as part of a universal childhood fantasy as posited by Freud after the first crisis in psychoanalytic thought, has been of concern not only to present-day analysts, but to the contemporaries of Freud.[30] The position of Johnson and Szurek, as well as others, is that certain sexual acting-out may be a function of unconscious provocation by the parents, serving to gratify their repressed desires which they project onto their children.[31] Since the acting-out of the children is often restricted to a single area of behavior—often nonsexual—Johnson and Szurek have labeled this phenomenon as superego lacunae.[32] Since it is the function of parents to provide and indeed call forth certain sexual functions in the child, the acting-out of the child who needs

therapy must be distinguished from the patterns of development of "normal" children who at least do not make the kinds of signs of distress that provoke the interest of treatment agencies. What is distinctive of the parents of the acting-out child is the openly sexual content of interactions between parent and child; and even though the parents may not be conscious of the consequences of the interaction, they remember (without analytic uncovering of repressed material) specifically sexual discussions and characterizations of the child's behavior.[33] It would seem that the distinction between these parents and those who do not have acting-out children is the fact that the latter are less likely to freely and aggressively define the children sexually. Indeed, it may be really impossible for any adult to consciously intervene in the sexual life of the child without a burden of guilt that will perhaps overwhelm both him and the child. Ferenczi suggests that in this situation the child will come to identify with the adult and will introject the adult's guilt and anxiety so that the child feels both innocent and culpable at the same time.[34] In the case of certain pathological adults, the calling forth of sexuality on the part of the child by the adult—a customary characteristic of the learning of sexual patterns—becomes a disorganizing and disruptive sexual experience.

The children's world

The capacity for specifically sexual pleasure (as defined by orgasm) has been observed in both male and female children as early as four months.[35] This is clearly not present in

[30] Bernard C. Glueck, Jr., "Early sexual experiences in schizophrenia," in *Advances in sex research*, edited by Hugo G. Beigel, New York: Harper and Row, 1963, pp. 248-255. Karl Abraham, "The experiencing of sexual traumas as a form of sexual activity," *Selected papers of Karl Abraham, M.D.*, London: Hogarth, 1927, pp. 47-63. Sandor Ferenczi, "Confusion of tongues between the adult and the child," *Internat. J. Psycho-Anal.* (1949) 30:225-230.
[31] Adelaide M. Johnson and S. A. Szurek, "The genesis of antisocial acting out in children and adults," *Psychoanal. Quart.* (1952) 21:323-343. Edward M. Litin, Mary E. Griffin, and Adelaide M. Johnson, "Parental influence in unusual sexual behavior in children," *Psychoanal. Quart.* (1956) 25:37-55.
[32] See Johnson and Szurek, in footnote 31, p. 323.
[33] See the case reports in Litin, Griffin, and Johnson, in footnote 31.
[34] See Ferenczi, in footnote 30, p. 228.
[35] Alfred C. Kinsey, Wardell B. Pomeroy, Clyde E. Martin, and Paul H. Gebhard, *Sexual behavior in the human female*, Philadelphia: Saunders, 1953, p. 103.

all children; however, the capacity seems to develop steadily over time, with more and more children at each age level being able to respond to specifically sexual stimuli. Shortly after puberty most males in the United States (90 percent by age 16) have had orgasmic experience, and this same figure is attained by age 29 among females.[36]

However, the development of the physical capacity to respond in a specifically sexual manner probably only complicates the already difficult situation in which children learn to deal with sexual information. As noted above, the phenomenon of nonlabeling or mislabeling leaves the young child without a vocabulary with which to describe his physical or psychic experiences.[37] This specific absence of terminology has two major consequences. The first is the tendency for fantasy to overrun the sexual life of the child. The mysterious penis that must exist behind the female pubic hair, the feeling that females have been castrated, and other childhood fantasies are common, because there has been no system of naming which will adequately control the child's nascent interest in his own or others' bodies.[38] The second consequence of the lack of a controlling set of symbols is probably related to the tendency for children to identify their sexual organs with excretory functions, and many psychoanalysts have noted that the emphasis on the dirtiness of the excretory function utilized to enforce sphincter control surely has consequences for the child's perception of the cleanliness of his own genitalia and of their sexual function. This may also be related to some of the sexual differences between girls and boys; since boys may get dirty—therefore dirt is not so bad—and girls may not, the association may be more firmly entrenched among the latter.

In addition to the fantasy-proneness of childhood, there is the tendency for the unsatisfied curiosity of children to lead them directly into sexual play. This is probably true of many aspects of childhood behavior where the child does not possess a meaningful vocabulary with which to communicate or to elicit information. From the data on adults in the United States gathered in the samples of the Institute for Sex Research, about 57 percent of the males and 48 percent of the females who were interviewed as adults remembered sociosexual play

prior to puberty, with most of it occurring between ages 8 and 13.[39] Of a small sample of males interviewed before puberty, about 70 percent reported such sex play, suggesting that it is an even more widespread phenomenon, and that the memory of it is apparently often repressed by adult respondents.[40] Most of the play was sporadic and primarily motivated by curiosity about the body of either the same or the opposite sex.[41] Similar to children's other patterns of behavior, the learning situation was usually initiated by a child slightly older either in age or experience, and most commonly the behavior did not continue. The lack of labeling may make experimental play more likely in that it creates a zone of the body about which there is some fundamental mystery and concern.[42]

Given this framework of repression and avoidance by parents, it is not surprising that

---

[36] See footnote 35, p. 717.
[37] This has also been discussed by Albert Bandura and Richard H. Walters in *Adolescent aggression: A study of the influence of child-training practices and family interrelationships*, New York: Ronald, 1959, pp. 184-187.
[38] I have already noted the lack of consensus about sexuality among adults who have at least had some sexual experience; how much more mysterious must sexual functions appear to the inexperienced child. The role of language as imposing order on the external world may be found explicitly in the works of Kenneth Burke and George Herbert Mead and implicitly in those of Erving Goffman.
[39] See footnote 35, p. 107. Also see footnote 6, pp. 165-167.
[40] See footnote 39, p. 167.
[41] See footnote 39, p. 182.
[42] There is a body of evidence that among young children there is a large amount of game and folklore material that is rapidly forgotten after puberty. A certain amount of this material is sexual; however, the folklorists who work with children usually fail to keep records of this, or if they do so, do not publish it. An interesting aspect of this material is its eternal character—that is, it is passed on from generation to generation; for example, children in England are currently singing a recognizable variant of a song about Bonaparte popular in the early nineteenth century. See Iona Opie and Peter Opie, *The lore and language of school children*, London: Oxford, 1959, pp. 98-99. This evidence for the historical continuity of children's culture makes the contention in the earlier part of the paper concerning the change in the modern consciousness about children somewhat more complex; however, what seems to have happened is that the culture of children existed despite parental ignorance, and it had traditions of some viability independent of the adult community. It is unclear to what extent an adequate vocabulary for children would influence their overt behavior, but most likely it would not stimulate additional activity. This fear that is often expressed by parents is a function of their own anxiety and not necessarily related to the motives and drives of their children. Thus the parent placing himself in the role of the child presumes that exposure to certain types of stimulation or knowledge of certain types of behavior would cause the child to react in the same way as an adult would.

the child gets the bulk of his sexual information, though not his attitudes, through peer relationships. Though the parents are not providing cognitive information about sexuality for the child, they are creating attitudes and orientations through which information from other children will be filtered. In the peer relationships, since no children—or, at most, few—have accurate information about even reproductive functions, they will systematically misinform each other, just as they are systematically misinformed by their parents about being brought by the stork, being brought in the doctor's bag, or having been found in a cabbage patch. Unfortunately these belief systems and their origins among children have not been systematically studied, and the most likely reason for this is that the research itself must be a form of sex education.[43] In the exchanges between child and interlocutor the child will not remain unchanged, and even if he is asked only the meaning of certain terms, he will be in that moment informed or made curious. In this case there can be nothing but action research.

In all of the American studies it is clear that the primary source of sex information is peers. This has been a stable characteristic of most populations studied beginning with the Exner study of 1915 (85 percent of 948 college men),[44] and continuing through Hughes in 1926 (78 percent of 1,029 schoolboys),[45] Ramsey in 1943 (90 percent of 291 high school students, either from peers or by self-discovery),[46] Gebhard and coworkers in 1965 (91 percent of 477 lower-class men, 89 percent of 888 incarcerated criminals, and 89 percent of 1,356 convicted sex offenders).[47]

In approximately one-half of the cases in all of the studies, neither parent contributed any information. In the Ramsey study of 1943, 60 percent of the mothers and 82 percent of the fathers had given no sexual information.[48] In the study by Gebhard and coworkers, approximately three-quarters of the parents of both sexes had failed to give any direct sexual information.[49]

The information that mothers give is usually related to menstruation and pregnancy; however, less than one boy in four in the Ramsey study received even this information from his mother. Learning about contraceptives, prostitution, and coitus was practically restricted to

peers (over 90 percent in each instance). The role of the father is most ambiguous in this whole area; the myth of the good heart-to-heart talk between father and son seems to be exactly that. The father even less than the mother serves as a source of sexual information, and this seems to be a surprising finding. Apparently the father either assumes the boy will learn in his own good time, or that he has no real role to play in this area.[50] Unfortunately the questions asked have not ascertained whether the father ever made an attempt to teach his children anything about sex and then found out he was too late.

The Ramsey study also focused upon the age at which learning took place, and it is clear that pregnancy was learned of first (69 percent by age 10), intercourse usually next (57 percent by age 10), and masturbation next (43 percent by age 10). By age 14, the point at which it is suggested that most sex education programs should start, nearly all (92 to 100 percent) of the boys had learned about the previous three categories, and as many had learned of female prostitution. They remained most ignorant of menstruation (38 percent) and venereal disease (57 percent).[51] However, there is nothing in this learning process which suggests that the children have any integrated body of sexual knowledge. The young boy with

---

43 A series of reports has appeared about a study of this sort conducted through the use of doll play and interviews with 200 children. The general good sense of these researchers is attested to in the following: ". . . no series of scientific terms can 'immunize' a child against the inevitable language of the street. The child may need both in order to become an effective member of his group." See the following papers by Jacob Conn: "Sexual curiosity of children." Amer. J. Diseases Children (1940) 60:1110-1119. "Children's reactions to the discovery of genital differences," Amer. J. Orthopsychiat. (1940) 10:747-754. "Children's awareness of the origins of babies," J. Child Psychiat. (1948) 1:140-176. See also Jacob Conn and Leo Kanner, "Children's awareness of sex differences," J. Child Psychiat. (1947) 1:3-57.
44 Cited in Glenn Ramsey, "The sex information of younger boys," Amer. J. Orthopsychiat. (1943) 13:347-352.
45 See footnote 44, p. 349.
46 See footnote 44, pp. 349-350.
47 Paul H. Gebhard, John H. Gagnon, Wardell B. Pomeroy, and Cornelia V. Christenson, Sex offenders: An analysis of types, New York: Harper and Row, 1965.
48 See footnote 44, pp. 350-351.
49 See footnote 47. Also, the data for 5,000 college males is currently being analyzed at the Institute for Sex Research; this should provide some evidence about the experience of this social level.
50 See footnote 37, pp. 150-154.
51 All figures from Ramsey, footnote 44.

experience in sex play may not associate his firsthand knowledge of the anatomical differences between boys and girls with the fact that babies grow inside of his mother, and the biological facts of fertilization may never dawn on him at all. Even though the large body of data on females in the files of the Institute for Sex Research has not been analyzed for these variables, it would seem safe to speculate that, except for menstruation, females are unlikely to have learned the facts in any more logical or coherent order. In the case of females it is clear that the mother may often play a more decisive role because it is more appropriate that she inform her daughter of the dangers of sexuality and the possibility of menstruation. This is certainly not always the case, since a fair number of females in our sample report that they first learned of menstruation when it occurred for them the first time.

What is learned is important; however, it is the context in which it is learned that is more important. The exchange of sexual information among children is clandestine and subversive, and the manner in which parents attempt to teach their children reinforces this learning structure. The admonitions of parents, since they are general and diffuse, do not result so much in cessation of either interest or behavior, but in their concealment and the provoking of guilt. It is clear that few males have been deterred by the horror stories attached to masturbation. Madness, degeneration, and physical stigmata have all at various times been attributed to this behavior in the face of the evidence that the majority of males, especially in adolescence, have masturbated and that they have suffered none of these consequences. Those they have suffered have been related to the anxiety produced by worrying about the nonexistent consequences.

Thus children interact and exchange information on a sporadic and unconnected basis, usually but not always with some guilt.[52] The novelist Richard Wright recalled in his autobiography that in his early childhood he repeated an obscenity to his grandmother and received a ferocious beating for it, but did not know why he had been beaten.[53] This seems to happen fairly often—that the child behaves in a manner an adult perceives as sexual, and the child is punished without being able to

make a connection between stimulus and response. The punitive action of the parent may have little inhibitory power since it is nonspecific to the child's behavior, but it may provoke intense anxiety.

The development of guilty knowledge occurs extremely quickly, and the children's world resembles a secret society keeping information from parents.[54] This secret society is under enormous strain from two sources, both of them pointed out by Simmel. One is the tendency of children to express spontaneously what they know or feel, and the second is the difficulty of keeping a secret in a "small and narrow circle."[55] There is a positive value set on the ability of adults to talk to children about their problems, and the quality of child-rearing is often judged by whether the child will go to the parents with his difficulties. Even with all of these tensions organized to force the communication of sexual attitudes and information between the parents and the child, the barriers of mutual distrust and anxiety are too high. Thus the sexual learning process contributes another element to the child's future character structure—the capacity and need to keep sexuality secret, especially from those one loves.

After adolescence a different set of sexual problems appears, many of which are more or less restricted to the United States and relate less to the areas of Western Europe. Free dating and open intersexual social contact result from very special American conditions. Even with these special conditions many of the preparatory attitudes and belief systems that originated in childhood and infancy continue to play a powerful role.

Despite a rapidly changing society, especially in the technological realm, the power of these early experiences may be attested to by the stability (for the last fifty years at least) in

[52] See footnote 42, pp. 93-97.
[53] Richard Wright, Black boy, New York: Signet, 1963, pp. 49-53.
[54] This also has been pointed out by Freud. "We are shown . . . above all, how the secret of sexual life begins to dawn on her indistinctly and then takes complete possession of the child's mind; how, in the consciousness of her secret knowledge, she at first suffers hurt, but little by little overcomes it." Sigmund Freud, Standard edition of the complete psychological works 14:341, London: Hogarth, 1963.
[55] Kurt H. Wolff, editor, The sociology of George Simmel, Glencoe, Ill.: Free Press, 1950, pp. 330-335.

patterns of overt sexual behavior. For the male the only basic overt behavioral change in his sexual repertoire has been a substantial decline in the frequency of coitus with prostitutes, although the proportion of men who have had at least once such experience seems not to have changed.[56] The use of prostitutes as a stable and substantial source of coitus seems to be a phenomenon of the past. Two attitudinal changes have occurred that are of some importance. First, the intensity and duration of anxiety about masturbation have declined (although the incidence and frequency of the behavior have remained remarkably constant) and, second, the proportion of males who seriously adhere to the "double standard" has declined, with a shift to a position described by Reiss as "permissiveness with affection." [57] The most radical change in sexual patterns has been the substantial increase in the incidence of premarital coitus among females born after 1900, who grew up during the 1920's, when contrasted with females born before 1900, who grew up before the first World War.[58] There has been no recent change similar to this, as surveys of college students have shown.[59] The bulk of this coitus is restricted to one male and to the year before marriage, indicating that premarital coitus in the female seems linked more directly to age at marriage and falling in love than it is to the attributes that are most important in determining male sexual behavior.[60] Attitudinal shifts have taken place among females, but often they are situation-specific, changing from a more permissive stance when the girl is in the process of courtship and is about to get married to a less permissive one when she has teen-age daughters.[61] The connection between these changes in attitudes and how they are translated into overt behavior is still obscure.

The long predicted change in American sexual patterns has not, in fact, occurred, despite the advent of the automobile and other artifacts of a changing technology. Since most of the sexual orientations of the adult personality are results of events that are not reversible through conventional means, there are no grounds for predicting that the sexual life can be easily changed. Given our difficulties in changing the behavior of schizophrenics, drug addicts, or juvenile delinquents, or even of changing the political party affiliation of others, there seems to be a curious contradiction in the belief that sexual behavior is immediately amenable to change from the slightest external impulse. This anxious belief may arise from the facts that practically all sexual behavior is taboo, that violations of the norms are widespread, and that the transgressions are systematically ignored. These violations, which are as constant as the norms, are assumed, when discovered, to be the product of changes in behavior rather than to represent the persistence of previous patterns.

Planning and the unplannable

The forces that mold childhood and thereby provide the structure around which the personality of the adult is formed are still only vaguely understood. Even such an insightful work as Erikson's *Childhood and Society* primarily provides a set of labels, albeit useful, and only intimations of possible explanations of process and change.[62] Even if these processes were understood at some high level of scientific sophistication, it does not follow that many parents would be able to utilize the available knowledge. A large portion of the actions of parents toward children is based upon irrational grounds, often repetitive of the experiences that the parents had as children. I am not suggesting a simplistic cyclical theory, but attempting to point out a differential amenability to change in various areas of both the personality and social life.

It is experiences in infancy and childhood that ready the child for integration of sexual knowledge and sexual behavior. This readiness is the consequence of systems of parental behavior that have no direct sexual bearing but spill over into the sexual area. The actions of the parents are not planned or rational, and, when there is an attempt to make them so,

---

[56] See footnote 6, pp. 394-417.
[57] See footnote 6. Ira Reiss, *Premarital sexual standards in America*, Glencoe, Ill.: Free Press, 1960, pp. 126-145.
[58] See footnote 35, pp. 298-302. Winston Ehrmann, *Premarital dating behavior*, New York: Holt, 1959, pp. 32-36.
[59] Mervin B. Freedman, "The sexual behavior of American college women: An empirical study and an historical survey," *Merrill Palmer Quart.* (1965) 11:33-48.
[60] See footnote 35, pp. 282-345.
[61] Robert R. Bell and Jack V. Buerkle, "Mother and daughter attitudes to premarital sexual behavior," *Marriage and family living* (1961) 23:390-392.
[62] Erik H. Erikson, *Childhood and Society*; New York, Norton, 1950.

the child often becomes confused—he must respond at one level to the habitual character of the parents and then at another to the parents' rational plans. In the midst of these plans the irrational components of the parents' character tend to erupt, and the child is unclear as to the actual nature of the parents' expectations.

These confusions on the part of parents and the consequent disorderliness of the child's life are now commonly placed at the door of permissive child-rearing. It is now suggested by psychiatrists as well as Dr. Spock that discipline—when not carried too far—is a good thing and that good discipline is needed for the child's own sense of security.[63] The sentiment of psychiatrists that parents should return to punishment—administered "wisely" is the usual codicil—is based on two disparate but mutually supporting experiences. The first is related to the stresses of the therapeutic life for the therapist, for whom treatment failure and changes in the presenting syndromes of new patients have endlessly complicated the problems of traditional psychoanalysis. (In contrast to Freud, it is possible to argue that the success or failure of psychoanalytic therapy is unconnected to the explanatory value of the theory in reference to human behavior; however, since psychoanalysis has been primarily used as part of a treatment program, this distinction is usually not made.) As Freudian analytic techniques are rejected, so are the pronouncements about the processes of normal childhood development and the role of permissiveness. This reaction is especially notable among those therapists who deal with criminal or other deviant populations or mass groups such as school children.[64] The intractability of the case or the dimensions of the problem (often simply in terms of size) are enough to make people suggest a return to techniques which are applicable in the mass and by the number.

The second experience is the difficulty which parents have in applying the suggested methodology and the responsibility that it implies. The popular literature is replete with anxious parents unhinged by the dangerousness and difficulty of the child-rearing task, and much talk to parents is bent upon reducing parental anxiety. The opening line of Dr. Spock is the summation of all such reassurance: "You know more than you think you do."[65] The

current mode is to tell parents to rely upon their common sense, whatever that might be. The import of these admonitions is to remove the onus from the parent of the terrifying (and rightly so) responsibility of rearing children, for this is often too much for the consciousness of the parent; he cannot reconcile the seriousness of his task, the lack of accurate guide rules (as opposed to clichés) for his behavior, and his emotional involvement in the child who is demanding his attention. The new literature even deflects from parental responsibility by pointing out elements such as inherent differences between children, as if this provided an exclusionary clause. It is not that the techniques of permissive child-rearing are necessarily indicted by the failures of parents in using them, but rather that parental incapacities have made adherence to the principles so sporadic and of such uneven intensity that they resulted only in confusion for the child.

In addition to the parents' incapacity to deal with the indirect elements which affect sexuality, they are also unable to deal with the problem of the supply of specifically sexual information. Since the parents persist in patterns of information control that are mostly composed of negative sanctions and nonlabeling and mislabeling of behavior, the child must search for information in the meager resources of his equally misinformed friends. As has been suggested earlier, given the troubled quality of adults when they deal with sexuality, it may be better for the children to learn through the informal channels of other children, since

---

[63] The revision of Spock's classic in 1957 to include a greater concern with discipline is noted in Martha Weinman, "Now 'Dr. Spock' goes to the White House," *The New York Times Magazine* (December 4, 1960), pp. 26, 120-121. The cause of the revision was "permissiveness running away with itself." The child-rearing column of the Magazine section of *The New York Times* is increasingly running to titles such as, "Relearning what permissiveness means," or "When discipline is called for." The column often translates psychiatric positions into layman's information.

[64] Many of these impressions come from personal interaction with psychiatrists, but the *J. Offender Therapy*, which is directed toward dealing with criminal populations explicitly, says what many therapists feel when confronted with these kinds of problems. See Ernst Schmidhofer, "Acting up or acting out," *J. Offender Therapy* (1964) 8:1-4, or Mark D. Altschule, "The alleged value of antisocial self expression," *J. Offender Therapy* (1963) 7:73-74.

[65] Benjamin S. Spock, *The pocket book of baby and child care*, New York: Pocket Books, 1946, p. 3.

material from parents that might be overloaded with anxiety is reduced in significance and impact.

The overwhelmingly unplanned and unplannable elements in the development of the sexual life of children make it extremely difficult to discuss the role that planning in sex education might play. It is, however, possible to suggest that information imparted to children in schools or in other educational contexts should be communicated in each grade as part of the general curriculum. While it may be too rapid for some children and too slow for others, in general, if there is a source of accurate information that the children may tap anonymously and which is presented in a nonpejorative manner, at least the methods of communicating the information to the children will not in themselves be particularly destructive.[66] The specific age at which a child receives this information, as well as the specific items of information to be imparted, are of less significance than the preparation of the child for receiving this knowledge. The child who is traumatized by the sight of a nude body, or by learning that intercourse occurs, or by learning that babies grow inside of the mother, has previously developed a background of experience such that sooner or later, in one context or another, he would have been unable to cope with similar sexual stimuli. The specific triggering event is less important than the accumulation of readying experiences that prepared the child for such responses.

Planning of sex education should then be viewed as a rather secondary force in the development of the sexual life of the child, and while humanitarian values suggest that such planning should be done, the bulk of the evidence suggests that it will play a minor role in setting patterns of sexual life. There may be some long-run value in the teaching of sex education in schools, since it reduces the role of the parent who may only reproduce his own anxieties in the child. Whatever patterns of sexual life are considered desirable to maintain in a society, or whatever changes men may seek to make in these patterns, it is certain that it will be more difficult to resist or accomplish these goals because of the roots of sexuality in childhood. Even the accumulation of scientific knowledge about human sexual behavior may not accelerate much the pace or direction of change, for in this area of behavior—as is probably true in others—the statement that "Ye shall know the truth, and the truth shall make you free," may not apply. In a society that is addicted to the ideology of limitless possibilities in human engineering it is perhaps important to focus on some of the refractory elements in human development. While it is possible to be more hopeful about the human capacity for change than was Freud in his later years, his statement about the limited potentials of sex education should be kept in mind. It occurs during his discussion of the limited consequences for mental health that either the purely intellectual discussion of instinctual conflicts or the reading of psychoanalytic writings have. Freud says of these activities:

We have increased his knowledge, but altered nothing else in him. . . . We can have analogous experiences, I think, when we give children sexual enlightenment. I am far from maintaining that this is a harmful or unnecessary thing to do, but it is clear that the prophylactic effect of this liberal measure has been greatly over-estimated. After such enlightenment, children know something they did not know before, but they make no use of the new knowledge that has been presented to them. We come to see that they are not even in so great a hurry to sacrifice for this new knowledge the sexual theories which might be described as a natural growth and which they have constructed in harmony with, and dependence on, their imperfect libidinal organization—theories about the part played by the stork, about the nature of sexual intercourse, and about the way in which babies are made. For a long time after they have been given sexual enlightenment they behave like primitive races who have had Christianity thrust upon them and who continue to worship their old idols in secret.[67]

---

66 *Symposium on sex education*, edited by E. C. Cumings, New York: Amer. Social Hygiene Assn., November, 1957.
67 Sigmund Freud, "Analysis terminable and interminable," *Standard edition of the complete psychological works* 23:216-253, London: Hogarth, 1964, pp. 233-234.

Parent-child conflict in sexual values

Observers of contemporary American society suggest that the "generation gap" has never been wider. Young people and their parents are finding it increasingly difficult to communicate with each other, and the question of acceptable sexual behavior is a major source of conflict. Robert Bell is Associate Professor of Sociology at Temple University and the author of several books on sexual behavior, including *Marriage and Family Interaction, Premarital Sex in a Changing Society,* and *Studies in Marriage and the Family.* In this article, Professor Bell describes some of the specific points of contention that exist between parents and their children concerning premarital sexual activity. The article describes both the nature and extent of these conflicts and presents a brief review of some relevant research findings.

The old cliché that as one grows older he becomes more conservative may be true, if premarital sexual values held by parents are compared with the values they held when they were younger. In this paper, the interest is in the nature of sex value conflict between parents and their unmarried late adolescent and young adult children. Our discussion will focus on values held by parents and by their unmarried children toward premarital sexual intimacy.

Conceptually, our approach focuses upon values related to a specific area of sexual behavior held by individuals from two very different role perspectives. The perspectives differ because parents and children are always at different stages in the life cycle, and while parents are highly significant in the socialization of their children, other social forces increasingly come to influence the child as he grows older. The various social values that

influence the child's sexual behavior are often complementary, but they may also be contradictory. Furthermore, various types of influences on the acceptance of a given set of values may operate on the child only during a given age period. For example, the youngster at age fifteen may be influenced by his age peers to a much greater extent than he will be at age twenty.

Given their different stages in the life cycle, parents and children will almost always show differences in how they define appropriate behavior for a given role. Values as to "proper" premarital sexual role behavior from the perspective of the parents are greatly influenced by the strong emotional involvement of the parent with his child. Youth, on the other hand, are going through a life cycle stage in which the actual behavior occurs, and they must relate the parent values to what they are doing or may do. There is a significant difference between defining appropriate role conduct for others to follow and defining proper role conduct to be followed by oneself. Even more important for actual behavior, there is often more than one significant group of role definers to which the young person can turn to as guides for his sex role behavior. Therefore, our discussion will focus more specifically on parent values related to premarital sexual intimacy, the peer group values of youth, and how these two different age groups, as role definers, influence the sexual values and behavior of unmarried youth.

From *Journal of Social Issues,* XXII, No. 2 (1966), 34-44. Reprinted by permission of The Society for the Psychological Study of Social Issues.

For several reasons, our discussion will center primarily on the middle class. First, this class level has been highly significant in influencing changes in general sexual values and behavior. Second, and on a more pragmatic level, what little research has been done on parent-child conflict over sexual values has been done with middle-class groups. Third, the general values of the middle class are coming to include an increasing proportion of the American population. This also suggests that the values and behavior of college youth are of increasing importance as this group continues to expand in size and influence within the middle class.

A further limit is that our main focus is on the generational conflict between mother and daughter. The history of change in sexual values in the United States has been completely interwoven with the attainment of greater sex equality and freedom by the female (2). Also, the relationship between the mother and daughter tends to be the closest of the possible parent-child relationships in the family socializing of the child to future adult sex roles. Furthermore, whatever the value system verbalized and/or applied by the girl, she often has more to gain or lose personally than the boy by whatever premarital sexual decisions she makes.

We also believe that any analysis of conflict over premarital sex between generations should center on *value* changes rather than *behavioral* changes. On the basis of available evidence, it appears that there have been no significant changes in the *frequency* of premarital sexual petting or coitus since the 1920's. Kinsey has pointed out that "there has been little recognition that the premarital petting and coital patterns which were established then (1920's) are. still with us" (15, p. 300). Therefore, it is important to recognize that the parents and even some of the grandparents of today were the youth who introduced the new patterns of premarital sexual behavior about forty years ago.

Parent values about premarital sex

The transmission of sexual values by parents to their children is only a small part of all parent values passed on during the family socialization process. Most parents do a more deliberate and comprehensive job of transmitting values to their children in such areas as educational attainment, career choice, religious beliefs, and so forth than they do with reference to any aspect of sexual values. Often when parents do discuss sex with their children it may be from a "clinical, physiological" perspective with overtones of parental embarrassment and a desire to get a distasteful task over with.

But perhaps more important than the formal confrontation between the parent and child in sexual matters are the informal values transmitted by the parent. In the past girls were often taught that premarital sexual deviancy was dirty and shameful, and that nonconformity to premarital sexual chastity values would mean suffering great personal and social shame. This highly negative view of premarital sex is undoubtedly less common today, but the newer, more "positive" values may also have some negative consequences. Very often today the mother continues to place great value on the daughter's virginity, and stresses to the daughter the great virtues of maintaining her virginity until marriage. But the "romatic" view of the rewards for the girl who waits for coitus until after marriage are often highly unrealistic and may sometimes create problems by leading the girl to expectations that cannot be realistically met in marital sex. Morton Hunt writes with regard to this approach that "if the woman has been assured that she will, that she ought, and she *must* see colored lights, feel like a breaking wave, or helplessly utter inarticulate cries, she is apt to consider herself or her husband at fault when these promised wonders do not appear" (13, 114). Whether or not the "romantic" view of marital sex is presented by her mother, the girl often encounters it in the "approved" reading list suggested by the adult world, which tells her about the positive delights of waiting for sex until after marriage. So, though premarital sexual control may be "positive" in that it is based on rewards for waiting, it can be "negative" if the rewards are unrealistic and unobtainable.

For many parents, a major problem as their child moves through adolescence and into early adult years centers around how much independence to allow the child. Because they often recall the child's younger dependency, it may be difficult to assess the independency of the same child who is now older. Also, over the years the growing child has increasingly become involved with reference groups outside—and sometimes competing with—the family. In other words, the self-role definitions by the child and the parents' definitions of the child's role undergo constant change as the child grows older. For example, "The daughter in her younger years has her role as daughter defined to a great degree by her mother. But as she grows older, she is influenced by other definitions which she internalizes and applies to herself in her movement toward self-determination. The mother frequently continues to visualize the daughter's role as it was defined in the past and also attaches the same importance to her function as mother in defining her daughter's role. But given the rapid social change associated with family roles the definer, as well as the definitions, may no longer be institutionally appropriate" (5, 388).

Parents may also be biased in their definitions of their child as less mature than they, the parents, were when they were the child's age. One can not recall experiences earlier in the life cycle free from influence by the events that have occurred since. This may result in many parents' thinking of their younger selves as being more mature than they actually were. At the same time the parents' view of their child's degree of maturity may be biased by their recall of him when he was younger and less mature. Thus, from the parents' perspective they may recall themselves as youngsters within the context of what has occurred since (more mature) and may see their offspring within the context of their earlier childhood (less mature).

There also may be some symbolic significance for parents who must define their children as having reached the age when something as "adult" as sexual behavior is of relevance. In part, viewing one's children as too young for sexual involvement may contribute to the parents' feeling young, while seeing their children as old enough to be involved in sexual activity may lead to some parents feeling forced to view themselves as aging. For example, the comment about a man seen out with a young woman that "she is young enough to be his daughter" may have implications for his self-role image if the young woman *is* his daughter. We have little research data on how

the aging process of parents influences their definitions of appropriate behavior for their young adult children.

In general, it is probable that most parents assume that their children, especially their daughters, accept the traditional restrictive values about premarital sexual behavior unless they are forced to do otherwise. Also, because of the great emotional involvement of parents with their own children, there is a common parental tendency to attribute sexual "immorality" to other youngsters. For many parents to face the possibility that their children do not conform to their values is to suggest some failure on the part of the parents. Often, rather than admit failure, the parents may define their children as having been forced to reject the parent values by other social influences or that their children have willfully let them down.

Youth views about premarital sex

The importance of age peer group influence on the values and behavior of young people has been shown by a number of social scientists (see: 6, 9, 10, 11, 12, 14, 19, 20, 21, 22). Because youth subcultures are to some degree self-developing, they often have conflict points in relation to some dominant adult values. However, the inconsistency and lack of effective adult definitions for adolescent behavior have also contributed to the emergence of youth subcultural values. That adults often view the adolescent with indecision as to appropriate behavior means that sometimes given adolescent behavior is treated one way at one time and in a different way at another time. Since the young person desires some decisiveness and precision in his role definitions, he often develops his role prescriptions. Often when he creates his own role expectations, he demands a high degree of conformity by other adolescents as "proof" of the rightness of his definitions. It is ironical that the adolescent often thinks of himself as a social deviant. What he fails to realize is that his adolescent group deviates from the adult world, but that the requirements for conformity within his youth subculture are very strong (1, 369-74).

Youth subcultures have developed great influence over many aspects of premarital male-female interaction. The patterns of dating and courtship, appropriate behavior, success and failure are for the most part patterns defined by the youth group and not by the adult world. Yet, heterosexual relationships of youth are often based on adult role patterns, and they are therefore an important part of the youth world because they are seen by the youth as symbolizing adult status. To many young people, who are no longer defined by the adult world as children, but are not yet given full status as adults, their involvement in what they see as adult roles is important to them in seeking for adult status and recognition.

A part of the American youth subculture has been the development of new values related to premarital sexual intimacy. Reiss suggests that "It might well be that, since the 1920's, what has been occurring is a change in attitudes to match the change in behavior of that era" [premarital sexual behavior] (16, 233). The evidence suggests that for at least some college students new sex norms are emerging at the various stages of dating and courtship. One study found that "on the dating level necking is the norm for females and petting for males. During going steady and engagement, petting seems to be acceptable for both sexes. This would suggest that the young people both act and accept a higher level of intimacy than has generally been suggested by courtship norms." (3, 63).

In the past, emphasis was placed on the girl's virginity at the time of marriage; but today, many young people may only emphasize her being a virgin until she is in love, which may mean at the stage of going steady or engagement (8, Ch. 5 and 16, Ch. 6). If the girl is in love, some premarital sexual relations may be acceptable by peer group standards, although the dominant adult values—that love *and* marriage are basic prerequisites for coitus —continue. In the United States love as a prerequisite for sexual relations has long been a necessary condition for most middle-class females. The condition has not changed; rather, the point in the courtship-marriage process where it may be applied to sexual involvement has shifted. Hence, the major point of parent-child conflict over premarital sex centers around the parent value that one should be in love *and* married before entering coitus and the modified value system of youth that an emotional and interpersonal commitment is important, but that this may occur before marriage.

There are two recent studies that provide some evidence on the nature of generational conflict; one study is of youth and adults in general and the other study is specifically concerned with mothers and their daughters. Reiss, in his extensive study of premarital sexual permissiveness, provides data on values held by adults as contrasted with values in a sample of high school and college students. The respondents were asked to express their beliefs about different combinations of intimacy and degree of interpersonal commitment for both unmarried males and females. Respondents were asked if they believed petting to be acceptable when the male or female is engaged. In the adult sample the belief that petting during engagement was acceptable for the engaged male was the response of 61 per cent, and for the engaged female the response was 56 per cent. Of the student responses 85 per cent approved for the engaged male and 82 per cent for the engaged female (17, 190-91); thus adult attitudes about petting during engagement were more conservative than those of the student population. It may also be noted that for both the adult and student groups there was a single standard—that is, the acceptance rates were essentially the same for both males and females.

Reiss also asked his respondents if they believed full sexual relations to be acceptable if the male or female were engaged. Approval was the response given by 20 per cent of the adult group for males and 17 per cent for females. In the student group acceptance was given by 52 per cent for the male and 44 per cent for the female (17, 190-91). Here, as with petting, there are significant differences between the adult and the student samples, and once again both respondent groups suggest a single standard of acceptance or rejection for both males and females.

A study by Bell and Buerkle compared the attitudes of 217 coeds with those of their mothers. Both mothers and daughters were asked to respond to the question, "How important do you think it is that a girl be a virgin when she marries?" Of the mothers, 88 per cent answered "very important," 12 per cent "generally important," and 0 per cent "not important"; compared to 55 per cent, 34 per cent and 13 per cent of the daughters (4, 391). Both the mothers and daughters were also asked: "Do you think sexual intercourse during engagement is: very wrong; generally wrong; right in many situations?" The percentages for each response category were 83 per cent, 15 per cent, and 2 per cent for the mothers; and 35 per cent, 48 per cent, and 17 per cent for the daughters (4, 391).

Both of the above questions show sharp differences between the value responses of the mothers and daughters with reference to premarital chastity. Many mothers were undoubtedly influenced in their responses by having a daughter in the age setting where the questions had an immediate and highly emotional application. Nevertheless, the differences in mother and daughter responses indicate that the area of premarital sexual behavior is one of potentially great conflict. One means of minimizing conflict is for the daughter not to discuss her sexual values or behavior with her mother. In the Bell and Buerkle study it was found that only 37 per cent of the daughters, in contrast with 83 per cent of the mothers, felt daughters should freely answer questions from their mothers in regard to attitudes toward sexual intimacy (4, 392).

The area of sexual values appears to be highly influenced by emotion, especially for the mother with reference to her daughter. Generational conflict with regard to premarital sexual intimacy has a variety of implications. First, the conflict in values clearly suggests that the traditional morality is often not socially effective as a meaningful determinant of behavior. Social values have behavioral influence when they emerge as social norms with significant rewards and punishments. In the case of sexual norms, however, there are rarely clearly-articulated rewards, or positive consequences, for the conforming individual. In almost all situations, the effectiveness of sexual norms is dependent upon their negative sanctions, or punishments. For example, the traditional norm of female premarital chastity bases its behavioral influence primarily on negative consequences for the girl who fails to conform. This negative means of control is most commonly found as a part of the adult value system. In effect, the major sanctions over premarital chastity are based upon punishments for the girl and for her family if she deviates. Yet, in most cases the girl who has premarital coitus is not discovered by her parents or by the community. The real danger for the girl often centers around premarital pregnancy, because if that occurs and becomes known there can be no denying premarital coitus. Vincent has suggested that an important part of the negative sanction toward premarital pregnancy is not the pregnancy itself, but rather that it symbolizes premarital coitus *and* getting caught (23, Ch. 1).

The available studies indicate that fear of pregnancy is not the major deterrent for most girls (7, 344 and 15, 315). The personal values of the girl appear far more important in restricting her from engaging in premarital coitus. Yet, within the privacy of the youth world, there may operate for some girls certain values positive toward premarital coitus. For example, there may be a strong emotional desire and commitment to the boy and a positive feeling by the girl of wanting to engage in greater sexual intimacy.

There is a tendency by parents, as well as by many who give professional advice, to overlook the pleasurable aspects of sex at all ages, especially for the young who are experiencing sexual pleasure for the first time. Undoubtedly many girls engage in premarital sexual intimacy to "compensate" for some need and many may suffer some negative consequences. But it is foolish to state categorically that the "artificial" setting of premarital sex always makes it negative and unpleasant for the girl. We would be much more honest if we recognized that for many girls premarital coitus is enjoyable and the participants suffer no negative consequences. This was illustrated in the Kinsey research; it was found that "69 per cent of the still unmarried females in the sample who had had premarital coitus insisted they did not regret their experiences. Another 13 per cent recorded some minor regrets" (15, 316). Kinsey also found that "77 per cent of the married females, looking back from the vantage point of their more mature experience, saw no reason to regret their premarital coitus" (15, 316).

The extent of generational conflict

With the evidence suggesting strong conflict between generations with regard to premarital sexual values, our final consideration is: how permanent is this generational conflict? We can provide some evidence on this question by examining the values of college-educated females of different ages. This appears justified because higher educated females are generally the most liberal in their views about sexual rights and expectations for women.

The evidence suggests that the premarital sexual liberalism of the college girl may be a temporary phenomenon. The coed's sexual liberalism must be seen as related to the interactional context of her being emotionally involved, and to a future commitment to an ongoing paired relationship. The Bell and Buerkle study (4) found that the values of daughters toward the importance of premarital virginity were very similar to those of their mothers, until they had spent some time in college. However, at "around age 20 there emerge sharp differences between mothers and daughters in regard to premarital sexual attitudes. Behavioral studies indicate that it is at this point that sexual activity is greatly intensified, perhaps because it is at this age that college girls are entering engagement. A suggested pattern is that the college girl of 20 or 21 years of age, in her junior or senior year and engaged, has a strong 'liberal' pattern toward premarital sexual behavior and attitudes" (4, 392 and 18, 696).

We can get some indication of the persistence of premarital sexual liberalism by comparing the values of mothers by education. In the mothers' views as to the importance of premarital virginity it was found that the college educated mothers were actually as "conservative" as those mothers with lower levels of education (4, 392). It is quite possible that in the future the coeds will become as conservative as the college educated mothers. This may occur when the coed's attitudinal rationales are not related to herself, but as a mother to her own daughter. It is therefore possible that the "sexual emancipation" of the college girl exists only for a short period of time, centering mainly around the engagement years.

Yet, even if the girl becomes more conservative as she grows older, and especially with reference to her own daughter, her temporary "liberalism" probably is contributing to some shift in adult values about premartial sexual intimacy. Certainly, today's parental generation accepts greater sexual intimacy as a part of the premarital heterosexual relationship. Probably most parents assume that their adolescent and young adult children are engaging in necking and even some petting. Most parents, as long as they don't actually see the sexual intimacy, don't concern themselves about it. However, to suggest that parents may be more liberal (or tolerant) of premarital sexual intimacy does not necessarily suggest that parents are liberal if the intimacy reaches coitus.

It also appears that there has been some reduction in the severity of negative sanctions by parents if the daughter deviates and is caught. Among middle-class parents today it may be less common to reject the unwed daughter if she becomes pregnant than in the past, and more common for the parents to help her. This is not to suggest that today's parents offer any positive sanctions for premarital pregnancy, but that they may be able to adapt (often painfully) to it, rather than respond with high rejection and anger.

If our suggestion is correct (that parents take a less totally negative view of "discovered" premarital coitus), then this further suggests that traditional sexual values are being altered, since, as we have suggested, in the past the values of premarital chastity were primarily based on the negative consequences for those who deviated and were caught. If these negative consequences have been reduced, then the social force of the traditional values has been reduced as a means utilized by parents to control premarital sexual deviancy.

Conclusions

Based on the available evidence, there are several general speculations that may be made about future generational conflict over premarital sex. In general we would suggest that conflict between parents and their adolescent-young adult children with regard to premarital sexual intimacy may decrease in the future, because of several trends.

1. The trend in the United States is toward a more liberal view of sexual behavior in general. This is reflected in the generally accepted professional opinion that the woman has a right to sexual satisfaction, and that sexual satisfaction is a desirable end in itself. The trend toward a belief in a single sexual standard for both men

and women, even though within the setting of marriage, is bound to influence the beliefs and behavior of the unmarried. For the unmarried, there may be an increasing tendency to attach less importance to the marriage act as the arbitrary dividing line between socially approved and socially disapproved sexual intimacy.

2. Since the evidence suggests that over the past three or four generations the rates of female premarital coital experience have not changed, and since the younger generation has developed some value frameworks for its behavior, modification of traditional values and behavior may increasingly influence the values of parents to be more liberal. That is, it may become increasingly difficult for many parents to hold their children to a set of conservative values which they, the parents, did not hold to when they were younger.

3. Parents seem increasingly unwilling to strongly punish their daughters who sexually deviate and are caught. This parental reduction of punishment may be influenced by the increasing public attention directed at such social problems as illegal abortion. For example, many parents may be more willing to accept and help an unmarried pregnant daughter than take the risk of her seeking out an illegal abortion. The possible negative consequences of abortion may appear more undesirable than the premarital pregnancy.

4. Less generational conflict will occur if parents know less about the sexual activities of their children. A great part of the social activity of young people is carried out in the privacy of their age peer setting; what they do in the way of sexual intimacy is increasingly less apt to be noted by their parents. With the development and marketing of oral contraceptives, the risks of premarital pregnancy will be greatly reduced. In the future the rates of premarital coitus may remain the same, but, with the chances of pregnancy reduced, parents may be less aware of their children's premarital coitus.

Over time, then, the values of parents and the adult community in general may become more liberal and the conflict between generations reduced. (There seems little possibility that the opposite will occur; i.e., the younger generation's reducing the conflict by becoming more conservative.) But in the meantime, and certainly in the near future, it appears that parents and their children will continue to live with somewhat different value systems with regard to premarital sexual values. Parents will probably continue to hold to traditional values, and assume that *their* child is conforming to those values unless his actions force them to see otherwise. The youth generation will probably continue to develop their own modified value systems and keep those values to themselves, and implicitly allow their parents to believe they are behaving according to the traditional values of premarital sexual morality. For many parents and their children, the conflict about premarital sex will continue to be characterized by the parent's playing ostrich and burying his head in the sand, and the youth's efforts to keep the sand from blowing away.

References

1. Bell, Robert R. *Marriage and family interaction*, Homewood, Ill.: The Dorsey Press, 1963.

2. Bell, Robert R. *Premarital sex in a changing society*, Englewood Cliffs, N.J.: Prentice-Hall (in press).

3. Bell, Robert R. and Leonard Blumberg. "Courtship stages and intimacy attitudes," *Family life coordinator*, 1960, 8, 60-63.

4. Bell, Robert R. and Jack V. Buerkle. "Mother and daughter attitudes to premarital sexual behavior," *Marriage and family living*, 1961, 23, 390-92.

5. Bell, Robert R. and Jack V. Buerkle. "Mother-daughter conflict during the 'launching stage,'" *Marriage and family living*, 1962, 24, 384-88.

6. Bernard, Jessie (Editor). "Teen-age culture," *Annals American academy of political and social science*, November, 1961, 338.

7. Burgess, Ernest and Paul Wallin. *Engagement and marriage*, Chicago: J. B. Lippincott, 1953.

8. Ehrmann, Winston. *Premarital dating behavior*, New York: Henry Holt, 1959.

9. Ginsberg, Eli. *Values and ideals of American youth*, New York: Columbia University Press, 1962.

10. Gottlieb, David and Charles Ramsey. *The American adolescent*. Homewood, Ill.: The Dorsey Press, 1964.

11. Grinder, Robert. *Studies in adolescence,* New York: Macmillan, 1963.

12. Hechinger, Grace and Fred. *Teen-age tyranny,* New York: Crest, 1962.

13. Hunt, Norton M. *The natural history of love,* New York: Alfred A. Knopf, 1959.

14. Kelley, Earl C. *In defense of youth,* Englewood Cliffs, N.J.: Prentice-Hall, 1962.

15. Kinsey, Alfred C., Wardell B. Pomeroy, Clyde E. Martin and Paul H. Gebhard. *Sexual behavior in the human female,* Philadelphia: W. B. Saunders, 1953.

16. Reiss, Ira L. *Premarital sexual standards in America,* Glencoe, Ill.: The Free Press, 1960.

17. Reiss, Ira L. "The scaling of premarital sexual permissiveness," *J. Marriage and the Family,* 1964, 26, 188-98.

18. Reiss, Ira L. "Premarital sexual permissiveness among negroes and whites," *Amer. Sociol. Review,* 1964, 29, 688-98.

19. Remmers, H. H. and D. H. Radler. *The American teenager,* New York: Charter, 1957.

20. Seidman, Jerome. *The Adolescent,* New York: Holt, 1960.

21. Smith, Ernest A. *American youth culture,* New York: The Free Press, 1963.

22. Symonds, P. M. *From adolescent to adult,* New York: Columbia University Press, 1961.

23. Vincent, Clark. *Unmarried mothers,* Glencoe, Ill.: The Free Press, 1961.

Sexual morality and the dilemma of the colleges[1]

DANA L. FARNSWORTH

Dana Farnsworth, M.D., is Henry K. Oliver Professor of Hygiene and Director of the University Health Services at Harvard University. He is the author of *Mental Health in College and University; Psychiatry, Education and the Young Adult,* a textbook on psychiatry, and numerous articles on psychiatric problems of the young adult.

In this article Dr. Farnsworth further documents the difference in value orientations that exists between the older and younger generations. The essay focuses on sexual morality and describes the characteristics associated with the "new morality," amorality, and traditional morality. The three systems are discussed in terms of their impact on the behavior and attitudes of both college students and older authority figures, such as parents, university administrators, and religious leaders.

During the last few years much interest has been focused on sexual practices in the colleges, an interest stimulated in part by the demands of students for greater freedom in this area together with confusion on the part of parents and college officials as to what should be the proper standards of behavior. It is quite difficult for parents and children to talk together frankly about sexual matters because of the great gulf in experience between the two generations. The background of our present college generation is very different from that of their parents. Social change was quite rapid during the time the parents of today were maturing but is even more so at present.

Communication between older and younger members of the college communities also is hampered by many influences, including lack of a consensus as to what the central issues are, criticism of those who become interested in the subject, and lack of persons competent to hold discussion groups.

From the *American Journal of Orthopsychiatry,* XXXV, No. 4 (July 1965), 676-681. Copyright, the American Orthopsychiatric Association, Inc. Reproduced by permission.

[1] Presented at the 1965 annual meeting of the American Orthopsychiatric Association, New York, New York.

The sexual behavior of college students may be changing in the direction of practices formerly attributed to members of lower socioeconomic groups [2]. Reliable data on which to base such an opinion is not yet conclusive, but all general observations suggest this to be true. Not only is there thought to be a qualitative change in sexual practices but also an acceleration in such behavior. What was thought to be characteristic behavior at 18 or 20 years of age may now be observed in persons 16 to 18 or even younger.

There appear to be three general points of view regarding sexual behavior which can be characterized as: (1) the traditional morality, (2) the new morality, and (3) amorality. In the first of these, the traditional morality, the following principles are considered important:

—Renunciation or control of instinctual gratification permits a reasonable degree of civilization (Freud).
—Restraint tends to aid in developing a capacity for thoughtfulness concerning the welfare of others, particularly in a parental sense. Restraint also is thought to aid in the sublimation of sexual energies.
—Marriage becomes one of life's most cherished institutions when sexual restraint is practiced.
—The total moral fiber of a society is strengthened if sexual standards are maintained and weakened when sexual standards are ignored.
—Young people need help in controlling their strong impulses during their formative years.

In the new morality:

—Fidelity and consideration of others occupy a very high place.
—Physical sex is supposed to occur only after the establishment of friendship and love.
—Exploitation of the sexual partner is very much opposed.
—A high ethical component is apparent in the thinking of those who adhere to this general view even though it may not be in accordance with views traditionally held, nor with the views of many religious groups.

In the third general viewpoint, which is in effect a somewhat amoral one, the central belief is that no restrictions are needed. If sexual impulses are allowed free rein, tension, anxiety, and frustration will be lowered, and happiness, satisfaction in living, and effectiveness increased. The main problem for those who hold this point of view is that of persuading other persons to accept this way of behaving.

Obviously, no one of these three viewpoints can be portrayed explicitly without some qualification. Any individual may move from one viewpoint to another, or he may adhere to one and act as if he upheld another. It is this discrepancy between outer appearance and private behavior that is confusing to many persons, young and old alike.

In the past, sexual behavior has been regulated in varying degrees by religious teachings and customs based on them and by fear of disaster if something goes wrong, such as detection, disease, or pregnancy. These deterrents to free sexual behavior have become somewhat weakened, especially during the last few decades for reasons familiar to everyone. At the same time there does not appear to have been any major moral breakdown. This suggests that the present generation of young people is fully as moral as any in the past although for different reasons.

College officials are very much concerned about certain key issues with respect to sexual behavior. For example, pressures toward experience which the young person does not wish and for which he is not yet ready may be unduly effective. A certain "bandwagon" effect occurs when peer group pressures push young people into such behavior. Frequently these pressures become so strong that a young person subject to them may feel guilty for *not* indulging in behavior currently popular, just as he may feel guilty *for* doing so if his training has been conventional or idealistic.

Illegitimate pregnancies pose problems which are virtually insoluble in terms of the social, cultural, and legal framework within which colleges must operate. It is probable that those persons who become pregnant are more disturbed emotionally than those who manage their lives without this complication. A recent study at a British university confirmed this thesis clearly [1]. The loss of any student because of the failure to manage sexual life successfully is always keenly felt by college officials as well as by the student's family.

Parental attitudes in general are not consistent enough for any guidelines or policy. Although opinions regarding sexual behavior are usually very firmly held, they are sometimes favorable and at other times unfavorable toward free sexual expression. Furthermore, when college administrators are called upon to take definite action in a given situation, there is a considerable tendency to blame such officials for their attempts at restoring order rather than looking at the original source of difficulty.

Freedom of choice is desired for all students, but when peer group pressures and the bandwagon effect become too strong, the individual may be deprived of this freedom.

I believe it is correct to assert that most college administrators do not wish to have a series of complicated and specific rules regarding behavior in this area; they realize that attempts at enforcement create many new problems. They do not wish to develop a spy system since the main purpose of the college experience is to enable students to develop the ability to make their own decisions—hopefully wise decisions. Most administrators are averse to impose on others their personal views, varying as these do from person to person, institution to institution, and section to section in the country. Administrators also cannot and do not wish to ignore public sentiment in the communities surrounding the colleges.

The excessive emphasis on all aspects of sex and obscenity which is now prevalent in novels, plays, and the mass media of communication may enable parents, teachers, and others to become more honest about sexual education than has been possible up to now.

At the present time it seems to me that the following problems that are well nigh insoluble prevent the promotion of a satisfactory kind of sexual education. Religious views vary among sects as well as in different parts of the country. Contraception is not completely reliable no matter what assurances some people may give. For college students this reliability may be impaired by conscious maneuvering on the part of one partner to produce pregnancy. The strong views of parents either in the direction of freedom of sexual behavior

or of control are not expressed in such a way as to be of much help. Those who have a vested interest in pornography are very ingenious in developing excellent arguments to prevent interference in their moneymaking activities. College administrators value freedom and dislike censorship. Drawing the line between these attitudes and the desire to be helpful in guiding the development of young people into channels which will not be destructive to their future is a very delicate matter. There is no consensus as to appropriate means of furthering sex education not only at the college level but at all stages of development. Variations in attitudes toward sexual education in different sections of the country make it almost impossible for any widespread program to be adopted. Not the least of the difficulties is that anyone working seriously for improved sexual adaptation almost invariably becomes the object of ridicule from his associates and others in the community.

Once a program is agreed upon, the question then arises as to who will carry it out. Should it be done by parents, physicians, members of the clergy, marital counselors, faculty members, or some other group? If persons in any of these groups are willing to undertake this task, then how shall they be trained? How is it possible to separate the giving of factual information from moralizing?

College officials may be reticent about imposing their views on others, but they do wish to make it crystal clear that they uphold high standards of personal behavior just as they uphold intellectual integrity. They want to encourage as much thoughtfulness in this area of behavior as in any other. They wish to develop the kind of behavior which will not bring unnecessary unhappiness or disaster to young people as they fashion a way of life which will strengthen rather than weaken family life.

In my opinion, no particular viewpoint can be forced on young people, but there should be full and frank discussion in families, in groups, between couples, and between older and younger colleagues in the colleges. If students are given answers without any real awareness of the issues, they will not be helped very much. If, however, a program is developed which will enable them to get a keen awareness of the issues that are involved, I believe that they will come up with better answers than our generation has been able to evolve.

After all, the problem is of more significance to young people than to those of the older generation. It is up to them to determine what kind of a world they want their children to live in. As they discuss sexual issues, it is desirable that they recall the nature of the training they experienced and the embarrassing situations they encountered in their childhood and to relate these experiences to their present problems. Finally, they should project their thoughts into the future in terms of developing attitudes toward sex which will be helpful as they begin to raise their own children. This three-dimensional approach to the problem helps bring some objectivity in place of the rather intense urgency with which most young adolescents and early adults view such problems.

Unfortunately, those who guide the policies of institutions get little help from parents, as I have already stated, because of the confusion and variety of their views, but I fear that they get even less help from the faculty. There is a tendency to leave all such matters to the dean's office and to give inadequate support to the idea that integrity confined to intellectual matters is quite insufficient and should be extended to all facets of behavior.

Even though the colleges are not *in loco parentis* to their students in the literal sense, they do have a responsibility to encourage them to adopt reasonable standards of behavior. There is no compelling reason for college administrators to be intimidated by the accusation that they are "upholding middle-class morals." The standards of morality and how they are determined and transmitted from one generation to another are proper and necessary subjects for continuing discussion between students and faculty members.

For parents, religious leaders, college officials, and all others who have a responsibility for late adolescents and young adults in secondary schools and colleges, some standards or ideals of behavior are desirable. Let us first examine the principle, "All premarital sexual intercourse is undesirable." Deviations from that code of behavior have every imaginable variety, ranging from rape or the production of a child with illegitimate parents (at the most regrettable end of the spectrum of undesirable

activities) to intercourse between engaged couples who expect to marry soon and who can marry at once if pregnancy occurs (at the least undesirable end). In each instance of departure from the ideal, the individual knows of its undesirability and is aware of possible consequences. If unpleasant developments follow, he is in a position to learn from his experience; there is no one on whom he can reasonably project blame.

Let us assume another principle: "Premarital sexual relations are undesirable for those who are immature or cannot undertake the responsibility for a possible child, but for those who are mature and responsible, they are enriching and ennobling." Immediately a couple considering such relations must classify themselves, just at the time when it is only logical that they should be optimistic. It is easy to guess what the decision will be. If tragedy ensues, as it occasionally does, who can wonder that they are confused about society's inconsistent attitudes toward them.

Until we resolve our own confusions, we will not be in a favorable position to help our younger colleagues thread their way through the devious paths of development to sexual maturity. The experiences in our college psychiatric and counseling services lead us to believe that those who ignore the conventional standards are no more happy or effective than those who observe them. In fact, I believe that they have more depression, anxiety, agitation, and other inhibiting emotional conflict than those who manage to adhere to their ideals.

A large proportion of the younger students who come from families with reasonable ideals feel more comfortable if limits are set, if some guidelines are evident, and if someone is present who cares enough about them to help them avoid disaster.

As college officials, we are more concerned with the quality of future marriages and the family life they make possible than with any particular physical act in which either partner may have been involved. Of course, this does not imply that the nature and extent of sexual activities before marriage is irrelevant to the success of that marriage.

If we are to progress in making sense out of this important area of personal development, we will need the sympathetic understanding and support of parents, faculty members, and the students themselves. There should then follow innumerable personal discussions, seminars, and other procedures for transmitting accurate information. At the same time, the complex issues associated with choice of behavior should be explored. Opinions concerning sexual behavior should be expressed, but not put forth as scientific facts.

Sexual education and the formation of standards of sexual morality are not separable from other aspects of personal maturation, nor should they be unduly circumscribed as they are pursued in the colleges. The goal should be that of aiding each student develop a healthy personality in which sexuality plays a constructive and satisfying part, rather than being considered undignified and regrettable.

References

1. Kidd, C. B., R. Giel and J. B. Brown. The antecedent mental health of pregnant unmarried women. Proceedings of the British Student Health Association. Oxford, 1964, For private circulation. Pp. 51-59.

2. Kinsey, A. C., W. B. Pomeroy, C. E. Martin and P. H. Gebhard. Sexual behavior in the human female. Philadelphia: W. B. Saunders Co., 1953. Pp. 293-296.

A special type of choice of object made by men (contributions to the psychology of love I)[1]

SIGMUND FREUD

Sigmund Freud, the founder of psychoanalysis, devoted much of his life to understanding the nature and origins of love and sexual behavior, and his ideas still influence much of the current psychological thinking on these topics. In this article, which was originally written in 1910, Freud describes some of the factors which contribute to the feeling of love in the adult male. He describes the basic characteristics that the woman must possess in order to arouse the feeling of love in the male and speculates about the relationship of love and sex. The ideas contained in the article are highly relevant for American society in view of the emphasis that is placed on love as an essential ingredient in the selection of a mate.

Up till now we have left it to the creative writer to depict for us the "necessary conditions for loving" which govern people's choice of an object, and the way in which they bring the demands of their imagination into harmony with reality. The writer can indeed draw on certain qualities which fit him to carry out such a task: above all, on a sensitivity that

Chapter XI, from COLLECTED PAPERS OF SIGMUND FREUD, edited by Ernest Jones, Basic Books, Inc., Publishers, New York, 1959. Published in Great Britain in Vol. XI, Standard Edition, THE COMPLETE PSYCHOLOGICAL WORKS OF SIGMUND FREUD. Reprinted by permission of Sigmund Freud Copyrights Ltd., The Estate of Mr. James Strachey, and The Hogarth Press Ltd.

[1] BEITRAGE ZUR PSYCHOLOGIE DES LIEBESLEBENS I
ÜBER EINEN BESONDEREN TYPUS DER OBJEKTWAHL BEIM MANNE
(a) German Editions:
1910 Fb. psychoan. psychopath. Forsch., 2 (2), 389-97. ('Beiträge zur Psychologie des Liebeslebens' I.)
1918 S.K.S.N., 4, 200-12. (2nd ed. 1922.)
1924 G.S., 5, 186-97.
1924 In Beiträge zur Psychologie des Liebeslebens, Leipzig, Vienna and Zurich: Internationaler Psychoanalytischer Verlag. (Pp. 3-14.)
1931 Sexualtheorie und Traumlehre, 69-80.
1943 G.W., 8, 66-77.
(b) English Translation:
'Contributions to the Psychology of Love: A Special Type of Choice of Object made by Men'

enables him to perceive the hidden impulses in the minds of other people, and the courage to let his own unconscious speak. But there is one circumstance which lessens the evidential value of what he has to say. Writers are under the necessity to produce intellectual and aesthetic pleasure, as well as certain emotional effects. For this reason they cannot reproduce the stuff of reality unchanged, but must isolate portions of it, remove disturbing associations, tone down the whole, and fill in what is missing. These are the privileges of what is known as "poetic license." Moreover, they can show only slight interest in the origin and development of the mental states which they portray in their completed form. In consequence, it becomes inevitable that science should concern herself with the same materials whose treatment by artists has given enjoyment to mankind for thousands of years, though her touch must be clumsier, and the yield of pleasure less. These observations will, it may be hoped, serve to justify us in extending a strictly scientific treatment to the field of human love. Science is, after all, the most complete renunciation of the pleasure principle of which our mental activity is capable.

In the course of psychoanalytic treatment there are ample opportunities for collecting impressions of the way in which neurotics behave in love; while at the same time, we can recall having observed or heard of similar behavior in people of average health or even in those with outstanding qualities. When the material happens to be favorable and thus leads to an accumulation of such impressions, distinct types emerge more clearly. I will begin here with a description of one such type of object-choice—which occurs in men—since it is characterized by a number of "necessary conditions for loving" whose combination is unintelligible, and indeed bewildering, and since it admits of a simple explanation on psychoanalytic lines.

(1) The first of these preconditions for loving can be described as positively specific: wherever it is found, the presence of the other characteristics of this type may be looked for. It may be termed the precondition that there should be "an injured third party"; it stipulates that the person in question shall never choose as his love-object a woman who is disengaged—that is, an unmarried girl or an unattached married woman—but only one to whom another man can claim right of possession as her husband, fiancé, or friend. In some cases this precondition proves so cogent that a woman can be ignored, or even rejected, so long as she does not belong to any man, but becomes the object of passionate feelings immediately she comes into one of these relationships with another man.

(2) The second precondition is perhaps a less constant one, but it is no less striking. It has to be found in conjunction with the first for the type to be realized, whereas the first precondition seems very often to occur independently as well. This second precondition is to the effect that a woman who is chaste and whose reputation is irreproachable never exercises an attraction that might raise her to the status of a love-object, but only a woman who is in some way or other of bad repute sexually, whose fidelity and reliability are open to some doubt. This latter characteristic may vary within substantial limits, from the faint breath of scandal attaching to a married woman who is not averse to a flirtation up to the openly promiscuous way of life of a *cocotte* or of an adept in the art of love; but the men who belong to our type will not be satisfied without something of the kind. This second necessary condition may be termed, rather crudely, "love for a prostitute."

While the first precondition provides an opportunity for gratifying impulses of rivalry and hostility directed at the man from whom the loved woman is wrested, the second one, that of the woman's being like a prostitute, is connected with the experiencing of *jealousy*, which appears to be a necessity for lovers of this type. It is only when they are able to be jealous that their passion reaches its height and the woman acquires her full value, and they never fail to seize on an occasion that allows

1925 C.P., 4, 192-202. (Tr. Joan Riviere.)

The present translation is a new one by Alan Tyson.

This and the two following papers, though they were written and published over a period of some years, were brought together by Freud in the fourth series of his shorter papers (S.K.S.N., 4, 1918) under the collective title printed above. We learn from Ernest Jones (1955, 333) that Freud had announced his intention of writing some such work at a meeting of the Vienna Psycho-Analytical Society on November 28, 1906. The gist of the present paper was given before the same society on May 19, 1909, and discussed a week later. But it was not actually written until the early summer of the following year.

them to experience these most powerful emotions. What is strange is that it is not the lawful possessor of the loved one who becomes the target of this jealousy, but strangers, making their appearance for the first time, in relation to whom the loved one can be brought under suspicion. In glaring instances the lover shows no wish for exclusive possession of the woman and seems to be perfectly comfortable in the triangular situation. One of my patients, who had been made to suffer terribly by his lady's escapades, had no objection to her getting married, and did all he could to bring it about; in the years that followed he never showed a trace of jealousy towards her husband. Another typical patient had, it is true, been very jealous of the husband in his first love affair, and had forced the lady to stop having marital relations; but in his numerous subsequent affairs he behaved like the other members of this type and no longer regarded the lawful husband as an interference.

So much for the conditions required in the love-object. The following points describe the lover's behavior towards the object he has chosen.

(3) In normal love the woman's value is measured by her sexual integrity, and is reduced by any approach to the characteristic of being like a prostitute.[2] Hence the fact that women with this characteristic are considered by men of our type to be *love-objects of the highest value* seems to be a striking departure from the normal. Their love-relationships with these women are carried on with the highest expenditure of mental energy, to the exclusion of all other interests; they are felt as the only people whom it is possible to love, and the demand for fidelity, which the lover makes upon himself, is repeated again and again, however often it may be broken in reality. These features of the love-relationships which I am here describing show their *compulsive* nature very clearly, though that is something which is found up to a certain degree whenever anyone falls in love. But the fidelity and intensity that mark the attachment must not lead one to expect that a single love-relationship of this kind will make up the whole erotic life of the person in question or occur only once in it. On the contrary, passionate attachments of this sort are repeated with the same peculiarities— each an exact replica of the others—again and

again in the lives of men of this type; in fact, owing to external events such as changes of residence and environment, the love-objects may replace one another so frequently that a *long series of them is formed.*

(4) What is most startling of all to the observer in lovers of this type is the urge they show to *"rescue"* the woman they love. The man is convinced that she is in need of him, that without him she would lose all moral control and rapidly sink to a lamentable level. He rescues her, therefore, by not giving her up. In some individual cases the idea of having to rescue her can be justified by reference to her sexual unreliability and the dangers of her social position: but it is no less conspicuous where there is no such basis in reality. One man of the type I am describing, who knew how to win his ladies by clever methods of seduction and subtle arguments, spared no efforts in the subsequent course of these affairs to keep the woman he was for the time being in love with on the path of "virtue" by presenting her with tracts of his own composition.

If we survey the different features of the picture presented here—the conditions imposed on the man that his loved one should not be unattached and should be like a prostitute, the high value he sets on her, his need for feeling jealousy, his fidelity, which is nevertheless compatible with being broken down into a long series of instances, and the urge to rescue the woman—it will seem scarcely probable that they should all be derived from a single source. Yet psychoanalytic exploration into the life-histories of men of this type has no difficulty in showing that there is such a single source. The object-choice which is so strangely conditioned, and this very singular way of behaving in love, have the same psychical origin as we find in the loves of normal people. They are derived from the infantile fixation of tender feelings on the mother, and represent one of the consequences of that fixation. In normal love only a few characteristics survive which reveal unmistakably the maternal prototype of the object-choice, as, for instance, the prefer-

[2] [The German *"Dirne,"* here and in several other passages in this paper, is not well rendered by "prostitute," which in English lays too much stress on the monetary side of the relation. "Harlot" would give the sense better, if the word had not today acquired an antiquated and even Biblical coloring.]

ence shown by young men for maturer women; the detachment of libido from the mother has been effected relatively swiftly. In our type, on the other hand, the libido has remained attached to the mother for so long, even after the onset of puberty, that the maternal characteristics remain stamped on the love-objects that are chosen later, and all these turn into easily recognizable mother-surrogates. The comparison with the way in which the skull of a newly born child is shaped[3] springs to mind at this point: after a protracted labor it always takes the form of a cast of the narrow part of the mother's pelvis.

We have now to show the plausibility of our assertion that the characteristic features of our type—its conditions for loving and its behavior in love—do in fact arise from the psychical constellation connected with the mother. This would seem to be easiest where the first precondition is concerned—the condition that the woman should not be unattached, or that there should be an injured third party. It is at once clear that for the child who is growing up in the family circle, the fact of the mother belonging to the father becomes an inseparable part of the mother's essence, and that the injured third party is none other than the father himself. The trait of overvaluing the loved one, and regarding her as unique and irreplaceable, can be seen to fall just as naturally into the context of the child's experience, for no one possesses more than one mother, and the relation to her is based on an event that is not open to any doubt and can not be repeated.

If we are to understand the love-objects chosen by our type as being above all mother-surrogates, then the formation of a series of them, which seems so flatly to contradict the condition of being faithful to one, can now also be understood. We have learned from psychoanalysis in other examples that the notion of something irreplaceable, when it is active in the unconscious, frequently appears as broken up into an endless series: endless for the reason that every surrogate nevertheless fails to provide the desired satisfaction. This is the explanation of the insatiable urge to ask questions shown by children at a certain age: they have one single question to ask, but it never crosses their lips.[4] It explains, too, the garrulity of some people affected by neurosis;

they are under the pressure of a secret which is burning to be disclosed but which, despite all temptation, they never reveal.

On the other hand the second precondition for loving—the condition that the object chosen should be like a prostitute—seems energetically to oppose a derivation from the mother-complex. The adult's conscious thought likes to regard his mother as a person of unimpeachable moral purity; and there are few ideas which he finds so offensive when they come from others, or feels as so tormenting when they spring from his own mind, as one which calls this aspect of his mother in question. This very relation of the sharpest contrast between "mother" and "prostitute" will, however, encourage us to enquire into the history of the development of these two complexes and the unconscious relation between them, since we long ago discovered that what, in the conscious, is found split into a pair of opposites often occurs in the unconscious as a unity.[5] Investigation then leads us back to the time in a boy's life at which he first gains a more or less complete knowledge of the sexual relations between adults, somewhere about the years of prepuberty. Brutal pieces of information, which are undisguisedly intended to arouse contempt and rebelliousness, now acquaint him with the secret of sexual life and destroy the authority of adults, which appears incompatible with the revelation of their sexual activities. The aspect of these disclosures which affects the newly initiated child most strongly is the way in which they apply to his own parents. This application is often flatly rejected by him, in some such words as these: *"Your parents and other people may do something like that with one another, but my parents can't possibly do it."* [6]

As an almost invariable corollary to this sexual enlightenment, the boy at the same time gains a knowledge of the existence of certain women who practice sexual intercourse as a means of livelihood, and who are for this reason

---

[3] [In the editions before 1924 this read "deformed."]
[4] [This point is also made by Freud in his essay on Leonardo da Vinci (1910c), above, p. 78.]
[5] [This fact had already been hinted at in Freud's *Interpretation of dreams* (1900a), *Standard Ed.*, 4, 318, and explicitly mentioned in Chapter VI of his book on jokes (1905c). See also above, p. 155 ff.]
[6] [Cf. the last paragraph of Freud's paper on the sexual theories of children (1908c).]

held in general contempt. The boy himself is necessarily far from feeling this contempt: as soon as he learns that he too can be initiated by these unfortunates into sexual life, which till then he accepted as being reserved exclusively for "grown-ups," he regards them only with a mixture of longing and horror. When after this, he can no longer maintain the doubt which makes his parents an exception to the universal and odious norms of sexual activity, he tells himself with cynical logic that the difference between his mother and a whore is not after all so very great, since basically they do the same thing. The enlightening information he has received has in fact awakened the memory-traces of the impressions and wishes of his early infancy, and these have led to a reactivation in him of certain mental impulses. He begins to desire his mother herself in the sense with which he has recently become acquainted, and to hate his father anew as a rival who stands in the way of this wish; he comes, as we say, under the dominance of the Oedipus complex.[7] He does not forgive his mother for having granted the favor of sexual intercourse not to himself but to his father, and he regards it as an act of unfaithfulness. If these impulses do not quickly pass, there is no outlet for them other than to run their course in phantasies which have as their subject his mother's sexual activities under the most diverse circumstances; and the consequent tension leads particularly readily to his finding relief in masturbation. As a result of the constant combined operation of the two driving forces, desire and thirst for revenge, phantasies of his mother's unfaithfulness are by far the most preferred; the lover with whom she commits her act of infidelity almost always exhibits the features of the boy's own ego, or more accurately, of his own idealized personality, grown up and so raised to a level with his father. What I have elsewhere [8] described as the "family romance" comprises the manifold ramifications of this imaginative activity and the way in which they are interwoven with various egoistic interests of this period of life.

Now that we have gained an insight into this piece of mental development we can no longer regard it as contradictory and incomprehensible that the precondition of the loved one's being like a prostitute should derive directly from the mother-complex. The type of male love which

we have described bears the traces of this evolution and is simple to understand as a fixation on the phantasies formed by the boy in puberty —phantasies which have later after all found a way out into real life. There is no difficulty in assuming that the masturbation assiduously practiced in the years of puberty has played its part in the fixation of the phantasies.

To these phantasies which have succeeded in dominating the man's love in real life, the urge to *rescue* the loved one seems to bear merely a loose and superficial relation, and one that is fully accounted for by conscious reasons. By her propensity to be fickle and unfaithful the loved one brings herself into dangerous situations, and thus it is understandable that the lover should be at pains to protect her from these dangers by watching over her virtue and counteracting her bad inclinations. However, the study of people's screen-memories, phantasies and nocturnal dreams shows that we have here a particularly felicitous "rationalization" of an unconscious motive, a process which may be compared to a successful secondary revision of a dream. In actual fact the "rescue-*motif*" has a meaning and history of its own, and is an independent derivative of the mother-complex, or more accurately, of the parental complex. When a child hears that he *owes his life* to his parents, or that his mother *gave him life,* his feelings of tenderness unite with impulses which strive at power and independence, and they generate the wish to return this gift to the parents and to repay them with one of equal value. It is as though the boy's defiance were to make him say: "I want nothing from my father; I will give him back all I have cost him." He then forms the phantasy of *rescuing his father from danger and saving his life;* in this way he puts his account square with him. This phantasy is commonly enough displaced on to the emperor, king, or some other great man; after being thus distorted it becomes admissible to consciousness, and may even be made use of by creative writers. In its application to a

---

[7] [This appears to be Freud's first published use of the actual term. The concept had, of course, long been familiar to him (cf. *Standard Ed., 4,* 263n.), and he had already spoken of the "nuclear complex," e.g., in the paper referred to in the last footnote and in his "Five Lectures," 1910a, above, p. 47.]

[8] In [a discussion included in] Rank's *The myth of the birth of the hero* (1909) [Freud (1909c)].

boy's father it is the defiant meaning in the idea of rescuing which is by far the most important; where his mother is concerned it is usually its tender meaning. The mother gave the child life, and it is not easy to find a substitute of equal value for this unique gift. With a slight change of meaning, such as is easily effected in the unconscious and is comparable to the way in which in consciousness concepts shade into one another, rescuing his mother takes on the significance of giving her a child or making a child for her—needless to say, one like himself. This is not too remote from the original sense of rescuing, and the change in meaning is not an arbitrary one. His mother gave him a life—his own life—and in exchange he gives her another life, that of a child which has the greatest resemblance to himself. The son shows his gratitude by wishing to have by his mother a son who is like himself: in other words, in the rescue-phantasy he is completely identifying himself with his father. All his instincts, those of tenderness, gratitude, lustfulness, defiance and independence, find satisfaction in the single wish *to be his own father*. Even the element of danger has not been lost in the change of meaning; for the act of birth itself is the danger from which he was saved by his mother's efforts. Birth is both the first of all dangers to life and the prototype of all the later ones that cause us to feel anxiety, and the experience of birth has probably left behind in us the expression of affect which we call anxiety. Macduff of the Scottish legend, who was not born of his mother but ripped from her womb, was for that reason unacquainted with anxiety.[9]

Artemidorus, the dream-interpreter of antiquity, was certainly right in maintaining that the meaning of a dream depends on who the dreamer happens to be.[10] Under the laws governing the expression of unconscious thoughts, the meaning of rescuing may vary, depending on whether the author of the phantasy is a man or a woman. It can equally mean (in a man) making a child, i.e. causing it to be born, or (in a woman) giving birth oneself to a child. These various meanings of rescuing in dreams and phantasies can be recognized particularly clearly when they are found in connection with water. A man rescuing a woman from the water in a dream means that he makes her a mother, which in the light of the preced-

ing discussion amounts to making her his own mother. A woman rescuing someone else (a child) from the water acknowledges herself in this way as the mother who bore him, like Pharaoh's daughter in the legend of Moses (Rank, 1909). At times there is also a tender meaning contained in rescue-phantasies directed towards the father. In such cases they aim at expressing the subject's wish to have his father as a son—that is, to have a son who is like his father.[11]

It is on account of all these connections between the rescue-*motif* and the parental complex that the urge to rescue the loved one forms an important feature of the type of loving which I have been discussing.

I do not feel that it is necessary for me to justify my method of work on this subject; as in my presentation of anal erotism [Freud (1908b)], so here too I have in the first place aimed at singling out from the observational material extreme and sharply defined types. In both cases we find a far greater number of individuals in whom only a few features of the type can be recognized, or only features which are not distinctly marked, and it is obvious that a proper appreciation of these types will not be possible until the whole context to which they belong has been explored.[12]

---

[9] [*Macbeth*, V, 7. This is Freud's first extended allusion to the relation between birth and anxiety. He had already referred to the question in a footnote added in the previous year (1909) to Chapter VI (E) of *The interpretation of dreams* (1900a), *Standard Ed.*, 5, 400-1, and had mentioned it in a discussion at the Vienna Psycho-Analytical Society on November 17, 1909 (Jones, 1955, 494). He dealt with it again at some length near the beginning of Lecture XXV of the *Introductory Lectures* (1916-17). But his longest discussion of it will, of course, be found in *Inhibitions, symptoms and anxiety* (1926d), especially in Chapters II, VIII and XI, A (b), where his former opinions are largely revised. At the beginning of his psychological studies Freud had connected the symptoms of anxiety not with the experience of birth, but with the accompaniments of copulation. Cf. the penultimate paragraph of Section III of his first paper on anxiety neurosis (1895b) and a passage near the end of the probably even earlier Draft E in the Fliess correspondence (Freud, 1950a).]
[10] [Cf. a passage in Chapter II of *The interpretation of dreams* (1900a), *Standard Ed.*, 4, 98, and a footnote to it added in 1914.]
[11] [Dreams of rescuing are mentioned in a paragraph added in 1911 to Chapter VI (E) of *The interpretation of dreams, Standard Ed.*, 5, 403. A woman's rescue dream is analyzed in Freud's paper on "Dreams and telepathy" (1922a), *Standard Ed.*, 18, 212 ff.]
[12] [In a paper (1920a) written many years after the present one, Freud demonstrated the occurrence of precisely the same type of object-choice in a homosexual girl, *Standard Ed.*, 18, 160 f.]

5

CRISIS AND RESPONSE: MAN REACTS TO STRESS

In an era of tranquilizers, LSD, Viet Nam, civil riots, and the Middle East crisis, the term stress needs little introduction. Nevertheless, the opinions of psychologists and psychiatrists vary considerably with regard to the nature of stress, how different individuals respond to it, and its effects on the person. Our task in this section is to review some of these issues.

Pepitone (1967) suggests that "there is no one correct definition of stress," and a review of the anthropological, psychological, physiological, psychiatric, and sociological literature tends to confirm his observation. Selye (1956), who has been instrumental in stimulating much of the present interest in the topic, defines stress as "the state manifested by a specific syndrome which consists of all the nonspecifically induced changes within a biologic system (p. 54)." In this context, the experiencing of stress is essentially a biological phenomenon which involves a pattern of well-defined physiological reactions that Selye labels the "General Adaptation Syndrome." While many situations (called *stressors* by Selye) are capable of inducing stress, Selye feels that the term should be reserved for the reaction itself. Lazarus (1966) indicates that four main classes of re-

sponses are usually used by researchers to indicate stress: 1) reports of upset emotions, such as anger, fear, guilt, and depression; 2) different forms of motor behavior, such as increased muscle tension, tremor, certain facial expressions, and speech disturbance; 3) impairment in cognitive functioning, which includes a variety of inefficiencies in thinking, problem solving, judgment, and perception; and, 4) a multitude of physiological changes.

Stress need not refer only to a response pattern. The term is often applied to the stimulus conditions, either external or internal, that produce the reactions.

Many situations are well known to be stress-inducing, and several of these have been carefully described. Specifically, stress and the responses to it have been studied in the context of life in a Nazi concentration camp (Bettelheim, 1943; 1960); anticipated surgery (Janis, 1948; Titchener & Levine, 1960); parachute training (Fenz, 1964; Basowitz, Persky, Korchin & Grinker, 1955); aerial combat (Grinker & Spiegal, 1945); decision-making by college students (Silber et al, 1961); patients with severe injuries (Hamburg, Hamburg & DeGoza, 1953); and parents with fatally ill children

(Chodoff, Friedman, & Hamburg, 1964). Hamburg and Adams (1967) list seventeen examples of stressful situations that have been emphasized in the recent research and clinical literature.

The different uses of the term stress have led to terminological confusion about what the concept refers to. Lazarus (1966) suggests that one way out of this difficulty is to use the concept of stress to refer generally to "the whole area of problems that includes the stimuli producing stress reactions, the reactions themselves and the various intervening processes (p. 27)." Although stress includes concepts representing physiological, sociological, and psychological variables, we shall restrict our discussion to the psychological aspects of stress.

Stress as anxiety

For many psychologists, stress is best understood as an example of anxiety. As Levitt (1967) notes: "A 'stress' or 'stressful situation' is one containing stimuli or circumstances calculated to arouse anxiety in the individual" (p. 12). Attempts to understand anxiety, in turn, frequently involve comparing it with fear. Both fear and anxiety have in common the awareness of certain well-known physiological changes, such as increased heartbeat, the sensation of "butterflies" in the pit of the stomach, and perspiration of the hands or other parts of the body. Whether these physiological sensations are called responses to fear or to anxiety is due to the circumstances surrounding the experience rather than to qualitative differences in the nature of the sensations themselves. As Levitt (1967) notes:

. . . no difference between anxiety and fear, no matter how they are conceptualized in theory, is reflected in physiological concomitants. The human body reacts in much the same fashion whether the anxiety is considered to be specific, diffuse, exaggerated, or realistic.

The distinction between anxiety and fear is no more than theoretical, at least at present. Experimentalists consider the terms to be interchangeable, with perhaps different shading of meaning (p. 10-11).

Not all psychologists would agree with this conclusion, and several hypotheses have been offered for differentiating fear and anxiety. Horney (1937) suggests that,

Fear and anxiety are both proportionate reactions to danger, but in the case of fear the danger is a transparent, objective one and in the case of anxiety it is hidden and subjective. That is, the intensity of the anxiety is proportionate to the meaning the situation has for the person concerned, and the reasons why he is thus anxious are essentially unknown to him (p. 43-44).

Goldstein (1939) differentiates fear from anxiety by suggesting that fear involves the conscious confrontation with an object which we can avoid or attempt to remove. When we are afraid, we can specify the cause of the fear and determine how we shall react to it. Anxiety, on the other hand, has no recognizable origin. It attacks, according to Goldstein (1939), "from the rear." Consequently, reassurance that the danger is nonexistent does not help to diminish the anxiety, and specific adaptive responses are not readily available. May (1950) considers fear more closely related to a specific event, whereas anxiety is more general or "free-floating." May (1950) writes that "the central difference between fear and anxiety is that fear is a reaction to a specific danger while anxiety is unspecific, 'vague,' 'objectless.' The special characteristics of anxiety are the feelings of *uncertainty* and *helplessness* in the face of danger" (p. 190-191). According to Sechrest and Wallace (1967), "Anxiety can be considered strong fear. However, it differs from fear in one important respect. In anxiety the *source* of fear is vague and poorly defined. Typically, the anxious individual is totally unaware of the reasons for his apprehensions. He can't identify the reasons why he feels 'at loose ends' " (p. 82).

This last distinction calls attention to the hypothesis that fear and anxiety occupy different levels of awareness. Fear is considered conscious or fully within awareness, but anxiety is thought to be either outside of awareness (unconscious) or at a very low level of awareness. As Horney (1937) notes:

The degree of awareness of a feeling does not indicate anything of its strength or importance. Concerning anxiety this means not only that we may have anxiety without knowing it, but that anxiety may be the determining factor in our lives without our being conscious of it.

In fact, we seem to go to any length to escape anxiety or to avoid feeling it (p. 45-46).

Anxiety experienced in this manner is often described as a general sense of "impending doom," an uncanny feeling of threat, or, as one Kentucky mountaineer once stated, "I'm as nervous as a long-tailed cat in a room full of rocking chairs."

The source of anxiety

Psychological theorists have probably devoted more attention to the source of anxiety than to its other characteristics. Freud had two theories of anxiety. In his original theory, Freud (1895) considered anxiety to be the result of certain sexual practices which failed to provide adequate outlets for accumulated sexual energy (libido). Specifically, "voluntary or involuntary abstinence, sexual intercourse with incomplete gratification, coitus interruptus, the deflection of psychical interest from sexuality" are some of the situations responsible for the development of anxiety (Freud, 1895b, p. 108). Freud hypothesized that this accumulated amount of libido was transformed into anxiety, although he never described the details of the conversion process. Later, Freud (1926) modified his theory of anxiety and related it to the occurrence of *traumatic situations* and *danger situations*.

According to Freud, traumatic situations occur when the individual is overwhelmed by excessive stimulation. The prototype for this is the experience of birth. Anxiety is experienced by the ego, and in the newborn infant, the ego is insufficiently developed to handle the tremendous amount of stimulation associated with entrance into the world. In later life, any situation which produces sufficient stimulation to overwhelm the person constitutes a traumatic event. Civilian disasters, combat experiences in times of war, and other danger situations which involve the immediate threat to one's life are examples of traumatic situations. It is important to note that the source of anxiety can be either external or internal. Although the source is external at birth, Freud (1926) indicated that most traumatic experiences result from internal stimulation. Specifically, anxiety originates from the child's or adult's inability

to satisfy biological drives emanating from the id. For example, sexual wishes directed toward a parent, member of the same sex, or other socially unacceptable objects are anxiety-producing.

A *danger situation* exists when the person is forewarned of a traumatic situation. In this regard, anxiety serves as a *signal* to warn the child of impending danger. Freud described several typical danger situations of childhood. The first situation the child interprets as dangerous is the separation from an important adult, such as the mother, who is an important source of gratification for the child. Next, is the fear of loss of love from a significant adult, even though the person is physically present. Finally, the fear of castration experienced by the young boy during the Oedipal conflict is a source of considerable anxiety. The little girl fears some analogous injury to her genitals during this state. These danger situations are usually overcome without difficulty. In fact, signal anxiety is an essential aspect of normal personality development, for it allows the ego to maintain control over id impulses. However, in excessive amounts, signal anxiety is the basis for the development of neuroses.

The basic source of anxiety for Horney (1937) is "an insidiously increasing, all-pervading feeling of being lonely and helpless in a hostile world" which can be caused by a variety of childhood experiences (p. 89). Specifically, this insecurity can be produced by "direct or indirect domination, indifference, erratic behavior, lack of respect for the child's individual needs, lack of real guidance, disparaging attitudes, too much admiration or the absence of it, lack of reliable warmth, having to take sides in parental disagreements, too much or too little responsibility, overprotection, isolation from other children, injustice, discrimination, unkept promises, hostile atmosphere, and so on and so on" (Horney, 1945, p. 41).

One of the most popular explanations of anxiety is the hypothesis that anxiety is learned from the association of a neutral stimulus with a painful experience. This approach has been most extensively explored by Dollard and Miller (1950), although the idea was originally introduced by Freud (1915a). A *phobia* is a specific fear of certain objects or situations in daily life even though they are not inherently dangerous. Freud (1915a) explained phobias on the basis of unacceptable impulses from the unconscious becoming attached to substitute ideas or objects. When the person is confronted by the substitute object, the object is likely to stimulate the anxiety which is experienced by the person in the form of a fear. For example, in the famous case of *little Hans,* Freud (1909) discovered that the five-year-old boy's fear of being bitten by a horse if he went out of the house was related to unconscious fears of castration.

Using a similar rationale, Dollard and Miller (1950) have investigated how anxiety or fear is learned. Their basic assumption, like Freud's, is that everyone is motivated to avoid pain. The avoidance of pain is considered to be a primary drive, and a person will learn to be afraid of anything that is associated with pain. The amount or intensity of the fear is directly related to both the number of painful experiences and the intensity of the pain associated with each experience. An important aspect of the Dollard and Miller theory is its emphasis on the role of generalization. Generalization occurs when the fear response, which has been learned in one situation, is evoked by a different situation. The likelihood of this occurring is a direct function of the similarity of the two situations. The more similar, the greater the probability that generalization will take place. The child who receives a painful injection from a doctor in a white coat is more likely to be afraid of a new doctor who wears a white coat than one who does not, other things being equal.

Although the pain-based concept of anxiety has considerable common sense appeal as well as support from research, there is reason to question its adequacy as a completely satisfactory explanation. Specifically, Kessen and Mandler (1961) point out that children with congenital analgesia, a rare condition involving total insensitivity to pain, also develop anxieties. The fact that these children, who are incapable of experiencing pain, still have anxiety suggests that pain is not the only source of anxiety. As an alternative hypothesis, Kessen and Mandler (1961) suggest that anxiety develops in association with conditions of *fundamental distress* in the newborn and young child. Distressful conditions include lack of food, changes in temperature, and other unpleasant stimulus conditions. Any drive state is capable of becoming associated with stress.

Anxiety has also been interpreted as a consequence of psychological conflict. A conflict situation exists when a person is simultaneously motivated to make two opposing responses. Introductory textbooks in psychology generally describe four basic types of conflict situations. *Approach-approach* conflicts involve the choice between two appealing alternatives, such as trying to decide on steak or roast beef for dinner. This kind of conflict is not terribly anxiety arousing since the person stands to gain regardless of his decision.

Approach-avoidance conflicts exist when a person has to decide about something which has both positive and negative characteristics. The student wanting to elect a course that has the reputation of being interesting but difficult is faced with this kind of conflict. Approach-avoidance conflicts are highly similar to what psychoanalysts call *ambivalence,* which is the simultaneous experiencing of opposing feelings, like love and hate, toward the same object. The child who feels anger toward a parent may experience considerable anxiety and guilt as a result of this feeling, particularly if the parent is outwardly loving and generous.

Avoidance-avoidance conflicts necessitate choosing between two undesirable alternatives. The college student majoring in English, who lacks a scientific aptitude, is likely to experience this conflict when he is faced with selecting a course in chemistry or a course in physics in order to satisfy graduation requirements. Finally, there are *double approach-avoidance* conflicts which require a choice between two alternatives, each of which has positive and negative characteristics. This type of conflict is probably most similar to the more difficult and complex decisions that occur in daily life, such as making a choice between two jobs, two automobiles, or two mates.

Despite the variation in the theories about its nature and source, the concept of anxiety is generally used to designate the psychological processes that occur between the stress stimulus and the person's response. Lazarus (1966) suggests that the term "threat" is better suited to "express the condition of the person or animal when confronted with a stimulus that he appraises as endangering important values and goals" (p. 28). It is interesting to note the similarity between Lazarus's definition of threat and May's (1950) definition of anxiety as,

"... the apprehension cued off by a threat to some value which the individual holds essential to his existence as a personality" (p. 191). Similarly, Thorne (1963) asserts that the threat of failure is the primary stimulus in anxiety and suggests that failure results whenever anything blocks the individual's tendency toward self-actualization. Regardless of its label or specific definition, the importance of anxiety as a human experience cannot be denied. As Fromm-Reichman (1955) notes: "The most unpleasant and at the same time the most universal experience, except loneliness, is anxiety. We observe both healthy and mentally disturbed people doing everything possible to ward off anxiety and keep it from awareness" (p. 113).

Psychological reactions to stress

The human responses to stress are extremely varied. Historically, the various forms of self-protective behavior used to cope with psychological stress have been discussed under the heading of *defense mechanisms* (Anna Freud, 1936). The notion of psychological defense against threat is generally traced back to Freud, although the specific use of the concept in the form of repression was first mentioned by Schopenhauer (1819). Nevertheless, Freud's ideas have been primarily responsible for stimulating most of the research and theory on psychological defense. In his early writings, Freud (1894, 1896) used the terms defense and repression interchangeably and pointed out that the defensive process was unintentional and not willfully motivated by the person. Initially, psychological defense was simply "an attempt to repress an unbearable idea which appeared in painful contrast to the ego of the patient" (S. Freud, 1896, p. 155). Later, Freud (1915b) described repression as an activity of the ego oriented toward keeping unwanted id impulses, or any of the id's derivatives, out of consciousness.

Anna Freud (1936) provided a more detailed theoretical and behavioral description of the notion of defense by introducing an expanded classification of defenses. She deviated from the writings of her father by stressing the multiplicity of defenses and the bi-directionality of ego-defense (against pain from without and against the instincts from within). In her own words: "At particular periods in life and according to its own specific structure the in-dividual ego selects now one defensive method now another—it may be repression, displacement, reversal, etc.—and these it can employ both in its conflict with the instincts and in its defense against the liberation of affect" (Anna Freud, 1936, p. 34).

Consistent with these specific formulations of Anna Freud is Fenichel (1945), who summarizes the defensive processes of the ego as follows: "The ego learns to ward off impulses that are either dangerous or inappropriate. Mechanisms that first were used against painful external stimuli now become turned against inner drives" (p. 51). More recently, Gero (1951) maintains that: "Today, the conception of defense is extremely complex. It refers to a set of unconscious activities of the ego which partake of all the puzzling qualities of unconscious processes and which occur without any intentional effort" (p. 565).

A number of defense mechanisms have been described by psychoanalytic theorists. Let us consider just a few as examples of this approach. In addition to repression, denial, projection, fixation, regression, and reaction formation are probably the most frequently cited defense mechanisms. *Denial,* as used originally by Anna Freud (1936), refers to the child's blocking of certain unpleasant perceptions of the outside world. This is usually accomplished by some form of wish-fulfilling fantasy. Brenner (1955) cites the example of the little boy who denies his fear of his father by claiming to be the heavyweight boxing champion of the world and by walking around the house wearing a belt symbolic of this strength. *Projection* is an attempt to remove anxiety arousing impulses by attributing them to someone or something in the external world. In projection, "I hate him" becomes "he hates me." *Reaction formation* consists of replacing an anxiety-producing feeling with its opposite. A frequently cited example is the overprotective mother whose excessive display of love for a child may represent unconscious feelings of rejection or hostility toward the child. *Fixation* and *regression* are closely related. Fixation refers to the maintenance of behavior corresponding to a particular age or stage of development. It represents a failure to pass on to the next stage as a result of excessive anxiety or frustration associated with either the present or anticipated stage. Regression is a return to a previous stage of development in the face of psychological stress. Temporary regression is often characteristic of children when a new baby is born into the same family. The older child may revert to soiling, baby talk, thumb sucking, or some other infantile behavior in order to obtain the attention of the mother.

Defense mechanisms refer to the specific behaviors which persons use to protect themselves against their unconscious conflicts and impulses. Like the conflicts themselves, the defenses are unconscious. They operate outside the awareness of the person even though the defensive behavior may be apparent to other people. Defense mechanisms also deny, falsify, or distort the individual's perception of reality. For this reason, they are essentially maladaptive. According to psychoanalytic theory, all of us use defense mechanisms. The psychologically healthy person can be differentiated from the neurotic or emotionally disturbed person on the basis of: 1) the number of defenses used; 2) the kinds of defenses used; and 3) the frequency or extent to which defenses are used. The use of defenses per se cannot be the only criterion for differentiating maladaptive from adaptive behavior.

It is perhaps the awareness of this last factor that has caused some psychologists to challenge the traditional psychoanalytic view of the concept of psychological defense. Many psychologists do not like the idea of the "healthy being less sick" and have attempted to introduce additional concepts that would account for more adaptive solutions to psychological threat. Typically, the word *coping* is used to differentiate these more adaptive behaviors from defense mechanisms. Mechanic (1967) describes his separation of the terms as follows:

Coping, as I use the term, refers to the instrumental behavior and instrumental capacities in meeting life demands and goals. It involves the application of skills, techniques, and knowledge that a person has acquired. The extent to which a person experiences discomfort in the first place depends on the adequacy or inadequacy of these skills or techniques to a very large extent. Defense, as I use the term, refers to the manner in which a person manages his emotional and affective states when discomfort is aroused or anticipated. Thus, dissonance reduction, the manipulation of self-evaluations, social comparison, and

the like, tend to be primarily problems of defense and not problems of coping (p. 201).

Hamburg and Adams (1967) suggest that behavior serves coping functions "when it increases the likelihood (from a specific vantage point with respect to a specific time unit) that a task will be accomplished according to standards tolerable to both the individual and the group in which he lives" (p. 280). Although they point out that there is much individual variability in patterns of coping behavior, Hamburg and Adams (1967) emphasize that the "seeking and utilizing of information" is an important characteristic of coping behavior by patients with severe illness, parents of fatally ill children, and adolescents adapting to the difficult psychosocial transition of high school to college.

Kroeber (1963) describes the person as having the capacity to act in either a defensive (maladaptive) or coping (adaptive) manner. Coping behavior represents an extension of the traditional concept of defense mechanisms and refers to "behaviors that are particularly relevant to an active, effective person dealing with demands, often conflicting, of a biological, psychological, or social nature" (p. 179). Specifically, Kroeber (1963) suggests that there are "ego mechanisms" which can serve a coping or defensive purpose. Defense mechanisms differ from coping mechanisms in the following ways: 1) Defense mechanisms are rigid, compelled, and possibly conditioned while coping mechanisms are more flexible, purposive, and involve a greater element of choice. 2) Defensive behavior is motivated by past events but coping behavior is more future-oriented. 3) Defense mechanisms distort the individual's perception of the situation; coping mechanisms accurately represent the reality characteristics of the situation. 4) Defense mechanisms include a greater amount of the illogical, emotional thinking characteristic of the unconscious, while coping mechanisms are more conscious and logical. 5) The person using defense mechanisms operates with the naive belief that it is possible and necessary to totally remove disturbing feelings. However, this attitude may involve unrealistic thinking. Coping behavior helps the individual to handle or control disturbing feelings to the extent the person feels this is necessary. 6) Coping mechanisms allow for the open, controlled, and moderated satisfaction of impulses. Defense mechanisms only allow for the indirect or vicarious satisfaction of impulses.

In recent years the concept of psychological defense has been extended beyond the idea of certain specific behavior reactions to include more general predispositions toward behavior. Much of the impetus for this development has come from the laboratory where research on the personality has suggested that individuals have characteristic modes of perceiving and appraising threat. Typically, these behaviors are discussed within the category of cognitive style. While a number of similar cognitive styles have been described, such as leveling-sharpening (Holzman & Gardner, 1959), facilitation-inhibition (Ullman, 1962), and externalization-internalization (Shannon, 1962), repression-sensitization is the behavioral dimension that has stimulated the most research. According to Altrocchi (1961):

Repressors are defined as those who tend to use avoidance, denial, and repression of potential threat and conflict as a primary mode of adaptation; sensitizers are defined as those who tend to be alerted to potential threat and conflict, to respond more readily with manifest anxiety, and to use intellectual and obsessive defenses (p. 528).

This definition parallels that of Byrne (1963) who states:

Repression-sensitization refers to a personality variable consisting of individual differences in ways of responding to threatening stimuli. At the repression extreme are predominantly avoiding behaviors (including denial and sweet-lemon rationalization) while the sensitizing end is made up of predominantly approaching mechanisms (including intellectualization, obsession-compulsion, and sour-grape rationalization).

Although the use of the term "repression-sensitization" is fairly recent, the denoted behavior has both theoretical and empirical antecedents. Theoretically, Hartman (1939) has noted that:

The single fact is decisive that every individual selects only certain of the possible defense-mechanisms and invariably employs those which he has selected. This suggests that each individual ego is endowed from the beginning with its own peculiar dispositions and tendencies, though we cannot predicate their nature and conditioning factors (p. 365).

Rosenzweig (1938) noted the consistency of an individual's reaction to threat, and his concepts of the *impunitive, extrapunitive,* and *intrapunitive* personality are direct forerunners of the contemporary repressor and sensitizer. It is interesting to note the similarity between Rosenzweig's (1938) earlier formulations and some of the present ideas on cognitive style:

The factor in question concerns the way in which individuals seemed, according to the impression of the experimenter, to vary in their *immediate reaction to frustration or failure.* These variations in reaction appeared to correlate with subsequent predominance in recall of successes or failures. Briefly, it seemed that individuals who at the time of experiencing failure were inclined to blame the external world (e.g. the puzzles, the experimenter) —a type of reaction later called "extrapunitive" —or to blame themselves—later called "intrapunitive"—tended characteristically to recall their failures, in contradiction to the repression hypothesis; only those who tended to gloss over their failures as if inevitable and tried to rationalize them away at the time of their occurrence—a type of reaction later called "impunitive"—recalled their successes better than their failures, i.e., displayed stimulus repression (p. 486).

There is increasing reason to believe that what is stressful for a given individual and what constitutes an adaptive response to stress will vary for different persons. Specific life situations may be much more influential in determining the characteristics of stress than we have previously thought. Despite these differences, however, it is possible for the individual to gain insight into possible sources of personal stress by becoming familiar with the experiences of others. The readings in this section present discussions of specific problems related to psychological stress and are intended to provide points of departure for the reader who desires to understand better his own anxieties.

References

Altrocchi, J. Interpersonal perceptions of repressors and sensitizers and component analyses of assumed dissimilarity scores. *J. abnorm. soc. Psychol.*, 1961, 62, 528-534.

Basowitz, H., Persky, H., Korchin, S. J., & Grinker, R. R. *Anxiety and stress.* New York: McGraw-Hill, 1955.

Bettelheim, B. Individual and mass behavior in extreme situations. *J. abnorm. soc. Psych.*, 1943, 38, 417-452.

Bettelheim, B. *The informed heart.* New York: Free Press, 1960.

Brenner, C. *An elementary textbook of psychoanalysis.* New York: International Universities Press, 1955. Also available in paperback published by Anchor Books, Doubleday (N.Y.).

Byrne, D., Barry, J., & Nelson, D. Relation of the revised repression-sensitization scale to measures of self-description. *Psychol. Reports,* 1963, 13, 323-334.

Chodoff, P., Friedman, S., & Hamburg, D. Stress, defenses, and coping behavior: Observations in patients of children with malignant disease. *American J. of Psychiatry,* 1964, 120, 743-749.

Dollard, J. & Miller, N. E. *Personality and psychotherapy.* New York: McGraw-Hill, 1950. Also available in paperback.

Fenichel, O. *The psychoanalytic theory of neurosis.* New York: Norton, 1945

Fenz, W. D. Conflict and stress as related to physiological activation and sensory, perceptual, and cognitive functioning. *Psychol. Monogr.,* 1964, 78, No. 8 (Whole No. 585), 33 pp.

Freud, Anna (1936) *The ego and the mechanisms of defense.* (Translated by C. M. Baines.) New York: International Universities Press, 1946.

Freud, S. (1894) The defense neuro-psychoses. (Translated by Joan Riviere.) *Collected Papers,* Vol. I. New York: Basic Books, 1959. Pp. 59-75. Also available in paperback published by Crowell-Collier, Inc. (N.Y.).

Freud, S. (1895a) The justification for detaching from neurasthenia a particular syndrome: The anxiety neurosis. (Translated by Joan Riviere.) *Collected Papers,* Vol. I. New York: Basic Books, 1959. Pp. 76-109.

Freud, S. (1895b) A reply to criticisms on the anxiety neurosis. (Translated by Joan Riviere.) *Collected Papers,* Vol. I. New York: Basic Books, 1959. Pp. 107-127.

Freud, S. (1896) Further remarks on the defense neuro-psychoses. (Translated by Joan Riviere.) *Collected Papers,* Vol. I. New York: Basic Books, 1959. Pp. 155-182.

Freud, S. (1909) Analysis of a phobia in a five-year-old boy. (Translated by Joan Riviere.) *Collected Papers,* Vol. III. New York: Basic Books. Pp. 149-295. Crowell-Collier (N.Y.).

Freud, S. (1915a) The unconscious. (Translated by Joan Riviere.) *Collected Papers,* Vol. IV. New York: Basic Books, 1959. Pp. 98-136. Crowell-Collier.

Freud, S. (1915b) Repression. (Translated by Joan Riviere.) *Collected Papers,* Vol. IV. New York: Basic Books, 1959. Pp. 84-97. Crowell-Collier.

Freud, S. (1926) *The problem of anxiety.* Translated by H. A. Bunker, New York: Norton, 1936.

Fromm-Reichman, F. *An outline of psychoanalysis.* New York: Random House, 1955.

Gero, G. The concept of defense. *Psychoanal. Quart.,* 1951, 20, 565-578.

Goldstein, K. *The organism.* New York: American Book Co., 1939. Also available in paperback published by Beacon Press.

Grinker, R. R. & Spiegal, J. P. *Men under stress.* New York: McGraw-Hill, 1945.

Hamburg, D. & Adams, J. E. A perspective on coping behavior. *Arch. gen. Psychiat.,* 1967, 17, 277-284.

Hamburg, D., Hamburg, B., & DeGoza, S. Adaptive problems and mechanisms in severely burned patients. *Psychiatry,* 1953, 16, 1-20.

Hartman, H. Ego-psychology and the problem of adaptation. In Rapaport, D. (Ed.) *The organization and pathology of thought.* New York: Columbia University Press, 1951.

Holzman, P. S. & Gardner, R. W. Leveling and repression. *J. abnorm. soc. Psychol.,* 1959, 59, 151-155.

Horney, K. *The neurotic personality of our time.* New York: Norton, 1937.

Horney, K. *Our inner conflicts.* New York: Norton, 1945.

Janis, I. L. *Psychological stress.* New York: Wiley, 1958.

Kessen, W. & Mandler, G. Anxiety, pain and the inhibition of distress. *Psychol. Rev.,* 1961, 68, 396-404.

Kroeber, T. C. The coping functions of the ego mechanisms. In R. W. White (Ed.) *The study of lives.* New York: Atherton Press, 1963. Pp. 178-199.

Lazarus, R. S. *Psychological stress and the coping process.* New York: McGraw-Hill, 1966.

Levitt, E. L. *The psychology of anxiety.* Indianapolis, Ind.: Bobbs-Merrill, 1967.

May, R. *The meaning of anxiety.* New York: Ronald Press, 1950.

Mechanic, D. Commentary on A. Pepitone's paper: Self, social environment, and stress. In Appley, M. H. & R. Trumbull (Ed.) *Psychological stress.* New York: Appleton-Century-Crofts, 1967. Pp. 199-202.

Pepitone, A. Self, social environment, and stress. In Appley, M. H. & R. Trumbull (Ed.) *Psychological stress.* New York: Appleton-Century-Crofts, 1967. Pp. 182-208.

Rosenzweig, S. The experimental study of repression. In H. A. Murray (Ed.) *Explorations in personality.* New York: Oxford Press, 1938. Pp. 472-490.

Schopenhauer, A. (1819) *The world as will and idea,* Vol. III. (Translated by R. B. Haldane & J. Kenp.) London: Trubner, 1886.

Sechrest, I. & Wallace, J., Jr. *Psychology and human problems.* Columbus, Ohio: Charles E. Merrill Books, Inc., 1967.

Selye, H. *The stress of life.* New York: McGraw-Hill, 1956.

Shannon, D. T. Clinical patterns of defense as revealed in visual recognition thresholds, *J. abnorm. soc. Psychol.,* 1962, 64, 370-377.

Silber, E. et al. Competent adolescents coping with college decisions. *Arch. gen. Psychiat.,* 1961, 5, 517-527.

Thorne, F. C. An existential theory of anxiety, *J. of clinical Psychol.,* 1963, 19, 35-42.

Titchener, J. L. & Levine, M. *Surgery as a human experience.* New York: Oxford University Press, 1960.

Ullman, L. P. An empirically derived MMPI scale which measures facilitation-inhibition of recognition of threatening stimuli, *J. clinical Psychol.,* 1962, 18, 127-132.

A theory of threat and defense

RICHARD A. HOGAN

Unsuccessful adjustment is often explained in terms of exposure to strong threat and excessive reliance on psychological defense mechanisms. The following article describes the basic strategy of this type of explanation by relating the concepts of threat and defense to self theory. The author illustrates his hypotheses with specific examples taken from the actual case histories of persons undergoing psychological treatment.

Richard Hogan, Ph.D., is presently engaged in the private practice of clinical psychology. He holds the Diploma in Clinical Psychology of the American Board of Examiners in Professional Psychology and was formerly Dean of Students and Associate Professor of Psychology and Education at Pepperdine College.

The writings of Maslow [4, 5], Rosenzweig [8], Rogers [7], Snygg and Combs [10] have in recent years emphasized the concept of threat. The phenomenon of threat, while it has been of general popular and psychological significance for many years, is being viewed more and more as essential in accounting for the psychology of maladjustment.

The theory proposed in this paper is an attempt to explore threat in two directions. It is designed to propose an explanation of threat in terms of a systematic theory of personality. It is formulated in specific terms to foster objective investigation of threat and defense.

The theory of personality is a derivation and expansion of that proposed by Rogers [7]. More particularly, it is related to that view of self and behavior which emphasized the concept of self and its structural properties [6].

An investigation of the measurement of the amount of defensiveness exhibited by clients in counseling stimulated the development of the

From *Journal of Consulting Psychology,* XVI (1952), 417-426. Reprinted by permission of the American Psychological Association and the author.

theory. In another paper, the writer has presented the method of measuring client defensiveness in terms of the theory [3].

Theory of self and behavior

A question that persists when one attempts rigorously to devise a conception of threat comes when the question is asked, threat to what? Current literature reflects conceptions of threat to the self, to the ego, to the integration of the self, to the security of the self, and so forth. This question, however, points up the need for a theory which might explain what the self is. Accordingly, the theory of threat to be presented is based upon a theory of self and behavior which may in briefest outline be presented as follows:

The self is defined as the organism experiencing relations with the environment. Within the first few years of life, the organism as a functioning unit becomes differentiated from the other units in the behavioral field. Self becomes, then, a frame of reference emphasizing the experiencing organism as a unit in the behavioral field.

Behavior is the result of the individual's attempts to reformulate his tension system adequately. Needs and emotions function as a system of tensions, which at a given moment is characterized by relative balance and imbalance. Imbalance in this tension system urges activity. Activity is an attempt to balance the tension system by increasing or reducing tensions to a subjectively defined state of satisfaction.

The individual attempts to reformulate his tension system in the behavioral field as he perceives it. His perceptions constitute his reality. In the course of interaction, conflicts arise—conflicts of goals, methods of interaction, expected rewards and punishments. Also varying bases of interpretation develop—different frames of reference for investing sensations with symbolic and affective connotations. An individual learns the consequences of different bases of interpretation and the effects of different choices at conflict points. Those that more adequately resolve the tension system, he tends to retain as acceptable; those that less adequately resolve the tension system, he tends to retain as unacceptable.

There are three important categories of perceptual data which determine the form of behavior in a given field. They are the individual's perception of the self's relation to the particular field, the capacities of the self in the field, and the desirability of various ways of behaving in the field. The individual's perception of self defines the nature of self and the field. His perception of his capacities defines the possible ways in which he can behave. His value system defines the appropriate way of behaving from among the possible ways of behaving. These perceptions are learned as suggested above.

A variety of such perceptions become abstracted and symbolized as self-definitions and evaluations. Numerous such self-definitions and evaluations arise, are confirmed, rejected, and altered in the life history of the individual. Those which have functionally persisted may be called the structure of the self—that picture of self which is carried around for ready reference. The structure of the self is the preferred frame of reference. It becomes a guide to interaction, designed to provide an orderly, predictable picture of life and behavior which is relied upon for adequate tension reformulation.

The structure of self is thus important motivationally. Since it is the platform for adequate tension reformulation, it can become important in its own right. Behavior inconsistent with this organization of concepts and values disturbs feelings that develop about the self. Behavior inconsistent with conceptions of self and environment questions the predictability of life, causing insecurity. Feelings of inadequacy result when performance does not match the self's conception of its ability. Worthlessness and guilt arise when behavior abrogates cherished values. These feelings of insecurity, inadequacy, and worthlessness—experienced varieties of anxiety—amount to imbalances in the tension system which must be resolved. There thus develops a need to maintain and enhance the self through behavior consistent with the structure of the self.

Any experienced change in the nature of self and the environment, the capacities of the self, and its insight into values places a pressure on the structure of the self. There are essentially two ways in which the individual may react: by changing his experiences to fit the structure of self, or by changing the structure of self to fit experience. Persistence in behavior consistent with older conceptions of self may foster a spurious balance in feelings of security, adequacy, and worth; clinging to the familiar and preferred is soothing. This process is here termed defense. But such action seldom satisfies all the new pressures set up by change in the tension system. Awareness of change and difference, together with an incorporation of the new perceptions in the structure of the self, does resolve new tension, as well as establish a firmer base for the self's adequacy, security, and worth. Continuing redefinition and reevaluations of the self with changing experience lead to a continuously revised structure of self which is more reliable in predicting and guiding behavior which adequately reformulates the tension system. This process may be described as self-realization or self-actualization.

Theory of threat

With this theory of the self and behavior in mind the theory of threat can be proposed. Threat occurs when the self perceives its experiences as being inconsistent with the structure of the self. In other words, when threat is spoken of, what is meant is threat to a related concept or value. In the first therapeutic interview with a student-client, Miss Ban [11], the following statements which she makes illustrate the concept of threat. Her fourth statement in the interview went like this:

(Statement 4, first interview): No, I don't stack up and I'm cognizant of the fact that I'm in greater competition now than I've ever been before because of the caliber of the students here and I realized that before I came and I've taken that into consideration and I still feel that my capacities aren't being—that I'm not learning what I should be and how much I should be.

A few statements later she says:

(Statement 12, first interview): I mean as one of my ideals I want social work very much, and if I'm not going to be a good social worker because of my own personal difficulties then I don't want to be one: I mean there is so much built up around social work as a symbol but . . . well . . . life isn't very interesting after that point, so I'm concerned.

In the fourth statement Miss Ban expresses a threat to a concept of capacity. She says: "I still feel that my capacities aren't being—I'm not learning what I should be and how much I should be." Here, on the one hand, is a particular level of performance as defined by Miss Ban, and on the other hand, the experience of not living up to this definition of capacity. In the twelfth statement Miss Ban evidences threat to one of her values. She says: "I mean as one of my ideals I want social work very much; and if I'm not going to be a good social worker because of my personal difficulties then I don't want to be one." In other words, her lack of academic performance is inconsistent with her ideal of being a social worker and thus threatens this value. Her expression of concern in these statements can be explained in somewhat the following way. First, a value, that of social work, is being threatened by lack of performance in the academic world. This is a threat to the value and disturbs whatever tensions it is designed to reduce. Secondly, the low performance she is experiencing threatens her concept of her capacity and disturbs the needs and feelings related to this concept. Thus she is threatened both with relation to her self-definition and her self-evaluation.

A few characteristics of threat may now be noted. First, that which is threatened is, basically, the individual's perception of his ability adequately to reformulate his tension system. At different levels of theoretical importance or interest one may speak of threat to concepts and values, threat to the self, threat to the security, adequacy, or worth of the self, or threat to its need satisfaction. All these expressions are accurate within the theory of self and behavior that has been presented. At the behavioral level the concepts and values in the structure of the self provide the background against which experiences are related to be interpreted as threatening or nonthreatening. Because the self is that which is defined by concepts and values, threat may be accurately conceived as occurring to the self. Since concepts and values are designed to guide behavior in meeting needs, threat may be spoken of in relation to adequate need satisfaction. Since lack of prediction and control foster insecurity, inadequacy, and worthlessness, unpredictable and uncontrollable experience increases these feelings, threatening the self's security, adequacy, and worth.

Second, threat is felt as perceived by the self; it is essentially phenomenological. Threat is felt when the incongruence is perceived, irrespective of what may be the nature of the situation as perceived by others or from other points of view. Thus a boy experiences an error in bridge as evidence of his incompetence, whereas another may shrug it off. A girl may view an affair with a boy as jeopardizing her work toward a career, whereas another will see it as evidence of her popularity. It is the interpretation of the experience from the accepted frame of reference that determines which experiences are threatening and which are not.

Third, the disturbance occasioned by threat requires that the individual do something to resolve the threat. Threat is a motivating factor of prime importance.

Fourth, there are essentially two reactions to such a threat; the individual may revise his concepts or values, and perhaps the attendant tensions, to include the new and different experience; in this way he would change his structure of self so that it was more consistent with his continuing experience. Also, the individual may deny or in some way distort the inconsistent experience in such a way so that he may see himself in the accustomed way. The first reaction is termed an accepting reaction in that it involves the admission of all relevant perceptions and the making of necessary revisions in concepts and values so that they are more consistent with one's total experience and more adequate to reformulate the tension system. The second reaction is termed the defensive reaction in that it involves the maintenance and enhancement of the self through clinging to familiar concepts and values of the self in the face of experiences which challenge them.

Theory of defense

Defense is defined as a sequence of behavior in response to threat, the goal of which is the maintenance of the structure of the self against the threat. The characteristics of defense may be illustrated by excerpts from the case of a client, Mr. Lew [12]. Mr. Lew defined himself as a shy, rather socially maladjusted person. Others saw him quite differently, which was threatening to him. In discussing this area, he said:

. . . my dad, for instance, (says) you've got personality, you've got looks, and then gives me good advice. Well, it irks me for the simple reason that the personality people perceive is not my personality and for that reason it irks me because *it isn't true*—what they're saying, only they don't know what they're talking about, and of course I can't explain it to them, it's impossible.

The attitudes of others toward Mr. Lew are inconsistent with his concept of himself. This threat instigates the defense of denying the perceptions of others and maintaining his own concept of self.

From this illustration, the characteristics of defensive behavior may be differentiated.

First, defense is a response to threat. The inconsistent perceptions of Mr. Lew and others challenge his conception of self and disturb his security. This feeling disturbance activates behavior to restore feelings of security.

Second, the purpose of defense is to maintain or enhance the self as perceived. From among the possible ways of reestablishing his security, Mr. Lew chose to support his current conception of self. He acted to continue perceiving himself as shy and unsociable.

Third, defense involves a denial or distortion of the offending experience. Mr. Lew vehemently denied the assertions of others concerning his personality.

Fourth, defense reduces the awareness of threat, but not the threat itself. By convincing himself the statements of others were untrue, Mr. Lew restored his shaken security. By discounting their veracity, he reduced the concern they gave him. But he did not resolve the threat; people still saw him as personable and good-looking. Nor did he preclude further threats; in the future, when others perceive him in this fashion, he will be threatened again.

Fifth, defense requires further defense. Mr. Lew was not content merely to deny others' perceptions, he had to justify his denial by saying people really don't see him as he is, that people don't know what they're talking about. Each of these justifications is in itself a distortion, which will require further defense if challenged. In effect, defense further widens the area of distorted perceptions within the self which must be defended.

Levels of defense

Since defense does not resolve threat, but merely reduces awareness of threat, each defense is subject to further threat. Threat then is followed by defense and further threat. This sequence tends to continue until challenges cease or the threat is resolved. In effect, as the self organizes its perceptions more in terms of defense, layer after layer of defense is built up around threatened areas. Defense is echeloned in depth, maintaining the sensitive area against experience, and the resulting conative-cognitive organization can be discussed in terms of levels of defense. As each level of defense is threatened, another level is added to strengthen the defense.

The sequence of threat and defense and the resulting levels of defense are well illustrated in the case of Miss Ban. In this case, the areas of marriage and a career were two threatened areas. In order to understand Miss Ban's perception of these areas, her expressions from various portions of the case are presented.

(Statement 246, fourth interview): . . . In fact, I mean—this is very pertinent—in that although I realized that a fellow-girl relationship with me would be very good for my entire emotional self, I think it would do a quite—very—a great deal for me, I fear it completely, and that's no good; I mean, I shouldn't. I mean, it's very normal, I mean, normal desire for girls to desire fellows and vice versa, and yet I think I'm beginning to fear it—in—I think it ultimately might prove detrimental to my entire personality. I fear it because the other experience, the *entire* relationship after a certain point was *so* disheartening. And as I said I think it was a very traumatic thing in my life. It was completely disheartening. But I mean every time I think of another relationship with a fellow, even with this nice fellow, I know, I figure, Oh, what's the use, and, uh. . . .

This material from the fourth interview—near the peak of catharsis, reveals the basic threat to the self, which is diagrammed below:

(1) *Structure of self*
". . . I realized that a fellow-girl relationship would be very good for my entire emotional self . . ."

(2) *Threatening experience*
". . . the other experience (with a fellow), the entire relationship after a certain point was so disheartening . . . a very traumatic thing . . ."

This threat was so great a blow to her emotional security, that Miss Ban, as will be seen below, reorganized the basis of her security so as to avoid "fellow-girl" relationships:

(3) *Revised structure of self*
Fellow-girl relationships are disheartening

The revised structure of self, in itself a defense, omitted the perceived desires for such relationships, and these kept threatening the self, requiring defense.

(3) *Threatening experience*
Fellow-girl relationships are disheartening

(4) *Threatening experience*
". . . everytime I think of another relationship with a fellow, even with this nice fellow (another one) . . ."

(5) *Defense of self against threat*
". . . I think, 'Oh, what's the use,' and, uh . . ."

In further defense of this and other areas of self, Miss Ban decided upon a career: social work. The following excerpt from the first interview indicates what this structure of self has come to mean and how it is threatened.

(Statement 12, first interview): . . . I mean, this is perhaps more critical than—in my growth process —than any other time in the past. I mean, so you either go this way, or this way—the wrong way or the right way—in learning, and in your philosophy of life and in your adjustment in general. I mean, being in social work your personal life, as you know, is so tied up with your work—with your ultimate work—that—I feel that if I'm not completely happy, and if I'm not completely satisfied, then I'm not going to do well—a good job. And I—that's a conflict, I know. I mean as one of my ideals I want social work very much, and if I'm not going to be a good social worker because of my own personal difficulties—then I don't want to be one. I mean if I don't want to be a social worker—I mean, there is so much built up around social work as a symbol. But well, life isn't very interesting after that point. So, I'm concerned.

Miss Ban finds her ideal of social work threatened by "personal difficulties," which include social maladjustment and low academic scholarship. Yet the basic threat outlined above, however well defended, is at the root of the maladjustment. This is brought out clearly in a few statements from the second interview which follow.

Miss Ban (Statement 83, second interview): [1] And the other factor of my make-up, personality . . . vocationally, I am not worried, too. *I think I've settled the conflict of . . . that most girls go through of marriage and career.*"

Counselor (84): "You have pretty well settled that for yourself."

Miss Ban (84): "Yeah. Quite well. I mean, as well as I can. *I've thought it through carefully. I mean, I read on it and talked on it, and I think I. . . .*"

Counselor (85): "You've thought a lot about this. . . ."

Miss Ban (85): "I think I was disturbed about that when I was about seventeen or eighteen, I mean, when I had to make the decision. I mean, in my thinking I had to make a decision, and I was disturbed about it. I think it's resolved itself."

Counselor (86): "At the time you had to make the decision it was a little hard to make, but now you are pretty well satisfied with the way things are in that area."

Miss Ban (86): "Yeah. *I mean, I don't know if I have a wholesome attitude of philosophizing, which is not perhaps wholesome,* but in a sense. . . . I mean, *I am able to philosophize about things and about situations.* I mean, about marriage and about men and possibilities and all. And . . . *oh, I mean, you worry about it,* I guess, occasionally. *Most young men and women, I guess, would tend to worry about it,* but that. . . ."

Counselor (87) "It comes up occasionally and . . . ."

Miss Ban (87): "Yeah, *it does occasionally. And when I was feeling real low a couple of months ago . . . Of course everything would bother you when you are feeling low.* I mean, every other problem bothered me too—*but now it's not bothering me. Now the main thing that seems to be bothering me is this adjustment to school,* and so on. And this well, the loneliness doesn't bother me on the surface as much now as the schooling. It's the main thing."

This discussion illustrates the sequential nature of threat and defense which is diagrammatically presented below:

(1) *Structure of self*
". . . I realize that a fellow-girl relationship would be very good for my entire emotional self. . . ." (246)

(2) *Threatening experience*
". . . the other experience (with a fellow), the entire relationship after a certain point was so disheartening . . . a very traumatic thing. . . ." (246)

(3) *Revised structure of self*
Fellow-girl relationships are disheartening. . . ". . . I want social work very much. . . ." (246)

(4) *Threatening experience*
". . . every time I think of another relationship with a fellow, even with this nice fellow (another one). . . ." (246)

(5) *Defense of self*
". . . I think, 'Oh, what's the use,' and uh. . . ." (246) "I think I've settled the conflict of . . . that most girls go through of marriage and career." (83)

(6) *Threatening experience*
Awareness that conflict is not completely settled, just "as well as I can" (84)

(7) *Further level of defense*
"I've thought it through carefully. I mean, I read on it and talked on it. . . ." (84)

(8) *Threatening experience*
". . . I don't know if I have a wholesome attitude of philosophizing, which is not perhaps wholesome. . . ." (86)

(9) *Further level of defense*
". . . I am able to philosophize about things and situations." (86)

(10) *Threatening experience*
". . . oh, I mean, you worry about it. . . ." (86)

(11) *Further level of defense*
"Most young men and women, I guess, would tend to worry about it. . . ." (86)

(12) *Threatening experience*
". . . it does (come up) occasionally. And when I was feeling real low a couple of months ago. . . ." (87)

(13) *Further level of defense*
". . . of course, everything would bother you when you are feeling low" (87)

(14) *Threatening experience*
- - - loneliness - - - (87)

---

[1] Italics mine.

(15) *Further level of defense*
". . . but, now it's not bothering me. Now the main thing that seems to be bothering me is this adjustment to school, and so on. And this, well, this loneliness doesn't bother me on the surface as much now as the schooling. It's the main thing." (87)

Miss Ban perceives the conflict as settled. She has it settled, not "pretty well" or "quite well," but "as well as I can." Evidently her continuing experience in the area causes her to doubt and be threatened by the consideration that it might not be definitely settled. She has thus talked about it, read on it, and philosophized to the point where her perception of it as conflictual and disturbing is justified. Nevertheless, she doubts the "wholesomeness" of philosophizing and does worry about (is still threatened by) the conflict. That this is not serious she rationalizes by viewing it as something that everyone does. Then she implies she worries a great deal about it, but she sees it as something which is not the main worry, the latter being school. She then proceeds to discuss the problems relating to school.

It will be noted throughout this sequence that the threat somehow would not be covered up, no matter how many reasons, platitudes and values, were brought to defense. The final defense was complete withdrawal of discussion to a less threatened area.

Implications of the theory

The theory of threat emphasizes the importance of the conceptual level of organization in behavior. In effect, needs become less crucial in the explanation of behavior. More and more significance is attached to the particular interpretation placed on needs by the self and the methods and goals held by the self as necessary for need satisfaction.

In light of this emphasis, certain problems arise. This magnified emphasis on conceptual organization runs counter to the equally significant implication of the theory that adjustment involves a continuous revision of the conceptual organization in light of adequate need satisfaction and continuing experience. Also, the evidence seems to suggest that extreme threat can cause a breakdown of the structure of self to provide need satisfaction under extreme conditions [9]. Each of the latter considerations points up the relatively greater importance of needs in the determination of behavior. This position must be questioned in view of tendencies toward suicide and self-sacrifice which appear as behavior in terms of conceptual organization rather than need satisfaction [6]. One issue presented by this evidence is that of the conditions under which the conceptual organization becomes inflexible and unresponsive to new conditions of need satisfaction (maladjustment). Another issue is the conditions under which the conceptual organization determines behavior which requires or promises need deprivation (heroism, etc.).

The theory proposes one way of resolving these issues by making a distinction between the basic needs and the needs for security, adequacy, and worth. Behavior directives based upon learnings from experience with basic need satisfaction cannot lead to maladjustment; conceptual organization representing a logical extension of these learnings tends to be reliable because satisfying and consistent with experience. Concern for self, however, motivates the individual to find a *sure* base for living, a *definite* notion of capacity, an *unassailable* standard of worth. The former approach looks to continuing experience with a "what's going to happen?"; the latter, with a "this *has* to happen?" Thus the self-concerned individual, organizing more and more of experience in terms of prior patterns, becomes maladjusted through denial and distortion of more and more experience. The suicide lives in reverse, dispatching himself consistent with his feeling of worthlessness, inadequacy, or insecurity. The hero (with qualms from the inevitable uncertainty of situations) behaves deftly as questions of value and capacity are settled surely and certainly because based on all experience and continuously satisfying. The martyr, on the other hand, may deprive or frustrate needs to recoup the feeling of worth or adequacy he has lost.

Such an emphasis on conceptual organization appears to call for a revision of psychopathological theory. Rosenzweig [8] has suggested a differentiation of reactions to frustration into need-persistive and ego-defensive categories. The need-persistive reaction "serves to fulfill the frustrated need in spite of momentary obstructions. . . ."; ego-defensive reactions "serve to protect the integration of the personality, if and when the latter is threatened by the frustrating situation." "Most behavior incident to frustration entails both types of reaction, but pure cases of each alone are found, and the theoretical distinction between the two appears justified as an aid to analysis." The distinction is between need deprivation and threat to self. The implication is that in some situations needs dominate behavior and in others, behavior is dominated by the conceptual organization of the self. Such a distinction raises a question concerning the conditions under which self-involvement does and does not occur. Also, it requires an accounting of the conditions under which threat to the self will be followed by defense or acceptance. The present theory suggests that self-involvement occurs when some value or concept becomes relevant to some experience. Self-involvement could occur without threat if the self is identified with its experience rather than being primarily self-concerned. Self-involvement with threat requires experience related to self-structure predicated on the maintenance of security, adequacy, or worth. Self-involvement with threat induces defense when behavior is directed at preserving matters of self-concern rather than finding a more effective measure of need satisfaction. The opposite of the latter process—self-involvement without threat—is seen in successful psychotherapy.

Undoubtedly tension is heightened by frustration, threat, or some combination of both. Yet the relative pathologic importance of the two is still in question. Is it need deprivation, or threat to the self, or some combination which is fundamentally pathological? Maslow, in his brief review of the concepts of frustration and conflict, concludes:

We may then proceed to a reclassification of our concepts in the general field of psychopathogenesis. We may speak first of deprivation and, secondly, of choice and consider them both to be nonpathogenic and, therefore, unimportant concepts for the student of psychopathology. The one concept that is important is neither conflict nor frustration but the essential pathogenic characteristic of both—namely, threat of thwarting of the basic needs of the organism.

. . . we may expand the above statement to read "danger to the basic needs or the necessary conditions upon which they rest for the individual."

If we had the space, this would involve a discussion not only of specifically individual defense mechanisms, e.g., identifying keeping a job with masculinity, but also broader conditions like freedom to speak, to complain, to be ambitious, to move away, to determine one's own fate. We may summarize by saying that, in general, all the following are felt as threatening in our sense; danger of thwarting of the basic needs, or the conditions upon which they rest, threat to life itself, threat to the general integrity of the organism, threat to the integration of the organism, and threat to the organism's basic mastery of the world [5, p. 82].

At the root of threat, to be sure, lies the possible thwarting of needs. Yet, if need satisfaction were of prime importance in maladjustment, need-persistive reactions would usually predominate; and occasions when they did to the detriment of cherished values would be viewed with less concern. Yet the conditions established for need satisfaction seem predominant in maladjustment. The individual is absorbed with defending his system of defenses. It appears that deprivation involving threat and not deprivation alone is responsible for maladjustment.

As Maslow suggests, no theory of threat is complete unless it provides an understanding of possible reactions to threat. In light of the present theory, these are essentially two. First, the individual may accept the threatening experience. This may be done by an admission of the total experience and consequent reorganization of the structure of the self. This appears outside the realm of possibility from the standpoint of Freudian psychology [1], in which personality is viewed in terms of more or less adequate defense systems. Such a view would imply each behavior pattern is motivated to an extent by anxiety and none solely by other needs; such an inclusive implication strains the facts of everyday living, though perhaps not the facts of neurosis and psychosis. Secondly, an individual may respond to threat by defense. Defense involves a denial or distortion of experience. Defense can include a denial of experience to permit behavior consistent with the structure of the self and a denial of experience to perceive behavior in terms of the structure of the self.

The implications for mental hygiene are

numerous. The values of self-determination for growth and adjustment seem clearly superior to those of introjection. The necessity of basing learning on all relevant aspects of the tension system rather than only upon the peculiarly susceptible self-feelings of insecurity, inadequacy, and worthlessness seems apparent. Also, the need for developing behavior-directing concepts and values on the basis of all relevant experience is indicated for the construction of the reliable self. Finally, a searching for and resolution of threat, rather than a defense of that which is threatened, leads to self-actualization.

Among possible research implications, a few will be mentioned. Varying levels of defense may well indicate areas of varying sensitivity to threat within the self. An investigation of this relationship could well reveal the soundness and the usefulness of the theory. The concepts of threat and defense might well be utilized as criteria for adjustment and maladjustment. Haigh's study applying these concepts to psychotherapeutic-interview protocols tends to confirm such an hypothesis [2]. The theory appears useful in level of aspiration studies, in the analysis of comments of subjects performing below their set levels of aspiration. In another paper, the writer has reported the development and evaluation of a method of analyzing interviews for client defensiveness [3].

Summary

A theory of threat and defense has been presented in terms of a theory of self-emphasizing cognitive determinants of behavior. Threat is understood as occurring when experience is perceived as inconsistent with learned conceptions and evaluations of self. Defense is conceived as a response to threat maintaining the self as conceived by denying or distorting the threatening experience. A defensive reaction reduces awareness of threat but does not resolve the threat. The self and its defense are susceptible to further threat. Threat and defense thus follow one another in successive levels. Implications of the theory for maladjustment, mental hygiene, and research have been briefly indicated.

References

1. Freud, S. *The problem of anxiety.* New York: Norton, 1936.

2. Haigh, G. Defensive behavior in client-centered therapy. *J. consult. Psychol.,* 1949, 13, 181-189.

3. Hogan, R. A. A measure of client defensiveness. In Werner Wolff (Ed.), *Success in psychotherapy.* New York: Grune & Stratton, in press.

4. Maslow, A. H. Deprivation, threat and frustration. *Psychol. Rev.,* 1941, 48, 364-366.

5. Maslow, A. H. Conflict, frustration and the theory of threat. *J. abnorm. soc. Psychol.,* 1943, 38, 81-86.

6. Raimy, V. C. Self-reference in counseling interviews. *J. consult. Psychol.,* 1948, 12, 153-163.

7. Rogers, C. R. *Client-centered therapy.* Boston: Houghton Mifflin, 1951.

8. Rosenzweig, S. Need-persistive and ego-defensive reactions to frustration as demonstrated by an experiment on repression. *Psychol. Rev.,* 1941, 48, 347-349.

9. Sherif, M., & Cantril, H. *The psychology of ego-involvements.* New York: Wiley, 1947.

10. Snygg, D., & Combs, A. W. *Individual behavior.* New York: Harper, 1949.

11. Case of Miss Ban. Counseling Center, Univer. of Chicago. (Dittoed)

12. Case of Mr. Lew. Counseling Center, Univer. of Chicago. (Dittoed)

Coping devices and defense mechanisms in relation to autonomous ego functions

LOIS B. MURPHY

The concept of defense mechanisms that individuals develop and utilize a variety of behaviors to protect themselves against anxiety is one of the most widely accepted aspects of the psychoanalytic theory of personality. Although a variety of defense mechanisms have been described in great detail, it is not always easy to recognize them, because the observable behavior can serve a variety of underlying motives. This point is illustrated in the following article which discusses defense mechanisms in the context of other psychological functions. The author describes the development of defense mechanisms in infants and young children and points out how children learn to cope with environment stresses.

Lois Murphy, Ph.D., is Director of the Research Department, Division of Developmental Studies, and a therapist in the Children's Service at the Menninger Foundation. She is the author of *Personality in Young Children, The Widening World of Childhood,* several other books, and a number of articles on personality development in infancy, childhood, and adolescence.

Doctor Heider's discussion of vulnerability included some consideration of the efforts made by an infant to manage its needs and its relation to the environment in such a way as to keep comfortable. In the present paper, I would like to suggest some relationships between coping devices, defense mechanisms, and autonomous functions of the ego in the early development of the child's capacity to handle its relation to the environment. In a short paper, it is not possible to present a full discussion of the development of any of these three groups of functions; but I shall try to indicate some of the lines such a discussion would have to follow.

The term "coping devices" can be used to refer to specific acts, however minimal or complex, which deal with stress, difficulties, challenges, new opportunities, and other situations, stimuli, or demands which cannot be handled by reflex, or other automatic reactions. By contrast, defense mechanisms are intrapsychic operations utilized by the child to reduce anxiety aroused by inner conflict or conflict between pressures from the outside and the inside.

I shall also want to keep in mind the distinction between "defensive behavior" (fighting, turning away), "defensive function" (struggling for cognitive mastery in order to reduce anxiety) and "defense mechanisms" which usually involve some distortion of reality —temporary, limited, superficial—or deep, permanent, or pervasive. Examples of the latter, common in even normal young children, are temporary denial or minimization of a threat. "Autonomous ego functions" include those activities made available by the developing potentialities of the child's equipment as an organism, activities such as seeing, hearing, remembering, exploring, which do not have to be motivated by conflict or obstacles, however much they may be shaped or colored by the affective experiences concomitant with their emergence or practice.

We saw in Doctor Heider's study of vulnerability that records of infants observed at the

Reprinted with permission from the *Bulletin of the Menninger Clinic*, Vol. 24, pp. 144-153. Copyright 1960 by The Menninger Foundation.

age of one month, two months, and three months provide evidence for activities which might be regarded as precursors of later coping devices and defense mechanisms. In common with very simple organisms such as worms and ants, a baby soon after birth will turn its face or body away from a threatening stimulus, shut its eyes to avoid such a threat, or curl into itself. Some neonates will also push away or in some other way crudely attack a stimulus which is a source of discomfort, such as an uncomfortable blanket pressing on its face. A baby's cry, at first a primitive discharge mechanism of the organism, soon becomes a technique or device for obtaining help. It is used as communication and demand, as well as an expression of anger, fear, discomfort, or pain and anxiety.

As soon as the development of motor skills and locomotion makes it possible for the baby to turn over, creep, or pull or push himself away from the stimulus, his primitive turning away or shutting his eyes is extended to removing his body. As fine motor control develops, his initial amorphous hitting out yields to more coordinated methods of hitting or throwing away. These are all active ways of defending one's self against discomfort or external stress—that is, defensive behavior.

As memory, imagery, and fantasy develop during the early months, the baby's resources are greatly extended so that it is no longer necessary for him to depend solely on physically active dealings with the external environment. We can see a series of steps between the earliest methods of coping and later methods of defending himself, some of which become patterned into defense mechanisms. For example: The baby turns away from a threatening stimulus. This makes it possible for him to forget; or parallel with forgetting, to deny the existence of the threat. When forgetting is maintained consistently, we might call it repression. It is hardly reasonable to assume that all forgetting is repression under emotional conflict since when the infant is very young such a multitude of stimuli are pressing upon him in succession that memory must be regarded as a positive development and an achievement in itself, and forgetting as a normal consequence of the shifting of attention from a previous stimulus to a new and more absorbing one.

Enduring memory, itself an achievement, very likely may depend upon the development of constellations of organized traces which can capture new impressions and integrate them into an already established configuration; but without conscious memory it is possible for massive, deeply disturbing experiences to leave an enduring impression, or for crucially significant events occurring at a time when thresholds are low, to be imprinted in an enduring way, later expressed in the form of expectations or attitudes. In the first two or three weeks, thousands of relatively irrelevant impressions from the point of view of the baby's early economy are only momentarily registered; it requires scores of exposures to make conditioning occur during the first two weeks of life. Probably only those impressions which are received repeatedly, or in a context of deeply significant or pervasive affect can be expected to endure. Thus we can speak of repression only when we are talking about traces which would otherwise be retained or remembered. Repression takes more energy than simple forgetting. It is easy to forget things of no consequence. It is hard to repress those which cause us deep conflict or anxiety.

When the baby reaches an age where the threat comes from the reaction of the environment to something he has done, whether it is a matter of biting the nipple of his mother while nursing or throwing something frustrating or annoying to him out of his play pen or high chair, we find the beginning of anger at the external person who punishes or reproves for the painful or socially destructive action.

It is not uncommon to see forceful spirited babies look angrily and defiantly at the grownup who has slapped the baby's hand or protested some action. It is as if the baby said, "It is you who are bad, not I." This quick exchange seems to serve the purpose of forestalling recognition or acceptance of guilty feelings by the baby, especially in those cases where the baby maintains a proud autonomy after such accusing looks at the grownup. In some instances a baby may follow such an angry accusation with a shy, withdrawing, retreating appeal as if for forgiveness or for reinstatement of love, a look expressive of reparation. This is a distinct next step, however. In a setting of exchanges of anger before a baby has clearly differentiated concepts of self and of mother, such responses may involve precursors of later projection.

By the age of two or three years such processes have gone far enough so that children (for example, Martin in our group) have developed a pattern of anticipating blame, protest, accusation, or punishment from the adult and forestalling it by (1) projecting threats to the adults, and (2) acting in a way which takes into account the possibility of their threatening behavior. Even when there is no objective evidence at all that a specific new adult is hostile, the child retreats to a safe area where dangerous activity will be avoided, in this way taking no risk. In other words, early experiences of exchange of hostilities leads to a pattern of anticipation of threat from the grownup. This can become an intrapsychic device which operates automatically and autonomously, finally emerging as a "defense mechanism."

In the early stages of turning away, denial, repression and projection, we can see the steps in the baby's actual behavior. After an end product such as projection has been repeated to the point where it becomes crystallized into a mechanism, the child does not go through these steps and the pattern can no longer be broken. In exactly the same way, other higher units are established which then become autonomous and capable of incorporation into still more complicated configurations of response; the defense mechanism has become an autonomous response pattern.

By the age of two to four years, all of the children in our study group had already developed a repertoire of such autonomous patterns—defense mechanisms which played their part in the total resources of coping used by each child. This was true regardless of the overall level of happiness, or adjustment, or prognosis of future comfortable development as seen by the psychiatrist.

Furthermore, the most normal and happy of our group of children drew upon defense mechanisms, as part of their total strategy for coping, with considerable flexibility and with changing emphases over the period during which we observe them.

An example of sequences [1] in coping with fear of thunder shows Molly's way of progressing by a series of steps in which defenses and overt efforts were combined:

As a two-year-old, Molly cried and was terrified during thunderstorms or when a jet plane passed overhead. At three years three months, she got into bed with her older sister during a thunderstorm and accepted comfort from her. At about the same time Molly began to reassure herself (and her baby brother) saying, "It's just a noise and it really won't hurt you a bit."

A month later Molly was again terrified as a jet plane flew unusually low overhead; she cried, and clung to her sister for comfort. A few hours later she repeated several times to herself, "Thunder really doesn't hurt you; it just sounds noisy. I'm not scared of planes, just thunder." The next month she opened the door into her parents' room during a thunderstorm saying that her younger brother was afraid (although he was really fast asleep).

Nine months later, at four years two months, she was awakened from a nap during a thunderstorm but remained quietly in bed. Afterward she said to her sister, "There was lots of thunder, but I just snuggled in my bed and didn't cry a bit."

Four months later, at four and one-half years, Molly showed no fear herself during a storm and comforted her frightened little brother, saying, "I remember when I was a little baby, I was scared of thunder and I used to cry every time it thundered."

Here we see the two-steps-forward-one-step-backward process:

1. Overt expression of fearful affect and helplessness;
2. to actively seeking comfort from a supporting person;
3. to internalizing the comfort and the image of the comforting person, acting as a comforter to herself;
4. to differentiating sources of the fear while still reverting to the need for physical comfort from her sister;
5. to projecting her fear to her baby brother (as a way of rationalizing getting the support she needed) and seeking a symbol of support (opening the door without demand for physical or other active comforting);
6. to combine actively comforting herself with

---

[1] This is a fuller discussion of a sequence noted in "Learning how children cope with their problems." *Children*, 1957, 4:132-136.

formulation of a self-image in terms of pride in control and mastery of her fears;

7. to reaction formation, achievement of bravery, and referral of the fear to her past.

It seems clear that in her total process of coping Molly is able to use denial (of her lingering fear) partly because of her increasing cognitive mastery (grasp of the difference between thunder, noise of planes, and other noises from objects closer at hand which might actually be realistically threatening) and, one might say that the denial is an active important step in the relinquishment of the fearful affect initially associated with the stimulus of thunder. In other words, denial is used in the service of mastery, and is supported by the cognitive processes which might in turn be regarded as contributing to the maintenance of the defense; or perhaps we can simply say the two go hand in hand. Certainly the cognitive mastery and the denial are both important in the total process of coping with fear of thunder. As we go through the sequences, one defense mechanism yields to another and her projection of fear onto her little brother is essentially another form of denial; or is used in the service of denial as part of the total process of outgrowing her fear.

As we follow the development of such efforts to master fears and other stresses on the part of our children, we are struck by the flexibility with which they use defense mechanisms along with overt defensive maneuvers as part of the total coping strategy. This flexibility includes the capacity to use one mechanism at one time and another later as well as the capacity to use different ones together, when they are needed. An important point in relation to Molly is that she is not an inhibited, withdrawn child who is unable to deal directly with the environment. She is very direct in her ability to seek comfort from her sister, to go to her parents' room, or to actively snuggle into bed herself. The intrapsychic defense mechanisms appear not as substitutes for these active efforts or as a result of failure to make active efforts but rather go hand in hand with her active efforts as part of her total progress in coping.

Up to this point we have dealt with the development of defense mechanisms in relation to defensive operations. We see a continuity between the baby's first efforts to turn away even through such a limited act as shutting his eyes or turning his head, and his later efforts to turn away bodily, efforts to deny and repress, and then his subsequent patterns of denial and projection. We can speak of the emergence of defense mechanisms as autonomous response patterns which have developed by a series of steps from primitive overt defense operations, but which, once reaching a state of effective operation at an intrapsychic level, function automatically without going through the preliminary steps.

We cannot see the whole process adequately, however, unless we also look at the defensive use of ego functions which are a natural part of the child's total cognitive, motor and affective development. Normal babies who are not hungry, sleepy, or in pain respond with varying degrees of vivid interest in visual, auditory, tactual stimuli as fast as their neurological development provides the equipment for responsiveness to the stimuli of the outside world. Babies differ widely in their use of such stimuli. The analysis of records of our children as infants shows wide differences between the tendencies of certain babies to pay more attention to faces and to people than to things, or to pay more attention to colorful, shiny, and in other ways interesting objects in contrast to faces. Our knowledge is not at a point where it is possible to stand on firm ground in any theory regarding the basis for such differences in eager excitement about and response to things as compared with faces. (Controlled studies of differences between babies whose first oral gratifications come through being nursed, or being fed while held cuddled and smiled at by the mother, as compared with babies who are played with very little, or are fed by bottles held on mechanical bottle holders, might contribute something to this distinction.)

One of the babies with a strong interest in impersonal objects was Abby who was born at a time when her family actually fostered such an interest. With her father busy completing an advanced professional degree, and her mother helping to support the home, neither parent had with the baby the time for play which subsequent children in the family received. Abby had a cradle gym and was very much interested in it, playing with the toys which dangled above her chest with great enthusiasm. This interest persisted until by the time she was in nursery school she was a child who enjoyed puzzles and other types of play with the objects and toys of nursery school very much. She did not make contact with other children readily. Her nursery school teacher felt this as a lack and may have expressed some of her dissatisfaction with Abby's limited use of the social opportunities of the nursery school. But by the time Abby was seven to eight years old in elementary school where her teacher expressed great appreciation of the intellectual skills she had by now developed, Abby began to expand into very much more active spontaneous social relationships with children, and was, at the age of eight, one of the most popular, if not the most popular, child in her group. This social ease utilized in fact the intellectual ease which had developed from early infancy and which was now accepted as important and praiseworthy in the school situation. This is a brief summary of many hundreds of pages of data; what we are interested in here is the fact that what began as an autonomous ego function—mainly observing, analyzing, making relationships between her perceptions and concepts of objects —was utilized by her in infancy more than it might otherwise have been in her early months, partly in lieu of the attention from parents which she would have been getting if they had not been so busy. Since she was in a family with intellectual interests, it contributed to her subsequent identification with her parents, and thus received constant reinforcement at home, and became a source of gratification and contact with people.

In nursery school it appears that this interest in puzzles was used defensively and with more conflict partly because of the lack of enthusiasm of the nursery school teacher; but whatever conflicts and unhappiness arose in nursery school around her intellectual interests were not deep enough to outweigh the positive gratifications which were intrinsic in the first place and reinforced by the family interests in the second place. By the time she got to school where intellectual performance was expected, she was able to retrieve and build on her foundations of autonomous ego functioning and her enthusiasm for intellectual activities.

It is particularly dramatic in this connection that her I.Q. increased twenty-four points between her test at nursery school age and the test when she was eight years old. At the latter stage, she was generally more spontaneous and outgoing, free from social inhibitions as well as functioning more enthusiastically in cognitive terms. During the preschool period of conflict and defensiveness in the use of cognitive functioning, she was constricted. Later, despite the fact that cognitive functions had been utilized defensively for a period, she was able to recapture the enthusiastic immediacy of satisfaction of spontaneous cognitive activity, and to blossom into richer intellectual cognitive functioning; and because of this, and parallel with its acceptance and appreciation in a social group, she blossomed likewise into more creative social activity.

It is interesting to note that along with her popularity and leadership in the group, traces of the unhappiness and insecurity she had had earlier in nursery school were expressed in her concern about insecure children in the school group, children who were different, as she might have felt different in nursery school, or left out as a baby. This sensitivity to difference included unusual social awareness and creativity in relation to Negro children or other minority groups in the school group, even at this age when many children handle sensitivity to difference by activities aimed toward protecting their own status.

At the period of her flowering, Abby's I.Q. was 146, indicating that all along this was a sensitive little girl whose perceptiveness might have contributed to a more than average vulnerability to her nursery school teacher's disapproval of intellectuality.

With many another child, knowledge and the desire to know, to have questions answered, to solve problems, are utilized defensively in certain situations parallel with their use as a spontaneous expression of childish response to the world about them when they are free from threat. At the same time in some children the defensive use of the drive for knowledge interferes with spontaneous autonomous delight in intellectual functioning. With Martin, the intellectual interest appeared to be pushed beyond his capacity because of a need to outstrip an older brother. In his case, the intellectual functioning rarely seemed to go on in the atmosphere of enthusiasm, mastery and ease characteristic of others. Typically Martin produced his answers and his thoughts in an atmosphere of anxiety and tension and a need to prove something.

We can see then, that in these normal children defense mechanisms develop out of and also parallel with autonomous ego functions. Moreover, children use defense mechanisms, defensive operations, and autonomous ego functions in a mutually supportive way. Further, we can see that the level of spontaneity attending cognitive functioning shifts from one period to another. While cognitive activities may serve a temporarily defensive function, they can be retrieved for more spontaneous and autonomous experiencing when the situation changes and a defensive role is no longer needed. Finally, in the case of one or two children under a chronic, persistent, competitive pressure, cognitive functions were used for defensive purposes so consistently as to become embedded in a defensive character structure, and thus became less accessible to a flexible and happy use than they were in most of the children in the study.

It is not possible to take space for a fuller discussion here; we shall have to be content with the final observation that when we compare the happier and the less happy children in our study group the difference does not lie in the kinds of defense mechanisms used in each group. Rather, the difference appears to be, first, in the flexibility with which defense mechanisms are used to eke out the child's coping resources when necessary and then relinquished when they are no longer needed. Second, the difference lies in the success of the overall coping pattern (including defense mechanisms) in protecting and facilitating the child's capacity for gratification, relationships, and growth.

References

1. Escalona, Sibylle, Leitch, Mary and others. *Early phases of personality development.* Monographs of the Society for Research in Child Development, Inc., Vol. 17, No. 54, 1952. Evanston, Ill.: Child Development Publications, 1953.

2. Leitch, Mary and Escalona, Sibylle. The reaction of infants to stress. 1949, *Psa. Study of the Child,* 3 & 4, 121-140.

3. Erikson, E. H. *Childhood and society.* New York: Norton, 1950.

4. Freud, Sigmund. *Beyond the pleasure principle.* New York: Liveright, 1950.

5. Bergman, Paul and Escalona, Sibylle. Unusual sensitivities in very young children. 1949, *Psa. Study of the Child.* 3 & 4, 333-352.

6. Shirley, M. M. *The First Two Years. Vol. II: Intellectual development.* Minneapolis: University of Minnesota, 1933.

7. Hoffer, Willie. Development of the body ego. 1950, *Psa. Study of the Child.* 5, 18-23.

8. Stevenson, Olive. The First Treasured Possession. *Psa. Study of the Child.* 9, 199-217, 1954.

9. Lerner, Eugene and Murphy, Lois B., eds. *Methods for the study of personality in young children.* Monographs of the Society for Research in Child Development, Vol. 6, No. 4. Washington, D.C.: Society for Research in Child Development, National Research Council, 1941.

10. Frank, L. K. Tactile communication. *Genet. Psychol. Monogr.* 1957, 56, 209-255.

11. Hellersberg, Elisabeth. Unevenness of growth in its relation to vulnerability, anxiety, ego weakness, and schizophrenic patterns. *Am. J. Ortho.* 1957, 27:577-586.

12. Schopenhauer, Arthur. *Complete essays of Schopenhauer.* (Translated by T. Bailey Saunders.) New York: Wiley, 1942.

13. Waals, H. G. Van Der. Le narcissisme. *Revue française de psychanalyse,* 1949, 13:501-525.

14. Lynd, Helen M. *On shame and the search for identity.* New York: Harcourt, Brace, 1958.

15. Erikson, E. H. *Young man Luther.* New York: Norton, 1958.

16. Murphy, Gardner *Personality.* New York: Harper, 1947.

17. Schachtel, E. G. *Metamorphosis.* New York: Basic Books, 1959.

18. Spitz, René *No and yes.* New York: International Universities, 1957.

19. Rado, Sandor *Psychoanalysis of behavior.* New York: Grune & Stratton, 1956.

20. Hendrick, Ives Instinct and the ego during infancy. *Psa. Quart.,* 1942, 11:33-58.

21. Fenichel, Otto *The psychoanalytic theory of neurosis.* New York: Norton, 1945.

22. Guernsey, Martha Summarized in *Experimental social psychology* by Gardner Murphy, L. B.

Murphy and T. M. Newcomb. New York: Harper, 1937.

23. Klein, Melanie Some theoretical conclusions regarding the emotional life of the infant. In *Developments in Psychoanalysis,* (Ed.) Joan Riviere. London: Hogarth, 1952.

24. Heimann, Paula Certain functions of introjection and projection in early infancy. In *Develop-*

ments in Psychoanalysis. (Ed.) Joan Riviere, London: Hogarth, 1952.

25. Mittelmann, Béla Motility in infants, children and adults. *Psa. Study of the Child,* 1954, 9:142-177.

26. Hartmann, Heinz *Ego psychology and the problem of adaptation.* (Translated by David Rapaport.) New York: International Universities, 1958.

Reaction patterns to severe, chronic stress in American army prisoners of war of the Chinese[1]

EDGAR H. SCHEIN

The popular term "brainwashing" refers to certain psychological techniques which are used to change a person's beliefs and attitudes. The expression is often misused and misunderstood and has frightening implications for many people. In this essay, Edgar H. Schein, Ph.D., Professor of Organizational Psychology and Management at the Massachusetts Institute of Technology and formerly a research psychologist in the Neuropsychiatry Division at the Walter Reed Army Institute of Research, describes some of the "brainwashing" procedures used by the Chinese Communists to indoctrinate prisoners of war during the Korean War. In addition to providing an informative view of some of the social psychological factors involved in the creation of stress, the article describes different adjustment reactions to stress and relates these to individual personality characteristics.

In this paper I will outline some of the constellations of stress which prisoners of war faced during the Korean conflict and describe some of the reaction patterns to these stresses. Rather than presenting a complete catalogue of their experiences (3), I have selected those aspects which seem to me to throw some light on the problem of collaboration with the enemy. I will give particular emphasis to the

social psychological factors, because the Chinese approach to treatment of prisoners seemed to emphasize control over groups, rather than individuals.

My material is based on a variety of sources. I was in Korea during the repatriation, and had the opportunity to interview extensively 20 unselected repatriates. This basic material was supplemented by the information gathered by three psychiatrists, Drs. Harvey Strassman, Patrick Israel, and Clinton Tempereau, who together had seen some 300 men. On board ship returning to the United States, I also had the opportunity to sit in on bull sessions among repatriates in which many of the prison experiences were discussed. Additional details were obtained from the Army dossiers on the men.

From *Journal of Social Issues,* XIII, No. 3 (1957), 21-30. Reprinted by permission of The Society for the Psychological Study of Social Issues.

[1] This work was completed while the author was a captain, U. S. Army Medical Service Corps, assigned to the Walter Reed Army Institute of Research. I would like to acknowledge the invaluable help and guidance of Dr. David McK. Rioch and Capt. Harold Williams as well as the staff of the Neuropsychiatric Division of the Walter Reed Army Institute of Research. Portions of this paper were read at the meetings of the Group for the Advancement of Psychiatry, Asbury Park, New Jersey, November, 1956.

The typical experience of the prisoner of war must be divided into two broad phases. The first phase lasted anywhere from one to six months beginning with capture, followed by exhausting marches to the north of Korea and severe privation in inadequately equipped temporary camps, terminating in assignment to a permanent prisoner of war camp.

The second phase, lasting two or more years, was marked by chronic pressures to collaborate and to give up existing group loyalties in favor of new ones. Thus, while physical stresses had been outstanding in the first six months, psychological stresses were outstanding in this second period.

The reactions of the men toward capture were influenced by their overall attitude toward the Korean situation. Many of them felt inadequately prepared, both physically and psychologically. The physical training, equipment, and rotation system all came in for retrospective criticism, though this response might have been merely a rationalization for being captured. When the Chinese entered the war they penetrated into rear areas, where they captured many men who were taken completely by surprise. The men felt that when positions were over-run, their leadership was often less than adequate. Thus, many men were disposed to blame the UN command for the unfortunate event of being captured.

On the psychological side, the men were not clearly aware of what they were fighting for or what kind of enemy they were opposing. In addition, the reports of the atrocities committed by the North Koreans led most men to expect death, torture, or nonrepatriation if captured.

It was in such a context that the soldier found his Chinese captor extending his hand in a friendly gesture and saying "Welcome" or "Congratulations, you've been *liberated.*" This Chinese tactic was part of their "lenient policy" which was explained to groups of prisoners shortly after capture in these terms: because the UN had entered the war illegally and was an aggressor, all UN military personnel were in fact war criminals, and *could* be shot summarily. But the average soldier was, after all, only carrying out orders for his leaders who were the real criminals. Therefore, the Chinese soldier would consider the POW a "student," and would teach him the "truth" about the

war. Anyone who did not cooperate by going to school and by learning voluntarily could be reverted to his "war criminal" status and shot, particularly if a confession of "criminal" deeds could be obtained from him.

In the weeks following capture, the men were collected in large groups and marched north. From a physical point of view, the stresses during these marches were very severe: there was no medicine for the wounded, the food was unpalatable and insufficient, especially by our standards, clothing was scarce in the face of severe winter weather, and shelter was inadequate and overcrowded. The Chinese set a severe pace and showed little consideration for weariness that was the product of wounds, diarrhea, and frostbite. Men who were not able to keep up were abandoned unless they were helped by their fellows. The men marched only at night, and were kept under cover during the day, ostensibly as protection against strafing by our own planes.

From a psychological point of view this situation is best described as a recurring cycle of fear, relief, and new fear. The men were afraid that they might die, that they might never be repatriated, that they might never again have a chance to communicate with the outside, and that no one even knew they were alive. The Chinese, on the other hand, were reassuring and promised that the men would be repatriated soon, that conditions would improve, and that they would soon be permitted to communicate with the outside.

One of the chief problems for the men was the disorganization within the group itself. It was difficult to maintain close group ties if one was competing with others for the essentials of life, and if one spent one's resting time in overcrowded huts among others who had severe diarrhea and were occasionally incontinent. Lines of authority often broke down, and with this, group cohesion and morale suffered. A few men attempted to escape, but they were usually recaptured in a short time and returned to the group. The Chinese also fostered low morale and the feeling of being abandoned by systematically reporting false news about United Nations defeats and losses.

In this situation goals became increasingly short-run. As long as the men were marching, they had something to do and could look forward to relief from the harsh conditions of the march. However, arrival at a temporary camp was usually a severe disappointment. Not only were physical conditions as bad as ever, but the sedentary life in overcrowded quarters produced more disease and still lower morale.

What happened to the men under these conditions? During the one- to two-week marches they became increasingly apathetic.[2] They developed a slow, plodding gait, called by one man a "prisoners' shuffle." Uppermost in their minds were fantasies of food: men remembered all the good meals they had ever had or planned detailed menus for years into the future. To a lesser extent, they thought of loved ones at home and about cars which seemed to them to symbolize freedom and the return home.

In the temporary camps, disease and exposure took a heavy toll in lives. But it was the feeling of many men, including some of the doctors who survived the experience, that some of these deaths were not warranted by a man's physical condition. Instead, what appeared to happen was that some men became so apathetic that they ceased to care about their bodily needs. They retreated further into themselves, refused to eat even what little food was available, refused to get any exercise, and eventually lay down as if waiting to die. The reports were emphatic concerning the lucidity and sanity of these men. They seemed willing to accept the prospect of death rather than to continue fighting a severely frustrating and depriving environment.

Two things seemed to save a man who was close to such "apathy" death: getting him on his feet and doing something, no matter how trivial, or getting him angry or concerned about some present or future problem. Usually it was the effort of a friend who maternally and insistently motivated the individual toward realistic goals which snapped him out of such a state of resignation. In one case such "therapy" consisted of kicking the man until he was mad enough to get up and fight.

Throughout this time, the Chinese played the role of the benevolent but handicapped captor. Prisoners were always reminded that it was their *own* Air Force bombing which was responsible for the inadequate supplies. Furthermore, they were reminded that they were getting treatment which was just as good as that which the average Chinese was getting.

One important effect of this was that a man could never give *full* vent to his hostility toward the Chinese, even in fantasy. In their *manner* and *words* they were usually solicitous and sympathetic. The Chinese also implied that conditions could be better for a prisoner if he would take a more "cooperative" attitude, if he would support their propaganda for peace. Thus a man was made to feel that he was himself responsible for his traumatic circumstances.

Arrival at a permanent camp usually brought relief from many of these physical hardships. Food, shelter, and medicine, while not plentiful, appeared to be sufficient for the maintenance of life and some degree of health. However, the Chinese now increased sharply their efforts to involve prisoners in their own propaganda program and to undermine loyalties to their country. This marks the beginning of the second phase of the imprisonment experience.

The Chinese program of subversion and indoctrination was thoroughly integrated into the entire camp routine and involved the manipulation of the entire social milieu of the prison camp. Its aims appeared to be to manage a large group of prisoners with a minimum staff of guards, to indoctrinate them with the Communist political ideology, to interrogate them to obtain intelligence information and confessions for propaganda purposes, and to develop a corps of collaborators within the prisoner group. What success the Chinese had stemmed from their *total* control of the environment, not from the application of any one technique.

The most significant feature of Chinese prisoner camp control was the systematic destruction of the prisoners' formal and informal group structure. Soon after arrival at a camp, the men were segregated by race, nationality, and rank. The Chinese put their own men in charge of the platoons and companies and made arbitrary selections of POW squad leaders to remind the prisoners that their old rank system no longer had any validity. In addition, the Chinese attempted to undermine *informal* group structure by prohibiting any kind of group meeting and by systematically fomenting mutual distrust by playing men off

---

[2] A more detailed discussion of the apathy reaction may be found in Strassman, Thaler, and Schein (4).

against one another. The most effective device to this end was the practice of obtaining from informers or Chinese spies detailed information about someone's activities, no matter how trivial, then calling him in to interrogate him about it. Such detailed surveillance of the men's activities made them feel that their own ranks were so infiltrated by spies and informers that it was not safe to trust anyone.

A similar device was used to obtain information during interrogation. After a man had resisted giving information for hours or days, he would be shown a signed statement by one of his fellow prisoners giving that same information. Still another device was to make prisoners who had not collaborated look like collaborators, by bestowing special favors upon them.

A particularly successful Chinese technique was their use of testimonials from other prisoners, such as the false germ-warfare confessions and appeals based on familiar contexts, such as peace appeals. Confessions by prisoners or propaganda lectures given by collaborators had a particularly demoralizing effect, because only if resistance had been *unanimous* could a man solidly believe that his values were correct, even if he could not defend them logically.

If the men, in spite of their state of social disorganization, did manage to organize any kind of group activity, the Chinese would quickly break up the group by removing its leaders or key members and assigning them to another camp.

Loyalties to home and country were undermined by the systematic manipulation of mail. Usually only mail which carried bad news was delivered. If a man received no mail at all, the Chinese suggested that his loved ones had abandoned him.

Feelings of social isolation were increased by the complete information control maintained in the camps. Only the Communist press, radio, magazines, and movies were allowed.

The weakening of the prisoner group's social structure is particularly significant because we depend to such an extent on consensual validation in judging ourselves and others. The prisoners lost their most important sources of information and support concerning standards of behavior and beliefs. Often men who attempted to resist the Chinese by means other than *outright* obstruction or aggression failed

to obtain the active support of others, often earning their suspicion instead.

At the same time, the Chinese did create a situation in which meaningful social relationships could be had through common political activity, such as the "peace" committees which served as propaganda organs. The Chinese interrogators or instructors sometimes lived with prisoners for long periods of time in order to establish close personal relationships with them.

The Communist doctrines were presented through compulsory lectures followed by compulsory group discussions for the purpose of justifying the conclusions given at the end of the lectures. On the whole, this phase of indoctrination was ineffective because of the crudeness of the propaganda material used in the lectures. However, its constant repetition seemed eventually to influence those men who did not have well-formed political opinions to start with, particularly because no counter-arguments could be heard. The group discussions were effective only if their monitor was someone who could keep control over the group and keep it on the topic of discussion. Attempts by the Chinese to use "progressive" POWs in the role of monitors were seldom successful because they aroused too much hostility in the men.

The Chinese also attempted to get prisoners to use mutual criticism and self-criticism in the fashion in which it is used within China.[3] Whenever a POW was caught breaking one of the innumerable camp rules, he was required to give an elaborate confession and self-criticism, no matter how trivial the offense. In general, the POWs were able to use this opportunity to ridicule the Chinese by taking advantage of their lack of understanding of slang and American idiom. They would emphasize the wrong parts of sentences or insert words and phrases which made it apparent to other prisoners that the joke was on the Chinese. Often men were required to make these confessions in front of large groups of other prisoners. If the man could successfully communicate by a linguistic device his lack of sincerity, this ritual could backfire on the Chinese by giving the men an opportunity to express their solidarity (by

---

[3] See the paper by Robert J. Lifton in this issue.

sharing a communication which could not be understood by the Chinese). However, in other instances, prisoners who viewed such public confessions felt contempt for the confessor and felt their own group was being undermined still further by such public humiliation.

Various tales of how prisoners resisted the pressures put on them have been widely circulated in the press. For example, a number of prisoners ridiculed the Chinese by playing baseball with a basketball, yet telling the Chinese this was the correct way to play the game. Such stories suggest that morale and group solidarity was actually quite high in the camps. Our interviews with the men suggest that morale climbed sharply during the *last six to nine months* of imprisonment when the armistice talks were underway, when the compulsory indoctrination program had been put on a voluntary basis, and when the Chinese were improving camp conditions in anticipation of the repatriation. However, we heard practically no stories of successful group resistance or high morale from the first year or so in the camps when the indoctrination program was seriously pursued by the Chinese. (At that time the men had neither the time nor the opportunity to play any kind of games, because all their time was spent on indoctrination activities or exhausting labor).

Throughout, the Chinese created an environment in which rewards such as extra food, medicine, special privileges, and status were given for cooperation and collaboration, while threats of death, nonrepatriation, reprisal against family, torture, decreases in food and medicine, and imprisonment served to keep men from offering much resistance. Only imprisonment was consistently used as an actual punishment. *Chronic* resistance was usually handled by transferring the prisoner to a so-called "reactionary" camp.

Whatever behavior the Chinese attempted to elicit, they always *paced* their demands very carefully, they always required some level of *participation* from the prisoner, no matter how trivial, and they *repeated* endlessly.

To what extent did these pressures produce either changes in beliefs and attitudes, or collaboration? Close observation of the repatriates and the reports of the men themselves suggest that the Chinese did not have much success in changing beliefs and attitudes. Doubt and confusion were created in many prisoners, as a result of having to examine so closely their own way of thinking, but very few changes, if any, occurred that resembled actual *conversion* to Communism. The type of prisoner who was most likely to become *sympathetic* toward Communism was the one who had chronically occupied a low status position in this society, and for whom the democratic principles were not very salient or meaningful.

In producing collaboration, however, the Chinese were far more effective. By collaboration I mean such activities as giving lectures for the Communists, writing and broadcasting propaganda, giving false confessions, writing and signing petitions, informing on fellow POWs, and so on; none of these activities required a personal change of belief. Some 10 to 15 per cent of the men chronically collaborated, but the dynamics of this response are very complex. By far the greatest determinant was the amount of pressure the Chinese put on a particular prisoner. Beyond this, the reports of the men permit one to isolate several sets of motives that operated, though it is impossible to tell how many cases of each type there may have been.

1) Some men collaborated for outright opportunistic reasons; these men lacked any kind of stable group identification, and exploited the situation for its material benefits without any regard for the consequences to themselves, their fellow prisoners, or their country.

2) Some men collaborated because their egos were too weak to withstand the physical and psychological rigors; these men were primarily motivated by fear, though they often rationalized their behavior; they were unable to resist any kind of authority figure and could be blackmailed by the Chinese once they had begun to collaborate.

3) Some men collaborated with the firm conviction that they were infiltrating the Chinese ranks and obtaining intelligence information which would be useful to UN forces. This was a convenient rationalization for anyone who could not withstand the pressures. Many of these men were initially tricked into collaboration or were motivated by a desire to communicate with the outside world. None of these men became ideologically confused; what Communist beliefs they might have professed were for the benefit of the Chinese only.

4) The prisoner who was vulnerable to the ideological appeal because of his low status in this society often collaborated with the conviction that he was doing the right thing in supporting the Communist peace movement. This group included the young and less intelligent men from backward or rural areas, the malcontents, and members of various minority groups. These men often viewed themselves as failures in our society, and felt that society had never given them a chance. They were positively attracted by the immediate status and privileges which went with being a "progressive," and by the promise of important roles which they could presumably play in the peace movement of the future.

Perhaps the most important thing to note about collaboration is the manner in which the social disorganization contributed to it. A man might make a slanted radio broadcast in order to communicate with the outside, he might start reading Communist literature out of sheer boredom, he might give information which he knew the Chinese already had, and so on. Once this happened, however, the Chinese rewarded him, increased pressure on him to collaborate, and blackmailed him by threatening exposure. At the same time, in most cases, his fellow prisoners forced him into further collaboration by mistrusting him and ostracizing him. Thus a man had to stand entirely on his own judgment and strength and both of these often failed. One of the most common failures was a man's lack of awareness concerning the effects of his own actions on the other prisoners, and the value of these actions for the Chinese propaganda effort. The man who confessed to germ warfare, thinking he could repudiate such a confession later, did not realize its immediate propaganda value to the Communists.

A certain percentage of men, though the exact number is difficult to estimate, exhibited chronic resistance and obstructionism toward Chinese indoctrination efforts. Many of these men were well integrated with secure, stable group identifications who could withstand the social isolation and still exercise good judgment. Others were chronic obstructionists whose histories showed recurring resistance to any form of authority. Still others were idealists or martyrs to religious and ethical principles, and still others were anxious, guilt-ridden individuals who could only cope with their own strong impulses to collaborate by denying them and over-reacting in the other direction.

By far the largest group of prisoners, however, established a complex compromise between the demands of the Chinese and their own value system. This adjustment, called by the men "playing it cool," consisted primarily of a physical and emotional withdrawal from the whole environment. These men learned to suspend their feelings and to adopt an attitude of watching and waiting, rather than hoping and planning. This reaction, though passive, was not as severe as the apathy described earlier. It was a difficult adjustment to maintain because some concessions had to be made to the Chinese in the form of trivial or well-timed collaborative acts, and in the form of a feigned interest in the indoctrination program. At the same time, each man had to be prepared to deal with the hostility of his buddies if he made an error in judgment.

Discussion

This paper has placed particular emphasis on the social psychological factors involved in "brainwashing" because it is my opinion that the process is primarily concerned with social forces, not with the strengths and weaknesses of individual minds. It has often been asserted that drugs, hypnotic techniques, refined "mental tortures" and, more recently, implanted electrodes can make the task of the "brainwasher" much easier by rendering the human mind submissive with a minimum of effort.[4] There is little question that such techniques can be used to elicit confessions or signatures on documents prepared by the captor; but so can withdrawal of food, water, or air produce the same results. The point is that the Chinese Communists do not appear to be interested in obtaining merely a confession or *transient* submission. Instead, they appear to be interested in producing changes in men which will be lasting and self-sustaining. A germ-warfare confession alone was not enough —the POW had to "testify" before an international commission explaining in detail how the bombs had been dropped and had to tell

---

[4] For example, see the paper by James G. Miller in this issue.

his story in other prison camps to his fellow POWs.

There is little evidence that drugs, post-hypnotic suggestion, or implanted electrodes can now or ever will be able to produce the kind of behavior exhibited by many prisoners who collaborated and made false confessions. On the other hand, there is increasing evidence (1, 2) that Russian and Chinese interrogation and indoctrination techniques involve the destruction of the person's social ties and identifications and the partial destruction of his ego. If this is successfully accomplished, the person is offered a new identity for himself and given the opportunity to identify with new groups. What physical torture and deprivation are involved in this process may be either a calculated attempt to degrade and humiliate a man to destroy his image of himself as a dignified human being or the product of fortuitous circumstances, i.e., failure of supply lines to the prison, loss of temper on the part of the interrogator, an attempt to inspire fear in other prisoners by torturing one of them, and so on. We do not have sufficient evidence to determine which of these alternatives represents Communist intentions; possibly all of them are involved in the actual prison situation.

Ultimately that which sustains humans is their personality integration born out of secure and stable group identifications. One may be able to produce temporary submission by direct intervention in cortical processes, but only by destroying a man's self-image and his group supports can one produce any lasting changes in his beliefs and attitudes. By concerning ourselves with the problem of artificially creating submission in man, we run the real risk of overlooking the fact that we are in a genuine struggle of ideas with other portions of the world and that man often submits himself directly to ideas and principles.

To understand and combat "brainwashing" we must look at those social conditions which make people ready to accept new ideas from anyone who states them clearly and forcefully and those social conditions which give people the sense of integrity which will sustain them when their immediate social and emotional supports are stripped away.

References

1. Hinckle, Lawrence E. and Wolff, Harold C. Communist interrogation and indoctrination of "enemies of the state." *Arch. neur. and Psychiat.* 1956, 76, 115-174.

2. Lifton, Robert L. "Thought reform" of Western civilians in Chinese communist prisons. *Psychiatry,* 1956, 19, 173-198.

3. Schein, Edgar H. The Chinese indoctrination program for prisoners of war. *Psychiatry,* 1956, 19, 149-172.

4. Strassman, Harvey D., Thaler, Margaret, and Schein, Edgar H. A prisoner of war syndrome: Apathy as a reaction to severe stress. *Amer. J. Psychiat.,* 1956, 112, 998-1003.

Culture patterns and human stress
a study in social psychiatry [1]

JOHN J. HONIGMANN

Psychological approaches to understanding stress often focus on the individual person. What is considered stressful is thought to vary from one person to the next, and stress is considered to be closely related to an individual's prior life experiences. Anthropological and sociological methods of inquiry have a different orientation and place more emphasis on social and cultural factors. This article represents an anthropological approach to a psychological problem. The author points out that cultural patterns contain inherent sources of stress to which all members of the society are exposed, and he suggests that the specific nature of the stress will vary from one culture to another. The article describes some of the specific kinds of stress characteristic of American culture, contrasts these with examples from other cultures, and explores some of the built-in mechanisms that cultures provide for the relief of stress.

John J. Honigan, Ph.D., is Professor of Anthropology at the University of North Carolina. His books include *Culture and Ethos of Kaska Society*, *The World of Man*, and *Personality in Culture*.

The principal purpose of this essay is to contribute additional insights in that area where the sciences of psychiatry and anthropology have their meeting ground. Specifically I hope to demonstrate the utility of the culture concept as a tool for understanding tension or stress in human beings, as well as the limitations which surround this approach. In order to achieve those ends it will be necessary, first, to illustrate how culture may induce stress in the individual. By going a step further I shall try to show that cultural pathways may also be utilized as mechanisms for relieving stress. Were a simple application of these principles possible, the anthropologist should thus be led to the point where he could, theoretically, excise those culture patterns which induce severe human tension and institute customary pathways of behavior along which accumulated organismic unrest might be discharged. However, this paper will show that the removal of stress-inducing customs cannot always be attempted without a fundamental reorganization of the life of the people—a price that the group may be reluctant to pay.

The culture concept

The word "culture," which in the past few decades has acquired a distinctive technical meaning that has also become fairly widespread in popular thinking, refers to the traditional way of life pursued by human beings. By "a culture" the anthropologist means the learned patterns of behavior characteristic of a particular, specifiable group of human beings. An example of such learned behavior patterns is to be found in the Wind River Shoshone, among whom 10- or 12-year-old boys formed gangs in which they played or hunted. "In the course

[1] For biographical data, see *Psychiatry* (1947) 10:37. For bibliography, see *Psychiatry* (1947) 10:117. The larger portion of this paper was delivered before the resident staff of the Psychiatric Department of Bellevue Hospital in New York.

of time, a definite unity would pervade a gang of boys . . . they would be antagonistic to, and abuse, newcomers. ·. . ." [2] It is the function of the anthropologist to study and describe the culture patterns by which men live. In doing so he attempts to relate particular sequences of interpersonal behavior to other behavior patterns which are a part of the cultural configuration. So, for example, he might designate a relationship between the aggressive gang life of the Shoshone adolescents and the aggressiveness that was expected of a compact body of Shoshone warriors going to meet the enemy. In another cultural context the social scientist might relate the teasing behavior which is expressed toward grandparents to the diminished social prestige suffered by oldsters who have been forced to retire from the active pursuit of making a living in sub-Arctic Indian tribes and now look to the younger generation for support. Conversely, the filial piety demanded of Chinese youth could be related to the patriarchal, age-dominated social system of China in which advanced age earns an increment of prestige for a man. Out of many such particular relationships, charted for specific cultural configurations, may emerge a generalization, a universal law of social interaction. Such laws are as yet a largely unrealized goal of social anthropology. An example of what appears to be a valid generalization derived from the study of many individual social systems is the following: ". . . the way in which parent-child relationships are patterned in respect to such behaviors as: succoring-dependence, dominance-submission and exhibitionism-spectatorship, provides a learning situation for the child which patterns his subsequent behavior in situations where these behaviors are involved." [3]

The procedure of interrelating aspects of culture is the essence of so-called "functionalism" in social anthropology. The theory of functionalism, in turn, leads to the conclusion that the behavior patterns which are regarded as "fitting" in one cultural context may have no place in the way of life of another group. As an illustration of what is here meant by "cultural fit" we might take behavior reported by Tomasic for the Dinaric pastoralists.[4] American society could not tolerate the custom found among these southeast European people according to which a newly married wife passed her wedding night sleeping not with her spouse but with the husband's brother (or cousin). Both participants were fully dressed. In Dinaric culture the ritual built up a close and trustful friendship between these two. In the course of the marriage the everyday male companionship and affection, which the wife could expect in her husband's household, would come not so much from her husband as from her husband's brother. Husband and wife avoided public affection in this pastoral group. Thus "bundling" of the woman and her brother-in-law was functional in Dinaric culture but would have small place in our contemporary way of life. Another example of cultural fit is to be found in the Dakota and other western Indians. Among these people, relatives expect to share in any surplus wealth which one of the kin group manages to accumulate.[5] Very clearly such behavior is not expected in our own social system. But the Indian is becoming more and more a part of our system. The traditional pattern of sharing is also beginning to lose its fit. It plays havoc with Indian rehabilitation programs. A man will not work hard, the Bureau of Indian Affairs has discovered, if ambition is regarded as a threat to the community and if the rewards for hard work act as a signal calling a man's relatives together to share in his good fortune. The white rancher or farmer, on the other hand, is motivated to greater effort partly by the thought that his income belongs to him and need not be shared among a large kin group.

So much for the concept of culture. If the exposition has seemed on the lengthy side, it might be pointed out that anthropology has sometimes been called the science of culture. Anthropologists are highly pleased with the culture concept and regard it as a fine tool with which to study human behavior. However, in the last few decades, anthropology has also interested itself in personality. With their interest in comparing social systems students of

[2] D. B. Shimkin, *Childhood and development among the Wind River Shoshone;* Anthropological Records, Vol. 5, No. 5; University of California Press, Los Angeles and Berkeley, 1947.

[3] Margaret Mead, "A case history in cross-national communication," in *The communication of ideas* (Ed.) L. Bryson, New York: Harper & Brothers, 1948, p. 213.

[4] Dinko Tomasic, *Personality and culture in Eastern European politics,* New York: George W. Stewart, 1948, pp. 74-75.

[5] See Gordon Macgregor, *Warriors without weapons,* Chicago: University of Chicago Press, 1946.

culture also came to realize that the distinctive life-ways of different social groups result in the patterning of a distinctive inner life for the majority of members of each such group. In other words societies are characterized by "personality types." Thus there are the mild and gentle Mountain Arapesh people, among whom the behavior of both sexes is said to be comparable to the behavior which we in our society expect from women.[6] Not far from the Arapesh are the vigorous and aggressive Mundugamor [7] whom we might compare with the withdrawn and isolated Balinese,[8] or to the danger-loving Dionysian warriors of the American Great Plains.[9] Out of this interest in comparative character structure has developed a new sub-discipline within the field of anthropology—namely, culture and personality. The workers in this area have been profoundly influenced by psychiatric thinking and it may be expected that even closer cooperation between psychiatrists and students of culture-personality relationships may be expected in the future.[10]

Culture and human stress

Culture and personality research, by focussing not on the gross outlines of group behavior but on the fate of the individual in the interpersonal network that constitutes a social system, has made anthropologists aware of the fact that the way of life of a particular group may be so designed as to make strong tension inevitable in particular areas of life. In order to demonstrate the proposition that culture patterns may induce human stress I shall consider, first, cultures as relatively self-contained systems of behavior—that is, cultures which are not in contact with foreign ways of life—and, second, I shall talk of what happens when a culture comes into contact with some other social system that embodies demands which are not congruent with the norms of the former.

For a first example, I will use Attawapiskat, a community of about 460 Cree Indians located on the west coast of James Bay in northern Ontario.[11] In this hunting and trapping economy, hard work and effort are highly evaluated and may be utilized by the men as prestige-gaining techniques. The industrious person is praised, while the one who neglects keeping his canoe in good repair, is lackadaisical about cutting wood or setting traps and fails to provide adequately for his family is

condemned as "lazy." The principal point I want to make is that aged men suffer under these customary demands. Respect is withdrawn from the old because they, of biological necessity, relax and cease trying. I heard a wife say this about her half-paralyzed and older husband: "Never does he do anything—never!" The culture of the Attawapiskat Cree holds in reserve no secondary rewards for old age; the oldsters are not the fountains of wisdom to which community deliberations are referred, nor are they selected as chiefs. They cannot be shamans because native ritualism has long since disappeared from this community. It is hardly an exaggeration to say that the old are left without any functions in Attawapiskat. Pushed to one side the aged eat the food that is not too willingly shared with them by secretly guilty relatives and dream of the time of their youth. Interviews with old men were always productive when I asked about the games and activities of young people in the past.

Psychological tension of a different order occurs among the people of Nakoroka village in Fiji.[12] Here the men are said to be obsessed with anxiety about their relative prestige and never does a man dare to cease trying to advance his status along the pathways laid out by Fijian culture. I believe that the late Ruth Benedict sometimes referred to cultures which

---

[6] Margaret Mead, *Sex and temperament. In—From the south seas*, New York: Morrow, 1939.
[7] Reference footnote 6.
[8] Gregory Bateson and Margaret Mead, *Balinese character*, New York: Special Publications of the New York Academy of Sciences, 1942, Vol. 12.
[9] Ruth Benedict, *Patterns of culture*, New York: Penguin Books, 1934.
[10] For examples of culture and personality studies drawing heavily on the thought of psychiatry, the reader is referred to the papers of Ruth Benedict, Cora Du Bois, Erik Homburger Erikson, Erich Fromm, John Gillin, Esther Goldfrank, Geoffrey Gorer, A. Irving Hallowell, Douglas G. Haring, Abram Kardiner, Clyde Kluckhohn, Weston LaBarre, Margaret Mead, Hortense Powdermaker, Géza Roheim, and others in the following two recently published source books: Douglas G. Haring (Ed.), *Personal character and cultural milieu*, Syracuse: Syracuse University Press, 1949; and Clyde Kluckhohn and Henry A. Murray (Eds.), *Personality in nature, society, and culture*, New York: Alfred A. Knopf, 1948. The Haring volume contains a particularly comprehensive and useful bibliography of the field.
[11] Data are largely contained in unpublished field notes and an as yet unpublished report deposited with the Department of National Health and Welfare, Ottawa. See, however, Honigmann, "Incentives to work in a Canadian Indian community," in *Human Organization* (1949) 8:23-28.
[12] Buell Quain, *Fijian village*, Chicago: University of Chicago Press, 1948.

never allow men to contentedly rest upon their laurels as "treadmill cultures." From a knowledge of human psychology it is reasonable to assume that a treadmill system poses a problem of fairly constant tension for the individuals living under its terms.

A third example to illustrate the thesis that cultures may be so designed as to produce personal stress in their human carriers comes from the Kaska Indians of northern British Columbia and southern Yukon Territory.[13] The Kaska Indian is, at least in some ways, remarkably close to Karen Horney's "detached personality type," which, she says, is governed by a "tendency to suppress all feeling." [14] Kaska adults have been enculturated to meet crisis situations with denial and minimization. One result of this is that illness is often neglected, because the threat in facing the disease is too great. For a person to openly admit fear in illness is also disturbing. Individuals are also unable to reveal themselves emotionally, and are provided with no techniques for psychologically getting close to other people.[15] There is, consequently, painful shyness with strangers and also profound reserve among familiar acquaintances. This general pattern of "emotional constriction" is further revealed in the sexual sphere. Coitus among unmarried adolescents is not solicited openly but through a prolonged routine of teasing, chasing, and other rapelike behavior. Such patterns reveal the ambivalence with which the Kaska personality regards sex. Hostility is likewise suppressed. At least when they are sober, people avoid any danger of quarrelling. The hostility which is inevitably generated in the social system is customarily deflected into gossip which again insures the atomization of the social system. Now these behavior patterns are extremely useful for getting along in Kaska society. They represent what is expected of a "good" Kaska Indian. Open emotional expression and demonstrativeness would be horribly unfit and disturbing. From one point of view the patterns of Kaska culture could only be called sociologically "normal." But familiarity with a number of Kaska individuals suggests that these patterns also impose a strain on and create anxieties for them. The evidence suggests that people carry within themselves an unfulfilled desire for emotional warmth—an impulse to which they dare not respond. In other words they could be char-acterized by David Levy's syndrome of "affect hunger." If this and other similar evidence were estimated by a psychiatrist, he would presumably be forced to the conclusion that certain aspects of Kaska culture—those behavior patterns specified above—are psychiatrically "abnormal," because they result in something less than mental health. To me this seems analogous to saying that certain ways of disposing of garbage or sewage are "unhealthy" because they lead to a condition of disease.[16]

Our own culture is certainly not without stress-producing patterns and the psychiatrist of our times may find it highly rewarding to pay close attention to these patterns. For instance there are the customary patterns that suppress spontaneity. Here we have, more specifically, the severe sanctions on childhood aggression found in many American social classes. It is also true that the severity of these controls leaves few legitimate channels through which childhood hostility can be drained off, while at the same time hostility is particularly likely to be aroused in the presence of many

---

[13] Honigmann, *Culture and ethos of Kaska society*, New Haven: Yale University Publications in Anthropology No. 40, 1949. See also "Cultural dynamics of sex," *Psychiatry*, 1947, 10:37-47.

[14] Karen Horney, *Our inner conflicts*, New York: Norton, 1945, p. 85.

[15] For the same personality trait in another group of northern forest Indians, the Ojibwa, see A. Irving Hallowell, "Psychosexual adjustment, personality and the good life in a nonliterate culture," in *Psychosexual development in health and disease*, Ed. by Paul Henry Hoch and Joseph Zubin, New York: Grune and Stratton, 1949, p. 123. Note this sentence from Hallowell's paper: "With so little real give and take or learning to know each other on an openly confident and genuinely friendly basis, there is a high degree of projection in interpersonal relations." See also, Ruth Landes, "The abnormal among the Ojibwa Indians," *J. abnorm. soc. Psychol.*, 1938, 33:14-33, p. 20.

[16] I find it necessary to point out that I am not offering a value judgment with respect to either the sociological normality or the psychiatric abnormality of these behavior patterns. On the contrary I am using yardsticks ("cultural fit" and "mental health") analogous to the yardsticks which the science of nutrition applies to diet, or traditional medicine to organismic functioning. There is, of course, theoretically no end to the yardsticks that might be called into operation for the purpose of comparing cultures but I do believe that cultures *can* be compared. For two divergent viewpoints on this question of cultural comparison see the relativistic position of Melville J. Herskovits in *Man and his works*, New York: Alfred A. Knopf, 1948, pp. 61-78, and the stand of John Gillin in *The ways of men*, New York: Appleton-Century-Crofts, 1948, pp. 163-171 and 198-220. For a brief discussion of the arbitrariness of all units of measurement, see Walter Coutu, *Emergent human nature*, New York: Alfred A. Knopf, 1949, pp. 4-11.

and strict inhibiting factors. Our mass education also contributes to suppressing spontaneity. With many to educate and no time for the individual pupil, schools are too often a place which children regard as a place of confinement. Then there are the patterns of impersonality determined by our complex urban civilization. Modern man spends a great portion of his working hours among strangers whom he doesn't really know, in whom he cannot confide, to whom he cannot turn for guidance. People in quandaries are not likely to receive as useful support from strangers as from close kin and a circle of intimate friends. It is likely that small quarrels will magnify when the isolated modern family is left to work through a solution *alone* in the three rooms of an apartment building that represents home.[17] One more source of human stress in modern culture lies in our patterns of industrial life. For example, modern industry appears to be geared in such a way that it encourages "supervisory anxiety" in almost every person who works with a boss above him. Industrial-relations sociologists have come to the conclusion that worrying about what the boss thinks takes up a large part of the worker's factory day and may also be carried home from the plant. Fear and anxiety may also arise out of the divergent orientations of management and labor, and each disagreement between the chronically maladjusted groups draws the battle lines more sharply. Executives and workers have their mental health impaired in this climate.

Human stress is particularly likely to arise when one culture enters into contact with a profoundly different way of life—that is, operationally speaking, when the persons who have been raised in one tradition are forced to interact with people brought up with different values and expectations. Intercultural relations of this order are extraordinarily facilitated in the modern world where space and time have been overcome by machines and overcome so quickly that time has not permitted new patterns of social relations to develop in order to bridge the gap. Often what happens under conditions of culture contact is this: The invading group fails to understand the way of life of the host population or makes demands on the hosts for which cultural solutions are lacking. The original population comprehends no

more clearly the visitor's customary behavior. However, so often it is the white European or American who is the invader. He comes with tremendous prestige that often instigates voluntary emulation of his customs by the native. Rapid change ensues in which cultural fit becomes impaired, while on the psychological level, uncertainty and tension are aroused.

The strain of living under culture-contact conditions is well revealed in this statement from a Solomon Islander: [18]

You white men give us orders. . . . The white man has come and tells us to behave like *his* father. Our own fathers, we must forget them. . . . In the olden days we did this thing, we did that thing. We did not stop and say to ourselves first, "This thing I want to do, is it right?" We always knew. Now we have to say, "This thing I want to do, will the white man tell me it is wrong and punish me?"

A very simple example of the unrest promoted by intercultural misunderstanding comes from Attawapiskat. The local Cree Indians regard summer as a time of relaxation after the winter trapping season. Missionaries and Indian agents, however, plague the natives to work, to earn money so as to reduce the relief load, to improve the community, to raise potatoes. These demands are a source of friction between the two social bodies. The Indians feel no unworthiness in accepting government relief and will not learn the shame that the administrators are trying to inculcate on this point. At the same time, the native will not abandon his definition of summer, particularly for work that lies outside the sphere of trapping, hunting, and fishing and therefore meets with little or no emotional appeal.

Another example of culture conflict is found in the Navaho Indians. The Navaho are eager for education and often enter mission schools. Missionaries, however, tend to follow a policy of trying to exterminate the indigenous way of life. Students in mission schools, for example,

---

[17] Honigmann, "There isn't a person," *Antioch Review*, 1949, 9:388-395.
[18] Quoted from A. Irving Hallowell, "Sociopsychological aspects of acculturation," in *The study of man in the world crisis*, (Ed.) by Ralph Linton, New York: Columbia University Press, 1945, p. 193.

are forbidden to attend native ceremonials. The result is that Navaho children in church schools are caught between the expectations of parents and the demands of missionaries. In turn, it is found that despite patterns of "good" infant care, Navaho children return home from school endowed with considerable anxiety.[19]

Among the Lovedu of South Africa, culture change is also at work. Here mission-educated natives return to the reserve and try to get along with European patterns of interpersonal relations. The social system in the reserve is founded on easy cooperation without any resort to force or direction. The work party is really a "party," with native beer flowing freely and friendly gossip usual. But the Europeanized native has learned another style of interpersonal life. He tries to get the cooperation of his neighbors via wage labor. Since he pays "good money" to those whom he hires, he also tries to boss and supervise and tries to reduce the time during which the workers rest. In this way he arouses resentment, earns the dislike of his neighbors, and becomes caught up in a far-reaching web of confusion.[20]

The most extreme development of intercultural conflict and resultant distress lies in "detribalization." The word means that the individual is lifted out of his circle of kin, friends, familiar environment, and traditional life-ways and is put down to work in an urban quarter or mining town surrounded by strangers who are similarly transplanted. He has not been prepared for living under these conditions. Carothers' study in Kenya discusses from the psychiatric point of view some of the consequences of detribalization in East Africa. For example, he points out that the certification rate to mental hospitals for urban natives is five times greater than that of the tribalized natives living on reserves.[21]

Culture and the relief of stress [22]

Having examined instances of culture patterns producing individual stress, I turn now to an examination of the thesis that in any social system customary channels may be found serving as avenues for reducing tension. Such channels may be very roughly divided into those which do not result in any seriously intensified personal disorganization or group disequilibrium and, second, those that are dys-

crasic in the sense that they promote problems which threaten group integration and which must cast their reflection in the form of personal distress.

In a sense, of course, all of culture constitutes a defense against helplessness, anxiety, and annihilation. This is only to say that culture is an adaptive mechanism enabling the human species to survive. With reference to specifying channels of release, however, one can be more analytical. One widespread category of "cultural defense mechanisms" is summed up in the word "magic." Magic provides a guarantee against insecurities which, in their turn, are culturally defined. Thus the Bantu Negro is enculturated to fear the drought which may destroy his crops. At the same time, Bantu culture provides numerous magical solutions for ending or avoiding drought and thereby helps to reduce personal tension. Magic, as Malinowski pointed out, is also a morale builder. The Moro of the Sudan are thought to have the "best" agricultural magic among their neighbors and they also have the best crops! [23] The knowledge that their magic is powerful no doubt gives them a zest and confidence to work on land that is better than average to begin with.

Ceremonies need not be exclusively magical to act as tension-reducing mechanisms. In Ashanti culture there occurred a regular ceremony which allowed the people in political power to hear the derision and reproaches of their subjects. These complaints were in retaliation for injustices committed. In part the ceremony was magical—it was designed to safeguard the souls of the rulers after their death. For the governed, however, it was an

[19] Dorothea Leighton and Clyde Kluckhohn, *Children of the people*, Cambridge: Harvard University Press, 1947, pp. 64-68.
[20] E. Jensen Krige and J. D. Krige, *Realm of a rain queen*, London: Oxford University Press, 1943, chapter 4.
[21] J. C. Carothers, "A study of mental derangement in Africans, and an attempt to explain its peculiarities, more especially in relation to the African attitude to life," *Psychiatry*, 1948, 11:47-86. The author has not ruled out the possibility of selective migration to urban areas, a thorny problem similar to the "selection" question faced in all investigations of this type.
[22] Ernest Beaglehole, "Emotional release in a Polynesian community," *J. abnorm. soc. Psychol.*, 1937, 32:319-328; and the same author's "A note on cultural compensation," *J. abnorm. soc. Psychol.*, 1938, 33:121-123.
[23] S. F. Nadel, *The Nuba*, London: Oxford University Press, 1947, p. 22.

opportunity to regularly work off accumulated tension.

Anthropologists have discovered that cult groups are often invented to relieve personal disturbances affecting large segments of a society. Often such movements accompany culture contact experiences. The Vailala Madness of New Guinea, occurring in 1919, may be taken as an example. This activity arose out of the helplessness of natives under foreign domination and was based on a belief in the early return of the dead. The cult was marked by violent dancing. People anticipated the day when the whites would be driven out of the country and when the old times would return.[24] The Ghost Dance founded among the American Indians was a comparable reaction against the tensions occasioned by the expansion of the American frontier. It is possible that such movements may be at least in part functionally equivalent to group therapy in Western psychiatry—that is, they may allow disturbed individuals to repair morale through an intense group experience.

Less spectacular cultural devices for relieving tension and uncertainty are to be found in entertainment patterns all over the world. The love story magazines of our time assure young women of the reality of the Cinderella myth so that the myth persists in spite of the almost daily denials of its reality that the workaday world presents. In other respects, too, it is likely that fiction compensates for frustration. The comic magazines probably allow our much sat-upon children to vicariously participate in the aggression and violence that is so closely damned up in the socialization process.

Another customary pattern for relieving distress consists in the preparation and drinking of alcoholic beverages. The use of alcohol is a very ancient custom closely tied up in time with the invention of agriculture.[25] With alcohol we approach the dyscrasic solutions to personal stress—not because alcohol is bad in itself but because of the breakdown in social cooperation and the resultant heightened stress that so often accompanies its use. The Kaska Indians learned the preparation and use of fruit wines and beers from the whites. Consumption by these normally introverted and inhibited people is accompanied by a release of many of the controls found in normal life. Aggression, direct sexual approach, self-pity—all these

accompany drunkenness. Sometimes we see an orgiastic display of uncontrolled emotion—behavior that is best described as "running amok." Psychotic episodes are said to resemble states of inebriated euphoria and depression. The emotional sprees associated with drunkenness are sometimes succeeded by intense experiences of guilt and by suicidal attempts. Also in the category of dyscrasic cultural solutions to tension is witchcraft—working sorcery against an enemy—or, what is probably more common in social life, witch-fear—the belief that somebody is working witchcraft against one. It has been noted that an increase in witchcraft belief often accompanies culture-contact conditions. Thus the Navaho after their period of captivity by the United States Army toward the end of the nineteenth century experienced an outbreak of sorcery fear. The Lovedu, also previously mentioned in this paper, are experiencing an increase of witch-fear as part of their program of culture change. The Kaska, after invasion of their territory by gold miners, were struck by an epidemic of witch-fear in which children were accused of being sorcerers, tortured, and in some cases put to death.[26] A complete explanation of such witch-fear outbreaks would require on-the-spot study by psychiatrists as well as anthropologists. Provisionally it seems that the people are experiencing anxiety from altered conditions of the social and natural environment. Hostility derives from the anxiety but cannot be expressed against the real sources of the insecurity—that is, the white man. Instead the hostility is released within the group, either in witchcraft or, as in projection, in the fear that somebody is working sorcery against one.

---

[24] Melville J. Herskovits, Man and his works, New York: Alfred A. Knopf, 1948, pp. 531-532.

[25] For the relevant social anthropological material on alcohol see: Alcohol, Science and Society, New Haven: Quart. J. Studies on Alcohol, 1945, pp. 153-200. Donald Horton, "The functions of alcohol in primitive societies: A cross-cultural study," Quart. J. Studies on Alcohol, 1943, 3:199-320. Donald Horton, "The functions of alcohol in primitive societies," in Personality in nature, society, and culture, ed. by Clyde Kluckhohn and Henry A. Murray, New York: Alfred A. Knopf, 1948, pp. 540-550. And John J. Honigmann and Irma Honigmann, "Drinking in an Indian-White community," Quart. J. Studies on Alcohol, 1945, 5:575-519. The last study should be supplemented by Culture and ethos of Kaska society (reference footnote 13).

[26] Honigmann, "Witch-Fear in post-contact Kaska society," Amer. Anthrop., 1947, 49:222-243.

The behavior may be regarded as dyscrasic because it creates an atmosphere of suspicion, intensified by anxiety, and promotes a breakdown of cooperation within the group thus adding to the problems of adaptation and adjustment.[27]

The difficulty of change

At this point it would seem that the reduction of stress depends largely on the substitution of less stressful for distressful behavior patterns. Two major considerations must be faced before any such program of social engineering can be seriously debated. The first of these is the concept of cultural fit—the proposition that specific patterns in culture are related to others and that reciprocity between behaviors is essential for the ongoingness of a social system. Stressful patterns *may* be in highly crucial integrative positions.[28] It follows that patterns in strategic positions cannot usually be altered without a fundamental reorganization of a people's way of life, a process of change which the group might not welcome and which must be accompanied by an increase in tension.[29] I can now introduce the second consideration that promises to limit the initiative of American social scientists of the present day who are engaged in social engineering—namely, the tenets of political democracy constituting part of *their* social system. Briefly, this dogma maintains that people generally enjoy the moral right of self-determination and that, in the absence of a willingness to change, authoritarian manipulation is as morally wrong as cultural genocide.[30] Administrators and applied social scientists who intend to adhere to this value premise must find themselves forced to resort to patient education before they can introduce any major dislocations in the life-ways of a group. It is immaterial at this point to debate whether voluntary change following upon education and undertaken with the cooperation of a people is not also the type of change most likely to take hold and with the least disturbance. The assumption may, however, be proposed for serious study and testing.

No matter how strikingly signs of stress may emerge from culture when sought for with the yardstick of mental health, social anthropologists—who are, after all, not primarily psychiatrists and keep in view a vista broader than mental health—do not find it easy to make any blanket statement regarding the undesirability of stress induced by culture. Nor are they easily led to make any simple valuational statements beyond the empirical statement that certain cultural situations induce stress.[31] Social anthropologists, while sharing with psychiatrists an interest in diagnosing tension-inducing situations, also remain cognizant of the many other and often conflicting values of the groups which they are studying. Thus witch-fear and witchcraft have been labelled as dyscrasic phenomena. At the same time that these behaviors disturb group functioning however, they enjoy certain cultural fits and functions. Among the Hopi the channelization of hostility into secret witchcraft results in the fact that open violence and aggression are submerged. This state in turn permits social cooperation to proceed without overt disorganization becoming the dominant problem. However covert disorganization leaves much to be desired in the mental health of the Hopi. Culture configurations like that of the Hopi warn the social scientist that he cannot easily impose his values on an exotic group with the certainty that change will make only for better mental health. The eradication of witchery patterns among the Hopi would probably seriously complicate social life before a new equilibrium was achieved.[32] Similarly, the stress which is

---

[27] Clyde Kluckhohn, *Navaho witchcraft*, Papers of the Peabody Museum of American Archaeology and Ethnology, 1944, Vol. 22, No. 2, Cambridge.

[28] For a comprehensive exposition of the theory of integration see John Gillin, *The ways of men*, New York: Appleton-Century-Crofts, 1948, chapter 24.

[29] Cf. Gluckman's statement that, considered sociologically, conflict may be "a mode of integrating groups and . . . hostility between groups is a form of social balance." Max Gluckman, *Malinowski's sociological theories*, Cape Town: The Rhodes-Livingston Papers, 1949, No. 16, p. 10.

[30] For remarks on the democratic dogma as it affects American anthropologists engaged in social action see: Margaret Mead, *And keep your powder dry*, New York: Morrow, 1942, chapter 11. "Professional problems of education in dependent countries," *J. Negro Educ.*, 1946, 15:346-357, p. 348. And *Final draft of the preliminary report of the committee on ethics, society for applied anthropology*, mimeographed, 1948.

[31] Note that measurement and evaluation are used here in specific senses, the former implying an empirical yardstick allowing for retest, reliability, and validity.

[32] I speak for argument's sake and to prove a logical thesis as though it were perfectly feasible to make cultural excisions and transplantations. Of course social science is by no means able to engage in such surgery. The techniques to be understood include propaganda and other applications of social pressure.

generated by the operation of the status system in Fiji is also the driving force that keeps the system operating. Fijians value their status system and are not likely to readily cooperate in a program of change. Anxiety is a vital part of the social system which, without that motivational spark, would probably stop dead. A serious problem of readjustment and morale would then face the native or his administrators. The situation is basically not different from that found, upon analysis, in our own society. The sense of social isolation engendered by our large and impersonal cities or factories is a necessary correlate of large numbers of people living together in a limited area or working together at highly specialized tasks. Management could not give orders in a modern factory to a series of discrete personal entities like John Smith, that nice-red-haired-guy-by-the-bench-near-the-window-on-the-ground-floor-with-the-wife-who. . . .

Modern production would break down if impersonality were dropped and few persons of our society appear willing to pay that price for a higher degree of personality which, after all, would very likely bring along its own tensions. All that social scientists can expect, then, is to reduce the degree of personal isolation *within* the modern urban social system and to remain ready to patch up adjustments as they arise until such a time as a group is willing to make major changes in its way of life.

Obviously I do not mean to imply that, for the sake of maintaining tradition, all tension-producing behavior patterns must be left untouched. In Kaska society 10 percent of children grow up in extreme emotional isolation as a result of the death of one or both parents. Adult mortality is at least partly related to customary behavior patterns involving diet, medication, hygienic routines, and so on. Innovations designed by medical and nutritional specialists and patiently introduced to the Indians could very likely alter this state of affairs without profoundly dislocating Kaska life. In cultures undergoing social change resulting from contact with other cultures, stress is a function of such change. It would seem as if human nature becomes conditioned to one set of values and finds it difficult to readily or quickly shift to different standards without some intermediate period of training or habituation. It does not follow that culture-contact

conditions cannot be eased at times. However, it is also probable that any such easing of the stress factor in a culture-contact situation may slow down or otherwise affect the rate of change—a condition that neither the administrating power nor the changing cultural group may at once desire. Hence their cooperation may be difficult to secure.

One other possible objection of psychiatrists to what I am saying comes to mind. Psychiatrists may reply: We are not concerned with the question of normal stress, which you have been largely concerned with and from which life can never be wholly free; we are concerned with severe, disorganizing stress. My reply to that is: There seems no way of clearly and inevitably differentiating between situations that promote "normal" stress and those that develop "disorganizing" stress. For example, the pressures on spontaneity and aggressiveness in our society undoubtedly play a part in the development of essentially healthy people who can accept the group's demands without losing their way. At the same time the selfsame patterns also contribute to the formation of people who are not adequately prepared for the problems that they must face and become seriously upset by the vicissitudes of living. Obviously in the latter category the psychiatrist will recognize not only the role of the culture patterns in question but also factors peculiar to the life history of the individual and possibly constitutional factors predisposing to breakdown. These, however, may also be distinguished in the life histories of healthy people. What is here emphasized is that the same culture patterns may be seriously disorganizing experiences for some individuals at the same time leaving other persons with rather momentary frustration but no lasting maladjustment.

Summary

To sum up, there are two main considerations and a resultant problem which emerge from this discussion:

1. Cultures induce personal anxieties and conflicts in their carriers. Personal stress is particularly likely to accompany conditions of culture contact which occur not only when exotic societies come into meeting with European systems but also in our own country when the rural person becomes exposed to

urban living or the immigrant to American living.

2. Cultures include mechanisms by which the members of a social group may obtain relief from tension. These mechanisms are sometimes injurious to the integrity of the group and the adjustment of its members.

The problem is this: How can social engineering create cultural climates which will not only induce a minimum of tension but which will also provide nondyscrasic channels for the relief of personal stress? It is assumed that only change will be attempted which meets with the implicit or explicit consent of the group and that no measure will be introduced which threatens the fundamental aspects of the life plan according to which the group is organized.

Student stress and the institutional environment

DONALD R. BROWN

The last decade has seen the stereotype of the college student vary from apathy to militant activism. Both kinds of behavior are considered to be in part psychological responses to stressful situations. The following article deals with stress as it occurs within the college community. The author is Professor of Psychology and Research Psychologist at the Center for Research on Learning and Teaching at the University of Michigan. He has published articles in the areas of cognition, personality, perception, and the social psychology of higher education and has edited a recent book, *Changing Role and Status of Women in Soviet Russia*. In this selection, Dr. Brown discusses student unrest in its historical context and relates the causes of student stress to discrepancies which exist between student perceptions of the university and the realities of contemporary college education.

Spencer Brown, whose recent article in the New York *Sunday Times Magazine* has helped many of us over thirty to recover enough perspective to hold our heads almost high again, reports a confrontation between television interviewers and Robert Frost:

Or we say, as did a group of reporters interviewing Robert Frost on television, that this is the worst or most dangerous or most difficult time Man has ever lived through. They kept trying to badger the octogenarian poet into saying what they wanted him to say; but at last he succeeded in out shouting them and making himself heard: "Yes, yes, yes, it's a terribly difficult time for a man to try to save his soul—about as difficult as it always has been" (Brown, 1966, 57).

Frost, who in his youth went through a protracted period of what we would now term alienation (see, for example, Keniston's discussion), brings, I think, a much needed balm to the troubled contemporary scene. There is student stress and unrest. There has always been unrest and considerable stress amongst university students. The upset follows in part from the nature of growth during late adolescence and, therefore, we should hope there always will be such unrest. The real question is not if student discontent is new, but rather what accounts for it as a natural phenomenon of growth and what new features of the present educational scene in America can account for its current manifestations and greater visibility.

From *Journal of Social Issues*, XXIII, No. 3 (1967), 92-107. Reprinted by permission of The Society for the Psychological Study of Social Issues.

Today's visible student

Consider the following quasi-descriptive statements which seem to me to account for the greater visibility on the national scene of students and their concerns.

. . . The college student population has grown astronomically since 1946. More students—more visibility.

. . . College attendance is increasingly seen as a necessity in present-day America. Student population has increased faster than the general population.

. . . Students come from a wider range of the population on all demographic dimensions than they previously did and, consequently, present new challenges to the colleges as socialization agencies.

. . . The post-Sputnik emphasis on the meritocracy and the seller's market consequent to the increased numbers has put students under great competitive stress for admission even to the less prestigeful institutions.

. . . In purely visibility terms, the news hungry media tend to fan the sparks of unrest by massive and immediate publicity which has no trouble in finding its own performers. Sampson's discussion of this factor, especially with reference to the events at Berkeley, is a good case in point.

. . . The increased sophistication of students, as in all other groups in our society, has produced greater concerns over issues of individual rights, both in the university and in the society.

. . . The better academic preparation in the secondary schools following the massive curricular reform movements which started in the middle '50's has resulted, in part, in students who have tasted good teaching and want more of it.

. . . A society in which affluence and freedom exist side by side with poverty and the enslavement of ignorance, discrimination and hopelessness, has produced contradictions and hypocrisies which all can see.

. . . An increased emphasis on the existential view of self-determination, responsibility and meaningful personal communication is gradually replacing the older pragmatism in action and privacy in personal matters as the mass ethic of the younger intelligentsia.

. . . The inherent loneliness of youth, as it seeks self-definition and clarity, has been increased by the rise in anonymity accompanying the moral blandness of a society in which guilt is hard to define and therefore impossible to expiate.

. . . The increasing technical mechanization of the societal means of dealing with large numbers, as personified in the phobia of the IBM card, threatens the less stout-hearted with an overwhelming crisis of depersonalization.

. . . The changing image of college life from the social to the intellectual has caused increasing numbers of entering students to have high expectations of the curriculum, the faculty, their peers and of the intellectual life itself, which are unfortunately rarely fulfilled.

Student conceptions of education as viewed historically

It is always helpful before one views with alarm the present situation, as outlined briefly in the preceding set of twelve statements, to look back with Robert Frost and try to understand the alarming situations of the past. Let me start by reference to a statement, called to my attention by Professor George Stern, written by one of the great Eton masters in the 1860's —a period when education of any sort, higher or otherwise, was reserved for the social, cultural and economic elite.

You go to school at the age of twelve or thirteen; and for the next four or five years you are not engaged so much in acquiring knowledge as in making mental efforts under criticism. A certain amount of knowledge you can, indeed, with average faculties acquire so as to retain; nor need you regret the hours that you have spent on much that is forgotten, for the shadow of lost knowledge at least protects you from any delusions. You go to a great school, not for knowledge as much as for arts and habits; for the habit of attention, for the art of expression, for the art of assuming at a moment's notice a new intellectual posture, for the art of entering quickly into another person's thoughts, for the habit of submitting to censure and refutation, for the art of indicating assent or dissent in graduated terms, for the habits of regarding minute points of accuracy, for the habit of working out what is possible in a given time, for taste, for discrimination, for mental courage and mental soberness. Above all, you go to a great school for self-knowledge (Cory, 1938, 208).

While what Cory described as the goals of a liberal arts education hold today as they did in the 1860's in upperclass England, nonetheless, the sociological derivations of our students in the university and college of the 1960's differ considerably, and twenty-five years from now will differ even more.

For many years our students came from much the same social class as those that Cory was describing; but sometime shortly after World War I the proportion of Americans attending high school increased astronomically, and this desire for education burst into the college scene about the time of World War II. It has been increasing ever since so that today we find it necessary to think at least twenty-five years ahead in order to be prepared for the ever-growing onslaught of students. This trend is bound to have far reaching consequences on the nature of education and the needs that students bring to our institutions of higher learning. How has this manifested itself since World War II?

After the war . . .

Immediately following the war, enrollments bulged with veterans flocking to our campuses. These were young men and women of above average college age who had been brought up during the great depression and then tempered in the fiery inferno of World War II. Their values and goals were clear. They knew who their enemies were. First, there were the problems of economic inequity and irresponsibility which could be defeated by the "new economics." Later there were the evils of totalitarianism and fascism over which they had waged a long and bitter struggle ending in total victory, or so it seemed. They retreated to the security of alma mater, with the help of a benevolent G. I. Bill, to prepare themselves for the fruits of a better life for which they had made so many sacrifices.

This is the generation of the "over thirties." They knew what they were doing in college; their devotion to their studies and pragmatic approach to the curriculum had profound effects on the university. Practically overnight the Hollywood rah-rah culture of the campuses was dealt its death blow and was ultimately finished off by the rise of the meritocracy following the launching of Sputnik. They had seen society marshal its resources and solve, at least for the time, economic and political problems of life or death proportions.

Faith in an ordered and continued use of intelligence and sustained effort within the social mechanism was the lesson which they brought out of their experience. By contrast, the present generation, *suffering* from the benefits of affluence, has been insulated from the opportunity (delusional as it may seem) to see society solve problems at first hand.

Children of an affluent society . . .

Following this post World War II generation on the campus, there came the children of the newly affluent society. They came to college in numbers larger than ever before and from much more diverse educational and cultural backgrounds. Our attention was called quite forcibly to their appearance and to the disparity from the good old days at "City College" when, as memory had it, no one but first class intellects with real commitment and social concern manifested on every side populated the campuses. Philip Jacob (1960), in his study on value change in college students, summarizes the orientation of this group of the new affluents as (a) an absorbing self-interestedness, directed essentially toward satisfying the desires for material well-being, privacy within one's own male-oriented family domain, and relief from boredom; (b) group dependence, which causes students to bring personal conduct and standards into line with the expectations of groups to whom they turn for a sense of belongingness or look upon as vehicles to self-advancement; (c) social and political indifference and irresponsibility; and (d) an instrumental approach to reason and morality which pulls both reason and moral code into the service of present personal goals rather than acknowledges them as guides of verity and controlling rules of conduct. Jacob was, of course, describing what we all came to think of as the age of student apathy—in many ways a most confronting age during which to be a member of the establishment. Contrast this description with a quote from an article which appeared in the University of Michigan student newspaper. *The American Student is Breaking Out of His Cocoon* is the lead.

The eruption started in the last 50's when students (where older brothers and sisters had thought the smooth move was to mind one's own business) were stirred by the civil rights movement and began to emerge from their study carrels and fraternity houses to make their dent on the world.

They were a new generation bred in prosperity. These students did not know the depression, they did not remember the war. To seek material reward—the house in Scarsdale, the pretty wife, and the steady job—was not enough because it was so obtainable. To be satisfied with a return to normalcy was not enough because normalcy was already the way of life.

They took their tactics from Gandhi, their idealism from philosophy class, their money from Daddy. They worked hand in hand with civil rights groups such as CORE, NAACP, SNCC and SCLC.

The results of the movement were civil rights acts, the voting rights bill, and the emergence of the American student.

Realizing they had the power to influence events, students broadened their involvement so that it ranged from criticizing foreign policy to organizing the poor.

Thus, the idealism of the civil rights movement led to an alienation from the multi-university and the hope for an idyllic "community of scholars" as the wave of the future. The democratic nature of the movement led students to hope that they could have a meaningful voice in governing their own affairs at their universities; and the success of the movement made students realize that they could implement their goals (Michigan Daily, February 20, 1966).

One is aware, naturally, that any attempt to describe all students at all institutions is a task fraught with folly. The above quote from the *Michigan Daily* makes it appear that the vast majority of students were caught up in the rising activism of the civil rights movement and ultimately in the concern about the nature of the university. We know from the work of Katz and Sanford (Katz, 1965) that at most only about 15 per cent of the students on an extremely active campus are so involved. These descriptions, which are applicable to historical periods over the last one hundred years, refer not to the modal situation but rather to the salient situation. They tend to represent the highly visible peaks of student behavior in the mass rather than individual students on the one hand or the majority of students on the other. These are the dominant images that characterized the periods, not necessarily the dominant behavior.

Student stereotypes of education and of the university

For the sake of argument, I will maintain that at present, students come to the university holding to varying degrees one of the following often mutually exclusive stereotypes about the process of education and the university's role in this process.

The question is of "being" or of "doing"

In the first case, the emphasis is upon broadening one's intellectual horizons and consequently maturing and stabilizing the personality. The liberal arts curriculum as classically defined is accepted as the road to these goals and the product is hopefully "cultured." The stress in this type of education is on *being* and not only on *doing*. The image is best represented by the statement quoted from the Eton schoolmaster. This image is today still represented by some of the prestigeful colleges—particularly by some of the members of the Seven Women's College Conference, which are prestigeful not so much because of their lofty educational aims but because these aims are generally supported by the upper classes, and in particular, for women.

College . . . to acquire occupational training

Secondly, there is the much more widely held image of the college as a place to acquire occupational training. As a society becomes both affluent and technologically advanced, the demand for highly trained personnel increases. The university, particularly the public university, experiences great pressure from its constitutents to fulfill the demands of the occupational marketplace. At the same time, these pressures heighten the demand for a college degree and cheapen it as a symbol of professionalization. The degree comes to cover a multitude of sins committed in the name of education. All sorts of occupational groups join in and demand college programs in their fields. The emphasis in this kind of education is on *doing* and on being able to *do* rather than on *being*. Students holding this point of view tend not to be attracted by movements espousing social change since their purpose is to join the mainstream at a step up the ladder.

College . . . a place to "have fun"

The third dominant image relates to the collegiate fun culture which is the one most often portrayed in the mass media image of college, particularly before the rise of the meritocracy. The idea of the college embodied in this viewpoint sees it as a never ending series of increasingly romantic social events. Perhaps this image never did exist to the extent that Hollywood and college fiction would have it.

Pluralistic society . . . pluralistic university

If we take a frankly sociological view of the matter and attempt to understand these seeming changes in the value orientation of university students as reflections of the population from which they are recruited, we must admit that from this view college going has not only increased numerically but has increasingly attracted segments of our population with different "life expectancies" from those to which the more traditional liberal arts curriculum was originally attuned. We are dealing here with what Joshua Aaron Fishman (1960) referred to as a population change rather than a value change. For example, the increasing numbers of veterans attending college on the G. I. Bill and its various revisions since World War II, working class children attending on government loans or state scholarship programs, the meritorious attending on National Merit Scholarships and similar competitive awards for students with outstanding high school attainment, Negro youth attending on the various new grants directed toward their recruitment, children of immigrants located by the nationwide searches—all of these groups bring new value constellations to our colleges, and the realities of their post-college lives will undoubtedly be different from those of the classical liberal arts college student who could postpone his vocational plans until graduate school and even sometimes forever.

It is interesting to speculate on the differences in the atmosphere of universities which follow from the obvious fact that, not only have the sources of students changed, as the well-established universities have increasingly culled off the cream of admissions and thereby gotten a much broader geographic representation in their student bodies, and the large state universities have dipped much further down to sample the real sources of intellectual quality in their states, but at the same time, the recruitment of faculty has been very much influenced by these previous population shifts in college attendance. It is not idle speculation to propose that a large per cent of faculty just now entering into senior positions come from the G. I. Bill crop which flooded graduate schools with the sort of Ph.D. material that rarely aspired to such educational heights before. As I look back on my own college experience, I am struck by how much more similar in social economic background current faculties are to their students than was my faculty, which tended to represent a kind of upper class, traditional, scholarly gentleman with considerable family wealth. All of this is bound to make for profound changes in our universities, in student roles and student stress.

The above merely indicates to me the striking pluralism of American society and the consequent pluralism that we can expect in universities.

The students, coming as they do from the larger society, bring with them one or another of these three views of higher education. Therefore, they start their college experience with views that are to varying degrees incongruent with the generally held values of the faculty and the high sounding official ideology of the institution. The faculty see themselves as seekers of knowledge in specialized areas and privileged critics of the culture. Indeed, they demand special privileges of tenure and academic freedom in order to permit the unhampered pursuit of these goals. In recent years because of the nature of the market, they have indeed demanded almost complete freedom even from teaching. At the same time they're asked to educate a semicaptive audience which holds values often widely discrepant from their own views and very often widely variant within any given classroom. Here are certainly then the seeds of conflict, and the resolution of conflict is often stressful. The students are not without resources of their own for avoiding the issues of this conflict. They can create a "peer culture" which largely perpetuates the general societal values held outside the college and turn to this subculture for their goals and for their rewards. Or, they can create a "peer-culture" which openly challenges the state of society and provides a comforting way to engage in social and individual revolt.

The society and, indeed, often the university, are not completely clear about the goals of higher education. It is not surprising that the students, unable to face the multiplicity of challenges to their self-image and the incongruity between their stereotypic expectation and the institutional ideology, find themselves forced to seek clarity in group identifications which reinforce the old and familiar or set new and often rebellious goals.

The entering freshman

Sanford, in *The American College* (1962), has put it well when he describes the freshman as follows:

The freshman tends to be like a convert to adulthood, an enthusiastic supporter and imitator of adult ways who knows what it is to backslide—which he sometimes does. The achievement of flexible control, the arrangement in which there is genuine freedom of impulses because there is little danger of their getting out of hand lies ahead; nevertheless, impulses are not inhibited or contained with sufficient effectiveness so that the young person can turn his attention to other matters. He is now ready to concentrate upon his relations with the external world—to improve his understanding of that world and to find a place within it (Sanford, 1962, 260).

Upon arrival at college, to some extent, the immediate support of family and community are withdrawn or at least become more distant, often as contact is made with a new set of values. On today's educational scene, the student faces considerable threat and consequent distress from several different sources: (a) highly selective admissions policies place the student into competition with a homogeneously intelligent group of peers in which doubt may be cast on his own academic competence; (b) the relative lack of structure or of the externally imposed structure, to which the student had become accustomed in high school, places him into a new and ambiguous situation; (c) the seemingly sophisticated environment of the university may cast doubts upon the student's own sense of social confidence; (d) the rapidly apparent discrepancy between the student's expectations about university life and its reality provides one further, especially important source of student stress.

The freshman understandably seeks new sources of support in the face of all these assaults. Easier than trying to go it alone is the choice of the readily available support of peers who can minimize the threat by offering subcultures in which the student can more readily determine his own stake in this new venture. If this identification with the peer culture which can exist within and on the periphery of an institution persists for four years in an unaltered form, education is apt to be a failure. It will fail because the student either keeps a value structure which developed before college and which will remain untested against the broader horizons of the university, or because, in his anxiety to avoid rejection by the valued group, he will adopt a set of values by simple imitation. It is important that the institution provide an open channel for its students to switch identities often during their college careers, both to avoid too narrow a range of choices and too early a commitment which will hamstring the individual for life.

The institution and student growth: a challenge

I would suggest that the problem that faces the university of today and one which will increase in the future is how can an increasingly diverse body of students, drawn more and more widely from all areas of the population as the economic wherewithal for education becomes more available, be brought together in the common pursuit of intellectual and personal goals.

To accomplish this challenging task, the university must bring student groups and their peer cultures into the service of their own education and development. Colleges must begin to operate on several levels at once. For example, it has long been assumed by the better residential colleges that students largely educate one another. While this may still be true in the small residential colleges, unfortunately with the rapid expansion and increasing specialization of knowledge and the cafeteria-like offerings of our universities, it is rare to find two students coming together outside of class who have a common academic experience to share.

A situation which throws people together in a university but provides little shared intellectual experience will quite naturally lead the students to seek ways of interacting that are not necessarily congruent with the purposes of the university. Therefore, the university should consider new ways of grouping students in the curriculum, in the residential arrangements and in scheduling so that larger numbers will have some common shared intellectual life which will serve as a foundation for intellectual and social interaction. Very often students are forced in their noncurricular groupings into nonintellective areas of concern by denying them easily integrated experiences which stem from the academic content of their institutional endeavor.

The Michigan projects

Two current projects at the University of Michigan are relevant here. Both of these projects owe a great deal in their original inception and in their ongoing administration to Professor Theodore Newcomb, who throughout his professional career has contributed so significantly to the area now known as the social psychology of higher education.

The first project is the "Pilot Program." It was conceived as a way of reducing the stresses inherent in the divorcement between intellectual values and the residential life of a large campus. This was most manifest in the lack of intellectual life in the residence halls at the University. The "Pilot Program" then is a community in revolt against the forces of anonymity and alienation which threaten to undermine the educational objectives of a large University. The program consists of approximately six hundred volunteer entering freshmen of both sexes in the College of Literature, Science, and the Arts. They are assigned to houses (subunits) within the larger dormitories, known as Pilot Houses. These students are permitted to register for sections of regular introductory freshmen courses which are reserved for members of the Pilot Program only. Thus the student might conceivably find himself in as many as three of his freshmen courses along with his immediate dormitory mates. There is no infringement in any way on the right of the student to choose his curriculum within the structure of the college rules. In addition, the instructors of these sections are made aware of the nature of the Pilot Program and are encouraged to have meals in the Pilot Houses with their students and, indeed, if at all possible, to schedule class meetings within the dormitory as well. A further aspect of the Pilot Program involves the selection of specially selected Resident Fellows who act as counselors and tutors to the students. These Fellows are selected from amongst the graduate students on the basis of their intellectual commitment and ability to serve as intellectual mentors rather than as disciplinarians in the dormitories.

The program is the responsibility of a committee of faculty from the College of Literature, Science, and the Arts and of representatives from the residence halls personnel of the University. This committee is somewhat unusual in that it attempts to institute policies in almost every area of undergraduate education, including staffing of residence halls, design of undergraduate courses, academic counseling, as well as registration and classification procedures. The committee reports directly to the Dean of the College.

So far the program does not sound startlingly different from what has occurred at other institutions in recent years. The program, however, does have some unique features. The program is considered frankly experimental and therefore is being continuously evaluated from a variety of points of view. The one that is of the most interest is the evaluation of the development of students and the implications for student stress and unrest. A study of a small number of pilot students with comparison students in the Literary College as a control shows that the pilot students tend to self-select themselves into the program on the basis of a greater need for contact with faculty. This need for contact with faculty seems to be based upon their recognition of a greater sense of dependency and requirement of intimacy on their part. They tend more often to come from smaller high schools and small towns than from large urban centers. They recognize before coming to the University the threat of size and consequent anonymity. The Pilot Program students at the end of the year express far greater satisfaction with the nature of residential life at the University and, in particular, with the quality of the residential staff. They are more critical and demanding of faculty and faculty performance but are also more satisfied with the progress they have made in the freshman year and the overall quality of the University.

The pilot program . . . a test for a residential college

Continuing longitudinal studies of these students are now in progress and very detailed data will be available in the near future. Aside from the evaluation of the effects on students, another unique aspect for the Pilot Program is that it is serving as a pilot test, in the literal meaning, for the opening of a residential college for 1200 students this fall (1967) at the University of Michigan. In its capacity as a pilot, special courses designed to be included in the core curriculum of the residential college have been developed and tried out in the pilot program. These courses have been evaluated as well by the committee.

One of the most striking conclusions from the evaluation of the pilot program so far is the amount that can be accomplished in reducing student stress and loneliness while increasing student dignity and competence, as measured by standardized instruments such as the Student Activities Index (Stern, 1958) and College Characteristics Index (Stern and Pace, 1958), by such relatively simple and inexpensive devices as the grouping and scheduling of students. Perhaps the major implication is the obvious working of a Hawthorne effect. If so, then along with Nevitt Sanford, I would say that we should maximize the new and the exciting in our educational arrangements, in order to increase this kind of involvement on the part of the faculty and students.

What freshmen expect

One reason for emphasizing techniques such as these for reducing stress can be found in the data which we at the Center for Research on Learning and Teaching at the University of Michigan have collected on nine hundred entering freshmen in fall 1966. In the course of a large number of paper and pencil questionnaires and inventories, the students were asked to complete the College and University Environment Scales (Pace, 1963). Our students filled out the CUES battery before they arrived at the University and were asked to complete the inventory as a description of the University as they expected and hoped it would be. The students under these instructions described

their expectations about the University on the five scales which Pace has developed from the instrument as follows:

They do not see the University as a place where practicality will be greatly emphasized. The practicality scale consists of a . . . combination of items which suggests a practical, instrumental emphasis in the college environment. Procedures, personal status and practical benefits are important. Status is gained by knowing the right people, being in the right groups and doing what is expected. Order and supervision are characteristic of the administration and of classwork. Good fun, school spirit and student leadership in campus social activities are evident (Pace, 1963, 24).

Interestingly enough those items which the students do choose in the scaled direction refer with great agreement to good fun, school spirit and student leadership in campus social activities. Other data from upper classmen would indicate that this part of the entering student's perception of the University is quite unrealistic in terms of present student life.

Similarly, the students score much higher than one would expect on the community scale, which consists of items portraying "a friendly, cohesive, group-oriented campus. The environment is supportive and sympathetic. There is a feeling of group welfare and group loyalty which encompasses the college as a whole. The campus is a community. It has a congenial atmosphere" (Pace, 1963, 24).

While it is true that there is a sense of community to be found on a campus such as that in Ann Arbor, it is almost a caricature to describe it in the above terms. Any student who seriously expects to find this kind of small college and small town atmosphere is bound to have to make some serious readjustments in his expectations, with consequent distress and unrest.

Pace's awareness scale is practically a description of my three dimensions of student growth mentioned above. The items included reflect

. . . a concern and emphasis upon three sorts of meaning—personal, poetic and political. An emphasis upon self-understanding, reflectiveness, and identity suggest the search for personal meaning. A wide range of opportunities for creative and appreciative relationships to painting, music, drama, poetry, sculpture, architecture, etc., suggest the search for poetic meaning. A concern about events around the world, the welfare of mankind and the present and future condition of man suggests the search for political meaning and idealistic commitment. What seems to be evident in this sort of environment is a stress on awareness, an awareness of self, of society, and of esthetic stimuli (Pace, 1963, 23).

On this scale the entering students see the University as being an environment totally of this sort. Of the thirty items on the scale, these pre-freshmen see their prospective campus in this light at least 70 per cent of the time or more on each item. Since the instructions ask the students to describe the University as they hoped and expected to find it, one can assume that the students are committed to the notion of self-development and intellectual growth, albeit, perhaps unrealistically or even romantically. While it is true that the University strives to be this sort of place and, as a function of the self-selection of students who share these expectations, is to a large extent such an environment, it falls far short of the hopes and aspirations of these entering students. Take, for example, the item which is agreed to by 99.7 per cent of the sample, "tutorial and honors programs available to qualified," or the near unanimous agreement with the expectation that "a noted philosopher-theologian would always draw a capacity crowd at a lecture." It seems unlikely that a student who shared the expectations on this scale would not find some disappointment and consequent unrest before the end of the freshman year.

On the other hand the students do seem to be aware of the general lack of conventional propriety on such a campus, since they score extremely low on this scale measuring "an environment that is polite and considerate."

And finally, on Pace's scholarship scale the entering students again score extremely high, agreeing over 75 per cent of the time with twenty-six of the thirty items. These items are descriptive of the state of scholarship they expect on the campus. They

describe an academic scholarly environment. The emphasis is on competitively high academic achievement and a serious interest in scholarship.

The pursuit of knowledge and theories, scientific or philosophical, is carried out rigorously and vigorously. Intellectual speculation and interest in ideas as ideas, knowledge for its own sake, and intellectual discipline—all these are characteristic of the environment (Pace, 1963, 25).

Here again one can't help but wonder whether those 80 per cent who expect most professors to be thorough teachers who will probe fundamentals, or those 97 per cent who expect that lectures by famous scientists will always be very well-attended, or those 80 per cent who hope that class discussion will typically be vigorous and intense will find their hopes realized.

One cannot help but be impressed by the stress which may well arise in students holding these expectations for their education, when they come up against the realities of academic life on a large, albeit good and exciting campus. Indeed, one wonders if any faculty could live up to the image that these students see as their hope for the next four years.

The University of Michigan's Residential College

The Pilot Program described above is one attempt by the University to find ways of maximizing its realization of this image for the students. Another such attempt at the University of Michigan is the planned residential college for 1200 students in the liberal arts. Here a faculty committee has had the opportunity to plan during a leisurely period of three years a total college complete with its own physical plant. The unique feature of this college, as compared to any other existing small residential college, is that this college is an integral part of a large university with all of the resources of a large university at its service. To maximize these resources, this college will not have a separate faculty but will draw upon the regular faculty of the University for its staff on a part-time basis.

In addition, this plan is unique in that the living arrangements and their relationship to the intellectual environment of the college were designed by faculty in complete coordination with the structure of the curriculum before the college started. Furthermore, there was the opportunity to pretest certain of the new core courses in the Pilot Program described above.

Finally, its uniqueness stems from a concerted effort to apply the knowledge of student development and evaluational techniques directly to the continuing evolution of this institution.

As the results of these studies become available, it is assumed that changes will be fed back, not only into the Residential College and the Pilot Program, but into the life of the University itself.

Unrest . . . a discrepancy between expectation and reality

The implication of these educational experiments for student unrest is quite clear. My assumption has been that a large part of student stress and unrest comes from the discrepancy between students' expectations and preparations for college today and the reality of our institutions. Hope for intimate contact with faculty and peers, the expectation of a sense of community, the existential hope for deep interpersonal and intrapersonal communication, and the need for true intellectual stimulation can make for an exciting student body, but it can also make for a restless college if the institution is not ready to meet these hopes for any other than a small segment of the student body.

It is interesting that in an earlier study (Brown, 1960) in which the faculty's perception of the ideal student was probed, it was found that what the current students seem to expect in terms of the nature of their university experience and of their own development at the university in this day and age was precisely what faculty responded to in their nominations of ideal students during the senior year at Vassar. If we could somehow arrange the mechanisms inherent in large complex environments such as ours so that these two sets of expectations and desires could be better matched, perhaps a very important source of student stress could be eliminated.

In conclusion . . .

I have tried to focus on some of the causes of student stress and unrest. These are seen to follow directly from the incongruity between the students' desires and expectations—based in large measure on the changing nature of the student population—and the increasing importance

personality and anonymity associated with growth in the structure and organization of the American university. Students are seen as undergoing major reorientations in their values as a natural consequence of growth and development within their four years at college. Such growth itself provides a ready source for stress and conflict which is further heightened by the typical incongruity between what the student expects and the reality of his education.

It is only through a thorough understanding of the range and patterns of student hopes and expectations and their ways of dealing with the stress and conflict produced in these four years, that educators can hope to devise the variety of educational environments that will help rather than hinder the emotional and intellectual development of their students.

References

Brown, Donald R. Non-intellective qualities and the perception of the ideal student by college faculty. *J. of educ. Sociol.,* 6, 33, 1960, 269-278.

Brown, Spencer We can't appease the younger generation. *The New York Times Magazine,* November 27, 1966.

Cory, William Eton reform. Quoted by G. Adan, "William Cory," *The Cornhill Magazine,* 1938, 208.

Fishman, Joshua Aaron In Brown, D. R. (Ed.) Social changes and the college student: a symposium. *The Educational Record,* 4, 41, 1960, 342-346.

Jacob, Philip Social change and student values. In Brown, D. R. (Ed.), Social changes and the college student: a symposium. *The Educational Record,* 4, 41, 1960, 338-341.

Michigan Daily February 20, 1966.

Pace, Charles Robert *College and university environment scales.* Educational Testing Service, Princeton, New Jersey, 1963.

Sanford, Nevitt *The American college.* New York: Wiley, 1962.

Stern, George Student activity index. Psychological Research Center, Syracuse University, 1958.

Stern, George, and Pace, Charles Robert College characteristics index. Psychological Research Center, Syracuse University, 1958.

6

A MODERN DILEMMA I: IDENTITY AND ALIENATION

One of the fundamental tasks of growing up in a society is to find one's place within that society. This process has been referred to in a variety of ways, such as "finding oneself," establishing an identity, or achieving self-realization. Whatever the label, psychologists generally agree that the process is an important and necessary step in developing a well-integrated personality. As Royce (1964) notes:

The man who has a clear view of himself is said to have a strong ego or a strong personality. We say that he knows who he is and that he knows where he has been and where he is going. The confused personality, on the other hand, does not know who he is. His self-concept is vague or chameleon-like. He shifts with the personalities or the events which surround him, and when one probes to the depths of his personality, one finds little or nothing there (p. 102).

Achieving a clear view of oneself is not an automatic process or one that is to be taken for granted. Even casual observation reveals that all persons in our society perform a variety of learned acts as an ordinary part of living.

Technically, these behaviors are referred to as social *roles*. The concept of role provides a link between the society and the individual and facilitates the understanding of this interaction. What a person thinks of himself and what others think of him is determined at least in part by the number and kind of social roles he fulfills. Problems may arise for an individual when he is called upon to play conflicting roles. To the extent that a modern, complex, and rapidly changing society such as our own places divergent demands on the person, he can be expected to have difficulty coming to grips with his identity as a unique individual. It is important to understand how each person defines himself and how he maintains a consistent self-image in the context of a heterogeneous society. This is the problem of personal identity. Our task in this section is to explore what identity is, how it develops, and what happens to the person when it is lost.

The nature of identity

The fact that others see us differently and make different demands upon us suggests that we are many things to many people. The concept of identity is based upon this funda-mental fact of social living. As Stone (1962) notes:

Almost all writers using the term imply that identity establishes *what* and *where* the person is in social terms . . . when one has identity, he is *situated*—that is, cast in the shape of a social object by the acknowledgment of his participation or membership in social relations. One's identity is established when others *place* him as a social object by assigning him the same words of identity that he appropriates for himself or *announces* (p. 93).

In keeping with Stone's (1962) observa-tions, Miller (1963) suggests that an individual has many *public identities*. *Objective public identities* consist of the "person's pattern of traits as they appear to members of groups" (Miller, 1963, p. 673). One's *subjective public identity* is the *person's* perception of how he appears to the group. According to Miller (1963), many of the characteristics of an individual's identity are subidentities and lie between the periphery and the core of the personality. Every man has a number of sub-identities and these are defined by the limita-tions of specific roles. Sexual identification, the feeling of masculinity or feminity, is an ex-ample of a subidentity and is discussed in de-tail by Cohen (1966) later in this section.

The notion of subidentity provides a useful conceptual tool for understanding the relation-ship between the social structure and the per-sonality. However, many psychologists feel that a more basic or central concept of identity is needed to account for the constancy and sta-bility of the individual as he confronts a variety of life situations. As Shibutani (1964) sug-gests: "Self-images vary from situation to situ-ation, but each man also has a stable sense of personal identity" (p. 231). We are often not aware of this sense of identity, perhaps because we take it for granted (Shibutani, 1964), or because it is largely unconscious (Rubins, 1961; Erikson, 1962). But we should be care-ful not to misinterpret any difficulty in recog-nizing our personal identity as evidence that it lacks psychological significance. To understand the nature of one's personal identity is to an-swer the question: Who am I? (Lynd, 1958; Rubins, 1961).

In recent years a number of attempts have been made to describe the nature of personal identity. Although these definitions differ in specific details, descriptive terminology, and theoretical biases, they all emphasize that per-sonal identity is a basic underlying concept that emanates from the core of the personality. Rokeach (1964) describes identity in terms of the primitive belief system that provides the individual with a feeling of trust in the depend-ability of the physical world, society, and him-self. The person is most emotionally committed to his primitive beliefs which are formed early in life and lie at the core of his total system of beliefs. This belief system enables the per-son to "maintain, insofar as possible, a sense of ego and group identity stable and continuous over time, an identity which experiences itself to be a part of, and simultaneously apart from, a stable physical and social environment" (Rokeach, 1964, p. 26).

Rubins (1961) states that identity possesses three characteristics: 1) it is an experiential state; 2) it places the person in a particular social context; and, 3) it maintains temporal constancy, involving the past and the present. Identity:

. . . includes all that has gone before, all ex-periences and personal attributes since birth, whether unconscious or conscious, even though some may have been rejected or eliminated on a conscious level. It is because of this that identity becomes more complex and formed with chron-ological growth. The adult has more of a past with which to define himself than does the child (Rubins, 1961, p. 137).

According to Wheelis (1958):

Identity is a coherent sense of self. It depends upon the awareness that one's endeavors and one's life makes sense, that they are meaningful in the context in which life is lived. It depends also upon stable values, and upon the conviction that one's actions and values are harmoniously related. It is a sense of wholeness, of integration, of knowing what is right and what is wrong and of being able to choose (p. 19).

It is important to note the emphasis that Wheelis places on the role of values in the formation of an identity concept. In this regard, his ideas are similar to those of May (1953, 1967), Maslow (1959), Bonner (1965), and other psychologists who have broken away from scientific psychology's traditional neglect of the study of values. For all of these writers, the problem of identity is to a large extent discovering a coherent and acceptable system of values by which one can live. As Bonner (1965) notes:

. . . the ills of modern man and the reasons for his despair, lie in a neglected dimension of psychological inquiry: the realm of the human spirit, the dimension of consciousness in which values and meanings are warring with one another. Man's troubles spring not only from his sexual, marital, and vocational difficulties and failures, but equally if not more from his spiritual frustrations (p. 61).

Probably the most well-known authority on the topic of identity is Erik Erikson whose writings have done much to popularize the related terms *identity* and *identity-crisis*. Despite the current tendency to use the terms with "faddish ease," Erikson (1962) points out that the concept of identity is quite complex, partly conscious but mostly unconscious, and involves social as well as psychological processes. As an example of the multiple meanings of the terms, Erikson (1956) notes that at different times identity can refer to a "conscious *sense of individual identity*," an "unconscious striving for a *continuity of personal character*," a criterion for the synthesis of the ego, or a "maintenance of an inner *solidarity* with a group's ideals and identity" (p. 57). Erikson (1962) defines identity as: "a double sense of personal self-sameness slowly accrued from infantile experiences and of shared sameness experienced in encounters with a widening part of the community" (p. 6) and "the accrued confidence that the inner sameness and continuity prepared in the past are matched by the sameness and continuity of one's meaning for others, as evidenced in the tangible promise of a 'career'" (Erikson, 1963, p. 261-262). Thus, for Erikson, the essence of identity is provided by the feeling of consistency or sameness that exists between the individual and the world around him. Achieving identity is tantamount to the popular expression of being "tuned in."

Although the basic sense of identity is established very early in life, probably during infancy, the quest for identity becomes most conspicuous during adolescence and the teenage years (Erikson, 1963; Rubins, 1961). As Rubins (1961) observes, adolescence is a period of test and rapid change, and the success of the adolescent in getting through this stage will be determined by the stability of the preceding self-identity. It is during this time that the person "through free role experimentation may find a niche in some section of his society, a niche which is firmly defined and yet seems to be uniquely made for him. In finding it the young adult gains an assured sense of inner continuity and social sameness which will bridge what he *was* as a child and what he is *about to become,* and will reconcile his *conception of himself* and his *community's recognition of him*" (Erikson, 1956, p. 66-67). It is necessary for each of us to have some idea about our worth as a person, our impact on others, and our general place in the world. The awareness of these factors provides the individual with a feeling of security. As Goodman (1960) notes: ". . . in normal conditions a large part of security comes from knowing your contribution is useful, and the rest from knowing it's uniquely yours: they need you" (p. 98).

Much of the significance of the identity concept and its relevance for modern man seems to be derived from the fact that we live in an increasingly impersonal world which provides few direct sources of feedback about our individual importance and uniqueness. Advocates of this view suggest that we have less opportunity to become aware of the extent to which we are needed. There is fairly common agreement among different writers that one's parents play a key role in the establishment of identity, although the specific nature of this role is attributed to different factors by different theorists. Using the parent-child interaction as a basis for understanding the origins of identity, Bettelheim (1962) offers an interesting explanation of the modern struggle for identity. He feels that the attainment of self-identity and self-realization is contingent upon the younger generation replacing the older generation in certain areas, primarily work and economic responsibility. Bettelheim (1962) points out that in pre-industrial society, the father was forced to turn over the economic responsibility of the household to the son because financial survival was based on physical strength. The father's increasing age and diminishing strength provided a natural and ideal basis for passing the dominant position in the household over to the son. In modern society, the advent of technology has reduced the need for physical labor, thus making the older generation less dependent on youth. By losing the opportunity to support his family, the son has lost a vital source of feedback about his capabilities as well as the chance to measure himself against his father. As Bettelheim (1962) notes: "Youth itself, feeling insecure because of its marginal position in a society that no longer depends on it for economic survival, is tempted to use the one power this reversal between the generations has conferred on it: to be accuser and judge of the parents' success or failure as parents" (p. 79). This, in turn, has stimulated the insecurity of both parent and child.

The importance of the parents in the establishment of a firm identity has also been noted by Erikson (1956). Like Bettelheim, Erikson feels that parents fail to provide their children with an adequate model against which the children can measure themselves. However, Erikson (1956) attributes this to different reasons. He feels that parents of children with identity problems look to their children to satisfy certain emotional needs that children typically expect from their parents. In other words, there is a role reversal between the child and the parent in terms of emotional dependency. Erikson (1956) describes the mothers of children experiencing identity crises as "so hungry for approval and for recognition" that they look to their children to justify their own existence. These mothers are so jealous and unsure of themselves that they constantly undermine the child's attempt to identify with his father. The mother bears the constant grudge, accurately perceived by the members of her family, that both the child and the father "failed to make a mother out of her" (Erikson, 1956, p. 92). The fathers, like their wives, are strongly jealous of their children. Although they are often highly successful in their occupation, these men are unable to stand up to their wives. Like children, the fathers look to their wives as mothers to satisfy their own excessive needs for dependency with the result that they sacrifice their integrity and initiative.

Keniston (1967) has also described a mother-dominated home situation in the genesis of students with identity problems. He describes the mothers as "over-solicitous and limiting" and indicates that: "The most common family environment of the alienated-student-to-be consists of a parental schism supplemented by a special mother-son alliance of mutual understanding and maternal control and depreciation of the father" (p. 113).

The consequences of failing to find an identity: alienation

The failure to achieve an adequate sense of identity may lead to serious consequences. A variety of terms, such as identity-crisis, apathy, and "dropping-out," have been used to describe what happens when a feeling of identity is not achieved, but the most popular term is *alienation*. For Rubins (1961), alienation is "an uncertainty about most life activities, a distorting or benumbing or repressing of inner emotional experiences, a blurring of self-identity" (p. 140). According to Keniston (1963), alienation is "the rejection of the roles and values and institutions" a young person sees "as typical of adult American life" (p. 42). Keniston (1965) describes alienation in detail as follows:

On every level, then, the alienated refuse conventional commitments, seeing them as unprofitable, dangerous, futile, or merely uncertain and unpredictable. Not only do they repudiate those institutions they see as characteristic of our society, but the belief in the possibility or utility of political and civic activities, closeness and intimacy with others, or even a resolute commitment to action or responsibility. The rejection of American society is but one part of a more global distrust of any commitment (p. 60).

Similarly, Erikson (1956) notes that: "The loss of a sense of identity often is expressed in a scornful and snobbish hostility toward the roles offered as proper and desirable in one's family or immediate community. Any part aspect of the required role, or all parts, be it masculinity or femininity, rationality or class membership, can become the main focus of the young person's acid disdain" (p. 85).

While it might appear from these comments that the most conspicuous symptom of alienation is the failure to accept the more conventional behaviors offered by society, this interpretation can be misleading. As Keniston (1967) points out, dissent itself is not necessarily indicative of alienation but can be placed on a continuum between two ideal types which he labels "the political activist or protester" and the "withdrawn, culturally alienated student" (p. 111). Keniston (1967) indicates that, contrary to popular opinion which tends to support a stereotype of the dissenter, there are many differences between these two ideal types of dissenters. For purposes of our discussion here, the most relevant difference is that "the protesting student is likely to accept the basic political and social values of his parents, the alienated student almost always rejects his parents' values" (p. 113). In other words, criticism per se of one's parents or other source of authority is not necessarily an indication of alienation. The culturally alienated student is not only critical of society but makes no attempt to change things because he is convinced that meaningful change is impossible. The only solution for this person is some form of withdrawal from society or "dropping-out."

If one of the basic characteristics of the alienated youth is the rejection of an elder's value system, it is important that we understand the basis for this rejection. Keniston (1967) and Bettelheim (1962) suggest that the culturally alienated student rejects the prevailing values of the society because he finds them meaningless, particularly in terms of the emphasis on achieving status and success. Bettelheim (1962) provides a vivid description of what the alienated youth may feel about his parents' values.

Why is this goal eluding modern young man in search of himself? If manhood, if the good life in the good community, is the goal of adolescence, then the goal is clear, and with it the direction and the path. But what if existing manhood is viewed as empty, static, obsolescent? Then becoming a man is death, and manhood marks the death of adolescence, not its fulfillment. The buoyancy of youth is fed by the conviction of a full life to come, one in which all great things are theoretically attainable. But one cannot believe in the good life to come when the goal is suburbia. One cannot realize one's values by climbing the ladder of the business community, nor probe one's manhood on the greens of the country club; neither

can one settle into security in an insecure world (p. 83).

It is not our task here to resolve the issue of whether or not the values of contemporary American society have in fact become meaningless, corrupt, insignificant, or unclear. What is important from the standpoint of psychological insight is to realize that the overt behavior of teenagers or young adults is often misleading and subject to misinterpretation. For example, one of the kinds of behavior which typically upsets parents, teachers, college administrators, and other authority figures is any form of open rebellion, be it passive or active. College students, in particular, who challenge or openly oppose the values of their elders, are often singled out and cited as proof that our system of values and morality is breaking down. Ironically, the politically active students, who have been condemned as alienated by some political leaders, may represent some of the least alienated members of our society from the standpoint of maintaining an idealistic value system. These students are often basically committed to some of the most traditional American values, such as justice, equal opportunity, free speech, and citizen's participation in decision making (Keniston, 1967). Rejection or criticism of the power structure based on the belief that American ideals are not being followed in practice is hardly a sound basis for the diagnosis of alienation.

It is important to distinguish the kind of protest that Keniston describes from what Erikson (1956) has called the "choice of the negative identity." In this case, the person's behavior is characterized by the rejection of and contempt for behavior considered desirable by one's family and the acceptance of negative, undesirable, or alien behaviors. The specific nature of the negative identity that is chosen by the individual is based upon all the identifications and roles which had previously been presented to him as undesirable or dangerous. For example, a teetotaler's son who has been continuously exposed to lectures on the evils of alcohol consumption might adopt a negative identity by becoming an alcoholic. According to Erikson (1956), the choice of a negative identity suggests that the individual may find it easier to accept what "one is least supposed to be than to struggle for a feeling of reality in acceptable roles which are unattainable with the patient's inner means" (p. 88). As an illustration of this, he cites the statements of a young man that: "I would rather be quite insecure than a little secure," and of a young woman: "At least in the gutter I'm a genius" (Erikson, 1956, p. 88). Apparently, in the midst of the struggle for identity, the choice of an unflattering but certain view of oneself is preferable to an unstable but flattering self-image.

There is little question that the formation of an adequate sense of personal identity, even if the process is still only partially known and understood, has profound implications for the psychological stability of the individual. The impact on man of the uncertainty of the times has been vividly depicted by Bonner (1965), who writes: "Today, man has no sure anchorage, no personal basis of values. His work is meaningless, he is disoriented, he has no sense of direction within it. This condition, not the inherent degeneracy of a people, is the source of the diabolic behavior of men" (p. 72). If this is an accurate view of the consequences of failing to establish a clear feeling of identity, then the understanding of this problem is a matter of the greatest urgency not only for the serious social scientist, but for every member of the society.

References

Bettelheim, B. The problem of generations. *Daedalus,* 1962, 91, 68-96.

Bonner, H. *On being mindful of man.* Boston: Houghton Mifflin, 1965.

Erikson, E. The problem of ego identity. *J. Amer. Psychoanalyt. Assoc.,* 1956, 4, 56-121.

Erikson, E. Youth, fidelity, and diversity. *Daedalus,* 1962, 91, 5-27.

Erikson, E. *Childhood and society.* Second edition. New York: Norton, 1963.

Goodman, P. Youth in organized society. *Commentary,* 1960, 29, 95-107.

Keniston, K. Inburn: An American Ishmael. In R. W. White (Ed.), *The study of lives,* New York: Atherton Press, 1963. Pp. 40-70.

Keniston, K. *The uncommitted: Alienated youth in American society.* New York: Harcourt, Brace & World, 1965.

Keniston, K. The sources of student dissent. *J. soc. Issues,* 1967, 23, 108-137.

Lynd, H. M. *On shame and the search for identity.* New York: Harcourt, Brace, 1958.

Maslow, A. *New knowledge in human values.* New York: Harper, 1959.

May, R. *Man's search for himself.* New York: Norton, 1953.

May, R. *Psychology and the human dilemma.* Princeton, N. J.: Van Nostrand, 1967.

Miller, D. R. The study of social relationships: Situation, identity, and social interaction. In S. Koch (Ed.), *Psychology: A study of a science,* Volume 5, New York: McGraw-Hill, 1963. Pp. 641-737.

Rokeach, M. *The three Christs of Ypsilanti.* New York: Alfred A. Knopf, 1964.

Royce, J. R. *The encapsulated man.* Princeton, N. J.: Van Nostrand, 1964.

Rubins, J. L. The self-concept, identity, and alienation from self. *Amer. J. Psychoanaly.,* 1961, 21, 132-143.

Shibutani, T. The structure of personal identity. In E. E. Sampson (Ed.), *Approaches, contexts, and problems of social psychology.* Englewood Cliffs, N. J.: Prentice-Hall, 1964. Pp. 231-235.

Stone, G. P. Appearance and the self. In A. M. Rose (Ed.), *Human behavior and social processes: An interactionist approach.* Boston: Houghton Mifflin, 1962. Pp. 86-118.

Wheelis, A. *The quest for identity.* New York: Norton, 1958.

On alienated concepts of identity

ERNEST G. SCHACHTEL

The terms identity and alienation often generate confusion and uncertainty because they are described in technical langauge and vague abstractions. This selection facilitates a clearer understanding of these concepts by minimizing the use of professional jargon. The author outlines the origins of the terms and describes their current meaning in the context of the psychoanalytic theory of personality. The article relates alienation to negative attitudes toward oneself and cites specific examples to illustrate how these attitudes develop and how they are expressed in actual behavior.

Ernest G. Schachtel, Ph.D., is in the private practice of psychoanalysis and psychotherapy in New York City, a Training and Supervising Analyst at the William Alanson White Institute of Psychiatry, Psychoanalysis, and Psychology and Adjunct Professor of Psychology in the Postdoctoral Training Program at New York University. He is the author of two books, *Metamorphosis: On the Development of Affect, Perception, Attention and Memory* and *Experiental Foundations of Rorschach's Test*.

In daily life the question of identity arises when we want to claim something from the post office, or when we want to pay by check in a store where we are not known, or in crossing a border. On such occasions we are asked: "Who are you, so that I can know for sure it is you and nobody else?" And we establish our identity by showing a driver's license or a passport or some similar document which tells our name, our address, the date of our birth, and perhaps some physical characteristics. Together, these will tell us apart from anybody else and will also establish that we are the same person that was born on such and such a date. We have *papers* to establish our identity, and this paper-identity is something fixed and definite. This is also the meaning of the word "identity," as applied to people, for the average person.

Such paper-identity seems far removed, at first glance, from the current concern of psychoanalysts, philosophers, and other students of the contemporary scene, with man's search for and doubt in his identity. But actually it is quite central to it. It is a telling symbol of alienated identity. It is a kind of identity which is the product of bureaucratic needs of commerce or administration. Its most gruesome and tragic manifestations occurred in our time when men's identities were reduced to numbers in concentration and extermination camps, and when countless people fleeing from the terror of the totalitarian states were shunted from country to country because they did not have the right paper-identities.

In the case of paper-identities, the person who demands and examines one's papers is the one who, in his role as an official, is alienated from the other person as a human being. Similarly, the guards in the concentration camps were alienated from their victims. However, many of these victims, systematically robbed of any meaningful purpose and dignity in their lives, succumbed to their tormentors and lost their sense of identity long before they lost their lives.

In our own and many other societies the loss

From *American Journal of Psychoanalysis*, XXIII (1961), 120-127. Reprinted by permission of the journal and the author.

of identity takes place without the terror of the concentration camps, in more insidious ways. I have described elsewhere how many people in our time tend to think of their lives as though they were answering the kind of questionnaire that one has to fill out when, for example, applying for a passport [1]. They tend to accept the paper-identity as their real identity. It is tempting to do so because it is something fixed and definite and does not require that the person be really in touch with himself. The paper-identity corresponds to the logical propositions concerning identity: A = A, and A is not non-A.

But man is not a logical proposition, and the paper-identity does not answer the question who this person, identified by some scrap of paper, is as a person. This question is not simple to answer. It has haunted many people increasingly in the last hundred years. They no longer feel certain who they are, because in modern industrial society, as Hegel and Marx first showed, they are alienated from nature, alienated from their fellow men, alienated from the work of their hands and minds, and alienated from themselves. I can only state here my belief that self-alienation, the doubt about and search for identity, always goes together with alienation from others and from the world around us.

The problem of identity and alienation from the self came to the attention of psychoanalysts in the last thirty years when they observed its role in an increasing number of patients. Karen Horney formulated it as the problem of the real self, as distinguished from the idealized self-image [2]; Fromm as the problem of the original, real self as distinguished from the conventional or pseudo-self; [1] [3], [4] Erikson, who has made the most detailed study in the development of the sense of identity, as the problem of ego-identity. [5]

Many patients who come to us suffer in one form or another from the lack of a sense of identity. This may take the form of feeling like impostors—in their work, or in relation to their background, their past, or to some part of themselves that they repress or consciously want to hide because they feel ashamed or guilty. Or else they feel that they *ought* to *have* something they lack or imagine they lack, such as material possessions, prestige, or certain personal qualities or traits; or they feel that a different husband or wife, or friends different from those they have, would give them the status they want and thereby, miraculously, transform them into full-blown persons. When the lack of a sense of identity becomes conscious, it is often experienced—probably always—as a feeling that, compared with others, one is not fully a person.

Among adults, one can observe two frequent reactions to the conscious or unconscious feeling of not being fully a person, of not having found an identity acceptable to oneself. One is an anxious retreat or depressive resignation, or a mixture of these. The other is a more or less conscious effort at disguise, at playing a role, at presenting an artificial façade to the world. These reactions are not mutually exclusive. They usually occur together, one of them being more emphasized or closer to consciousness than the other. The fear of exposure is present in both, but especially strong in people who rely on a façade. They tend to feel that they travel with a forged passport, under an assumed identity. When their disguise and the reasons for it have been analyzed, the sense of a lack of identity often comes to the fore as strongly as in those who, to begin with, have been aware of and suffered from the feeling of not really or fully being a person with a meaningful place in life. Both tend to feel that they do not really know who they are, what they want, or how they feel about other people.

When these people consult an analyst, they often expect, implicitly or explicitly, that he will tell them who they are or who they should be. Their wish and search is for a *definite, fixed identity*. They want to be a *personality*. Often these are people who suffer from over-adaptation to whatever situation they are in, and to whomever they are dealing with at the moment. They have been described pointedly in several plays and stories by Pirandello. They long for a definite, fixed, circumscribed personality. "Having" such a personality, as one has a possession, they hope will solve their dilemma. Having such a personality, they feel, is good; not having it, bad. Their wish to "possess" a definite identity does not and cannot solve the problem of their alienation from themselves,

---

[1] In his latest book he seems to see the real self in what he calls "universal man" and considers the conscious self, especially the social self, as alienated from this universal man who, in turn, is repressed.

because it actually is the continuation of alienation. They want to substitute a fixed, reified personality for the on-going process of living, feeling, acting, and thinking in which they alone could find themselves. They search for a definite, stable shell called "personality" to which they want to cling. Their quest is self-defeating, because what they search for is an alienated concept of a thing, rather than a living, developing person. Their wish is a symptom, not a cure. In this symptom, however, both the malady of alienation and the longing for a more meaningful life find expression, even though in a way which perpetuates the ill from which they seek to escape. The self-conscious preoccupation with this wished-for magic object called "personality" interferes with the actual experience of living.

In calling the object of these people's search an alienated "concept" of identity, I do not mean a scientific or even an explicit concept. I am describing an implicit concept, which becomes apparent only in the analysis of the underlying, often not conscious, assumptions that direct this kind of search. This applies equally to the following examples of alienated concepts of identity.

There is one psychoanalytic term that has gained wide popularity and in popular use has changed its meaning. Such popular use always indicates a significant fact about a society and therefore deserves our attention. I refer to the term "ego." People say that something is good or bad for their "ego." They mean by this that their self-feeling—in the sense of the status which they accord to themselves—rises when something is good and falls when something is bad for their ego. In this usage ego is only part of the person.[2] My "ego" is not identical with "I" or "self." It is not identical with the I who is well or ill, who sees and hears and touches and tastes and smells, who acts, walks, sits, stands, lies, who is moved by others, by what is seen and experienced. Moreover, what is "good" or "bad" for my ego is not at all necessarily good or bad for me, although I may be inclined to think so. The popular "ego" gains from success, winning in competition, status, being admired, flattered, loved; it does not gain from facing the truth, from loving somebody else, from humility. It behaves like a stock or a piece of merchandise endowed with self-awareness; if it is much in demand

it rises, is blown up, feels important; if not, it falls, shrinks, feels it is nothing.[3] Thus, it is an *alienated* part of the self, it has the tendency to become the *focal point* of the feeling of identity and to dominate the whole life of the people who are involved with their "ego" to a significant degree. Their mood fluctuates with their "ego." They are haunted by their "ego" and preoccupied with its enhancement or its downfall. They no longer seem to feel that they have a life apart from their "ego," but they stand or fall with it. The "ego" has become their identity and at the same time the main object of their worry, ambition, and preoccupation, crowding out any real concern with themselves and with others. The popular ego can serve as the most important model of an alienated concept of identity, even though it may be surpassed in rigidity and fixedness by some other examples of such concepts, to which I shall turn now.

In her thoughtful book, *On Shame and the Search for Identity,* Helen Lynd quotes Dostoevsky's Mitya Karamazov who, on trial for the murder of his father, suffers his worst misery when the prosecutor asks him to take off his socks.

They were very dirty . . . and now everyone could see it. All his life he had thought both his big toes hideous. He particularly loathed the coarse, flat, crooked nail on the right one and now they would all see it. Feeling intolerably ashamed. . . . [6]

The accidental, unchangeable appearance of his feet, of the nail of his right big toe, here becomes the focal point of his identity. It is on this that he feels the peasants who stand around him and look at him will judge him and that he judges himself. Very often real or imagined physical attributes, parts of the body image or the entire body image, become focal points of identity. Many people build

___

[2] The psychoanalytic concept of ego also is not identical with the whole person, but its relation to the total personality is radically different from the relation of the popular ego to the total personality, and most of the ego-processes, in the psychoanalytic meaning of the term, are not part of the popular "ego."
[3] Some psychologists who speak of "ego involvement" adopt in this phrase the described popular meaning of "ego." The term usually means that a person's ambition is involved in wanting to be successful in some task or situation.

around such a negative identity the feeling that this particular feature unalterably determines the course of their lives, and that they are thereby doomed to unhappiness. Usually, in these cases, qualities such as attractiveness and beauty are no longer felt to be based on the alive expression and flux of human feelings, but have become fixed and dead features, or a series of poses, as in so many Hollywood stars or fashion models. These features are cut off from the center of the person and worn like a mask. Unattractiveness is experienced as not possessing this mask.

In the same way, other real or imagined attributes, or the lack of them, become focal points for a reified, alienated, negative identity. For example: feeling not sufficiently masculine or feminine, being born on the wrong side of the tracks, being a member of a minority group against which racial or religious prejudices are directed, and, in the most general form, feeling intrinsically inadequate or "bad." I do not imply, of course, that in our society the accidental circumstance of being born as the member of one social, national, or religious group or class rather than another does not result in very real, objective difficulties, disadvantages or privileges. I am concerned here only with the *attitude* which the person takes toward such handicaps or advantages, which is important for his ability to deal with them. In this attitude the structure of the sense of identity and the way in which such factors as the social background and innate advantages or handicaps are incorporated in the sense of identity play a decisive role.

What are the dynamics of such alienated concepts of identity? Sometimes they crystallize around repeated parental remarks which, rather than referring to the particular act of the child, say or imply that the child *is* or *lacks,* by its very nature, such and such; that Tom is a lazy good-for-nothing or that he is "just like Uncle Harry," who happens to be the black sheep in the family. Frequently they develop from an ego-ideal that is alien to the child's own personality, but about which he has come to feel that, unless he is such and such, he is nothing.[4] Whatever their genetic origin, I shall consider here mainly the phenomenological structure of alienated identity concepts and the dynamics of this structure which tend to perpetuate self-alienation.

By making some quality or circumstance, real or exaggerated or imagined, the focal point of a reified identity, I look upon myself as though I were a thing (res) and the quality or circumstance were a fixed attribute of this thing or object.[5] But the "I" that feels that I am this or that, in doing so, distances itself from the very same reified object attribute which it experiences as determining its identity and very often as a bane on its life. In feeling that I am such and such, I distinguish between the unfortunate I and the presumably unalterable quality or lack which, for all time, condemns me to have this negative identity. I do not feel that *I am doing* this or that or failing to do it, but that there *is* a something in me or about me, or that I lack something and that this, once and for all, *makes* me this or that, fixes my identity.

The person who has this attitude toward himself usually is unaware of its being a particular attitude with concrete and far-reaching implications. He takes his attitude for granted as a natural, inevitable one and is aware only of the painful self-consciousness and self-preoccupation it involves. He can not imagine how anyone with his "fate" could have any other attitude.

The two most significant implications of this attitude to oneself are 1) the severance from the living I of the reified attribute which is experienced as a fixed, unchangeable quality, and 2) the severance of this reified attribute from its dynamic and structural connection with other qualities, needs, acts, and experiences of the person. In other words, the reified attribute is cut off from the living, developing, fluctuating I in *time,* since it is experienced as immutable. But it is also cut off from being experienced as an *integral* part of the living

---

[4] I cannot discuss here the genetic individual and social causes of self-alienation and of the formation of alienated identity concepts. Regarding the social roots of alienation, compare Erich Fromm, The sane society, N. Y.: Rinehart & Company, 1955. Regarding the individual vicissitudes of the development of the sense of identity, compare Erik H. Erikson, Identity and the life cycle, N. Y.: International Universities Press, 1959 (Monograph 1, Psychological Issues); Edith Jacobson, The self and the object world, *The psychoanalytic study of the child,* 1954, Vol. IX, 75-127. Compare also the sections on perception and on memory in Ernest Schachtel, op. cit.

[5] The significance of such fixation has been emphasized by D. J. van Lennep, The fourteenth test. In Harold H. and Gladys L. Anderson (Eds.), An introduction to projective techniques, N. Y.: Prentice-Hall, 1951, 153-154.

personality, connected with the totality of the person's strivings, attitudes, perceptions, feelings, with his acting, and failing to act.

In reality, of course, we can observe that certain actions, moods, and experiences cause changes in the role of the negative identity in the conscious feelings and thoughts of the person. However, he usually does not experience the reified attribute which forms the core of his negative self-feeling as something connected with, and due to, his own actions and attitudes, but as something fixed on which he has no influence. Furthermore, just as the person's feeling about himself may fluctuate with the ups and downs of his "ego," so it also varies with the intensity of the negative self-feeling based on some reified attribute which, at times, may disappear altogether from the conscious thoughts of the person. However, when it reappears, it is "recognized" as the same unfortunate quality that throughout the past has tainted—and will forever taint—the person's life. Thus, in spite of such fluctuations, the alienated attribute is experienced as a "something" that basically does not and can not change.

To be saddled with a reified, negative identity seems, on the face of it, nothing but a painful burden. Yet one often can see people cling to such negative self-images with a great deal of stubbornness and in the face of contradictory evidence. In psychoanalytic therapy, it is often seen that the patient who comes for help tries to convince the therapist that nothing can be done for him, since he is born with such and such a handicap or without such and such an advantage. On closer scrutiny, one may find that such insistence by the patient on the hopelessness of the situation has a way of occurring at a point when the patient is afraid to face an issue, or when he wants to be pitied rather than helped. Thus, the reified identity concept often provides a protection against an anxiety-arousing challenge, a way out of a feared situation, and thereby a certain relief.

This relief is dynamically similar to the relief observable in certain hypochondriacal and paranoid patients. It sounds paradoxical to speak of relief in the case of patients who are so obviously beset by worry, suffering, and fear as the hypochondriac and the paranoid. However, as Sullivan has pointed out, the hypochondriacal patient who is preoccupied with imagined, anticipated, or real ailments sees himself as the "customarily handicapped" one and thereby avoids the anxiety-provoking prospect of facing and dealing with his real problems. His hypochondriacal preoccupation gets the patient, in Sullivan's words, "off the spot with himself"—namely, off the spot where he would have to deal with his realistic personality problems.[6]

The person living with an alienated and reified, negative identity concept of himself closely resembles the hypochondriacal patient, except that his unhappy preoccupation concerns not a physical ailment but a reified physical or psychic quality that has become the focal point of his self-image. The relief he gains from his burdensome preoccupation is due to the fact that the reified "bad" quality no longer is viewed as part of the on-going process of living and of goal-directed thought and action. It has been severed from the "I" that acts with foresight and responsibility and is looked upon as an inherent, unalterable, unfortunate something, an ossified part of oneself that no longer participates in the flux, growth, and development of life. It is experienced as an unchangeable fate whose bearer is doomed to live and die with it. The relief this brings is that the person no longer feels *responsible* for the supposed consequences of this fixed attribute; he is not *doing* anything for which he can be blamed, even though he may feel ashamed and unacceptable for *being* such and such. The preoccupation with the reified identity directs attention away from what he *does* to what he supposedly *is*. Furthermore, he now no longer has to do anything about it because, obviously, he can't do anything about it. Thus, the anxiety, fear, and effort that would be connected with facing and acting upon the real problem is avoided by putting up with the negative, fixed identity which, in addition, may be used to indulge self-pity and to enlist the sympathy of others.

The similarity in the dynamics of hypochondria and paranoia, on the one hand, and the alienated, reified self-concept, on the other, lies in this *shift of responsibility and of focus*

---

[6] For this analysis of the dynamics of hypochondria and for the close relation between hypochondria and paranoia see Harry Stack Sullivan. The interpersonal theory of psychiatry, N. Y.: W. W. Norton, 1953, 355-358, 362-363.

from my own actions and conduct of life to something else over which I have no control. In the alienated self-concept, this something else is a reified quality, or the lack of such a quality; in hypochondria an ailment, real or imagined; in paranoia the delusional persecutors. The difference between paranoia and the alienated self-concept lies in the fact that in paranoia the shift in responsibility is brought about by delusions distorting reality, while in the alienated, negative identity concept it is brought about by an attitude which excludes part of oneself from the process of living and freezes it into a cancer-like, uncontrollable, and unalterable thing. This "thing" very often also becomes the focus, in the paranoid neuroses, of the imagined judgments, observation, and talk of other people about the patient. He believes that, just as his own thoughts tend to revolve around some reified and alienated quality, other people will be similarly preoccupied with this quality in him.

So far I have discussed mainly negative self-images. However, alienated identity concepts may be positive as well as negative. Alienated identity of the positive variety occurs in vanity, conceit and—in its more pathological form—in delusions of grandeur, just as in its negative counterpart the "I" of the vain person is severed from a fixed attribute on which the vanity is based. The person feels that he *possesses* this quality. It becomes the focal point of his identity and serves as its prop. Beauty, masculinity or femininity, being born on the right side of the tracks, success, money, prestige, or "being good" may serve as such a prop. While in the negative identity feeling a reified attribute haunts the person, such an attribute serves the positive self-image as a support. Yet it is equally alienated from the living person. This is expressed nicely in the phrase "a stuffed shirt." It is not the person in the shirt but some dead matter, some stuffing that is used to bolster and aggrandize the self-feeling. It often becomes apparent in the behavior of the person that he *leans* on this real or imagined attribute, just as it often is apparent that a person feels pulled down by the weight of some alienated negative attribute.

The reliance on an identity, on a self-image based on the prop of some reified attribute remains precarious even where it seems to work, after a fashion, as it does in the self-satisfaction of the vain. This precariousness is inevitable, since the positive self-evaluation of such a person does not rest on a feeling of wholeness and meaningfulness in life, in thought, feeling, and deed. He is always threatened with the danger of losing this "thing," this possession, on which his self-esteem is based. This is the theme of Oscar Wilde's novel, *The Picture of Dorian Gray*. Dorian Gray exchanges his identity with the portrait of his youthful charm. He becomes the picture of himself as the beautiful youth, alienated from his actual life, which affects the portrait he has hidden in the attic, marking it over the years with his cruelty, selfishness, and greed, and with his advancing age. The portrait is the skeleton in the closet, the secret threat that hangs over the unchanging mask. Today, especially in this country where youth has become a public fetish, many thousands try to preserve its alienated mask while terrified by the prospect of suddenly growing old, when the mask can no longer be worn or will become grotesque.

I believe that in every case of alienated identity concepts there is a secret counterimage. In Dorian Gray, this is the actual, living person, transplanted to the portrait. Very often such a hidden self announces itself merely in a vague background feeling that the person would be lost, would be nothing if it were not for the alienated, reified quality on which the feeling of being something, somebody, or the feeling of vanity, is based. In this feeling both a truth and an irrational anxiety find expression. The truth is that no man who looks upon himself as a thing and bases his existence on the support of some reified attribute of this thing has found himself and his place in life. The irrational anxiety is the feeling that without the prop of such an attribute he could not live.

Similarly, in the negative alienated identity concepts there usually is a positive counterimage. It may take a generalized, vague form: If it were not for such and such (the reified attribute forming the focus of the negative identity), I would be all right, successful, wonderful, etc. Or it may take the more concrete form of some grandiose, exaggerated fantasy about one's positive qualities. These positive counterimages, too, express both an irrational hope and a truth. The irrational hope is that one may have some magical quality which will transport him into a state of security, or even superiority, because then he will possess that attribute which, instead of haunting him, will save him. But actually it is nothing but the equally reified counterpart of what at present drags him down. The truth is that man has potentialities for overcoming his alienation from himself and for living without the burden and the artificial props of alienated, reified identity concepts.

Goethe, in an interpretation of the Delphic word, "Know thyself," distinguishes between helpful self-awareness and futile and self-tormenting rumination. He opposes the "ascetic" interpretation he finds among "our modern hypochrondrists" and those who turn their vengeance against themselves. Instead, he sees the real meaning of self-knowledge in taking notice of oneself and becoming aware of one's relation to other people and to the world [7]. The pseudo-self-knowledge against which he speaks foreshadows the widespread present-day self-preoccupation which is concerned, fruitlessly, with an alienated, negative sense of identity. In contrast to this, Goethe counsels a productive self-knowledge: to pay attention to what one is actually doing in his relation to others, to the world and—we might add—to himself.

References

1. Schachtel, E. Metamorphosis: On the development of affect perception, attention and memory, New York: Basic Books, 1959, 287-8.

2. Horney, Karen Neurosis and human growth, New York: W. W. Norton, 1950.

3. Fromm, Erich Escape from Freedom, New York: Farrar & Rinehart, 1941, 195-206.

4. Fromm, Erich Psychoanalysis and Zen Buddhism. In D. T. Suzuki, Erich Fromm and Richard De Martino, Zen Buddhism and psychoanalysis, New York: Harper, 1960, 106-109.

5. Erikson, Erik H. Identity and the life cycle, New York: International University Press, 1959.

6. Dostoevski, Fyodor The Brothers Karamazov, New York: Modern Library, 1950, 587.

7. Goethe, J. W. Maximen und reflexionen, in Sämmtliche werke, Stuttgart and Tübingen: 1853, I. G. Cotta'scher Verlag, Vol. 3, 225-6.

Social change and youth in America

KENNETH KENISTON

Belief in the value of dynamic change and innovation is one of the most striking characteristics of American culture. This emphasis on the desirability of rapid change has permitted the United States to progress in the development of its economy to the extent that this country now claims the industrial leadership of the world. However, change does not occur without some undesirable consequences. This article deals with the effects of unrestrained change on society and the individual. The author analyzes the impact of change on both the young and old in our society and discusses change in relation to the formation of identity, alienated behavior, and individual motivations.

Kenneth Keniston is Associate Professor of Psychology and Psychiatry at the Yale University Medical School. A former Rhodes Scholar, his research on the psychological characteristics of young adults has been published in two books,

From *Daedalus*, XCI (1962), 145-171. Reprinted by permission of the American Academy of Arts and Sciences.

The Uncommitted: Alienated Youth in America and Young Radicals: Notes on Committed Youth.

Every society tends to ignore its most troublesome characteristics.[1] Usually these remain unfathomed precisely because they are taken for granted, because life would be inconceivable without these traits. And most often they are taken for granted because their recognition would be painful to those concerned or disruptive to the society. Active awareness would at times involve confronting an embarrassing gap between social creed and social fact; at other times, the society chooses to ignore those of its qualities which subject its citizens to the greatest psychological strain. Such pluralistic ignorance is usually guaranteed and disguised by a kind of rhetoric of pseudo-awareness, which, by appearing to talk about the characteristic and even to praise it, prevents real understanding far more effectively than could an easily broken conspiracy of silence.

Such is often the case with discussions of social change in America. From hundreds of platforms on Commencement Day, young men and women are told that they go out into a rapidly changing world, that they live amidst unprecedented new opportunities, that they must continue the innovations which have made and will continue to produce an ever-improving society in an ever-improving world. Not only is social change here portrayed as inevitable and good, but, the acoustics of the audience being what it is, no one really hears, and all leave with the illusory conviction that they have understood something about their society. But it occurs to none of the graduating class that their deepest anxieties and most confused moments might be a consequence of this "rapidly changing world."

More academic discussions of social change often fail similarly to clarify its meaning in our society. Most scholarly discussions of innovation concentrate either on the primitive world or on some relatively small segment of modern society. No conference is complete without panels and papers on "New Trends in X," "Recent Developments in Y," and "The New American Z." But commentators on American society are usually so preoccupied with specific changes—in markets, population patterns, styles of life—that they rarely if ever consider the over-all impact of the very fact that our entire society is in flux. And however important it may be to understand these specific changes in society, their chief importance for the individual is in that they are merely part of the broader picture of social change in all areas.

Even when we do reflect on the meaning of change in our own society, we are usually led to minimize its effects by the myth that familiarity breeds disappearance—that is, by the belief that because as individuals and as a society we have made an accommodation to social change, its effects have therefore vanished. It is of course true that the vast majority of Americans have made a kind of adaptation to social change. Most would feel lost without the technological innovations with which industrial managers and advertising men annually supply us: late-model cars, TV sets, refrigerators, women's fashions, and home furnishings. And, more important, we have made a kind of peace with far more profound nontechnological changes; new conceptions of the family, of sex roles, of work and play cease to shock or even to surprise us. But such an adaptation, even when it involves the expectation of and the need for continuing innovation, does not mean that change has ceased to affect us. It would be as true to say that because the American Indian has found in defeat, resentment, and apathy an adaptation of the social changes which destroyed his tribal life, he has ceased to be affected by these changes. Indeed, the acceptance and anticipation of social change by most Americans is itself one of the best indications of how profoundly it has altered our outlooks.

Thus, though barraged with discussions of "our rapidly changing world" and "recent developments," we too easily can remain incognizant of the enormous significance, and in many ways the historical uniqueness, of social change in our society. Rapid changes in all aspects of life mean that little can be counted on to endure from generation to generation, that all technologies, all institutions, and all values are open to revision and obsolescence. Continual innovation as we experienced it in this country profoundly affects our conceptions

---

[1] An earlier version of parts of this paper was presented at the Annual Conference of Jewish Communal Services, May 1961, and was published in *The Journal of Jewish Communal Services* (Fall 1961).

of ourselves, our visions of the future, the quality of our attachment to the present, and the myths we construct of the past. It constitutes one of the deepest sources of strain in American life,[2] and many characteristically "American" outlooks, values, and institutions can be interpreted as attempts to adapt to the stress of continual change.

Social change in America

Many of the outlooks and values of American youth can be seen as responses to the social changes which confront this generation.[3] But merely to point out that society is changing and that youth must cope with the strains thus created is to state a truth so universal as to be almost tautological. Social change is the rule in history: past ages which at first glance appear to have been static usually turn out on closer study to have been merely those in which conflicting pressures for change were temporarily canceled out. Indeed, the very concept of a static society is usually a mistake of the short-sighted, a hypothetical contract which facilitates the analysis of change, or a myth created by those who dislike innovation.[4] All new generations must accommodate themselves to social change; indeed, one of youth's historic roles has been to provide the enthusiasm—if not the leadership—for still further changes.

And even if we add the qualifier "rapid" to "social change," there is still little distinctive about the problems of American youth. For though most historical changes have been slow and have involved little marked generational discontinuity, in our own century at least most of the world is in the midst of rapid, massive, and often disruptive changes, and these may create even greater problems for the youth of underdeveloped countries than they do for Americans. Thus, to understand the responses of American youth to the problems of social change, we must first characterize, however tentatively and impressionistically, the most striking features of social change in this country.

Social change in America is by no means *sui generis;* in particular, it has much in common with the process of innovation in other industrialized countries. In all industrially advanced nations, the primary motor of social change is technological innovation: changes in nontechnological areas of society usually follow the needs and effects of technological and scientific advances. But though our own country is not unique in the role technology plays, it is distinguished by the intensity of and the relative absence of restraint on technological change. Probably more than any other society, we revere technological innovation, we seldom seek to limit its effects on other areas of society, and we have developed complex institutions to assure its persistence and acceleration. And, most important, because of the almost unchallenged role of technology in our society, our attitudes toward it spread into other areas of life, coloring our views on change in whatever area it occurs. This country closely approximates the ideal type of unrestrained and undirected technological change which pervades all areas of life; and, in so far as other nations wish to or are in fact becoming more like us, the adaptations of American youth may augur similar trends elsewhere.

Our almost unqualified acceptance of technological innovation is historically unusual. To be sure, given a broad definition of technology, most major social and cultural changes have been accompanied, if not produced, by technological advances. The control of fire, the domestication of animals, the development of irrigation, the discovery of the compass— each innovation has been followed by profound changes in the constitution of society. But, until recently, technological innovation has been largely accidental and usually bitterly resisted by the order it threatened to supplant. Indeed, if there has been any one historical attitude toward change, it has been to deplore it. Most cultures have assumed that change was for the worse; most individuals have felt that the old ways were the best ways. There is a certain wisdom behind this assumption, for

---

[2] It need hardly be added that our society's capacity for innovation and change is also one of its greatest strengths.
[3] Among the other major factors creating stresses for American youth are (1) the discontinuities between childhood and adulthood, especially in the areas of sex, work, and dependency; (2) the great rise in the aspirations and standards of youth, which create new dissatisfactions; and (3) the general intellectual climate of skepticism and debunking, which makes "ideological" commitment difficult. In this essay, however, I will concentrate on the stresses created by social change.
[4] One should not confuse static with stable societies. American society is extremely stable internally despite rapid rates of change. Similarly, other societies, though relatively static, are unstable internally.

it is indeed true that technological change and its inevitable social and psychological accompaniments produce strains, conflicts, and imbalances among societies as among individuals. Were it not for our own and other modern societies, we might ascribe to human nature and social organization a deep conservatism which dictates that changes shall be made only when absolutely necessary and after a last-ditch stand by what is being replaced.

But in our own society in particular, this attitude no longer holds. We value scientific innovation and technological change almost without conscious reservation.[5] Even when scientific discoveries make possible the total destruction of the world, we do not seriously question the value of such discoveries. Those rare voices who may ask whether a new bomb, a new tail fin, a new shampoo, or a new superhighway might not be better left unproduced are almost invariably suppressed before the overwhelming conviction that "you can't stop the clock." And these attitudes extend beyond science and technology, affecting our opinions of every kind of change—as indeed they must if unwillingness to bear the nontechnological side effects of technological innovation is not to impede the latter. Whether in social institutions, in ideology, or even in individual character, change is more often than not considered self-justifying. Our words of highest praise stress transformation—dynamic, expanding, new, modern, recent, growing, current, youthful, and so on. And our words of condemnation equally deplore the static and unchanging—old-fashioned, outmoded, antiquated, obsolete, stagnating, stand-still. We desire change not only when we have clear evidence that the status quo is inadequate, but often regardless of whether what we have from the past still serves us. The assumption that the new will be better than the old goes very deep in our culture; and even when we explicitly reject such notions as that of progress, we often retain the implicit assumption that change *per se* is desirable.

Given this assumption that change is good, it is inevitable that institutions should have developed which would guarantee change and seek to accelerate it. Here as in other areas, technology leads the way. Probably the most potent innovating institution in our society is pure science, which provides an ever-increasing repertoire of techniques for altering the environment. An even greater investment of time and money goes into applied science and technology, into converting abstract scientific principles into concrete innovations relevant to our industrialized society. The elevation of technological innovation into a profession, research and development, is the high point of institutionalized technological change in this country and probably in the world. And along with the institutionalized change increasingly goes planned obsolescence to assure that even if the motivation to discard the outmoded should flag, the consumer will have no choice but to buy the newest and latest, since the old will have ceased to function.

But the most drastic strains occur only at the peripheries of purely technological innovation, because of changes in other social institutions which follow in the wake of new commodities and technologies. Consider the effects of the automobile, which has changed patterns of work and residence, transformed the countryside with turnpikes and freeways, all but destroyed public transportation, been instrumental in producing urban blight and the flight to the suburbs, and even changed techniques of courtship in America. Further examples could be adduced, but the point is clear: unrestrained technological change guarantees the continual transformation of other sectors of society to accommodate the effects and requirements of technology. And here, too, our society abounds with planning groups, special legislative committees, citizens' movements, research organizations, community workers, and consultants of every variety whose chief task is, as it were, to clean up after technologically induced changes, though rarely if ever to plan or coordinate major social innovations in the first place. Thus, citizens' committees usually worry more about how to relocate the families dispossessed by new roadways than about whether new roads are a definite social asset. But by mitigating some of the more acute stresses indirectly created by technological change, such organizations add to social stability.

---

[5] Unconsciously, however, most Americans have highly ambivalent feelings about science and technology, usually expressed in the myth of the (mad) scientist whose creation eventually destroys him.

One of the principal consequences of our high regard for change and of the institutionalization of innovation is that we have virtually assured not only that change will continue, but that its pace will accelerate. Since scientific knowledge is growing at a logarithmic rate, each decade sees still more, and more revolutionary, scientific discoveries made available to industry for translation into new commodities and techniques of production.[6] And while social change undoubtedly lags behind technological change, the pace of social innovation has also increased. An American born at the turn of the century has witnessed in his lifetime social transformations unequaled in any other comparable period in history: the introduction of electricity, radio, television, the automobile, the airplane, atomic bombs and power, rocketry, the automation of industry in the technological area, and equally unprecedented changes in society and ideology: new conceptions of the family, of the relations between the sexes, of work, residence, leisure, of the role of government, of the place of America in world affairs. We correctly characterize the rate of change in terms of self-stimulating chain reactions—the "exploding" metropolis, the "upward spiral" of living standards, the "rocketing" demands for goods and services. And unlike drastic social changes in the past (which have usually resulted from pestilence, war, military conquest, or contact with a superior culture), these have taken place "in the natural course of events." In our society at present, "the natural course of events" is precisely that the rate of change should continue to accelerate up to the as-yet-unreached limits of human and institutional adaptability.

The effects of this kind of valued, institutionalized, and accelerating social change are augmented in American society by two factors. The first is the relative absence of traditional institutions or values opposed to change. In most other industrialized nations, the impact of technology on the society at large has been limited by pre-existing social forces—aristocratic interests, class cleavages, or religious values—opposed to unrestrained technological change. Or, as in the case of Japan, technological changes were introduced by semifeudal groups determined to preserve their hegemony in the new power structure. Technologically induced changes have thus often been curbed or stopped when they conflicted with older institutions and values, or these pretechnological forces have continued to exist side by side with technological changes. The result has been some mitigation of the effects of technological innovation, a greater channeling of these changes into pre-existing institutions, and the persistence within the society of enclaves relatively unaffected by the values of a technological era.[7] But America has few such antitechnological forces. Lacking a feudal past, our values were from the first those most congenial to technology—a strong emphasis on getting things done, on practicality, on efficiency, on hard work, on rewards for achievement, not birth, and on treating all men according to the same universal rules.

A second factor which increases the effect of technological change is our unusual unwillingness to control, limit, or guide directions of industrial and social change—an unwillingness related to the absence of institutions opposing innovation. Most rapid changes in the world today involve far more central planning or foreknowledge of goal than we are willing to allow in America. At one extreme are countries like China and Russia, which attempt the total planning of all technological, industrial, and social change. While unplanned changes inevitably occur, central planning means that the major directions of change are outlined in advance and that unplanned changes can frequently be redirected according to central objectives. Furthermore, most underdeveloped nations are aiming at developing a highly technological society; in so far as they succeed, the direction of their changes is given by the model they seek to emulate. Given three abstract types of change—planned, imitative, and unguided—our own society most closely approximates the unguided type. We do little to limit the effects of change in one area of life on other aspects of society, and prefer to let social transformations occur in what we consider a "free" or "natural" way, that is, to be determined by technological innovations.

---

[6] See Walter Rosenblith, "On some social consequences of scientific and technological change," *Daedalus* (Summer 1961), pp. 498-513.
[7] Obviously, the existence of institutions and values opposed to technological change in a technological society is itself a major source of social and individual tension.

As a result, we virtually guarantee our inability to anticipate or predict the future directions of social change. The Russian knows at least that his society is committed to increasing production and expansion; the Nigerian knows that his nation aims at increasing Westernization; but partly by our refusal to guide the course of our society, we have no way of knowing where we are headed.

The phenomenology of unrestrained technological change

Man's individual life has always been uncertain: no man could ever predict the precise events which would befall him and his children. In many ways we have decreased existential uncertainty in our society by reducing the possibilities of premature death and diminishing the hazards of natural disaster. But at the same time, a society changing in the way ours is greatly increases the unpredictability and uncertainty of the life situation shared by all the members of any generation. In almost every other time and place, a man could be reasonably certain that essentially the same technologies, social institutions, outlooks on life, and types of people would surround his children in their maturity as surrounded him in his. Today, we can no longer expect this. Instead, our chief certainty about the life situation of our descendants is that it will be drastically and unpredictably different from our own.

Few Americans consciously reflect on the significance of social change; as I have argued earlier, the rhetoric with which we conventionally discuss our changing society usually conceals a recognition of how deeply the pace, the pervasiveness, and the lack of overall direction of change in our society affect our outlooks. But nonetheless, the very fact of living amidst this kind of social transformation produces a characteristic point of view about the past and future, a new emphasis on the present, and above all an altered relationship between the generations which we can call the phenomenology of unrestrained technological change.[8]

The major components of this world view follow from the characteristics of change in this country. First, the past grows increasingly distant from the present. The differences between the America of 1950 and that of 1960 are greater than those between 1900 and 1910; because of the accelerating rate of innovation, more things change, and more rapidly, in each successive decade. Social changes that once would have taken a century now occur in less than a generation. As a result, the past grows progressively more different from the present in fact, and seems more remote and irrelevant psychologically. Second, the future, too, grows more remote and uncertain. Because the future directions of social change are virtually unpredictable, today's young men and women are growing into a world that is more unknowable than that confronted by any previous generation. The kind of society today's students will confront as mature adults is almost impossible for them or anyone else to anticipate. Third, the present assumes a new significance as the one time in which the environment is relevant, immediate, and knowable. The past's solutions to life's problems are not necessarily relevant to the here-and-now, and no one can know whether what is decided today will remain valid in tomorrow's world; hence, the present assumes an autonomy unknown in more static societies. Finally, and perhaps of greatest psychological importance, the relations between the generations are weakened as the rate of social innovation increases. The wisdom and skills of fathers can no longer be transmitted to sons with any assurance that they will be appropriate for them; truth must as often be created by children as learned from parents.

This mentality by no means characterizes all Americans to the same degree. The impact of social change is always very uneven, affecting some social strata more than others, and influencing some age groups more than others. The groups most affected are usually in elite or vanguard positions: those in roles of intellectual leadership usually initiate innovations and make the first psychological adaptations to them, integrating novelty with older values and institutions and providing in their persons models which exemplify techniques of adaptation to the new social order. Similarly,

---

[8] Other types of social change also have their own characteristic world views. In particular, the mentality of elite youth in underdeveloped countries now beginning industrialization differs from that in transitional countries like Japan, where technological and pretechnological elements coexist. American society probably comes closest to a "pure" type of exclusively technological change.

social change subjects different age groups to differing amounts of stress. Those least affected are those most outside the society, the very young and the very old; most affected are youths in the process of making a lifelong commitment to the future. The young, who have outlived the social definitions of childhood and are not yet fully located in the world of adult commitments and roles, are most immediately torn between the pulls of the past and the future. Reared by elders who were formed in a previous version of the society, and anticipating a life in a still different society, they must somehow choose between competing versions of past and future. Thus, it is youth that must chiefly cope with the strains of social change, and among youth, it is "elite" youth who feel these most acutely.

Accordingly, in the following comments on the outlooks of American youth, I will emphasize those views which seem most directly related to the world view created by unrestrained change,[9] and will base my statements primarily on my observations over the past decade of a number of able students in an "elite" college. While these young men are undoubtedly more articulate and reflective than most of their contemporaries, I suspect they voice attitudes common to many of their age mates.

Outlooks of elite youth

One of the most outstanding (and to many members of the older generation, most puzzling) characteristics of young people today is their apparent *lack of deep commitments to adult values and roles*. An increasing number of young people—students, teenagers, juvenile delinquents, and beats—are alienated from their parents' conceptions of adulthood, disaffected from the main streams of traditional public life, and disaffiliated from many of the historical institutions of our society. This alienation is of course one of the cardinal tenets of the Beat Generation; but it more subtly characterizes a great many other young people, even those who appear at first glance to be chiefly concerned with getting ahead and making a place for themselves. A surprising number of these young men and women, despite their efforts to get good scholarships and good grades so that they can get into a good medical school and have a good practice, nonetheless view the world they are entering

with a deep mistrust. Paul Goodman aptly describes their view of society as "an apparently closed room with a rat race going on in the middle." [10] Whether they call it a rat race or not is immaterial (though many do): a surprising number of apparently ambitious young people see it as that. The adult world into which they are headed is seen as a cold, mechanical, abstract, specialized, and emotionally meaningless place in which one simply goes through the motions, but without conviction that the motions are worthy, humane, dignified, relevant, or exciting. Thus, for many young people, it is essential to stay "cool"; and "coolness" involves detachment, lack of commitment, never being enthusiastic or going overboard about anything.

This is a bleak picture, and it must be partially qualified. For few young people are deliberately cynical or calculating; rather, many feel forced into detachment and premature cynicism because society seems to offer them so little that is relevant, stable, and meaningful. They wish there were values, goals, or institutions to which they could be genuinely committed; they continue to search for them; and, given something like the Peace Corps, which promises challenge and a genuine expression of idealism, an extraordinary number of young people are prepared to drop everything to join. But when society as a whole appears to offer them few challenging or exciting opportunities—few of what Erikson would call objects of "fidelity"—"playing it cool" seems to many the only way to avoid damaging commitment to false life styles or goals.

To many older people, this attitude seems to smack of ingratitude and irresponsibility. In an earlier age, most men would have been grateful for the opportunities offered these contemporary young. Enormous possibilities are open to students with a college education, and yet many have little enthusiasm for these opportunities. If they are enthusiastic at all, it is about their steady girl friend, about their role in the college drama society, about writing

---

[9] Once again I omit any discussion of other sources of strain on youth (see reference 3). Furthermore, I do not mean to suggest that these outlooks are the only possible responses to unrestrained change, or that they are unaffected by other historical and social forces in American life.

[10] Paul Goodman, *Growing up absurd*, New York: Random House, 1960.

poetry, or about a weekend with their buddies. Yet, at the same time, the members of this apparently irresponsible generation are surprisingly sane, realistic, and level-headed. They may not be given to vast enthusiasms, but neither are they given to fanaticism. They have a great, even an excessive, awareness of the complexities of the world around them; they are well-read and well-informed; they are kind and decent and moderate in their personal relations.

Part of the contrast between the apparent maturity and the alienation of the young is understandable in terms of the phenomenology of unrestrained change. For the sanity of young people today is partly manifest in their awareness that their world is very different from that of their parents. They know that rash commitments may prove outmoded tomorrow; they know that most viewpoints are rapidly shifting; they, therefore, find it difficult to locate a fixed position on which to stand. Furthermore, many young men and women sense that their parents are poor models for the kinds of lives they themselves will lead in their mature years, that is, poor exemplars for what they should and should not be. Or perhaps it would be more accurate to say, not that their parents are poor models (for a poor model is still a model of what not to be), but that parents are increasingly irrelevant as models for their children. Many young people are at a real loss as to what they should seek to become: no valid models exist for the as-yet-to-be-imagined world in which they will live. Not surprisingly, their very sanity and realism sometimes leads them to be disaffected from the values of their elders.

Another salient fact about young people today is their relative *lack of rebelliousness* against their parents or their parents' generation. Given their unwillingness to make commitments to the "adult world" in general, their lack of rebellion seems surprising, for we are accustomed to think that if a young man does not accept his parents' values, he must be actively rejecting them. And when the generations face similar life situations, emulation and rejection are indeed the two main possibilities. But rebellion, after all, presupposes that the target of one's hostility is an active threat: in classical stories of filial rebellion, the son is in real danger of being forced to become like his father, and he rebels rather than accept this definition of himself. But when a young man simply sees no possibility of becoming like his parents, then their world is so remote that it neither tempts nor threatens him. Indeed, many a youth is so distant from his parents, in generational terms if not in affection, that he can afford to "understand" them, and often to show a touching sympathy for their hesitant efforts to guide and advise him. Parents, too, often sense that they appear dated or "square" to their children; and this knowledge makes them the more unwilling to try to impose their own values or preferences. The result is frequently an unstated "gentleman's agreement" between the generations that neither will interfere with the other. This understanding acknowledges a real fact of existence today; but just as often, it creates new problems.

One of these problems appears very vividly in the *absence of paternal exemplars* in many contemporary plays, novels, and films. One of the characteristic facts about most of our modern heroes is that they have no fathers— or, when they do have fathers, these are portrayed as inadequate or in some other way as psychologically absent. Take Augie March or Holden Caulfield, take the heroes of Arthur Miller's and Tennessee Williams' plays, or consider the leading character in a film like *Rebel Without A Cause*. None of them has a father who can act as a model or for that matter as a target of overt rebellion. The same is true, though less dramatically, for a great many young people today. One sometimes even hears students in private conversations deplore the tolerance and permissiveness of their exemplary parents: "If only, just once, they would tell me what *they* think I should do." Young people want and need models and guardians of their development; and they usually feel cheated if they are not available. The gentleman's agreement seldom works.

It would be wrong, however, to infer that parents have suddenly become incompetent. On the contrary, most American parents are genuinely interested in their children, they try hard to understand and sympathize with them, they continually think and worry about how to guide their development. In other, more stable times, these same parents would have been excellent models for their children, nourishing their growth while recognizing their individuality. But today they often leave their children with a feeling of never really having had parents, of being somehow cheated of their birthright. The explanation is not hard to find; even the most well-intentioned parent cannot now hope to be a complete exemplar for his children's future. A man born in the 1910's or 1920's and formed during the depression already finds himself in a world that was inconceivable then; his children will live in a world still more inconceivable. It would be unrealistic to hope that they would model their lives on his.

Another aspect of the psychology of rapid change is the *widespread feeling of powerlessness*—social, political, and personal—of many young people today. In the 1930's, there was a vocal minority which believed that society should and, most important, *could* be radically transformed; and there were more who were at least convinced that their efforts mattered and might make a difference in politics and the organization of society. Today the feeling of powerlessness extends even beyond matters of political and social interest; many young people see themselves as unable to influence any but the most personal spheres of their lives. The world is seen as fluid and chaotic, individuals as victims of impersonal forces which they can seldom understand and never control. Students, for example, tend not only to have a highly negative view of the work of the average American adult, seeing it as sterile, empty, and unrewarding, but to feel themselves caught up in a system which they can neither change nor escape. They are pessimistic about their own chances of affecting or altering the great corporations, bureaucracies, and academies for which most of them will work, and equally pessimistic about the possibility of finding work outside the system that might be more meaningful.

Such feelings of powerlessness of course tend to be self-fulfilling. The young man who believes himself incapable of finding a job outside the bureaucratic system and, once in a job, unable to shape it so that it becomes more meaningful will usually end up exactly where he fears to be—in a meaningless job. Or, a generation which believes that it cannot influence social development will, by its consequent lack of involvement with social issues, in fact end up powerless before other forces, personal or impersonal, which *can* affect social change. In a generation as in individuals, the conviction of powerlessness begets the fact of powerlessness.[11] But, however incorrect, this conviction is easy to comprehend. The world has always been amazingly complex, and with our widening understanding comes a sometimes paralyzing awareness of its complexity. Furthermore, when one's vantage point is continually shifting, when the future is in fact more changeable than ever before, when the past can provide all too few hints as to how to lead a meaningful life in a shifting society— then it is very difficult to sustain a conviction that one can master the environment.

The most common response to this feeling of helplessness is what David Riesman has called *privatism*. Younger people increasingly emphasize and value precisely those areas of their lives which are least involved in the wider society, and which, therefore, seem most manageable and controllable. Young men and women today want large families, they are prepared to work hard to make them good families, they often value family closeness above meaningful work, many expect that family life will be the most important aspect of their lives. Within one's own family one seems able to control the present and, within limits, to shape the future. Leisure, too, is far more under the individual's personal control than his public life is; a man may feel obliged to do empty work to earn a living, but he can spend his leisure as he likes. Many young people expect to find in leisure a measure of stability, enjoyment, and control which they would otherwise lack. Hence their emphasis on assuring leisure time, on spending their leisure to good advantage, on getting jobs with long vacations, and on living in areas where leisure can be well enjoyed. Indeed, some anticipate working at their leisure with a dedication that will be totally lacking in their work itself. In leisure, as in the family, young people hope to find some of the predictability and control that seem to them so absent in the wider society.

---

11 It is ironic that this generation, which is better prepared than any before it, which knows more about itself and the world and is thus in a better position to find those points of leverage from which things can be changed, should feel unable to shape its own destiny in any public respect.

Closely related to the emphasis on the private spheres of life is the *foreshortening of time span*. Long-range endeavors and commitments seem increasingly problematical, for even if one could be sure there will be no world holocaust, the future direction of society seems almost equally uncertain. Similarly, as the past becomes more remote, in psychological terms if not in actual chronology, there is a greater tendency to disregard it altogether. The extreme form of this trend is found in the "beat" emphasis on present satisfactions, with an almost total refusal to consider future consequences or past commitments. Here the future and the past disappear completely, and the greatest possible intensification of the present is sought. In less psychopathic form, the same emphasis on pursuits which can be realized in the present for their own sake and not for some future reward is found in many young people. The promise of continuing inflation makes the concept of a nest egg obsolete, the guarantee of changing job markets makes commitment to a specialized skill problematical, the possibility of a war, if seriously entertained, makes all future planning ridiculous. The consequence is that only the rare young man has life goals that extend more than five or ten years ahead; most can see only as far as graduate school, and many simply drift into, rather than choose, their future careers. The long-range goals, postponed satisfactions, and indefinitely deferred rewards of the Protestant Ethic are being replaced by an often reluctant hedonism of the moment.

A corollary of the emphasis on the private and the present is the *decline in political involvement* among college youth. To be sure, American students have never evinced the intense political concerns of their Continental contemporaries, and admittedly, there are exceptions, especially in the "direct-action" movements centered around desegregation. But the general pattern of political disengagement remains relatively unchanged, or if anything has become more marked. Those familiar with elite college students in the 1930's and in the late 1950's contrast the political activity of a noisy minority then with the general apathy now before world problems of greater magnitude. Instead of political action, we have a burgeoning of the arts on many campuses, with hundreds of plays, operas, poems, and short stories produced annually by college students. Underlying this preference of aesthetic to political commitment are many of the outlooks I have mentioned: the feeling of public powerlessness, the emphasis on the private and immediate aspects of life, the feeling of disengagement from the values of the parental generation. But most important is the real anxiety that overtakes many thoughtful young people when they contemplate their own helplessness in the face of social and historical forces which may be taking the world to destruction. It is perhaps significant that Harvard students began rioting about Latin diplomas the evening of a relatively underattended rally to protest American intervention in Cuba, a protest to which most students would have subscribed. So high a level of anxiety is generated by any discussion of complex international relations, the possibilities of nuclear war, or even the complicated issues of American domestic policies, that all but the extraordinarily honest or the extraordinarily masochistic prefer to release their tensions in other ways than in political activity. And in this disinvolvement they are of course supported by the traditional American myth of youth, which makes it a time for panty raids but not for politics.

In general, then, many college students have a kind of *cult of experience,* which stresses, in the words of one student, "the maximum possible number of sense experiences." Part of the fascination which the beat generation holds for college students lies in its quest for "kicks," for an intensification of present, private experiences without reference to other people, to social norms, to the past or the future. Few college students go this far, even in the small group that dresses "beat," rides motorcycles, and supports the espresso bars; for most, experience is sought in ways less asocial than sex, speed, and stimulants. But travel, artistic and expressive experience, the enjoyment of nature, the privacy of erotic love, or the company of friends occupy a similar place in the hierarchy of values. Parallel with this goes the search for self within the self rather than in society, activity or commitment, and a belief that truth can be uncovered by burrowing within the psyche. The experience sought is private, even solipsistic; it involves an indifference to the beckonings of the wider society.

To be sure, Teddy Roosevelt, too, was in his way a seeker after experience; but unlike most contemporary American youths, he sought it in frantic extroversion, in bravado and heroic action; and its rewards were eventual public acclaim. But for most college students today, T.R. and the values of his era have become merely comic.

Youth culture and identity

Many of these outlooks of youth can be summed up as a sophisticated version of the almost unique American phenomenon of the "youth culture," [12] that is, the special culture of those who are between childhood and adulthood, a culture which differs from both that of the child and that of the adult. To understand the youth culture, we must consider not only the increasing gap between the generations but the discontinuity between childhood and adulthood. [13] Generational discontinuities are gaps in time, between one *mature* generation and the next; but age group discontinuities are gaps between different age groups at the *same* time. The transition from childhood to adulthood is never, in any society, completely continuous; but in some societies like our own there are radical discontinuities between the culturally given definitions of the child and of the adult. The child is seen as irresponsible, the adult responsible; the child is dependent, the adult is independent; the child is supposedly unsexual, the adult is interested in sex; the child plays, the adult works, etc. In societies where these age-group discontinuities are sharpest, there is usually some form of initiation rite to guarantee that everyone grows up, that the transition be clearly marked, and that there be no backsliding to childish ways.

But in our society we lack formalized rites of initiation into adulthood; the wan vestiges of such rites, like bar mitzvah, confirmation, or graduation day exercises, have lost most of their former significance. Instead, we have a youth culture, not so obviously transitional, but more like a waiting period, in which the youth is ostensibly preparing himself for adult responsibilities, but in which to adults he often seems to be armoring himself against them. Of course, the years of the youth culture are usually spent in acquiring an education, in high school, college, vocational or professional training. But it would be wrong to think of the youth culture as merely an apprenticeship, a way of teaching the young the technical skills of adulthood. For the essence of the youth culture is that it is not a rational transitional period—were it one, it would simply combine the values of both childhood and adulthood. Instead, it has roles, values, and ways of behaving all its own; it emphasizes disengagement from adult values, sexual attractiveness, daring, immediate pleasure, and comradeship in a way that is true neither of childhood nor of adulthood. The youth culture is not always or explicitly anti-adult, but it is belligerently *non*-adult. The rock'n' roller, the Joe College student, the juvenile delinquent, and the beatnik, whatever their important differences, all form part of this general youth culture.

To understand this subculture we must consider its relation to both the discontinuities between age groups and the discontinuities between generations. I have noted that young people frequently view the more public aspects of adult life as empty, meaningless, a rat race, a futile treadmill; only in private areas can meaning and warmth be found. Childhood contrasts sharply with this image: childhood is seen as (and often really is) a time for the full employment of one's talents and interest, a time when work, love, and play are integrally related, when imagination is given free play, and life has spontaneity, freedom, and warmth. Adulthood obviously suffers by comparison, and it is understandable that those who are being rushed to maturity should drag their feet if this is what they foresee. The youth culture provides a kind of way-station, a temporary stopover in which one can muster strength for the next harrowing stage of the trip. And for many, the youth culture is not merely one of the stops, but the last stop they will really enjoy or feel commitment to. Thus, the youth culture is partially a consequence of the discontinuity of age groups, an expression of the

---

[12] Talcott Parsons, "Age and sex grading in the United States," reprinted in Parsons, *Essays in sociological theory, pure and applied* (Glencoe, Illinois: The Free Press, 1949). The beginnings of a youth culture are appearing in other highly industrialized countries, which suggests that this institution is characteristic of a high degree of industrialization.

[13] Ruth Benedict, "Continuities and discontinuities in cultural conditioning." In Clyde Kluckhohn and Henry A. Murray (Eds.), *Personality in nature, society, and culture,* New York: Norton, 1948.

reluctance of many young men and women to face the unknown perils of adulthood.

But the gap between childhood and adulthood will not explain why in our society at present the youth culture is becoming more and more important, why it involves a greater and greater part of young men and women's lives, or why it seems so tempting, compared with adulthood, that some young people increasingly refuse to make the transition at all. Rock'n'roll, for example, is probably the first music that has appealed almost exclusively to the youth culture; catering to the teenage market has become one of the nation's major industries. And, as Riesman has noted, the very word "teenager" has few of the connotations of transition and growing up of words like "youth" and "adolescent," which "teenager" is gradually replacing.[14]

The youth culture not only expresses youth's unwillingness to grow up, but serves a more positive function in resolving generational discontinuities. Erik H. Erikson would characterize our youth culture as a psychosocial moratorium on adulthood, which provides young people with an opportunity to develop their identity as adults.[15] One of the main psychological functions of a sense of identity is to provide a sense of inner self-sameness and continuity, to bind together the past, the present, and the future into a coherent whole; and the first task of adolescence and early adulthood is the achievement of identity. The word "achieve" is crucial here, for identity is not simply given by the society in which the adolescent lives; in many cases and in varying degrees, he must make his own unique synthesis of the often incompatible models, identifications, and ideals offered by society. The more incompatible the components from which the sense of identity must be built and the more uncertain the future for which one attempts to achieve identity, the more difficult the task becomes. If growing up were merely a matter of becoming "socialized," that is, of learning how to "fit into" society, it is hard to see how anyone could grow up at all in modern America, for the society into which young people will some day "fit" remains to be developed or even imagined. Oversimplifying, we might say that socialization is the main problem in a society where there are known and stable roles for children to fit into; but

in a rapidly changing society like ours, identity formation increasingly replaces socialization in importance.

Even the achievement of identity, however, becomes more difficult in a time of rapid change. For, recall that one of the chief tasks of identity formation is the creation of a sense of self that will link the past, the present, and the future. When the generational past becomes ever more distant, and when the future is more and more unpredictable, such continuity requires more work, more creative effort. Furthermore, as Erikson emphasizes, another of the chief tasks of identity formation is the development of an "ideology," that is, of a philosophy of life, a basic outlook on the world which can orient one's actions in adult life. In a time of rapid ideological change, it seldom suffices for a young man or woman simply to accept some ideology from the past. The task is more difficult; it involves selecting from many ideologies those essential elements which are most relevant and most enduring. Such an achievement takes time, and sometimes the longest time for the most talented, who usually take the job most seriously.

The youth culture, then, provides not only an opportunity to postpone adulthood, but also a more positive chance to develop a sense of identity which will resolve the discontinuity between childhood and adulthood on the one hand, and bridge the gap between the generations on the other. Of course, a few young men and women attempt to find an alternative to identity in other-direction. Unable to discover or create any solid internal basis for their lives, they become hyperadaptable; they develop extraordinary sensitivity to the wishes and expectations of others; in a real sense, they let themselves be defined by the demands of their environment. Thus, they are safe from disappointment, for having made no bets on the future at all, they never have put their money on the wrong horse. But this alternative is an evasion, not a solution, of the problem of identity. The other-directed man is left internally empty; he has settled for playing the

---

[14] David Riesman, "Where is the college generation headed?" Harper's Magazine, April 1961.
[15] Erik H. Erikson, "The problem of ego identity," in Identity and the life cycle, published as Vol. I, No. 1 of Psychol. Issues (1959). See also his "Youth: Fidelity and diversity," in this issue.

roles that others demand of him. And role-playing does not satisfy or fulfill; letting the environment call the shots means having nothing of one's own. Most young people see this very clearly, and only a few are tempted to give up the struggle.

There is another small group, the so-called beats and their close fellow-travelers, who choose the other alternative, to opt out of the "system" altogether and to try to remain permanently within the youth culture. In so doing, some young people are able to create for themselves a world of immediate, private and simple enjoyment. But leaving the "system" also has its problems. The search for self which runs through the youth culture and the beat world is not the whole of life, and to continue it indefinitely means usually renouncing attainments which have been traditionally part of the definition of a man or a woman: intimacy and love for others; personal creativity in work, ideas, and children; and that fullness and roundedness of life which is ideally the reward of old age. So, though many young people are tempted and fascinated by the beat alternative, few actually choose it.

The vast majority of young people today accept neither the other-directed nor the beat evasion of the problem of identity. In many ways uncommitted to the public aspects of adult life, they are willing nonetheless to go through the motions without complete commitment. They have a kind of "double consciousness," one part oriented to the adult world which they will soon enter, the other part geared to their version of the youth culture. They are not rebellious (in fact they like their parents), but they feel estranged and distant from what their elders represent. They often wish they could model themselves after (or against) what their parents stand for, but they are sensible enough to see that older people are often genuinely confused themselves. They feel relatively powerless to control or to influence the personal world around them, but they try to make up for this feeling by emphasizing those private aspects of life in which some measure of predictability and warmth can be made to obtain. They often take enthusiastic part in the youth culture, but most of them are nonetheless attempting to "graduate" into adulthood. And though many hesitate on the threshold of adulthood, they do so not

simply from antagonism or fear, but often from awareness that they have yet to develop a viable identity which will provide continuity both within their lives and between their own, their parents', and their future children's generations. And in each of these complex and ambivalent reactions young people are in part responding to the very process of unrestrained change in which they, like all of us, are involved.

Evaluations and prospects

In these comments so far I have emphasized those attitudes which seem most directly related to the stresses of unrestrained change, neglecting other causal factors and painting a somewhat dark picture. I have done this partly because the more sanguine view of youth—which stresses the emancipations, the sociological understandability of youth's behavior, the stability of our society despite unprecedented changes, and the "adaptive" nature of youth's behavior—this more encouraging view has already been well presented.[16] But furthermore, if we shift from a sociological to a psychological perspective and ask how young people themselves experience growing up in this changing society, a less hopeful picture emerges. Rightly or wrongly, many young people experience emancipations as alienations; they find their many freedoms burdensome without criteria by which to choose among equally attractive alternatives; they resent being "understood" either sociologically or psychologically; and they often find the impressive stability of our society either oppressive or uninteresting. Furthermore, what may constitute an "adaptation" from one sociological point of view (e.g., the American Indian's regression in the face of American core culture) may be not only painful to the individual but disastrous to the society in the long run. A sociological and a psychological account of youth thus give different though perhaps complementary pictures, and lead to different evaluations of the outlook of American youth. Despite the stability of American society and the undeniable surfeit of opportunities and freedoms available to young people today,

---

[16] Talcott Parsons, "Youth in the context of American society," in this issue.

many of youth's attitudes seem to me to offer little ground for optimism.

The drift of American youth, I have argued, is away from public involvements and social responsibilities and toward a world of private and personal satisfactions. Almost all young people will eventually be *in* the system—that is, they will occupy occupational and other roles within the social structure—but a relatively large number of them will never be *for* the system. Like the stereotypical Madison Avenue ad-man who works to make money so that he can nourish his private (and forever unrealized) dream of writing a novel, their work and their participation in public life will always have a somewhat half-hearted quality, for their enthusiasms will be elsewhere—with the family, the home workshop, the forthcoming vacation, or the unpainted paintings. Their vision and their consciousness will be split, with one eye on the main chance and the other eye (the better one) on some private utopia. This will make them good organizational workers, who labor with detachment and correctness but without the intensity or involvement which might upset bureaucratic applecarts. And they will assure a highly stable political and social order, for few of them will be enough committed to politics to consider revolution, subversion, or even radical change. This orientation also has much to commend it to the individual: the private and immediate is indeed that sphere subject to the greatest personal control, and great satisfaction can be found in it. The "rich full life" has many virtues, especially when contrasted with the puritanical and future-oriented acquisitiveness of earlier American generations. And I doubt if commitment and "fidelity" will disappear; rather, they will simply be transferred to the aesthetic, the sensual, and the experiential, a transfer which would bode well for the future of the arts.

Yet the difficulties in this split consciousness seem to me overwhelming, both for the individual and for the society. For one, few individuals can successfully maintain such an outlook. The man who spends his working day at a job whose primary meaning is merely to earn enough money to enable him to enjoy the rest of his time can seldom really enjoy his leisure, his family, or his avocations. Life is of a piece, and if work is empty or routine, the rest will inevitably become contaminated as well, becoming a compulsive escape or a driven effort to compensate for the absent satisfactions that should inhere in work. Similarly, to try to avoid social and political problems by cultivating one's garden can at best be only partly successful. When the effects of government and society are so ubiquitous, one can escape them only in the backwaters, and then only for a short while. Putting work, society, and politics into one pigeonhole, and family, leisure, and enjoyment into another creates a compartmentalization which is in continual danger of collapsing. Or, put more precisely, such a division of life into nonoverlapping spheres merely creates a new psychological strain, the almost impossible strain of artificially maintaining a continually split outlook.

Also on the demerit side, psychologically, is the willful limitation of vision which privatism involves, the motivated denial of the reality or importance of the nonprivate world. Given the unabating impact of social forces on every individual, to pretend that these do not exist (or that, if they do exist, have no effect on one) qualifies as a gross distortion of reality. Such blindness is of course understandable: given the anxiety one must inevitably feel before a volatile world situation, coupled with the felt inability to affect world events, blinders seem in the short run the best way to avoid constant uneasiness. Or similarly, given the widespread belief that work is simply a way of earning a living, refusal to admit the real importance to one's psychic life of the way one spends one's working days may be a kind of pseudo-solution. But a pseudo-solution it is, for the ability to acknowledge unpleasant reality and live with the attendant anxiety is one of the criteria of psychological health. From a psychological point of view, alienation and privatism can hardly be considered ideal responses to social change.

From a social point of view, the long-range limitations of these "adaptations" seem equally great. Indeed, it may be that, through withdrawal from concern with the general shape of society, we obtain short-run social stability at the price of long-run stagnation and inability to adapt. Young people, by exaggerating their own powerlessness, see the "system," whether at work, in politics, or in international affairs, as far more inexorable and unmalleable than it really is. Consider, for example, the attitude of most American youth (and most older people as well) toward efforts to direct or restrain the effects of social change. Partly by a false equation of Stalinism with social planning, partly on the assumption that unrestrained social change is "natural," and partly from a conviction that social planning is in any case impossible, young people usually declare their lack of interest. Apart from the incorrectness of such beliefs, their difficulty is that they tend to be self-confirming in practice. Given a generation with such assumptions, social changes will inevitably continue to occur in their present haphazard and unguided way, often regardless of the needs of the public. Or again, it seems likely that if any considerable proportion of American students were to demand that their future work be personally challenging and socially useful, they would be able to create or find such work and would revolutionize the quality of work for their fellows in the process. But few make such demands. Or, most ominous of all, if the future leaders of public opinion decide that they can leave the planning of foreign policy to weapons experts and military specialists, there is an all too great chance that the tough-minded "realism" of the experts will remain unmitigated by the public's wish to survive.

In short, an alienated generation seems too great a luxury in the 1960's. To cultivate one's garden is a stance most appropriate to times of peace and calm, and least apposite to an era of desperate international crisis. It would be a happier world than this in which men could devote themselves to personal allegiances and private utopias. But it is not this world. International problems alone are so pressing that for any proportion of the ablest college students to take an apolitical stance seems almost suicidal. And even if world problems were less horrendous, there is a great deal to be done in our own society, which to many, young and old, still seems corrupt, unjust, ugly, and inhuman. But to the extent that the younger generation loses interest in these public tasks, remaining content with private virtue, the public tasks will remain undone. Only a utopia can afford alienation.

In so far as alienation and privatism are dominant responses of the current college generation to the stresses of unrestrained change, the prospects are not bright. But for several reasons, I think this prognosis needs qualification. For one, I have obviously omitted the many exceptions to the picture I have sketched—the young men and women who have the courage to confront the problems of their society and the world, who have achieved a sense of identity which enables them to remain involved in and committed to the solution of these problems. Furthermore, for most students alienation is a kind of *faute de mieux* response, which they would readily abandon, could they find styles of life more deserving of allegiance. Indeed, I think most thoughtful students agree with my strictures against privatism, and accept withdrawal only as a last resort when other options have failed. But, most important, I have omitted from my account so far any discussion of those forces which do or might provide a greater sense of continuity, despite rapid change. Discussion of these forces may correct this perhaps unnecessarily discouraged picture.

Throughout this account, I have suggested that Americans are unwilling to plan, guide, restrain, or coordinate social change for the public good. While this is true when America is compared with other industrialized nations, it is less true than in the past, and there are signs that many Americans are increasingly skeptical of the notion that unrestrained change is somehow more "free" or more "natural" than social planning. We may be beginning to realize that the decision not to plan social changes is really a decision to allow forces and pressures other than the public interest to plot the course of change. For example, it is surely not more natural to allow our cities to be overrun and destroyed by the technological requirements of automobiles than to ask whether humane and social considerations might not require the banning or limiting of cars in major cities. Or to allow television and radio programming to be controlled by the decisions of sponsors and networks seems to many less "free" than to control them by public agencies. If we are prepared to guide and limit the course of social change, giving a push here and a pull there when the "natural" changes in our society conflict with the needs of the public, then the future may be a less uncertain prospect for our children.

Indeed, if but a small proportion of the energy we now spend in trying to second-guess the future were channelled into efforts to shape it, we and our children might have an easier task in discovering how to make sense in, and of, our changing society.

I have also neglected the role that an understanding of their situation might play for the younger generation. Here I obviously do not mean that students should be moralistically lectured about the need for social responsibility and the perversity of withdrawal into private life. Such sermonizing would clearly have the opposite effect, if only because most young people are already perfectly willing to abandon privatism if they can find something better. But I do mean that thoughtful students should be encouraged to understand the meaning and importance of their own stage in life and of the problems which affect them as a generation. The emphasis on individual psychological understanding which characterizes many "progressive" colleges can provide only a part of the needed insight. The rest must come from an effort to end the pluralistic ignorance of the stresses confronting all members of the current younger generation. Here colleges do far too little, for courses dealing with the broad social pressures that impinge on the individual often deliberately attempt to prevent that personal involvement which alone gives insight. But one can imagine that a concrete understanding of the psychosocial forces that affect a generation might have some of the same therapeutic effects on the more reflective members of the generation that insight into psychodynamic forces can give the thoughtful individual.

And finally, I have underplayed the importance the values and principles can and do play in providing continuity amid rapid change. If one is convinced that there are guiding principles which will remain constant—and if one can find these enduring values—life can be meaningful and livable despite rapid change. But here we need to proceed cautiously. Technologies, institutions, ideologies, and people—all react by extremes when faced with the fear of obsolescence. Either they firmly insist that *nothing* has changed and that they are as integrally valid as ever before or—and this is equally disastrous—they become so eager to abandon the outmoded that they abandon essential principles along with the irrelevant. Thus, parents who dimly fear that they may appear "square" to their children can react either by a complete refusal to admit that anything has changed since their early days or (more often) by suppressing any expression of moral concern. The second alternative seems to me the more prevalent and dangerous. An antiquated outlook is usually simply ignored by the young. But person or institution that abandons its essential principles indirectly communicates that there are no principles which can withstand the test of time, and thus makes the task of the young more difficult.

Yet the bases for the continuity of the generations must of necessity shift. Parents can no longer hope to be literal models for their children; institutions cannot hope to persist without change in rite, practice, and custom. And, although many of the essential principles of parents, elders, and traditional institutions can persist, even those who seek to maintain the continuity of a tradition must, paradoxically, assume a creative and innovating role. We need not only a rediscovery of the vital ideals of the past, but a willingness to create new ideals—new values, new myths, and new utopias—which will help us to adapt creatively to a world undergoing continual and sweeping transformations. It is for such ideals that young people are searching: they need foundations for their lives which will link them to their personal and communal pasts and to their present society but which at the same time will provide a trustworthy basis for their futures. The total emulation or total rejection of the older generation by the young must be replaced by a re-creation in each generation of the living and relevant aspects of the past, and by the creation of new images of life which will provide points of constancy in a time of rapid change.

Personal identity and sexual identity [1]

MABEL BLAKE COHEN

Mabel Blake Cohen, Ph.D., M.D., a former editor of *Psychiatry,* is a Training Analyst of the Washington Psychoanalytic Institute and is engaged in the private practice of psychoanalysis. In this article, Dr. Cohen describes the differences between personal identity and sexual identity. Using research on pregnant mothers as a basis for her analysis, Dr. Cohen cites specific case histories to illustrate some of the consequences which can arise from the failure to develop and integrate both types of identity. The article traces the origins of sexual identity and challenges the validity of society's traditional definition of masculine and feminine roles.

It sometimes seems to me that the roles of both male and female, as popularly defined in our culture, are impossible to play. There are a number of catchwords applied—for instance, courage, strength, activity, leadership to the male; or receptivity, passivity, nurturance, giving, to the female. When one strives to contemplate the task of being always, or almost always, brave, one becomes rebellious and weary with its naïveté. Who would claim that his doubts and fears detracted in any way from Adlai Stevenson's masculinity? Yet a boy of fourteen, if asked to confess his fear of anything or anybody, would equate it in his mind and feelings with that terrible thing—being a sissy. Similarly, a woman of complete receptivity or passivity would be not only a startling phenomenon, but also an unpleasing one to contemplate. It may amuse you to have me take these crude stereotypes seriously, yet I hope to show how important they are as influences on the development of our children, and how they linger in the background of the adult's mind, influencing the members of the next generation as they in turn become parents.

Alongside the widely-held notion of some essence of masculinity and femininity exists the startling belief among many of us that most of the neurotic illness in our population is mother-generated. Such a potency attributed to the mother can only amaze one when put alongside the theory of the female as the weaker vessel. It arouses questions as to the whereabouts of the other parent, and about the depths of dependency on a mother image generated by our philosophy of child-rearing. The psychoanalytic theories of infant and early childhood development have certainly played an influential part in introducing a sense of guilty responsibility into the transactions between mother and child, which goes far toward undermining the spontaneity of their relationship. The more recent efforts to look at the family as an organic unit should in the long run help us to a better balance in our scientific approach. But how long will it take for

[1] The Ninth Annual Frieda Fromm-Reichmann Memorial Lecture, given on November 19, 1965, at the Clinical Center, National Institute of Health, Bethesda, Maryland, under the auspices of the Washington School of Psychiatry.

Much of the material on pregnancy presented in this article was gathered by a research group consisting, in addition to the author, of John M. Fearing, M.D., Robert G. Kvarnes, M.D., Edward M. Ohaneson, M.D., Edith Weigert, M.D., and Naomi K. Wenner, M.D., assisted by Sara Saltzman, Ph.D., and Joseph Margolin, Ph.D., psychologists. I am grateful to them for permission to use their work.

such efforts to affect the folklore of masculinity and femininity, their powers and their duties, their deeds and their misdeeds?

My use of the term *identity* in this paper needs some clarification. The term was popularized in psychoanalytic circles by Erikson, who found it useful in describing the social development of the person from child to adult.[2] He saw the developing child as moving through a series of self-concepts and developmental crises. At each level the self-concept differs from the previous one, and the critical issues which must be solved also change with time. In this sense, the person could be seen as passing through a series of identities, as in libidinal terms he is seen as passing through a series of libidinal stages. Erikson emphasized a point which Sullivan had made decades earlier—namely, that the essentials of development are not completed, as previously supposed, by the end of the childhood Oedipal period.[3] Sullivan had stressed the importance of preadolescent and adolescent experiences. Erikson focused a good deal of attention on the adolescent era, with its particular threats to identity as the personality struggles for independence from old authorities. Maturity, with the establishment of adult sexuality, a career, a home, a family, represents the next crisis in development, and is the one on which I shall focus.

What, exactly, is meant by the term identity? This is a rather difficult question to answer, partly because it is a loose term and partly because it has come to be used, like aspirin, for everything. It is an outgrowth in psychoanalysis of the interest in ego psychology which was initiated by Hartmann's essay, *Ego Psychology and the Problem of Adaptation,* published in 1939. Hartmann said that

. . . a concept of health which is conceived solely as the negative of neurosis and disregards the state of conflict-free sphere (of the ego) is too narrow, if only because without taking this sphere into account, the concepts of ego-strength, rank order, and equilibrium cannot be satisfactorily delineated. Another reason why some theoretical concepts of health are too narrow is that they usually underestimate the great variety of personality types which must, practically speaking, be considered healthy and the many personality types which are socially necessary.[4]

In other words, Hartmann viewed the ego as an active element in the personality, with positive, adaptive functions as well as the more negative, defensive ones previously described. Rappaport[5] and later Gill[6] have continued to discuss, describe, and attempt to define the functions of the ego with particular interest in its synthetic and active elements. From the structural point of view, the task of maturation can be thought of as the building of psychic structures which represent a composite of instinctual drive, defense, reappearance of drive in an altered, hopefully more mature form, and so on. Gill has recently reminded us that ego and id represent a continuum, that which is called the id being the more primitive levels of structure and the ego the more complex ones.[7]

Identity, then, could be thought of as an ego-id-superego complex or continuum, or as the personality-as-a-whole. However, Erikson's more useful contribution, it seems to me, comes from looking at it in social or behavioral terms, and that is the way I shall use it. It could be thought of as the self as it is experienced and as it functions in life situations. It would, then, include conscious motivations and also the less conscious identifications, drives, and defenses which give it some of its individual coloring. It would be formed by the interaction of heredity, constitution, and experience, over time. This view gives a great deal of weight to learning experiences throughout the life cycle in influencing behavior and improving adaptation.

It seems to me no coincidence that this concept has come into popularity at the same time that psychoanalysis has been moving out of the consulting room and into the community by way of both the vast increase in the number of those exposed to psychoanalytic concepts and also the greater activity of

[2] Erik Erikson, *Childhood and society,* New York: Norton, 1950.
[3] Harry Stack Sullivan, *Conceptions of modern psychiatry,* New York: Norton, 1953.
[4] Heinz Hartmann, *Ego psychology and the problem of adaptation,* New York: Internat. Univ. Press, 1958, p. 81.
[5] David Rappaport, "The structure of psychoanalytic theory: A systematizing attempt," *Psychol. Issues,* Vol. 2, No. 2, New York: Internat. Univ. Press, 1960.
[6] Merton M. Gill, "Topography and systems in psychoanalytic theory," *Psychol. Issues,* Vol. 3, No. 2, New York: Internat. Univ. Press, 1963.
[7] See footnote 6, p. 164.

analysts themselves in tackling the problems of society. One of the tasks of community psychiatry, as it works toward goals of social change, is to develop knowledge about what constitutes learning experiences for either groups or individuals, for it is clearly true that experiences themselves are not necessarily contributory to learning, no matter how good they are. Here, too, questions regarding identity come to have a significant bearing upon whether an experience is going to have a learning effect or not.

My thesis in this paper is that there is a considerable incompatibility between many people's sense of identity as persons and as sexual beings, or, to put it another way, between society's traditional definition of the persons's sexual role and the optimal development of his assets as a person.

There is, at present, and has been for the past generation or so, a great deal of confusion about principles of child-rearing. Philosophies and approaches have ranged from extremes of permissiveness to various kinds of limit-setting, as far as discipline is concerned. Attitudes toward the sexual aspects of the child's development have also varied, especially in regard to girls, where there has been a range from completely egalitarian treatment to attempts to redefine femininity in terms of the requirements of modern life. As children grow up, they almost seem to have two identities, the sexual one and the personal one. Since the indoctrination as to sexual role comes earliest, beginning in the very first days of life, it tends to color, and at times to overwhelm, the later development of social skills and intellectual capacities. I shall hope to show, by quoting from observations of early infancy and from longitudinal studies of child development, how some of the various influences on development manifest themselves. Then I shall turn to a current study of pregnancy for material on some of the results of these various developmental influences on adults who are now mothers and fathers.

First, I should like to consider the contrasts between the traditional definitions of masculinity and femininity, on the one hand, and actual adult male or female functioning, on the other. Kagan and Moss, in their recent report of a longitudinal study of children's development,[8] define the traditional masculine model as active sexually, athletic, independent, dominant, courageous, and competitive. His choice of career is not highly intellectual, but is more likely to be that of salesman, businessman, athletic coach, or the like. The feminine model is passive and dependent, showing both sexual timidity and social anxiety, fearing and avoiding problem situations, and pursuing homemaking activities rather than career ones. The actuality of these concepts as models for development of many children in our culture is supported by a number of studies of children's attitudes toward the sexes. For instance, Bandura, Ross, and Ross noted in testing children's tendency to imitate adults that the boys normally regarded the male figure as the source of power and the female figure more as the distributor, regardless of the actual power structure of the experimental situation.[9] And Ruth Hartley's studies of children's concepts of male and female roles showed that the shifts in feminine behavior in our society in recent years have not yet affected these concepts.[10]

The traditional concepts of masculinity and femininity undergo many vicissitudes, of course. From the beginning there is constant pressure on the boy to be active, athletic, and competitive; however, in school, and especially in the high-school years, the pressures to develop intellectually, to go to college, and to prepare for a career become more insistent and tend to replace the high valuation of physical activity. But adolescence is also the courtship period, and in this area the older traditions continue to take first place. With the girl, there is considerable indulgence of tomboy behavior up until puberty. After that time, the pressures for traditional femininity, prettiness, ladylike behavior, and apparent passivity in courtship become very strong. Attitudes toward intellectual development in the girl are more ambivalent; in some families intellectual achievements are highly regarded, while in others they are either disapproved or

[8] Jerome Kagan and Howard A. Moss, *Birth to maturity: A study in psychological development*, New York: Wiley, 1962.
[9] Albert Bandura, Dorothea Ross, and Sheila A. Ross, "A comparative test of the status, envy, social power, and secondary reinforcement theories of identificatory learning," *J. abnorm. soc. Psychol.*, 1963, 67:527-534.
[10] Ruth Hartley, "Children's concepts of male and female roles," *Merrill-Palmer Quart.*, 1960, 6:83-91.

regarded with neutrality. Probably the stereotypes reach their peak in intensity of impact during adolescence and from then on become ameliorated by the necessities of education, careers, and marriage.

It is not until after marriage and the establishment of a family that the carrying out of male and female functions has a weighty impact on behavior. Until the children come, the man and wife can be very much alike, both working, both playing at homemaking, both saving toward the purchase of a home and furniture, and so on. It is only with the conception, gestation, and birth of the baby that a decisive division of labor must occur. Now the man becomes in reality the support of the family, and concomitant with this comes an increased feeling of responsibility. The woman, under the ordinary circumstances of raising her children herself, now must withdraw from her career activities, or at least relegate them to second place. She and her child have to become the supported, and hence she must assume a relatively passive and receptive position in relation to her husband in such important areas as money matters, career interests, and coming and going. She also needs to accept the giving or service role in the family, in such matters as baby-tending, meal-supplying, and so forth. Now the stereotypes of childhood and adolescence must give way before the realities of everyday adult life, in which neither the masculine nor the feminine one has a chance of success. This brave, strong, dominant male is expected to get up at night with a colicky infant, and this passive, helpless, and dependent woman is expected to deal courageously and with common sense with all the accidents and upsets of life with a small baby. Neither compliance with the cultural stereotypes nor rebellion against them and insistence on differences will solve the problems of the adult marriage partners.

A good deal of new information on childhood development has recently become available from two sources: First, carefully controlled observations of the earliest days of infancy, and, second, longitudinal studies such as those from Berkeley and from the Fels Institute. Most of this work has been done by psychologists and is in the form of statistical statements of probabilities rather than individual case material. The psychologists are notably reluctant to embody their findings in anybody's theory of personality, even Freud's, but prefer to let the facts stand for themselves. For instance, Kagan and Moss are still uncertain as to the propriety of admitting the concept of repression into their system.[11] The psychologists' reluctance to theorize is, one might say, the psychoanalyst's opportunity, and with an apologetic glance in their direction, I shall feel free to take their observations as starting points for my speculations.

The observations of early infancy point to some patterns of response present from birth which are related to subsequent development. One of the most interesting of these, described by Bell, is the arousal level of the infant.[12] There appears to be a wide range, with two extreme types. One type of infant is characterized as a newborn by quiescent sleep and lean body build, and at a month's age by low waking arousal, lack of assertion of needs in the face of brief deprivation, and a strong positive response to maternal contact. At two and a half years, this type showed cautious, restless, shifting play and positive orientation toward contact with supportive adults. The other type manifested chubby body build, strong appetite, a high level of arousal during sleep in the newborn period, and a high level of responsiveness and arousal coupled with aversive response to maternal contact at the end of the first month. At two-and-a-half years this type showed intense, fearless play with inanimate objects and low orientation toward adult supportive figures and peers.

Such innate patterns may be argued as being the precursors of passive versus active orientations later in life. It is of interest that the two extreme types show differences in positive response to maternal cuddling which may have much to do with constitutional make-up. It would seem highly probable that the difference in the baby's response would in turn have considerable influence on what the mother offers. Both types of arousal pattern occur in each sex, although there is a greater proportion of the first, or cuddly, type among girls.

---

[11] See footnote 8, p. 283.
[12] Richard Q. Bell, "Activity, arousal and early object relations," unpublished manuscript presented to the Washington Psychoanalytic Institute.

There are other innate differencs in the two sexes: The obvious anatomical ones, larger size and greater strength in the male, greater mortality rate of male infants, more rapid rate of maturation for females. Differences in general intelligence cannot be shown early in life and during the preschool years. As the school years progress, the differences in type of ability, level of activity, motivation, interests, and so on become more and more apparent. One difference between the sexes which shows up quite early is the amount of aggressive behavior, which even in nursery school is higher for boys than for girls. However, the influence of social teaching in this type of behavior—manhood being equated with fighting—is hard to rule out.

Differential handling of boys and girls is apparent from birth on. Moss has observed that mothers tend to be more responsive to male infants, holding them proportionately more time and generally attending to them more than do mothers of female infants. Somewhat later, at seven months, both parents use more sugary and baby-talk terms to girl babies and work harder to get them to smile and vocalize. These differential ways of handling the two sexes were independent of the activity level of the infant.[13]

Longitudinal studies so far provide only partial information about influences on child development, since they have in the past only used observations and ratings of the behavior of the mother and the child and have overlooked the father, yet they have found some exciting correlations between experiences early in life and later behavior. The child's behavior up to the age of three does not tend to carry on in similar form to later ages, with some exceptions. Of the exceptions, the passivity-activity level of the child seems to be the most enduring. Following the three-year-old level, more behavior tends to show itself in enduring patterns, but the first three or four grades of school are still periods of rapid change. After that, relative stability of many behavior patterns emerges.

The Berkeley study rated maternal behavior in two aspects—the degree of affection and the degree of control exercised by the mother.[14] The investigators found the predictable better development in infancy and early childhood when the mother was affectionate and not too controlling, but surprisingly also found that with girls the positive correlation between good development and loving maternal behavior dropped out after the age of four. This suggests that the mother-daughter relationship undergoes some troubling changes from about the age of four onward which affect the development of the girl. This is confirmed by some of the findings of Kagan and Moss in the Fels longitudinal study.[15] They observed that strong intellectual strivings in boys were correlated positively with maternal protection in the first six years, while strong intellectual strivings in girls were correlated positively with critical maternal attitudes in the same years. One gets the picture, for the girls, of a mother who is in opposition to the traditional feminine stereotype, and who urges and drives her daughter in the direction of intellectual development.

The boys who showed strong intellectual strivings continued, as adults, to show the same tendencies, but these were also associated with high sexual and social anxiety and a general lack of traditional masculine-type behavior. When the striving girls reached adulthood, they exhibited intellectual competitiveness and masculine-type interests.

Two other groupings showed opposite trends. Those boys who were most active in childhood became as adults strongly masculine, actively sexual, but weaker in intellectual strivings. The girls who were passive and maternally protected in childhood tended to become passive women, dependent on their families, withdrawing from problem situations, showing high social anxiety, and involved in traditional feminine pursuits.

It might be well to be somewhat critical of the traditional masculine and feminine role definitions used in this and other studies. Admittedly they represent extremes and are far from average or typical behavior. It seems to me that they may well represent pathological overexaggerations rather than pictures of some ideal, as far as their mental-health aspects are

13 Howard A. Moss, communicated at the Conference on Mental Health in Pregnancy, National Institute of Mental Health, Bethesda, Md., April 1965.
14 Earl Schaefer and Nancy Bayley, "Maternal behavior, child behavior and their intercorrelations from infancy through adolescence," Monogr. Soc. Rsc. in Child Development, 1963, Vol. 28, 3, No. 87.
15 See footnote 8.

concerned. However, one can not get around the fact that they come up over and over again in studies, for example, of how the child looks at male and female differences.

To continue with some of the other findings, Kagan and Moss compared the vocational choices of the ten boys who were given the highest ratings on masculine activities at three to six years of age with the choices of the seven boys who were rated lowest.[16] They showed no overlap. The ten rated most masculine had become three businessmen, two farmers, two athletic coaches, a carpenter, a machinist, and an engineer. The seven who were rated lowest became three teachers, a chemist, a biologist, a physicist, and a psychiatrist! Their recreational choices showed the same dichotomy; the men in the first group built amplifiers, worked with machines, and engaged in sports, while the men in the other preferred art, music, and reading. It is important to add that these differences were not correlated with intelligence level. The developmental course for the girls was less consistent, for many of the active and competitive ones dropped these behaviors during adolescence and assumed more feminine interests. The girls also showed a rapid increase during early school years of withdrawal from challenging problem situations, and the I.Q. levels of the achieving girls did not increase through the early years of school as did those of the boys.

The overall pattern which emerges from this study is that of cultural disparagement of passivity and dependency in the boys and a gradual diminution in the frequency and intensity of these characteristics. However, a substitution occurs of behavior which is less obvious but related in kind, such as a low level of sexual activity, social anxiety, and the choice of a more sedentary and intellectual career, rather than an active and manipulative one. With the girls, aggression and activity were discouraged, while dependency and passivity were rewarded, with a resulting alteration in these behaviors which was most conspicuous in preadolescence and adolescence when heterosexual interests begin to flower. However, even prior to that the girls began to show timidity and withdrawal from challenging tasks and also a tendency toward stability or stagnation of intellectual development.

If the greatest value is placed on successful development of so-called typical masculine and feminine types of behavior, then creativity and maximum intellectual development seem to suffer in both sexes. With girls, there seems to be greater sexual and social anxiety. If the greatest value is placed on high achievement, then sex-typical behavior is less developed, and, with boys, there is greater evidence of sexual and social anxiety.

To illustrate some of the results of these childhood developmental processes, I would like to turn now to some material from an exploratory and descriptive study of pregnant women and their husbands in which a group of colleagues and I have been engaged for the last several years. When we started, our thought was that the later phases of maturing —marriage, the establishment of adult occupations, and the setting up of new family units —had had little attention. Pregnancy and the early postpartum period highlight the maturational challenges for both wife and husband, since with the establishment of the family comes the necessity to assume a caretaking responsibility and to devise a division of labor which may or may not have been accomplished before. For this reason, conflicts about both feminine and masculine roles tend to be more sharp and hence more available to study.

We have quite full material on more than fifty subjects, which includes weekly interviews with the wives, beginning in the third or fourth month of pregnancy and continuing through the first three months of the postpartum period. This interview material, which we discussed in weekly seminars, was supplemented by psychological examinations, one in the sixth month of pregnancy and a second one at the end of the subject's participation. In addition, we had two interviews with each husband, one before and one after the child was born. Our subjects came to us by referral from obstetricians in private practice and from local mental hygiene clinics. Women with problems were, therefore, in the majority, although there were also some well-adjusted ones who volunteered because they were interested in learning about themselves and their children.

On scrutinizing our cases, we were surprised to note that more of the multipara in the study were having pregnancy-connected emotional

---

[16] See footnote 8.

problems than primipara, by roughly fifty percent. It looked as though these mothers had learned from experience that pregnancy and child-raising were sources of conflict and dissatisfaction. Eleanor Pavenstadt, who studied a lower-income group in Boston, made a similar observation—namely, that an evaluation of these women after they had had two or three children showed them to be at a lower level of maturity and adjustment than had the initial testing early in their first pregnancies.[17] Because of their social and economic situation, Pavenstadt's subjects were, she felt, without much hope for the future, looking forward to a life of drudgery and involuntary childbearing. This might account for their apparent downhill course. Our subjects, on the other hand, were mainly middle-class Protestants with reasonable financial security and considerable fredom of choice about their family size. If, despite this, there was an increase in emotional disability with the birth of additional children, we would need to look to other conditions of their lives for an explanation.

When we began our study, we made the obvious assumption that the more emotionally unstable women would have the most trouble during their pregnancies. This turned out to be true in the majority of cases, but to our surprise there was a substantial proportion of quite neurotic women who were no worse or, in some cases, even felt and functioned better during their pregnancies than before or after. We finally distinguished five principal groups: First, those who seemed mentally healthy and had no problems during pregnancy; a second small group who were emotionally well-adjusted but had other problems, such as physical illness; a third group who had obvious neurotic difficulties but were not worse during pregnancy; a fourth group of neurotic women who improved during pregnancy; and the fifth and largest group of those who showed signs of neurotic illness and felt and functioned worse during pregnancy.

I must make it clear that I am not referring, when I use the word neurotic, to clinical illness, but rather to psychological problems of adjustment sufficiently severe to be handicapping. Some of our subjects had been in psychiatric treatment earlier; some had not. Some of them went on to psychotherapy after their time with us; most did not.

In general, the more maladjusted subjects had had a history of greater tension and conflict in the childhood home and had more difficulties in their marriages. Most of our first group of problem-free women had come from harmonious childhood homes and were happily adjusted in their marriages, with feelings of affection and security on the part of both husband and wife. It was particularly notable that these subjects all had had good relationships with their mothers, although in some cases the relationships with their fathers had been more conflicted. Also notable was the fact that these women were mature, competent, and quite free of conflicts about femininity. Whether they pursued careers or not, they and their husbands had established a relationship which was satisfying to both, not only sexually but also in their workaday living. In contrast, a high proportion of our fifth group, the most troubled ones, had come from unhappy, frustrated, conflictful childhood homes, and inevitably there were marital problems.

Group three, those who were not worse during pregnancy, is particularly interesting to contrast with group five. Despite serious childhood trauma, almost all of them had made successful marriages. In some, it seemed that the happy fortune of marrying a stable and supportive husband had had a curative effect in a woman who otherwise might have gone on toward increasing maladjustment.

Group four, those whose adjustment improved during pregnancy, also had a particular coloring. For these women the states of being pregnant and of being a mother were so intensely satisfying that other relationships and conflicts faded into the background. One of them had been rejected by her husband and was living alone, but was very content, wrapped up in the phenomena of gestation and in daydreams about her wonderful baby. She was quite efficient in coping with the realistic problems involved in living alone and being pregnant, as though she and the fetus formed an entirely complete unit. Another, who was lonely and bored with her marriage to an overly busy professional man, found in her pregnancy her chief source of satisfaction. A third regarded

[17] Eleanor Pavenstadt, communicated at the Conference on Mental Health in Pregnancy, National Institute of Mental Health, Bethesda, Md., April 1965.

the pregnancy as proof of her adequacy as a woman, something her marriage had not provided her with. We wondered whether in some of these cases the satisfaction with pregnancy and motherhood would evolve into a damaging symbiotic relationship with the child as time went on.

We found the sharpest identity conflicts in the most problem-ridden group. I shall be speaking of our subjects primarily within the frame of reference of socially conditioned impairments of ego development, rather than in terms of their unconscious conflicts. Looking at them in this way, it soon became apparent that issues around comfortable acceptance of the feminine role, adequacy of personal development, and satisfaction of dependent needs were intimately interwoven and were of prime importance in success or failure during pregnancy. Without due foresight, we had initially focused our attention almost exclusively on the woman, imagining that pregnancy had to do primarily with what went on inside her. But the husband's part was forcibly brought to our attention with our first cases, and we became more and more aware of his crucial effect on his wife's well-being. The issues which determined the adequacy of his collaboration were similar to those in his wife—namely, his feeling about himself as a man, his adequacy as a person, and his handling of his dependent needs *vis-à-vis* his wife.

We found the problem of dependency to be intimately related to questions of masculine and feminine identity. Dependency is a somewhat confused concept; as most often used, it describes a pathological state of childish demandingness. There is a tendency to overlook interdependency as a part of healthy human relations, both those of husband and wife and also those of people in general. Sometimes we talk of material dependency for goods and services, and sometimes of emotional dependency, without clearly distinguishing them. On the whole, we are more comfortable with the objective, material types of dependency, as when we depend on the fire department to put out our fires. The emotional type of dependency is more problematic. It involves needs for reassurance, support, proof of love or concern, approval, confirmation of our worth, and so on. This kind of experience is a daily necessity for us, and yet we do not clearly know what is an adequate and "normal" dose and what goes beyond that point.

An added difficulty is the high value we place on self-sufficiency or independence, considering it to be one of the qualities of healthy maturity. Could it be more correctly stated that self-sufficiency consists in knowing how to get one's dependency needs met without blood, sweat, and tears? One criterion of suitable degrees of dependency is that of the willingness of the other to be involved. One reacts against a patient's or friend's dependency needs if he seems to ask more than one is willing to give. Perhaps a bargain is inherent in the relationship between two adequate, self-sufficient, successfully dependent adults—namely, that the giving goes both ways. It would be best, then, to look for a dependency balance or equilibrium between two people, or to look for the unbalancing factors in cases of conflict.

Part of the mythology of the sexes is that the man is independent and the woman dependent, but this is only a myth. The man's dependency needs are largely cloaked beneath the masculinity image, while those of the woman are more in the open, and indeed are exaggerated by the popular stereotype of femininity. The need to feel cared for is present in both and undoubtedly goes back to early experience with the mother. A central condition for satisfaction is that the caring-for, whatever it may be, must be freely given by the other, rather than extracted from him. For the more maladjusted, in whom there is a grave lack of trust in the self and the other, gratification of dependency needs is difficult if not impossible of attainment. On the one hand, the freedom of the giving is doubted, and on the other the needs are frequently not expressed. The person tends to believe that if he asks for something, this invalidates the worth of the gift. He tends to rely, then, on the hope that the other will guess his needs and supply them in such a way as to resolve his doubts, a hope which is forever being frustrated. In those whose self-esteem is sturdier, the need for proof is less intense, requests can be verbalized, and a gift offered by the other is accepted at face value.

Another type of conflict regarding dependency occurs when such needs have to be denied, a situation frequent in those whose serious doubts of their own worth are covered up by compensatory strivings for strength and self-sufficiency. Such a defensive structure is seen most often in men, but it certainly occurs frequently in women too. We then see the person playing the role of bountiful provider, manager, or dictator to the other, but underneath the pseudo self-sufficiency is the expectation of the reward of love on the basis of good deeds or heroic character.

In any marriage, there are initially a good many illusions, both as to the perfection of the other and also as to the promise of fulfillment of all needs. Conflicts and disappointments are inevitable, but in fortunate instances a compromise eventually emerges in which there is sufficient satisfaction for each to make the relationship stable. The particular compromise varies with the characters of the two involved. In the so-called ideal, typical marriage the man carries more of the responsibility; he is the more active one, the initiator or, as current terminology puts it, the instrumental one. The woman tends to be more passive and is responsive rather than initiating. Her role has recently been relabeled by the social psychologists as that of being the expressive one. However, this balance may not suit the particular personalities involved, and it is easy to see instances of a more equal balance, a sort of comradeship arrangement, and, on the other side of the scale, examples of relationships in which the woman exhibits the greater degree of initiative, energy, and decision-making, while the man is relatively passive. The active-passive balance between the two is not congruent with the dependency-need balance, since an active person's dependency needs are met when he receives confirmation and appreciation for his actions. In terms of dependency needs, the equilibrium must be flexible enough to allow for shifts in situations of stress, and there must be ways of communicating requests between the two.

Especially during pregnancy and the early postpartum period, there is an increase in the woman's dependency needs. In the early stages of the pregnancy, of course, the stresses are largely symbolic, stemming from fears of the pregnancy, of the ordeal of the delivery, and of the increased responsibility after the baby is born. Fear of loss of attractiveness, physical damage, pain, and death, as well as concern about the welfare of the fetus, all make the woman turn toward her husband with increased demands. Later on, in the third trimester and the postpartum period, there are realistic needs for more care and attention from the husband. Our subjects quite frequently asked for a kind of mothering care from their husbands, wanting sympathy, small favors, interest in the developing child, reassurance about their attractiveness, help with planning, and so forth. Bibring and her group have documented the lack in modern, small-family life of easy ways of meeting the increased emotional and realistic needs of the pregnant woman—something which was provided by the larger kinship group of other societies and our earlier generations.[18] In the present day in our culture these pressures fall primarily on the husband's shoulders, and the wife's success in getting her needs met and her consequent feelings of well-being depend very much on her way of asking—whether open and appropriate or devious and inappropriate—and his way of responding.

The women in our study showed a readiness to accept help from us and to change habitual patterns of behavior which was perhaps related to their increased vulnerability during pregnancy. This state of loosening or increased permeability often affected the husband too. Where the husbands were able to offer a more sensitive response to their wives, and where the wives could become more open and realistic in their demands, the relationships improved in ways that promised well for the future. We found that counseling in this area paid big dividends in assuring less traumatic pregnancies and a more comfortable start for the babies.

In our most troubled group, we found patterns of interaction between husband and wife which often represented extreme exaggerations of those in the more normal marriages. Like Jack Sprat and his wife, the two have formed a combination which has all-or-nothing qualities about it, and when the pregnancy demands flexibility and shifts in the various aspects of the relationship, the adjustment breaks down. There are three rather typical groups of maladjustment—those in which sexual identity

[18] Grete L. Bibring, "Some considerations in the psychological processes of pregnancy," Psychoanalytic study of the child, 14:113-121, New York: Internat. Univ. Press, 1959, p. 113.

problems are foremost, those in which personal identity issues predominate, and those in which immaturity in both respects is so abysmal that constructive mutuality is impossible. Of course, not all troubled couples fit into one or the other of these clusters. There are, for instance, cases in which one or the other is borderline neurotic, or otherwise seriously ill, and the partner has to develop unusual qualities of giving or caretaking in order that the marriage may endure at all. However, in spite of these and other exceptions, there is a rather remarkable sameness about the interactions of members of the more typical clusters when viewed in terms of their identity and dependency struggles. I would like to illustrate them with some brief examples.

The first type of couple provides a sort of caricature of ideal, typical masculinity and femininity. The women are usually attractive, feminine in manner, and impeccably groomed. The men are active, energetic, ambitious, and closely follow the masculine model. The women are usually rather idle, with little to do except to run a small apartment and occasionally sew for themselves. The men are usually ambitious and overworked, often going to school at night as well as working hard at their jobs and their hobbies. The women show an increasing trend toward inadequacy, in the sense of leaving more and more up to their husbands; they are often demanding and irritable. The men are increasingly occupied with outside interests and activities and consequently are less and less committed to satisfaction in family life. Both partners accept the idea of the woman as dependent child and the man as active protector. Subjects in this group illustrate one of the imbalances between sexual development and personal development. Although the women are successfully feminine, as the culture defines it, they are limited if not infantile in their growth in the intellectual, social, and mastery aspects of living. The men are successful masculine types but are limited as human beings by rigidity, fear of and avoidance of emotion, and inability to participate in a comfortable intimate relationship.

For example, Mrs. A, who was in her second pregnancy, came to us because she was collapsing in weeping spells with increasing frequency. One obstacle to her participation in this study appeared in the beginning—namely,

how was Mrs. A to get to my office since her husband was afraid to let her drive while she was pregnant? The problem was solved when he was able to figure out a way of adjusting his schedule so that he could accompany her to all appointments, wait for her, and drive her home again. Mrs. A brought out this concern of her husband's with some pride as an illustration of how careful he was of her. She was an exceptionally pretty, typically feminine woman who described herself as very contented, loving to keep house and have children, tremendously admiring of her strong and handsome husband, yet afflicted with these strange spells of tearfulness and depression which came on her, it seemed, without warning.

Her husband was exceedingly busy, working in a demanding job and also going to night school. He was very ambitious and was pursuing a five-year plan for the family's advancement. In addition, he was an enthusiastic golfer and spent at least one of the weekend days on the golf course. He had to have the car for his work and his school, which meant that Mrs. A, who lived in an apartment well away from the shopping center, was stuck at home with her small child all day and most evenings. Even grocery shopping could only be done Saturday afternoons after her husband returned from the golf course.

The young couple accepted as a matter of course the concept that the man did almost everything, only excepting the cooking and child-rearing. He did the housecleaning, hired the domestic help, and made all the plans. Yet he was very impatient with his wife's childishness. He felt that she was demanding, wanting to tie him down to domesticity, and always expecting him or her family to bail her out of her difficulties. She was growing increasingly helpless and felt unable to do things for herself. It developed that her spells of depression would come on when she was unable to get some desired behavior out of her husband or her child.

The wife's story was that of a pretty, popular teenager who had been a cheer-leader, a camp counselor, and prominent in her class, but whose developmental course had been downhill since her great success in high school. There was no trouble with pregnancy and childbirth on a physiological level, but in the business of living, in the meeting of even minor crises, there was the unquestioning assumption that her proper role was helplessness.

In some pairs who follow this pattern, the division between the two is even greater, for the husband is oblivious of his wife's emotional needs, acting as though achieving success in the material world and taking total responsibility for the mechanics of living were his only functions. Child-rearing is then left up to an exceedingly infantile wife, with disastrous results. Quite commonly such pairs come to child-guidance clinics with problem children, and then it is the experience of the therapists that the husband resists getting involved in the treatment situation and cannot be convinced that he has anything to do with the problem.

The balance of dependency is seen in reverse in another group of subjects in which the wife is the active, efficient one and the husband is quiescent, passive, often openly dependent. Here the woman has often developed herself as an educated, able person and has strong strivings for independency and mastery, while she is more uncertain of herself as an attractive woman and often regards the female as inferior to the male, or has to deny that the female is inferior. The man seems uncertain of himself as a male and tends to demand a good deal of mothering care from his wife. He may be intellectually developed and successful professionally, but on the defensive at home, or he may be relatively unsuccessful and leaning on his wife for practical or emotional support. In these marriages there is more open strife between the two, because the wife, while acting quite independently, at the same time resents the husband's passivity. It seems to outrage her sense of what is due her as a woman. It is as though she still retains an ideal of feminine passivity, while her own needs or the requirements of the marriage push her simultaneously in the direction of activity. The husband, too, while lethargic and inactive, shows signs of ambivalence. He resents his wife's managerial efforts and tends to blame or condemn her for them. He also resists her dependency demands, withholding himself from her. Quite frequently in this combination the husband's potency is impaired, adding yet another reason for resentment and frustration in the wife.

One of our subjects, Mrs. B, was a successful private secretary who had always earned more than her salesman husband until she stopped work at the time of the birth of her first child. She had, by then, grown contemptuous of her husband's inadequacy and had considered leaving him before she learned that she was pregnant. Because of the child, she attempted to accept the marriage, but her sense of grievance and abandonment by him brought about a postpartum depression after her first delivery. Now in a second, unwanted pregnancy, she was fearful of a recurrence of the psychosis and filled to overflowing with resentment. She was preoccupied with a vast array of grievances against her husband, including his lack of sexual prowess, his silent and uncommunicative behavior, his failure to make minor household repairs, and his not noticing her and her needs. She would do household tasks that were too heavy or risky for her, rather than ask his help. Then there would be an accumulation of resentment which would come out in a wild torrent as the result of some minor irritation. He was repelled by her aggressiveness and bounciness and imagined that he wanted a docile, agreeable wife. He opposed her working because it did not agree with his fantasies of a proper family life. She, on her side, was hurt by his lack of interest in her and longed to feel more comfortable as a woman.

Marriages such as this in which the problem is some sort of reversal of the usual sexual roles occur frequently in the patients who find their way to a psychiatrist's office, actually more so than the first type of difficulty which I described. There seems to be a constant dissatisfaction which presses both partners to struggle for a better solution. In part, I would presume that the pressure of discontent comes from the violation of cultural norms. Not many men settle down contentedly to let their wives assume leadership, nor do many women accept with equanimity a passive husband. Hence in these marriages there is more open combat, more neurotic symptomatology, and more rebellion against their lot in life. The woman may be primarily aggressive, demanding, complaining, or reproaching, or she may develop various phobias or depression. The man may show passive resistance, rigidity, moral condemnation, or withdrawal; he may sometimes be impotent and sometimes alcoholic. In the more customary vocabulary of psychiatry, this type of marital pair is frequently referred to as "the castrating wife and castrated husband." The surface appearance does indeed support this description, but the epithets obscure the dynamic interplay of needs and frustrations which leads to this result.

A third style of marital disharmony might be called the sibling-rivalry relationship. Here it seems that both people are intent on having their own needs met without regard to the other. Wife and husband are both immature, not only in their adolescent view of sexuality but also in their inability to assume responsibility, control their impulses, and plan for the future. Sometimes they are in competition as to who will be the dependent one, receiving support, reassurance, and care from the other. There is more concern with competition than cooperation, more interest in outward appearances than inner experiences, and each is preoccupied with getting his own way and with his own grievances.

Mrs. C, for example, had always been relatively irresponsible, putting good times and lots of dates above school achievement. After a year of college she married a man who was as immature as herself. He was a college dropout, working in a low-paid job and anxious to marry in order to feel like a man. Marital trouble beset them from the start. She was insistent on having her own way, he equally determined to have his, and there were frequent noisy quarrels and physical battles. In a moment of relative peace they discontinued contraception and she became pregnant. She was delighted at the prospect of having a little baby to play with. He reacted by quitting his job, intending after a few weeks' rest to get a new and better one. The whole pregnancy was a game to her and an event which Mr. C ignored. Postpartum she was cared for by her over-indulgent mother. Nursing was attempted but promptly discontinued because it tied her down too much. When the baby was about two months old, the husband and wife resumed their rivalrous bickering, and Mrs. C left him, returning to her parental home with the baby.

One combination which is interesting by its absence in our study is that of the domineering husband and submissive wife, a pattern which is of fairly common occurrence in some European cultures. Its infrequency in this country may to some extent account for the oft-repeated complaint that American culture is woman-dominated.

Summarizing our study of pregnancy, I believe that we have shown the importance for the welfare of the family unit of, first, a sense of security on the part of both man and woman as to their worth as sexual beings and as to their development as persons, and, second, a balance or equilibrium between the two people as to their dependency needs, a balance which can take account of the varying intensity of such needs in various kinds of personalities, and which also can shift with the vicissitudes of living. If these two conditions are not present, the pregnancy may be fulfilling to the woman and confirming of her femininity, but a threat to the man, who may be too doubtful of himself to be able to meet his wife's increased needs, assume the responsibilities of fatherhood, and accept without anxiety her absorption in the child and consequent withdrawal from himself. Equally, the woman whose doubts of her worth go deep may find more threat than confirmation in the low-prestige mothering role, so that the pregnancy is fraught with anxiety, and her dependency on her husband rises so high as to render futile any reasonable efforts to support her. For the man, defensive needs to prove his masculinity, or lack of confidence in it, can lead either to overprotection and overcontrol of his wife or to abdication of his supportive and integrating functions in the family.

I believe the evidence presented here shows the invalidity of either activity-passivity or independence-dependence as indices of masculine-feminine development. Unfortunately, these are embedded in the culture. They are passed on to children by mothers and fathers uncertain of their own feminine or masculine worth, reinforced by schooling, by storybooks, by TV programs, and by peer-group attitudes. Regrettably, they are also held by many professional workers in the behavioral sciences. Sometimes the assumption is made that such qualities are inborn, as sexually determined characteristics. The material from observations of children contradicts this. Others assume that these qualities are either taught or reinforced as part of the acculturation process. Again, the evidence from longitudinal studies indicates that such acculturation is far from successful.

The constitutional tendencies toward activity and passivity do not reverse themselves under the pressures of socialization. Rather they linger on in one guise or another, and the anxieties which are aroused by social disapproval of passivity in boys or activity in girls can be seen in the multitudinous fears experienced by both sexes about not being thought appropriately masculine or feminine. Much of the castration anxiety in men and its counterpart, penis envy, in women seems to spring from fear of condemnation if one does not conform to the model. The overemphasis on so-called masculine traits throws the boy into conflict regarding the feeling aspects of experience and labels as suspect the development of intellectual and artistic interests. Similarly, the girl is made to feel uneasy in striving toward competence, intellectual development, and independence.

As they reach adulthood and marry, conflicts regarding the division of functions, the dependency balance, and the sharing of responsibility arise. For the woman, emphasis on dependency, passivity, and even inadequacy interferes with her functioning as homemaker, wife, and mother just as severely as with her functioning in a career. Despite the low prestige attached to the career of housewife, doing the job well requires competence, good judgment, and ability to take responsibility. Indeed, constructive use of the long hours alone, which are part of the experience of the housewife, requires a considerable degree of inner richness if retrogression and inertia are not to set in. For the man, the overemphasis on strength, courage, initiative, and leadership does violence to his appropriate needs for rest, receiving emotional support, and getting rid of the tensions of the market place.

I would not be thought to be an advocate of abolishing maleness and femaleness in favor of one uniform sex, as Simone de Beauvoir seems to do.[19] Rather, my aim would be to encourage a more critical scrutiny of our assumptions about sex-typical behavior. Freud's description of feminine masochism, it must be remembered, was based on a Victorian type of female who, when viewed from the twentieth century, looks like a rather hysterical specimen. But even nowadays, Ralph Greenson is reported in the press as describing the feminization of the United States.[20] He sees women becoming increasingly secure, sexually and socially, and men becoming economically and psychologically more insecure. Although he is careful to state that he is only observing and not condemning, the application of the adjectives "feminized" and "emasculated" to the male are not entirely devoid of value judgment. Also, the idea that, as women become more secure, men become more insecure, and vice versa, makes one wonder. Is it really true that we are on a teeter-totter and that only one sex can be secure at a time? The evidence from our study contradicts this assumption, as does common sense. Forty years ago, in a letter to Romain Rolland, Freud wrote, "Given our drive dispositions and our environment, the love for fellow man must be considered just as indispensable for the survival of mankind as is technology." [21] He was referring, of course, to the powerful influence the social value system, "love for fellow man," has over our instinctual life, serving to moderate our aggression. In a parallel fashion to man's other ills, our narrow conceptions of what is manly and hence not womanly, of what is womanly and hence not manly (conceptions which exclude large areas of thought and feeling which might appropriately be considered as human rather than narrowly sex-bound) can be seen to give rise to difficulties in our development and our relations with each other and with our children. They need to be modified by cultural expectations more flexibly in accord with individual needs as they are actually found in males and females.

---

[19] Simone de Beauvoir, *The second sex*, New York: Knopf, 1957.
[20] Ralph Greenson, in a talk to the Southern California Psychiatric Society, reported in the *Medical Tribune*, September 1965.
[21] Sigmund Freud, "An Romain Rolland," *Gesammelte Werke* (1948) 14:553.

Modern man's loss of significance

ROLLO MAY

Some persons will go to extremes in order to get attention and publicity. Although this type of behavior is often viewed as evidence of emotional disturbance the increasing incidence of nonconforming acts may be an indication that the need to be noticed is becoming more prevalent. This article focuses on the problem of achieving significance as an individual in contemporary society. The author discusses recent social crises, such as student revolts on college campuses, and raises serious questions about the psychological consequences of living in an impersonal society.

Rollo May, Ph.D., practices psychoanalysis in New York City, is a Supervising and Training Analyst of the William Alanson White Institute of Psychiatry, Psychoanalysis, and Psychology and is Adjunct Professor at New York University. His books include *Art of Counseling, The Meaning of Anxiety, Man's Search for Himself, Psychology and the Human Dilemma,* and *Love and Will.* He has edited a volume of readings on existential psychology entitled *Existence: A New Dimension in Psychiatry and Psychology.*

Man is only a reed, the feeblest reed in nature, but he is a thinking reed. There is no need for the entire universe to arm itself in order to annihilate him: a vapor, a drop of water, suffices to kill him. But were the universe to crush him, man would yet be more noble than that which slays him, because he knows that he dies, and the advantage the universe has over him; of this the universe knows nothing. Thus all our dignity lies in thought. By thought we must raise ourselves, not by space and time, which we cannot fill. Let us strive, then, to think well—therein is the principle of morality.—Blaise Pascal, *Pensées*

In a period of transition, when old values are empty and traditional mores no longer viable, the individual experiences a particular difficulty in finding himself in his world. More people experience more poignantly the problem of Willie Loman in *The Death of a Salesman,* "He never knew who he was." The basic dilemma, inhering in human consciousness, is part of all psychological experience and present in all historical periods. But in times of radical cultural change, as in sexual mores and religious beliefs, the particular dilemmas which are expressions of the basic human situation become harder to negotiate.[1]

To begin with, I pose the question, Is not one of the central problems of modern Western man that he experiences himself as without significance as an individual? Let us focus on that aspect of his image of himself which is his doubt whether he can act and his half-aware conviction that even if he did act it would do no good. This is only one side of contemporary man's picture of himself, but it is a psychologically critical aspect—a self-doubt which reflects the

From *Psychology and the Human Dilemma* by Rollo May (New York: D. Van Nostrand Company, Inc., 1967), pp. 25-39. Reprinted by permission of the publisher.

[1] It is easy, of course, to make prophetic generalities about one's age, the purpose often of which is to obfuscate and evade the concrete realities of our immediate daily experience. But we should not allow our weariness with such generalities to lead us to dull our awareness of what *is* going on around us, to cover up our consciousness of the meaning and implications of our historical time, or to hide behind the comfortable and secure stockade of *ex post facto* statistics. I shall try to make my own beliefs and assumptions as clear as possible as we go along, in the confidence that the reader can best disagree and arrive at his own beliefs in this dialogue if he has no confusion about mine.

tremendous technological power that surges up every moment about him to dwarf overwhelmingly his own puny efforts.

This is a cultural evolution of the problem of "identity" which was brought out with special cogency in the 1950's in the writings of such analysts as Erickson and Wheelis. Persons of all sorts these days, especially younger people, diagnose their trouble when they come to a counselor or therapist as an "identity crisis" —and the fact that the phrase has become trite should not lead us to overlook the fact that it may also be importantly true. "Nowadays the sense of self is deficient. The questions of adolescence—'Who am I?' 'Where am I going?' 'What is the meaning of life?'—receive no final answers. Nor can they be laid aside. The uncertainty persists," wrote Allen Wheelis in 1958.[2] He goes on with respect to the technological progress in our day in culture and in health, "But as our span of years has increased, our span of significant time has diminished."

My thesis is that the problem of identity in the 1950's has now become, more specifically, the crisis of the loss of the sense of significance. It is possible to lack a sense of identity and still preserve the hope of having influence—"I may not know who I am, but at least I can make them notice me." In our present stage of loss of sense of significance, the feeling tends to be, "Even if I did know who I am, I couldn't make any difference as an individual anyway."

I wish to cite as an example of this loss of individual significance, a series of incidents which expressed something important for persons all over the country. I refer to the "revolt" as its enemies labeled it, or "passive resistance" as the students called it, on the Berkeley campus of the University of California. Whatever the complex and subtle factors underlying this protest, it seems agreed on all sides that it was a welling up in students of profound and powerful resistance against the "facelessness of students in the modern factory university." The mood is shown excellently in the fiery rhetoric of Mario Savio, the senior in philosophy who led the massive sit-in which was the occasion for the arrests:

There is a time when the operation of the machine [of collectivized education] becomes so odious, makes you so sick at heart that you can't take part . . . you've got to put your bodies upon the gears and upon the wheels, upon the levers, upon all the apparatus and you've got to make it stop. . . .

Further evidence that the deep substratum of students' emotions coming then into eruption was the protest against their being treated as anonymous cogs in the wheels of a tremendous system is seen in the reasons many students gave for the value of the protests. After the demonstrations several persons who had participated remarked to me with considerable emotion, "Everybody now speaks to everybody else on the campus." No clearer statement could be made of the fact that what was at stake was the unbearable situation of "nobody knows my name," "I am without significance." It is, indeed, one of the clear values of being a rebel, as Camus and countless others in human history have said and as I shall try to indicate later in this book, that by the act of rebelling I force the impersonal authorities or the too systematic system to look at me, to recognize me, to admit that I *am,* to take account of my *power.* That last word is not underlined for purposes of rhetoric: I mean, literally, that unless I can have some effect, unless my potency can be exercised and can matter, I inevitably will be the passive victim of outside forces and I shall experience myself as without significance.

Since this experience of student insignificance is of importance for what follows in this book, let us note some evidence that the "facelessness of the education factory" is not at all a projection of students' neurotic or subjective phantasy.

At Berkeley, as on so many other state university campuses, the image of a "factory" is no longer a joke. Berkeley's student population totals nearly 27,500. With a full time faculty of 1,600, some of whom are on leave or engaged in research, the effective student-faculty ratio is approximately 18 to 1, according to university officials.

The most eminent members of Berkeley's faculty are frequently so absorbed in research that they have little time for students. The younger professors, facing a "publish or perish" battle to stay on at Berkeley, likewise have little time for students. The teaching burden falls heavily on teach-

[2] Allen Wheelis, *The quest for identity.* Norton: New York, 1958, pp. 18 and 23.

ing assistants who are usually inexperienced graduate students working toward their degrees. . . .

One of the many ironies of the Berkeley situation is that much of what has developed was clearly foreseen by President Kerr in his book, "The Uses of the University," published in 1963. Dr. Kerr, an expert in industrial relations with a national reputation as a labor mediator, warns against the "incipient undergraduate revolt," against the "faculty in absentia" and the frustration of students smothering "under a blanket of impersonal rules." In what now reads like the understatement of the Berkeley crisis, Dr. Kerr, who has been university president since 1958, warned, "The students also want to be treated as distinct individuals." [3]

It should be clear also that the contemporary phenomenon of student revolt is not "caused" by some special evil men sitting in the Presidents' offices or on the Boards of Trustees of the universities. That the students themselves see the impersonal source of the evil is shown in many student editorials like the following:

A University of Illinois student columnist, writing in the Daily Illini, called for more student participation in the planning of a new building to be paid for in part by student funds. "It is our job, as concerned students . . . to help save this wonderful organism, the university, from its own efficiency," he wrote, adding, ". . . the loss of a building is nothing compared to the loss of the sense of community here." [3]

What is occurring is an inescapable phenomenon of our times, the inevitable result of the collectivism, mass education, mass communication, mass technology, and the other "mass" processes which form modern people's minds and emotions.

That these are no flash-in-the-pan episodes is shown by the fact that despite the all-university committees' recommendation of the reforms the students demanded, a new apathy has come over the campus, according to Dr. Kerr, from which he warns new protests will spring.[4]

What is the deeper conflict underlying the profound student unrest? Dr. Kerr formulates it as the dilemma arising from the increasing withdrawal of faculty into specialized research at a time when "more students . . . want to

gain from their education a personal and social philosophy as well as or even instead of a vocational skill." Dr. Rosemary Park, President of Barnard College, describes the "dangerous times" the university is now in "when student dissatisfaction with education has never been more strident nor faculty disinterest in the institution they serve more apparent." [4] No wonder present graduate students at Berkeley are proclaiming that the only way to restore a meaningful tradition in university life is for the students to conduct "intellectual guerrilla warfare"—a curiously contradictory but significant phrase—against those universities that were set up solely to meet the "operational needs of the corporations and government" rather than "the needs of the moral man." [4] The upshot of all of this is a new and highly important form of the battle for human values against the sophisticated mechanical Moloch of education which threatens to devour what is most precious to each one of us, our imagination and our consciousness itself. It is indeed interesting that in this battle the *moral* demand and cry comes from the students and not the faculty!

Now it is important to recall that these students were brought up, as all of us were in this country from the time of the frontiersman on, to believe that the individual is the one who counts, that his power is decisive in the long run, and that in a democracy it is the individual's say which determines policy. Now they find themselves part of vast factorylike processes which seem to run autonomously and under their own satanically impersonal power. The "mass" processes are a characteristic of the transitional historical period in which we live, and I see no simple detour around the crises which have resulted and the revolts which will still occur. They are symptomatic of the dislocation of human consciousness in our time; they express the struggle of human beings—in this case particularly the students—to resolve the dilemmas so far as possible or to come to terms with them when resolution is impossible.

---

[3] From an editorial, "Berkeley's Lesson," in the *New England Association Review*, the official publication of the New England Association of Colleges and Secondary Schools, Winter 1965, pp. 14-15.

[4] Report of consultation on "The university in America," sponsored by the Center for the Study of Democratic Institutions, *New York Times*, May 10, 1966.

The dilemmas we confront, thus, are sharpened by the contemporary cultural and historical upheavals of Western civilization, upheavals which make it inevitable that the self-image of the individual will be greatly shaken. Robert and Helen Lynd wrote about the confusion of role of the individual in *Middletown* three decades ago; the citizen is "caught in a chaos of conflicting patterns, no one of them wholly condemned, but no one of them clearly approved and free from confusion; or where the group sanctions are clear in demanding a certain role of a man or woman, the individual encounters cultural requirements with no immediate means of meeting them." The Lynds related this to socioeconomic upheaval in Middletown in the 1930's, but I believe a greater and more fundamental conflict of roles—an experience of *absence* of any viable roles—is occurring in our present world three decades later. Lacking positive myths to guide him, many a sensitive contemporary man finds only the model of the machine beckoning him from every side to make himself over into its image. The protests we hear are the clashing sounds of struggle—agonizing, often despairing, but never relinquished—against this latter-day Circe.

The most striking symbol for the individual's sense of insignificance is, of course, the ever-present specter of thermonuclear war. So far as I can observe, people in New York City and over the East—and there is no reason to assume the mood is any different in other parts of the country if we make allowance for cultural lags and pockets of encapsulation—have the belief that they are impotent before this possibility of nuclear war; and the impotence leads to confusion, apathy, and the gnawing conviction, no matter how covered up by diversions or frantic togetherness, "I do not matter." This in turn leads to several vicious circles which we shall now examine. I choose the following example because it so well illustrates the psychological dynamics in this dilemma.

In the fall of 1961 there developed in the East in the face of the threat of thermonuclear war, a curious panic centering around fallout shelters. I say "curious" not because the anxiety itself was unexpected—it followed the panic over the only too real threat of the Berlin crisis—but because of certain psychological symptoms which emerged. During those weeks I participated in several public discussions and debates over radio and television, and I received the weird impression that for many people the fallout shelters represented a crawling back into caves in the earth as an acting out of the conviction that in our helplessness we could only revert to a new womb, our only concern an infantile preoccupation with saving our own skins. Understandably overweighed with their impotence in the crisis, people tended to act as though they could do no more than hope and pray for the luck to avert the holocaust while they themselves, ostrichlike, could only hide underground. Unfortunately, the stand of the government in recommending that those who could afford it—which meant the suburban rich—build their private shelters added to the impotence.[5]

I recall that one of my opponents in a radio debate at the time of that panic, an eminent political economist with considerable experience in government, said in answer to a question from one of the several hundred people in the hall, "You cannot have any influence whatever on the question of whether or not there will be war. This is decided entirely by the councils of the few high political leaders who gather in Berlin." This, of course, was exactly what people tended to believe anyway.[6] If they had been a little more convinced of the significance of their own acts, they wouldn't have bothered to come out to public discussions like this or even to flick the radio on.

The point I wish to make is that when people feel their insignificance as individual persons, they also suffer an undermining of their sense

[5] President Kennedy became aware that this advocacy of private shelters was a mistake, and the recommendation was rescinded in two months. I do not have the impression very many private shelters were actually built, partly no doubt because people got caught in the same psychological vicious circle we are about to explore.

[6] My own stand and that of many other people in the audience was, of course, radically against my opponent. Let me here only say that the reader will see that the point my opponent was raising is one of those questions that depends, in its ultimate truth or falsehood, exactly on whether or not we *do act*. If we had accepted my opponent's statement, we would remain passive; and his statement would become true by virtue of our accepting it. If, on the other hand, we refused to accept it, but did what little we could to influence Congress, the President, and other leaders, then even a group as small as this several hundred—and certainly the thousands listening on the radio—could have some significance, infinitesimally small as it may be to begin with. This is the point where political freedom begins, as I shall indicate later.

of human responsibility. Why load yourself with responsibility if what you do doesn't matter anyway, and you must be on edge every moment ready to flee? What vivid symbols of our impotence were these ghastly wounds in the ground! And what a testimony to the disintegration of social values was our being adjured to dig the caves at night to keep our neighbors from knowing where they were, so that in the time of peril one man, with two or three of his family gathered around him, could crawl into the cave and there gain some sort of isolated protection! (The protection was mostly illusory anyway, so we were later informed by the physicists who knew about the inevitable fire storms.) Or a cement ready-made shelter could be purchased, as it was pictured in *Life* and on television, with ventilation tubes from the world above, all the food stored in the walls, coke and a record-player furnished for the teenager and light reading to divert the adults while the bombs fell above on the earth —all for the bargain price of $20,000.

But the most staggering thing of all was that this crawling back into the earth was a protection purchased at the price of the destruction of human love and trust. We all too vividly recall the comforting reassurances from some clergymen and other respectable guardians of the nation's morals that it was ethical to shoot down your neighbors and his children if these unfortunates tried to push into your shelter in their moment of danger and panic.

Thus the impotence in the face of thermonuclear war *moved into anxiety, the anxiety into regression and apathy, these in turn into hostility, and the hostility into an alienation of man from man*. This is the vicious circle that is acted out when our sense of significance is undermined. The only way we can then move is backwards in a psychological regression to an infantile state, a self-chosen encapsulation in our latter-day combination womb-tomb, in which no umbilical cord is necessary since food is stored within the tomb as in the burial caves which Neolithic man built for his journey to the land of the dead.

But the human being never gives up his potency lightly or simply. Anxiety is generated within him in direct proportion to his conviction of his own impotence. What is important here is to emphasize the well-known vicious circle of panic which we have already touched upon—anxiety to apathy to increased hatred to greater isolation of the person from his fellowmen—an isolation which, finally, increases the individual's sense of insignificance and helplessness. Suspicion and enmity toward the neighbor in such times become acceptable and "moral" in ways that would horrify us (and are therefore repressed) in conventional periods. And the hatred and readiness to destroy our own neighbors become in a strange, reverse way—"strange" conventionally but not clinically—an outlet for our own anxiety and impotence. What happens in such moments of anxiety is only the extreme expression of the breakdown of man's sense of significance as an individual and consequently his loss of capacity for individual decision and responsibility.

The war in Vietnam—the most "unwanted war in history," as it has been called—did nothing to dispel the moods of earlier crises or lighten the sense of a profound and troubling impotence. The feeling of impotence was not at all limited to those who were opposed to the conflict but seemed to affect just as insidiously those who believed in and prosecuted the war.

I want to examine this crisis as an illustration of the fact that all of us, whether for or against the war, are caught in a historical situation of upheaval in which there is no clear right and wrong, in which psychological confusion is therefore inescapable, and—a fact which is most frightening of all—no one person or group of persons is in a position to exercise the significant power. Power takes on an anonymous, automatic, and impersonal character.

My purpose here is not political, but to describes as clearly as I can a situation which bears on psychological insignificance, so that we can return to an analysis of that problem. In hearings of the Senate Foreign Relations Committee the same questions were directed over and over to Secretary of State Rusk, Secretary of Defense McNamara, and other persons in the Government, Why were we in Vietnam? What were our real goals? What were our powers there, and what could we realistically expect to accomplish? After reams of testimony (our data is at least plentiful and ready at hand thanks to the mass communication of television and press) Senator Fulbright and other senators, who could by no means be considered stupid or biased about the war, still reported that these questions remain unanswered. "Mr. Fulbright said he had the greatest difficulty," so the *New York Times* reported,[7] "in understanding what the Administration's real objectives were and 'whether what we seek is achievable.' " As Senator Fulbright continually pointed out, and as the representatives of the government did not deny, it was an "open-ended" war; more and more power was poured, always with possibility of the ultimate power of the nuclear bomb in the offing, into a situation in which *by definition we did not and could not have control over the critical decisions.* Newsmen tried in vain to get McNamara to state the long-range plans for the commitment of troops, but he assiduously refused to state more than the pragmatic immediate fact that the Defense Department was "filling the requests of General Westmoreland," and the President, when pushed with similar questions, replied, "I have no unfulfilled requests on my desk."

Now the irony of this situation, not to be obscured by moralistic imputations against this or that Secretary, was that that was all they *could* say. For by the very structure of the situation they did not have control over long-range plans: China and other powers could change these at any moment. The citizen of Minneapolis or Denver who experienced his own lack of significance in this situation might assume, out of an anachronistic psychology of several decades ago, that at least others in Washington were making the significant decisions. But when we looked to Washington we found that *no one* in any final sense had the significant power; everyone, including the President, could plan only within a limited time range and within uncertain variables, for the critical data were simply not available; and the *pragmatic* answer, given by the immediate situation, was about all that could be arrived at.

The dilemma was starkly and tragically real. This dilemma was an inescapable result of the nature of our transitional historical period, when impersonal power has taken on such vast implications and meanings, and human consciousness, responsibility and intentions have not kept up, and probably could not have kept up. I am not making a statement of historical doom, nor do I at all imply that nothing could be done to improve the situation in the Vietnamese war; apathy and passivity are the last

things in the world I am proposing.[8] My point is that if our historical situation, and the psychological implications this has for those of us living at this moment, is recognized, we shall be helped to shift our approaches from self-defeating policies to others which at least have some chance of ultimately constructive results. I believe that we have played ostrich with the issue of power, resorting on the one hand to an anachronistic nineteenth-century military psychology, and on the other to self-righteous pacifism. Both were oversimplifications—and to oversimplify in the age of the nuclear bomb is highly dangerous. A widened and deepened consciousness, and a sense of responsibility infused with an imagination which could conceive of new ways of relating to the Orient, seem to me necessary for a constructive solution to our problems. But this possibility rests on our confronting the deeper dilemma between the impersonal power of technology on one hand and human values on the other.

In this vacuum of power—that is, the application of greater and greater power (in this case military) to a situation in which one did not have the ultimate significant choice—the real danger was that we would retreat to the only answer available, namely the *pragmatic* answer, the answer that can be given by logistics, the answer that can be arrived at by our computers, the impersonal answer, the answer furnished by the very technology whose unlimited and magnificent spawning had been central in bringing us into the situation in which our force for destruction so vastly exceeded our capacity for significant decision. As I shall indicate below, it is as absurd to "blame" technology—and as scientifically illiterate—as it is absurd morally to blame some "evil" government leaders in other countries—a kind of

<hr>

[7] *New York Times*, March 4, 1966.
[8] I have myself been continually concerned with action on these issues, because I believe that social apathy is our central danger. My own personal opinion was that, regardless of how and why we got into Vietnam, we could not simply pull out. I believe power confers responsibility, and it would have been irresponsible for a nation of our power to play ostrich in the East, or to fail to realize that we have tremendous influence in every section of the world whether we choose to exercise it in an enlightened way or not. I believe that our perpetual nonrecognition of Communist China was an example of playing ostrich. The widened and deepened consciousness which will be necessary for solutions to our problems will have to include, in my judgment, a fresh way of perceiving other nations like China, as well as other races.

self-righteousness which leads one into the illusion, so common in psychotherapy, that if only some other persons would change, we would be spared our great problems.

My purpose in this book, to repeat, is not political, but to make as clear as I can how certain important psychological problems arise. A situation of impotence and lack of significance such as has been presented above leads understandably to *confusion* and then to *apathy*. These in turn lead into the vicious circle in psychological dynamics which we have mentioned, and which we shall now explore more deeply.[9]

When the individual loses his significance, there occurs a sense of apathy, which is an expression of his state of diminished consciousness. Is not the real danger this surrender of consciousness—the danger that our society will move in the direction of the man who expects the drugs to make him comfortable and the machine not only to satisfy all his needs but in the form of psychoanalytic mechanisms, to make him happy and able to love as well? When Karl Jaspers talks about the danger of modern man losing his self-consciousness, he is not speaking in hyperbole: we need to take him quite seriously. For this loss is no longer simply a theoretical possibility dreamt up by psychoanalysts or the "morbid existentialist" philosophers.

This diminution of consciousness, I believe, is central to the deepest form of the loss of the sense of significance. What is implied is that this may be the last age of the historical man, that is, the last age in which man *knows* he has a history. Not the last age in which there is a factual history—that is not the point—but the last age in which I can self-consciously stand as a human being who knows that he stands at this point in history, and taking responsibility for this fact, can use the wisdom of the past to illuminate the life and world around me. Such action requires a self-consciousness that can affirm and assert itself, and that in turn requires that I believe in my own significance. It *does* matter then whether I act, and I act in faith that my actions can have some influence.

We have said that the devil of this drama is not technology, and it is absurd to think that if we could throw out technology, we should escape our human dilemmas. On the obvious level, technology is a set of tools, and the im-

portant question is, For what purpose are these tools used? On a less obvious level, it is true that technology does shape our image of ourselves in conditioning the kind of information we listen for. But the critical threat with respect to technology does not lie in those two: it is that we succumb to the temptation to use technology as a way of avoiding confronting our own anxiety, our alienation, and our loneliness. When a man is anxious about thermonuclear war, he can hope that with a few more missiles we shall be safe. When anxious about loneliness he can go to a psychoanalyst or learn some new operant conditioning technique, or take some drug, so that, at so much an hour or a dose, he can be changed into the man who will love and be happy. But technology used as a way to evade anxiety makes man even more anxious, more isolated, alienated in the long run, for it progressively robs him of consciousness and his own experiencing of himself as a centered person with significance.

The ultimately self-destructive use of technology consists of employing it to fill the vacuum of our own diminished consciousness. And conversely, the ultimate challenge facing modern man is whether he can widen and deepen his own consciousness to fill the vacuum created by the fantastic increase of his technological power. It seems to me that, and not the outcome of a particular war, is the issue on which our survival hinges.

There is, however, a particular dilemma we need to mention which is made more difficult by modern technology. This is the phenomenon of the "organization man." Increasingly in our time—this is an inevitable result of collectiviza-

---

[9] Though later in this book we shall be discussing the possible answers to these psychological problems, it may be clarifying here briefly to indicate that bringing the political problem into awareness, identifying it, and then frankly confronting it, is already the first step in developing the deepened consciousness that can meet the problem. A sense of responsibility infused with imagination seems to me the first essential. Second, a forming of policy based on *human* goals rather than those given by pragmatic, technological power. Third, a rigorous refusal to let the difficulty of forming long-term goals, as well as the ease of letting our computers form our short-term goals, keep us from devoting thought and energy to the project of long-term aims. We need "some sense of proportion in relating means to ends," write the editors of the journal *Christianity and Crisis*. "What is lacking so far is the willingness to look at realities and the moral imagination to seek better methods than the present contradictory mixture of peaceful rhetoric and stubborn policy"—March 5, 1966.

tion—it is the organization man who succeeds. And he is characterized by the fact that *he has significance only if he gives up his significance.* A curious paradox is present in some patients we get in New York City: one gains his status on Madison Avenue at the price of giving up his originality. One becomes the man who works well in an organization, the harmonistic "team man," the worker who maintains a protective coloring so that he won't be singled out and shot at. To this extent you are said to be significant, but it is a significance that is bought precisely at the price of giving up your significance.

The loss of the experience of one's own significance leads to the kind of anxiety that Paul Tillich called the anxiety of meaninglessness, or what Kierkegaard terms anxiety as the fear of nothingness. We used to talk about these things as psychological theories, and a couple of decades ago when I was undergoing my psychoanalytic training, we discussed them as psychological phenomena shown by "neurotic" people. Now such anxiety is endemic throughout our whole society. These are some of the considerations which impel me to suggest that there is "no hiding place" with respect to the psychological dilemmas of our time. We may as well, then, confront them directly. This we shall now essay to do.

7

A MODERN DILEMMA II: MAN'S BASIS FOR SELF-JUDGMENT

In our society, people are generally eager to avoid being considered abnormal, maladjusted, or mentally ill. Yet, we seldom ask ourselves what these terms really mean or what criteria they are based upon. We are quick to label others as "sick," "crazy" or "kooky," but we are often remiss in fully appreciating the many complexities and consequences involved in making such decisions. The lack of serious attention by the general public to the question of what constitutes normal behavior is not completely surprising in view of the fact that professional psychiatrists and psychologists have spent much less time studying normal behavior than they have investigating abnormal behavior. Kaplan (1967) suggests that this lack of attention to normal psychological functioning stems from the "trained incapacity" of psychiatrists who tend to view people as objects for their therapeutic techniques or examples of abstract categories of psychological symptoms. According to Kaplan (1967), psychiatrists, like other behavioral scientists, have become victims of "the law of the instrument." In its simplest form this law states: "If you give a small boy a hammer, it will turn out that everything he runs into needs pounding" (Kaplan, 1967, p.

325). Similarly, if you give a psychiatrist a diagnostic tool, it may turn out that everyone he runs into needs diagnosing.

The relatively small amount of professional concern may simply be due to the fact that the need to understand normal people is less pressing than the need to understand persons exhibiting more deviant behavior. Although normal persons are able to get along in society somehow, persons considered abnormal have difficulty. They frequently disrupt their own lives or the lives of others and require professional attention in order to modify their behavior. Nevertheless, the lack of an adequate definition of mental health is, according to Ginsburg (1963), one of the great theoretical shortcomings in present mental hygiene activity. It invariably results, he states, "in a confusion of goals and an uncertainty of means; it creates a situation like that of a hunter stalking an unknown prey with weapons which may turn out to be quite unsuitable" (Ginsburg, 1963, p. 8).

A number of attempts have been made to understand better what is acceptable behavior and to suggest various criteria of optimal psychological functioning. These behaviors are usually included under the heading of one of three concepts: normality, adjustment, or mental health. Although these terms reflect minor differences in meaning, they are highly similar, and all have two characteristics in common: 1) they emphasize the more positive or adaptive aspects of man's behavior in contrast with his less adaptive actions; and, 2) they represent attempts to provide meaningful criteria which man can use as a basis for evaluating himself and others. As London and Rosenhan (1968) note, normality is "not so much descriptive as evaluative . . . the meanings attributed to it are not intended merely to compare, but are ways of passing judgment, especially negative judgment, on behavior" (p. 4). In this section we shall review some of the specific attempts that have been made to define each of these concepts in trying to reach a better understanding of man's basis for self-judgment.

The concept of normality

Many people take the concept of normality for granted and arbitrarily accept certain behavior as normal while rejecting other actions as abnormal. Others simply consider the normal person as one who is free from abnormal traits, which only creates the problem of defining what is abnormal. The fact is that normality is not so easily defined. On the contrary, there are many ways to define normality, and this is well documented by the variety of specific characteristics that have been suggested in the psychological literature. For example, Shakow (1967) suggests that normal psychological functioning is characterized by curiosity, spontaneity, and alertness to new activities. The normal person is stable, flexible, and able to generalize easily. He is neither very similar to others nor very different from others and can discriminate between the personal and impersonal. The normal person is able to evaluate situations accurately and can handle uncertainty. He can disregard irrelevant stimulation, and his perception is realistic and accurate. According to McLaughlin (1950), the normal or "emotionally mature" person is, among other things: emotionally independent and self-reliant; able to achieve a balance between giving and receiving; relatively free from egotism, inferiority feelings, and excessive competitiveness; flexible and adaptable; constructively aggressive; and has a set of internal standards which facilitate psychological

growth. Bond (1952) lists the ability to work and love easily and the capacity to obtain happiness and efficiency in proportion to one's circumstances as characteristics of normality. Shoben (1957), in an article which appears later in this section, describes five essential ingredients of normality: self-control, personal responsibility, social responsibility, democratic social interest, and ideals.

Clearly, not all psychologists are in agreement about what is normal behavior, suggesting that the certainty which often exists among lay persons is not well-founded. Part of the lack of consensus about what is normal results from the fact that the various subgroups within a large society do not share the same values and consequently do not agree on similar standards of acceptable behavior. As Wile (1940) points out: "Abnormality varies according to the frame of reference—personal, familial, state, civil, economic, social or religious. Normality and abnormality are based upon prevailing concepts concerning physical, intellectual, ethical, and moral elements with judgments concerning their social, asocial or antisocial implications" (p. 216). Strauss (1967) also notes that large societies fail to provide the individual with a consistent set of expectations about what is considered deviant or abnormal. He writes:

The implication of our position is that nation is pluralistic, composed of many groups with divergent values; that some of those groups sometimes engage in public contests the results of which become written into law which defines—for a time, but not forever—what a deviant act is and who shall be punished for committing it. Implicit in this position is that the deviancy is a continual, never-ending process (Strauss, 1967, p. 265).

According to Simpson (1965), the individual who conforms to the standards of some groups will automatically violate the standards of other groups. Simpson (1965) challenges the assumption, prevalent among many social theorists, that society consists of a large majority of persons who conform to a general normative standard and a small percentage of deviant "boat-rockers." On the contrary, Simpson (1965) feels that social definitions of deviance and acceptable behavior are quite unclear.

Even if society's standards of acceptable behavior were completely consistent and clear, there is reason to believe that this would not provide a satisfactory basis for defining normality. For example, Mainord (1968), on the basis of evidence of man's sexual behavior (Kinsey et al., 1948) and dishonesty (Hartshorne and May, 1928), concludes that: ". . . much rule breaking is typical of the normal man but . . . it is done in such a way as to remain undetected" (p. 187). According to Mainord (1968), society acts either to restrain or encourage certain behaviors, and he postulates a continuum for describing behavior in these terms. At one end of the continuum are "socially restricted" persons, such as inmates of prisons or mental hospitals. At the other end are "socially encouraged" persons, such as corporate executives or public officials in high office. But the middle of the continuum is occupied by "the great majority of mankind whose total behaviors hardly impel society to respond at all" (Mainord, 1968, p. 183). These persons are "socially invisible" and it is this invisibility that characterizes the normal man. It is not that normal persons act in a different, better, or more acceptable manner than deviates. They are merely less conspicuous in their deviancy. This point of view is shared by Strauss (1967), who points out that highly visible acts are more likely to be labeled as abnormal or deviant, and, to some extent, by Kaplan (1967). For Kaplan (1967), a normal person is "someone who doesn't make trouble—trouble, that is, for whoever is doing the classifying" (p. 325).

Not all psychologists attempt to define normal behavior by listing specific characteristics of the person. For instance, London and Rosenhan (1968) suggest that normality, which is an attempt to describe what is acceptable behavior, can be defined in three ways. *Socially oriented* concepts of normality are rooted in conformity. From this standpoint, the normal person is one whose behavior is conventional and acceptable *to others*. The underlying assumption of this approach is that conventional behavior is by definition acceptable. In *self-oriented,* definitions, the individual provides his own standards of acceptable behavior. Behavior is considered normal from this perspective if it meets three criteria: (1) *intelligibility*—we feel we understand the nature and motives of our behavior; (2) *consistency*—we feel that our be-

havior is predictable on the basis of what we know about ourselves; and (3) *control*—we feel that our behavior is subject to our wishes so that we may either produce or prevent a particular behavior at will (London & Rosenhan, 1968, p. 4). The *idealized moral* concept of normality is based on the idea that people *ought* to behave in a particular way and defines normality in terms of the extent to which people behave as they ought to.

An example of a socially oriented concept of normality is provided by Mowrer (1953) who defines normality in terms of the organization and development of society. In his opinion, normality is best understood in the context of the historical development of the principles or "social ethics" upon which the organization of the society is based. Society places some pressure on every individual to accept and adapt to certain approved ways of behaving. "To the extent that an individual is able in his lifetime to assimilate the historically hard-won wisdom of society and to experience the fruits thereof, he may be said to be normal; to the extent that he fails, he is abnormal" (Mowrer, 1953, p. 167). Rosen (1962) also emphasizes the importance of society in assessing normal psychological functioning. For Rosen, normality is best defined in terms of the ability to get along with others. The normal person is "one who conforms within the limits of social tolerance. This definition includes both the individual who conforms tolerably without thinking much about it, and the individual who manages to conform outwardly, despite his nonconformist tendencies" (Rosen, 1962, p. 6). Sabshin (1967) suggests that the various definitions of normality can be summarized under four separate categories. First, *normality as health* consists of an application to psychological functioning of the traditional medical view of physical health as the absence of unfavorable symptoms. Second, *normality as Utopia* is based on the ideal of optimal functioning. In this view, normality is defined in terms of an ideal which is seldom achieved in actuality. Third, *normality as average* is a statistical solution which defines normal behavior on the basis of the principle of greatest frequency. From this standpoint, normal behavior is that which characterizes the greatest number of persons. Finally, *normality as process* emphasizes the capacity to change over time as an alternative to using specific behaviors as criteria. As the culture changes, the concept of what is normal also changes.

Kisker (1964) describes five models for determining normal behavior. In the *subjective model* the person uses himself as a standard of comparison. People who are seen as different are considered abnormal. This particular approach suffers from a lack of objectivity, since a person with a serious personality disturbance is likely to be the very one to deny it. The *normative model* is based on the establishment of an ideal, and normality is defined in terms of the extent to which this ideal is approximated. For example, the great religious leaders such as Buddha, Christ, Confucius, Mohammed, and Moses are likely to serve as ideals. This approach, like Sabshin's (1967) concept of *normality as Utopia,* suffers from the limitation that ideals are abstractions which are seldom reached in reality. The *cultural model* is based on the assumption that normality is defined by the majority of the people in the particular country. This approach is rather unwieldy in large, melting pot kinds of societies like our own in which a great number of subcultures are intermingled. The *statistical model* derives from the concept of the arithmetical average and is essentially the same as the one described by Sabshin (1967). The adequacy of both the cultural and statistical models are examined in detail by Wegrocki (1938) later in this section. Finally, Kisker (1964) describes the *clinical model* of normality which emphasizes the effectiveness of the individual personality. In this view, normality is measured by the internal organization and functioning of the individual personality. Freedom from symptoms is the main criterion for normality.

Both Sabshin's (1967) and Kisker's (1964) categories suggest that the task of arriving at any universal or commonly accepted definition of normality is likely to meet with considerable difficulty. Not only can we expect persons to disagree about the specific features of normal behavior, but we can expect variability in deciding what is the best basis for making comparisons. As Szasz (1960) points out, whatever a norm is, it involves "psychosocial, ethical, and legal concepts" (p. 114). Any approach which fails to take into consideration the wide spectrum of relevant considerations will clearly be oversimplifying the problem.

Just as different psychologists vary in their opinions of what it means to be normal, so do they vary in their estimates of how useful the concept of normality is. In fact, the concept of normality has been criticized in several ways. Some of the criticism has been as a very general level and has centered around the question of whether there is or can be such a thing as a normal personality. For example, both Darrah (1939) and Jones (1942) question whether such a thing as the normal personality exists. McLaughlin (1950) feels that the concept of normality is and will continue to be nebulous for several reasons: 1) there is considerable variation due to cultural and ethnic differences both across cultures and within the same culture; 2) the complexity of the human organism as a "psychobiologic and sociobiologic unit" defies any single concept of normality; 3) the rapid changes characteristic of childhood prevent the concept from being meaningfully applied to children; and, 4) what most people do is not a good criterion for normality since "what is prevalent is not necessarily optimal" (p. 22).

Based on a comprehensive review of the literature, Friedes (1960) presents a well-documented critique of the concept of the normal personality. He is particularly critical of the idealist notion of normality primarily because it attempts to establish specific values, characteristic of a particular culture at a particular time in history, as absolute or universal criteria. In his opinion, this view erroneously assumes that "what is good for us is good for everybody elsewhere" (Friedes, 1960, p. 28). Friedes (1960) suggests that a truly objective and scientific definition of normality may be impossible to attain. Consequently, a desirable alternative is to eliminate the concept of normality and replace it with a more viable perspective. Specifically, Friedes (1960) advocates replacing the idea that man is normal or abnormal with an attitude that sees man as having certain potentialities and limitations that vary according to different conditions. As an illustration of his rationale, Friedes (1960) offers the following examples: The qualities of suspicion and mistrust may contribute to one's success as a tax inspector or counter-intelligence agent, but, from the standpoint of abnormality, they may be considered undesirable or deviant traits. Similarly, a distant, withdrawn person may make a highly successful astronaut or competent research worker in a laboratory, yet these same characteristics might be used to describe the individual as psychologically unfit. To automatically label a person as abnormal on the basis of possessing certain personality traits is to deny the complexity of the interaction that characterizes the individual and his environment.

A final source of criticism to be considered here is based on the clinical observations of patients undergoing psychiatric treatment. Rieder (1950) suggests that the increasing familiarization of the general public with the various criteria of normality, made available through the popularization of psychiatry and psychoanalysis, has produced a double effect. For some, the notion of normality constitutes a "threat and accusation" (pp. 50-51). Other persons use their newly acquired knowledge of normality to develop "pseudonormal" attitudes and behaviors in an attempt to cover up their underlying emotional disturbance, which is often quite severe. As an illustration of this latter phenomenon, Rieder (1950) describes the emotionally disturbed mothers seen in a psychiatric clinic who have learned to conceal their problems through their exposure to mental hygiene courses, nursery school conferences, PTA programs, and reading of child psychology books. At the outset, the staff can find little wrong with how these disturbed women handle their children, and this syndrome is jokingly referred to among the staff as "the mother who makes like normal" (p. 45). Implicit in this behavior, according to Rieder (1950), is the fact that for a certain portion of our population the meaning of normality is derived from the concept of "good." Conversely, Szasz (1961) suggests that being mentally ill denotes behavior which is considered socially deviant or unpleasant.

The concept of adjustment

In recent years it has become increasingly popular to talk of being "well-adjusted." The notion of adjustment represents an extension of a biological concept to the realm of psychology and refers to the person's efforts to adapt to the stresses and strains of his environment. However, concepts of adjustment, like those of normality, are fundamentally evaluative. What is considered effective adjustment for a given individual will depend on criteria established by specific goals and values. According to Haas (1965), the notion of adjustment has been proposed because of the difficulties inherent in reaching a satisfactory definition of normality. White (1966) attributes the popularity of adjustment, along with the related ideas of mental health and emotional maturity, to the attempt to fill an "ideological vacuum" that has resulted from two major sources: 1) the decline of religion and ethics as guides to personal behavior; and, 2) the confusion and uncertainty in secular values other than those derived from science. Whatever the basis for its origin, the notion of being "well-adjusted" is presently a highly desirable goal for many persons in our society.

Like normality, definitions of adjustment vary considerably. Mathews (1960) maintains that successful adjustment consists of man's freedom "to join his fellow man in a loving, creative, and productive way" (p. 670). Haas (1965) defines adjustment as "the ability to get along with others" (p. 157). This is based upon having the necessary skills to "fit ourselves in with others and respond as desired by those with whom we associate" (Haas, 1965, p. 157). Coleman (1960) suggests three criteria for effective adjustment: 1) the behavior of the individual meets the objective requirements of the situation; 2) an individual's behavior satisfies his overall needs; and, 3) the behavior of the individual is compatible with the welfare of the group.

Sawrey and Telford (1963) describe five common meanings of adjustment. Three of these share an external frame of reference and include: 1) becoming accustomed to new conditions so that we are no longer disturbed by them (e.g., changes in temperature); 2) learning to accept and live with certain social conditions; 3) conforming to social demands. This last characteristic is closely related to compromising differences of opinion. Two additional criteria have a more personal connotation; 4) adjustment is indicated by harmony within the individual (the well-adjusted person is "integrated, self-consistent, self-accepting," and happy); and, 5) the self-realization or self-actualization concept which consists of the maximum realization of one's potential.

In his review of the literature on adjustment, Tindall (1955) concludes that the majority of writers generally regard the following seven characteristics as desirable.

1. *Maintaining an integrated personality.* This involves the coordination of one's needs and goal seeking behavior into smoothly functioning interaction with the environment.

2. *Conforming to social demands.* Emphasis here is upon harmony with the standards of the cultural group without surrendering individual spontaneity.

3. *Adapting to reality conditions.* This facet is characteristic of the ability to expose oneself to present hardship conditions in order to make gains toward long range goals.

4. *Maintaining consistency.* A qualitative facet which makes possible prediction for behavior and permits hopes for the assessment of adjustment.

5. *Maturing with age.* Allowance is made for maturation and development of the individual with concomitant growth of more complex adjustment processes.

6. *Maintaining an optimal emotional tone.* In the face of emotionally loaded situations the well-adjusted person is neither constricted in emotional involvement nor overwhelmed by his reactions.

7. *Contributing optimally to society through an increasing efficiency.* Here is an insurance that adjustive behavior reaches beyond self-centered goals (pp. 153-154).

Despite the popularity the goal of being well-adjusted has achieved in our society, the concept of adjustment is not without its critics. Tindall (1955) concludes that a global concept of adjustment is of limited usefulness and that we need more clear definitions of adjustment. White (1966) feels that the concept of adjustment disregards the significance of individuality. In White's opinion, adjustment has degenerated into a "doctrine of conformity" which is based on the assumption that a person should conform to the expectations of his social environment. White (1966) feels that this is a misapplication of the biological concept of adjustment which allows for the individual to change his environment to suit his own needs. This criticism is consistent with the observations of Barron (1968) who points out that the healthy person is often identified by his refusal to adjust or go along with social roles at the price of de-emphasizing the importance of the self and of his individuality.

The utility of the concept of adjustment seems to be based on two assumptions: 1) that an individual's environment presents a consistent set of standards which he can adjust to; and, 2) that these standards of behavior are desirable. We have already seen in our discussion of normality that the validity of the first assumption has been strongly challenged (Wile, 1940; Simpson, 1965). The individual, unless he restricts his life's activities to a relatively small and well-defined group of people, is not likely to come into contact with homogeneous and consistent standards of acceptable behavior. The second assumption is untenable. Although the majority rules, it is not necessarily correct. Anyone who has ever witnessed a lynch mob in action or viewed the atrocities of Nazi Germany realizes that the social environment does not always represent optimum criteria for living. Contrary to popular opinion, 50,000 Frenchmen *can* be wrong. As Ginsburg (1963) notes:

Adjustment itself has by now become a highly regarded value in our culture, along with happiness, success, fun, mental health, and others. But it is time to ask: who adjusts to what and according to whose standards and values; under what conditions is adjustment a strength and when is it only a pleasant term for the weakness of too easy and uncritical compliance; are all mavericks, crusaders, and their unfortunately diminishing like, inevitably to be considered maladjusted and is that necessarily something bad and to be avoided? (p. 47).

The concept of mental health

Closely related to the concepts of adjustment and normality and equally as popular is the notion of mental health. Concepts of mental health arise out of the historical context of physical medicine and are based on the "medical model" of personality functioning. Very simply, this view sees disordered behavior as a form of mental illness analogous to physical illness. This approach assumes that disordered psychological behavior can be defined in terms of specific symptoms in the same way that bodily disease is diagnosed. Concepts of mental health represent an extension of this philosophy and are defined as either the absence of symptoms or the presence of other more positive (healthy) characteristics. Typical definitions include "the ability to function effectively and happily as a person in one's expected role" (Bowman, 1965, p. 33), and "the ability to hold a job, have a family, keep out of trouble with the law, and enjoy the usual opportunities for pleasure" (Ginsburg, 1963, p. 9). Klein (1960) defines mental health in terms of three distinct properties. First, it refers to certain enduring aspects of the personality which he calls the "soundness" of the individual. These aspects are usually assessed in the context of the ideals of a particular culture. In our culture, soundness might include such characteristics as adaptability, initiative, and well-developed social skills. Second, mental health depicts the person's immediate state of health or "well-being." This includes the "current state of equilibrium between the individual and the social emotional environment impinging upon him" at a given time (p. 289). Third, mental health indicates the "emotional stability" of the individual which is reflected by his ability to "avoid illness even when exposed to illness-producing agents" (p. 289).

Like the concepts of normality and adjustment, definitions of mental health bear a strong general resemblance to each other but often differ in their specific nature. For example, Grinker (1967) describes the general qualities of a healthy personality as: ". . . realistic self-esteem, good affectional relations with consistency, continued accretion of a reservoir of internalized roles, a flexible sense of identity, and a capacity to organize behavior relative to the situational requirements" (p. 322). For Jourard (1963), the healthy person is one ". . . who has been able to gratify his basic needs through acceptable behavior so that his own personality is no longer a problem to him. He can take himself more or less for granted and devote his energies and thoughts to socially meaningful interests and problems beyond security, or lovability, or status" (p. 21). Bowman (1965) lists seven criteria for the healthy adult personality. In his opinion, the healthy person: 1) works for human betterment but accepts people and situations as he finds them; 2) feels part of the group and derives satisfaction from contributions he makes to others rather than from "selfish, self-centered gain or pleasure" (p. 39); 3) is aware of his relation to the universe and is interested in religious values; 4) knows his own abilities and limitations, has a reasonable amount of

self-confidence, and does not need to make excuses to protect himself; 5) has a consistent pattern of sound values and is not torn by internal conflict; 6) does not try to evade problems but approaches them realistically and constructively; and, 7) looks to the future without resting on past accomplishments. Similar lists have been compiled by Kalish (1966), Maslow (1962), and others, but by far the most extensive list is presented by Tyson (1951) who describes a total of 2,394 mental health suggestions taken from 228 references.

Not all of the attempts to understand mental health are represented by lists of specific personal qualities. Shoben (1967) offers the notion of the "examined life" as a fruitful conception of mental health. The examined life is an informed and critical life and involves the acceptance of responsibility for one's own actions and the continuing inquiry into the bases upon which a person acts. The examined life evolves out of the process of criticism and self-evaluation. This means that the specific criteria which characterize the individual change with time and experience. In this context, psychological growth is attained to the extent that the process of self-examination leads to increased self-knowledge and a "widened sense of self-determination" (p. 386).

One of the most comprehensive approaches to understanding mental health has been outlined by Jahoda (1953, 1958). Jahoda (1953) recommends eliminating those usual but inappropriate uses of the term which include: the absence of mental disease, statistical normality, psychological well-being, and successful survival. These criteria are inappropriate because "they neglect the social matrix of human behavior" (Jahoda, 1953, p. 351). As an alternative, Jahoda (1953, 1958) recommends substituting the following six criteria: 1) the individual's *attitudes toward his own self* (including self-awareness, self-acceptance, sense of identity, and accurate perception of oneself); 2) *growth, development, or self-actualization;* 3) *integration* (resistance to stress, balanced psychic forces within the person, and a unifying outlook on life); 4) *autonomy* (regulation of one's actions from within and independent behavior); 5) *perception of reality* (perception free from need-distortion and social sensitivity); 6) and mastery over the environment (the ability to love, adequacy in interpersonal relations and other activities, efficiency in problem-solving, capacity for adaptation, and efficiency in meeting situational requirements).

The concept of mental health is useful to the extent that it provides guidelines by which individuals may assess the adequacy of their psychological functioning. Although this is a commendable goal, there are definite limitations and disadvantages associated with this approach. There is reason to question the validity of looking at psychological disturbance as a form of mental illness in the traditional view of physical illness. As London and Rosenhan (1968) point out, deviant behavior does not necessarily or even typically stem from infectious disease. Although all behavior represents an interaction at some level of physical and psychological processes, not all persons engaging in deviant behavior can be demonstrated to have any signs of infectious or physical illness. Consequently, it is of dubious value to consider deviant acts as indications of mental illness requiring medical treatment. In keeping with this hypothesis, a recent textbook in psychiatry (Redlich & Freedman, 1966) omits the concept of mental illness and defines psychiatry as "the medical specialty concerned with the study, diagnosis, treatment, and prevention of behavior disorders" (p. 1). The authors go on to state that: "Whereas many cerebral diseases produce a behavior disorder, and while we believe that cerebral processes must be related fundamentally to behavior, medically recognizable diseases of the brain cannot, for the most part, be demonstrated in behavior disorders" (p. 2). An alternative explanation is to view disturbed behavior as the result of faulty learning experiences requiring corrective education. The issue of whether deviant behavior can be properly understood in terms of mental illness is a complex one involving many factors and is debated in detail by Szasz (1960) and Ausubel (1961) in their papers. The problem is of relevance here, because the validity of the concept of mental health is, to a large extent, dependent upon the notion of mental illness.

Another serious drawback of the mental health concept is related to the tendency of unsophisticated persons to adopt a particular conception of mental health as absolute. This is particularly undesirable in view of the fact that lists of mental health characteristics may represent arbitrary value systems or unrealistic ideals. As White (1966) observes, lists of qualities that comprise notions of mental health often bear little resemblance to any actual person: "Neurotics are not neurotic with respect to every feature of their lives; conversely, healthy people cannot be expected to be equally healthy in every department" (White, 1966, p. 373). Ideally, mental health criteria should only be applied in relation to a variety of other considerations and in the context of each person's life and background.

The characteristics of the mentally healthy person, whatever they may be, can not be interpreted apart from a particular value orientation. Even if the qualities are determined empirically—by the scientific study of persons considered to be mentally healthy—there remains the decision of which group of persons to study. This decision is clearly based on value judgments. The idea that notions of mental health and values are closely intertwined is not new and has been cited by more than one writer. For example, Scott (1958) notes:

The mental hygiene movement has traditionally been identified with one or another set of values—ideal standards from which behavior could be assessed as appropriate or inappropriate. The particular set of values adopted probably depends to a considerable degree on who is doing the judging. Such a diversity of evaluative judgments leads to chaos in the popular literature and to considerable confusion in the usage of the term "mental health" in scientific research (pp. 41-42).

It can be argued that values are an integral part of all psychological concepts. It is particularly important to realize their significance here because of the bases of the mental health approach. Medical diagnoses, upon which psychological diagnoses are based within the mental illness model, are scientific decisions that are relatively free from value considerations. However, the application of medical terminology or principles to behavior does not automatically free the psychological diagnoses from value entanglements. Mental health sounds much more objective than either adjustment or normality, but it is subject to many of the same pitfalls. The general problem of the relation of values to mental health is considered in more detail and from several perspectives in the papers by Becker (1958), Korner (1956), Lowe (1959), Smith (1961), and Rogers (1964).

In Section 6, we discussed how living in a complex society characterized by rapid change can undermine the individual's sense of security and identity. Perhaps the modern emphasis on being normal, well-adjusted, or mentally healthy represents a further search for specific criteria whereby man can judge himself. However, the final decision about what it means to be normal, healthy, or well-adjusted has not been reached. The individual is free to search for meaningful criteria by which he can evaluate his behavior. The success of this process, like the success of any pursuit of knowledge, is based on the gathering of information from as many different points of view as possible. The following papers represent a wide sampling of opinion that will hopefully facilitate the search.

References

Ausubel, D. Personality disorder is disease. *Amer. Psychologist,* 1961, 16, 69-74.

Barron, F. *Creativity and personal freedom.* Princeton, N.J.: Van Nostrand, 1968.

Becker, R. J. Links between psychology and religion. *Amer. Psychologist,* 1958, 13, 566-568.

Bond, E. D. The student council study: An approach to the normal. *Amer. J. Psychiat.,* 1952, 109, 11-16.

Bowman, H. A. The nature of mental health. In R. I. Sutherland & B. K. Smith (Eds.) *Understanding mental health.* Princeton, N. J.: Van Nostrand, 1965, pp. 33-39.

Coleman, J. C. *Personality dynamics and effective behavior.* Glenview, Ill.: Scott, Foresman, 1960.

Darrah, L. The difficulties of being "normal." *J., nerv. and mental Disease,* 1939, 90, 730-739.

Friedes, D. Toward the elimination of the concept of normality. *Journal of cons. Psychol.,* 1960, 24, 128-133.

Ginsburg, S. W. *A psychiatrist's views on social issues.* New York: Columbia University Press, 1963.

Grinker, R. R., Sr. Normality viewed as a system. *Arch. gen. Psychiat.,* 1967, 17, 320-324.

Haas, K. *Understanding ourselves and others.* Englewood Cliffs, N. J.: Prentice-Hall, 1965.

Hartshorne, H. & May, M. A. *Studies in deceit.* New York: Cromwell-Collier and Macmillan, 1928.

Jahoda, Marie The meaning of psychological health. *Social Casework,* 1953, 34, 349-354.

Jahoda, Marie *Current concepts of positive mental health.* New York: Basic Books, 1958.

Jones, E. The concept of the normal mind. *Int. J. Psychoanal.,* 1942, 23, 1-8.

Jourard, S. M. *Personal adjustment,* Second Edition. New York: Macmillan, 1963.

Kalish, R. A. *The psychology of human behavior.* Belmont, Calif.: Wadsworth, 1966.

Kaplan, A. A philosophic discussion of normality. *Arch. of gen. Psychiat.,* 1967, 17, 325-330.

Kinsey, A. C., Pomeroy, W. B., & Martin, C. E. *Sexual behavior in the human male.* Philadelphia: W. B. Saunders, 1948.

Kisker, G. *The disorganized personality.* New York: McGraw-Hill, 1964.

Klein, D. C. Some concepts concerning the mental health of the individual. *J. cons. Psychol.,* 1960, 24, 288-293.

Korner, I. N. Of values, value lag, and mental health. *Amer. Psychologist.* 1956, 11, 543-546.

London, P. & Rosenhan, D. The meaning of abnormality. In P. London & D. Rosenhan. (Eds.) *Foundations of abnormal psychology,* New York: Holt, Rinehart, & Winston, 1968. Pp. 3-27.

Lowe, C. M. Value orientations—an ethical dilemma. *Amer. Psychologist,* 1959, 14, 687-693.

Mainord, W. A. People at midpoint: The search for normality. In P. London & D. Rosenhan (Eds.) *Foundations of abnormal psychology.* New York: Holt, Rinehart, & Winston, 1968. Pp. 177-200.

Maslow, A. *Toward a psychology of being.* Princeton, N. J.: Van Nostrand, 1962.

Mathews, W. M. Successful adjustment: A frame of reference. *Amer. J. Orthopsychiat.,* 1960, 30, 667-675.

McLaughlin, J. T. Normality and psychosomatic illness. *Mental Hygiene.* 1950, 34, 19-33.

Mowrer, O. H. What is normal behavior? In A. Weider (Ed.) *Contributions toward medical psychology,* Vol. 1. New York: Ronald Press, 1953.

Redlich, R. C. & Freedman, D. X. *The theory and practice of psychiatry.* N.Y.: Basic Books, 1966.

Rieder, N. The concept of normality. *Psychoanalyt. Quart.,* 1950, 19, 43-51.

Rogers, C. R. Toward a modern approach to values: The valuing process in the mature person. *J. abnorm. soc. Psychol.,* 1964, 68, 160-167.

Rosen, J. N. *Direct psychoanalytic psychiatry.* New York: Grune & Stratton, 1962.

Sabsin, M. Psychiatric perspectives on normality. *Arch. gen. Psychiat.,* 1967, 17, 258-264.

Sawrey, J. M. & Telford, C. W. *Dynamics of mental health: The psychology of adjustment.* Boston: Allyn & Bacon, 1963.

Scott, W. A. Research definitions in mental health and mental illness. *Psychol. Bull.,* 1958, 55, 29-45.

Shakow, D. Understanding normal psychological function. *Arch. gen. Psychiat.,* 1967, 17, 306-319.

Shoben, E. J., Jr. Toward a concept of the normal personality. *Amer. Psychologist.* 1957, 12, 183-189.

Shoben, E. J., Jr. The examined life as mental health. In Mowrer, O. H. (Ed.), *Morality and mental health.* Chicago: Rand McNally, 1967.

Simpson, J. L. Public stereotypes of deviants. *Social Problems,* 1965, 13, 225.

Smith, M. B. Mental health reconsidered: A special case of the problem of values in psychology. *Amer. Psychologist,* 1961, 16, 299-306.

Strauss, A. L. A sociological view of normality. *Arch. gen. Psychiat.,* 1967, 17, 265-270.

Szasz, T. The myth of mental illness. *Amer. Psychologist,* 1960, 15, 113-118.

Szasz, T. The uses of naming and the origin of the myth of mental illness. *Amer. Psychologist,* 1961, 16, 59-65.

Tindall, R. H. Relationships among measures of adjustment. *Educational and Psychological Measurement,* 1955, 15, 152-162.

Tyson, R. Current mental hygiene practice. *J. clin. Psych.,* 1951, 7, 1-100.

Wegrocki, H. J. A critique of the cultural and statistical concepts of normality. *J. abnorm. soc. Psychol.,* 1939, 34, 166-178.

White, R. W. *Lives in progress.* Second Edition. New York: Holt, Rinehart and Winston, 1966.

Wile, I. S. What constitutes abnormality? *Amer. J. Orthopsychiat.,* 1940, 10, 216-228.

The myth of mental illness

THOMAS S. SZASZ

Mental illness is based on the belief that people can become psychologically sick in the same way that they develop a physical illness. Despite the familiarity, apparent simplicity, and widespread acceptance of this idea, mental illness is not an easily defined concept. In this article, Thomas Szasz, M.D., a frequent critic of modern attitudes toward disordered behavior, reviews some of the uses of the term, challenges the utility of the concept, and points out some of the difficulties that can arise from adopting a physical disease model to account for behavioral problems.

Dr. Szasz, who is Professor of Psychiatry at the Upstate Medical Center of the State University of New York, is the author of *Pain and Pleasure; The Myth of Mental Illness; Law, Liberty, and Psychiatry; The Ethics of Psychoanalysis; Psychiatric Justice;* and more than one hundred and fifty articles and book reviews in medical, legal, psychiatric, philosophical, and sociological journals and popular magazines.

My aim in this essay is to raise the question, "Is there such a thing as mental illness?" and to argue that there is not. Since the notion of mental illness is extremely widely

From *American Psychologist,* XV (1960), 113-118. Reprinted by permission of the American Psychological Association and the author.

used nowadays, inquiry into the ways in which this term is employed would seem to be especially indicated. Mental illness, of course, is not literally a "thing"—or physical object—and hence it can "exist" only in the same sort of way in which other theoretical concepts exist. Yet, familiar theories are in the habit of posing, sooner or later—at least to those who come to believe in them—as "objective truths" (or "facts"). During certain historical periods, explanatory conceptions such as deities, witches, and miscroorganisms appeared not only as theories but as self-evident *causes* of a vast number of events. I submit that today mental illness is widely regarded in a somewhat similar fashion, that is, as the cause of innumerable diverse happenings. As an antidote to the complacent use of the notion of mental illness—whether as a self-evident phenomenon, theory, or cause—let us ask this question: What is meant when it is asserted that someone is mentally ill?

In what follows I shall describe briefly the main uses to which the concept of mental illness has been put. I shall argue that this notion has outlived whatever usefulness it might have had and that it now functions merely as a convenient myth.

Mental illness as a sign of brain disease

The notion of mental illness derives its main support from such phenomena as syphilis of the brain or delirious conditions—intoxications, for instance—in which persons are known to manifest various peculiarities or disorders of thinking and behavior. Correctly speaking, however, these are diseases of the brain, not of the mind. According to one school of thought, *all* so-called mental illness is of this type. The assumption is made that some neurological defect, perhaps a very subtle one, will ultimately be found for all the disorders of thinking and behavior. Many contemporary psychiatrists, physicians, and other scientists hold this view. This position implies that people *cannot* have troubles—expressed in what are *now called* "mental illnesses"—because of differences in personal needs, opinions, social aspirations, values, and so on. *All problems in living* are attributed to physicochemical processes which in due time will be discovered by medical research.

"Mental illnesses" are thus regarded as basically no different than all other diseases (that is, of the body). The only difference, in this view, between mental and bodily diseases is that the former, affecting the brain, manifest themselves by means of mental symptoms; whereas the latter, affecting other organ systems (for example, the skin, liver, etc.), manifest themselves by means of symptoms referable to those parts of the body. This view rests on and expresses what are, in my opinion, two fundamental errors.

In the first place, what central nervous system symptoms would correspond to a skin eruption or a fracture? It would *not* be some emotion or complex bit of behavior. Rather, it would be blindness or a paralysis of some part of the body. The crux of the matter is that a disease of the brain, analogous to a disease of the skin or bone, is a neurological defect, and not a problem in living. For example, a *defect* in a person's visual field may be satisfactorily explained by correlating it with certain definite lesions in the nervous system. On the other hand, a person's *belief*— whether this be a belief in Christianity, in Communism, or in the idea that his internal organs are "rotting" and that his body is, in fact, already "dead"—cannot be explained by a defect or disease of the nervous system. Explanations of this sort of occurrence—assuming that one is interested in the belief itself and does not regard it simply as a "symptom" or expression of something else that is *more interesting*—must be sought along different lines.

The second error in regarding complex psychosocial behavior, consisting of communications about ourselves and the world about us, as mere symptoms of neurological functioning is *epistemological*. In other words, it is an error pertaining not to any mistakes in observation or reasoning, as such, but rather to the way in which we organize and express our knowledge. In the present case, the error lies in making a symmetrical dualism between mental and physical (or bodily) symptoms, a dualism which is merely a habit of speech and to which no known observations can be found to correspond. Let us see if this is so. In medical practice, when we speak of physical disturbances, we mean either signs (for example, a fever) or symptoms (for example, pain). We speak of mental symptoms, on the other hand, when we refer to a patient's *communications about himself, others, and the world about him*. He might state that he is Napoleon or that he is being persecuted by the Communists. These would be considered mental symptoms *only* if the observer believed that the patient was *not* Napoleon or that he was *not* being persecuted by the Communists. This makes it apparent that the statement that *"X is a mental symptom"* involves rendering a judgment. The judgment entails, moreover, a covert comparison or matching of the patient's ideas, concepts, or beliefs with those of the observer and the society in which they live. The notion of mental symptom is therefore inextricably tied to the *social* (including *ethical*) *context* in which it is made in much the same way as the notion of bodily symptom is tied to an *anatomical* and *genetic context* (Szasz, 1957a, 1957b).

To sum up what has been said thus far: I have tried to show that for those who regard mental symptoms as signs of brain disease, the concept of mental illness is unnecessary and misleading. For what they mean is that people so labeled suffer from diseases of the brain; and, if that is what they mean, it would seem better for the sake of clarity to say that and not something else.

Mental illness as a name for problems in living

The term "mental illness" is widely used to describe something which is very different than a disease of the brain. Many people today take it for granted that living is an arduous process. Its hardship for modern man, moreover, derives not so much from a struggle for biological survival as from the stresses and strains inherent in the social intercourse of complex human personalities. In this context, the notion of mental illness is used to identify or describe some feature of an individual's so-called personality. Mental illness—as a deformity of the personality, so to speak—is then regarded as the *cause* of the human disharmony. It is implicit in this view that social intercourse between people is regarded as something *inherently harmonious,* its disturbance being due solely to the presence of "mental illness" in many people. This is obviously fallacious reasoning, for it makes the abstraction "mental illness" into a *cause,* even though this abstrac-

tion was created in the first place to serve only as a shorthand expression for certain types of human behavior. It now becomes necessary to ask: "What kinds of behavior are regarded as indicative of mental illness, and by whom?"

The concept of illness, whether bodily or mental, implies *deviation from some clearly defined norm.* In the case of physical illness, the norm is the structural and functional integrity of the human body. Thus, although the desirability of physical health, as such, is an ethical value, what health *is* can be stated in anatomical and physiological terms. What is the norm deviation from which is regarded as mental illness? This question cannot be easily answered. But whatever this norm might be, we can be certain of only one thing: namely, that it is a norm that must be stated in terms of *psychosocial, ethical,* and *legal* concepts. For example, notions such as "excessive repression" or "acting out an unconscious impulse" illustrate the use of psychological concepts for judging (so-called) mental health and illness. The idea that chronic hostility, vengefulness, or divorce are indicative of mental illness would be illustrations of the use of ethical norms (that is, the desirability of love, kindness, and a stable marriage relationship). Finally, the widespread psychiatric opinion that only a mentally ill person would commit homicide illustrates the use of a legal concept as a norm of mental health. The norm from which deviation is measured whenever one speaks of a mental illness is a *psychosocial and ethical one.* Yet, the remedy is sought in terms of *medical* measures which—it is hoped and assumed—are free from wide differences of ethical value. The definition of the disorder and the terms in which its remedy are sought are, therefore, at serious odds with one another. The practical significance of this covert conflict between the alleged nature of the defect and the remedy can hardly be exaggerated.

Having identified the norms used to measure deviations in cases of mental illness, we will now turn to the question: "Who defines the norms and hence the deviation?" Two basic answers may be offered: (*a*) It may be the person himself (that is, the patient) who decides that he deviates from a norm. For example, an artist may believe that he suffers from a work inhibition; and he may implement this conclusion by seeking help *for* himself from a psychotherapist. (*b*) It may be someone other than the patient who decides that the latter is deviant (for example, relatives, physicians, legal authorities, society generally, etc.). In such a case a psychiatrist may be hired by others to do something *to* the patient in order to correct the deviation.

These considerations underscore the importance of asking the question "Whose agent is the psychiatrist?" and of giving a candid answer to it (Szasz, 1956, 1958). The psychiatrist (psychologist or nonmedical psychotherapist), it now develops, may be the agent of the patient, of the relatives, of the school, of the military services, of a business organization, of a court of law, and so forth. In speaking of the psychiatrist as the agent of these persons or organizations, it is not implied that his values concerning norms, or his ideas and aims concerning the proper nature of remedial action, need to coincide exactly with those of his employer. For example, a patient in individual psychotherapy may believe that his salvation lies in a new marriage; his psychotherapist need not share this hypothesis. As the patient's agent, however, he must abstain from bringing social or legal force to bear on the patient which would prevent him from putting his beliefs into action. If his *contract* is with the patient, the psychiatrist (psychotherapist) may disagree with him or stop his treatment; but he cannot engage others to obstruct the patient's aspirations. Similarly, if a psychiatrist is engaged by a court to determine the sanity of a criminal, he need not fully share the legal authorities' values and intentions in regard to the criminal and the means available for dealing with him. But the psychiatrist is expressly barred from stating, for example, that it is not the criminal who is "insane" but the men who wrote the law on the basis of which the very actions that are being judged are regarded as "criminal." Such an opinion could be voiced, of course, but not in a courtroom, and not by a psychiatrist who makes it his practice to assist the court in performing its daily work.

To recapitulate: In actual contemporary social usage, the finding of a mental illness is made by establishing a deviance in behavior from certain psychosocial, ethical, or legal norms. The judgment may be made, as in medicine, by the patient, the physician (psychiatrist), or others. Remedial action, finally, tends to be sought in a therapeutic—or covertly medical—framework, thus creating a situation in which *psychosocial, ethical,* and/or *legal deviations* are claimed to be correctible by (so-called) *medical action*. Since medical action is designed to correct only medical deviations, it seems logically absurd to expect that it will help solve problems whose very existence had been defined and established on nonmedical grounds. I think that these considerations may be fruitfully applied to the present use of tranquilizers and, more generally, to what might be expected of drugs of whatever type in regard to the amelioration or solution of problems in human living.

The role of ethics in psychiatry

Anything that people *do*—in contrast to things that *happen* to them (Peters, 1958)—takes place in a context of value. In this broad sense, no human activity is devoid of ethical implications. When the values underlying certain activities are widely shared, those who participate in their pursuit may lose sight of them altogether. The discipline of medicine, both as a pure science (for example, research) and as a technology (for example, therapy), contains many ethical considerations and judgments. Unfortunately, these are often denied, minimized, or merely kept out of focus; for the ideal of the medical profession as well as of the people whom it serves seems to be having a system of medicine (allegedly) free of ethical value. This sentimental notion is expressed by such things as the doctor's willingness to treat and help patients, irrespective of their religious or political beliefs, whether they are rich or poor, etc. While there may be some grounds for this belief—albeit it is a view that is not impressively true even in these regards —the fact remains that ethical considerations encompass a vast range of human affairs. By making the practice of medicine neutral in regard to some specific issues of value need not, and cannot, mean that it can be kept free from all such values. The practice of medicine is intimately tied to ethics; and the first thing that we must do, it seems to me, is to try to make this clear and explicit. I shall let this matter rest here, for it does not concern us specifically in this essay. Lest there be any vagueness, however, about how or where ethics and medicine meet, let me remind the reader of such issues as birth control, abortion, suicide, and euthanasia as only a few of the major areas of current ethicomedical controversy.

Psychiatry, I submit, is very much more intimately tied to problems of ethics than is medicine. I use the word "psychiatry" here to refer to that contemporary discipline which is concerned with *problems in living* (and not with diseases of the brain, which are problems for neurology). Problems in human relations can be analyzed, interpreted, and given meaning only within given social and ethical contexts. Accordingly, it *does* make a difference—arguments to the contrary notwithstanding—what the psychiatrist's socioethical orientations happen to be; for these will influence his ideas on what is wrong with the patient, what deserves comment or interpretation, in what possible directions change might be desirable, and so forth. Even in medicine proper, these factors play a role, as for instance, in the divergent orientations which physicians, depending on their religious affiliations, have toward such things as birth control and therapeutic abortion. Can anyone really believe that a psychotherapist's ideas concerning religious belief, slavery, or other similar issues play no role in his practical work? If they do make a difference, what are we to infer from it? Does it not seem reasonable that we ought to have different psychiatric therapies—each expressly recognized for the ethical positions which they embody—for, say, Catholics and Jews, religious persons and agnostics, democrats and communists, white supremacists and Negroes, and so on? Indeed, if we look at how psychiatry is actually practiced today (especially in the United States), we find that people do seek psychiatric help in accordance with their social status and ethical beliefs (Hollingshead & Redlich, 1958). This should really not surprise us more than being told that practicing Catholics rarely frequent birth control clinics.

The foregoing position which holds that contemporary psychotherapists deal with problems in living, rather than with mental illnesses and their cures, stands in opposition to a currently prevalent claim, according to which mental illness is just as "real" and "objective" as bodily illness. This is a confusing claim since it is never known exactly what is meant by such words as "real" and "objective." I suspect, however, that what is intended by the proponents of this view is to create the idea in the popular mind that mental illness is some sort of disease entity, like an infection or a malignancy. If this were true, one could *catch* or *get* a "mental illness," one might *have* or *harbor* it, one might *transmit* it to others, and finally one could get *rid* of it. In my opinion, there is not a shred of evidence to support this idea. To the contrary, all the evidence is the other way and supports the view that what people now call mental illnesses are for the most part *communications* expressing unacceptable ideas, often framed, moreover, in an unusual idiom. The scope of this essay allows me to do no more than mention this alternative theoretical approach to this problem (Szasz, 1957c).

This is not the place to consider in detail the similarities and differences between bodily and mental illnesses. It shall suffice for us here to emphasize only one important difference between them: namely, that whereas bodily disease refers to public, physicochemical occurrences, the notion of mental illness is used to codify relatively more private, sociopsychological happenings of which the observer (diagnostician) forms a part. In other words, the psychiatrist does not stand *apart* from what he observes, but is, in Harry Stack Sullivan's apt words, a "participant observer." This means that he is *committed* to some picture of what he considers reality—and to what he thinks society considers reality—and he observes and judges the patient's behavior in the light of these considerations. This touches on our earlier observation that the notion of mental symptom itself implies a comparison between observer and observed, psychiatrist and patient. This is so obvious that I may be charged with belaboring trivialities. Let me therefore say once more that my aim in presenting this argument was expressly to criticize and counter a prevailing contemporary tendency to deny the moral aspects of psychiatry (and psychotherapy) and to substitute for them allegedly value-free medical considerations. Psychotherapy, for example, is being widely practiced as though it entailed nothing other than restoring the patient from a state of mental sickness to one of mental health. While it is generally accepted that mental illness has something to do with man's social (or interpersonal) relations, it is paradoxically maintained that problems of values (that is, of ethics) do not arise in this process.[1] Yet, in one sense, much of psychotherapy may revolve around nothing other than the elucidation and weighing of goals and values—many of which may be mutually contradictory—and the means whereby they might best be harmonized, realized, or relinquished.

The diversity of human values and the methods by means of which they may be realized is so vast, and many of them remain so unacknowledged, that they cannot fail but lead to conflicts in human relations. Indeed, to say that human relations at all levels—from mother to child, through husband and wife, to nation and nation—are fraught with stress, strain, and disharmony is, once again, making the obvious explicit. Yet, what may be obvious may be also poorly understood. This I think is the case here. For it seems to me that—at least in our scientific theories of behavior—we have failed to *accept* the simple fact that human relations are inherently fraught with difficulties and that to make them even relatively harmonious requires much patience and hard work. I submit that the idea of mental illness is now being put to work to obscure certain difficulties which at present may be inherent—not that they need be unmodifiable—in the social intercourse of persons. If this is true, the concept functions as a disguise; for instead of calling attention to conflicting human needs, aspirations, and values, the notion of mental illness provides an amoral and impersonal "thing" (an "illness") as an explanation for *problems in living* (Szasz, 1959). We may recall in this connection that not so long ago it was devils and witches who were held responsible for men's problems in social living. The belief in mental illness, as something other than man's trouble in getting along with his fellow man, is the proper heir to the belief in demonology and witchcraft. Mental illness exists or is "real" in exactly the same sense in which witches existed or were "real."

Choice, responsibility, and psychiatry

While I have argued that mental illnesses do not exist, I obviously did not imply that

the social and psychological occurrences to which this label is currently being attached also do not exist. Like the personal and social troubles which people had in the Middle Ages, they are real enough. It is the labels we give them that concerns us and, having labelled them, what we do about them. While I cannot go into the ramified implications of this problem here, it is worth noting that a demonologic conception of problems in living gave rise to therapy along theological lines. Today, a belief in mental illness implies— nay, requires—therapy along medical or psychotherapeutic lines.

What is implied in the line of thought set forth here is something quite different. I do not intend to offer a new conception of "psychiatric illness" nor a new form of "therapy." My aim is more modest and yet also more ambitious. It is to suggest that the phenomena now called mental illnesses be looked at afresh and more simply, that they be removed from the category of illnesses, and that they be regarded as the expressions of man's struggle with the problem of *how* he should live. The last mentioned problem is obviously a vast one, its enormity reflecting not only man's inability to cope with his environment, but even more his increasing self-reflectiveness.

By problems in living, then, I refer to that truly explosive chain reaction which began with man's fall from divine grace by partaking of the fruit of the tree of knowledge. Man's awareness of himself and of the world about him seems to be a steadily expanding one, bringing in its wake an ever larger *burden of understanding* (an expression borrowed from Susanne Langer, 1953). *This burden, then, is to be expected and must not be misinterpreted.* Our only *rational* means for lightening it is *more understanding,* and appropriate *action* based on such understanding. The main alternative lies in acting as though the burden were not what in fact we perceive it to be

---

[1] Freud went so far as to say that: "I consider ethics to be taken for granted. Actually I have never done a mean thing" (Jones, 1957, p. 247). This surely is a strange thing to say for someone who has studied man as a social being as closely as did Freud. I mention it here to show how the notion of "illness" (in the case of psychoanalysis, "psychopathology," or "mental illness") was used by Freud—and by most of his followers—as a means for classifying certain forms of human behavior as falling within the scope of medicine, and hence (by *fiat*) outside that of ethics!

and taking refuge in an outmoded theological view of man. In the latter view, man does not fashion his life and much of his world about him, but merely lives out his fate in a world created by superior beings. This may logically lead to pleading nonresponsibility in the face of seemingly unfathomable problems and difficulties. Yet, if man fails to take increasing responsibility for his actions, individually as well as collectively, it seems unlikely that some higher power or being would assume this task and carry this burden for him. Moreover, this seems hardly the proper time in human history for obscuring the issue of man's responsibility for his actions by hiding it behind the skirt of an all-explaining conception of mental illness.

Conclusions

I have tried to show that the notion of mental illness has outlived whatever usefulness it might have had, and that it now functions merely as a convenient myth. As such, it is a true heir to religious myths in general, and to the belief in witchcraft in particular; the role of all these belief-systems was to act as *social tranquilizers,* thus encouraging the hope that mastery of certain specific problems may be achieved by means of substitutive (symbolic-magical) operations. The notion of mental illness thus serves mainly to obscure the everyday fact that life for most people is a continuous struggle, not for biological survival, but for a "place in the sun," "peace of mind," or some other human value. For man aware of himself and of the world about him, once the needs for preserving the body (and perhaps the race) are more or less satisfied, the problem arises as to what he should do with himself. Sustained adherence to the myth of mental illness allows people to avoid facing this problem, believing that mental health, conceived as the absence of mental illness, automatically insures the making of right and safe choices in one's conduct of life. But the facts are all the other way. It is the making of good choices in life that others regard, retrospectively, as good mental health!

The myth of mental illness encourages us, moreover, to believe in its logical corollary: that social intercourse would be harmonious, satisfying, and the secure basis of a "good life" were it not for the disrupting influences of mental illness or "psychopathology." The

potentiality for universal human happiness, in this form at least, seems to me but another example of the I-wish-it-were-true type of fantasy. I do believe that human happiness or well-being on a hitherto unimaginably large scale, and not just for a select few, is possible. This goal could be achieved, however, only at the cost of many men, and not just a few being willing and able to tackle their personal, social, and ethical conflicts. This means having the courage and integrity to forego waging battles on false fronts, finding solutions for substitute problems—for instance, fighting the battle of stomach acid and chronic fatigue instead of facing up to a marital conflict.

Our adversaries are not demons, witches, fate, or mental illness. We have no enemy whom we can fight, exorcise, or dispel by "cure." What we do have are *problems in living*—whether these be biologic, economic, political, or sociopsychological. In this essay I was concerned only with problems belonging in the last mentioned category, and within this group mainly with those pertaining to moral values. The field to which modern psychiatry addresses itself is vast, and I made no effort to encompass it all. My argument was limited to the proposition that mental illness is a myth, whose function it is to disguise and thus render more palatable the bitter pill of moral conflicts in human relations.

References

Hollingshead, A. B., & Redlich, F. C. *Social class and mental illness.* New York: Wiley, 1958.

Jones, E. *The life and work of Sigmund Freud.* Vol. III. New York: Basic Books, 1957.

Langer, S. K. *Philosophy in a new key.* New York: Mentor Books, 1953.

Peters, R. S. *The concept of motivation.* London: Routledge & Kegan Paul, 1958.

Szasz, T. S. Malingering: "Diagnosis" or social condemnation? *AMA Arch Neurol. Psychiat.,* 1956, 76, 432-443.

Szasz, T. S. *Pain and pleasure: A study of bodily feelings.* New York: Basic Books, 1957. (a)

Szasz, T. S. The problem of psychiatric nosology: A contribution to a situational analysis of psychiatric operations. *Amer. J. Psychiat.*, 1957, 114, 405-413. (b)

Szasz, T. S. On the theory of psychoanalytic treatment. *Int. J. Psycho-Anal.*, 1957, 38, 166-182. (c)

Szasz, T. S. Psychiatry, ethics and the criminal law. *Columbia law Rev.*, 1958, 58, 183-198.

Szasz, T. S. Moral conflict and psychiatry, *Yale Rev.*, 1959.

Personality disorder *is* disease

DAVID P. AUSUBEL

The complexity of the concept of mental illness is further illustrated in this rebuttal to the Szasz essay. The author reviews the arguments of Szasz and others who oppose the disease concept of personality disorder. He questions their rationale and offers some alternative conclusions which are more consistent with traditional medical beliefs. The article emphasizes the importance of viewing behavior as the product of both mental and physical functioning and is critical of approaches that separate these two spheres. This essay, considered together with the Szasz paper, demonstrates how much controversy still surrounds the topic of mental illness.

David Ausubel, M.D., Ph.D. is Professor in the Doctoral Program of Educational Psychology at the City University of New York. He has edited and written many articles and books including, *Ego Development and the Personality Disorders; Theory and Problems of Adolescent Development; Theory and Problems of Child Development; Drug Addiction: Physiological, Psychological, and Sociological Aspects; The Psychology of Meaningful Verbal Learning;* and *Educational Psychology: A Cognitive View.*

In two recent articles in the *American Psychologist,* Szasz (1960) and Mowrer (1960) have argued the case for discarding the concept of mental illness. The essence of Mowrer's position is that since medical science lacks "demonstrated competence . . . in psychiatry," psychology would be wise to "get out" from "under the penumbra of medicine," and to regard the behavior disorders as manifestations of sin rather than of disease (p. 302). Szasz' position, as we shall see shortly, is somewhat more complex than Mowrer's, but agrees with the latter in emphasizing the moral as opposed to the psychopathological basis of abnormal behavior.

For a long time now, clinical psychology has both repudiated the relevance of more judgment and accountability for assessing behavioral acts and choices, and has chafed under medical (psychiatric) control and authority in diagnosing and treating the personality disorders. One can readily appreciate, therefore, Mowrer's eagerness to sever the historical and professional ties that bind clinical psychology to medicine, even if this means denying that psychological disturbances constitute a form of illness, and even if psychology's close working relationship with psychiatry must be replaced by a new rapprochement with sin and theology, as "the lesser of two evils" (pp. 302-303). One can also sympathize with Mowrer's and Szasz' dissatisfaction with prevailing amoral and nonjudgmental trends in clinical psychology and with their entirely commendable efforts to restore moral judgment and accountability to

From *American Psychologist*, XVI (1961), 69-74. Reprinted by permission of the American Psychological Association and the author.

a respectable place among the criteria used in evaluating human behavior, both normal and abnormal.

Opposition to these two trends in the handling of the behavior disorders (i.e., to medical control and to nonjudgmental therapeutic attitudes), however, does not necessarily imply abandonment of the concept of mental illness. There is no inconsistency whatsoever in maintaining, on the one hand, that most purposeful human activity has a moral aspect the reality of which psychologists cannot afford to ignore (Ausubel, 1952, p. 462), that man is morally accountable for the majority of his misdeeds (Ausubel, 1952, p. 469), and that psychological rather than medical training and sophistication are basic to competence in the personality disorders (Ausubel, 1956, p. 101), and affirming, on the other hand, that the latter disorders are genuine manifestations of illness. In recent years psychology has been steadily moving away from the formerly fashionable stance of ethical neutrality in the behavioral sciences; and in spite of strident medical claims regarding superior professional qualifications and preclusive legal responsibility for treating psychiatric patients, and notwithstanding the nominally restrictive provisions of medical practice acts, clinical psychologists have been assuming an increasingly more important, independent, and responsible role in treating the mentally ill population of the United States.

It would be instructive at this point to examine the tactics of certain other medically allied professions in freeing themselves from medical control and in acquiring independent, legally recognized professional status. In no instance have they resorted to the devious stratagem of denying that they were treating diseases, in the hope of mollifying medical opposition and legitimizing their own professional activities. They took the position, instead, that simply because a given condition is defined as a disease, its treatment need not necessarily be turned over to doctors of medicine if other equally competent professional specialists were available. That this position is legally and politically tenable is demonstrated by the fact that an impressively large number of recognized diseases are legally treated today by both medical *and* nonmedical specialists (e.g., diseases of the mouth, face, jaws, teeth, eyes, and feet). And there are few convincing reasons for believing that psychiatrists wield that much more political power than physicians, maxillofacial surgeons, ophthalmologists, and orthopedic surgeons, that they could be successful where these latter specialists have failed, in legally restricting practice in their particular area of competence to holders of the medical degree. Hence, even if psychologists were not currently managing to hold their own vis-à-vis psychiatrists, it would be far less dangerous and much more forthright to press for the necessary ameliorative legislation than to seek cover behind an outmoded and thoroughly discredited conception of the behavior disorders.

The Szasz-Mowrer position

Szasz' (1960) contention that the concept of mental illness "now functions merely as a convenient myth" (p. 118) is grounded on four unsubstantiated and logically untenable propositions, which can be fairly summarized as follows:

1. Only symptoms resulting from demonstrable physical lesions qualify as legitimate manifestations of disease. Brain pathology is a type of physical lesion, but its symptoms properly speaking, are neurological rather than psychological in nature. Under no circumstances, therefore, can mental symptoms be considered a form of illness.

2. A basic dichotomy exists between *mental* symptoms, on the one hand, which are subjective in nature, dependent on subjective judgment and personal involvement of the observer, and referable to cultural-ethical norms, and *physical* symptoms, on the other hand, which are allegedly objective in nature, ascertainable without personal involvement of the observer, and independent of cultural norms and ethical standards. Only symptoms possessing the latter set of characteristics are genuinely reflective of illness and amenable to medical treatment.

3. Mental symptoms are merely expressions of problems of living and, hence, cannot be regarded as manifestations of a pathological condition. The concept of mental illness is misleading and demonological because it seeks to explain psychological disturbance, in particular, and human disharmony, in general, in

terms of a metaphorical but nonexistent disease entity, instead of attributing them to inherent difficulties in coming to grips with elusive problems of choice and responsibility.

4. Personality disorders, therefore, can be most fruitfully conceptualized as products of moral conflict, confusion, and aberration. Mowrer (1960) extends this latter proposition to include the dictum that psychiatric symptoms are primarily reflective of unacknowledged sin, and that individuals manifesting these symptoms are responsible for and deserve their suffering, both because of their original transgressions and because they refuse to avow and expiate their guilt (pp. 301, 304).

Widespread adoption of the Szasz-Mowrer view of the personality disorders would, in my opinion, turn back the psychiatric clock twenty-five hundred years. The most significant and perhaps the only real advance registered by mankind in evolving a rational and humane method of handling behavioral aberrations has been in substituting a concept of disease for the demonological retributional doctrines regarding their nature and etiology that flourished until comparatively recent times. Conceptualized as illness, the symptoms of personality disorders can be interpreted in the light of underlying stresses and resistances, both genic and environmental, and can be evaluated in relation to *specifiable* quantitative and qualitative norms of appropriately adaptive behavior, both cross-culturally and within a particular cultural context. It would behoove us, therefore, before we abandon the concept of mental illness and return to the medieval doctrine of unexpiated sin or adopt Szasz' ambiguous criterion of difficulty in ethical choice and responsibility, to subject the foregoing propositions to careful and detailed study.

Mental symptoms and brain pathology

Although I agree with Szasz in rejecting the doctrine that ultimately some neuroanatomic or neurophysiologic defect will be discovered in *all* cases of personality disorder, I disagree with his reasons for not accepting this proposition. Notwithstanding Szasz' straw man presentation of their position, the proponents of the extreme somatic view do not really assert that the *particular nature* of a patient's disordered beliefs can be correlated with "certain definite lesions in the nervous system" (Szasz, 1960, p. 113). They hold rather that normal cognitive and behavioral functioning depends on the anatomic and physiologic integrity of certain key areas of the brain, and that impairment of this substrate integrity, therefore, provides a physical basis for disturbed ideation and behavior, but does not explain, except in a very gross way, the particular kinds of symptoms involved. In fact, they are generally inclined to attribute the *specific* character of the patient's symptoms to the nature of his pre-illness personality structure, the substrate integrity of which is impaired by the lesion or metabolic defect in question.

Nevertheless, even though this type of reasoning plausibly accounts for the psychological symptoms found in general paresis, various toxic deleria, and other comparable conditions, it is an extremely improbable explanation of *all* instances of personality disorder. Unlike the tissues of any other organ, brain tissue possesses the unique property of making possible awareness of and adjustment to the world of sensory, social, and symbolic stimulation. Hence by virtue of this unique relationship of the nervous system to the environment, diseases of behavior and personality may reflect abnormalities in personal and social adjustment, quite apart from any structural or metabolic disturbance in the underlying neural substrate. I would conclude, therefore, that although brain pathology is probably not the most important cause of behavior disorder, it is undoubtedly responsible for the incidence of *some* psychological abnormalities, *as well as* for various neurological signs and symptoms.

But even if we completely accepted Szasz' view that brain pathology does not account for any symptoms of personality disorder, it would still be unnecessary to accept his assertion that to qualify as a genuine manifestation of disease a given symptom must be caused by a physical lesion. Adoption of such a criterion would be arbitrary and inconsistent both with medical and lay connotations of the term "disease," which in current usage is generally regarded as including any marked deviation, physical, mental, or behavioral, from normally desirable standards of structural and functional integrity.

Mental versus physical symptoms

Szasz contends that since the analogy between physical and mental symptoms is patently fallacious, the postulated parallelism between physical and mental disease is logically untenable. This line of reasoning is based on the assumption that the two categories of symptoms can be sharply dichotomized with respect to such basic dimensions as objectivity-subjectivity, the relevance of cultural norms, and the need for personal involvement of the observer. In my opinion, the existence of such a dichotomy cannot be empirically demonstrated in convincing fashion.

Practically all symptoms of bodily disease involve some elements of subjective judgment —both on the part of the patient and of the physician. Pain is perhaps the most important and commonly used criterion of physical illness. Yet, any evaluation of its reported locus, intensity, character, and duration is dependent upon the patient's subjective appraisal of his own sensations and on the physician's assessment of the latter's pain threshold, intelligence, and personality structure. It is also a medical commonplace that the severity of pain in most instances of bodily illness may be mitigated by the administration of a placebo. Furthermore, in taking a meaningful history the physician must not only serve as a participant observer, but also as a skilled interpreter of human behavior. It is the rare patient who does not react psychologically to the signs of physical illness; and hence physicians are constantly called upon to decide, for example, to what extent precordial pain and reported tightness in the chest are manifestations of coronary insufficiency, of fear of cardiac disease and impending death, or of combinations of both conditions. Even such allegedly objective signs as pulse rate, BMR, blood pressure, and blood cholesterol have their subjective and relativistic aspects. Pulse rate and blood pressure are notoriously susceptible to emotional influences, and BMR and blood cholesterol fluctuate widely from one cultural environment to another (Dreyfuss & Czaczkes, 1959). And anyone who believes that ethical norms have no relevance to physical illness has obviously failed to consider the problems confronting Catholic patients and/or physicians when issues of contraception, abortion, and preferential saving of the mother's as against the fetus' life must be faced in the context of various obstetrical emergencies and medical contraindications to pregnancy.

It should now be clear, therefore, that symptoms not only do not need a physical basis to qualify as manifestations of illness, but also that the evaluation of *all* symptoms, physical as well as mental, is dependent in large measure on subjective judgment, emotional factors, cultural-ethical norms, and personal involvement on the part of the observer. These considerations alone render no longer tenable Szasz' contention (1960, p. 114) that there is an inherent contradiction between using cultural and ethical norms as criteria of mental disease, on the one hand, and of employing medical measures of treatment on the other. But even if the postulated dichotomy between mental and physical symptoms were valid, the use of physical measures in treating subjective and relativistic psychological symptoms would still be warranted. Once we accept the proposition that impairment of the neutral substrate of personality can result in behavior disorder, it is logically consistent to accept the corollary proposition that other kinds of manipulation of the same neutral substrate can conceivably have therapeutic effects, irrespective of whether the underlying cause of the mental symptoms is physical or psychological.

Mental illness and problems of living

"The phenomena now called mental illness," argues Szasz (1960), can be regarded more forthrightly and simply as "expressions of man's struggle with the problem of how he should live" (p. 117). This statement undoubtedly oversimplifies the nature of personality disorders; but even if it were adequately inclusive it would not be inconsistent with the position that these disorders are a manifestation of illness. There is no valid reason why a particular symptom cannot both reflect a problem in living *and* constitute a manifestation of disease. The notion of mental illness, conceived in this way, would not "obscure the everyday fact that life for most people is a continuous struggle . . . for a 'place in the sun,' 'peace of mind,' or some other human value" (p. 118). It is quite true, as Szasz points out, that "human relations are inherently fraught with difficulties" (p. 117), and that most people manage to cope with such difficulties without becoming mentally ill. But conceding this fact hardly precludes the possibility that some individuals, either because of the magnitude of the stress involved, or because of genically or environmentally induced susceptibility to ordinary degrees of stress, respond to the problems of living with behavior that is either seriously distorted or sufficiently unadaptive to prevent normal interpersonal relations and vocational functioning. The latter outcome—gross deviation from a designated range of desirable behavioral variability—conforms to the generally understood meaning of mental illness.

The plausibility of subsuming abnormal behavioral reactions to stress under the general rubric of disease is further enhanced by the fact that these reactions include the same three principal categories of symptoms found in physical illness. Depression and catastrophic impairment of self-esteem, for example, are manifestations of personality disorder which are symptomologically comparable to edema in cardiac failure or to heart murmurs in valvular disease. They are indicative of underlying pathology but are neither adaptive nor adjustive. Symptoms such as hypomanic overactivity and compulsive striving toward unrealistically high achievement goals, on the other hand, are both adaptive and adjustive, and constitute a type of compensatory response to basic feelings of inadequacy, which is not unlike cardiac hypertrophy in hypertensive heart disease or elevated white blood cell count in acute infections. And finally, distortive psychological defenses that have some adjustive value but are generally maladaptive (e.g., phobias, delusions, autistic fantasies) are analogous to the pathological situation found in conditions like pneumonia, in which the excessive outpouring of serum and phagocytes in defensive response to pathogenic bacteria literally causes the patient to drown in his own fluids.

Within the context of this same general proposition, Szasz repudiates the concept of mental illness as demonological in nature, i.e., as the "true heir to religious myths in general and to the belief in witchcraft in particular" (p. 118) because it allegedly employs a reified abstraction ("a deformity of personality") to

account in causal terms both for "human disharmony" and for symptoms of behavior disorder (p. 114). But again he appears to be demolishing a straw man. Modern students of personality disorder do not regard mental illness as a cause of human disharmony, but as a co-manifestation with it of inherent difficulties in personal adjustment and interpersonal relations; and in so far as I can accurately interpret the literature, psychopathologists do not conceive of mental illness as a cause of particular behavioral symptoms but as a generic term under which these symptoms can be subsumed.

Mental illness and moral responsibility

Szasz' final reason for regarding mental illness as a myth is really a corollary of his previously considered more general proposition that mental symptoms are essentially reflective of problems of living and hence do not legitimately qualify as manifestations of disease. It focuses on difficulties of ethical choice and responsibility as the particular life problems most likely to be productive of personality disorder. Mowrer (1960) further extends this corollary by asserting that neurotic and psychotic individuals are responsible for their suffering (p. 301), and that unacknowledged and unexpiated sin, in turn, is the basic cause of this suffering (p. 304). As previously suggested, however, one can plausibly accept the proposition that psychiatrists and clinical psychologists have erred in trying to divorce behavioral evaluation from ethical considerations, in conducting psychotherapy in an amoral setting, and in confusing the psychological explanation of unethical behavior with absolution from accountability for same, *without* necessarily endorsing the view that personality disorders are basically a reflection of sin, and that victims of these disorders are less ill than responsible for their symptoms (Ausubel, 1952, pp. 392-397, 465-471).

In the first place, it is possible in most instances (although admittedly difficult in some) to distinguish quite unambiguously between mental illness and ordinary cases of immorality. The vast majority of persons who are guilty of moral lapses knowingly violate their own ethical precepts for expediential reasons— despite being volitionally capable at the time, both of choosing the more moral alternative and of exercising the necessary inhibitory control (Ausubel, 1952, pp. 465-471). Such persons, also, usually do not exhibit any signs of behavior disorder. At crucial choice points in facing the problems of living they simply choose the opportunistic instead of the moral alternative. They are not mentally ill, but they are clearly accountable for their misconduct. Hence, since personality disorder and immorality are neither coextensive nor mutually exclusive conditions, the concept of mental illness need not necessarily obscure the issue of moral accountability.

Second, guilt may be a contributory factor in behavior disorder, but is by no means the only or principal cause thereof. Feelings of guilt may give rise to anxiety and depression; but in the absence of catastrophic impairment of self-esteem induced by *other* factors, these symptoms tend to be transitory and peripheral in nature (Ausubel, 1952, pp. 362-363). Repression of guilt, is more a consequence than a cause of anxiety. Guilt is repressed in order to avoid the anxiety producing trauma to self-esteem that would otherwise result if it were acknowledged. Repression per se enters the causal picture in anxiety only secondarily—by obviating "the possibility of punishment, confession, expiation, and other guilt reduction mechanisms" (Ausubel, 1952, p. 456). Furthermore, in most types of personality disorder other than anxiety, depression, and various complications of anxiety such as phobias, obsessions, and compulsion, guilt feelings are either not particularly prominent (schizophrenic reactions), or are conspicuously absent (e.g., classical cases of inadequate or aggressive antisocial psychopathy).

Third, it is just as unreasonable to hold an individual responsible for symptoms of behavior disorder as to deem him accountable for symptoms of physical illness. He is no more culpable for his inability to cope with sociopsychological stress than he would be for his inability to resist the spread of infectious organisms. In those instances where warranted guilt feelings *do* contribute to personality disorder, the patient is accountable for the misdeeds underlying his guilt but is hardly responsible for the symptoms brought on by the guilt feelings or for unlawful acts committed during his illness. Acknowledgment of guilt may be therapeutically beneficial under these circumstances but punishment for the original misconduct should obviously be deferred until after recovery.

Lastly, even if it were true that all personality disorder is a reflection of sin and that people are accountable for their behavioral symptoms, it would still be unnecessary to deny that these symptoms are manifestations of disease. Illness is no less real because the victim happens to be culpable for his illness. A glutton with hypertensive heart disease undoubtedly aggravates his condition by overeating, and is culpable in part for the often fatal symptoms of his disease, but what reasonable person would claim that for this reason he is not really ill?

Conclusions

Four propositions in support of the argument for discarding the concept of mental illness were carefully examined, and the following conclusions were reached:

First, although brain pathology is probably not the major cause of personality disorder, it does account for *some* psychological symptoms by impairing the neural substrate of personality. In any case, however, a symptom need not reflect a physical lesion in order to qualify as a genuine manifestation of disease.

Second, Szasz' postulated dichotomy between mental and physical symptoms is untenable, because the assessment of *all* symptoms is dependent to some extent on subjective judgment, emotional factors, cultural-ethical norms, and personal involvement of the observer. Furthermore, the use of medical measures in treating behavior disorders—irrespective of whether the underlying causes are neural or psychological—is defensible on the grounds that if inadvertent impairment of the neural substrate of personality can have distortive effects on behavior, directed manipulation of the same substrate may have therapeutic effects.

Third, there is no inherent contradiction in regarding mental symptoms both as expressions of problems in living *and* as manifestations of illness. The latter situation results when individuals are for various reasons unable to cope with such problems, and react with seriously distorted or maladaptive behavior. The three principal categories of behavioral symptoms—manifestations of impaired functioning, adaptive compensation, and defensive over-reaction—are also found in bodily disease. The concept of mental illness has never been advanced as a demonological cause of human disharmony, but only as a co-manifestation with it of certain inescapable difficulties and hazards in personal and social adjustment. The same concept is also generally accepted as a generic term for all behavioral symptoms rather than as a reified cause of these symptoms.

Fourth, the view that personality disorder is less a manifestation of illness than of sin, i.e., of culpable inadequacy in meeting problems of ethical choice and responsibility, and that victims of behavior disorder are therefore morally accountable for their symptoms, is neither logically nor empirically tenable. In most instances immoral behavior and mental illness are clearly distinguishable conditions. Guilt is only a secondary etiological factor in anxiety and depression, and in other personality disorders is either not prominent or conspicuously absent. The issue of culpability for symptoms is largely irrelevant in handling the behavior disorders, and in any case does not detract from the reality of illness.

In general, it is both unnecessary and potentially dangerous to discard the concept of mental illness on the grounds that only in this way can clinical psychology escape from the professional domination of medicine. Dentists, podiatrists, optometrists, and osteopaths have managed to acquire an independent profes-sional status without rejecting the concept of disease. It is equally unnecessary and dangerous to substitute the doctrine of sin for illness in order to counteract prevailing amoral and non-judgmental trends in psychotherapy. The hypothesis of repressed guilt does not adequately explain most kinds and instances of personality disorder, and the concept of mental illness does not preclude judgments of moral accountability where warranted. Definition of behavior disorder in terms of sin or of difficulties associated with ethical choice and responsibility would substitute theological disputation and philosophical wrangling about values for specifiable quantitative and qualitative criteria of disease.

References

Ausubel, D. P. *Ego development and the personality disorders.* New York: Grune & Stratton, 1952.

Ausubel, D. P. Relationships between psychology and psychiatry: The hidden issues. *Amer. Psychologist,* 1956, 11, 99-105.

Dreyfuss, F. & Czaczkes, J. W. Blood cholesterol and uric acid of healthy medical students under the stress of an examination. *AMA Arch. intern. Med.,* 1959, 103, 708.

Mowrer, O. H. "Sin," the lesser of two evils. *Amer. Psychologist,* 1960, 15, 301-304.

Szasz, T. S. The myth of mental illness. *Amer. Psychologist,* 1960, 15, 113-118.

"Mental health" reconsidered: a special case of the problem of values in psychology [1]

M. BREWSTER SMITH

For a long time many psychologists and psychiatrists have labored under the misconception that the maintenance of scientific objectivity requires that they ignore questions of value. It is becoming increasingly clear that values cannot be removed from the serious consideration of human problems. In this article, M. Brewster Smith, Ph.D., Chairman of the Psychology Department at the University of Chicago, and former Director of the Institute for Human Development at the University of California, Berkeley, discusses the psychologist's role with respect to questions of value and mental health. Professor Smith compares the function of the psychologist with that of other professionals who have been more traditionally concerned with values and recommends ways in which psychologists can deal with values. The article reviews some current definitions of mental health and concludes with recommendations for more satisfactory mental health criteria.

Dr. Smith is the author of *Social Psychology and Human Values* and has coauthored *The American Soldier* and *Opinions and Personality*.

The signs are increasingly clear that "mental health" and its complement, "mental illness," are terms that embarrass psychologists. Many of us do not like them (cf. APA, 1959). Unable to define or to conceptualize them to our satisfaction, we use the terms in spite of ourselves, since they label the goals, however nebulous, of many of our service activities and the auspices of much of our research support. Even when we try to avoid them, we are swept along in the social movement of which they are shibboleths, and our scruples make little dif-

ference. Little wonder, then, that we and our colleagues in the other "mental health professions" seek to clear our consciences by continuing to engage in sporadic attempts to give them more precise and explicit meaning.

Having contributed from time to time to this discussion, I feel entitled to some skepticism about where it has got us. True, we have made some gains in disposing of several unprofitable ways of thinking about mental health that used to be prevalent. We have come to see that statistical notions of "normality" are no real help in giving psychological meaning to mental health and illness: they beg the question or fail to come to grips with it. We have become suspicious of the once regnant concept of adjustment, as it has fallen into disrepute at the hands of social critics and moralists (e.g., Riesman, 1950) who see it as a pseudoscientific rationalization for conformist values, and of psychological theorists (e.g., White, 1959) who are challenging the sufficiency of the equilibrium model in which it is rooted. And from many quarters we encounter the call for a more positive view of mental health than is involved in the mere absence of manifest mental disorder. Since the appearance of Jahoda's

From *American Psychologist,* XVI (1961), 299-306. Reprinted by permission of the American Psychological Association and the author.

[1] Adapted from a paper prepared for the Work Conference on Mental Health-Teacher Education Research Projects, Madison, Wisconsin, November 10-18, 1960. I am indebted to Barbara Biber, Robert Peck, Fred Wilhelms, John Withall, Nicholas Hobbs, Erich Lindemann, Ronald Lippitt, Ralph Ojemann, Hildegard Peplau, Carl Rogers, and the other participants in the conference for their reactions to the earlier version of the paper.

useful book (1958) that reviewed the considerable array of proposals toward such a conception of optimal human functioning, the flow of suggestions has not abated. The discussion goes on in articles, conferences, and symposia, with little evidence of consensus in the offing.

The various lists of criteria that have been proposed for positive mental health reshuffle overlapping conceptions of desirable functioning without attaining agreement—or giving much promise that agreement can be reached. The inventories repeat themselves, and indeed it is inevitable that they should, since each successor list is proposed by a wise psychologist who scrutinizes previous proposals and introduces variations and emphases to fit his own values and preferences. Some give greater weight to the cognitive values of accurate perception and self-knowledge (e.g., Jahoda, 1955); some to moral values, to meaningful commitment, to social responsibility (e.g., Allport, 1960; Shoben, 1957); some to working effectiveness (e.g., Ginsburg, 1955); some to the blander social virtues (e.g., aspects of Foote & Cottrell, 1955); some to zest, exuberance, and creativity (e.g., Maslow, 1954). The terms recur, but in different combinations and with connotations that slant in divergent directions. By way of illustration, Table 1 gives the six headings under which Jahoda (1958) organized the proposals for mental health criteria that she encountered in her review of the literature, and Allport's most recent proposal (1960), rearranged to bring out correspondences and discrepancies in the two lists. While it is an advance that psychologists are now looking for multiple criteria of good functioning rather than seeking the single touchstone of a unitary definition of mental health, we may well ask: How are psychologists to decide what items belong in such a list? By what warrant may we assign priorities to alternative criteria? Surely we need something closer to *terra firma* on which to build our research, from which to guide our practice.

There is little to be gained, I think, from adding to these competing lists. Conceptual clarification, on the other hand, may be more profitable, and my attempt in the present essay lies in that direction. Starting from the now prevalent recognition that mental health is an evaluative term, that personal and social values as standards of the preferable are somehow

TABLE 1

Two Illustrative Conceptions of Positive Mental Health
in Terms of Multiple Criteria

Jahoda (1958)	Allport (1960)
attitudes toward the self	self-objectification
growth and self-actualization	ego-extension
integration	unifying philosophy of life
autonomy	
perception of reality	realistic coping skills, abilities, and perceptions
environmental mastery	
	warm and deep relation of self to others
	compassionate regard for all living creatures

Note.—Rubrics rearranged to bring out parallels.

crucially involved in any discourse about mental health, I try first to show that this intrusion of values into psychology, lamented by some, applauded by others, is entirely legitimate. But I question, secondly, whether there is any profit in the argument about which evaluative criteria for appraising human personality and behavior are to be included in a concept of mental health. Rather, I suggest that, at least in the present stage of personality theory, "mental health" should not be regarded as a theoretical concept at all, but as a rubric or chapter heading under which fall a variety of evaluative concerns. I try to show that such a view of the term may help to clear the ground for both practical and theoretical purposes.

In an earlier effort (1959) at clarification in this area, I observed that at the crux of the difficulty of assimilating "mental health" to psychology is the fact that "science has not yet learned how to deal surefootedly with values" (p. 673). Any progress toward clarity in psychological thinking about mental health, I am increasingly convinced, depends on our becoming clearer, as psychologists, about how we are to think about values. Whatever advances we make on the problem of values in this setting should also stand us in good stead in other contexts where issues of value confront psychology. The value problem is worth a close and sustained look.

Why the search for a value-laden conception of positive mental health?

While evaluative criteria and judgments are involved in the notion of mental disorder, our consensus about what is *un*desirable is close enough for practical purposes that the role of values tends to remain implicit. It is when we want to talk about positive criteria of psychological functioning that we encounter the value problem head on. A good starting point for the present discussion, then, is to ask why we ever got ourselves into this difficult, intellectually treacherous business of positive mental health. Are not the problems of mental disorder enough? Why should the mental health movement be impelled, as it has been since the days of Clifford Beers (cf. Joint Commission on Mental Illness and Health, 1961), to extend itself to concern with the "mental hygiene" of promoting positive mental health—in the absence of firm knowledge or clear guidelines?

The answer to such a question cannot be simple. But I think a generally critical onlooker from England, R. S. Peters (1960), has hit the essential point when he addressed the BBC audience thus:

We have a highly specialized society and we are often warned that we are developing not merely two nations but a league of nations without a common culture and shared ideals. This should not surprise us; for where are such unifying ideals to be fostered? The study of literature, history, and the classics has had to be cut down to make room for the vast expansion in scientific education without which our society cannot survive, and the Church is rapidly losing the authority it once had as a source of unifying ideals. We tend to treat the doctor who looks after our bodies and the psychiatrist who advises us about our minds with more respect than we treat the priest who advises us about our souls—if we still think we have one. For they are scientists; and it is scientists who are now coming to be thought of as the repositories of wisdom about the mysteries of life.

This general trend explains why the educationist sometimes inclines his ear towards a new expert, the psychologist, when he is at a loss to find new unifying educational ideals to replace the old religious ones. There is thus much talk in educational circles of "the mental health of the child," "wholeness," "integration," "adjustment," and all that sort of thing. We no longer talk of turning out Christian gentlemen; we talk of letting people develop mental health or mature personalities. Indeed in America Freud's priestly role is much more explicitly acknowledged. . . . Nevertheless the general trend is [also] with us, as is shown in the frequent references to psychological notions such as "mental health" in discussion about educational ideals (p. 46).

Discount the bias of perspective arising from Peters' assured stance in the tradition of British class education, and hold in abeyance reaction to his critical undertones: his point remains that a good many thoughtful people have turned, appropriately or otherwise, to notions of mental health in order to fill a void left by the attrition of traditionally or religiously sanctioned values. There is consumer demand for psychologists to enter the discussion of goals and aspirations for human behavior; but we had better be clear about our warrant for doing so.

The demand for a psychologically informed phrasing of objectives—for conceptions of positive mental health—comes most compellingly from those concerned with the rearing and education of children. The psychologist or psychiatrist who mainly deals with hospitalized psychotics has enough to do in trying to treat severe mental disorder and get his patients to function at some minimally adequate level; since consensus on these objectives is immediately given, the value problem hardly rises to the surface. But responsibility for the raising of children calls for positive criteria against which the success of one's efforts on their behalf can be measured. Perhaps a counselor may appropriately leave it to his adult client to set the goals for his therapy; the case can hardly be extended to the child as ward of teacher and parent—who in turn look to the psychologist for guidance.

Of course there are intellectual positions from which the responsibility appears to be minimized. If you take a Rousseau-like view that regards optimal development as the unfolding of a benign inner potential, you can at least pretend to leave goal setting entirely to the child's own nature. This doctrine of benign potentiality, which is still very much alive in educational and psychological theory (witness Maslow, 1954), strikes me as involving psychological half-truths and philosophical error. It is we ourselves, in terms of our tacit values, who single out, as optimal, one of an infinite set of possible environments for the development child, and distinguish the way he develops in such an auspicious setting as the actualization of a naturally given potential. We ignore the infinite variety of other developmental trends that he simultaneously has the potential to actualize, many of which we would not think highly of—and ignore the silent and therefore not fully responsible intrusion of our own values involved in distinguishing one class of possible trends as self-actualizing.

Another way of minimizing responsibility for educational goal setting in terms of mental health is to accept as ultimate the values of the culture, to define the function of education as cultural transmission and, in effect, leave matters of value-choice to parents and school board. The trouble is that this option is no longer really available, even if we prefer it. The state of affairs evoked by Peters is with us: there is no longer such a solid traditional consensus for us to fall back on. Parents and school boards too are confused and involved in the fray. Under these circumstances, education can hardly avoid a complex role that combines and balances cultural transmission, on the one hand, and social criticism and reconstruction on the other. This characteristic American philosophy of education has thus become virtually a policy of necessity. It calls for clear-headedness about goals and has tended to draw on psychology for their formulation.

Insofar as we take the requirements of education seriously, then, we cannot help trying to grapple with conceptions of optimal human functioning. We also need them in planning and assessing programs of counseling and of environmental change. In the face of a waning consensus on traditional values, we join our lay clientele in hoping that psychology can help in this endeavor. But hope does not guarantee success. The strength of our needs may head us the more rigidly down blind alleys, unless we have our wits about us.

The value problem

The skeptical reader imbued with the distinction between scientific objectivity, on the one hand, and the humanistic cultivation of values on the other will have balked at an earlier point, and stayed with the question: By what warrant do psychologists assume the right to posit any set of human values, as we do when we propose criteria of positive mental health? The psychologist has no more right to do so, he will say, than anyone else. Let him stick to his last, and recognize the limits of his competence. My serious rejoinder, which requires somewhat of a detour to develop, reverses this conventional view: the psychologist has *as much* right to posit values as anyone else, in some important respects more. It is time to dispel the shopworn bromide that the humanist (or moralist or philosopher) has a corner on pronouncements about values, while the psychologist (or sociologist or scientist generally) must restrict himself to facts. Things are just not that simple.

For most of us, the two sources to which everyone once looked for what were then regarded as "absolute" values—Tradition and Theology—speak only equivocally if at all. We are still suffering from the crisis of personal and social readjustment occasioned by this loss. As we regain our bearings, our nostalgia for the old illusion of Absoluteness, of givenness in the eternal scheme of things, begins to fade. But in spite of the pessimism of those who hunger after Absoluteness, we still have values, in the sense of personal standards of desirability and obligation. We see them, now, as committing choices that people make (often unwittingly) in the interplay of cultural tradition and individual experience. We see them as "relative," yes, but relative not only to culture (an exclusive focus on *cultural* relativism was the mistake of the last generation of anthropologists). They are relative also to human nature—in the diverse varieties of this nature that have emerged in human history with a degree of continuity and cumulativeness—and relative to the opportunities and limitations of human situations. Thus the warrior virtues held validity for the traditional Sioux; for the reservation Sioux they no longer make any sense (MacGregor, 1946). And one can fairly doubt whether the petty competitive values of the Alorese studied by Cora DuBois (1944) ever made much sense: she showed them to be part and parcel of a wretched and demeaning way of life that I doubt whether any Alorese would choose were some magic to give him a wider range of opportunity.

If values are social products, they rest, ultimately, on a personal commitment. Everybody, scientist or humanist, or man in the street, has the right to posit values. And, since people in society are interdependent, everyone has a right to try to persuade others to his ways of valuing: *de gustibus non disputandum est* may apply to tastes and preferences, but it has never prevented controversy about values, as the course of human history well reveals. We *all* have the right to dispute values, and most of us do it. The humanist and the humane scientist nevertheless have potentially different specialized roles in the argument.

Their roles arise from the peculiar nature of argument about values that follows from the basis of values in an optional personal commitment. If you want to persuade someone to value something as you do, you can follow one of at least two strategies (assuming that physical or social coercion is ruled out, which historically has, unfortunately, not been the case): You can, first, try to open his eyes to new ways of seeing things—increase the range of possibilities of which he is aware, create the conditions for differentiations and restructurings in his experience from which it is possible (not necessary) that, seeing things like yourself, he may come to value them likewise. Or, second, you can give him evidence that the position he takes on a particular value has consequences for other values to which he is also committed. For the fact that values rest on a personal option does not make them arbitrary in the sense of being detached from cause or consequence. If you show a person that his chosen value of racial purity conflicts with the values of the American Creed that he also embraces, he *may* reconsider it (Myrdal, 1944). Or if you show him that his prejudiced value rests causally on evasive covert tactics of defense against inner weakness, you again have a chance to win out (Adorno, Frenkel-Brunswik, Levinson, & Sanford, 1950). The *ad hominem* argument, in ill favor as it is, is fair play in this peculiar and important realm, so long as it is not taken as conclusive. Since values rest on personal option, *no* argument is conclusive, though many can be persuasive, and appropriately so.

I am thus suggesting that the humanist and the moral philosopher are especially equipped to employ the first of these strategies: drawing on the fund of human history and culture, with its stock of transmitted discriminations, they can sensitize us to differentiations and potentialities of human experience which, un-

aided, we could never attain individually. Our value choices are enriched and modified by this exposure. The second strategy, that of displaying the causal network in which value choice is embedded, is one for which the humane or behavioral scientist is uniquely qualified.

The old myth had it that man lost his pre-cultural innocence when, biting the fruit of the Tree of Knowledge, he became aware of Good and Evil. In becoming modern, Man has taken a second portentous bite of the same fruit. There are alternative versions of Good and Evil, he discovers to his discomfiture, and it is up to him to choose the commitments he is to live by. From this emerging view that can no longer turn to authoritative interpretations of tradition or divine revelation to resolve questions of value, it makes no sense at all for us to encyst ourselves behind a pass-the-buck notion that we can leave value judgments to some other discipline that specializes in them. There is no discipline that has this mythical competence: the humanist and the theologian speak with no greater authority than we. We are all in it together.

The list problem

I think I have shown the legitimacy, the clear warrant, for psychologists to concern themselves with values, as we do when we involve ourselves with mental health. But my argument gives no help at all on the other problem: what value dimensions are to get on our lists of mental health criteria, and why? If anything, it makes things more difficult. For if values are matters of a committing personal option, how are psychologists—let alone people at large—to come to agree on any particular list any more closely than the limited extent to which they already do? Even with a richer exposure to the humanistic tradition than is customary for psychologists, even with a far more adequate fund of causal knowledge than is presently available, psychological "experts" are not going to agree on the proper goals for human nature, and these are what we are talking about.

The actual situation is well typified by the experience of the Cornell Conference (National Assembly on Mental Health Education, 1960). To quote the conference report:

Everyone at Cornell seemed to agree that the good life for all was to be desired. They split, however, on what the good life was—as they had split on the definition of mental health, and they split on who, if anyone, should have the right to try to "impose" it on others (p. 20).

The definition of mental health, of course, *involves* a conception of the good life, which nobody *can* impose on anyone else (barring "brainwashing" and physical coercion), though, at least among colleagues and equals, it is fair enough for each of us to try to persuade the rest.

But the time has come to cut the Gordian knot, to restructure the problem along more profitable lines. The place to cut, I think, is the notion that the lists we have been considering itemize criteria of some entity called "positive mental health," and are equivalent to a definition of it. Even though we may have forsaken the view of mental health as a unitary phenomenon, and may have no intention of adding up a single score across our multiple criteria, we remain beguiled by the assumption that an articulate theoretical concept or construct of mental health lurks somewhere ready to be discovered. It is the pursuit of this will-o'-the-wisp that has made the procession of lists of mental health criteria so fruitless.

As we actually study effective functioning —or commit ourselves to social or educational programs that seek in various ways to promote it—our focus then becomes, not "mental health" variously indexed, but any or all of a number of much more specific evaluative dimensions of human functioning: any that we are ready to commit ourselves to take seriously as relevant and valued potential psychological outcomes of the programs that we are working with, any that we can begin to pin down in operational terms, as many of them as seem important to us and as we can feasibly cope with. Here I find myself in essential agreement with the position recently taken by Levine and Kantor (1960).

From the standpoint of research, the problem of attaining consensus on criteria is thus scaled down to the workaday dimensions we are used to: the practical difficulty of trying to convince at least some of our colleagues to study some of the same things we are studying by similar methods, so that our results can dovetail or add up. There is no reason at all why study of the causes, consequences, and interrelations of standing on various mental health dimensions has to await consensus on a common list that may never be attained— and by my personal value commitments would not even be desirable!

In the long run, it is possible that our understanding of interrelated system properties of personality may advance to a point that warrants a more theoretical conception of mental health—one related, say, to empirically based estimates of such properties as self-maintenance, growth, and resilience (cf. Smith, 1959). We are certainly still far from being able to envision such a conception except in the most schematic terms. But, if it is to be attained at all, the road to it should lie through nonevaluative research on personality development and functioning, on the one hand, and, on the other, through the strategy I have just been advocating: modestly exploring the empirical correlates of valued attributes of personality.

But what of the public demands for mental health "expertise" with which we started? What implications does our analysis have for the role of the psychologist in school, clinic, or consulting room? The very fact that no simple rule book of prescribed conduct seems to follow from it gives me greater confidence in the appropriateness of the approach we have taken.

Knowing that he lacks a scientifically sanctioned single set of mental health criteria, the psychologist in his consulting or service or educational relationships will hesitate to prescribe the nature of the good life to others in the name of psychology. Since values rest on a personal option, he will find it easiest to keep a clear scientific and professional conscience when he can use his knowledge and skill to help others identify, clarify, and realize their value commitments—provided that he can reconcile them with the values that he himself is committed to. Yet his own psychologically informed personal commitments about the nature of good human functioning cannot exist in a vacuum. They may lead him to avoid or to terminate service relationships that appear to violate them, to seek relationships that promote them. When his role as teacher or therapist vests him with more direct and personal responsibility for goal setting, he will not hesitate to act in terms of his convictions about what is desirable in the relationship and of the best knowledge and wisdom he can muster. But he will seek to move such relationships in the direction of increasing the responsibility of the other party for choosing his own goals. To his colleagues in and out of psychology and to various publics, he may often appear as an advocate of particular values. But his advocacy will consist in displaying the nature of his personal commitment and of using his psychological knowledge and insight to explore the linkage between holding or attaining a value and its conditions and consequences. In a word, explicitness about values goes with responsible scientific and professional behavior, and when we are explicit about such values as truthfulness, competence, care, responsibility, creativity, we add nothing consequential by labeling them as dimensions or criteria of positive mental health.

Mental health as a rubric

If "mental health" is to lose its presumptive conceptual standing, what does its status become? I see it rather as a rubric, a chapter title, a label for the common concern of various disciplines involved in evaluating human functioning from the perspective of the psychology of personality. Its usefulness in this respect does not depend on its dubious status as a theoretical concept. As chapter title, "mental health" is analogous to "mechanics" in classical physics: a rubric under which we treat a number of theoretical constructs (e.g., mass, force, velocity) and the laws relating them. You do not argue very violently about where chapter boundaries should be drawn.

There remain many meaningful problems concerning the contents and organization of such a chapter, even about its name. Personally, I agree with Levine and Kantor (1960) and with Szasz (1960) that the term "mental health" is unfortunate for our present purposes, biasing the issues as it does toward a model of physical health and illness that seems quite inappropriate to the analysis of effective and disordered conduct. But with the focus shifted to specific evaluative dimensions, I do not find myself caring very much about this argument, any more than I worry about the chapter titles

in a book of applied science. This is an editorial problem, not a substantive one.

As for the contents of the mental health chapter, a variety of pragmatic considerations come to mind to assist in culling, augmenting, and refining the items in the available lists. Candidates for treatment as dimensions of mental health or of goodness of psychological functioning might be expected to meet most of the following criteria, none of which seems to require elaborate justification:

1. They should be serious contenders in the arena of human values (though an impossible consensus is of course not required). The posited value should be explicit.

2. They should be capable of measurement or of inference from identifiable aspects of behavior.

3. They should articulate with personality theory (a weak requirement, since the proviso must be added immediately that personality theories will probably need to be extended and modified to make contact with value dimensions chosen on other grounds).

4. They should be relevant to the social context for which the chapter is being written. In the context of education, for instance, this is to ask: What kinds of psychological assets would we like to see the schools develop in our children? Quite different considerations would come to the fore in the context of a correctional agency.

Considerations such as these make it unlikely that the entire range of moral, esthetic, and cognitive values will vie for inclusion in the mental health chapter. But no harm is done if a venturesome soul decides to study the natural history of some utterly "unpsychological" value under mental health auspices.

A more fundamental choice concerns short vs. long versions of the chapter: in other words, minimal vs. extended conceptions of mental health. I can illustrate this choice best if I introduce at the same time a possible principle for organizing the chapter. Jahoda (1958) observed that "one has the option of defining mental health in at least two ways: as a relatively constant and enduring function of the personality . . . ; or as a momentary function of personality and situation" (pp. 7-8). Klein (1960) makes a similar point in his distinction between soundness or general stability, and well-being. We want, that is, to distinguish, on the one hand, the person's present state and behavior as an interactive resultant of his personality and features of the momentary situation that he confronts, and, on the other, the corresponding dispositions of his present personality, with situational effects discounted. Add a time dimension—here in terms of an assessment of mental health in childhood with prognosis to adulthood, since a primary ingredient of our interest in the mental health of children is the foundation it is assumed to provide for adult functioning—and minimal vs. extended views of mental health may be illustrated as in Table 2.

To me, this way of mapping the contents of the chapter seems clarifying. As I look at the top row, the narrow conception of the scope of mental health seems thoroughly viable. I am led to think that Jahoda (1958) may have dismissed this version too quickly, that the psychiatrist Walter Barton in his postscript to her volume was certainly right about its relevance and adequacy for the context of institutional psychiatry. But as I compare the top and bottom lines, I agree with her that the narrow version of the chapter is not in itself

TABLE 2

Illustration of Narrow and Broad Conceptions of Mental Health

| Scope | Mental Health of Child | | Adult Prognosis |
	Present Behavior	Present Disposition	
Minimal Conception	Freedom from incapacitating symptoms	Good resistance to stress	Absence of mental disorder in adulthood
Extended Conception	Momentary well-being (in specified respects)	Capacities for competent, happy, zestful, etc. child life	Capacities for competent, happy, zestful, etc. adult life

adequate to the evaluative concerns of education—to pick one relevant context with which psychologists are involved. And it is of course the bottom line, the extended version, that potentially expands greatly as various dimensions of good functioning are specified. Comparison of the two lines reminds me to agree with Clausen (1956) that we know very little

about their relationship to one another: no longer regarding mental health as a theoretical concept, we have no particular reason to expect resistance to mental disorder to correlate with various aspects of positive functioning, but the problem calls for research. And finally, the presence of the right-hand column calls to mind how little we know about the continuities of behavior seen in evaluative terms.

So long as we grope futilely toward a *concept* of "mental health," minimal or maximal, the advantages of specificity and researchability appear to be on the side of the minimal conception. Viewing these versions as different locations of chapter boundary lines, however, we can be as specific as we want about our positively valued criteria. It may well turn out to be the case, then, that the extended version includes the valued dimensions of behavior and personality that are most responsive to our interventions. "Mental health promotion" in this sense may not be as impractical as some of us have come to assume.

Conclusion

Where has this analysis of "mental health" as a problem of values led us? It may free us, I hope, from some of the embarrassment that has motivated psychologists' attempts to treat it as a theoretical concept—attempts that have not been additive and have not made the term theoretically respectable. If we understand "mental health" not as an unsatisfactory and vague theoretical concept but as a reasonably adequate rubric or label for an evaluative psychological perspective on personality—even though the term is not of our own choosing—we can get about our business without wasting our efforts on the search for consensus on a unique set of mental health criteria when consensus is not to be had.

Under this rubric, our business, be it research or service, is properly concerned with specific valued dimensions or attributes of behavior and personality. In our focus on these dimensions we are not at all handicapped by the lack of a satisfactory conceptual definition of mental health.

Nor need we be embarrassed by the intrusion of values in our focus on various specified aspects of desirable or undesirable psychological functioning. What is to be avoided is the *surreptitious* advocacy of values disguised under presumptive scientific auspices. The lists of psychological desiderata that psychologists have continued to propose, each reflecting the value commitments of its proponent, have this drawback insofar as they are offered as "criteria of positive mental health." But there is nothing surreptitious, nothing illegitimate, in using evaluative dimensions such as those that appear on these lists to appraise behavior and personality, so long as the value position one takes is explicit. And there is much to be gained from psychological study of the empirical antecedents, consequences, and interrelations of realizing different values in the sphere of personality.

In the study of optimal human functioning, I have argued, behavioral and social scientists can put their special qualifications to work toward the clarification of values among which people must choose and of the causal relations that are relevant to value choice. From it we should not only increase our knowledge about ways and means of attaining the values we agree on; we should also bring to light factual relationships that have a bearing on our choice of what values to pursue, individually and socially. To the extent that the behavioral sciences develop in this direction, they contribute to providing a badly needed bridge between what C. P. Snow (1959) has called "the two cultures" of the scientists and the humanistic intellectuals.

References

Adorno, T. W., Frenkel-Brunswik, Else, Levinson, D., & Sanford, N. *The authoritarian personality.* New York: Harper, 1950.

Allport, G. W. Personality: Normal and abnormal. In *Personality and social encounter.* Boston: Beacon, 1960, Pp. 155-168.

American Psychological Association Ad Hoc Planning Group on the Role of the APA in Mental Health Programs and Research. Mental health and the American Psychological Association. *Amer. Psychologist,* 1959, 14, 820-825.

Clausen, J. A. *Sociology and the field of mental health.* New York: Russell Sage Foundation, 1956.

DuBois, Cora *The people of Alor.* Minneapolis: Univer. Minnesota Press, 1944.

Foote, N. N., & Cottrell, L. S., Jr. *Identity and interpersonal competence.* Chicago: Univer. Chicago Press, 1955.

Ginsburg, S. W. The mental health movement: Its theoretical assumptions. In Ruth Kotinsky & Helen Witmer (Eds.), *Community programs for mental health.* Cambridge: Harvard Univer. Press, 1955. Pp. 1-29.

Jahoda, Marie Toward a social psychology of mental health. In Ruth Kotinsky & Helen Witmer (Eds.), *Community programs for mental health.* Cambridge: Harvard Univer. Press, 1955. Pp. 296-322.

Jahoda, Marie *Current conceptions of positive mental health.* New York: Basic Books, 1958.

Joint Commission on Mental Illness and Health *Action for mental health: Final report of the joint commission.* New York: Basic Books, 1961.

Klein, D. C. Some concepts concerning the mental health of the individual. *J. consult. Psychol.,* 1960, 24, 288-293.

Levine, L. S., & Kantor, R. E. Psychological effectiveness and imposed social position: A descriptive framework. Paper presented at the symposium, Positive conceptions of mental health: Implications for research and service, American Psychological Association, Chicago, September 5, 1960.

MacGregor, G. *Warriors without weapons.* Chicago: Chicago Univer. Press, 1946.

Maslow, A. H. *Motivation and personality.* New York: Harper, 1954.

Myrdal, G. *An American dilemma.* New York: Harper, 1944.

National Assembly on Mental Health Education *Mental health education: A critique.* Philadelphia: Pennsylvania Mental Health, Inc., 1960.

Peters, R. S. Private wants and public tradition. *Listener,* 1960, July 14, 46-47.

Riesman, D. *The lonely crowd.* New Haven: Yale Univer. Press, 1950.

Shoben, E. J., Jr. Toward a concept of the normal personality. *Amer. Psychologist,* 1957, 12, 183-189.

Smith, M. B. Research strategies toward a conception of positive mental health. *Amer. Psychologist,* 1959, 14, 673-681.

Snow, C. P. *The two cultures and the scientific revolution.* New York: Cambridge Univer. Press, 1959.

Szasz, T. S. The myth of mental illness. *Amer. Psychologist,* 1960, 15, 113-118.

White, R. W. Motivation reconsidered: The concept of competence. *Psychol. Rev.,* 1959, 66, 297-333.

Of values, value lag, and mental health

IJA N. KORNER

Adaptive psychological functioning is dependent to some extent on a stable system of values. Nevertheless, psychologists have tended to pay more attention to mechanisms of adjustment than they have to value orientations. This paper discusses the relationship of values to mental health and personal adjustment. The author, who is Professor of Psychology at the Green Bay campus of the University of Wisconsin and the author of more than forty articles on psychological topics and research, describes some of the difficulties of formulating and maintaining a viable set of values in a rapidly changing society. Dr. Korner comments on the consequences of compromising one's values and questions the role and responsibility of the mental health scientist with regard to personal values.

When the Committee on Mental Health of the APA met in New York last September, it so happened that the first five minutes of conference were spent agreeing unanimously that we would not define the term "mental health." This was a relief to all of us, and we quickly settled down to some productive work.

I would like to ask you for the same favor. Let us assume a few things. First, let us agree that mental health is necessary, virtuous, and good. Second, let us assume that social sciences have realized that they have the responsibility of being agents in the fight for conditions of mental health. Three, let us agree that the most important phase of mental health activity is the prophylactic one. By the latter, we mean the creation of conditions within the individual which will render him sufficiently capable to withstand the various stresses and pressures to which he will be subject during his lifetime.

One of the social scientists, the anthropologist, has raised the prophylactic aspects of mental health to an important hypothesis in his field. Ralph Linton (1) in the Introduction to Kardiner's *The Frontiers of Society*, says:

The basic personality type for any society is that personality configuration which is shared by the bulk of the society members as a result of the early experiences which they have in common. It does not correspond to the total personality of the individual, but rather to the project system, or in different phraseology, the value attitude system which is basic to the individual's personality configuration. Thus, the same basic personality type may be reflected in many different forms of behavior and may enter into many different total personality configurations.

What makes Linton an anthropologist, not a mental health expert, is the fact that he confines himself to the *study* of the processes. He is an onlooker whose responsibility is looking and understanding. He is, so to speak, a diagnostician primarily. The mental health scientist, on the other hand, is interested not only in understanding, but also in amending, reshaping, altering—his aim is not only diagnosis, but therapeutic activity in the widest sense of the word. The anthropologist is interested in the past and present of a culture; the mental health scientist in its present, as well as its future. Both work on the same continuum, though on different ends of it.

The mental health expert is interested in

From *American Psychologist*, XI (1956), 543-546. Reprinted by permission of the American Psychological Association and the author.

good functioning personality mechanisms, as well as in the value system within which these mechanisms operate. The interrelationship between these two, personality mechanism and value system, is complex. Suffice it to emphasize that the mechanisms and their structure not only serve to maintain the value structure, but also to alter the latter according to the dictates of reality.

When the anthropologist studies the value structure of a culture, he declares himself most competent to do so where the society under study is small and its institutions stable. "Basic personality" types can be established best when the elusive forces of cultural activity have had time to develop stable and consistent patterns. It is the stability of a society which aids an anthropologist to hunt down the sensitive patterns of the unconscious shaping of values.

We have some historical evidence that some time-epochs are characterized by rapid, others by slow, cultural changes. It is speculated that the former is deterrent, the latter conducive to good mental health conditions. If the change in values becomes noticeable but within a span of two to three generations, our social system can take care of the situation. An individual who is past middle age and who is out of step with the contemporary value system can be called "old-fashioned," "reactionary," and allowances will be made for his backwardness. This would be the case when a man believes that woman's function is the bearing and raising of children and the preoccupation with domestic duties. If, though, he adds to these, that woman has never been able to do well in the sciences and should not meddle with them, he may lose some of the protection granted to him by his "old-fashionedness."

When the values change so rapidly as to make an individual out of step with the value system within one generation, the repercussions may be deep and severe. They may not be noticeable in the surface behavior of a particular individual. The mechanisms take care of not letting the problem interfere with the individual's social interactions. The damage of the individual's "out-of-stepness" with contemporary value systems is often obliterated by their "good adjustment." Let us take as an example a young woman. She obtained up-to-date coeducational and liberal schooling. She went through college with the intention of becoming a journalist. Following graduation, she obtained a job and had good chances of making a career of it. Unfortunately, she was not only a woman, but also a female. She fell in love and compounded the error by marriage and two children. She is a good and conscientious mother—she is well adjusted. Everyone—even she, herself—believes in it. Still, to the observer, she is different—she lost many qualities which made her outstanding. She lost lustre, some of her sparkle and *joie de vivre*. She is not and never will be a psychiatric patient. Only rarely will she be bitter—even less complaining. She has excellent mechanisms of adjustment and she uses them to advantage. Her ego has effectuated a compromise, and compromise is considered to be the acme of adjustment.

In other instances where the adjustment mechanisms are less perfect than in our hypothetical woman, the result may be a deeply disturbed patient. In the case of the young woman, it was the value judgment, "a girl has the same opportunity and can do the same as a man," which was replaced rather suddenly by the value, "housewife," etc. Our present age does not emphasize the value "housewife" either in education or in school. To the contrary, there is a thorough indoctrination that being a housewife is a fate and not a call. Becoming a housewife requires considerable value adjustments from any woman.

This example is only one illustration of the many value changes which occurred within a short span of time. In the '30's, it was pacifism and isolationism; in the '40's, war and some internationalism; in the '50's, democracy versus security. In the '30's, we learned depression and the need for economic security; in the '50's, we must believe in eternal prosperity, and any comparison to the economic events of the '30's is decried as heresy and prophecy of gloom.

The scientist in the '30's lived close to the laboratory and far away from Washington. He moved into government in the '40's and in the '50's is quite confused about his move. In psychology, we came from academic to applied, from strictly scientific subjects in the '30's to such practical themes as "learning in psychotherapy." While we stressed catharsis and the necessity to lift repression in the '30's, we now extol ego psychology and accept dicta like "in therapy we replace ill-fitting repressions with more adequate ones."

One of the reasons why our time and our specific culture fosters rapid value changes is explained by the growth of the media of communication, which are unique in that they can spread as well as create new values within short spans of time (2). In this respect, our culture has less value stability than many contemporary non-Western cultures.

When an individual faces the necessity either to give up, devaluate, or exchange one value for another, the personality mechanisms are called into action. These, when functioning successfully, should but cannot always take care of all the necessary value changes. The chief instrument of value adjustment is primarily the ego's capacity for making compromises. This point of view, though essentially correct, does not take into account two important factors. First, not all compromises are good. In fact, only few are. Well-chosen and well-executed compromises often leave hurt and pain as the residue; on some levels of personality functioning, any compromise is damaging. Last, not least, the number of compromises any given individual is capable of making is limited. It is questionable that all values can be compromised with. Some values are so fundamental to personality structure that any attempt at compromise weakens that part of the personality structure referred to as superego, resulting in considerable damage to the total personality structure.

Parenthetically, how much of a child's personality structure is damaged by overhearing his parents discuss the pending income tax returns?

Second, the transforming and changing of values requires a great deal of time. Because of their irrational character, values are little amenable to reasoning and to volition. If, as mentioned earlier, the changes are slow, the adjustments are difficult but possible. If they are fast, the individual falls further and further behind; instead of assimilation and integration there is superimposition of layer upon layer of nonintegrable values. The new values often exist side by side with older values, resulting in an overt or covert conflict. Frequently then, the end result resembles a cancelling-out process in which the new and old values are kept in suspense by both being inactivated. This phenomenon of coexistence of superego-imposed values as a result of rapid value changes is what is meant by "value lag." The argument that the problem of value lag should be solved by better ego functioning is fallacious. The argument is fallacious because it assumes that the ego is all-powerful and capable, that it can be groomed and made to cover all human stresses and strains. The ego *does* deal with "value lag," but at a price. It is exactly this price in which the mental health expert is interested. My opinion is that it is too high already, and it has not yet reached its peak.

The matrix of the superego is values. Stability of values is necessary for superego formation. The price of tampering with the superego is considerable, as we all so well know. When values are required to change too rapidly, the superego as a whole is under stress. The result is either increased rigidity, with commensurate increase in resistance to change, or disorganization and too little resistance to change. The outcome lies somewhere on a continuum between zealot and psychopath.

The capacity of the superego to reorganize its own structure, to alter its own processes, is relatively unknown. There is some evidence that under favorable circumstances changes can and do occur. On the other hand, we also know that this capacity is limited. The superego can be stretched to the point of breaking. Value compromises leave behind severe superego scar tissue which frequently requires multiple therapeutic surgery.

The task of the mental health scientist is to provide means and ways by which value lag can be kept at a minimum or avoided altogether. What can be done?

First, we, the social scientists, must overcome our deep-seated resistances to dealing with values. Second, we must accept values as the matrix within which the adjustment processes function, and not elevate the mechanisms to the position of mastery over values. Third, we must apply research to the problem of value formation, the process of value change. There needs to be more research on optimal conditions for value change, value lag, value integration, and value disintegration. All this will take time. What can we do at the present?

Above all, let us recognize and face the problem of value and value lag. Then let us impress its importance upon others. We can only speculate as to how to cope best with value lag. The following avenues appear promising:

We cannot slow down the process of value change. Can we by the method of logic and/or research discern between stable and relatively immutable values and others which are liable to short-time change? "Motherhood," as well as acceptance of one's sex role, appear to be stable values. Earlier an instance was reported where this value was inadequately integrated. The stable values should be made subject to intense study. We could investigate some European countries, Switzerland for example. Here a number of values are made synonymous with being Swiss. There exists a national value structure, intensively indoctrinated in the home, at school, and at play. It is held that this basic value stability has a beneficial effect upon the individual. It is often postulated that mental health is good in societies with stable value structure. Do statistics bear this out?

We must distinguish at this point between a structure of stable values, and a value structure which is arteriosclerotic in character. Often the latter is mistaken for a stable one. Stable values which persist over generations would have to be investigated with the aim of weeding out those values which are still "on the books," so to speak, but which fail to have any functional meaning for our society. Rugged individualism, a value still much in evidence in our society, a remnant of the frontier value system, may be one of those hindering, pseudo-stable, sclerotic values. In a time of increased federalization, planned economy, and mechanization, this value to many an individual would be more of a hindrance than a help. Thus we may discern between stable values which help the individual, representing contemporariness, and those pseudo-stable values which have lost their functional meaning, which are deadwood in the "superego." Mental health scientists may face the necessity to take a stand concerning the advisability of supporting stable, opposing "pseudo-stable, sclerotic," values.

The insistence upon integration of basic values in early childhood and school education would be one of the functions of the mental health scientist. This appears a matter of commonsense, but acting in its behalf is not an easy matter. In order to propagate childhood indoctrination of "motherhood," etc., we may well come into painful conflict through misunderstanding with the emancipation movement of women. It would even be misunderstood by many of the teaching profession who may feel that this could not be part of "liberal education." Still the curriculum is built around stressing the woman's role as equal and alike, rather than as equal but different.

Speaking about schools, what about the value clash between the educator's attempt to give his students a humanistic view of the world, and industry's increased demand for the mechanized man?

Some values may emerge as sensitive to change within one to two generations. Such a value may be represented by the earlier mentioned "housewife," or "scientist," or "sentimentalist." The unstable values often are incompatible with the more basic values, counterpointing the difference between generations rather than the likeness which the basic values emphasize. Should it be the task of the mental health scientist to oppose in word and deed those unstable values which are detrimental to development? Can we dare to advise and/or act against a value by predicting its potential as a source of conflict? So far everyone who attempted to deal actively with values rather than to submit to them did so by his conviction that he presented "right." Can we scientists invade critically the area of values with no convictions, no moral banners, no preaching of gloom, no concept of right and wrong, invoking only the operational concept of "adjustment"? Even if that were possible it would precipitate upon us the wrath of a considerable segment of society. The social scientist would be accused of propaganda, thought and feeling control, Fascism, Communism, to name only a few. The physicist, less wise in the ways of the world than some of us, is learning the lesson of his mistake, which consisted of having discovered sin. Can we, the social scientists, permit the creation and perpetuation of maladjustment, which in our language is equal to sin, by averting our eyes from the problem of values?

I cannot give an answer to this question. I think I am apprehensive about having to make up my mind to be actively against sin, meaning to speak up about values and the virus of conflict which attacks them. Together with others, though, I could tolerate the discomfort.

Maybe the first task of the social scientist is to create a mental health scientist who, among others, is not afraid of society.

My subject was the problem of value and value lag, which I consider a serious one. What is required for its solution from us social scientists is primarily insight, courage, and research skill. All these we possess. I, therefore, see no reason why we cannot deal with this problem successfully.

References

1. Kardiner, A. *The psychological frontiers of society.* N. Y.: Columbia Univer. Press, 1945.

2. Ruesch, J., & Bateson, G. *Communication.* N. Y.: W. W. Norton, 1951.

Links between psychology and religion

RUSSELL J. BECKER

Responsibility for the psychological well-being of the individual person has traditionally been the concern of several disciplines, including religion, medicine, and psychology. In recent years more persons appear to be turning to psychologists and psychiatrists for help with their personal problems than to the clergy. The question of who is in the best position to help persons solve their personal dilemmas is of great practical significance. This article addresses itself to this issue and to the relative roles of psychology and religion in responding to the needs of the individual. Dr. Becker, who is Associate Professor of Pastoral Theology in the Yale Divinity School, traces the historical relationship of psychology and religion and describes how the increasing use of certain modern treatment techniques has altered the relationship between the clergyman and the psychologist.

There are two important ways in which modern psychology has been related to religion in the Western world. The first of these arose when psychologists took the data of religious life as relevant material for empirical study. This fact gave birth to the "psychology of religion." This development since 1895 is no different in principle from other applications of psychological theory and methodology which brought into being the fields of educational psychology, industrial psychology, social psychology, clinical psychology, vocational psychology, and the like. The second relationship emerged as clinical psychology became more directly involved in psychotherapy during the past two decades. Because of this turn of events we are now witnessing a more fundamental convergence of psychology and religion.

The working relationship of religion and psychology based on the psychological study and analysis of religious data has been a fruitful one. William James' classic work on the *Varieties of Religious Experience* (4), relying as it did on classification as its method, set the stage for objective analysis and study of the subjective and seemingly sacrosanct religious aspects of life. The course of the last 60 years has been one of progressive refinement in the tools of analysis as well as in the religious problems analyzed. It will suffice here simply

From *American Psychologist*, XIII (1958), 566-568. Reprinted by permission of the American Psychological Association and the author.

to suggest that there was a pioneering leap which occurred between the Starbuck and Leuba questionnaire studies of conversion in the 1890's and the situational testing used by Hartshorne and May in their studies of the character building role of religious education in the 1920's. Similarly, it is a great leap from there to the recent analysis of the incidence of mental illness in a closed religious community (the Hutterites in South Dakota) by Eaton and Wiles (1) and by Kaplan (5), as well as to the current report of Festinger and others (2) on what happens when a prophesying sect has its prophecy proven wrong. When the psychologist takes his methods of empirical investigation (be they questionnaire, experimental situation, epidemiological survey, participant observation, or whatever) to the data of religious life, the result is a welcome increase in the body of human knowledge. One can only hope that the use of research instruments more refined than simple classification and the questionnaire will be an accelerating one.

Both the psychologist and the informed religious person have felt satisfied with the growth of a psychology of religion. To the psychologist it is an extension of a science of psychology. To the informed religious person it is an increase in our knowledge of the truth.

The second area of relationship between psychology and religion raises some deeper issues. Within the past two decades psychology and psychologists have found themselves drawn in an ever increasing degree to the work of psychotherapy. This involvement has been not merely as the research adjunct to medical treatment but increasingly as practitioners and theoreticians, as well as research investigators of psychotherapy. With this expansion of the clinical aspects of psychology there has come a new family of relationships. Psychology and medicine have had to give absorbing time and attention to the relationships between themselves as fields of clinical practice. On the more theoretical side, psychology has found that the relationship with religion, which was neatly kept in check so long as the psychologist was the detached, experimental investigator, has become all "muddied up" now that psychotherapists are deeply involved in the business of changing persons. The goals of psychotherapy and the real concerns of psy-

chotherapists place psychotherapists in juxtaposition to the goals and work of religion relative to the individual person. Thus psychology and religion, which entered into a state of legal separation during the early part of this century, in order to allow psychology to thrive as a science unfettered by doctrinal restraints, have fallen in love again and are at least cohabiting, if not fully married to each other, because of the influence of psychotherapy on psychology.

The unity of aim shared by religion and psychotherapy is twofold: concern for the individual person and a value orientation relative to his true well-being. It need hardly be argued that the patience involved in spending 50 or 100 or 200 hours with a single individual plus the depth of permissiveness, acceptance, and respect involved in the therapist's capacity to be open to the emotional complexities of another person's life provide a new definition of what "caring" for another person means, of what charity or true "love" means, of what creative personal relationships may be, of what the ethical demands of religion upon daily living are. This may be said of psychotherapy in general and is not limited to one "school" or another. It does not detract from the depth of concern for the individual by psychotherapists to say that they are paid for their services. No religious institution exists as a social fact without some "payment" or provision for its own survival. What we have in the evolving field of psychotherapy is a new conception of the ethic of love and a new understanding of the worth of persons that has grown up largely outside of organized religion. Now that it exists, we can recognize this fact and allow it to take its place alongside of similar views differently expressed within our historic religious traditions of Judaism and Christianity.

That psychotherapists hold a framework of value relative to the life of man and act upon that framework has been a disconcerting fact to many psychologists in search of a value-free science. To suggest that there is a view of man's nature and destiny present in the work of psychotherapists disturbs the "scientific," "nonreligious" demeanor of many. Nonetheless, there exists either explicitly or implicitly a view of man's nature and destiny, what he is and what his true well-being may be, in every psychologist's understanding of emotional illness and in what he sees as curative of that illness.

In the process of defining emotional illness and emotional maturity, psychotherapists present their views of man and their conceptions of his highest good. Let us consider one or two examples. In his *Collected Papers*, Freud (3) states:

The patient's symptoms and pathological manifestations, like all his mental processes, are of a very elaborately organized nature; their elements at bottom consist of motives, of instinctual impulses. But the patient knows nothing of these elemental motives or not nearly enough. Now we teach him to understand the structure of these highly complicated formations in his mind; we trace the symptoms back to the instinctual impulses which motivate them; we point out to the patient these instinctual motives in his symptoms of which he has hitherto been unaware . . . (p. 393).

Psychological sickness according to Freud is due to elaborate mental processes, largely instinctual, of which we know all too little. Psychological health, maturity, and personal well-being lie in the direction of increasing rational understanding, insight, and awareness relative to these little known forces within us.

Whitaker and Malone (6) see the sick person as one whose

. . . intrapersonal organization of affect breaks down. The structuring of personality occurs around the organization of affect (anxiety) through the developing sequence of interpersonal relations. The good parent-child relation is the interpersonal situation which provides the best opportunity for the structuring interpersonally of the affects (primarily anxiety). The process of psychotherapy represents an effort to restore or improve the structure of personality through the organization of affect between patient and therapist (p. 121).

In the Freudian analytic view of illness and of the maturing factor in persons, there is a more rational-cognitive emphasis than in the Whitaker and Malone outlook which emphasizes that affective relationships between persons are the source of disturbed living as well as the avenue by which personal growth must be sought. Notwithstanding this very real difference, the points being made are that each

is a view of man and each contains a set of values by which life should be guided for its fulfillment of given potentialities.

As corroborating evidence of the centrality of a value orientation to the work of the psychotherapists, we need only note the ease with which psychotherapists move from the clinical situation working with one person to the larger fabric of society with analyses and remedies for the ills of society. Works such as Franz Alexander's *Our Age of Unreason,* Erich Fromm's *The Sane Society,* Robert Lindner's *Must We Conform?* come to mind.

What this paper is suggesting is that psychotherapy, by virtue of the obvious ethical implications involved in its "caring" for or "treating" persons and because of its unavoidable espousal of some view of man and some value orientation as to his true well-being, has brought psychology and religion into a contiguity and interlacing of work where it is no longer possible to distinguish neatly the psychologist from his religious colleague. The earlier established field of the psychology of religion had kept the religious and the scientific order of things identifiably distinct. This new phase of relationship blurs those distinctions to the point where many have found it satisfying to have a religion of psychotherapy.

At this point it is enough to recognize that psychology and religion are linked arm in arm in the depths and in the implications of psychotherapeutic practice. It is to be hoped that we may one day have a symposium in which psychology asks of the student of religion what problems he sees as historically recurring in this business of holding a value orientation and a given goal for the good of man. It will presage a new level of growth in psychology when its psychotherapists are ready to inquire what relevant wisdom may have been gained in the experience of religious history. This symposium itself is an important enough step for today toward a new-found proximity of religion and psychology.

References

1. Eaton, J., & Weil, R. J. *Culture and mental disorders.* Chicago: Free Press, 1955.
2. Festinger, L., Riecken, H. W., & Schachter, S.

When prophecy fails. Minneapolis: Univer. Minnesota Press, 1956.

3. Freud, S. *Collected papers.* London: Hogarth, 1924.

4. James, W. *Varieties of religious experience.* New York: Modern Library, 1902.

5. Kaplan, B., & Plant, T. P. A. *Personality in a communal society.* Lawrence: Univer. Kansas Press, 1956.

6. Whitaker, C., & Malone, T. *The roots of psychotherapy.* New York: McGraw-Hill, 1953.

Value orientations—an ethical dilemma [1]

C. MARSHALL LOWE

All professional disciplines require their members to conform to ethical standards of behavior. This responsibility is particularly difficult for the psychologist because of the diversity of his interests and the conflicts which may emerge between personal and professional goals. This article describes some of the problems and ethical dilemmas facing psychologists today. The author classifies the value systems used by different kinds of psychologists into four categories and illustrates each type of value orientation by citing the work of a well-known psychologist. The article critically discusses the advantages and limitations of adopting a particular set of values and raises important questions for all persons to consider.

C. Marshall Lowe, B.S., Ph.D., has completed formal training in both theology and psychology. He is Assistant Professor in the Division of Counseling Psychology in the School of Education at the University of California, Berkeley, and the author of *Value Orientations in Counseling Psychotherapy: The Meaning of Mental Health.*

The psychologist is being called upon today to play a new role. Society is asking him to leave his laboratory and to move out into the world to be of practical service to mankind. While the psychologist must, of necessity, play this new role, he does so with certain difficulties, for he must divest himself of the robes of scientific impartiality. The psychologist as a scientist limits himself to what is; his choice of field of inquiry in his quest for truth involves values which are purely personal. But as a practitioner, the psychologist must be concerned with what should be; his personal tastes now affect the lives of others and so become social values.

The point of this article is that the involvement of the psychologist's own values in the applied field creates an ethical dilemma. The dilemma exists because the psychologist as a scientist cannot know to which of mankind's brave new worlds he is to be beholden. The educational psychologist facilitates learning; but learning involves understanding, whose nature is determined only by a philosophy of education. The industrial psychologist is employed by a company which seeks a profit, and only personal choice can help him reconcile loyalty to the employer with a broader loyalty to society as it is represented by the consumer and by the fellow employee.

With the counselor and the clinician, the ethical dilemma becomes more severe, for they serve not an organization but rather a particular

From *American Psychologist,* XIV (1959), 687-693. Reprinted by permission of the American Psychological Association and the author.

[1] Based upon a master's thesis submitted to the Ohio State University in 1958. The author is indebted for guidance to John R. Kinzer and Collins W. Burnett of the Department of Psychology.

individual. The clinician is of service by striving to bring back one who is mentally unhealthy to psychic health, and yet his science can scarcely tell him what mental health and psychological maturity really are. The counselor provides guidance for effective living, and yet it is scarcely as a psychologist that he describes the good life.

In therapy, the psychologist works toward ends which he calls "adjustment," "self-realization," "relearning," etc. These words do not even approximately describe the same thing. Further, it is impossible for research to enter the breach and describe the ends of effective counseling. The therapist remembers the words of Williamson (1958) that "every choice and every action must be based upon explicit or implicit acceptance of a value" (p. 524). He recalls the admonition of Rogers (1947) that a person is always controlled by the one upon whom he is dependent. And if the therapist is experimentally minded, he finds scarcely any comfort in the findings of Rosenthal (1955) that those clients who improve in therapy tend to revise certain of their values so that they more closely resemble those of the therapist.

In the counseling interview, it does not matter whether or not the therapist is consciously aware of a value orientation. If he is aware of his value orientation, he finds it often impossible to be loyal both to his own highest values and those of the client. If he has not systematized his beliefs, the therapist will assume his own values to be self-evident, and in ignorance he will project his own values onto the client.

The dilemma of the practicing psychologist is compounded by the existence of a multiplicity of competing sets of values, for one value orientation tends to exclude all others. As we present the controversy over values, we will assemble them into four main orientations: naturalism, culturalism, humanism, and theism. We shall see that each makes a demand for loyalty, setting at the same time its own criterion or goal. We shall see also that every orientation has critics who oppose its claims.

Naturalism

Naturalism, the first value orientation that we shall consider, has taken several current forms. One of these is logical positivism. Insofar as positivism seeks to throw out of the cultural vocabulary all notions that are not susceptible to empirical validation, it implies a naturalistic world view by assuming that scientific laws can account for all phenomena. Since reality is limited to what is defined operationally, naturalism limits psychology to the study of behavior, the mind being reduced to the physiological and physical, which can be measured. The result is Behaviorism and a limited scientific vocabulary that prevents the erection of any hierarchy of values that will transcend the physical. Both Behaviorism and classical psychoanalysis in turn imply a physical hedonism by placing emphasis on physical laws which reduce the life of the mind to the needs of the body.

Today the foremost naturalist in psychology is B. F. Skinner, who is an exceedingly bold social thinker. The common theme of his social treatises is that the psychologist possesses the means of social control and must use these means effectively for the welfare of society. The function of the psychologist is then to be a behavioral engineer who manipulates behavior in such a way as to insure cultural survival. It is part of his orientation that Skinner chooses not to state values. When forced by critics to state a moral position, he took the position that the criterion for good was to be the survival value for the culture. The psychologist is permitted to do anything and everything that will allow his fellow men to keep breathing (Skinner, 1956).

Skinner's values for psychology are picturesquely stated in his utopian novel *Walden Two* (1948). Skinner's conception of paradise is a large rural colony where democracy is replaced by behavioral engineering. If the means are scientific control, the end is physical comfort, which is provided by the short work day which the elimination of cultural anachronisms permits. While a small autocracy controls life in the colony, the only technique available to it is positive reinforcement, lest members avail themselves of their one freedom, which is to leave. If at first glance man is a slave, in Skinner's view he is free from the tyranny of chance and free to take advantage of the best that cultural engineering can provide.

Criticisms of Naturalism. Naturalism in its many manifestations has been attacked both on ontological and on epistemological grounds. Axiology, however, is our concern in this paper, and understandably there is criticism of naturalism here too. For the sake of brevity, we will let the criticism focus upon the utopian social world of B. F. Skinner. Thus, Carl Rogers (1956) has charged that Skinner completely abandoned scientific method in *Walden Two*. In Rogers' view, Skinner confuses what is with what should be. Science can compare two values only in terms of a criterion, or third value, which must lie outside science. When science is itself the criterion, or final value, it is miscontrol. It is "locked in the rigidity of initial choice" and "can never transcend itself to seek new goals" (p. 1062). Rogers concludes that *"Walden Two* and *Nineteen Eighty Four* are at a deep philosophical level indistinguishable" (p. 1062).

The reaction by humanist philosophy has been even more violent. Joseph Wood Krutch has written *The Measure of Man* (1954) to refute *Walden Two*. Krutch is concerned because there is no clear way of differentiating between the positivistic control of *Walden Two* and the fascist control of a Nazi labor camp. He worries because social control is passing from the hands of philosophers and theologians who are aware of moral issues into the hands of experimentalists who are less aware of the value judgments that they make and whose methods are such as to prevent others from questioning them. In Krutch's view, survival is not the ultimate aim of man. Cockroaches have survived for 250,000,000 years, but Krutch feels that it is not enough merely to exist as an animal.

A final criticism is made of *Walden Two* as a novel. It is claimed that the characters have no real personality, but are only puppets whose strings are pulled by the author for polemic purposes. Physical hedonism and literary art are indeed incompatible, for the novel can speak to the reader only by allowing him to identify with characters who do not eliminate their hardships, but surmount them even in the face of tragedy.

Walden Two has significance not as a novel but as a statement of those values by which Skinner seeks to give coherence to life. Skinner's credo raises the problem that psychology now comes forth and claims that it can determine the conduct of a public whose highest value seemingly is that it is free to choose for itself.

Culturalism

Just as the naturalists take their cue from the physical world and make the physiological processes of the body the final criterion in psychotherapy, so there is another group of thinkers who are oriented to man's social nature. We term this second value orientation "culturalism" and include in the group those who take their cue from the social world and who see man's problems as arising more from his social needs than from his physical wants.

Culturalism makes loyalty to the culture from which man is derived the supreme value. In psychology, it has an explicit pronouncement in the APA's "Ethical Standards of Psychologists," which states: "The psychologist's ultimate allegiance is to society and his professional behavior should demonstrate an awareness of his social responsibilities" (1953, Paragraph 1.12-1). The APA doubtless sought for a code that would speak to its time; but we should not overlook the fact that at other times such a code might have stated that "ultimate allegiance" is to God, or in another period to the "rights of man."

Applying culturalism to the field of mental health, we find those who see wholeness only in relating to other people. We see this emphasis first in such social psychoanalysts as Adler, Sullivan, and Horney who see the cause of neurosis in isolation from other people and who see the cure in being led back to other people.

We see this emphasis secondly in those psychologists who subordinate the individual to the social through emphasis on "adjustment." Adjustment psychology carries social psychoanalysis one step further: one must not only be able to relate to other people, but must also be able to adapt to what others are doing. Thus Shaffer and Shoben in their *Psychology of Adjustment* (1956) compare the process of social adjustment in humans with that of biological adjustment in animals. They recommend for man the following procedure:

In response to your need for approval, you may act so as to gain favor in the future or you may display other abilities that bring you recognition. *These are quite sensible things to do under the circumstances* [Italics added] (p. 4).

As Shoben writes in the journals to a more sophisticated readership, his position becomes more complex. While he rejects the notion that the "normal" is the average, he (1957) considers pathology as being nonconformity to group norms. And like Skinner he has a utopia:

What kind of world would be ours if we were less concerned about achievement and fully occupied with understanding each other, participating more wholeheartedly in the corporate venture of building a society . . . and developed a sense of worthwhileness of intimate relationships marked by a high degree of cherishing and the mutual pursuit of essentially private interests? (Shoben, 1956, pp. 330-331)

Criticism of Culturalism. The critical problem of culturalism involves the choice of particular cultural values. Man cannot choose to accept or reject social values; his only option is to select particular social values. Arnold Green (1946) writes:

the history of psychotherapy can be viewed as an unsuccessful struggle to evaluate the role of social values [for] it is safe to say that all behavior resulting in the need for psychotherapy is social [in the sense that] it involves a conflict between self-and-others and between self-values and other(s) values (pp. 199-200).

Culturalism must seek to reduce diverse social values to a least common denominator, but the result is dissatisfying to many.

First, voices are raised against subservience to a "democratic" ideology which, as Green (1946) points out, is rapidly changing and which at the present time is rather vague, as Walker and Peiffer (1957) remind us in their criticism of Shoben. To provide orientation by the values of midcentury America is thus to build upon sand while the rain is already falling.

Other voices cry out that what is most common is very far from being the best. The popular press reminds us that to be normal is nothing to brag about, and every social reformer has as his bugaboo the person who is too well adjusted to things as they are. Erich Fromm (1955) sees adjustment as destroying what is distinctive in human personality and postulates a *folie á millions* where multitudes share the same vices. Another psychoanalyst, Robert

Lindner (1952), sees man as exchanging the freedom that is his to work out his own destiny for the doped security of accepting things as they are.

And finally, there are psychologists who raise their voices in concern for the abdication of moral responsibility that culturalism implies. In the view of M. Brewster Smith (1954), psychology has helped to destroy values traditionally related to the Western world and, by then abdicating responsibility for values, has added "to the crescendo urging total conformity, a trend which in the long run may not be at all conservative of our traditional values" (p. 515). C. Gilbert Wrenn (1952) points out that the counselor can never be really loyal to society until he is loyal to something more than society. The psychologist to be ethical must do more than observe a code of ethics: "He must be great within himself because he relates himself to God and the greatness of the Infinite" (p. 176).

The conformitizing of the "other directed" person is being accelerated by the "organization man." The dilemma of culturalism is that it allows itself to be caught in a vicious circle —our society can be like a dog following its own tail. If there is nothing external that it can follow, it is doomed to meander meaninglessly in circles. The hope for the world is in following after the most sublime, and not after the most painfully obvious.

Humanism

While the culturalist looks outside of man to what is in the social world, there is another group of thinkers, whom we term the humanists, who believe that the criteria for ethical values lie within certain native human characteristics. In the broad sense, anyone concerned with the dignity of man is a humanist. However, as we use the term, humanism is belief in the self-sufficiency of man to control his own destiny and to realize his inherent potentialities through rational thought processes. Man's final moral obligation is to strive continually to realize all the unique potentialities which are inherent in human nature, the ultimate value being man. Among humanist psychologists, the aim is the same whether the object of therapy be termed "self-actualization" as by Goldstein, "emergent value-attributes" by Cantril, the positive "emotional tone" by Cole, or the "growth potential" by Rogers; each one equates activism with mental health.

The philosophical underpinnings of humanism in psychotherapy is seen in Erich Fromm. Fromm's slogan is *Man for Himself* (1947), the title of his best known book. He finds that "man cannot live statically because his inner contradictions drive him to seek for an equilibrium, for a new harmony instead of the lost animal harmony of nature" (1955, p. 28). Thus: "The whole life of the individual is nothing but the process of giving birth to himself" (1955, p. 26). The life of man consists in *The Art of Loving* (1956), Fromm's most recent book. To love others, one must first love himself and have faith in himself, for man must respect his own self before he can have respect for someone else.

The humanist methodology in therapy is seen in Carl Rogers, who has published his credo in the *Humanist* (1957b):

The good life, from the point of view of my experience, is the process of movement in a direction which the human organism selects when it is inwardly free to move in any direction (p. 293).

Rogers' conception of therapy seems to be almost identical with his ideal of the good life, for he believes in a "process conception of psychotherapy" (1958), which seems to be a microcosm of the good life outside. Rogers' humanistic concern determines both what he does and does not do as a counselor: the therapist plays a relatively passive role, because man is inherently able to solve his own problems. The task of therapy is to let the rational self shine forth through a constricting fog in all its logic: "The tragedy for most of us is that our defenses keep us from being aware of this rationality" (1957b, p. 299). The client is a human being whose feelings are worthy of complete respect. Thus the counselor empathizes with the client and respects his emotions. Should the counselor be an unbeliever in the worth of the true self and should lack an "unconditional positive regard" for the client, the client's inner personality will not dare emerge, and therapeutic change will not occur (1957a). Therapy takes place as the self finds shelter and feasts on its own experience until it becomes the fully developed onion with its concentric layers. Rogers and the client form "a mutual admiration society" whose purpose is clear: the human personality is to be magnified and praised.

Criticism of Humanism. Humanistic psychology can first of all be criticized for absolutizing American activism when it is only a cultural phenomenon. Rogers may tell us quite open-mindedly that he has discovered a drive towards self-assertiveness in all his clients, but he does not tell us how many of these clients were unrelated in any way to the middle class, which judges personal worth by the amount of achievement. What Rogers boasts of so proudly as self-actualization may be but the pathology of a culture whose members are frightened at being cut off from past traditions and rush pellmell into the future, as if they were animals in stampede. Today the absolute nature of self-actualization seems threatened on the one hand by the corporation, which, in the organization man, grinds out its own cultural type, and on the other hand, by increasing contact with other cultures, which are in many ways superior to our own even if they produce little change over many centuries.

Humanism also lays itself open to the charge that man is not so perfectly rational as he sometimes likes to conceive himself as being. The social criticism of Reinhold Niebuhr (1941) is too complex to be quickly summarized; but, starting from premises similar to Fromm's, he sees man as being anxious. Man resolves this anxiety by deluding himself into thinking that he is really in control of life. He deceives himself into thinking that he is more perfect than he really is, erring because he is unaware of his own ignorance. Having charted the disastrous historical debacles that have been caused by self-inflated prigs, Niebuhr concludes that it is the man who thinks that he is most like God who is the most completely depraved.

Humanists frequently surround themselves with the sanctimonious glow of those who can "intuit" experiences to which the tough minded remain impervious. But being optimistic about human nature does not make a man more saintly, any more than Niebuhr's ability to see the manifestations of human sinfulness wherever he looks makes him less of a believer in God. Humanism represents the Enlightenment. But set against the Enlightenment is the pessimism of Freudian psychoanalysis and Pauline theology, for these two movements span the history of the Western world like the legs of a caliper and provide their own measure for man.

Self-actualization does not seem to be enough. Some men seem so bereft of personality that they have few powers to realize; while others, such as F. Scott Fitzgerald and Françoise Sagan, have drained a rich humanity to the dregs and have felt only *ennui* in the process of living. Man is a creature caught between the need of individuality and the need of belonging, plagued by contradictory loyalties to the self and to others; burdened by the guilt inherent in the realization that he has not fulfilled his potentialities; and inwardly frightened as he seeks to build up walls of meaning out of sand in a delirious attempt to enshrine the human self which he knows the incoming tide of time will surely wash away.

In contradiction to humanism, there are some who believe that man has some other end than merely to feel dignified. They would say that man has the greatest dignity when he feels his own inward wretchedness and that he is the creature of the greatest progress when "his richest gain he counts but loss, and pours contempt on all his pride."

Theism

The final value orientation, theism, believes that man's loyalty is to God and that man is totally dependent upon God. Believers in other value orientations can also be religious in a broad sense of the word. The theist, however, differs from all who believe in the self-sufficiency of man by his belief in a personal God before whom he stands in need of redemption.

While theists have a diversity of beliefs, there is one value that is central: "You shall love the Lord your God with all your heart, and with all your soul, and with all your might." This great commandment involves the theist with the will of God in interpersonal relations, including marriage and family problems; in the choice and resolution of conflicts; in finding a philosophy of life; and in vocational choice.

Theism is distinctive in its belief that man is lost until he has found God. In words which Augustine addresses to God: "Thou hast made us for Thyself, and the heart never rests until it finds its rest in Thee." Man is a creature dependent past, present, and future upon the God who created him. While the humanist believes that man is made in the image of God in

a way that enables him to become a little god, the theist believes that man is made in the image of God as one set of gears is made in the image of another set, so that it can receive power in order to pass it on.

The theist believes that the problems that men face are such that they have a solution in religious faith. When despair over the apparent meaninglessness and monotony of life causes a depressed state, the cure is through faith in a God who creates all life for a unique purpose. In the melancholy of change of life and in the despair of old age, he finds in religion that path of transition from physical to spiritual goals. When man is fearful, he finds strength through the spirit of God; and, when he is anxious within, he finds inner reassurance in the love of the Heavenly Father, whose love can bear his inner weaknesses. In loneliness and in isolation from other people, he enters into harmonic relationships with those who seek to radiate a forgiving love that understands all things.

Gordon W. Allport (1950) thus notes that "love is incomparably the greatest psychotherapeutic agent" (p. 80). He notes that religion needs to become a part of psychotherapy, for it "offers an interpretation of life and a rule of life that is based wholly upon love" (p. 82). Allport also notes that religion is needed to give meaning to life, a need also noted by Carl Jung (1933), who, speaking of his patients over 35, claims that

It is safe to say that everyone of them fell ill because he had lost that which the living religions of every age have given to their followers, and none of them has been really healed who did not regain his spiritual outlook (p. 264).

Criticism of Theism. There are certain objections that are raised against theism. If man is anxious and upset because he has difficulty in believing in anything deeply, then religious faith becomes the problem. While the vast majority of Americans believe in God according to the opinion polls, theism requires a committed faith that rather few people have had in any age.

A second objection takes into account the wrong use of religion. Finding an awakening of religious interest in the postwar era, a number of America's most prominent churchmen have spoken out against a religious revival, which, lacking any deep-seated devotion to God, is centered in a self-serving religious faith that is interested only in comfort by the bland assurance that everything is really all right. Prophetically, at the very start of the post-war era, Arnold Green (1946) saw the dangers in superficial religion, pointing out that "faith cannot be consciously designed to meet a personality need any more than it can be established by fiat or legislative action" (p. 205). He concluded that religion can be therapeutic only when it is not so regarded.

A third objection is that theism keeps man in infantile dependence. Psychoanalysis believes that authoritarian religion is the internalized voice of authority, having the same restrictive effect as had the father. Fromm (1947) thus lists ways in which he feels organized religion has impeded human progress. Somewhat similarly, Rollo May (1953) objects to "the divine right of being taken care of" which blocks growth towards maturity. May further brands as neurotic the use of religion in helping to obviate that loneliness and anxiety which is vital to *Man's Search for Himself*.

There are certain irreconcilable differences between theism and the other value orientations at critical choice-points. For the humanist, man gains his life by holding it close to him, cherishing it, and feeling the self develop within him. The theist on the other hand believes that man finds his life only by losing his life and by emptying the self for others, being filled with a love which is ultimately of God. These are two contrasting ways to mental health, and the psychologist must choose between them.

Conclusion

If the psychologist is by definition to be ethical, he must conform to professional standards of conduct. Having described different value orientations, we can now conclude that there is no single professional standard to which his values can conform. If psychology declares by fiat that one set of values is to become absolute, it ceases to be science and becomes a social movement. If it chooses a syncretistic blend, it has arbitrarily decided in favor of a culturalism that attempts to adapt to as many viewpoints as possible. But when a value is compromised, it has become the means to some other end. Finally, psychology can choose to hide its head in the sand of scientific research. However, the only result

of such a move would be a regression to ethical superstitions exceeding even those of the so-called primitives. To do research without intending it to serve a particular value orientation is to build a high speed automobile without any steering wheel.

Williamson has already made a start in untieing the ethical knot by suggesting that value orientations be removed from under the proverbial bushel and, once out in the open, be dealt with as objectively as possible. We would suggest in addition that each area in psychology become more fully aware of the implications of its efforts, much as education does through a philosophy of education. We would further suggest that, as psychologists familiarize themselves with the value orientation under which they operate, they confess their philosophic biases and then turn those biases to fullest advantage by being of professional assistance to the special interest groups with which their values coincide. In such ways as these the public will receive more of what psychology has to contribute and, dealing with psychology at a more objective level, will be able to put that contribution to better use.

We conclude that differences in value orientations cannot be resolved, each orientation having adherents whose beliefs should be respected. We suggest that each counselor have an understanding of the values both of himself and others and that his values be known by all who are personally affected by his professional behavior.

References

Allport, G. W. *The individual and his religion.* New York: Macmillan, 1950.

American Psychological Association *Ethical standards of psychologists.* Washington, D. C.: APA, 1953.

Fromm, E. *Man for himself.* New York: Rinehart, 1947.

Fromm, E. *The sane society.* New York: Rinehart, 1955.

Fromm, E. *The art of loving.* New York: Harper, 1956.

Green, A. Social values and psychotherapy. *J. Personality,* 1946, 14, 199-228.

Jung, C. G. *Modern man in search of a soul.* New York: Harcourt Brace, 1933.

Krutch, J. W. *The measure of man.* New York: Bobbs-Merrill, 1954.

Lindner, R. *Prescription for rebellion.* New York: Rinehart, 1952.

May, R. *Man's search for himself.* New York: Norton, 1953.

Niebuhr, R. *The nature of man.* New York: Scribners, 1941.

Rogers, C. R. Divergent trends in methods of improving adjustment. *Harvard Educ. Rev.,* 1947, 18, 209-219.

Rogers, C. R. Some issues concerning the control of human behavior. *Science,* 1956, 124, 1060-1064.

Rogers, C. R. Necessary conditions of therapeutic change. *J. consult. Psychol.,* 1957, 21, 95-103. (a)

Rogers, C. R. A therapist's view of the good life. *Humanist,* 1957, 17, 291-300. (b)

Rogers, C. R. A process conception of psychotherapy. *Amer. Psychologist,* 1958, 13, 142-149.

Rosenthal, D. Changes in some moral values following psychotherapy. *J. consult. Psychol.,* 1955, 19, 431-436.

Shaffer, L. F., & Shoben, E. J. *The psychology of adjustment.* Cambridge: Riverside, 1956.

Shoben, E. J. Work, love, and maturity. *Personal guid. J.,* 1956, 34, 326-332.

Shoben, E. J. Toward a concept of the normal personality. *Amer. Psychologist,* 1957, 12, 183-189.

Skinner, B. F. *Walden two.* New York: Macmillan, 1948.

Skinner, B. F. Some issues concerning the control of human behavior. *Science,* 1956, 124, 1057-1065.

Smith, M. B. Toward scientific and professional responsibilities. *Amer. Psychologist,* 1954, 9, 513-516.

Walker, D. E., & Peiffer, H. C. The goals of counseling. *J. counsel. Psychol.,* 1957, 4, 204-209.

Williamson, E. G. Value orientation in counseling. *Personnel guid. J.,* 1958, 36, 520-528.

Wrenn, C. G. The ethics of counseling, *Educ. psychol. Meas.,* 1952, 12, 161-177.

A critique of cultural and statistical concepts of abnormality

HENRY J. WEGROCKI

It is difficult to establish guidelines which can consistently and accurately differentiate normal behavior from abnormal behavior. This article critically reviews the adequacy of two of the most common bases for assessing abnormality, the cultural and statistical models. The author considers the rationale and evidence for each approach in an attempt to evaluate the merits of a relative versus an absolute basis for determining abnormality. Despite the length of time that has passed since its original publication, the article retains its relevance and raises some fundamental questions for which no totally satisfactory solutions have yet been found.

Before his death in 1967, Henry Wegrocki, Ph.D., was engaged in the private practice of psychiatry and was Associate Clinical Professor of Psychiatry at the University of Southern California Medical School.

One of the most significant contributions to a proper orientation and envisagement of human behavior has been the body of data coming in the past few decades from the field of ethnological research. Human behavior had so

From *Journal of Abnormal and Social Psychology,* XXXIV (1939), 166-178. Reprinted by permission of the American Psychological Association and Mrs. H. J. Wegrocki.

long been seen in terms of the categories of Western civilization that a critical evaluation of cultures other than our own could not help exercising a salutary effect on the ever-present tendency to view a situation in terms of familiar classifications. The achievement of a realization that the categories of social structure and function are ever plastic and dynamic, that they differ with varying cultures, and that one culture cannot be interpreted or evaluated in terms of the categories of another, represents as tremendous an advance in the study of social behavior as did the brilliant insight of Freud in the field of depth psychology.

Wundt (20) to some extent, but especially Boas (3), have emphasized this approach continuously. One may say that most of the "mistakes" of earlier anthropologists have been due to the tendency of seeing the features of other cultures simply in terms of the categories of Western civilization and forming, consequently, a distorted impression of those features, whether they relate to religion, marriage, or some other aspect of social life.

In connection with this modern ethnological conception of the relativity of interpretations and standards, there has arisen the problem of whether the standard of what constitutes abnormality is a relative or an absolute one. Foley (10) infers from the ethnological material at hand that abnormality is a relative concept and criticizes Benedict (1), who seems to present evidence for the "statistical or relativity theory" yet "at times appears inconsistent in seeking for an absolute and universal criterion of abnormality." Briefly, the evidence from Benedict can be subsumed under three headings: (a) behavior considered abnormal in our culture but normal in other societal configurations; (b) types of abnormalities not occurring in Western civilization; and (c) behavior considered normal in our society but abnormal in others.

(a) Of "our" type of abnormal behavior considered normal in other cultures, Benedict gives, as an example, that of the Northwest Coast Indians whom Boas has studied at first hand. "All existence is seen in this culture in terms of an insult-complex." This complex is not only condoned but culturally reënforced. When the self-esteem and prestige of the chief is injured, he either arranges a "potlatch" ceremony or goes head-hunting. The injury to his prestige is a function of the prevalent insult-complex. Almost anything is an insult. It may be the victory of a rival chief in a potlatch competition; it may be the accidental death of a wife, or a score of other situations, all of which are interpreted as having a reference to the individual.

If, on the other hand, he has been bested in competition with a rival chief, he will arrange a potlatch ceremony in which he gives away property to his rival, at the same time declaiming a recitative in which there is "an uncensored self-glorification and ridicule of the opponent that is hard to equal outside of the monologue of the abnormal"; "either of the two mentioned above procedures are meaningless without the fundamental paranoid reading of bereavement."

Among other "abnormal" traits which are an integral part of some culture patterns, ethnological literature mentions the Dobuans (11), who exhibit an "unnatural" degree of fear and suspicion; the Polynesians, who regard their chief as tabu to touch, allegedly because of a prevalent "défense de toucher" neurosis; the Plains Indians with their religiously colored visual and auditory hallucinations; the Yogis with their trance states; and the frequent institutionalizations of homosexuality, whether in the religions of different cultures (e.g., shamans of North Siberia or Borneo) or in their social structures (e.g., the berdache of American Indian tribes or the homosexual youth of Grecian-Spartan antiquity).

(b) The second argument in favor of the cultural envisagement of abnormality is the existence of "styles" of abnormalities which presumably do not occur in our Western type of cultures. The "arctic hysteria" noted by Czaplicka (8) and its tropical correlative "lâttah" (Clifford, 6, 7) with their picture of echolalia, echopraxia and uncontrolled expression of obscenities, as well as the "amok" seizure of the Malayan world, are given as examples.

(c) Of normal behavior in our culture considered abnormal in others, Benedict mentions as most conspicuous the role of personal initiative and drive in our own, as compared with the Zuñi culture. Among the Zuñi Indians, for example, "the individual with undisguised initiative and greater drive than his fellows is apt to be branded a witch and hung up by his thumbs." Similarly, what seems to us a perfectly normal pattern of behavior—acquisitiveness, for example—would be looked upon by the potlatch celebrants as just a little "queer." For them, possession of property is secondary to the prestige they acquire when they distribute it.

These are then, briefly, the bases for the assertion that abnormality is a relative concept, differing from culture to culture, that no particular efficacy attaches to the expression, and that it gains meaning only in terms of the social milieu in which it is considered.

The question of what are the differentia of normality and abnormality is of course the crux of the problem. Is the concept of abnormality culturally defined? Is that which is *regarded* as abnormal or normal in a particular culture the *only* criterion for calling a behavior pattern such? Foley, for whom abnormality is a purely statistical concept, would answer in a positive manner and points to Benedict's example of the Northwest Coast Indians who institutionalize "paranoia." Let us, however, consider this "institutionalization of paranoia," as well as some of the other bits of evidence, critically.

Is it not stretching the point to call the Indians' megalomaniac activities and beliefs delusions in the sense that the paranoiac in the psychopathic institution has his beliefs called delusions? Macfie Campbell (5) states that "the delusions of the ill-balanced and the beliefs of the orthodox are more closely akin than is usually recognized," and we cannot separate the two as sharply as we would wish to do. The abnormal delusion proper is, however, an attempt of the personality to deal with a conflict-producing situation, and the delusion "like fever, becomes an attempt by nature at cure." The patient's delusion is an internal resolution of a problem; it is his way of meeting the intolerable situation. That is why it is abnormal. It represents a spontaneous protective device of the personality, something which is not learned. It is a crystallization of something which hitherto had been prepotent. The individual's personality thereafter refracts and reflects in terms of a distorted slant.

The Haida chief, upon the death of a member of his family, also experiences a certain tension. He resolves this tension, however, in a way which is not only socially sanctioned but socially determined. His reaction is not some-thing spontaneous arising out of the nuclear substrate of his instinctive life. It is not a crystallization in a certain direction of some previously unrealized protective potentialities of the psyche. His reaction is predetermined socially. Since his milieu expects that reaction of him, he acts upon that expectation when the situation arises. Of course it is possible that historically the behavior may have had and must have had some spontaneous protective significance—most likely imbedded deeply in a web of primitive beliefs about magic practices. Yet the modern Alaskan chief, unlike his distant prototype, has no conflicts of doubt about the likelihood that malignant forces have caused the death of some member of his family; he *knows,* and he acts upon that knowledge by venting his emotions. There is no permanent change in his personality when a tension-producing situation arises. Emotions are aroused and appeased with no change in the personality profile.

In the personality of one who is labelled "abnormal" this change is, however, to be found. There is always "the way he was before" and "the way he is now," regardless of the fact that a present symptomatological picture had its roots in a prepotent substrate which would make for a particular personality outline. This is not true of the Haida chief, in whom the "delusions" of reference and grandeur are externally imposed patterns. A Northwest Coast Indian, if given the opportunity for a naturalistic investigation of the situations that provoke his "paranoid" reactions—as, for example, through an education—could unlearn his previous emotional habits or at the least modify them. He is capable of insight; the true paranoiac is usually beyond it. The latter, if he kills the person who he thinks is persecuting him, only temporarily resolves his difficulty; the Indian chief who kills another family "to avenge the insult of his wife's death" achieves a permanent affective equilibration with regard to that incident. His prestige restored, he once more enjoys his self-respect. The Haida defends imagined assaults against his personal integrity only when some violent extra-personal event occurs. The paranoid psychotic defends himself against imagined assaults even though there is no objective evidence of any.

The point that the writer would then emphasize is that the delusions of the psychotic and the delusions of the Northwest Coast

Indian cannot by any means be equated. Mechanisms like the conviction of grandeur are abnormal not by virtue of unique, abnormal qualia but by virtue of their *function in the total economy of the personality.* The true paranoiac reaction represents a *choice of the abnormal;* the reaction of the Haida chief represents no such choice—there is but one path for him to follow. If one of the chief's men showed paranoid symptoms by proclaiming that *he* really was the chief of the tribe and that his lawful place was being usurped, the institutionalization of paranoid symptoms within that culture would not, I am sure, prevent the rest of the tribe from thinking him abnormal.

Fundamentally the same criticism might be applied to the "défense de toucher" neurosis supposedly exemplified by the Polynesian tabu on touching the chief. Here, as in paranoia, we must consider whether the mechanism is a cultural habit reënforced by emotional associations or whether it is a true morbid reaction. Obviously it is the former. Thus by reason of that fact it *is not* abnormal. As in the paranoia of the Haida, there is no choice here and consequently no conflict. If a person is brought up with the idea that to touch the chief means death, his acting upon that idea in adulthood is not a neurosis but simply a habit. There is, in other words, the genetic aspect to true abnormality which cannot be evaded but which is overlooked when we speak of "abnormal" symptoms. The explanation of the delusion of persecution of the Dobu is of course subject to the same criticism, which would hold likewise for trances, visions, the hearing of voices, and hysterical seizures. When these are simply culturally reënforced pattern-suggestions, they are not abnormal in the true sense of the word. When the Plains Indian by a rigid physical regimen of exhaustion and fatigue plus a liberal dose of suggestion achieves a vision, that achievement is not an abnormal reaction in the same sense that the visual hallucination of the psychotic is.

A similar example presented as an argument for the cultural definition of abnormality is the supposed institutionalization of homosexuality among different cultures. The difficulty with all discussions of this enormously complex topic is the lack of agreement among investigators as to the sense in which the homosexual is abnormal. Obviously, homosexuality is not the same type of morbid mental reaction as paranoia; in fact, it is not a morbid mental reaction at all. The abnormality of homosexuality exists at a different level; it is social and biological rather than psychological.[1] Homosexuality as an abnormal form of behavior cannot be spoken of in the same sense in which one speaks of visual and auditory hallucinations or grandiose delusions. Sex inversion is rather a statistical type of abnormality. It represents extreme deviations from the norm and makes for the nonconformity which engenders social antagonism and ostracism in certain societies. We are not justified, then, in saying that certain cultures institutionalize this abnormality; because, when we call homosexuality an abnormality in the same sense in which we speak of a delusion as abnormal, we are misusing the term and being inconsistent about its application.

The second point of view from which the cultural definition is sometimes argued is that there occur among different cultures abnormalities which are peculiar to them, as, for example, "arctic hysteria," "amok," "lâttah," *et al.* The untenability of this hypothesis becomes evident when a little analytic insight is applied to the phenomena considered. In his masterly analysis of the lâttah reaction, Van Loon (19) has also, the writer thinks, given a good explanation of "arctic hysteria." "Lâttah," he writes, "is chiefly a woman's complaint. The symptoms appear in consequence of a fright or some other sudden emotion; the startled patient screams" and exhibits echolalia, echopraxia, shouting of obscenities and a strong feeling of fear and timidity. "The immediate cause of becoming lâttah the patients report to be a dream of a highly sexual nature which ends in the waking up of the dreamer with a start. The waking up is here a substitute for the dream activity, protecting the dreamer's consciousness against the repressed complex." The same analysis might be applied to "arctic hysteria," which seems to show all the lâttah symptoms, although the occurrence of a sudden waking from sleep

---

[1] By this it is meant that homosexuality is not a compromise symptom due to a conflict, as is the case with paranoid manifestations. Whatever abnormality attaches to it is a secondary function due to the conflicts it creates in a social milieu. In short, it creates conflicts; it is not created by them. Only in those cases where it is used as an escape mechanism can it truly be called abnormal.

as the beginning of the complaint is nowhere reported.

The amok type of seizure, Van Loon explains, is due to hallucinations of being attacked by men or animals and seems to be confined to men. Clifford (7), on the other hand, considers amok from a genetic standpoint as having a background of anger, grudge, excitement and mental irritation, what the Malay calls "sâkit hâti" (sickness of the liver). "A Malay loses something he values, his father dies, he has a quarrel—any of these things cause him 'sickness of the liver.' The state of feeling which drives the European to suicide makes the Malay go amok." In the heat of the moment "he may strike his father, and the hatred of self which results, causes him to long for death and to seek it in the only way which occurs to a Malay, viz. by running amok." The psychoanalyst with his theories of the introjective process in melancholia would doubtless find "amok" a fertile field for interesting speculative analogies.

From the above discussion it is evident that the various "unique types of mental disorder" probably would yield readily to an analysis in terms of the categories of psychopathology. The mental disturbance can, to be sure, be understood only in terms of the cultural and social pattern within which it occurs, but the form that it does take is a secondary function of the abnormality. Only in this sense does culture condition abnormality. The paranoid reaction can occur in almost any culture, but the form that it takes is culturally modifiable. Although the psychotic can feel himself persecuted in almost any culture, in the one the persecutor may be the sorcerer, in another a usurping chief, and in still another the President of the United States.

The third argument for the cultural definition of abnormality is one which infers that, inasmuch as traits considered normal in our society are considered abnormal in other cultures, abnormality can be looked upon as simply that form of behavior which a group considers aberrant.

As previously mentioned with reference to homosexuality, the term "abnormality" cannot with exactitude be applied to *all* those forms of behavior which fail to meet with social sanction. That would be making the term meaningless. The same criticism might be applied to this third argument. There is no element of internal conflict in the Zuñi, for instance, who, feeling full of energy, gives vent to that energy. His behavior is aberrant, because it conflicts with the prevailing pattern. That, however, *does not* constitute abnormality. Such a Zuñi is not abnormal; he is delinquent (13). He is maladjusted to the demands of his culture and comes into conflict with his group, not because he adheres to a different standard but because he violates the group standards which are also his own (to paraphrase Mead). Edwards (9) pointed out this very frequent confusion concerning abnormality when he differentiated four standard types of individuals: "The average individual is the fictitious individual who ranks at the midpoint in all distributions of test results. The normal individual is one who is integrated, healthy and without any great variation from the average. The adjusted individual is one who is reasonably well-fitted into his environment and to its demands. The effective individual is one who, whether he is adjusted or normal, accomplishes his purposes."

From the above criticisms we can readily see that a relativity or statistical theory of abnormality which argues from the ethnological material at hand cannot stand a close analysis. From Benedict's writings one might get the impression that she also, like Foley, believes that what is abnormal depends simply on whether or not it is regarded as such by the greater majority of individuals in a specific culture. In various parts of her book (2) though, as well as in her articles, there are statements which run counter to any such belief. That is what Foley had in mind when he stated that Benedict seemed "inconsistent in seeking for an absolute and universal criterion of abnormality." In a private communication, Benedict explains this seeming paradox as follows. "In 1930-1931 when I wrote the article you refer to and the bulk of the book, writers in abnormal psychology constantly confused adequate personal adjustment and certain fixed symptoms. I wanted to break down the confusion, to show that interculturally adequate functioning and fixed symptoms could not be equated." When Benedict showed that the Northwest Coast Indians exhibited paranoid-like symptoms, she did not wish to prove that what the psychopathologist would call abnormal has no universal validity, but rather that, in spite of the fact the Northwest Coast Indians acted *like* paranoids, they were actually well-adjusted and "adult" individuals. What she was really arguing against was the confusion between fixed symptoms and adequate personal adjustment.

There is, of course, one way in which culture *does* determine abnormality and that is in the number of possible conflicts it can present to its component individuals. (In this sense "determine" has, however, a different meaning from that used above.) In a civilization like that of Samoa, for example, there is a minimum of possible aberrant behavior because of the rarity of situations which can produce conflicts in individuals. Even there, however, as Mead points out (13), Christianity with its introduction of a different set of standards is bringing to the islands that choice which is the forerunner of conflict and neurosis. A similar source of abnormality is the destruction of native culture and the production of new stresses. Profound depression and the absence of the will-to-live are among some of the abnormalities produced (15). McDougall (12) suggests that there may be temperamental differences in ability to adapt oneself to varying environments. He mentions, for example, the American Indian as being unadaptable because of his introverted disposition, as opposed to the care-free adaptable Negro with his extravert temperament. Seligman (16) voices the same opinion when he speaks of the extraverted Papuan and the introverted Malayan.

Benedict speculates that possibly the aberrant may represent "that arc of human capacities that is not capitalized in his culture" and that "the misfit is one whose disposition is not capitalized in his culture." She concludes that "the problem of understanding abnormal human behavior in any absolute sense independent of causal factors is still far in the future." "When data are available in psychiatry, this minimum definition of abnormal human tendencies will be probably quite unlike our culturally conditioned, highly elaborated psychoses such as those described, e.g., under the terms schizophrenic and manic-depressive." Keeping away from any committal to a relativity theory of abnormality, she is criticized therefor by Foley (10) for whom,

"it is obvious that deviation implies relative variability of behavior; the responses of the individual must be considered in relation to the responses of other individuals." For Foley, therefore, deviation from normative mean and abnormality are synonymous. In that sense, then, abnormality is for him a statistical concept.

There are, however, many objections to this aspect of the statistico-relative formulation. The most important one is probably the fact that a statistical theory considers only the actual observable behavior of an individual without delving into its meaning. Thus an erroneous identification is established between behavior patterns which are similar but do not have the same causal background. For example, the paranoid behavior of the schizophrenic and the "paranoid" behavior of the Northwest Coast Indian are equated; because the latter does not represent a deviation from the norm of that culture's behavior pattern while the former does, they are accepted as substantiating the statistical relativity theory. Of course we may arbitrarily define *abnormality* in such a way that it will mean the same as *deviation;* if, however, we proceed from an empirical point of view, it is obvious that we are not justified in equating such abnormalities as the psychoneuroses, the psychoses, sex inversion and amentia, and in speaking of them as deviations from a norm.

A statistical norm implies a graduated scale in which the items can be ranged on the basis of the possession of a "more" or "less" of a certain property. In that sense we can see that only sex inversion and amentia can be spoken of as deviations from a norm, inasmuch as it would have some meaning to speak of a "more" or "less" of development of cortical neurones or a "more" or "less" of a sex-determining hormone. It would, however, have only a qualitative significance if we spoke of one person's being "more" deluded than another or "less" paranoid. In this sense, therefore, we are not justified in speaking of abnormality as a statistical concept. There are rather certain abnormalities which, because of their nature, can be ranged on graduated scales and others which, because of a different substrate, cannot be similarly measured. A proximate graduation scale similar to one used in attitude testing can of course be utilized, but its use is bound up with all the prejudice that subjective judgments embody when topics of wide personal opinion-variance are considered. Besides, there is no real basis for comparative evaluation. Should, for example, a paranoid trait such as the conviction of persecution, be measured by judges with respect to the degree in which it inhibits the satisfactory functioning of the total personality and causes personal unhappiness, or with respect to the degree in which it interferes with an adequate adjustment to the social group and creates opposition within the environment? Should the frequency with which it manifests itself in life situations be the determining criterion, or the intensity with which it is adhered to? Finally, should the degree of insight a person has into it be the standard? The bases for judging the "more" or "less" of a paranoid trait are, as is obvious, very divergent. No single criterion is any more justifiable than any other. A "paranoid scale" would, therefore, be of slight operational significance.

Skaggs (18) was aware of this difficulty when he said: "It is the writer's view that abnormality is, of necessity, a qualitative and not a quantitative concept at the present time. While definitions of abnormality which involve statistical norms are commendable in their aim, the soundness of such definitions appears to be questionable."

Realizing further that only confusion results when we try to generalize about different abnormalities, he even suggests that "the terms sub-normal and super-normal be kept strictly apart from the term 'abnormality'." Bridges (4) places all abnormalities not of a sub-normal or super-normal type in the category of the "para-normal," a group which, for Skaggs, is really the only one deserving of the name "abnormal." Because this group cannot be quantitatively ranged it is small surprise that, for Skaggs, the normative definition of abnormality as a lack of integration and balance of the total personality seems the most logical one.

Of the three types of possible definitions of abnormality mentioned by Morgan—(1) the normative, (2) the pathological, and (3) the statistical (15)—we can see that when we take all those types of behavior which are referred to as abnormal, there will be some which will fall more readily into one category,

others which will more easily fit into another.[2] Thus all the symptoms associated with the psychoneuroses seem best defined by a normative approach which arbitrarily postulates, on the basis of the best psychiatric opinion, a theoretical integrated balanced personality, wide deviations from which would be looked upon as "abnormal." The functional psychoses also fit into this group, shading, however, into the pathological where the organic psychoses, behavior disturbances due to cerebral lesions or malfunctionings, and extreme amentias belong; the statistical can really claim only the less decidedly pathological aments and those sex-inverts where the presumption of constitutional involvement is strong.

The confusion arises, of course, from subsuming different types of abnormalities under one heading "abnormality" and speaking of them as if they were homogeneous entities. Obviously abnormal behavior is *called* abnormal because it deviates from the behavior of the general group. It is not, however, the *fact* of deviation which makes it abnormal but its causal background. That is why the hallucinations of the Plains Indians are not abnormal, while those of the schizophrenic are. It is not the *fact* of social sanction in Plains Indian society which makes that bit of behavior normal, but the fact that it does not have the background of a symptomatic resolution of an inner conflict such as produces that phenomenon in the schizophrenic. The "abnormal" behavior of the Indian is analogous to the behavior of the psychotic *but not homologous*. Just because it is analogous, the confusion has arisen of identifying the two.

If, therefore, behavior anomalies which are at bottom constitutionally or pathologically conditioned be excluded or subsumed as a different group under the category of the non-normal, we could state the quintessence of abnormality (Bridges' "para-normality"), as *the tendency to choose a type of reaction which represents an escape from a conflict-producing situation instead of a facing of the problem.*[3]

---

[2] It might be remarked that these three types are not equivalent logically for the statistical and normative answer to the question: "What kind of behavior should we *call* abnormal?" while the pathological, in reality, says: "We grant that this bit of behavior is abnormal, but *why* is it abnormal?"

[3] Sublimation would not fit into this category because, as Alexander states, "the process represents a legitimate activity directed outwards, with an aim lying outside of the

An essential element in this type of problem-resolution is that the conflict does not seem to be on a conscious level, so that the strange bit of behavior resulting is looked upon as an abnormal intruder and, at least in its incipient stage, is felt as something which is not ego-determined.[4] Inasmuch as pathological and, above all, constitutional factors cannot be partialled out in the aetiology of a behavior anomaly, however, the above definition has only an ideal value of slight practical significance.[5]

It does clarify though, to some extent, the confusion which arises from labelling any bit of behavior "abnormal." It is obvious, for example, that masturbation *per se* is not abnormal and represents a quite normal, i.e., usual, growing-up phenomenon. In certain instances, however, its great frequency or its inappropriateness point to the use of it as an escape mechanism. What holds true for masturbation is true of all "abnormal mechanisms." *It is not the mechanism that is abnormal; it is its function which determines its abnormality.* It is precisely for this reason that the institutionalized "abnormal" traits in various cultures are not properly called "abnormal" entities. Because this distinction is not kept in mind and because a primarily statistico-relative conception of abnormality is adhered to, the unwarranted conclusion is drawn that standards of "abnormality" differ with cultures and are culturally determined.

References

1. Benedict, R. Anthropology and the abnormal. *J. gen. Psychol.*, 1934, 10, 59-82.

2. Benedict, R. *Patterns of culture.* Boston: Houghton Mifflin, 1934.

3. Boas, F. *Mind of primitive man.* New York: Macmillan, 1919.

4. Bridges, J. W. *Psychology—normal and abnormal.* New York: Appleton, Century, 1930.

5. Campbell, C. M. *Delusion and belief.* Cambridge: Harvard Univ. Press, 1926.

6. Clifford, H. *Studies in brown humanity.* London: G. Richards, 1898.

7. Clifford, H. *In court and kampong.* London: G. Richards, 1897.

8. Czaplicka, M. A. *Aboriginal Siberia: a study in social anthropology.* Oxford: Clarendon Press, 1914.

9. Edwards, A. S. A theoretical and clinical study of so-called normality. This *Journal*, 1934, 28, 366-376.

10. Foley, J. P. Jr. The criterion of abnormality. This *Journal*, 1935, 30, 279-290.

11. Fortune, R. F. *Sorcerers of Dobu.* New York: Routledge, 1932.

12. McDougall, W. *Outline of abnormal psychology.* New York: Scribners, 1926.

13. Mead, M. *Coming of age in Samoa.* New York: Morrow, 1928.

14. Mead, M. *Growing up in New Guinea.* New York: Morrow, 1930.

15. Morgan, J. J. B. *The psychology of abnormal people.* New York: Longmans Green, 1928.

16. Pitt-Rivers, G. H. *The contact of races and the clash of cultures.* London: Routledge, 1927.

17. Seligman, C. G. Temperament, conflict and psychosis in a stone age population. *Brit. J. Psychol.*, 1929, 9, 187-202.

18. Skaggs, E. B. The meaning of the term "abnormality" in psychology. This *Journal*, 1933, 28, 113-118.

19. Van Loon, F. H. G. Amok and lâttah. This *Journal*, 1926, 21, 434-444.

20. Wundt, W. *Völkerpsychologie.* 10 vols. Leipzig: W. Engelmann, 1900-1920.

personality, and, secondly, it has a social quality. It is a normal modification of impulses not adapted to reality." "In contrast, the neurotic supplants outwardly directed activity by bodily changes which have a purely subjective significance, or by commonplace activities which do not essentially get beyond the bounds of the personality, or by purely psychological quantities of imaginative activity." (Healy, Brenner and Bowers, *The structure and meaning of psychoanalysis*, 251.)

[4] In a letter commenting upon the above, Benedict writes: "I couldn't use this definition in 1931—I have always felt that the final answer must be in these terms."

[5] In a monograph now in preparation, A. Angyal approaches the problem of abnormality from a different point of view and substitutes for the latter the concept of "bio-negativity." "A process is bio-negative if it is in, but directed against, the organism"—"the same factors may be bio-positive in certain types of personality organization and bio-negative in others." His conception neither opposes nor affirms the above formulation of abnormality, for it rests upon a different conceptual basis.

Toward a concept of the normal personality [1]

EDWARD JOSEPH SHOBEN, JR.

It is difficult to arrive at a meaningful definition of the normal personality that is not merely an arbitrary list of traits reflecting a particular set of values. This article reviews some of the problems of defining normality and the criticisms that have been made of previous solutions. The author develops a model of positive adjustment based on what he considers to be the unique attributes of the human being. The resulting conception of normality considers man's shortcomings, as well as his more positive attributes. In this way, the essay attempts to provide a realistic description of normality which reflects some of the difficulties inherent in adapting to a complex and troublesome world.

E. J. Shoben, Jr., Ph.D., is Director of the Center for Higher Education and Coordinator of Academic Planning at the Buffalo campus of the State University of New York. He has previously held positions as Director of the Commission on Academic Affairs of the American Council on Education, Director of the Center for Research and Training in Higher Education and Professor of Higher Education and Psychology at the University of Cincinnati. Dr. Shoben holds the Diploma in Clinical Psychology of the American Board of Examiners in Professional Psychology, is the coauthor of two books, *Perspectives in Psychology* and *The Psychology of Adjustment*, and is the author of a forthcoming book *College and the Cultural Crisis*.

Clinical practice and the behavioral sciences alike have typically focused on the pathological in their studies of personality and behavior dynamics. While much of crucial importance remains to be learned, there is an abundant empirical knowledge and an impressive body of theory concerning the deviant and the diseased, the anxious and the neurotic, the disturbed and the maladjusted. In contrast, there is little information and even less conceptual clarity about the nature of psychological normality. Indeed, there are even those (5, 13) who argue that there is no such thing as a normal man; there are only those who manage their interpersonal relationships in such a way that others are strongly motivated to avoid them, even by committing them to a mental hospital or a prison, as opposed to those who do not incite such degrees of social ostracism.

This argument has two characteristics. First, it disposes of the issue by simply distributing people along a dimension of pathology. All men are a little queer, but some are much more so than others. Second, it has affinities with the two major ideas that have been brought to bear on the question of what constitutes normal or abnormal behavior: the statistical conception of the usual or the average and the notion of cultural relativism. If pathology is conceived as the extent to which one is tolerated by one's fellows, then any individual can theoretically be described in

From *American Psychologist*, XII (1957), 183-189. Reprinted by permission of the American Psychological Association and the author.

[1] This paper is revised from versions read on March 26, 1956, at the convention of the American Personnel and Guidance Association in Washington, D. C., and on November 16, 1956, at a conference on mental health research at Catholic University in Washington, D. C., under the joint sponsorship of Catholic University, the University of Maryland, and the U. S. Veterans Administration.

terms of some index number that reflects the degree of acceptability accorded him. The resulting distribution would effectively amount to an ordering of people from the least to the most pathological. Similarly, if the positions on such a continuum are thought of as functions of one's acceptance or avoidance by others, then they can only be defined by reference to some group. The implications here are twofold. First, the conception of pathology is necessarily relativistic, varying from group to group or culture to culture. Second, the degree of pathology is defined as the obverse of the degree of conformity to group norms. The more one's behavior conforms to the standards of the group, the less one is likely to be subject to social avoidance; whereas the more one's behavior deviates from the rules, the greater is the probability of ostracism to the point of institutional commitment.

Statistical and relativistic concepts of normality

Yet it is doubtful that the issues are fully clarified by these statistical and culturally relativistic ideas. Is it most fruitful to regard normality or integrative behavior as merely reflecting a minimal degree of pathology, or may there be a certain merit in considering the asset side of personality, the positive aspects of human development? This question becomes particularly relevant when one is concerned with the socialization process or with the goals and outcomes of psychotherapy or various rehabilitative efforts.

It seems most improbable that the family, the church, and the school, the main agents of socialization, exist for the minimizing of inevitable pathological traits in the developing members of the community. Rather, parents, priests, and educators are likely to insist that their function is that of facilitating some sort of positive growth, the progressive acquisition of those characteristics, including skills, knowledge, and attitudes, which permit more productive, contributory, and satisfying ways of life. Similarly, while psychotherapists may sometimes accept the limited goals of simply trying to inhibit pathological processes, there are certainly those (11, 16) who take the position that therapy is to be judged more in terms of how much it contributes to a patient's ability to achieve adult gratifications rather than its sheer efficiency in reducing symptoms or shoring up pathological defenses.

A general concern for such a point of view seems to be emerging in the field of public mental health (26). Beginning with an emphasis on treatment, the concept of community mental health swung to a preventive phase with the main interest focused on identifying the antecedents of mental disease and on reducing morbidity rates by attacking their determinants. The vogue of eugenics was one illustrative feature of this stage. More recently, there has been a considerable dissatisfaction with the whole notion of interpreting psychological states in terms of disease analogues (15, 23). Maladjustive behavior patterns, the neuroses, and—perhaps to a lesser extent—the psychoses may possibly be better understood as disordered, ineffective, and defensive styles of life than as forms of sickness. In consequence, there seems to be a growing tendency to conceive of the public mental health enterprise as emphasizing positive development with the prevention and treatment of pathology regarded as vital, but secondary.

But in what does positive development consist? The statistical concept of the average is not very helpful. Tiegs and Katz (27), for example, reported a study of college students who had been rated for fourteen different evidences of "nervousness." By and large, these traits were normally distributed, suggesting that those subjects rated low must be considered just as "abnormal" (unusual) as those rated high. This conception seems to provide a superficial quantitative model only at the expense of hopeless self-contradiction and violence to the ordinary categories of communication. Even in a case that at first blush seems to cause no difficulty, the problem remains. Criminal behavior, for example, is distributed in a J-shaped fashion with most cases concentrated at the point of zero offenses, ranging to a relatively few instances of many-time offenders. Few would argue that the usual behavior here is not also the most "positive." But one suspects that the sheer frequency of law-abiding behavior has little to do with its acknowledged integrative character. If conformity to social rules is generally considered more desirable than criminality, it is not because of its rate of occurrence but because of its consequences for both society and the individual.

Thus, a statistical emphasis on the usual as the criterion of positive adjustment or normality shades into a socially relativistic concept with an implied criterion of conformity. The terms "usual" or "most frequent" or "average" are meaningless without reference to some group, and this state of affairs poses two problems. First, conformity in itself, as history abundantly demonstrates, is a dubious guide to conduct. Innovation is as necessary to a culture's survival as are tradition and conservation, and conformity has frequently meant acquiescence in conditions undermining the maturity and positive development of human beings rather than their enhancement. On more personal levels, conformity sometimes seems related in some degree to personality processes that can quite properly be called pathological (2, 24). Second, relativistic conceptions of normality pose serious questions as to the reference group against which any individual is to be assessed. Benedict (3), for example, has made it quite clear that behavior which is considered abnormal in one culture is quite acceptable in others, that certain forms of abnormalities which occur in some societies are absent in others, and that conduct which is thought completely normal in one group may be regarded as intensely pathological in another. Such observations, while descriptively sound, can lead readily to two troublesome inferences. One is that the storm trooper must be considered as the prototype of integrative adjustment in Nazi culture, the members of the Politburo as best representing human normality Soviet-style, and the cruelest adolescent in a delinquent gang as its most positively developed member. The other is that any evaluative judgment of cultures and societies must be regarded as inappropriate. Since normality is conceived only in terms of conformity to group standards, the group itself must be beyond appraisal. Thus, the suspicion and mistrust of Dobu (10), the sense of resigned futility that permeates Alor (6), and the regimentation that characterizes totalitarian nations can logically only be taken as norms in terms of which individual behavior may be interpreted, not as indications of abnormal tendencies in the cultures themselves.

Wegrocki (28), in criticizing such relativistic notions, argues that it is not the form of behavior, the actual acts themselves, that defines its normal or pathological character. Rather, it is its function. What he calls the "quintessence of abnormality" lies in reactions which represent an escape from conflicts and problems rather than a facing of them. This formulation, implying that integrative adjustments are those which most directly confront conflicts and problems, seems essentially free of the difficulties inherent in statistical conceptions and the idea of cultural relativism. But it presents troubles of its own. For instance, what does it mean to "face" a problem or conflict? On what ground, other than the most arbitrarily moralistic one, can such confrontations be defended as more positive than escape? Finally, does this facing of one's problems have any relationship to the matter of conformity in the sense of helping to clarify decisions regarding the acceptance or rejection of group standards?

To deal with such questions requires coming to grips with certain problems of value. It is at this point that the behavioral sciences and ethics meet and merge, and it seems unlikely that any conception of normality can be developed apart from some general considerations that are fundamentally moral. Once the purely relativistic ideas of normality are swept away, it becomes difficult to avoid some concern for the issues of happiness and right conduct (*i.e.,* conduct leading to the greatest degree of human satisfaction) that are the traditional province of the literary interpreter of human experience, the theologian, and the moral philosopher. A primary challenge here is that of providing a rational and naturalistic basis for a concept of integrative adjustment that is at once consistent with the stance and contributions of empirical science and in harmony with whatever wisdom mankind has accumulated through its history.

Symbolic and social aspects of human nature

One way to meet this challenge is by frankly postulating a basic principle of value. The fundamental contention advanced here is that behavior is "positive" or "integrative" to the extent that it reflects the unique attributes of the human animal. There are undoubtedly other ways of approaching a fruitful concept of normality. Nevertheless, this assertion is consistent with the implications of organic evolution, escapes the fallacy of the survival-of-the-fittest doctrine in its various forms, and permits a derivation of more specific criteria of positive adjustment from the distinctive characteristics of man. No discontinuity within the phylogenetic scale need be assumed. It seems clear, however, that man, while certainly an animal, can hardly be described as "nothing but" an animal; and his normality or integration seems much more likely to consist in the fulfillment of his unique potentialities than in the development of those he shares with infra-human organisms.

Foremost among these uniquely human potentialities, as Cassirer (4) and Langer (14) make clear, is the enormous capacity for symbolization. What is most characteristic of men is their pervasive employment of *propositional* language. While other organisms, especially dogs (22) and the higher apes (29), react to symbols, their faculty for doing so indicates only an ability to respond to mediate or representative as well as direct stimuli. Man, on the other hand, uses symbols designatively, as a vehicle for recollecting past events, for dealing with things which are not physically present, and for projecting experience into the future. Goldstein (12) makes the same point in his discussion of the "attitude toward the merely possible," the ability to deal with things that are only imagined or which are not part of an immediate, concrete situation. In patients whose speech has been impaired because of brain damage, this attitude toward the possible is disrupted. Thus, aphasics are typically unable to say such things as, "The snow is black" or "The moon shines in the daytime"; similarly, they are incapable of *pretending* to comb their hair or to take a drink of water, although they can actually *perform* these acts. Such patients appear to have lost the uniquely human capacity for thinking *about* things as well as directly "thinking things."

It is his symbolic ability, then, that makes man the only creature who can "look before and after and pine for what is not." Propositional speech makes it possible for him to learn from not only his own personal experience but from that of other men in other times and places, to forecast the consequences of his own behavior, and to have ideals. These three symbol-given attributes—the aptitude for capitalizing on experience, including the experience of others, over time, the capacity for foresight and the self-imposed control of behavior through the anticipation of its outcomes, and the ability to envision worlds closer than the present one to the heart's desire—constitute a basic set of distinctively human potentialities.

A second set of such potentialities seems related to the long period of helpless dependence that characterizes infancy and childhood. Made mandatory by the relative biological incompleteness of the human baby, this phase of development is likely to be lengthened as cultures become more complex. Thus, in such simpler societies as the Samoan (18), children can achieve a higher degree of independence at an earlier age than in the civilizations of the West, for example, where the necessity for learning complicated and specialized economic skills extends the period of dependence through adolescence and even into chronological young adulthood. The central point, however, is that unlike the young of any other species, human children in *all* cultural settings must spend a long time during which the gratification of their most basic needs is mediated by somebody else and is dependent on their relationship to somebody else.

This state of affairs exposes youngsters during their earliest and most formative stages of development to two fundamental conditions of human life. The first is that one's survival, contentment, and need fulfillment involve an inevitable element of reliance on other people. The second is that the relative autonomy, authority, and power that characterize the parent figures and others on whom one relies in childhood are always perceived to a greater or lesser extent in association with responsibility and a kind of altruism. That is, the enjoyment of adult privileges and status tends to occur in conjunction with the acceptance, in some degree, of responsibility for mediating, in some way, the need gratifications of others. Mowrer and Kluckhohn (20) seem to be speaking of a similar pattern when they describe the socialization process as progressing from childhood *dependency* through *independence* to adult *dependability*.

Moreover, this reciprocal relationship between reliance and responsibility seems to obtain on adult levels as well as between children and parents, with the degree of reciprocity a partial function of the complexity of the culture. In simpler societies, a relatively small number of persons may assume primary responsibility for virtually all of the needs of the group in excess of its bare subsistence demands. Under civilized conditions, however, the specialization made necessary by technology and the pattern of urban living means that each adult is dependent on some other adult in some way and that, conversely, he is responsible in some fashion for the welfare of some other adult. The difference between the simpler and the more complex cultures, however, is only one of degree. The crucial point is that, throughout human society, men are in one way or another dependent on each other both in the familiar situation of parents and children and in the course of adult living. This pattern of interdependency gives to human life a social character to be found nowhere else in the animal kingdom. Even among the remarkable social insects, the patterns of symbiosis found there seem to be a result of a genetically determined division of labor rather than the fulfillment of a potentiality for the mutual sharing of responsibilities for each other.

It is in this notion of the fulfillment of distinctively human potentialities that a fruitful conception of positive adjustment may have its roots. From the symbolic and peculiarly social character of human life, it may be possible to derive a set of potential attributes the cultivation of which results in something different from the mere absence of pathology and which forms a standard against which to assess the degree of integration in individual persons. To accept this task is to attempt the construction of a normative or ideal model of a normal, positively developed, or integratively adjusted human being.

A model of integrative adjustment

In the first place, it would seem that, as the symbolic capacity that endows man with foresight develops in an individual, there is a concomitant increase in his ability to control his own behavior by anticipating its probable long-range consequences. The normal person is, first of all, one who has learned that in many situations his greatest satisfaction is

gained by foregoing the immediate opportunities for comfort and pleasure in the interest of more remote rewards. He lives according to what Paul Elmer More, the Anglican theologian, calls "the law of costingness":

. . . the simple and tyrannical fact that, whether in the world physical, or in the world intellectual, or in the world spiritual, we can get nothing without paying an exacted price. The fool is he who ignores, and the villain is he who thinks he can outwit, the vigilance of the nemesis guarding this law of costingness . . . all [one's] progress is dependent on surrendering one interest or value for a higher interest or value (19, p. 158).

Mowrer and Ullman (21) have made the same point in arguing, from the results of an ingenious experiment, that normality results in large part from the acquired ability to subject impulses to control through the symbolic cues one presents to oneself in the course of estimating the consequences of one's own behavior. Through symbolization, the future outcomes of one's actions are drawn into the psychological present; the strength of more remote rewards or punishments is consequently increased; and a long-range inhibitory or facilitating effect on incipient conduct is thereby exercised.

This increase in self-control means a lessened need for control by external authority, and conformity consequently becomes a relatively unimportant issue. The integratively adjusted person either conforms to the standards of his group because their acceptance leads to the most rewarding long-range consequences for him, or he rebels against authority, whether of persons or of law or custom, on *considered* grounds. This considered form of revolt implies two things. The first is an honest conviction that rules or the ruler are somehow unjust and that the implementation of his own values is likely to lead to a more broadly satisfying state of affairs. Such an attack on authority is very different from revolts that occur out of sheer needs for self-assertion or desires for power or as expressions of displaced hostility. The main dimension of difference is that of honesty as opposed to deception. The normal person is relatively well aware of his motives in either conforming or rebelling. The pathological rebel, on the other hand, tends to deceive himself and others about his goals. His reasons for nonconformity amount to rationalizations, and his justifications are typically projections. This kind of self-defeating and socially disruptive deceptiveness is seen daily in clinical practice.

The second characteristic of nonconformity in the normal person is that it is undertaken with an essential acceptance of the possible consequences. Having considered the risks beforehand, he is inclined neither to whine nor to ask that his rebellious conduct be overlooked if he runs afoul of trouble. In keeping with the "law of costingness," he is willing to pay the price for behaving in accordance with his own idiosyncratic values. "We have the right to lead our own lives," John Erskine (8) makes Helen of Troy say to her daughter Hermione, "but that right implies another— to suffer the *consequences*. . . . Do your best, and if it's a mistake, hide nothing and be glad to suffer for it. That's morality." A psychological paraphrase of this bit of belletristic wisdom is not inappropriate: The assumption of responsibility [2] for one's actions is one of the attributes of personal integration.

But if personal responsibility and self-control through foresight can be derived as aspects of integrative adjustment from man's symbolic capacity, a third characteristic of interpersonal responsibility can be deduced from his social nature. If interdependency is an essential part of human social life, then the normal person becomes one who can act dependably in relation to others and at the same time acknowledge his need for others. The roots of the former probably lie, as McClelland (17) has pointed out, in the role perceptions which developing children form of parent figures and other agents of the socialization process. By conceiving of such people as at least in some degree the nurturant guides of others and through identification with them, the integratively adjusted individual "wants to be" himself trustworthy and altruistic in the sense of being dependable and acting out of a genuine concern for the welfare of others as he can best conceive it. Altruism in this context, therefore, means nothing sentimental. It certainly includes the making and enforcement of disciplinary rules and the imposition of behavioral limits, but only if these steps are motivated by an interest in helping others and express concern and affection rather than mere personal annoyance or the power conferred by a superior status.

Similarly, the acknowledgment of one's needs for others implies a learned capacity for forming and maintaining intimate interpersonal relationships. Erikson (7) refers to this aspect of the normal personality as the attitude of "basic trust," and it is not far from what can be meaningfully styled in plain language as the ability to love. One suspects that the origins of this ability lies in the long experience during childhood of having need gratifications frequently associated with the presence of another person, typically a parent figure. By this association and the process of generalization, one comes to attach a positive affect to others. But as the youngster develops, he gradually learns that the need-mediating behavior of others is maintained only by his reciprocating, by his entering into a relationship of mutuality with others. If this kind of mutuality is not required of him, he is likely to perpetuate his dependency beyond the period his biological level of development and the complexity of his culture define as appropriate; whereas if he is required to demonstrate this mutuality too soon, he is likely to form the schema that interpersonal relationships are essentially matters of traded favors, and that, instead of basic trust, the proper attitude is one of getting as much as possible while giving no more than necessary. The pursuit in research and thought of such hypotheses as these might shed a good deal of light on the determinants of friendship, marital happiness, and effective parenthood, the relational expressions of effective personal integration.

But there is still another interpersonal attitude relevant to a positive conception of adjustment that is somewhat different from that

---

[2] This conception of responsibility is by no means antideterministic. As Fingarette (8) points out, one can *understand* his own or another's behavior, in the sense of accounting for it or rationally explaining it, by the retrospective process of examining the past. Responsibility, on the other hand, is neither retrospective in orientation nor explanatory in function. It is future oriented and refers to the *act* of proclaiming oneself as answerable for one's own conduct and its consequences. Thus, "responsibility," in this context, is not a logical term, implying causation, but a behavioral and attitudinal one, descriptive of a class of human actions.

bound up with relationships of an intimate and personal kind. There is a sense in which each individual, even if he regards himself as unfortunate and unhappy, owes his essential humanity to the group which enabled him to survive his helpless infancy. As studies of feral children (25) have shown, even the humanly distinctive and enormously adaptive trait of propositional speech does not become usable without the stimulation and nurture of other people. A kind of obligation is therefore created for the person to be an asset rather than a burden to society. It is partly to the discharging of this obligation that Adler (1) referred in developing his concept of social interest as a mark of normality. While the notion certainly implies the learning of local loyalties and personal affections, it also transcends the provincial limits of group and era. Because man's symbolic capacity enables him to benefit from the record of human history and to anticipate the future, and because his pattern of social interdependency, especially in civilized societies, reaches across the boundaries of political units and parochial affiliations, it seems reasonable to expect the positively developed person to behave in such a fashion as to contribute, according to his own particular lights, to the general welfare of humanity, to take as his frame of reference mankind at large as best he understands it rather than his own group or clan.

Ideologies are at issue here, but there need be neither embarrassment nor a lack of room for debate regarding the specifics of policy and values in the hypothesis that democratic attitudes are closely bound up with personality integration. After all, democracy in psychological terms implies only a concern about others, a valuing of persons above things, and a willingness to particpiate in mutually gratifying relationships with many categories of persons, including those of which one has only vicarious knowledge. Departures from democratic attitudes in this psychological sense mean a restriction on the potentiality for friendship and imply both a fear of others and a valuation of such things as power over people, thus endangering the interpersonal rewards that come from acting on the attitude of basic trust. Democratic social interest, then, means simply the most direct route to the fulfillment of a distinctively human capacity derived from man's symbolic character and the inevitability of his social life.

Finally, man's ability to assume an attitude toward the "merely possible" suggests that the normal person has ideals and standards that he tries to live up to even though they often exceed his grasp. For an integrative adjustment does not consist in the attainment of perfection but in a striving to act in accordance with the best principles of conduct that one can conceive. Operationally, this notion implies that there is an optimum discrepancy between one's self-concept and one's ego ideal. Those for whom this discrepancy is too large (in favor, of course, of the ideal) are likely to condemn themselves to the frustration of never approximating their goals and to an almost perpetually low self-esteem. Those whose discrepancies are too low, on the other hand, are probably less than integratively adjusted either because they are failing to fulfill their human capacity to envision themselves as they could be or because they are self-deceptively overestimating themselves.

This model of integrative adjustment as characterized by self-control, personal responsibility, social responsibility, democratic social interest, and ideals must be regarded only in the most tentative fashion. Nevertheless, it does seem to take into account some realistic considerations. It avoids the impossible conception of the normal person as one who is always happy, free from conflict, and without problems. Rather, it suggests that he may often fall short of his ideals; and because of ignorance, the limitations under which an individual lives in a complex world, or the strength of immediate pressures, he may sometimes behave in ways that prove to be shortsighted or self-defeating. Consequently, he knows something of the experience of guilt at times, and because he tries to be fully aware of the risks he takes, he can hardly be entirely free from fear and worry. On the other hand, a person who is congruent to the model is likely to be one who enjoys a relatively consistent and high degree of self-respect and who elicits a predominantly positive and warm reaction from others. Moreover, it is such a person who seems to learn wisdom rather than hostile bitterness or pathologically frightened withdrawal from whatever disappointments or suffering may be his lot. Guilt, for example, becomes a challenge to his honesty, especially with himself but also with others; and it signalizes for him the desirability of modifying his behavior, of greater effort to live up to his ideals, rather than the need to defend himself by such mechanisms as rationalization or projection. Finally, the model permits a wide variation in the actual behaviors in which normal people may engage and even makes allowance for a wide range of disagreements among them. Integrative adjustment does not consist in the individual's fitting a preconceived behavioral mold. It may well consist in the degree to which his efforts fulfill the symbolic and social potentialities that are distinctively human.

References

1. Adler, A. *Social interest: A challenge to mankind.* London: Faber & Faber, 1938.

2. Adorno, T. W., Frenkel-Brunswik, Else, Levinson, D. J., & Sanford, R. N. *The authoritarian personality.* New York: Harper, 1950.

3. Benedict, Ruth Anthropology and the abnormal. *J. gen. Psychol.,* 1934, 10, 59-82.

4. Cassirer, E. *An essay on man.* New Haven: Yale Univer. Press, 1944.

5. Darrah, L. W. The difficulty of being normal. *J. nerv. ment. Dis.,* 1939, 90, 730-739

6. DuBois, Cora *The people of Alor.* Minneapolis: Univer. Minnesota Press, 1944.

7. Erikson, E. H. *Childhood and society.* New York: Norton, 1950.

8. Erskine, J. *The private life of Helen of Troy.* New York: Bobbs-Merrill Co., 1925.

9. Fingarette, H. Psychoanalytic perspectives on moral guilt and responsibility: A re-evaluation. *Phil. phenomenol. Res.,* 1955, 16, 18-36.

10. Fortune, R. F. *Sorcerers of Dobu.* London: Routledge, 1932.

11. Fromm, E. *The sane society.* New York: Rinehart, 1955.

12. Goldstein, K. *Human nature in the light of psychopathology.* Cambridge, Mass.: Harvard Univer. Press, 1940.

13. Hacker, F. H. The concept of normality and its practical significance. *Amer. J. Orthopsychiat.,* 1945, 15, 47-64.

14. Langer, Susanne K. *Philosophy in a new key.* Cambridge, Mass.: Harvard Univer. Press, 1942.

15. Marzolf, S. S. The disease concept in psychology. *Psychol. Rev.,* 1947, 54, 211-221.

16. May, R. *Man's search for himself.* New York: Norton, 1953.

17. McClelland, D. *Personality.* New York: William Sloane Associates, 1951.

18. Mead, Margaret *Coming of age in Samoa.* New York: William Morrow, 1928.

19. More, P. E. *The Catholic faith.* Princeton: Princeton Univer. Press, 1931.

20. Mowrer, O. H., & Kluckhohn, C. A dynamic theory of personality. In J. McV. Hunt (Ed.), *Personality and the behavior disorders.* New York: Ronald Press, 1944. Pp. 69-135.

21. Mowrer, O. H., & Ullmann, A. D. Time as a determinant in integrative learning. *Psychol. Rev.,* 1945, 52, 61-90.

22. Pavlov, I. P. *Conditioned reflexes.* London: Oxford Univer. Press, 1927.

23. Riese, W. *The conception of disease.* New York: Philosophical Library, 1953.

24. Riesman, D. *The lonely crowd.* New Haven: Yale Univer. Press, 1950.

25. Singh, J. A. L., & Zingg, R. M. *Wolf-children and feral man.* New York: Harper, 1942.

26. Subcommittee on Evaluation of Mental Health Activities. *Evaluation in mental health.* Bethesda, Md.: Public Health Service, 1955.

27. Tiegs, E. W., & Katz, B. *Mental hygiene in education.* New York: Ronald Press, 1941.

28. Wegrocki, H. J. A critique of cultural and statistical concepts of abnormality. *J. abnorm. soc. Psychol.,* 1939, 34, 166-178.

29. Yerkes, R. M. *Chimpanzees: A laboratory colony.* New Haven: Yale Univer. Press, 1943.

Toward a modern approach to values: the valuing process in the mature person

CARL R. ROGERS

The concepts of normality, psychological adjustment, and emotional maturity cannot be fully understood apart from human values. Whereas most attempts to define emotional maturity emphasize *what* the individual values, this article focuses on *how* the person values. Dr. Rogers describes some of the changes that occur in the valuing orientation of the individual between infancy and adulthood and illustrates some of the specific value directions adopted by his clients in psychotherapy as they approach greater psychological maturity. This article presents some hypotheses on the origins of values and provides a timely discussion of one of the major problem areas confronting contemporary society.

A description is given of the change in the value orientation of the individual from infancy to average adulthood, and from this adult status to a greater degree of psychological maturity attained through psychotherapy or fortunate life circumstances. On the basis of these observations, the theory is advanced that there is an organismic basis for the valuing process within the human individual; that this valuing process is effective to the degree that the individual is open to his experience; that in persons relatively open to their experiencing there is an important commonality or universality of value directions; that these directions make for the constructive enhancement of the individual and his community, and for the survival and evolution of his species.

There is a great deal of concern today with the problem of values. Youth, in almost every country, is deeply uncertain of its value orientation; the values associated with various religions have lost much of their influence; sophisticated individuals in every culture seem unsure and troubled as to the goals they hold in esteem. The reasons are not far to seek. The world culture, in all its aspects, seems increasingly scientific and relativistic, and the rigid, absolute views on values which come to us from the past appear anachronistic. Even more important, perhaps, is the fact that the modern individual is assailed from every angle by divergent and contradictory value claims. It is no longer possible, as it was in the not too distant historical past, to settle comfortably into the value system of one's forebears or one's community and live out one's life without ever examining the nature and the assumptions of that system.

In this situation it is not surprising that value orientations from the past appear to be in a state of disintegration or collapse. Men question whether there are, or can be, any universal values. It is often felt that we may have lost, in our modern world, all possibility of any general or cross-cultural basis for values. One natural result of this uncertainty and confusion is that there is an increasing concern about, interest in, and a searching for, a sound or meaningful value approach which can hold its own in today's world.

I share this general concern. As with other issues the general problem faced by the culture

From *Journal of Abnormal and Social Psychology*, LXVIII (1964), 160-170. Reprinted by permission of the American Psychological Association and the author.

is painfully and specifically evident in the cultural microcosm which is called the therapeutic relationship, which is my sphere of experience.

As a consequence of this experience I should like to attempt a modest theoretical approach to this whole problem. I have observed changes in the approach to values as the individual grows from infancy to adulthood. I observe further changes when, if he is fortunate, he continues to grow toward true psychological maturity. Many of these observations grow out of my experience as therapist, where I have had the mind stretching opportunity of seeing the ways in which individuals move toward a richer life. From these observations I believe I see some directional threads emerging which might offer a new concept of the valuing process, more tenable in the modern world. I have made a beginning by presenting some of these ideas partially in previous writings (Rogers, 1951, 1959); I would like now to voice them more clearly and more fully.

Some definitions

Charles Morris (1956, pp. 9-12) has made some useful distinctions in regard to values. There are "operative values," which are the behaviors of organisms in which they show preference for one object or objective rather than another. The lowly earthworm, selecting the smooth arm of a Y maze rather than the arm which is paved with sandpaper, is giving an indication of an operative value.

There are also "conceived values," the preference of an individual for a symbolized object. "Honesty is the best policy" is such a conceived value.

There is also the term "objective value," to refer to what is objectively preferable, whether or not it is sensed or conceived of as desirable. I will be concerned primarily with operative or conceptualized values.

Infant's way of valuing

Let me first speak about the infant. The living human being has, at the outset, a clear approach to values. We can infer from studying his behavior that he prefers those experiences which maintain, enhance, or actualize his organism, and rejects those which do not serve this end. Watch him for a bit:

Hunger is negatively valued. His expression of this often comes through loud and clear.

Food is positively valued. But when he is satisfied, food is negatively valued, and the same milk he responded to so eagerly is now spit out, or the breast which seemed so satisfying is now rejected as he turns his head away from the nipple with an amusing facial expression of disgust and revulsion.

He values security, and the holding and caressing which seem to communicate security.

He values new experience for its own sake, and we observe this in his obvious pleasure in discovering his toes, in his searching movements, in his endless curiosity.

He shows a clear negative valuing of pain, bitter tastes, sudden loud sounds.

All of this is commonplace, but let us look at these facts in terms of what they tell us about the infant's approach to values. It is first of all a flexible, changing, valuing *process,* not a fixed system. He likes food and dislikes the same food. He values security and rest and rejects it for new experience. What is going on seems best described as an organismic valuing process, in which each element, each moment of what he is experiencing is somehow weighed, and selected or rejected, depending on whether, at that moment, it tends to actualize the organism or not. This complicated weighing of experience is clearly an organismic, not a conscious or symbolic function. These are operative, not conceived values. But this process can, nonetheless, deal with complex value problems. I would remind you of the experiment in which young infants had spread in front of them a score or more of dishes of natural (that is, unflavored) foods. Over a period of time they clearly tended to value the foods which enhanced their own survival, growth, and development. If for a time a child gorged himself on starches, this would soon be balanced by a protein "binge." If at times he chose a diet deficient in some vitamin, he would later seek out foods rich in this very vitamin. The physiological wisdom of his body guided his behavioral movements, resulting in what we might think of as objectively sound value choices.

Another aspect of the infant's approach to values is that the source or locus of the evaluating process is clearly within himself. Unlike many of us, he *knows* what he likes and dislikes, and the origin of these value choices lies strictly within himself. He is the center of the valuing process, the evidence for his choices being supplied by his own senses. He is not at this point influenced by what his parents think he should prefer, or by what the church says, or by the opinion of the latest "expert" in the field, or by the persuasive talents of an advertising firm. It is from within his own experiencing that his organism is saying in nonverbal terms, "This is good for me." "That is bad for me." "I like this." "I strongly dislike that." He would laugh at our concern over values, if he could understand it.

Change in the valuing process

What happens to this efficient, soundly based valuing process? By what sequence of events do we exchange it for the more rigid, uncertain, inefficient approach to values which characterizes most of us as adults? Let me try to state briefly one of the major ways in which I think this happens.

The infant needs love, wants it, tends to behave in ways which will bring a repetition of this wanted experience. But this brings complications. He pulls baby sister's hair, and finds it satisfying to hear her wails and protests. He then hears that he is "a naughty, bad boy," and this may be reinforced by a slap on the hand. He is cut off from affection. As this experience is repeated, and many, many others like it, he gradually learns that what "feels good" is often "bad" in the eyes of significant others. Then the next step occurs, in which he comes to take the same attitude toward himself which these others have taken. Now, as he pulls his sister's hair, he solemnly intones, "Bad, bad boy." He is introjecting the value judgment of another, taking it in as his own. To that degree he loses touch with his own organismic valuing process. He has deserted the wisdom of his organism, giving up the locus of evaluation, and is trying to behave in terms of values set by another, in order to hold love.

Or take another example at an older level. A boy senses, though perhaps not consciously, that he is more loved and prized by his parents when he thinks of being a doctor than when he thinks of being an artist. Gradually he introjects the values attached to being a doctor. He comes to want, above all, to be a doctor. Then in college he is baffled by the fact that he repeatedly fails in chemistry, which is absolutely necessary to becoming a physician, in spite of the fact that the guidance counselor assures him he has the ability to pass the course. Only in counseling interviews does he begin to realize how completely he has lost touch with his organismic reactions, how out of touch he is with his own valuing process.

Perhaps these illustrations will indicate that in an attempt to gain or hold love, approval, esteem, the individual relinquishes the locus of evaluation which was his in infancy, and places it in others. He learns to have a basic *dis*trust for his own experiencing as a guide to his behavior. He learns from others a large number of conceived values, and adopts them as his own, even though they may be widely discrepant from what he is experiencing.

Some introjected patterns

It is in this fashion, I believe, that most of us accumulate the introjected value patterns by which we live. In the fantastically complex culture of today, the patterns we introject as desirable or undesirable come from a variety of sources and are often highly contradictory. Let me list a few of the introjections which are commonly held.

Sexual desires and behaviors are mostly bad. The sources of this construct are many—parents, church, teachers.

Disobedience is bad. Here parents and teachers combine with the military to emphasize this concept. To obey is good. To obey without question is even better.

Making money is the highest good. The sources of this conceived value are too numerous to mention.

Learning an accumulation of scholarly facts is highly desirable. Education is the source.

Communism is utterly bad. Here the government is a major source.

To love thy neighbor is the highest good. This concept comes from the church, perhaps from the parents.

Cooperation and teamwork are preferable to

acting alone. Here companions are an important source.

Cheating is clever and desirable. The peer group again is the origin.

Coca-Colas, chewing gum, electric refrigerators, and automobiles are all utterly desirable. From Jamaica to Japan, from Copenhagen to Kowloon, the "Coca-Cola culture" has come to be regarded as the acme of desirability.

This is a small and diversified sample of the myriads of conceived values which individuals often introject, and hold as their own, without ever having considered their inner organismic reactions to these patterns and objects.

Common characteristics of adult valuing

I believe it will be clear from the foregoing that the usual adult—I feel I am speaking for most of us—has an approach to values which has these characteristics:

The majority of his values are introjected from other individuals or groups significant to him, but are regarded by him as his own.

The source or locus of evaluation on most matters lies outside of himself.

The criterion by which his values are set is the degree to which they will cause him to be loved, accepted, or esteemed.

These conceived preferences are either not related at all, or not clearly related, to his own process of experiencing.

Often there is a wide and unrecognized discrepancy between the evidence supplied by his own experience, and these conceived values.

Because these conceptions are not open to testing in experience, he must hold them in a rigid and unchanging fashion. The alternative would be a collapse of his values. Hence his values are "right."

Because they are untestable, there is no ready way of solving contradictions. If he has taken in from the community the conception that money is the *summum bonum* and from the church the conception that love of one's neighbor is the highest value, he has no way of discovering which has more value for *him*. Hence a common aspect of modern life is living with absolutely contradictory values. We calmly discuss the possibility of dropping a hydrogen bomb on Russia, but find

tears in our eyes when we see headlines about the suffering of one small child.

Because he has relinquished the locus of evaluation to others, and has lost touch with his own valuing process, he feels profoundly insecure and easily threatened in his values. If some of these conceptions were destroyed, what would take their place? This threatening possibility makes him hold his value conceptions more rigidly or more confusedly, or both.

Fundamental discrepancy

I believe that this picture of the individual, with values mostly introjected, held as fixed concepts, rarely examined or tested, is the picture of most of us. By taking over the conceptions of others as our own, we lose contact with the potential wisdom of our own functioning, and lose confidence in ourselves. Since these value constructs are often sharply at variance with what is going on in our own experiencing, we have in a very basic way divorced ourselves from ourselves, and this accounts for much of modern strain and insecurity. This fundamental discrepancy between the individual's concept and what he is actually experiencing, between the intellectual structure of his values and the valuing process going on unrecognized within—this is a part of the fundamental estrangement of modern man from himself.

Restoring contact with experience

Some individuals are fortunate in going beyond the picture I have just given, developing further in the direction of psychological maturity. We see this happen in psychotherapy where we endeavor to provide a climate favorable to the growth of the person. We also see it happen in life, whenever life provides a therapeutic climate for the individual. Let me concentrate on this further maturing of a value approach as I have seen it in therapy.

As the client senses and realizes that he is prized as a person [1] he can slowly begin to value the different aspects of himself. Most importantly, he can begin, with much diffi-

---

[1] The therapeutic relationship is not devoid of values. When it is most effective it is, I believe, marked by one primary value, namely, that this person (the client) has *worth*.

culty at first, to sense and to feel what is going on within him, what he is feeling, what he is experiencing, how he is reacting. He uses his experiencing as a direct referent to which he can turn in forming accurate conceptualizations and as a guide to his behavior. Gendlin (1961, 1962) has elaborated the way in which this occurs. As his experiencing becomes more and more open to him, as he is able to live more freely in the process of his feelings, then significant changes begin to occur in his approach to values. It begins to assume many of the characteristics it had in infancy.

Introjected values in relation to experiencing

Perhaps I can indicate this by reviewing a few of the brief examples of introjected values which I have given, and suggesting what happens to them as the individual comes closer to what is going on within him.

The individual in therapy looks back and realizes, "But I *enjoyed* pulling my sister's hair—and that doesn't make me a bad person."

The student failing chemistry realizes, as he gets close to his own experiencing, "I don't like chemistry; I don't value being a doctor, even though my parents do; and I am not a failure for having these feelings."

The adult recognizes that sexual desires and behavior may be richly satisfying and permanently enriching in their consequences, or shallow and temporary and less than satisfying. He goes by his own experiencing, which does not always coincide with social norms.

He recognizes freely that this communist book or person expresses attitudes and goals which he shares as well as ideas and values which he does not share.

He realizes that at times he experiences cooperation as meaningful and valuable to him, and that at other times he wishes to be alone and act alone.

Valuing in the mature person

The valuing process which seems to develop in this more mature person is in some ways very much like that in the infant, and in some ways quite different. It is fluid, flexible, based on this particular moment, and the degree to which this moment is experienced as enhancing and actualizing. Values

are not held rigidly, but are continually changing. The painting which last year seemed meaningful now appears uninteresting, the way of working with individuals which was formerly experienced as good now seems inadequate, the belief which then seemed true is now experienced as only partly true, or perhaps false.

Another characteristic of the way this person values experience is that it is highly differentiated, or as the semanticists would say, extensional. The examples in the preceding section indicate that what were previously rather solid monolithic introjected values now become differentiated, tied to a particular time and experience.

Another characteristic of the mature individual's approach is that the locus of evaluation is again established firmly within the person. It is his own experience which provides the value information or feedback. This does not mean that he is not open to all the evidence he can obtain from other sources. But it means that this is taken for what it is—outside evidence—and is not as significant as his own reactions. Thus he may be told by a friend that a new book is very disappointing. He reads two unfavorable reviews of the book. Thus his tentative hypothesis is that he will not value the book. Yet if he reads the book his valuing will be based upon the reactions it stirs in *him*, not on what he has been told by others.

There is also involved in this valuing process a letting oneself down into the immediacy of what one is experiencing, endeavoring to sense and to clarify all its complex meanings. I think of a client who, toward the close of therapy, when puzzled about an issue, would put his head in his hands and say, "Now what *is* it that I'm feeling? I want to get next to it. I want to learn what it is." Then he would wait, quietly and patiently, trying to listen to himself, until he could discern the exact flavor of the feelings he was experiencing. He, like others, was trying to get close to himself.

In getting close to what is going on within himself, the process is much more complex than it is in the infant. In the mature person it has much more scope and sweep. For there is involved in the present moment of experiencing the memory traces of all the relevant learnings from the past. This moment has not only its immediate sensory impact, but it has meaning growing out of similar experiences in the past (Gendlin, 1962). It has both the new and the old in it. So when I experience a painting or a person, my experiencing contains within it the learnings I have accumulated from past meetings with paintings or persons, as well as the new impact of this particular encounter. Likewise the moment of experiencing contains, for the mature adult, hypotheses about consequences. "It is not pleasant to express forthrightly my negative feelings to this person, but past experience indicates that in a continuing relationship it will be helpful in the long run." Past and future are both in this moment and enter into the valuing.

I find that in the person I am speaking of (and here again we see a similarity to the infant), the criterion of the valuing process is the degree to which the object of the experience actualizes the individual himself. Does it make him a richer, more complete, more fully developed person? This may sound as though it were a selfish or unsocial criterion, but it does not prove to be so, since deep and helpful relationships with others are experienced as actualizing.

Like the infant, too, the psychologically mature adult trusts and uses the wisdom of his organism, with the difference that he is able to do so knowingly. He realizes that if he can trust all of himself, his feelings and his intuitions may be wiser than his mind, that as a total person he can be more sensitive and accurate than his thoughts alone. Hence he is not afraid to say, "I feel that this experience [or this thing, or this direction] is good. Later I will probably know *why* I feel it is good." He trusts the totality of himself, having moved toward becoming what Lancelot Whyte (1950) regards as "the unitary man."

It should be evident from what I have been saying that this valuing process in the mature individual is not an easy or simple thing. The process is complex, the choices often very perplexing and difficult, and there is no guarantee that the choice which is made will in fact prove to be self-actualizing. But because whatever evidence exists is available to the individual, and because he is open to his experiencing, errors are correctable. If this chosen course of action is not self-enhancing, this will be sensed, and he can make an adjustment or revision. He thrives on a maximum feedback interchange, and thus, like the gyroscopic compass on a ship, can continually correct his course toward his true goal of self-fulfillment.

Some propositions regarding the valuing process

Let me sharpen the meaning of what I have been saying by stating two propositions which contain the essential elements of this viewpoint. While it may not be possible to devise empirical tests of each proposition in its entirety, yet each is to some degree capable of being tested through the methods of psychological science. I would also state that though the following propositions are stated firmly in order to give them clarity, I am actually advancing them as decidedly tentative hypotheses.

Hypothesis I. There is an organismic base for an organized valuing process within the human individual.

It is hypothesized that this base is something the human being shares with the rest of the animate world. It is part of the functioning life process of any healthy organism. It is the capacity for receiving feedback information which enables the organism continually to adjust its behavior and reactions so as to achieve the maximum possible self-enhancement.

Hypothesis II. This valuing process in the human being is effective in achieving self-enhancement to the degree that the individual is open to the experiencing which is going on within himself.

I have tried to give two examples of individuals who are close to their own experiencing: the tiny infant who has not yet learned to deny in his awareness the processes going on within; and the psychologically mature person who has relearned the advantages of this open state.

There is a corollary to this second proposition which might be put in the following terms. One way of assisting the individual to move toward openness to experience is through a relationship in which he is prized as a separate person, in which the experiencing going on within him is empathically understood and valued, and in which he is given the freedom to experience his own feelings and those of others without being threatened in doing so.

This corollary obviously grows out of therapeutic experience. It is a brief statement of the essential qualities in the therapeutic relationship. There are already some empirical studies, of which the one by Barrett-Lennard (1962) is a good example, which give support to such a statement.

Propositions regarding the outcomes of the valuing process

I come now to the nub of any theory of values or valuing. What are its consequences? I should like to move into this new ground by stating bluntly two propositions as to the qualities of behavior which emerge from this valuing process. I shall then give some of the evidence from my experience as a therapist in support of these propositions.

Hypothesis III. In persons who are moving toward greater openness to their experiencing, there is an organismic commonality of value directions.

Hypothesis IV. These common value directions are of such kinds as to enhance the development of the individual himself, of others in his community, and to make for the survival and evolution of his species.

It has been a striking fact of my experience that in therapy, where individuals are valued, where there is greater freedom to feel and to be, certain value directions seem to emerge. These are not chaotic directions but instead exhibit a surprising commonality. This commonality is not dependent on the personality of the therapist, for I have seen these trends emerge in the clients of therapists sharply different in personality. This commonality does not seem to be due to the influences of any one culture, for I have found evidence of these directions in cultures as divergent as those of the United States, Holland, France, and Japan. I like to think that this commonality of value directions is due to the fact that we all belong to the same species—that just as a human infant tends, individually, to select a diet similar to that selected by other human infants, so a client in therapy tends, individually, to choose value directions similar to those chosen by other clients. As a species there may be certain elements of experience which tend to make for inner development and which would

be chosen by all individuals if they were genuinely free to choose.

Let me indicate a few of these value directions as I see them in my clients as they move in the direction of personal growth and maturity.

They tend to move away from façades. Pretense, defensiveness, putting up a front, tend to be negatively valued.

They tend to move away from "oughts." The compelling feeling of "I ought to do or be thus and so" is negatively valued. The client moves away from being what he "ought to be," no matter who has set that imperative.

They tend to move away from meeting the expectations of others. Pleasing others, as a goal in itself, is negatively valued.

Being real is positively valued. The client tends to move toward being himself, being his real feelings, being what he is. This seems to be a very deep preference.

Self-direction is positively valued. The client discovers an increasing pride and confidence in making his own choices, guiding his own life.

One's self, one's own feelings come to be positively valued. From a point where he looks upon himself with contempt and despair, the client comes to value himself and his reactions as being of worth.

Being a process is positively valued. From desiring some fixed goal, clients come to prefer the excitement of being a process of potentialities being born.

Sensitivity to others and acceptance of others is positively valued. The client comes to appreciate others for what they are, just as he has come to appreciate himself for what he is.

Deep relationships are positively valued. To achieve a close, intimate, real, fully communicative relationship with another person seems to meet a deep need in every individual, and is very highly valued.

Perhaps more than all else, the client comes to value an openness to all of his inner and outer experience. To be open to and sensitive to his own *inner* reactions and feelings, the reactions and feelings of others, and the realities of the objective world—this is a direction which he clearly prefers. This openness becomes the client's most valued resource.

These then are some of the preferred directions which I have observed in individuals moving toward personal maturity. Though I am sure that the list I have given is inadequate and perhaps to some degree inaccurate, it holds for me exciting possibilities. Let me try to explain why.

I find it significant that when individuals are prized as persons, the values they select do not run the full gamut of possibilities. I do not find, in such a climate of freedom, that one person comes to value fraud and murder and thievery, while another values a life of self-sacrifice, and another values only money. Instead there seems to be a deep and underlying thread of commonality. I believe that when the human being is inwardly free to choose whatever he deeply values, he tends to value those objects, experiences, and goals which make for his own survival, growth, and development, and for the survival and development of others. I hypothesize that it is *characteristic* of the human organism to prefer such actualizing and socialized goals when he is exposed to a growth promoting climate.

A corollary of what I have been saying is that in *any* culture, given a climate of respect and freedom in which he is valued as a person, the mature individual would tend to choose and prefer these same value directions. This is a significant hypothesis which could be tested. It means that though the individual of whom I am speaking would not have a consistent or even a stable system of conceived values, the valuing process within him would lead to emerging value directions which would be constant across cultures and across time.

Another implication I see is that individuals who exhibit the fluid valuing process I have tried to describe, whose value directions are generally those I have listed, would be highly effective in the ongoing process of human evolution. If the human species is to survive at all on this globe, the human being must become more readily adaptive to new problems and situations, must be able to select that which is valuable for development and survival out of new and complex situations, must be accurate in his appreciation of reality if he is to make such selections. The psychologically mature person as I have described him has,

I believe, the qualities which would cause him to value those experiences which would make for the survival and enhancement of the human race. He would be a worthy participant and guide in the process of human evolution.

Finally, it appears that we have returned to the issue of universality of values, but by a different route. Instead of universal values "out there," or a universal value system imposed by some group—philosophers, rulers, priests, or psychologists—we have the possibility of universal human value directions *emerging* from the experiencing of the human organism. Evidence from therapy indicates that both personal and social values emerge as natural, and experienced, when the individual is close to his own organismic valuing process. The suggestion is that though modern man no longer trusts religion or science or philosophy nor any system of beliefs to *give* him values, he may find an organismic valuing base within himself which, if he can learn again to be in touch with it, will prove to be an organized, adaptive, and social approach to the perplexing value issues which face all of us.

References

Barrett-Lennard, G. T. Dimensions of therapist response as causal factors in therapeutic change. *Psychol. Monogr.*, 1962, 76 (43, Whole No. 562).

Gendlin, E. T. Experiencing: A variable in the process of therapeutic change. *Amer. J. Psychother.*, 1961, 15, 233-245.

Gendlin, E. T. *Experiencing and the creation of meaning.* Glencoe, Ill.: Free Press, 1962.

Morris, C. W. *Varieties of human value.* Chicago: Univer. Chicago Press, 1956.

Rogers, C. R. *Client-centered therapy.* Boston: Houghton Mifflin, 1951.

Rogers, C. R. A theory of therapy, personality and interpersonal relationships. In S. Koch (Ed.), *Psychology: A study of a science.* Vol. 3. *Formulations of the person and the social context.* New York: McGraw-Hill, 1959. Pp. 185-256.

Whyte, L. L. *The next development in man.* New York: Mentor Books, 1950.